Investments
Alternate Edition

Herbert B. Mayo
Rider College

The Dryden Press

Chicago New York Philadelphia San Francisco Montreal Toronto London Sydney Tokyo Mexico City Rio de Janeiro Madrid

Address orders to:
383 Madison Avenue
New York, New York 10017

Address editorial correspondence to:
901 North Elm Street
Hinsdale, Illinois 60521

ISBN: 0-03-059937-7
Printed in the United States of America
012 056 987654321

CBS College Publishing
The Dryden Press
Holt, Rinehart and Winston
Saunders College Publishing

To Sharon—Wife and Friend

Preface

Most textbooks in investments today are written for students with some background (and in some cases an extensive background) in accounting, finance, and economics. Unfortunately, not every student who takes an investment course has completed these courses. Many four-year colleges and community colleges offer investment courses that may be taken early in the student's career. While many teachers bemoan this fact, it still remains that these students cannot cope with (or be expected to cope with) the material in many fine, but advanced, textbooks in investments. This text, then, is aimed at bridging the gap. The book covers the basics of investing, while assuming that the student has little, if any, background in business.

The text does assume that the student has a desire to tackle a fascinating subject that may have real impact on his or her well-being. Thus, while the presentation may be at an elementary level, in some cases the concepts are very sophisticated. No attempt is made to make the material unnecessarily difficult, but the very nature of evaluating investments and choosing among competing uses for the saver's funds is not easy, nor should it be. Investing requires determining one's goals and taking actions now to fulfill those goals.

Investing also requires an ability to forecast future events, or at least to anticipate the expected future. If one knew what was going to happen, investing would be easy. But the future can only be expected, and these expectations in many cases are not fulfilled. During the 1960s few individuals anticipated the inflation of the 1970s. During the 1960s the economy experienced a long period of stable economic growth, and economists believed that the problem of the business cycle had been overcome. They thought that by careful manipulation of fiscal and monetary policy, an era of continuous growth and prosperity would be upon us. That expectation certainly was not fulfilled.

If professional economists and others trained in forecasting have problems anticipating the future, one can imagine the problems besetting the typical saver who seeks to invest a moderate sum to help fulfill some future financial goal, such as putting a child through college. For the vast majority of individuals, investing is by its very nature a difficult problem. The security world is one of special jargon and terms, sophisticated professionals, and an almost limitless number of possible investments. It is a primary aim of this text to make investing a little less difficult by explaining the terms and jargon, by elucidating the possible investments available to the individual investor, and by explaining many of the techniques used by the professionals to value an asset.

This text uses a substantial number of examples and illustrations that employ data that are generally available to the investing public. It is believed that this information is accurate; however, the reader should not assume that any mention of a specific firm and its securities is a recommendation to buy or sell those securities. The examples have been chosen to illustrate specific points and not to pass judgment on individual investments.

Textbooks require the input of many individuals in addition to the author. I would like to acknowledge in particular the following people who contributed their time and thoughts to this text: Edward Krohn (Miami-Dade Community College), Craig Thompson (Rider College), Stuart Wood (Tulane University), Richard Howe (Orange Coast College), Edward Greiger (Browder College), and J. Daniel Williams (University of Akron). In addition, the many people in the editorial staff (including Wayne Koch, Jack Neifert, Lorraine Battista, and Elizabeth Warden) contributed much assistance and guidance that facilitated completion of the text. My thanks go to all.

Contents

PART TWO

THE TOOLS OF
INVESTING

PART FIVE

INVESTING IN OPTIONS

Part One

The Environment
of Investing

To ease the learning process, this text has been divided into distinct sections. The first considers the environment in which investment decisions are made, since it can have considerable impact on which assets the investor chooses to include in his or her portfolio.

The investor should start by specifying his or her goals of investing. Investing is a means to an end, such as financial security during retirement or the ability to make the down payment on a house. These ends should be specified before the individual acquires a portfolio, because not all assets will serve to meet the particular financial goals.

Once these goals are established, the investor should be aware of the environment and the mechanics of investing, including the process by which securities are issued and subsequently bought and sold, the regulations and tax laws that have been established by the various levels of government, and the necessity for the individual to bear risk. An understanding of this environment, along with the tools discussed in Part Two, lays the foundation for the process of analyzing specific assets for possible inclusion in one's portfolio.

chapter 1
AN INTRODUCTION TO BASIC INVESTMENTS

Once an individual has received income, there are two choices: to spend it or to save it. If the individual chooses to save, an additional decision must be made: What is to be done with the savings? This is an extremely important question because Americans earned $1,682.4 billion and saved $76.3 billion in the second quarter of 1978.* The saver must decide where to invest this command over goods and services that is currently not being used. In effect, the saver must decide on a portfolio of assets to own. This is an important decision for the individual because these assets are the means by which today's purchasing power is trans-

---

*Source: *Federal Reserve Bulletin,* November 1978, p. A53.

ferred to the future. A portfolio is a combination of assets designed to serve as a store of value. Poor management of these assets may destroy the portfolio's value, and the individual will not achieve his or her investment goals.

There are many assets that the investor may include in the portfolio and this book will discuss many of them. The stress, however, will be on long-term financial assets. While the saver may hold a portion of the portfolio in short-term assets, such as savings accounts, these assets do not seem to present the problem of choice that accompanies the decision to purchase a stock or a bond. Understanding the nature of long-term assets, i.e., how they are bought and sold, how they are valued, and how they may be used in portfolio construction, is the primary thrust of this text.

PORTFOLIO CONSTRUCTION AND SECURITY ANALYSIS

Investment goals

Several factors affect the construction of a portfolio. These include the goals of the investor, the risk involved, the taxes that will be imposed on any gain, and a knowledge of the available opportunities and alternative investments. This text will cover the range of these alternative investments, their use in a portfolio, the risks associated with owning them, and their valuation.

The investor's goals should largely determine the construction and management of the portfolio. Investing must have a purpose, for without a goal a portfolio is like a boat without a rudder. There must be some objective that offers a guide to the composition of the portfolio.

There are many reasons for saving and accumulating assets. Planning for retirement and preparing for the education of one's children are only two of the many reasons for saving. Other motives include the desire to meet financial emergencies, to leave a sizable estate, or even to accumulate wealth for the sake of accumulating. These are among the many reasons that people accumulate a portfolio of assets rather than spend all of their current income.

Their effect on the portfolio

These motives for saving should dictate, or at least affect, the composition of the portfolio. Savings that are held to meet emergencies should not be invested in assets on which the potential return involves substantial risk; instead, emphasis should be placed on assets on which the return is assured and which may be readily converted to cash, such as savings accounts. A portfolio that is designed to help finance retirement can stress long-term assets, such as bonds that will mature many years in the future or stocks that offer potential growth in value.

Willingness to bear risk

In addition to the individual's goal, his or her capacity or willingness to bear risk plays an important role in constructing the portfolio. Some individuals are more willing to bear risk, and these persons will tend to select assets on which the return involves greater risk to obtain the specified investment goals. If the saver wants to build a retirement fund, he or she can choose from a variety of possible investments. However, not all investments are equal with regard to risk and potential return. Those investors who are more willing to accept risk may construct portfolios with assets involving greater risk that may earn higher returns. Although conservative investors may select securities issued by the more financially stable firms, investors who are less averse to taking risk may select stocks issued by younger, less seasoned firms that may offer better opportunities for growth over a period of years.

Taxes also help to decide the composition of an individual's portfolio. Investments are subject to a variety of different taxes. The income that is generated is taxed as is the capital appreciation that is realized. Some states levy personal property taxes on one's securities. When a person dies, the federal government taxes the value of the estate, which includes the portfolio. In addition to the federal estate tax, several states tax the distribution of the wealth (i.e., they levy a tax on an individual's inheritance). Such taxes and the desire to reduce them affect the composition of each person's portfolio.

Taxes

Although decisions regarding the portfolio's construction and management as a whole are certainly important, the investor's primary decisions center around the acquisition of one asset at a time. The selection of a specific asset is the domain of security analysis. Security analysis considers individual assets by themselves, whereas portfolio management takes the aggregate view. Security analysis then considers the merits of the specific asset, while portfolio management determines the effect that the individual asset has on the whole portfolio.

The purchase of an asset

A large portion of this text is devoted to security analysis because it is impossible to know an asset's effect on the portfolio as a whole without first knowing its characteristics. Stocks and bonds differ greatly with regard to risk, potential return, and valuation. Even within a single type of asset such as bonds, there can be considerable variation. For example, a corporate bond is different from a municipal bond. The investor needs to know and to understand these differences as well as the relative merits and risks associated with each of the assets. After understanding how individual assets are valued, the investor may then construct a portfolio that will aid in the realization of his or her financial goals.

SOME PRELIMINARY DEFINITIONS

The term *investment* can have more than one meaning. In economics it refers to the purchase of a physical asset, such as a firm's purchase of a plant, equipment, or inventory, or an individual's purchase of a house. To the lay person the word denotes buying stock or bonds (or maybe even a house), but it probably does not mean purchasing a plant, equipment, or inventory.

The economic definition of investment

From the viewpoint of the aggregate economy, an individual's buying stocks or bonds is not an investment. For every investment by the buyer there is an equal *dis*investment by the seller. These buyers and sellers are trading one asset for another: The seller trades the security for cash, and the buyer trades cash for the security. These transactions occur in second-hand markets, and for that reason security markets are often referred to as secondary markets. Only when the securities are initially issued and sold in the primary market is there an investment in an economic sense. Then and only then does the firm receive the money that it, in turn, may use to purchase a plant, equipment, or inventory.

The lay person's definition of investment

In this text, the word *investment* is used in the lay person's sense. Purchases of an asset for the purpose of storing value will be called an investment, even if in the aggregate there is only a transfer of ownership from a seller to a buyer. The purchases of stocks, bonds, speculative options, commodity contracts, and even antiques, stamps, and real estate are all considered to be investments if the individual's intent is to transfer purchasing power to the future. If these assets are acting as stores of value, they are investments for that individual.

The present value depends on the future

Assets have *value* because of the benefits they offer. An investor appraises the asset and assigns a current value to it based on the belief that the asset will generate income or a flow of services or will appreciate in price. After computing this value, the individual compares it with the current market price in order to determine if the asset is currently over-priced or underpriced.

In some cases this valuation is relatively easy. For example, the bonds of the federal government pay a fixed amount of interest each year and mature at a specified date. Thus, the future benefits are known. However, the future benefits of other assets are not so readily identified. For example, while the investor may anticipate future dividends, neither their payment nor their amount can be known with certainty. Forecasting future benefits may be very difficult, but forecasts are still crucial to the process of valuation. Without them and an evaluation of the asset, the investor cannot know if the asset should be purchased or sold.

Different goals and forecasts produce different valuations

The valuation of some assets is complicated, and two people may have different estimates of the future benefits. It is therefore easy to understand why these two people may have completely divergent views on the worth of a particular asset. One person may believe that an asset is overvalued and hence seek to sell it, while another may seek to buy it in the belief that it is undervalued. Valuation may be very subjective, which leads to such inconsistencies as one person's buying while the other is selling. That does not mean that one person is necessarily irrational or incompetent. People's goals and perceptions (or estimates) of an asset's potential may change, which affects their valuation of the specific asset.

The return: Income and price appreciation

An investment is made because the investor anticipates a *return*. The return on an investment is what the investor earns. This may be in the form of income, such as dividends and interest, or in the form of capital appreciation if the asset's price rises. Not all assets offer both income and capital appreciation. Some stocks pay no current dividends but may appreciate in value. Other assets, including savings accounts, do not appreciate in value, and the return is solely the interest income.

Return is frequently expressed in percentages. It is then referred to as the *rate of return*, which is the return that is earned by the investment relative to its cost. Before purchasing an asset, the investor anticipates that the rate of return will be greater than that of other assets of similar risk. Without this anticipation, the purchase would not be made. The realized rate of return may, of course, be quite different from the anticipated rate of return. That is the element of risk.

Risk is the uncertainty that the anticipated return will be achieved. As is discussed in the next section, there are many sources of risk. The investor must be willing to bear this risk in order to achieve the expected return. Even relatively safe investments involve some risk; there is no completely safe investment. For example, savings accounts that are insured still involve some element of risk of loss. If the rate of inflation exceeds the rate of interest that is earned on these insured accounts, the investor suffers a loss of purchasing power.

All investments involve risk

A term that is frequently used in conjunction with risk is *speculation*. Many years ago virtually all investments were called speculations. Today the word implies only a high degree of risk. However, risk is not synonymous with speculation. Speculation has the connotation of gambling in which the odds are against the player. Many securities are risky, but over a period of years the investor will reap a positive return. The odds are not really against the investor, and such investments are not speculations.

Bearing risk is not speculating

The term *speculation* is rarely used in this text, and when it is employed, the implication is that the investor runs a good chance of losing the funds invested in the speculative asset (e.g., a commodity contract). Although a particular speculation may pay off handsomely, the investor should not expect that many such gambles will reap large returns. After the investor adjusts for the larger amount of risk that must be borne to own such speculative investments, the anticipated return may not justify the risk involved.

Besides involving risk and offering an expected return, stores of value have marketability or liquidity or both. *Marketability* means that the asset can readily be bought and sold. Frequently this is confused with *liquidity*, which is ease of converting the asset into cash *without significant loss*. An asset, such as stock, that is traded on the New York Stock Exchange, may be very marketable but not liquid if its value has declined since it was purchased. Other assets may be very liquid but not marketable. For example, a savings account may be readily converted into cash, but there is no market. Instead the saver just withdraws the funds from the account.

Assets may be sold

All stores of values possess some combinations of marketability, liquidity, and the potential for price change. However, the extent to which they possess each quality varies. If an asset lacks one or two of these characteristics, it must be strong with regard to the remaining characteristic(s) in order for it to be attractive as an investment. For example, money

The characteristics common to all assets

is the essence of liquidity. All other assets must be converted into money before the investor can exercise the purchasing power that is contained in the portfolio. Although money is the most liquid of all assets, it earns nothing for the owner (unless prices are declining). Other assets may provide their owners with a flow of income or services but do not have the liquidity of money. Bonds and savings accounts pay interest, stocks may pay dividends, and physical goods such as antiques provide enjoyment and service. For money to be attractive as a store of value, its liquidity must offset the advantages that are offered by other assets. If investors anticipate that security prices will fall, then money may be an attractive investment. But during periods of high interest rates, rising security prices, or inflation, money is a poor store of value, and savers should minimize the amount of money held as a store of value.

RISK

Uncertainty creates risk

All investments involve risk. Risk is the uncertainty that one's expectations will be fulfilled. When an investor purchases a particular asset, there is an expected return. The adjective *expected* is important because the return is not assured. That is the element of risk: The return that is actually earned will differ from the expected return. Even the holding of cash is not risk free, for an investor who is holding cash is forgoing income and risking the depreciation of that dollar through inflation. Risk is a part of life and a large part of investing.

Sources of risk:
1. Business risk

There are several types of risk, the most important of which are business risk, financial risk, market risk, and inflation. *Business risk* is the risk that is associated with the nature of the enterprise itself. All businesses are not equally risky. Drilling for new oil deposits is considerably more risky than running a commercial bank. The chances of finding oil may be slim and only one of many new wells may actually produce oil and earn a positive return. Commercial banks, however, can make loans that are secured by particular assets, such as homes or inventories. While these loans are not risk free, they may be relatively safe because even if the debtor defaults, the creditor (i.e., the bank) can seize the security to meet its claims. Some businesses are by their very nature riskier than others, and therefore investing in them is inherently riskier.

2. Financial risk

All assets must be financed. Either creditors or owners or both provide the funds to start and to sustain the business. The second major source of risk is *financial risk*. Borrowing funds to finance a business may increase the element of risk because creditors require that the borrower meet certain terms in order to obtain the funds. The most common of these requirements is the paying of interest and the repayment of principal. The creditor can (and usually does) demand other terms, such as collateral or restrictions on dividend payment, that the borrower must meet. These restrictions mean that the firm that uses debt financing bears more risk because it must meet these obligations in addition to its other obligations. When sales and earnings are rising, these constraints may not be burdensome, but during periods of financial stress the firm must meet the obligations required by its debt financing. Failure of the firm to meet these terms may result in financial ruin and bankruptcy. A firm that does not use borrowed funds to acquire its assets does not have these additional responsibilities and does not have the element of financial risk.

Investors also have to bear the element of *market risk*. The market value of assets can rise or decline. While it may be frustrating to invest in a firm that has a minimal degree of business and financial risk and then to watch the price of the security fall, that is the nature of market risk. Security prices do fluctuate, and the investor must accept the risk associated with this fluctuation. Thus, an investment in what appears to be a financially strong firm may still result in a loss if security prices as a whole decline.

3. Market risk

This market risk also applies to other assets, such as stamps and real estate, because their prices also fluctuate. If the value of houses rises in general, then the value of a particular house will tend to rise. But the converse is also true because prices of houses can decline, and thus market risk applies to that type of investment. While the investor may be able to reduce the impact of some sources of risk, market risk cannot be avoided.

In addition to the previously mentioned risks, the investor must also bear the risk associated with *inflation*. Inflation is the loss of purchasing power through a general rise in prices. If the prices of goods and services increase, the purchasing power of the investor's assets is reduced. It is this reduction in the purchasing power of money that inflicts losses and is an important type of risk.

4. Inflation

Investors will naturally seek to protect themselves from this risk by constructing a portfolio of assets with an anticipated return that is higher than the rate of inflation. It is important to note the word *anticipated*, because it influences the selection of particular assets. If inflation is expected to be only 4 per cent, a savings account offering 5 per cent will produce a gain and thereby "beat" inflation (at least before taxes). However, if the inflation rate were to increase unexpectedly to 7 per cent, the savings account will result in a loss. If the higher rate of inflation had been anticipated, the investor would not have chosen the savings account but might have purchased some other asset with a higher potential yield. Presumably this alternative investment would involve greater risk if it offered the anticipation of a higher return. The investor might have allowed for the risk of loss resulting from inflation by increasing the potential yield (and thereby the risk) from other sources.

By now it should be obvious that all investors bear risk. Even an investor who does nothing cannot avoid risk. By "doing nothing" and holding cash, the investor is still doing something and is bearing some element of risk. The very nature of transferring purchasing power from

The investor cannot avoid risk

today to tomorrow requires accepting some risk because the future is uncertain. An individual's financial status will often be such that consumption must be postponed to the future; the investor must select those assets that will help him or her to meet financial obligations and thereby overcome this situation. Risk simply cannot be avoided, as any choice will involve at least one of the major types of risk: business risk, financial risk, market risk, or inflation. The aim is to minimize these risks for a given potential return.

THE PLAN AND PURPOSE OF THIS TEXT

This text seeks to help the investor, especially the individual with little knowledge and understanding of investments, to increase the potential return from investments and to reduce the risk of loss. Perhaps because investing deals with the individual's money, it has a mysteriousness that is not justified. By introducing the various investments and the methods of their acquisition, analysis, and valuation, the text seeks to remove the mystery associated with investing.

While investments may be treated as a complex subject, the approach here will be to describe the various assets, the risks associated with them, and the advantages and disadvantages they offer. This is essential information that all investors need to know whether they have large or small portfolios.

The divisions of the text

The book is divided into several parts, the first two of which lay the foundation on which security selection is based. Part One covers the environment of security selection. This encompasses how securities come into existence (Chapter 2), the mechanics of purchasing stocks and bonds (Chapter 3), risk and its measurement (Chapter 4), and the impact of taxation on portfolio construction (Chapter 5). Part Two discusses the basic tools and information necessary to make investment decisions, including an explanation of the processes of compounding and discounting (Chapter 6), the sources of information for particular investments (Chapter 7), and the analysis of accounting statements (Chapter 8).

Parts Three and Four of the text are devoted to the analysis of more traditional investments: bonds and stocks. Chapter 9 describes the features common to all debt instruments, and Chapter 10 discusses the pricing or valuation of debt. Chapter 11 deals with corporate debt, and Chapter 12 is devoted to government securities. Part Four is concerned with common stocks. Chapter 13 examines the past performance of investments in stocks. Chapter 14 discusses models for the valuation of corporate stock; this is followed by a discussion of the firm's dividend policy (Chapter 15). The next two chapters deal with the techniques that are used to analyze stocks: the fundamental approach (Chapter 16 and the technical approach (Chapter 17).

Parts Five and Six discuss other assets that are possible investments. Part Five is devoted to options. Chapter 18 serves as a general introduction to options, and Chapters 19 and 20 cover warrants, puts and calls, and convertible bonds. Part Six explains a variety of miscellaneous assets, some of which have been more popular in the past and some of which appear to be becoming more popular as investments. Chapter 21 deals with investment companies, which provide an alternative to investing directly in stocks and bonds. Commodities, which are perhaps the riskiest of all investment opportunities that are covered in this text (Chapter 22), are discussed next. The last chapters in this section cover investing in real assets. Chapter 23 is devoted to collectables, such as art and gold coins, and Chapter 24 discusses investments in real estate.

The text concludes with a discussion of the efficient market hypothesis and portfolio construction. This conclusion of the text is a capstone chapter that stresses the need for financial planning and suggests certain assets that meet specific financial goals.

Learning Objectives

After completing this chapter you should be able to

1. Explain the role of a financial intermediary.

2. Illustrate the flow of funds from savers to firms.

3. Contrast and compare commercial banks and other savings banks.

4. Define the role of the investment banker.

5. Differentiate between an underwriting and a best effort agreement.

6. Identify the source of risk and the party that bears this risk in an underwriting.

7. Explain the role that is played in an underwriting by the originating house, the syndicate, the red herring, and the financial prospectus.

chapter 2

THE FINANCING OF BUSINESS

There are many diverse types of businesses in many industries, but they all have at least two things in common: Somebody had to provide the funds to start them, and someone must supply the funds to sustain them. From the modest corner store to the large corporate giant, each must have a source of capital. This capital comes from owners who have equity in the firm and from creditors who have lent funds to the firm.

It is through the financing of business that securities come into existence. Firms issue securities such as stocks or bonds or partnership shares, and these are bought by the general public and by financial institutions such as pension funds or mutual funds. Once in existence, many of these securities may be traded in the secondary markets, such as the New York Stock Exchange. These secondary markets make securities more attractive to individuals because investors know there is a place to sell the securities should the need arise.

This chapter is concerned with financing the needs of business. It begins with a general discussion of transferring funds from the general public to business. This transfer occurs either directly or through financial intermediaries. The second section describes the types of savings instruments that are issued by various financial intermediaries (e.g., commercial bonds) to attract the funds of savers. The chapter ends with a discussion of the mechanics of selling new securities to the general public through the underwriting of securities by investment bankers.

THE TRANSFER OF FUNDS TO BUSINESS

Direct and indirect transfers

Although there are many possible investments, there are basically only two methods for transferring funds to firms. One is the *direct* investment of savings by the general public into businesses. This occurs when business firms issue corporate securities, which are purchased by investors, or when individuals invest in sole proprietorships or partnerships. The second method is the *indirect* transfer through a financial institution, which transfers to firms the funds that are not currently being used (i.e., that are being saved) by individuals.

The role of secondary markets

From the viewpoint of the aggregate economy, the indirect transfer of funds from savers to firms is more important than the sale of new securities or investments in partnerships. Most individual households do not invest their savings directly in business. In addition, many firms retain earnings and never distribute them to owners. These firms sell new securities only on an intermittent basis, and many years may lapse between issues. Most purchases of securities by households do not transfer savings to businesses; instead, such purchases transfer securities from one individual owner to another. The primary role of organized security markets is to facilitate this transfer of securities among investors. It is, in part, the existence of these secondary markets that makes securities attractive to investors. Secondary markets make it easier for firms to issue additional securities when they believe that it is advantageous to sell directly to the investing public.

T-accounts

The process by which funds flow from savers to firms can be illustrated by the use of T-accounts. In the following examples, these accounts are abbreviated balance sheets. Whereas balance sheets enumerate (1) the assets of a firm or a household, (2) its liabilities (i.e., what it owes), and (3) its equity or net worth, T-accounts show only those assets and liabilities that are being discussed. All other assets, liabilities, and equity are omitted to simplify the transaction.

When a corporation issues a new security, such as a bond, and sells it to the general public, the following transaction occurs:

The saver purchases the bond with funds that are held in a checking account, thereby trading one asset (the funds in the account) for another asset (the bond). The firm acquires the funds by issuing and selling the security. Thus, there is a direct transfer of money from the saver to the firm.

The indirect transfer is a little more complicated because an intermediary operates between the saver and the firm. The intermediary acquires funds from savers by issuing a claim on itself, such as a savings account or a life insurance policy. The intermediary then lends the funds or buys new stock, which is issued by a company that is in need of money.

The flow of funds through a financial intermediary may also be illustrated by the use of T-accounts. In the following example the saver buys an ordinary whole life insurance policy. Such a policy includes not only life insurance but also a savings program. Since the buyer of the life insurance policy is saving, the insurance company is serving as a financial intermediary when it uses the proceeds from the policy to buy new securities that are issued by firms.

When the saver buys and pays for the insurance, the following transaction occurs:

INSURANCE COMPANY		SAVER
Checking Account ↑	Insurance Outstanding ↑	Checking Account ↓
		Insurance ↑

The insurance company acquires the money by issuing a liability on itself, i.e., the insurance. The life insurance is a liability because it is a promise to pay the insured's beneficiaries. The saver trades one asset, money in a checking account, for another asset, the life insurance.

The insurance company then lends the funds to a firm (i.e., it buys a security, such as a bond), at which time the following transaction occurs:

FIRM		INSURANCE COMPANY
Checking Account ↑	Debt ↑	Checking Account ↓
		Debt of Firm ↑

The insurance company gives up one asset, funds in the checking account, to acquire another asset, the bond. The borrower acquires the funds by promising to return them in the future and to pay interest while the loan is outstanding.

The preceding T-accounts may be combined to illustrate the process of transferring funds from the ultimate lender to the ultimate borrower.

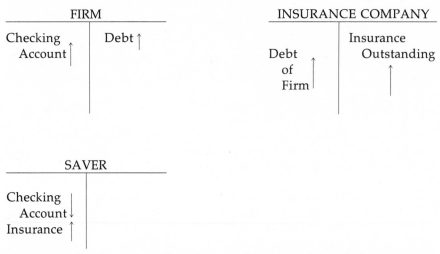

The saver's funds are transferred to the borrower through the insurance company. Through this process the borrower is able to acquire the funds because the insurance company was able to issue a debt (i.e., the policy) that the saver would purchase.

Private placements
    The sale of an issue of bonds or stock to a financial institution, such as a pension fund or a life insurance company, is called a *private placement*. The primary advantages of private placement to the firm are the elimination of the cost of selling securities to the general public and the ready availability of large amounts of cash. In addition, the firm does not have to meet the disclosure requirements that are necessary to sell securities to the general public. This disclosure of information is for the protection of the investing public; it is presumed that the financial institution can protect itself by requiring information as a precondition for granting the loan.* The disclosure requirements are both a cost to the firm when securities are issued to the public and a possible source of information to its competitors that the firm may wish to avoid divulging. An additional advantage to both the firm and the financial institution is that the terms of securities may be tailored to meet the needs of both parties. For example, the firm may be able to sell a bond of intermediate length (e.g., five years) to a financial institution, whereas the general public may prefer bonds of longer duration.

---

*Private lenders frequently negotiate for and receive a seat on the borrowing firm's board of directors.

The advantages of private placement are similar for the financial institution and for the firm that is obtaining the funds. A substantial amount of money may be invested at one time, and the maturity date can be set to meet the lender's needs. In addition, brokerage fees associated with purchasing securities on an organized exchange are avoided. The financial intermediary can gain more control over the firm that receives the funds by building restrictive covenants into the agreement. These covenants may restrict the firm from issuing additional securities without the prior permission of the lender and may limit the firm's dividends, its merger activity, and the types of investments that it may make. All of these restrictive covenants are designed to protect the lender from risk of loss and are part of any private sale of securities from a firm to a financial institution. Since each sale is separately negotiated, the individual terms vary with the bargaining powers of the parties and the economic conditions at the time of the agreement.

THE VARIETY OF FINANCIAL INTERMEDIARIES

In advanced economies, various financial intermediaries have developed that facilitate the indirect transfer of savings to borrowers. These intermediaries include commercial banks, savings and loan associations, mutual savings banks, credit unions, life insurance companies, and pension plans. Whenever these firms borrow from one group to lend to another, they are acting as financial intermediaries. However, if they purchase already existing financial assets such as stocks that are traded on the New York Stock Exchange or existing mortgages, they are not acting as financial intermediaries. Instead they are investing the funds in secondary markets. Many investment companies, such as mutual funds, are not financial intermediaries in the strictest sense because they purchase primarily secondhand assets.

Financial intermediaries and the direct transfer of savings

The differences between these financial intermediaries are related to the types of assets that each acquires and the types of claims (e.g., accounts) that each issues to obtain funds from savers. A variety of assets, ranging from loans of short duration to long-term bonds and corporate stock, are available to financial intermediaries. The differences in the portfolios of the various financial institutions are related primarily to the nature of each business or to the legal environment. For example, a savings and loan association specializes in granting mortgages because its depositors tend to leave funds with the institution for many years. Thus, the savings and loan association may grant loans that tie up the funds for many years. Commercial banks, however, offer a broader spectrum of loans but stress loans that mature rapidly. Since commercial banks must be able to meet withdrawals from checking accounts, they cannot have a portfolio limited to long-term investments such as mortgages. Their assets include short-term loans to businesses and short-term debt of the federal government.

Differences among financial intermediaries

While the variety of loans offered by financial intermediaries is important to the aggregate economy, the investor is concerned primarily with the various types of claims issued by financial intermediaries. These intermediaries offer a diversity of instruments to attract the funds of savers. Although each of these instruments is differentiated from the others, this differentiation is minimal in some cases. Savers must then select from these competing instruments (as well as from the securities and other investments that are discussed subsequently in this text).

Commercial banks

Commercial banks differ from all other financial intermediaries because they issue demand deposits (i.e., checking accounts), which are so called because they are payable to the holder on demand. Although this type of account does not pay interest, it offers the following two very important advantages to the saver: Funds in these accounts may be transferred by check, and the canceled checks are proof of payment. A saver may temporarily place funds that will soon be used to make payments in these accounts. While the funds are in the account, the commercial bank may lend them to firms, individuals, and governments that need to borrow money. Even after the saver writes checks and draws on the account, the recipients of the checks may continue to hold the funds in checking accounts before they, in turn, make payments. All of the deposits in checking accounts, of course, represent the potential to make payments, but as long as they remain in checking accounts and are not withdrawn for cash, the funds may be used by commercial banks to acquire income-earning assets.

Savings and time deposits

Commercial banks also issue a variety of savings accounts and time deposits. As their name implies, the purpose of these accounts is to provide a place to store savings for a period of time. A regular savings account (i.e., a passbook account) not only earns interest but also offers the saver the option to withdraw the funds on demand. These accounts are an extremely liquid asset. Time deposits, which include savings certificates or certificates of deposit, lack this last feature. These certificates pay more interest than do regular savings accounts; however, the saver must leave the funds with the bank for the duration of the certificate in order to collect this higher interest.

The variety of certificates that are available from one bank is shown in Exhibit 2–1. As may be seen from this exhibit, the shorter the term or time period, the lower is the rate of interest earned by the certificate. If the saver is willing to invest the funds for longer periods, the interest that is earned is greater. For example, 6 per cent is earned on funds that are invested in one-year certificates. However, 7.75 per cent is earned on a certificate of deposit with a maturity of eight to ten years. In addition, owing to daily compounding, the yield is increased to 8.17 per cent. (For a discussion of "compounding," see Chapter 6.)

%interest.
Instead of shouting it,
we're explaining it.

Savings Plan	Effective Annual Yield (1)	Initial Deposit	Maturity Date	Withdrawals	Interest Compounded	Interest Credited	Additional Deposits	Special Features
5% Passbook Savings Account	5.09%	$1 or more	None	Anytime	Quarterly	Quarterly (3)	Any amount, anytime	Interest calculated from day-of-deposit to day-of-withdrawal (If $25 balance is maintained). Interest credited to account quarterly.
5% Statement Savings Account	5.13%	$1 or more	None	Anytime	Daily	Quarterly (3)	Any amount, anytime	Interest calculated from day-of-deposit to day-of-withdrawal (If positive balance is maintained). Interest credited automatically on quarterly statement.
5½% Pyramid Passbook Account	5.65%	$10 or more	90 Days	First 10 days of calendar quarter after funds have been on deposit for a full calendar quarter (2)	Daily	Quarterly (3)	Any amount, anytime	Interest credited automatically into account (If $10 balance is maintained).
6% Certificate of Deposit	6.27%	$500 plus any multiple of $100	1 or 2 Years	At maturity (2)	Daily	Quarterly or annually at customer's choice.	None	Interest paid by check or credited to another account.
6½% Certificate of Deposit	6.81%	$500 plus any multiple of $100	3 Years	At maturity (2)	Daily	Quarterly or annually at customer's choice.	None	Interest paid by check or credited to another account.
7¼% Certificate of Deposit	7.63%	$1,000 plus any multiple of $100	4 Years	At maturity (2)	Daily	Quarterly or annually at customer's choice.	None	Interest paid by check or credited to another account.
7½% Investment Certificate of Deposit	7.90%	$1,000 plus any multiple of $100	6 Years	At maturity (2)	Daily	Quarterly or annually at customer's choice.	None	Interest paid by check or credited to another account.
7¾% Certificate of Deposit	8.17%	$1,000 plus any multiple of $100	8 Years	At maturity (2)	Daily	Quarterly or annually at customer's choice.	None	Interest paid by check or credited to another account.

(1) Annual Yield on Funds if interest is paid annually

(2) Federal law and regulation prohibit early withdrawal of a time deposit, except with consent of the bank and then only after reduction of the rate of interest to the bank's saving rate and a loss of three months' interest.

(3) Provided that the account remains open at the end of the quarter.

United Jersey Banks

The First National Bank of Princeton
Member FDIC

90 Nassau Street, Princeton, N.J. 08540

Main: 90 Nassau Street. **Branches:** East Nassau Office, 370 East Nassau (Near Harrison) • West Windsor Office, 40 Washington Road • Lawrence Township Office, Princeton Pike • Princeton Commerce Center, 29 Emmons Drive, Bldg. E (off Rt. 1) • Plainsboro Office, 607 Plainsboro Road • Windsor Plaza Office, Princeton-Hightstown Road, Princeton Junction.

phone: (609) 921-6100 *drive-in facilities*

Member bank of United Jersey Banks, a $2.3 billion Financial Services Organization with offices throughout New Jersey

EXHIBIT 2-1. Savings accounts offered by a commercial bank.

Negotiable certificates of deposit

Besides the savings certificates that are shown in Exhibit 2–1, commercial banks offer certificates of deposit in large denominations of $100,000 or more. These are called negotiable certificates of deposit because the rate of interest and the maturity date are negotiated between the bank and the borrower. The certificates that are shown in Exhibit 2–1 are not negotiated individually but instead are offered to the general public by the commercial bank. The interest rate on these certificates is subject to the maximum rate that is set by the banking laws (Regulation Q). The negotiable certificates of deposit are not subject to this regulation; hence, the interest that is paid varies with conditions in the money markets and may exceed the limits that are set on savings and time deposits.

Since the maturity date and interest rate are negotiated individually, these certificates of deposit have become popular with corporate financial managers. When the firm has excess cash, this is one possible means of investing the funds and earning interest. Because the terms are negotiated individually, the length of time can be set to meet the needs of the lending firm. Unfortunately, the large denomination has virtually excluded individuals from investing funds in these certificates. However, there are mutual funds that specialize in investing in such money market instruments. The individual saver may purchase shares in these funds and thereby participate in the market for negotiable certificates of deposit. (These mutual funds are discussed in more detail in Chapter 21.)

Savings and loan associations

In addition to commercial banks, other types of banks seek to attract the deposits of savers. These include savings and loan associations, mutual savings banks, and credit unions. All three are similar in that they offer a place for savers to deposits funds, which are subsequently lent by the financial intermediary. There are, however, differences between the various savings institutions.

After commercial banks, savings and loan associations are the most important in terms of total deposits. As of August 1978, they had total deposits of $420.4 million, which compares to time deposits of $580.6 million in commercial banks. Mutual savings banks had $139.3 million, and credit unions had $51.8 million in savings accounts.*

The savings accounts that are offered by savings and loan associations and mutual savings banks are similar to those offered by commercial banks. However, since not all of these savings banks can currently offer checking accounts to attract deposits, it is argued that they are not able to compete with commercial banks for deposits. Thus, these savings banks are permitted by law to offer slightly higher rates of interest than those that are permitted on comparable accounts with commercial

---

* Source: *Federal Reserve Bulletin*, November 1978, pp. A16 and A29.

EXHIBIT 2–2. Maximum Interest Rates Allowed by Law on Savings and Time Deposits (in Effect June 30, 1979)*

Type of Account	Commercial Banks	Interest Rate Savings and Loan Associations and Mutual Savings Banks
Savings account	5 %	5¼%
Time deposit		
90 days to 1 year	5½	5¾
1 to 2.5 years	6	6½
2.5 to 4 years	6½	6¾
4 to 6 years	7¼	7½
More than 6 years	7½	7¾

*Source: *Federal Reserve Bulletin*, August, 1979, p. A10.

banks. These differences in the maximum allowable interest rates are illustrated in Exhibit 2–2. As may be seen in the exhibit, the difference in the maximum interest rates is at most 0.5 per cent. In addition, as of November 1, 1978, savings and loan associations and other thrift institutions were permitted to issue six-month certificates that pay 0.25 per cent more than can be earned on short-term federal government debt (e.g., treasury bills).

Actually, the distinction between commercial banks and savings banks is becoming blurred. Savings banks in several northern states are permitted to issue a "negotiable order of withdrawal" (called a NOW account). A NOW account functions like a checking account, since the holder may write orders of withdrawal against funds in the account. While the funds are on deposit, they earn interest. The saver has the convenience of a checking account but still earns interest on the deposit.*

Some commercial banks and savings and loan associations offer a service that is similar to NOW accounts. These banks permit the transfer of funds between savings and checking accounts by telephone. By planning disbursements, the saver may keep funds in the savings account, where they earn interest, and then conveniently transfer them by phone to the checking account when payments are to be made.

Some savings banks offer another service that has obscured the distinction between them and commercial banks: They make payments for the individual. For example, savings and loan associations in several states can pay bills for the depositor by phone. The saver deposits funds in the savings account and provides the bank with information

NOW accounts

---

*In some states (e.g., Florida), even credit unions are permitted to let their depositors write drafts drawn on accounts with the credit union.

concerning frequent disbursements (e.g., telephone bill or an electricity bill) that must be made. The bank then makes the payments on orders from the saver. While the funds are in the savings account, the individual collects interest but still has the convenience of a checking account. The fee for this service is usually less than the price of postage.

Automatic transfers from savings to checking accounts

The innovation that will perhaps completely blur the distinction between commercial banks and savings banks is the regulation allowing commercial banks, in effect, to pay interest on checking accounts. This makes checking accounts a type of savings account and thereby ends the rigid distinction between the types of accounts. As of November 1, 1978, commercial banks were granted the right to make automatic transfers from savings to checking accounts. The effect of this ruling is the same as that which would occur if banks were permitted to pay interest on checking accounts. This innovation may be beneficial to investors, since it permits them to earn interest on funds that are temporarily idle. Whether these transfers are in fact beneficial to the *individual* investor depends upon the fees that are charged by the bank for the service. Since these fees vary, the investor should shop for the service that best suits his or her needs.*

THE ISSUING AND SELLING OF NEW SECURITIES

Firms, in addition to acquiring funds from financial intermediaries, may issue new securities and sell them to the general public through investment bankers. Firms employ this option when internally generated funds are insufficient to finance the desired level of investment spending and when the firm believes it to be advantageous to obtain outside funding from the general public instead of from a financial intermediary. Such outside funding may increase public interest in the firm and its securities and may also bypass some of the restrictive covenants that are required by financial institutions.

The following section deals with the sale of new securities to the general public through an investment banker. It covers the role played by the investment banker, the mechanics of selling new securities, and the potential volatility of the new issue market.

THE ROLE OF INVESTMENT BANKER

The role of middlemen

A firm can market securities directly to the public in several ways: by contacting its current stockholders and creditors and asking them to purchase the new securities, by advertising the securities, or even by

---

*This service will require Congressional approval by 1980.

peddling them from door to door. Although this last scenario is exaggerated, it illustrates that there is a cost to selling new securities, which may be considerable if the firm itself undertakes the task. For this reason, firms employ help in marketing new securities; they use the services of investment bankers, which sell new securities to the general public. In effect, an investment banker serves as a middleman to channel money from investors to the firm that needs the capital.

Investment banking is an important financial institution, but confusion exists concerning it, part of which may be attributable to the misnomer *investment banker*. An investment banker is rarely a banker and does not generally invest. Instead, the investment banker is usually a brokerage firm like Merrill Lynch Pierce Fenner and Smith or First Boston Corporation. Although these brokerage firms own securities, they do not necessarily buy and hold the newly issued securities for investment purposes.

Investment bankers perform a middleman function that brings together individuals who have money to invest and firms that need financing. Since brokerage firms have many customers, they are able to sell new securities without the costly search that the individual firm may have to make to sell its own securities. Thus, although the firm in need of financing must pay for the services, it is able to raise external capital at less expense through the investment banker than it could by selling the securities itself.

THE MECHANICS OF UNDERWRITING

If a firm needs funds from an external source, it can approach an investment banker to discuss an underwriting. The term *underwriting* refers to the process of selling new securities. In an underwriting the firm that is selling the securities, and not the firm that is issuing the shares, bears the risk associated with the sale. When an investment banker agrees to underwrite a sale of securities, it is agreeing to supply the firm with a specified amount of money. If it fails to sell the securities, the investment banker must still pay the agreed upon sum to the firm at the time of the offering (i.e., the sale) of the securities. Thus, the risk of selling rests with the underwriter and not with the firm issuing the securities. Failure to sell the securities imposes significant losses on the underwriter, who must remit funds for securities that have not been sold.

An underwriting

The firm that is in need of financing and the investment banker discuss the amount of funds needed, the type of security to be issued, the price and any special features of the security, and the cost to the firm of issuing the securities. All of these factors are negotiated by the firm that is seeking capital and the investment banker. If mutually acceptable terms are reached, the investment banker will be the middleman through which the securities are sold by the firm to the general public.

The participants

Because an underwriting starts with a particular brokerage firm, which manages the underwriting, that firm is called the *originating house*. The originating house need not be a single firm if the negotiation involves several investment bankers. In this case, several firms can join together to manage the underwriting and the selling of securities to the general public.

The originating house does not usually try to sell all of the securities by itself but forms a syndicate to market them. The *syndicate* is a group of brokerage houses that have joined together to underwrite a specific sale of securities. Each member of the syndicate is then allotted a specified number of the securities and is responsible for their sale.

The use of a syndicate has several advantages. First, the syndicate has access to many potential buyers for the securities. Second, by using a syndicate the number of securities that each brokerage firm must sell is reduced. This increase in the number of potential customers and the decrease in the amount that each broker must sell increase the probability that the entire issue of securities will be sold. Thus, syndication makes possible both the sale of a large offering of securities and a reduction in the risk borne by each member of the selling group. Third, since members of the syndicate are likely to be in different geographic locations, the new securities will be sold to a geographically dispersed public. Such geographic dispersion of ownership of the securities is a requirement for trading on the New York Stock Exchange.

TYPES OF AGREEMENTS

The guarantee of sale or best effort agreements

The agreement between the investment bankers and the firm may be one of two types. The investment bankers may agree to purchase (i.e., to underwrite) the entire issue of securities and to sell them to the general public. This guarantees a specified amount of money to the firm that is issuing the securities. The alternative is a *best effort* agreement in which the investment bankers make the best effort to sell the securities but do not guarantee that a specified amount of money will be raised. The former agreement places the risk of selling the securities on the investment bankers, and most sales of new securities are of this type. The underwriters purchase all of the securities, pay the expenses, and bear the risk of selling the securities, with the anticipation of recouping the expenses through the sale. Since they have agreed to purchase the entire issue, the underwriters must pay the firm for all of the securities even if the syndicate is unable to sell them.

The importance of the price of a new issue

It is for this reason that the pricing of securities is crucial. If the initial offer price is too high, the syndicate will be unable to sell the securities. When this occurs, the investment bankers have two choices: (1) to maintain the offer price and to hold the securities in inventory until they are sold or (2) to let the market find a lower price level that will induce investors to purchase the securities. Neither choice benefits the investment bankers. If the underwriters purchase the securities and hold them in inventory, they either must tie up their own funds, which could be earning a return elsewhere, or must borrow funds to pay for the securities. Like any other firm, the investment bankers must pay interest on these borrowed funds. Thus, the decision to support the offer price of the securities prevents the investment bankers from investing their own capital or (and this case is the more likely) requires that they borrow substantial amounts of capital. In either case, the profit margins on the underwriting are substantially decreased, and the investment bankers may even experience a loss on the underwriting.

Instead of supporting the price, the underwriters may choose to let the price of the securities fall. The inventory of unsold securities can then be sold, and the underwriters will not tie up capital or have to borrow money from their sources of credit. If the underwriters make this choice, they force losses on themselves when the securities are sold at less than cost. But they also cause the customers who bought the securities at the initial offer price to lose. The underwriters certainly do not want to inflict losses on these customers, because if they experience losses continually, the underwriters' market for future security issues will vanish. Therefore, the investment bankers do not try to overprice a new issue of securities, for overpricing will ultimately result in their suffering losses.

There is also an incentive to avoid underpricing new securities. If the issue is underpriced, all of the securities will be readily sold and their price will rise because demand will have exceeded supply. The buyers of the securities will be satisfied, for the price of the securities will have increased as a result of the underpricing. The initial purchasers of the securities reap windfall profits, but these profits are really at the expense of the company whose securities were underpriced. If the underwriters had assigned a higher price to the securities, the company would have raised more capital. Underwriting is a very competitive business, and each security issue is individually negotiated; hence, if one investment banker consistently underprices securities, firms will employ competitors to underwrite their securities.

MARKETING SECURITIES

Once the terms of the sale have been agreed upon, the managing house may issue a *preliminary prospectus*. This is often referred to as a *red herring* because of the red lettering on the title page. This lettering informs the prospective buyer that the securities are being registered with the Securities and Exchange Commission (SEC) and may subsequently be offered for sale. *Registration* refers to the disclosure of information concerning the firm, the securities being offered for sale, and the use of the proceeds from the sale.

The cost of printing the red herring is borne by the underwriters,

The red herring

PRELIMINARY PROSPECTUS DATED DECEMBER 12, 1978

350,000 Shares

 JAMES RIVER CORPORATION

OF VIRGINIA

Common Stock
($.10 par value)

The Common Stock is traded in the over-the-counter market. On December 11, 1978, the representative bid and asked prices per share of Common Stock as reported by NASDAQ were $21.50 and $22.50, respectively.

THESE SECURITIES HAVE NOT BEEN APPROVED OR DISAPPROVED BY THE SECURITIES AND EXCHANGE COMMISSION NOR HAS THE COMMISSION PASSED UPON THE ACCURACY OR ADEQUACY OF THIS PROSPECTUS. ANY REPRESENTATION TO THE CONTRARY IS A CRIMINAL OFFENSE.

	Price to Public	Underwriting Discount (1)	Proceeds to Company (2)
Per Share	$	$	$
Total	$	$	$

(1) See "Underwriting".

(2) Before deducting expenses estimated at $

The shares of Common Stock are offered by the several Underwriters when, as and if delivered to and accepted by them, and subject to prior sale, withdrawal of such offer without notice and certain other conditions. It is expected that delivery of certificates for such shares will be made on or about January   , 1979.

Kidder, Peabody & Co.
Incorporated

Scott & Stringfellow, Inc.

Wheat, First Securities, Inc.

The date of this preliminary prospectus is January   , 1979

EXHIBIT 2–3. Preliminary and final prospectus for an issue of shares of James River Corporation.

Exhibit continued on following pages.

TABLE OF CONTENTS

No person has been authorized to give any information or to make any representation not contained in this Prospectus and, if given or made, such information or representation must not be relied upon as having been authorized. This Prospectus does not constitute an offer of any securities other than those to which it relates, or an offer of those to which it relates to any person in any jurisdiction where such offer would be unlawful. The delivery of this Prospectus at any time does not imply that the information herein is correct as of any time subsequent to its date.

JAMES RIVER CORPORATION
OF VIRGINIA

350,000 Shares

Common Stock
($.10 par value)

PROSPECTUS

Kidder, Peabody & Co.
Incorporated

Scott & Stringfellow, Inc.

Wheat, First Securities, Inc.

EXHIBIT 2–3 *Continued.*

420,000 Shares

 JAMES RIVER CORPORATION

OF VIRGINIA

Common Stock
($.10 par value)

The Common Stock is traded in the over-the-counter market. On January 16, 1979, the representative bid and asked prices per share of Common Stock as reported by NASDAQ were $22.50 and $24.00, respectively.

THESE SECURITIES HAVE NOT BEEN APPROVED OR DISAPPROVED BY THE SECURITIES AND EXCHANGE COMMISSION NOR HAS THE COMMISSION PASSED UPON THE ACCURACY OR ADEQUACY OF THIS PROSPECTUS. ANY REPRESENTATION TO THE CONTRARY IS A CRIMINAL OFFENSE.

	Price to Public	Underwriting Discount (1)	Proceeds to Company (2)
Per Share	$23.00	$ 1.50	$21.50
Total	$9,660,000	$630,000	$9,030,000

(1) See "Underwriting".
(2) Before deducting expenses estimated at $230,000.

The shares of Common Stock are offered by the several Underwriters when, as and if delivered to and accepted by them, and subject to prior sale, withdrawal of such offer without notice and certain other conditions. It is expected that delivery of certificates for such shares will be made on or about January 24, 1979.

Kidder, Peabody & Co.
Incorporated

Scott & Stringfellow, Inc.

Wheat, First Securities, Inc.

The date of this final prospectus is January 17, 1979

EXHIBIT 2–3 *Continued.*

JAMES RIVER CORPORATION
OF VIRGINIA

420,000 Shares

Common Stock
($.10 par value)

PROSPECTUS

Kidder, Peabody & Co.
Incorporated

Scott & Stringfellow, Inc.

Wheat, First Securities, Inc.

EXHIBIT 2–3 *Continued.*

who recoup this cost through the underwriting fees. This preliminary prospectus describes the company and the securities to be issued; it includes the firm's income statement and balance sheets, its current activities (such as a pending merger or labor negotiation), the regulatory bodies to which it is subject, and the nature of its competition. The preliminary prospectus is thus a detailed document concerning the company and is, unfortunately, usually tedious reading.

The preliminary prospectus does not include the price of the securities. That will be determined on the day that the securities are issued. If security prices decline or rise, the price of the new securities may be adjusted for the change in market conditions. In fact, if prices decline sufficiently, the firm has the option of postponing or even canceling the underwriting.

The final prospectus

After the shares have been approved for issue by the SEC, a final prospectus is published. Except for changes that are required by the SEC, it is virtually identical to the preliminary prospectus. The red lettering is removed, and information regarding the price of the security, the underwriting discount, and the proceeds to the company, along with any more recent financial data, is added. Exhibit 2–3 illustrates the title pages for both the red herring and the final prospectus for an issue of 420,000 shares of James River Corporation. The names of the managing underwriters are in large print at the bottom of the page. These managing underwriters formed the syndicate that sold the shares to the general public. In this example, more than 40 firms participated in the selling group.

Underwriting fees

The cost of the underwriting, which is the difference between the price of the securities to the public and the proceeds to the firm, is also given in the prospectus shown in Exhibit 2–3. In this example, the cost is $1.50 per share, which is 6.97 per cent of the proceeds received by the firm for each share. The total cost is $630,000 for the sale of these shares. Underwriting fees tend to vary with the dollar value of the securities being underwritten and the type of securities being sold. Since some of the expenses are fixed (e.g., preparation of the prospectus), the unit cost for a large underwriting is smaller. Also, it may be more difficult to sell speculative bonds than quality bonds. Thus, underwriting fees for speculative issues tend to be higher.

Indirect compensation

In addition to the fee, the underwriter may receive indirect compensation, which may be in the form of the right (or option) to buy additional securities or membership on the firm's board of directors. Such indirect compensation may be as important as the monetary fee because it unites the underwriter and the firm. After the initial sale, the underwriter often becomes a market maker for the securities, which is particularly important to the investing public. Without a secondary market in which to sell the security, investors would be less interested in buying the securities initially. By maintaining a market in the security, the brokerage firm eases the task of selling the securities originally.

VOLATILITY OF THE NEW ISSUE MARKET

The new issue market (especially for common stock) is extremely volatile. There have been periods when the investing public seemed willing to purchase virtually any security that was being sold on the market. There have also been periods during which new companies were simply unable to raise money, and large companies did so only under onerous terms.

The new issue market is not only volatile regarding the number of securities that are offered but also regarding the price changes of the new issues. When the new issue market is "hot," it is not unusual for the prices to rise dramatically. In many cases, however, prices subsequently decline even more remarkably. The dramatic but short life of Four Seasons Nursing Homes is illustrated in Graph 2–1, which shows

"Hot" new issues

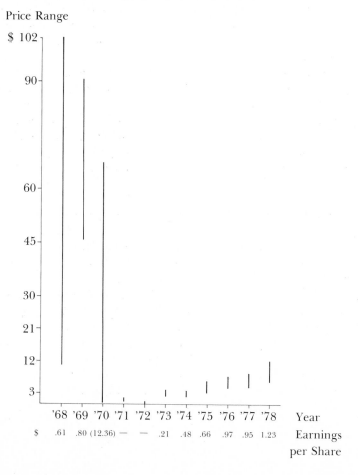

GRAPH 2–1. Annual Price Range and Earnings per Share of Stock of Four Seasons Nursing Homes (Anta Corporation)

the annual price range of the stock and the firm's earnings per share. The firm went public on May 10, 1968. The price rose dramatically from the initial price of $11 to $102. Only two years later the firm was bankrupt, and the price of the stock declined to $.16 (i.e., $^3/_{16}$ in the fractional prices that are used in the security markets).

A price of $102 for a share of Four Seasons Nursing Homes was indeed excessive. The company had 3.4 million shares outstanding, and, at a price of $102, the firm was worth $346.8 million ($102 × 3.4 million) according to the market. Since the firm had revenues of only $19.3 million and earnings of less than $2 million, it made no sense in terms of the firm's earning capacity to value the company in excess of $300 million.

Today, Four Seasons Nursing Homes has been reorganized as Anta Corporation. Although the stock has not regained its former value, the firm is profitable and even pays a dividend. As may be seen in Graph 2–1, the price of the stock has risen from the extremely low prices at which it was valued during the years of bankruptcy.

Not all new issues perform like that of Four Seasons Nursing Homes. Despite the fact that some firms do not fulfill their development potential and fail, others succeed and grow steadily. For example, James River Corporation went public on March 16, 1973, at $12 per share and has done quite well. This performance is illustrated in Graph 2–2, which plots the annual range of the stock's price and the firm's earnings per share. As may be seen from the graph, there has been a steady increase in the firm's earnings and in the price of the stock. Although the stock has not reached the heights achieved by that of Four Seasons Nursing Homes (and many other "high fliers" of the late 1960s), it is an expanding firm that continues to offer growth potential to investors. It is, however, still a small firm and thus may be viewed as a speculative investment.

GRAPH 2–2. Annual Price Range and Earnings per Share of Stock of James River Corporation

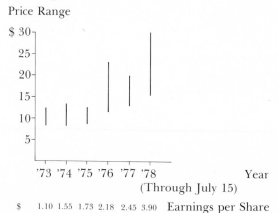

All firms, of course, were small at one time, and each one had to go public to have a market for its shares. Someone bought the shares of IBM, Xerox, and Johnson & Johnson when these firms went public. The ability to spot the companies that promise the greatest growth for the future is rare. However, the new issue market has offered and continues to offer the opportunity to invest in emerging firms, some of which may achieve substantial returns for those investors or speculators who are willing to accept the risk. It is the possibility of such large rewards that makes the new issue market so exciting. However, if the past is an indicator of the future, many firms that go public will fail and will inflict significant losses on those investors who have accepted this risk by purchasing securities issued by the small, emerging firms.

SUMMARY

All firms must have a source of funds with which to buy assets. These funds come from savers who are not currently using all of their income to buy goods and services.

A sophisticated financial system has emerged to transfer these savings to firms. Various financial intermediaries transfer the funds of savers to borrowers. These intermediaries are a kind of go-between; they obtain funds from savers by issuing liabilities on themselves, such as savings accounts, and then use the funds to make loans and to buy the new securities that are issued by firms. There are several types of financial intermediaries, such as savings and loan associations and commercial banks. They are differentiated from one another by the liabilities that they issue to savers and the portfolio of assets that they acquire. These intermediaries are subject to a considerable number of regulations, including a law governing the maximum amount of interest that they may pay savers.

In addition to obtaining funds from financial intermediaries, a firm may obtain money by selling securities, such as stocks and bonds, to the general public through investment bankers. These bankers act as middlemen between the firm and the savers. In many cases they underwrite an issue of new securities, which means that they guarantee a specified amount of money to the firm. The underwriters then sell the securities to the public. Since the underwriters are obligated to pay the specified amount for the securities to the firm, they bear the risk of the sale.

Terms to Remember

Secondary market

T-account

Private placement

Savings and loan
association

Mutual savings bank

Certificate of deposit

NOW account

Financial intermediary

Underwriting

Originating house

Syndicate

Best effort

Red herring

Prospectus

Underwriting fees

Registration

SEC

Questions

1. What is a financial intermediary and what role does it play?

2. What is the difference between demand deposits (checking accounts) and savings accounts?

3. What is the relationship between the interest rates that are paid on time deposits and the length of time to maturity of the certificates?

4. What are the advantages to the firm of selling securities privately to a financial institution instead of to the general investing public?

5. What is the role of an investment banker?

6. What is a syndicate, and what role does it play?

7. Why is it important that an underwriting not be overpriced? If it is overpriced, who will suffer losses?

8. Why do investors buy new issues of securities? What is the risk associated with buying shares of firms that are selling stock for the first time?

SELECTED READINGS

Dougall, Herbert E., and Jack E. Gaumnitz: *Capital Markets and Institutions,* 3rd ed. Englewood Cliffs, N.J., Prentice-Hall, Inc., 1975.

Gup, Benton E.: *Financial Intermediaries: An Introduction.* Boston, Houghton Mifflin Co., 1976.

Henning, Charles N., William Pigott, and Robert Haney Scott: *Financial Markets and the Economy.* Englewood Cliffs, N.J., Prentice-Hall, Inc., 1975.

Hutchison, G. Scott (ed.): *Why, When and How To Go Public*. New York, Presidents Publishing House, Inc., 1970.

Jones, Frank J.: *Macrofinance – The Financial System and the Economy*. Cambridge, Mass., Winthrop Publishers, Inc., 1978.

Kaufman, George G.: *Money, the Financial System and the Economy*, 2nd ed. Chicago, Rand McNally & Co., 1977.

Moore, Basil J.: *An Introduction to the Theory of Finance*. New York, The Free Press, 1968.

Robinson, Roland I., and Dwayne Wrightsman: *Financial Markets: The Accumulation and Allocation of Wealth*. New York, McGraw-Hill Book Co., 1974.

Learning Objectives

After completing this chapter you should be able to

1. Explain the role of market makers.

2. Distinguish between security exchanges and over-the-counter markets.

3. Illustrate how security transactions are reported in the financial press.

4. List the services provided by brokers.

5. Differentiate between the types of security orders.

6. Identify the costs of investing in securities.

7. Contrast cash and margin accounts.

8. State the purpose of the SIPC.

chapter 3

SECURITY MARKETS

There is a certain mystique to the novice and to the seasoned investor alike in the buying and selling of securities. This is due partially to the jargon that is used in the world of securities and partially to the fact that many dollars are earned and lost through these investments.

This chapter should eliminate some of the mystery by explaining the mechanics of buying and selling securities. The first section discusses security dealers and the role of security exchanges. The bulk of the chapter describes how the individual buys securities. The role of the broker, the types of orders and accounts, the delivery of the securities, and the brokerage cost of buying and selling are explained. The chapter ends with a brief discussion of the Securities Investor Protection Corporation (SIPC), which insures investors against losses incurred from the failure of a brokerage firm.

MARKET MAKERS

How securities are traded

Securities are bought and sold every day by investors who never meet each other. The market impersonally transfers securities from individuals who are selling to those who are buying. This transfer may occur on an *organized exchange*, such as the New York Stock Exchange, or on an unorganized, informal market that is called the *over-the-counter* (OTC) market. In either case there exist professional security dealers who make markets in securities and facilitate their transfer from sellers to buyers. Market makers for securities that are listed on the New York and American stock exchanges are called *specialists*. Market makers for over-the-counter securities are called *dealers*. These market makers offer to buy the securities from any seller and to sell the securities to any purchaser.

Round lots and odd lots

Transactions are made in either round lots or odd lots. A *round lot* is the basic unit for trading. For stock, it is usually 100 shares. Smaller transactions, e.g., 37 shares, are called *odd lots*. The round lot does not have to be 100 shares for all stocks. For example, for very cheap stocks (sometimes called cats and dogs), a round lot may be 500 or 1000 shares. For bonds, a round lot may be five $1000 bonds (i.e., $5000) or bonds totaling $10,000 or even $100,000 in face value. Odd lots are less profitable for brokerage firms and markets makers because the paperwork and the time involved in executing a trade are the same for ten shares or 100 shares, but the dollar volume of the trade is smaller for the odd lot. Thus, the price per share that the buyer is charged for an odd lot is usually higher than the price per share for a round lot. This additional fee may be hidden in a higher asking price for the security rather than being explicitly stated.

Bid and ask prices

Both specialists and dealers quote prices on a *bid and ask* basis; they buy at one price and sell at the other. For example, a market maker may be willing to purchase a specific stock for $20 per share and sell it for $21. The security is then quoted "20–21," which are the bid and ask prices. Selected quotes for over-the-counter stocks are illustrated in Exhibit 3–1. As can be seen in the exhibit, the market makers in Olympia Brewing are willing to purchase (bid for) the stock at $14 and to sell (ask) the stock for $14.50.

EXHIBIT 3–1. Selected Bid and Ask Quotes for Over-the-Counter Securities as of January 11, 1979*

Company	Price in Dollars	
	Bid	*Ask*
Beehive International	$4\frac{1}{2}$	5
Bob Evans	$22\frac{1}{2}$	$23\frac{1}{2}$
Olympia Brewing	14	$14\frac{1}{2}$
Southern Airways	$13\frac{1}{4}$	14
Wendys	$22\frac{1}{4}$	23

*Source: *The Wall Street Journal*, January 12, 1979, p. 28.

The difference between the bid and the ask is the *spread* (i.e., the $.50 difference between $14 and $14.50 for Olympia Brewing). Although the value of the security is the bid price, the investor pays the asking price. The spread, like brokerage commissions, is part of the cost of investing. These two costs should not be confused. The spread is one source of compensation for maintaining a market in the security. The broker's commission is compensation for executing the investor's purchase or sale order.

The spread may be quite large (at least as a percentage of the bid price). In Exhibit 3–1, for example, the spread is ½ point for Olympia Brewing, which is 3.6 per cent of the bid price. The spread for Beehive International is also ½ point, but that is 11.1 per cent of the bid. The proportional cost for the transaction of buying the stock of Beehive International is larger; although the value of one share of Beehive International is less than that of one share of Olympia Brewing, the cost of the paperwork associated with the transfer is about the same for the two stocks, regardless of the price of the shares.

The size of the differential between the bid and the ask is affected by various factors. If there are several market makers in a particular security, the spread tends to be smaller because of competition. The difference is also affected by the volume of transactions in the security and the number of shares that the firm has outstanding. If the volume of transactions or the number of outstanding securities is large, then the spread between the bid and the ask is small. AT&T's stock may be used as an example. If the stock is quoted 63–63⅛, the spread is only ⅛ of a point (i.e., 0.2 per cent of the bid). The spread is small because AT&T has 647.6 million shares outstanding and thousands of shares are traded daily. When the number of outstanding securities is small (i.e., the issue is *thin*), the spread is usually larger. In the case of Beehive International in Exhibit 3–1, the firm has 1.3 million shares outstanding, only a few hundred of which may be traded on a given day.

The spread is one source of profit for dealers as they turn over the securities in their portfolios. The market makers also earn income when they receive dividends and interest from the securities they own. Another source of profit is an increase in security prices, for the value of the dealer's portfolio rises. These profits are a necessary element of security markets because they induce the market makers to serve the crucial functions of buying and selling securities and of bearing the risk of loss from unforeseen price declines. These market makers guarantee to buy and sell at the prices they announce. Thus, an investor knows what the securities are worth at any given time and is assured that there is a place to sell current security holdings or to purchase additional securities. For this service, the market makers must be compensated, and this compensation is generated through the spread between the bid and ask prices, dividends and interest earned, and profits on the inventory of securities should their prices rise. (Of course, the market makers must bear any losses on securities that they hold when prices fall.)

Sources of profit for security dealers

**The determination
of security prices**

Although the bid and ask prices are quoted by market makers, the security prices are set by the demand from all buyers and the supply from all sellers of securities. Market makers try to quote prices that equate the supply with the demand (equilibrium price). If market makers bid too low a price, too few shares will be offered to satisfy the demand. If they ask too high a price, too few shares will be purchased, which will result in a glut, or excess shares, in their portfolios.

Could market makers set a security's equilibrium price? The answer is probably no. If the market makers tried to establish a price above the equilibrium price that is set by supply and demand, they would have to absorb all of the excess supply of securities that would be offered at the artificially higher price. Conversely, if the market makers attempted to establish a price below the equilibrium price, they would have to sell a sufficient number of securities to meet the excess demand that would exist at the artificially lower price. The buying of securities requires the delivery of the securities sold. Market makers do not have an infinite well of money with which to purchase the securities nor an unlimited supply of securities to deliver. They may increase or decrease their inventory, but they cannot indefinitely support the price by buying securities, nor can they prevent a price increase by selling them.

**Market makers
maintain an orderly
market**

Although market makers cannot set the market price, they perform an extremely important role: They maintain an orderly market in the security so that buyers and sellers will have an established market in which to trade securities. To establish this orderly market, the market makers offer to buy and sell at the quoted bid and ask prices. The market maker guarantees to make only one transaction at these prices. If a market maker sets too low a price for a certain stock, a large quantity will be demanded by investors. The market maker is required to sell only one round lot at this price and then may increase the bid and ask prices. The increase in the price of the stock will (1) induce some holders of the stock to sell their shares and (2) induce some investors who wanted to purchase the stock to drop out of the market.

If the market maker sets too high a price for the stock, a large quantity of shares will be offered for sale, but these shares will remain unsold. If the market maker is unable to or does not want to absorb all of these shares, the security dealer may purchase a round lot and then lower the bid and ask prices. The decline in the price of the stock will (1) induce some potential sellers to hold their stock and (2) induce some investors to enter the market by purchasing the shares, thereby reducing any surplus inventory of the market maker.

SECURITY EXCHANGES

Listed securities

When a company first sells its securities to the public, the securities are traded in the over-the-counter market. However, the firm may subsequently desire to have its securities listed on one of the major organized exchanges: the New York Stock Exchange (NYSE, or "the big board") or the American Stock Exchange (AMEX, or "the curb"). (Although the inclusion of the word *stock* in the names implies a market that deals solely in stock, some bond issues are also traded on these exchanges.) The listing of a firm's securities on a major exchange has an element of prestige, for it indicates that the company has grown above local importance and has attained a specified level of size and profitability. Listing may also facilitate selling securities in the future, for investors may be more willing to purchase the securities of companies whose stocks or bonds are publicly traded on an exchange.

In addition to these national exchanges, there are several regional stock exchanges, including the Philadelphia Exchange, the Midwest Exchange, and the Pacific Exchange. These regional exchanges list companies of particular interest to their geographic areas. For example, Aloha Airlines, Silver Dollar Mining, and Pacific Resources are primarily regional companies and are appropriately listed on the Pacific Exchange. Other firms in the region (e.g., Georgia Pacific), are listed on several exchanges. This company has a national market for its stock but is also of particular interest to investors living on the West Coast, since it has large timber holdings there. Its securities are actively traded on both the New York and the Pacific stock exchanges.*

Regional exchanges

The NYSE is the largest exchange and lists the securities of companies of national interest that are expected to maintain their relative position in their respective industry. The AMEX is smaller than the NYSE, but unlike the regional exchange, lists smaller firms with national followings. Many of the firms listed on the NYSE were originally listed on the AMEX. After achieving larger earnings and size, these firms transferred their securities from the AMEX to the NYSE.

The NYSE and the AMEX

The listing requirements for both exchanges are presented in Exhibit 3-2. As may be seen in the exhibit, the criteria that must be ful-

The listing requirements

---

*An investor may prefer to have orders executed on a regional exchange, because such execution will avoid the transfer taxes that are levied by New York.

EXHIBIT 3-2.   Listing Requirements

Requirements	New York Stock Exchange	American Stock Exchange
Number of shares held by the general public	1,000,000	400,000
Number of stockholders owning 100 or more shares	2,000	1,200, of which 500 must own 100 to 500 shares
Pretax income for latest fiscal year	$2,500,000	$750,000
Pretax income for preceding two years	$2,000,000	
Minimum aggregate value of shares publicly held	$16,000,000	$300,000
Tangible assets	$16,000,000	$4,000,000

filled in order to be listed are essentially the same for both exchanges, but the required sums are larger for the NYSE. In addition to the conditions stated in Exhibit 3–2, listing requires the firm to conform to certain procedures, including publishing quarterly reports, soliciting proxies, and announcing publicly any developments that may affect the value of the securities.

Once the securities are accepted for trading on an exchange, the firm must continue to meet the listing requirements. The exchange may delist the securities if the firm is unable to continue to meet the criteria for listing. Such delistings do occur, but over a period of years the number of listed securities has increased. Whereas 1253 stocks were traded on the NYSE in 1965, the number had grown to 2177 issues of 1575 companies in 1977.*

The reporting of listed stock transactions

Daily transactions on the listed exchanges are reported by the financial press (e.g., *The Wall Street Journal*). Weekly summaries are also reported in several publications (e.g., *The New York Times* and *Barron's*). Although there is variation in this reporting, the typical entry appears as follows:†

high	low	company	dividend	yield	PE	volume	high	low	last	net change
$64\frac{3}{4}$	$43\frac{1}{4}$	CBS	2.60	4.9	8	47	$53\frac{1}{2}$	53	$53\frac{1}{2}$	$-\frac{1}{2}$

"High" and "low" at the far left indicate the high and low prices ($64\frac{3}{4}$ and $43\frac{1}{4}$ respectively, for CBS) of the security during the preceding fifty-two weeks. Then the name of the company is given, usually in an abbreviated form, followed by the amount of the dividend ($2.60), which is generally the annual rate that the firm is paying. If the amount is not the annual rate, a symbol is placed after the dividend that refers the reader to a key explaining the particular exceptions. After the dividend the yield is given, which is the amount of the dividend divided by the price of the stock (4.9 per cent for CBS). This dividend yield is a measure of the flow of income that is produced by an investment in that particular stock. (Dividends are discussed in more detail in Chapter 15.) The PE ratio (8 for CBS) is the ratio of the price of the stock to the earnings per share of the firm. This ratio receives particular attention in investment analysis and is explained in detail in Chapter 16. For the purpose of this chapter, the PE ratio may be interpreted as a measure of what the market is willing to pay for the stock.

The last five entries pertain to the trading in that particular security on the preceding day. The first is the volume of transactions, which, for stocks, is expressed in hundreds of shares (i.e., 47 means 4700). (For

---

*Source: Maurice L. Farrell (ed.), *1978 Dow Jones Investor's Handbook,* (Princeton, N.J., Dow Jones Books, 1978), p. 70
†Data are taken from *The Wall Street Journal,* January 12, 1979.

bonds the volume is expressed in terms of the face value in denominations of $1000 of the bonds traded, e.g., 7 means that the face value of
the bonds that changed hands was $7000.) Next follow the price statis-
tics, which include the high, low, and closing prices. If the stock is
traded for a new high for the preceding 12 months, a "u" is placed next
to the value. If it is traded at a new low, a "d" is placed next to the
price. The last entry is the change in price from the closing price of the
previous day of trading.

Securities that are not traded on an exchange are traded over-the-
counter. The prices of many of these securities are also reported daily in
the financial sections of newspapers. However, these entries are usually
limited to the name of the company, the dividend, the volume of transactions, the closing bid and ask prices, and the net change in the *bid*
price from the previous day. Thus, a typical over-the-counter entry
would read as follows:

**The reporting of
OTC stock
transactions**

company	dividend	volume	bid-ask	net change
XYZ	.60	2	10–10½	–⅛

A share of XYZ pays a dividend of $.60 annually. The "2" in column 3
means that 200 shares were traded on the preceding trading day. The
closing bid and ask prices were $10 and $10.50 per share, and this closing bid price had decreased (was down) by $0.125 (⅛) from the preced-
ing day.

Quotes for over-the-counter securities are as readily available as
prices for securities that are traded on the organized exchanges. There
is an impressive system of communication for over-the-counter price
quotations called the National Association of Security Dealers Automat-
ed Quotation (NASDAQ) system. All major unlisted stocks are included
in this system. A broker may thereby readily obtain the bid and ask
prices of many over-the-counter stocks and bonds.

The distinction between the various exchanges and the over-the-
counter market is gradually being erased. For example, the financial
publications no longer report only NYSE transactions; they now report
the NYSE-Composite transactions, which include transactions in a particular security on many regional exchanges (e.g., the Midwest Exchange and the Pacific Exchange) as well as those on the NYSE.

**Movement toward a
national market
system**

The trend is in the direction of a national market system, and Congress has encouraged the formation of such a system. In September
1975, the Securities and Exchange Commission established the National
Market Advisory Board. The purpose of this board was to review the
current market structure and to recommend appropriate actions to facilitate the establishment of a national market system. There seems to be
no question that a national market system will emerge; the speculation
involves what form will it take and when will it be established.

THE MECHANICS OF
INVESTING IN SECURITIES

BROKERS

Individual investors purchase securities through brokers. Whereas some securities may be purchased directly from firms, the majority of purchases are made through brokerage firms such as Merrill Lynch Pierce Fenner and Smith or E. F. Hutton. These firms have salespersons who service the individual's account. In order to be permitted to buy and sell, these salespersons must pass a proficiency examination that is administered by the National Association of Security Dealers. Once the individual has passed the test, he or she is referred to as a registered representative and can buy or sell securities for customers' accounts.

Brokers are not experts

Although registered representatives must pass this proficiency examination, the investor should not assume that the broker is an expert. There are many aspects of investing, and even an individual who spends a considerable portion of the working day servicing accounts cannot be an expert on all of the aspects of investing. Thus, many recommendations are based on research that is done by analysts employed by the brokerage firm rather than by individual sales people.

Compensation through commissions

The individual should also realize that brokers make their living through selling. There are essentially two types of working relationships between the brokerage firm and the salesperson. In one case the firm pays a basic salary but the salesperson must bring in a specified amount in commissions, which go to the firm. After the minimum amount of sales have been met, the registered representative's salary is increased in proportion to the amount of additional commissions generated. In the second type of relationship, the salesperson's income is entirely related to the commissions generated. In either case the investor should realize that the broker's livelihood depends on the sale of securities. Thus, the broker's advice on investing may be colored by the desire to secure commissions. However, the investor is ultimately responsible for the investment decisions. Although advice may be requested from the broker, and it is sometimes offered even though unsolicited, the investor must weigh the impact of a specific investment decision in terms of fulfilling his or her personal goals.

Selecting a brokerage firm

Selecting a brokerage firm can be a difficult task. Various firms offer different services; for example, some may specialize in bonds, and others may deal solely in the securities of corporations located in a particular geographic region. The best source of information on stocks of local interest (e.g., local commercial banks) is often the small regional brokerage firm. Other brokerage firms offer a variety of services, including estate planning and life insurance, as well as the trading of stocks and bonds. Still other firms offer virtually no services other than executing orders at discount, (i.e., lower) commissions. Each investor therefore needs to identify his or her personal investment goals and decide on the strategies to attain those goals in order to select the firm that is best suited to that individual's needs.

Choosing a registered representative is perhaps a more difficult task than selecting a brokerage firm. This individual will need to know specific information, including the investor's income, other assets and outstanding debt, and financial goals, in order to give the best service to the account. Since people are reluctant to discuss, let alone disclose, some of this information, trust and confidence in the registered representative are probably the most important considerations in selecting a broker. Although any broker is capable of servicing the account, a rapport between the broker and the investor is particularly important if the relationship is going to be mutually successful. If the investor feels uncomfortable with a particular registered representative, he or she should ask to have the account transferred to another individual.

Selecting a broker

THE LONG POSITION

An investor has essentially only two courses of action, and these involve opposite positions. They are frequently referred to as the bull and bear positions and are symbolized by a statue, which is located outside the NYSE, of a bull and a bear locked in mortal combat.

If an investor expects a security's price to rise, the security is purchased. The investor takes a "long position" in the security in anticipation of the price increase. The investor is "bullish" because he or she believes that the price will rise. The long position earns profits for the investor if the price rises after the security has been purchased. For example, if an investor buys 100 shares of AT&T for $55 (i.e., $5500 plus brokerage fees) and the price rises to $60, then the profit on the long position is $5 per share (i.e., $500 on 100 shares before commissions).

The bullish position

Opposite the bullish position is the "bearish" position, in which the investor anticipates that the security's price will fall. The investor sells the security and holds cash or places the funds in interest-bearing short-term securities, such as treasury bills or a savings account. Some investors who are particularly bearish or who are willing to speculate on the decline in prices may even "sell short," which is a sale for future delivery. Since few investors do sell short, a detailed discussion of it is deferred until Chapter 18, which is concerned with some of the more speculative investment alternatives.

The bearish position

TYPES OF ORDERS

After an investor decides to purchase a security, a buy order is placed with the broker. The investor may ask the broker to buy the

The market order

security at the current price, which is the asking price set by the market maker. Such a request is a *market order*. The investor is not assured of receiving the security at the currently quoted price, since that price may change by the time the order is executed. However, the order is generally executed at or very near the asking price.

Purchase orders with specified prices

The investor may specify a price below the current asking price and wait until the price declines to the specified level. Such an order may be placed for one day (i.e., a *day order*), or the order may remain in effect indefinitely (i.e., a *good-till-canceled* order). Such an order remains on the books of the broker until it is either executed or canceled. If the price of the security does not decline to the specified level, the purchase is never made. Such an order may then become a nuisance for the broker, who must periodically inform the customer that the order is still in effect.

The stop loss order

After purchasing the security an investor may place a sell order, which may be at a higher or a lower price. An investor who desires to limit potential losses may place a *stop loss* order which specifies the price below the cost of the security at which the broker is authorized to sell. For example, if an investor buys CBS stock for $50 a share, a stop loss order at $45 limits the loss to $5 a share, plus the commission fees for the purchase and the sale. If the price of the stock should fall to $45, the stop loss order becomes a market order, and the stock is sold for $45. Such a sale protects the investor from riding the price of the stock down to $40 or lower. Of course, if the stock rebounds from $45 to $50, the investor has sold out at the bottom price.

The investor may also place a sell order above the purchase price. For example, the investor who purchases CBS stock at $50 may place a sell order at $60. Should the price of the stock reach $60, the order becomes a market order, and the stock is sold. Such an order puts a limit on the potential profit, for if the stock's price continues to rise, the investor who has already sold the stock does not continue to gain. However, the investor has protected the profit that resulted as the price increased from $50 to $60. In many cases the investor watches the stock's price rise, decides not to sell, and then watches the price subsequently decline. Sell orders are designed to reduce the possibility of this occurring.

The use of sell orders may be good strategy

The placing of sell orders can be an important part of an investor's strategy. For example, in the previous case the investor who purchased CBS stock at $50 may place sell orders at $45 and $60. If the price of the stock subsequently rises, this investor may change these sell orders. For example, if the price rises to $56 per share, the investor may change the sell orders to $52 and $64. This will preserve the capital invested, for the price of the stock cannot fall below $52 without triggering the sell order, but the price can now rise above $60 which was the previous upper limit for the sell order. By continuously raising the prices for the sell orders as the stock's price rises, the investor can continue to profit

Scott & Stringfellow Inc.
909 EAST MAIN STREET RICHMOND, VIRGINIA 23219
(804) 643-1811
MEMBERS
NEW YORK, AMERICAN (ASSOC.) AND RICHMOND STOCK EXCHANGES

OFFICES IN
BLUEFIELD, W. VIRGINIA 24701 (304) 325-3631
CULPEPER, VIRGINIA 22701 (703) 825-0783
STAUNTON, VIRGINIA 24401 (703) 886-2396
WARRENTON, VIRGINIA 22186 (703) 347-2820
WINCHESTER, VIRGINIA 22601 (703) 667-3311

PLEASE RETAIN THIS COPY FOR YOUR INCOME TAX RECORDS

WE CONFIRM THE FOLLOWING TRANSACTION SUBJECT TO CONDITIONS ON REVERSE SIDE.

YOU BOUGHT	YOU SOLD	SECURITY DESCRIPTION	PRICE
100		CLEVEPAK CORP	12 1/8

TRADE DATE AND NUMBER	SECURITY NUMBER	PRINCIPAL	COMMISSION		STATE TAX OR INTEREST	S.E.C. FEE	POSTAGE MISCELLANEOUS
04/12/77 112	179408	1,212.50	31.76				

ACCOUNT NUMBER	TYPE	✓	BRANCH	REG. REP.	CODES A	B	C	D
46078	1	8	01	19	1	1	2	

SEE REVERSE SIDE FOR EXPLANATION OF CODES.

8 223-54-4369

SETTLEMENT DATE	NET AMOUNT DUE *
04/19/77	1,244.26

CUSIP 186756102

EXHIBIT 3–3. Confirmation statement for the purchase of 100 shares of Clevepak Corporation.

from any price increase and at the same time protect the funds invested in the security against price declines.

The confirmation statement

Once the purchase has been made, the broker sends the investor a confirmation statement, an example of which is shown in Exhibit 3–3. This confirmation statement gives the number of shares and name of the security purchased (100 shares of Clevepak Corporation), the unit price ($12⅛), and the total amount that is due ($1244.26). The amount that is due includes both the price of the securities and the transactions fees. The major transaction fee is the brokerage firm's commission, but there may also be state transfer taxes and other miscellaneous fees. The investor has five business days after the date of purchase (April 12, 1977) to pay the amount that is due; the date by which payment must be made (April 19, 1977) is called the *settlement date*.

TYPES OF ACCOUNTS

A cash account

The investor must pay for the securities as they are purchased. This can be done either with cash or with a combination of cash and borrowed funds. The latter is called buying on *margin*. The investor then has either a cash account or a margin account. A cash account is what the name implies: The investor pays the entire cost of the securities (i.e., $1244.26 in Exhibit 3–3) in cash.

A margin account

When an investor uses margin, i.e., purchases the security partially with cash and partially with credit supplied by the brokers, he or she makes an initial payment that is similar to a down payment on a house and borrows the remaining funds that are necessary to make the purchase. To open a margin account, the investor signs an agreement with the broker that gives use of the securities and some control over the account to the broker. The securities serve as collateral for the loan.

The margin requirement

Should the amount of collateral in the account fall below a specified level, the broker can require that the investor put more assets in the account. This is called a *margin call*, and it may be satisfied by cash or additional securities. If the investor fails to meet a margin call, then the broker will sell some securities in the account to raise the cash needed to protect the loan.

The margin requirement is the minimum percentage of the total price that the investor must pay and is set by the Federal Reserve Board. Individual brokers, however, may require more margin. The minimum payment required of the investor is the value of the securities times the margin requirement plus the commission. Thus, if the margin requirement is 60 per cent and the price plus the commission on 100 shares of Clevepak Corporation is $1244.26, then the investor must supply $759.26 in cash ($727.50 + $31.76) and borrow $485 from the broker, who in turn borrows the funds from a commercial bank. The investor pays interest to the broker on $485. The interest rate will depend on the rate that the broker must pay to the lending institution. The investor, of course, may avoid the interest charges by paying the entire $1244.26 and not using borrowed funds.

The use of margin may increase the rate of return

Investors use margin to increase the potential return on the investment. When they expect the price of the security to rise, some investors pay for part of their purchases with borrowed funds. How the use of borrowed funds increases the potential return is illustrated in Exhibit 3–4. If the price of shares of Clevepak Corporation rises from $12\frac{1}{8}$ to 15, the profit is $255.74 (excluding commissions on the sale). If the investor pays the entire $1244.26, the percentage return is 20.5 per cent ([$255.74 ÷$1244.26]×100%). However, if the investor uses margin and pays for the stock with $759.26 in equity and $485 in borrowed funds, the investor's percentage return is increased (before the interest expense) to 33.7 per cent ([$255.74÷$759.26]×100%). In this case, the use of margin is favorable because it increases the investor's return on the invested funds.*

The use of margin may increase the percentage lost

Of course, if the price of the stock falls, the reverse occurs, i.e., the percentage loss is greater, as is illustrated in Exhibit 3–5. If the price

---

*How a firm may increase its earnings through the use of borrowed funds is explained in Chapter 14.

EXHIBIT 3–4. Potential Return Earned on Cash and Margin Purchases

	Cash Purchase, No Margin	*Margin Purchase*
Purchase price	$1244.26	$1244.26 cash — $759.26 debt — $485.00
Sale price	$1500.00	$1500.00
Profit on sale	$ 255.74	$ 255.74
Per cent earned	$\frac{\$ 255.74}{\$1244.26} \times 100\% = 20.5\%$	$\frac{\$ 255.74}{\$ 759.26} \times 100\% = 33.7\%$

EXHIBIT 3–5. Potential Loss From Cash and Margin Purchases

	Cash Purchase, No Margin	Margin Purchase
Purchase price	$1244.26	$1244.26 cash—$759.26 debt—$485.00
Sale price	$1000.00	$1000.00
Loss on sale	$ 244.26	$ 244.26
Per cent lost	$\frac{\$244.26}{\$1244.26} \times 100\% = 19.6\%$	$\frac{\$244.26}{\$759.26} \times 100\% = 32.2\%$

falls to $10, the investor loses $244.26 ($1244.26–$1000) before commissions on the sale. The percentage loss is 19.6 per cent ([$244.26 ÷$1244.26]×100%). However, if the investor uses margin, the percentage loss is increased to 32.2 per cent ([$244.26÷$759.26]×100%). Since the investor has borrowed money and thus reduced the amount of funds that he or she has committed to the investment, the percentage loss is greater. The use of margin magnifies not only the potential gain but also the potential loss. Because the potential loss is increased, buying securities on credit increases the element of risk that must be borne by the investor.

DELIVERY OF SECURITIES

Once the shares have been purchased and paid for, the investor must decide whether to leave the securities with the broker or to take delivery. (In the case of a margin account, the investor *must* leave the securities with the broker.) If the shares are left with the broker, they will be registered in the broker's name (i.e., in the *street name*). The broker then becomes custodian of the securities and is responsible for them. The broker sends a monthly statement of the securities that are being held in the street name to the investor. The monthly statement also includes any transactions that have taken place during the month, and any dividends and interest that have been received. The investor may either leave the dividends and interest payments to accumulate with the broker or receive payment from the broker.

Securities may be left with the broker

An example of a monthly statement is shown in Exhibit 3–6. The statement is divided into two parts. The top half enumerates all of the transactions during the month. According to this monthly statement, the investor made no purchases, deposited 158 shares of Martha Manning in the account on March 16, sold those shares on March 22 for $2\frac{5}{8}$, and received dividend payments from six firms. The investor also withdrew $633.80 from the account. The bottom half of the statement enumerates the investor's security position at the end of the month. In this exhibit the broker is holding ten stocks in nine companies for the cus-

The monthly statement

**Merrill Lynch
Pierce Fenner & Smith Inc.**
Member, Securities Investor Protection Corporation (SIPC)

**Statement of
Security Account**

ACCOUNT # 876 55352	A/E # 4265	PAGE # 1
SS OR ID # 000-00-0000	PERIOD ENDING 03 31 1978	
ACCOUNT EXECUTIVE NAME POOLED ACCOUNT		

DATE	BOT/RECD	SOLD/DELD	DESCRIPTION	PRICE	AMOUNT
			US FDS BALANCE FEB 24		$77.75CR
02 27			100 AMER FILTRONA CORP	* DIV	$18.00CR
03 15			325 CONTL GRP $2CVPF SRA	* DIV	$162.50CR
03 15			150 CONTINENTL GROUP INC	* DIV	$82.50CR
03 16	158		MANNING MARTHA CO	RCD	
03 17			100 MAGIC CHEF INC	* DIV	$12.50CR
03 20			905 VIRGINIA ELECT POWER	* DIV	$280.55CR
03 22			CHECK F		$383.52
03 22		158	MANNING MARTHA CO	2 5/8	$383.52CR
03 27			CHECK F 03/23		$633.80
03 27			100 LENOX INC	* DIV	$28.00CR
			US FDS CLOSING BALANCE		$28.00CR

LONG	SHORT	POSITION IN YOUR ACCOUNT	PX AS OF 03 30
100		AMER FILTRONA CORP	9.625
100		ATLANTA NATL R&T SBI	N/A
325		CONTL GRP $2CVPF SRA	24.750
150		**CONTINENTL GROUP INC	29.750
100		**GENERAL MEDICAL CORP	12.000
100		**LENOX INC	25.500
100		**MAGIC CHEF INC	8.625
100		NEW JERSEY NATL CORP	23.250
71		**S C M CORP	15.875
905		**VIRGINIA ELECT POWER	14.125

--------YEAR TO DATE DIVIDEND, INTEREST AND/OR CHARGE INFORMATION--------

TOTAL DIV REPORTABLE TO IRS: $672

MERRILL LYNCH RESEARCH FOCUSES ON THE MARKET OUTLOOK IN THIS MONTH'S
STATEMENT ENCLOSURE. FOR RECOMMENDATIONS, CALL YOUR ACCOUNT EXECUTIVE.

CODE 7076 REV. 11/77 PRINTED IN U.S.A.

EXHIBIT 3-6. Monthly statement for account with Merrill Lynch Pierce Fenner & Smith Inc.

FOR AN EXPLANATION OF SYMBOLS, PLEASE SEE REVERSE SIDE
PLEASE ADVISE YOUR ACCOUNT EXECUTIVE IMMEDIATELY OF ANY DISCREPANCIES ON YOUR STATEMENT.
WHEN MAKING INQUIRIES, PLEASE MENTION YOUR ACCOUNT NUMBER AND ADDRESS ALL CORRESPONDENCE TO THE OFFICE SERVICING YOUR ACCOUNT.
WE URGE YOU TO PRESERVE THIS STATEMENT FOR USE IN PREPARING INCOME TAX RETURNS.

tomer. The investor owns both the common and the preferred stock of Continental Group.

This monthly statement gives additional information that may be useful to the investor. Besides enumerating the securities held, it gives their prices as of a certain date. This may help in planning one's portfolio. The total dividends collected to date during the year are also given ($672). Since the total for the year must be reported to the Internal Revenue Service, the yearly total to date may aid in tax planning.

Advantages of leaving securities with the broker

The primary advantage of leaving the securities with the broker is convenience. The investor does not have to worry about storing the securities and can readily sell them, since they are in the broker's possession. The accrued interest and dividends may be viewed as a kind of forced savings program, for they may be immediately reinvested before the investor has an opportunity to spend the money elsewhere. The monthly statements are a readily accessible source of information for tax purposes.

There are, however, several important disadvantages in leaving the securities in the broker's name. If the brokerage firm fails or becomes insolvent, the investor may encounter difficulty in transferring the securities into his or her name and even greater difficulty in collecting any accrued dividends and interest.* In addition, since the securities are registered in the brokerage firm's name, interim financial statements, annual reports, and other announcements that are sent by the firm to its stockholders are mailed to the brokerage firm and not to the investor. The brokerage firm should forward this material to the investor but may not. To circumvent this problem an investor may write to the firm and ask to be placed on its mailing list. The firm may choose not to do so, for it sends the material to the brokerage firm and may view the additional mailing as an unnecessary expense. Another disadvantage is that shares held by the broker are voted by the broker.† However, since voting corporate shares is frequently only a formality, this disadvantage usually does not offset the potential custodial advantages of leaving the securities with the broker.

Disadvantages of leaving securities with a broker

Whether the investor ultimately decides to leave the securities with the broker or to take delivery depends on the individual investor. However, if the investor frequently buys and sells securities (i.e., is a *trader*), then the securities ought to be left with the broker in order to facilitate the transactions. If the investor is satisfied with the services of the broker and is convinced that the firm is financially secure, leaving the securities registered in the street name may be justified for reasons of convenience.

If the investor chooses to take delivery of the securities, that individual receives the stock certificates or bonds. Since the certificates may become negotiable, the investor may suffer a loss if they are stolen. Therefore, care should be taken to store them in a safe place (e.g., a lockbox or safe-deposit box in a bank). If the certificates are lost or destroyed, they can be replaced, but only at considerable expense in terms of money and time.

The storage of securities

THE COST OF INVESTING

Investing, like everything else, is not free. The individual must pay certain costs, the most obvious of which is commission fees. There may also be transfer fees, and some states tax the transfer of securities.

Commissions

---

*The Securities Investor Protection Corporation (SIPC) has reduced the investor's risk of loss from the failure of a brokerage firm. The SIPC is discussed later in this chapter.
†The investor may instruct the broker on how to cast the votes.

These last expenses tend to be small, but they do add up as the dollar value or the number of trades increases. (The investor may be able to avoid transfer taxes by trading on a local exchange instead of on the NYSE or AMEX.)

Commission costs are not insignificant, and for small investors they may constitute a substantial portion of the total amount spent on the investment. Commission rates are supposed to be set by supply and demand, but in reality only large investors (e.g., financial institutions such as insurance companies or mutual funds) are able to negotiate commissions with brokerage firms. These institutions do such a large dollar volume that they are able to negotiate lower rates. For these institutions, the commission rates (as a percentage of the dollar amount of the transaction) may be quite small.

Individuals, however, do not have this influence and generally have to accept the rate that is offered by the brokerage firm. Although the fee schedule may not be made public by the brokerage firm, the registered representative will generally tell the investor what the fee will be before executing the transaction.

In general, commission rates are quoted in terms of round lots of 100 shares. Most firms also set a minimum commission fee (e.g., $30) that may cover all transactions involving $1000 or less. Then, as the value of the 100 shares increases to greater than $1000, the fee also increases. However, this commission fee as a percentage of the dollar value of the transaction will usually fall. Such a hypothetical schedule is illustrated in Graph 3–1, which plots the dollar amount of the transac-

GRAPH 3–1.   Commission Fees to Purchase or Sell Stock

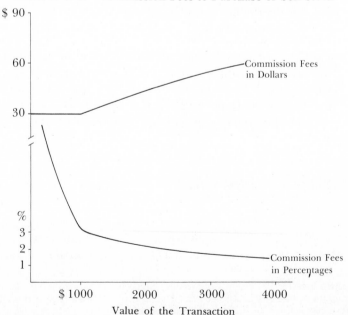

tion on the horizontal axis and the commission costs in dollars and as a percentage of the transaction on the vertical axis. Although the dollar cost of the commissions rises, the percentage cost declines as the amount invested increases.

Discount brokers

There are some brokerage firms that offer discount commission rates. However, these firms do not offer some of the services that are provided by the nondiscount houses. Research facilities and advisory services cost money and therefore are not available through discount brokers. If the individual does not need these services, the discount brokers may be a means to reduce the cost of investing by decreasing the commission fees.

Most discount houses require a minimum of transactions during a specified period. The more the individual buys and sells, the larger will be the discounts. However, if the investor does not anticipate trading securities, the discount brokers may prove to be just as expensive as the brokerage firms that offer research facilities and other services to their customers.

Implicit costs

Whereas commissions and other fees are explicit costs, there is also an important *implicit cost* of investing. This cost is the spread between the bid and the ask price of the security. As was explained earlier in this chapter, the investor pays the ask price but receives only the bid price when the securities are sold. This spread should be viewed as a cost of investing. Thus, if an investor wants to buy 100 shares of a stock quoted 20–21, the investor will have to pay $2100 plus commissions to buy stock that is currently worth (if it were to be sold) only $2000. If the commission rate is 2.5 per cent on purchases and sales, the cost of a *round trip* in the security (i.e., a purchase and a subsequent sale) is substantial, as is illustrated in Exhibit 3–7. First, the investor pays 2.5 per cent of $2100 to buy the stock, for a total cost of $2152.50 ($2100 + $52.50). If the stock is then sold, the investor will receive $1950 ($2000 − [0.025 × $2000] = $1950). Although the investor paid $2152.50, only $1950 will be received in the event that the stock must be liquidated at the bid price.

The cost of this purchase and the subsequent sale exceeded $200. This loss through the spread is regarded as a capital loss for income tax

EXHIBIT 3–7. Effect of the Spread on the Cost of Investing

Purchase		
Price	Commission	Total Cost
$2100.00	$52.50	$2152.50
Sale		
Price	Commission	Total Received
$2000.00	$50.00	$1950.00
Net Loss		
Total Cost Minus Total Received = Net Loss		
$2152.50 − $1950.00 = $202.50		

purposes. It is not considered to be part of the actual cost of investing. However, the individual investor should view this spread as an implicit cost of investing and should consider its impact on the total cost. As the previous example illustrates, the investor loses the difference in value between the bid and ask prices (the spread) upon purchasing the security. Thus, the bid price of the security must rise sufficiently to cover both the commission fees and the spread before the investor realizes any capital appreciation.

SIPC

FDIC insures commercial bank deposits

Most investors are aware that accounts in virtually all commercial banks are insured by the Federal Deposit Insurance Corporation (FDIC). Should an insured commercial bank fail, the FDIC reimburses the depositor for any losses up to $40,000. If a depositor has more than $40,000 on account at the time of the commercial bank's failure, the depositor becomes a general creditor for the additional funds.

This insurance has greatly increased the stability of the commercial banking system. Small depositors know that their funds are safe and therefore do not panic if a commercial bank fails (as one occasionally does). This stability simply did not exist prior to the formation of the FDIC. When panicky depositors tried to make withdrawals, some commercial banks could not meet the sudden requests for cash. Many had to close, which only increased the panic that caused the initial withdrawals. Since the advent of the FDIC, however, such panic withdrawals should not occur because the FDIC reimburses depositors (up to the limit) for any losses they sustain.

SIPC insures accounts with brokers

Like commercial banks, brokerage firms are also insured by an agency that was created by the federal government — the Securities Investor Protection Corporation (SIPC). The SIPC is managed by a seven-member board of directors. Five members are appointed by the President of the United States, and their appointments must be confirmed by the Senate. Two of the five represent the general public, and three represent the securities industry. The remaining two members are selected by the Secretary of the Treasury and the Federal Reserve Board.

The SIPC performs a role similar to that of the FDIC. Its objective is to preserve public confidence in the securities markets and industry. Although the SIPC does not protect investors from losses resulting from fluctuations in security prices, it does insure investors against losses arising from the failure of a brokerage firm. The insurance provided by the SIPC protects a customer's cash and securities up to $50,000. If a brokerage firm fails, the SIPC reimburses the firm's customers up to this specified limit. If a customer's claims exceed the $50,000 limit, that customer becomes a general creditor for the remainder of the funds.

The cost of this insurance is paid for by the brokerage firms that are members of the SIPC. All brokers and dealers that are registered with the Securities and Exchange Commission (SEC) and all members of national security exchanges must be members of the SIPC. Most security dealers are thus covered by the SIPC insurance. Some firms have even chosen to supplement this coverage by purchasing additional insurance from private insurance firms.

SUMMARY

This chapter has covered security markets and the mechanics of buying securities. Securities are traded on organized exchanges, such as the NYSE or in the informal over-the-counter markets. Securities are primarily bought through brokers, who buy and sell for their customers. The brokers obtain the securities from dealers, who make markets in them. These dealers offer to buy and sell at specified prices (i.e., quotes), which are called the bid and the ask. Brokers and investors obtain these prices through a sophisticated electronic system that transmits the quotes from the various dealers.

After securities are purchased, the investor must pay for them. This may be done with either cash or a combination of cash and borrowed funds. When the investor uses borrowed funds, that individual is buying on margin. Buying on margin increases both the potential return and the potential risk of loss for the investor.

Investors may take delivery of their securities or leave them with the broker. Leaving securities registered in the street name offers the advantage of convenience because the broker becomes the custodian of the certificates. Since the advent of the SIPC and its insurance protection, there is little risk of loss to the investor from leaving securities with the broker.

Terms to Remember

Organized exchange

Over-the-counter
   market

Specialist

Round lot

Odd lot

Bid and ask

Thin issue

Spread

Equilibrium price

"Big board"

AMEX

NASDAQ

SIPC

Registered
   representative

Bullish

Bearish

Long position

Market order

Day order

Good-till-canceled order

Stop loss order

Settlement date

Margin

Street name

Discount broker

Questions

1. What is the role of market makers, and how do they earn profits?

2. What is the difference between listed securities and securities traded in over-the-counter markets?

3. How is the market price of a security determined?

4. What is the difference between a market order, a good-till-canceled order, and a stop loss order?

5. In addition to commission fees, are there any costs of investing?

6. What are the advantages of leaving securities registered in the street name?

7. Why is it riskier to buy stocks on margin?

8. How is the SIPC similar to the FDIC?

SELECTED READINGS

New York Stock Exchange: Fact Book, issued annually.

Sobel, Robert: *The Big Board: A History of the New York Stock Market.* New York, The Free Press, 1965.

Sobel, Robert: *The Curbstone Brokers: The Origins of the American Stock Exchange.* New York, Macmillan Publishing Co., Inc., 1970.

Zarb, Frank, and Gabriel Kerekes: *The Stock Market Handbook.* Homewood, Ill., Dow Jones-Irwin, Inc., 1970.

Learning Objectives

After completing this chapter you should be able to

1. Identify the sources of risk.

2. State the advantage of diversification.

3. Construct a diversified portfolio.

4. Contrast the sources of expected return on an investment.

5. Define *beta coefficient.*

6. Understand how beta coefficients can be used in portfolio construction.

chapter 4
RISK

Investing involves risk and return. Until the 1950s investors dealt with these factors on an intuitive basis; there were no theoretical models to indicate the interrelationship between risk and return. However, with the pioneering work of several financial analysts, a theory of portfolio behavior and of the measures of risk and return developed.

This chapter gives a brief introduction to the modern portfolio theory, which is important because it establishes a framework with which to evaluate possible investments. This theory and its techniques require some understanding of mathematics and statistics; however, the explanations given here use only simple mathematics and stress intuitive reasoning.

The sources of risk are reviewed, followed by a discussion of the reduction of risk through diversification. The bulk of the chapter is devoted to measuring risk and expected return. Risk may be measured in several ways, but two methods will be emphasized: The first is the dispersion or variation from an investment's expected return, and the second is the responsiveness of the price of a specific asset relative to the prices of the market as a whole.

SOURCES OF RISK

The word *risk* is used frequently throughout this text. As was explained in the first chapter, there are several sources of risk. First, there is

Systematic risk

the risk arising from fluctuations in security prices. Asset values tend to move together. If security prices rise in general, the price of a specific security tends to rise in sympathy with the market. If market prices as a whole fall, the price of the specific security also tends to decline. This tendency for security prices to move together is referred to as systematic risk.

Unsystematic risk

In addition to systematic risk, there is the risk associated with the security itself. Since the individual buys specific securities, he or she must bear the risk associated with that investment. The investor may be unable to anticipate events that will affect a certain firm, such as a strike or a natural disaster, but these events may cause the value of the firm's securities to decline even when the prices for the majority of securities on the market rise. Other occurrences, such as a new discovery or an attempted take-over, may cause the price of a particular security to rise while those of the market in general decline. Such risk, which results from the dealings of the specific company, is referred to as unsystematic risk to differentiate it from the systematic risk associated with market movements.

The combined factors of systematic and unsystematic risk compose the total risk associated with the security. In addition, the investor must bear the risk of inflation. The rising prices of goods and services erode the purchasing power of the investor's assets. If the investor cannot earn a return that exceeds the rate of inflation, that individual may benefit more from spending the funds and consuming goods and services now.

Diversification reduces unsystematic risk

Unsystematic risk may be significantly reduced through diversification. This occurs when the investor purchases the securities of firms in different industries. Buying the stock of five telephone companies is not considered diversification, because the events that affect one company tend to affect the others. A diversified portfolio may consist of stocks and bonds issued by a telephone company, an electric utility, an insurance firm, a commercial bank, an oil refinery, a retail business, and a manufacturing firm. This is a diversified mixture of industries, and the impact of particular events on the earnings and growth of one firm need not apply to all of the firms; therefore, the risk of loss in owning the portfolio is reduced.*

How diversification reduces risk is illustrated in Graph 4–1, which shows the price performance of three stocks. Stock A's price rises each year, stock B's price fluctuates, and stock C's price is relatively stable. If the investor had bought stock A, the return would have been substantial, while stock C would have earned only a modest return. Purchasing stock B, however, could have resulted in a positive or a negative return, depending on the time that the security had been bought and sold.

The last quadrant illustrates what happens if the investor buys an equal dollar amount of each stock (i.e., buys a diversified portfolio). First, the value of the portfolio as a whole rises even though the value of an

---

*Since individual stock prices move together, even a diversified mixture of securities is not a completely diversified portfolio.

GRAPH 4-1. Prices of Three Stocks

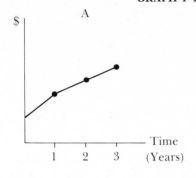

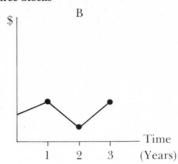

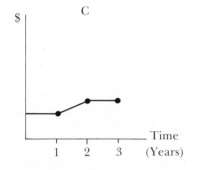

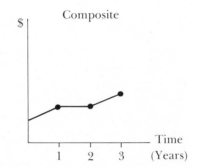

individual security may not. Second, and most importantly, the fluctuation in the value of the portfolio is less than the fluctuations in individual security prices. By diversifying the portfolio, the investor is able to reduce the risk of loss. Of course, the investor also gives up the possibility of a large gain (as was achieved by stock A).

In effect, a diversified portfolio reduces the element of unsystematic risk. The risk associated with each investment is reduced by accumulating a diversified portfolio of assets. Even if one company fails (or does extremely well), the impact on the portfolio as a whole is reduced through diversification. Distributing investments among different industries, however, does not eliminate systematic or market risk. The value of a group of securities will tend to follow the market values in general. The price movements of securities will be mirrored by the diversified portfolio; hence the investor cannot eliminate this source of risk.

How many securities are necessary to achieve a diversified portfolio that reduces and almost eliminates unsystematic risk? The answer is, surprisingly few. Several studies have found that risk has been significantly reduced in portfolios consisting of from ten to 15 securities.*

*For further discussion, see the following: John Evans and Stephen Archer, "Diversification and the Reduction of Dispersion: An Empirical Analysis," *Journal of Finance* (December 1968), pp. 761–767; Bruce D. Fielitz, "Indirect Versus Direct Diversification," *Financial Management* (Winter 1974), pp. 54–62; H. Latane and W. Young, "Tests of Portfolio Building Rules," *Journal of Finance*, (September 1969), pp. 595–612; and William Sharpe, "Risk, Market Sensitivity and Diversification," *Financial Analysts Journal*, (January–February 1972), pp. 74–79.

This reduction in unsystematic risk is illustrated in Graph 4–2. The vertical axis measures units of risk, and the horizontal axis gives the number of securities. Since market risk is independent of the number of securities in the portfolio, this element of risk is illustrated by a line, *AB*, that runs parallel to the horizontal axis. Regardless of the number of securities that an individual owns, the amount of market risk remains the same.

Portfolio risk

Portfolio risk, which is the sum of systematic and unsystematic risk, is indicated by line *CD*. The difference between line *AB* and line *CD* is the unsystematic risk associated with the specific securities in the portfolio. The amount of unsystematic risk depends on the number of securities held. As this number increases, unsystematic risk diminishes; this reduction in risk is illustrated in Graph 4–2 where line *CD* approaches line *AB*. For portfolios consisting of ten or more securities, risk involves primarily market (i.e., systematic) risk.

Such diversified portfolios, of course, do not consist of ten public utilities but of a cross section of American businesses. Investing $20,000 in ten stocks (i.e., $2000 for each) may achieve a reasonably well diversified portfolio. While such a portfolio may cost somewhat more in commissions than two $10,000 purchases, the small investor does achieve a diversified mixture of securities, which should reduce the risk of loss associated with an investment in a specific security. Unfortunately, the investor must still bear the systematic risk associated with investing and the risk of loss in purchasing power that results from inflation.

THE EXPECTED RETURN ON AN INVESTMENT

The portfolio theory is primarily concerned with systematic and unsystematic risk. Its purpose is to determine that combination of return and risk that will produce optimal results for the individual investor. To do this, a means for measuring return and risk must be devised. Such measurement is the focus of the next two sections of this chapter.

Sources of return: Income and price appreciation

An investment may offer a return from either of two sources. The first source is the flow of income that may be generated by the investment. A savings account yields the holder a flow of interest income while the account is held. The second source of return is capital appreciation. If an investor buys stock and its price subsequently increases, the investor will receive a capital gain. All investments offer the investor either potential income or capital appreciation. Some investments, like the savings account, offer only income, whereas other investments may offer only capital appreciation. For example, an investment in land may result in capital appreciation but produce no income. In fact, such an investment may require expenditures (e.g., property tax) on the part of the investor.

Return is anticipated

When the individual makes an investment, a return is *anticipated*. The yield that is achieved on the investment is not known until after the

GRAPH 4–2.   Portfolio Risk Consisting of Systematic and Un-
     systematic Risk

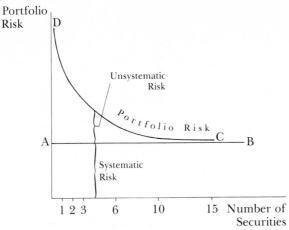

investment is sold and converted to cash. It is important to differentiate between the expected return and the realized return: The expected return induces a response (i.e., to purchase an asset), and the realized return is the result of making the investment. Frequently these are not equal, for events occur that alter the value of an investment and thus affect its return. Only in a world of certainty would the realized and expected yields be equal. Under those circumstances, of course, there would be no risk.

    Return or yield is frequently expressed as a percentage. Equation 1 is a formula for determining the anticipated return on an investment.

(1)   Expected return = expected income + expected capital appreciation

The total return that is anticipated is the sum of the two components: the expected flow of income and the expected capital gain. For example, if an investor buys stock for $20 per share that is expected to pay a dividend of $1 per share and if the investor expects the value of the stock to increase by 7 per cent annually, then the anticipated return for one year is 12 per cent. This is illustrated in the following equation: **The total anticipated return**

$$\text{Expected return} = \frac{\$1}{\$20} + .07 = 12\%$$

    The realized return on the investment may be expressed by the same general equation: **The realized return**

(2)   Realized return = income return + capital gain or loss

For example, if an investor purchases the stock in the previous example and sells it after a year for $30 per share, the realized annual yield is 55 per cent.

$$\text{Realized return} = \frac{\$1}{\$20} + \frac{(\$30 - \$20)}{\$20} = 55\%$$

In this case the realized rate of return exceeds the expected rate of return. If, however, the price of the stock declines from $20 to $15 per share, the realized rate of return is −20 per cent, which is less than the expected rate of return on the investment.

$$\text{Realized return} = \frac{\$1}{\$20} + \frac{(\$15 - \$20)}{\$20} = -20\%$$

Virtually all investments involve risk of loss. The expected return is an incentive for accepting this risk. An investor's required rate of return on an investment is the return that is necessary to induce that investor to bear the risk associated with a particular investment. Since each investor's willingness to bear risk is different, the required rate of return differs from one investor to another.

The investor's attitude toward risk   Despite this difference, virtually all investors have the same attitude toward risk — they do not like to bear it. In order to induce them to bear additional risk, the potential return from the investment must be increased. Such a relationship between risk and expected return is consistent with the investor's aversion to risk taking. A greater anticipated return is necessary to induce the investor to bear an increased risk of loss.

MEASURES OF RISK

THE RANGE

High and low prices   The range refers to an asset's high and low prices for a particular period, e.g., a year. The investor often encounters references to the range in a security's price, as illustrated by the following statements: "The stock is trading near its low for the year," or "The shares reached a new high."

The high and low prices of a stock are readily available in many financial newspapers (e.g., *The Wall Street Journal*). Some investors plan their strategy *as if* a stock trades within a price range. If the stock is near the low for the year, it may be a good time to purchase. Correspondingly, if it is trading near the high for the year, it may be a good time to sell. The range in the stock's price, then, can be used as a guide to strategy, because the price tends to gravitate to a mean between these two extremes. In other words, there is a "central tendency" for the price of the stock. The range in a stock's price then becomes a measure of risk. Stocks with wider ranges are "riskier" because their prices tend to deviate further from the average (mean) price.

One problem with using the range as a measure of risk is that two securities of different prices can have the same range. For example, a stock whose price ranges from $10 to $30 has the same range as a stock whose price varies from $50 to $70. The range is $20 in both cases, but an increase from $10 to $30 is a 200 per cent increment, whereas the increase from $50 to $70 is only a 40 per cent increase. The price of the latter stock appears to be more stable; hence, less risk is associated with this security, even though both stocks involve equal risk according to the range.

DISPERSION AROUND THE EXPECTED PRICE

The problem that is inherent in using the range to determine risk may be avoided by analyzing the dispersion around the expected price. Unlike the range, this technique considers not only the two extreme prices but all of the prices at which the stock may trade. If there is not much difference between most of these prices, i.e., they are close together, then the dispersion will be small. If most of these prices are near the extremes (near the high or the low price), then the dispersion will be large. The larger this dispersion, the greater is the risk associated with a particular stock. (A statistical measure of dispersion, the standard deviation, is presented in the appendix to this chapter, p. 75–77.)

This concept is perhaps best illustrated by a simple example. An investor believes that the expected price of two stocks is $15, but they could have the following prices:

Dispersion illustrated

Stock A	Stock B
13\frac{1}{2}$	$11
14	11$\frac{1}{2}$
14$\frac{1}{4}$	12
14$\frac{1}{2}$	12$\frac{1}{2}$
15	15
15$\frac{1}{2}$	17$\frac{1}{2}$
15$\frac{3}{4}$	18
16	18$\frac{1}{2}$
16$\frac{1}{2}$	19

Although the expected price is the same for both stocks, there is considerable difference in the possible prices. Stock A's prices are very close to the expected price, whereas stock B's prices are closer to the possible high and low prices. The possible prices of stock A cluster around the expected price. Since there is considerably less fluctuation in its prices, it is the less risky of the two securities.

These differences in risk are illustrated in Graph 4–3, which plots the various stock prices on the horizontal axis and the frequency of their occurrence on the vertical axis. This is basically the same informa-

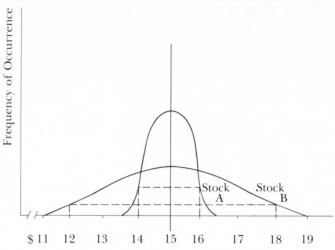

GRAPH 4–3. Distribution of the Prices of Two Stocks

tion that was previously given for stocks A and B, except that more price observations would be necessary to construct such a graph. Most of stock A's anticipated prices are close to the expected price, so the frequency distribution is higher and narrower. The frequency distribution for stock B's prices is lower and wider, which indicates a greater dispersion in that stock's price.

Larger dispersion means more risk

The larger dispersion around the expected price implies that the stock involves greater risk because the investor can be less certain of the stock's future price. The larger the dispersion, the greater is the chance of loss from the investment, and, correspondingly, the greater is the chance of gain. However, this potential for increased gain is concomitant with bearing more risk. Stock A involves less risk; it has the smaller dispersion. But it also has less potential for a large gain. A reduction in risk also means a reduction in possible return on the investment.

The expected return on the portfolio

Just as expected return and dispersion apply to individual securities, they may also be applied to an entire portfolio. A group or portfolio of securities also has an expected return and a dispersion around that expected return. Of concern to the investor are not only the anticipated return and the risk associated with each investment but also the expected return and the risk associated with the portfolio as a whole. This aggregate is, of course, the result of the individual investments and of each one's weight in the portfolio (i.e., the value of each asset, expressed in percentages, in proportion to the total value of the portfolio).

Consider two portfolios consisting of the following three stocks:

Stock	Expected Return
1	8.3%
2	10.6
3	12.3

In the first portfolio, equal amounts (e.g., $3333.33) are invested in each stock. The average expected return when the weight of each stock is equal is the sum of the expected returns divided by the number of stocks in the portfolio.

$$\frac{31.2}{3} = 10.4\%$$

Now consider the second portfolio. If 25 per cent of the total value of the portfolio is invested in stocks 1 and 2 and 50 per cent is invested in stock 3, the expected return is more heavily weighted in favor of stock 3. The expected return is a weighted average of each return times its proportion in the portfolio.

Expected return	×	weight (percentage value of stock in proportion to total value of portfolio)	=	weighted average
8.3	×	.25	=	2.075
10.6	×	.25	=	2.650
12.3	×	.50	=	6.150

The expected return is the sum of these weighted averages.

$$
\begin{array}{r}
2.075\% \\
2.650 \\
\underline{6.150} \\
10.875\%
\end{array}
$$

Thus, the expected return has been increased from 10.4 per cent to 10.875 per cent by weighting the portfolio in favor of stock 3.

Portfolio risk

Unfortunately an aggregate measure of the portfolio's risk is difficult to construct. Security prices tend to move together, but there can be considerable differences in these price movements. For example, construction stock prices may decline rapidly during a recession while retailing stock prices may decline only moderately. The relationship among the assets in the portfolio must also be considered in the construction of a measure of risk associated with the entire portfolio. In more advanced texts, this inner relationship among assets in a portfolio is called *covariation*.

The impact of prices moving together

Although the development of a measure of covariation and a discussion of its effect on the measurement of risk go beyond the scope of this text, the idea may be illustrated by a simple graph. The price movements of two stocks in three different instances are shown in Graph 4–4. In the first case the price movements are exactly opposite. In essence, in a portfolio whose value is divided equally between the two stocks, the effect of the fluctuations is canceled. In the second case the

GRAPH 4–4.   Stock Price Movements, Individually and Combined

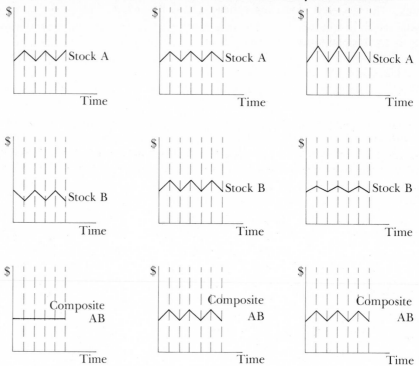

prices move exactly together. In a portfolio consisting of equal amounts of funds invested in these two securities, the effect of the price fluctuations is not reduced, and hence there is no reduction in risk. In the third case the price of stock A fluctuates more than that of stock B, so the impact of the fluctuations on the portfolio as a whole is reduced as the investor increases holdings of stock B relative to stock A. Risk is reduced but not erased by this substitution.

An investor should not consider a specific investment solely in terms of that asset; instead, the potential impact of the asset on the portfolio as a whole should influence the investing process. Without such consideration, a particular investment could prove to be counterproductive if it were to reduce the potential return on the portfolio as a whole without reducing the element of risk.

BETA COEFFICIENTS

Beta coefficients: Responsiveness of the stock's price to changes in the market

Another measure of risk is the responsiveness of a stock to changes in the market. This responsiveness may be measured by the ratio of the percentage change in the price of the stock relative to the percentage change in the market.

$$\frac{\text{Percentage change in the price of stock X}}{\text{Percentage change in the market}}$$

The price movement of the market may be measured by an index, such as Standard & Poor's 500 stock index or any other broad-based measure of stock prices.

This measure of risk, which has been given the name *beta coefficient*, has become widely used. Since a beta coefficient measures a stock's price relative to the prices of the market, it is measuring the systematic risk associated with the particular stock.

A beta coefficient of 1 means that the stock's price moves exactly with an index of the market as a whole. A 10 per cent increase in the market produces a 10 per cent increase in the price of the specific stock. Correspondingly, a 10 per cent decline in the market results in a 10 per cent decline in the value of the stock. A beta coefficient of less than 1 implies that the price of the stock tends to fluctuate less than the market as a whole. A coefficient of 0.7 indicates that the stock's price will rise only 7 per cent as a result of a 10 per cent increase in the market but will fall by only 7 per cent when the market declines by 10 per cent. A coefficient of 1.2 means that the price of the stock will rise by 12 per cent if market values increase by 10 per cent, but the price of the stock will decline by 12 per cent when market values decline by 10 per cent.

The numerical value of beta coefficients

The greater the beta coefficient, the more risk is associated with the individual stock. High beta coefficients may indicate exceptional profits during rising market prices, but they also indicate greater losses during declining market prices. Stocks with high beta coefficients are referred to as aggressive. The converse is true for stocks with low beta coefficients, which should underperform the market during periods of rising stock prices but outperform the market as a whole during periods of declining prices. Such stocks are referred to as defensive.

The higher the beta coefficient, the greater the risk

This relationship between the price of a specific security and the market index as a whole is illustrated in Graphs 4–5 and 4–6. In each graph the horizontal axis represents the percentage change in the market index and the vertical axis represents the percentage change in the price of the individual stock. The line *AB*, which represents the market, is the same in both graphs. It is a positive-sloped line that runs through the point of origin and is equidistant from both axes (i.e., it makes a 45-degree angle with each axis).

Graph 4–5 illustrates the case of a stock with a beta coefficient of greater than 1. Line *CD* represents a stock the price movements of which rise (and decline) more rapidly than those of the market. It has a beta coefficient of 1.2, so when the market index rises by 10 per cent, this stock's price rises by 12 per cent.

Graph 4–6 illustrates a stock with a beta coefficient of less than 1. Line *EF* represents a stock the price movements of which rise (and decline) more slowly than those of the market. In this case the beta coeffi-

GRAPH 4–5. Stock with a Beta Coefficient of Greater Than 1.0

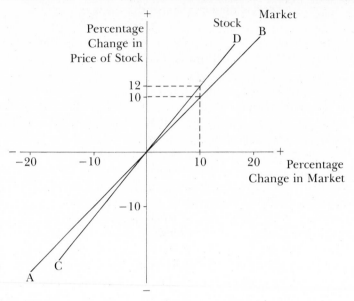

GRAPH 4–6. Stock with a Beta Coefficient of Less Than 1.0

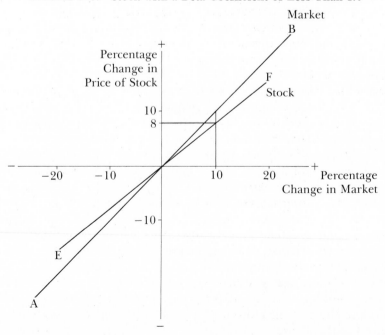

TABLE 4–1. *Selected Beta Coefficients*

COMPANY	BETA COEFFICIENT
AT&T	0.54
Exxon	0.67
Johnson & Johnson	0.72
Philip Morris, Inc.	0.77
IBM	0.84
Revlon, Inc.	0.97
GE	1.01
E. I. DuPont	1.08
Boeing	1.14
CBS, Inc.	1.20
Alcoa	1.23
K-Mart	1.30
RCA	1.35
McDonalds	1.40

Source: The beta coefficients were computed by Wilshire Associates, as reported in *Forbes,* (June 12, 1978), p. 48.

cient is 0.8, so when the market index rises by 10 per cent, this stock's price increases by only 8 per cent.

Beta coefficients vary among firms. This is illustrated in Table 4–1, which presents the beta coefficients for selected firms as computed by Wilshire Associates. As may be seen in the table, some firms (e.g., AT&T and Exxon) have relatively low beta coefficients, while the coefficients for other firms (e.g., McDonalds and RCA) are much higher. Investors who are willing to bear more risk may be attracted to these stocks with the higher beta coefficients, because when stock market prices rise, these stocks tend to outperform the market. Investors who are less inclined to bear risk may prefer the stocks with low beta coefficients. Although these investors forgo some potential return during rising market prices, they should suffer milder losses during periods of declining stock prices.

Variations in beta coefficients

Computing percentage changes for a significant number of securities over a reasonably long period is an extremely time-consuming and tedious job. Fortunately, the investor may obtain beta coefficients from several sources. The *Value Line Investment Survey* supplies beta coefficients for all securities covered by the service. The information may also be available through the investor's brokerage firm. Although not all brokers compute beta coefficients, the research departments of the larger brokerage firms determine beta coefficients, and these are available to the firm's customers.

Beta coefficients are available

The assumption that beta coefficients are reliable predictors of future stock price behavior may present a problem for investors. For example, a conservative investor who desires stocks that will be stable will probably purchase stocks with a low beta coefficient. An investor selecting a stock with a beta coefficient of 0.6, will certainly be upset if the market prices decline by 10 per cent and this stock's price falls by 15 per cent, since a beta coefficient of 0.6 indicates that the stock price

Beta coefficients may be unreliable predictors

should decline by only 6 per cent when market prices decline by 10 per cent.

Unfortunately, beta coefficients are constructed with historical price data. Although such data may be accumulated and tabulated for many years, it still does not mean that coefficients based on historical data will be accurate predictors of future price movements in individual stocks. Beta coefficients can and do change over time. Empirical studies have shown that beta coefficients for individual securities tend to be very unstable.* Therefore, the investor should not rely solely on these coefficients for selecting a particular security. However, beta coefficients do give the investor some indication of the systematic risk associated with specific stocks and thus can play an important role in the selection of a security.

Beta coefficients may help an investor construct a portfolio

Unlike the beta coefficient for individual securities, the beta coefficient for a portfolio composed of several securities is fairly stable over time. Changes in the different beta coefficients tend to average out; while one stock's beta coefficient is increasing, the beta coefficient of another stock is declining. A portfolio's historical beta coefficients, then, can be used as a tool to forecast its future beta coefficient, and this projection should be more accurate than forecasts of an individual security's beta coefficient.

Since a portfolio's beta coefficient is stable, the investor can construct a portfolio that responds in a desired way to market changes. For example, the average beta coefficient of the portfolio illustrated in Table 4–1 is approximately 1.† If an equal dollar amount were invested in each security, the value of the portfolio should follow the market values fairly closely, even though individual beta coefficients are greater or less than 1. This tendency of the portfolio to mirror the performance of the market should occur even though selected securities may achieve a return that is superior (or inferior) to that of the market as a whole. Hence, the beta coefficient for the portfolio may be a more useful tool than the beta coefficient for individual securities.

Beta coefficients may also be used in portfolio construction if the investor believes that the market prices will move in a particular direction. For example, if the individual anticipates an increase in prices, the investor may construct an aggressive portfolio consisting solely of securities with high beta coefficients. However, if the anticipated price increases do not occur and the market prices decline, such a strategy may result in a considerable loss.

SUMMARY

All investments involve risk because the future is uncertain. Although the individual anticipates income or capital appreciation, the

---

*See Robert A. Levy, "Stationarity of Beta Coefficients," *Financial Analysts Journal,* (November–December 1971), pp. 55–62.
†The average for the 14 stocks in Table 4–1 is 1.02.

realized return on an investment may be considerably different from the expected return.

There are several sources of risk. First, there is the risk associated with the particular asset. This risk is often called nonmarket or unsystematic risk because it relates only to the specific asset. This source of risk can be virtually eliminated by diversification. By owning a variety of assets (e.g., stocks in several companies in different industries), the investor reduces the risk associated with a particular asset.

Asset prices tend to move together. This second source of risk is called market or systematic risk. It cannot be erased by diversifying the portfolio. A diversified portfolio's prime source of risk is price movements in the market as a whole.

The investor must also bear the risk of loss that results from inflation. Unless the return on an investment exceeds the rate of inflation, the investor suffers a loss of purchasing power.

Since all investments involve risk, there should be a method to measure risk. A simple method utilizes the range in an asset's price. The wider the range, the greater is the element of risk.

A more sophisticated technique to measure risk is the dispersion around the expected price. If the possible prices of an investment are many and vary considerably from the anticipated return, the dispersion is large, and the risk associated with the asset is increased.

Another measure of risk determines the responsiveness of a particular asset's price to market prices as a whole. This measure is called a beta coefficient. The higher the beta coefficient, the greater is the risk associated with the asset, because its price will rise and decline faster than market prices as a whole.

During the 1970s, beta coefficients become an important tool in the construction of portfolios. Although the coefficients change for individual securities, they are stable for the portfolio as a whole. Hence, they may be used by investors as a means to help construct a portfolio that is consistent with the investor's willingness to bear risk.

Terms to Remember

Systematic risk	Diversification	Dispersion
Unsystematic risk	Expected return	Beta coefficient
Portfolio risk	Range	

Questions

1. What is the difference between market or systematic risk and nonmarket or unsystematic risk?

2. What is a diversified portfolio? What source of risk is reduced through diversification? How many securities are necessary to achieve this reduction in risk?

3. What are the sources of return on an investment? What is the difference between the expected and the realized return?

4. Why are a stock's high and low prices a poor measure of risk?

5. What is a beta coefficient? What do beta coefficients of 0.5, 1, and 1.5 mean?

6. How may beta coefficients be used by investors to aid in the construction of a portfolio?

SELECTED READINGS

Brealey, Richard A.: *An Introduction To Risk and Return From Common Stocks*. Cambridge, Mass., M.I.T. Press, 1969.

Fischer, Donald E., and Ronald I. Jordan: *Security Analysis and Portfolio Management*. Englewood Cliffs, N.J., Prentice-Hall, Inc., 1975.

Levy, Robert A.: "Stationarity of Beta Coefficients." *Financial Analysts Journal*. November–December 1971, pp. 55–62.

Lorie, James H., and Mary T. Hamilton: *The Stock Market: Theories and Evidence*. Homewood, Ill., Richard D. Irwin, Inc., 1973.

Malkiel, Burton G.: *A Random Walk Down Wall Street*, college edition revised. New York, W. W. Norton & Co., Inc., 1975, chapter 8 (pp. 176–203).

Rosenberg, Barr, and James Guy: Prediction of beta from investment fundamentals. *Financial Analysts Journal*, May–June 1976, pp. 60–72.

Sharpe, William F.: *Investments*. Englewood Cliffs, N.J., Prentice-Hall, Inc., 1978.

APPENDIX: Standard Deviation as a Measure of Risk

One measure of risk is the standard deviation, which is a measure of dispersion around a central tendency. The larger the dispersion (i.e., the greater the standard deviation), the greater is the risk. How this measure is constructed and interpreted may be illustrated by the possible prices for stocks A and B, which were presented in the body of this chapter. Their prices were as follows:

Stock A	Stock B
13\frac{1}{2}$	$11
14	11$\frac{1}{2}$
14$\frac{1}{4}$	12
14$\frac{1}{2}$	12$\frac{1}{2}$
15	15
15$\frac{1}{2}$	17$\frac{1}{2}$
15$\frac{3}{4}$	18
16	18$\frac{1}{2}$
16$\frac{1}{2}$	19

As was previously discussed, stock B's prices are more widely dispersed than stock A's prices; hence, this security involves more risk.

The standard deviation is calculated as follows:
1. For the range of prices observed, subtract the individual price of the particular stock from the average or expected price.
2. Square this difference.
3. Add these squared differences.
4. Divide this sum by the number of observations less 1.
5. Take the square root.
   For stock A the standard deviation is determined as follows:

How standard deviation is computed

Average Price	Individual Price	Difference	Difference Squared
$15	$13.50	1.5	2.2500
15	14	1	1.0000
15	14.25	.75	.5625
15	14.50	.5	.25
15	15	0	0
15	15.50	−.5	.25
15	15.75	−.75	.5625
15	16	−1	1.0000
15	16.50	−1.5	2.2500

The sum of the squared differences: 8.1250

GRAPH 4–7. Distribution of the Prices of Two Stocks

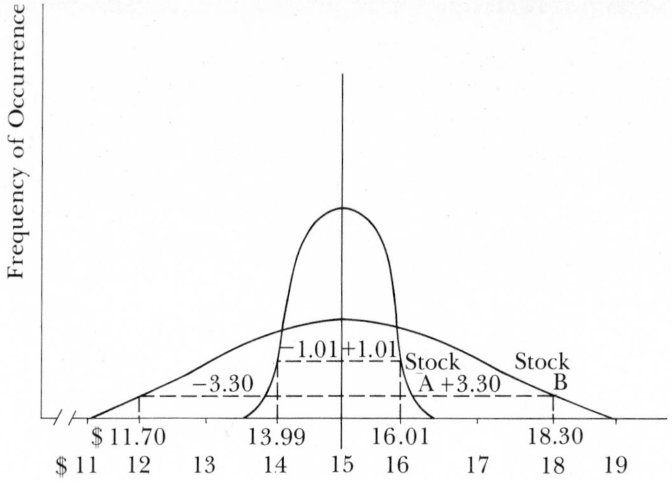

The sum of the squared differences divided by the number of observations less 1: $\dfrac{8.1250}{8} = 1.0156$

the square root: $\sqrt{1.0156} = \pm 1.01$

thus, the standard deviation is ± 1.01

Interpretations of the standard deviation

The investor must then interpret this result. Plus and minus one standard deviation has been shown to encompass approximately 66 per cent of all observations (in this case that is 66 per cent of the prices). The standard deviation for stock A is ± 1.01, which means that approximately two thirds of the prices fall between $13.99 and $16.01. These prices are simply the expected average price ($15) plus $1.01 and minus $1.01 (i.e., plus and minus the standard deviation).

For stock B the standard deviation is ± 3.30, which means that approximately two thirds of the expected prices fall between $11.70 and $18.30. Stock B's prices have a wider dispersion from the average price, and this fact is indicated by the greater standard deviation.

These differences in the standard deviations are illustrated in Graph 4–7, which reproduces Graph 4–3 but adds the standard deviations. The average price for both stocks is $15, but the standard deviation is greater for stock B than for stock A (i.e., ±$3.30 for B versus ±$1.01 for A). By computing the standard deviation, the analyst quantifies risk. This will help in the selection of individual securities, since the investor usually will consider only those assets with the least risk for a given expected return.

Learning Objectives

After completing this chapter you should be able to

1. Identify the taxes that affect investment decision making.

2. Define progressive tax.

3. Distinguish between ordinary income and capital gains.

4. Explain how pension plans are tax shelters.

5. Differentiate between estate and inheritance taxes.

6. Explain the role of security regulation and the SEC.

chapter 5
THE TAX AND REGULATORY ENVIRONMENT

There are many laws that affect investments, but two general classes predominate: taxation and the regulation of security markets. Taxation influences investment decisions because it alters the potential return on an asset. Regulation affects investing by altering the environment in which the decisions are made.

Taxation is imposed by all levels of government. Investment income, profits from price appreciation, and even the assets themselves may be subject to taxation. For this reason, considerable time and effort are devoted to reducing taxes and sheltering income.

This chapter briefly covers the main sources of taxation and offers several illustrations of tax shelters. Tax laws change virtually every year. This is unfortunate in that much of the specific information (e.g., tax rates) contained in this chapter may already be outdated. However, the basic tax principles tend to remain the same, even though specific laws may have changed.

The regulation of security markets is designed to provide the investor with information. Both the federal and state governments have passed "disclosure laws." This chapter includes a short discussion of the regulatory environment of investment. Like the tax laws, security laws change over time.

The investor needs to be aware of the most recent laws and how they may affect specific investment decisions. For this reason the individual should consult a lawyer or an accountant for the most recent laws and their application.

INCOME TAXATION

Personal and corporate income is subject to taxation. These taxes are levied both by the federal government and by many state governments. Some states also permit the taxation of income by their municipalities. For example, the income of New York City residents is subject to federal, state, and city taxes.

Tax rates are not evenly applied

In general, the income taxes apply to all sources of income. Thus, dividend and interest income is subject to this taxation. However, the tax is not applied evenly to the returns from all investments. For example, dividend income is taxed at a higher rate than are long-term capital gains. This difference in taxation may alter an investor's choice of assets by encouraging the purchase of securities with a higher potential for growth and capital gain in preference to securities that offer higher current income.

Progressivity

Income taxes levied by the federal government and by many state governments are progressive. A tax is *progressive* if the tax *rate* increases as the tax base (e.g., income) rises. If the tax rate declines as the base increases, the tax is *regressive*. If the tax rate remains constant, the tax is *proportionate*.

A normative question

Many individuals believe that taxes should be progressive, so that individuals with higher incomes or more wealth bear a larger proportion of the cost of government. It is on this basis that many regressive taxes are criticized. Regressive taxes place a greater share of the cost of government on those individuals with the least ability to afford the burden. This argument for progressive taxes, however, is based on ethical or normative beliefs: It is a moral judgment that some people should pay a proportionately higher amount of tax.

Illustration of progressivity

The progressivity of the federal income tax is illustrated by Table 5–1, which presents the federal income tax for a married couple filing a joint return. The first column gives selected taxable incomes (i.e., gross income reduced by itemized deductions in excess of the standard deduction set by the government and exemptions). The second column gives the tax rate on income earned in that tax bracket (i.e., the tax rate on the marginal or additional income), which is frequently referred to as the individual's marginal tax rate. The third column gives the total taxes paid on the taxable income,

TABLE 5–1. *Marginal and Average Federal Income Tax Rates in Effect for 1978 for Taxable Income of a Married Couple Filing a Joint Return*

TAXABLE INCOME	TAX ON THE LAST DOLLAR* (THE MARGINAL TAX RATE)	TOTAL TAXES PAID	AVERAGE TAX RATE (TAXES PAID DIVIDED BY TAXABLE INCOME)
$ 4,200	14%	$ 140	3.3%
5,200	15	290	5.6
6,200	16	450	7.3
•	•	•	•
•	•	•	•
•	•	•	•
23,200	28	4,380	18.9
27,200	32	5,660	20.8
31,200	36	7,100	22.8
35,200	39	8,660	24.6
•	•	•	•
•	•	•	•
•	•	•	•
55,200	50	18,060	32.7
67,200	53	24,420	36.3
•	•	•	•
•	•	•	•
•	•	•	•
123,200	62	57,580	46.7
143,200	64	70,380	49.1
•	•	•	•
•	•	•	•
•	•	•	•

*Last dollar indicates any additional income up to the next tax bracket.

and the fourth column gives the average tax rate paid by the family on its taxable income (i.e., the total taxes paid divided by the level of taxable income). As may be seen in the second and fourth columns, the marginal and average tax rates increase as income increases, which indicates that the federal income tax is progressive.

It is the marginal tax rate that influences an individual's investment decision making. Since investments alter the individual's marginal income, they also affect the amount that the individual nets from the investment. This can play an important role in the selection of which assets to include in the portfolio.

TAX SHELTERS

Since many taxes are progressive and investors may desire to minimize the amount of taxes paid, much effort is directed toward sheltering income from taxes. The term *tax shelter* evokes a variety of emotions and misunderstandings. In the minds of some people, *tax shelter* means all those taxes that other people (especially the "rich") are not paying. For some investors, the possibility of sheltering income from taxation may be

The desire to reduce taxes

sufficient to make irrational (and costly) investments. Still other investors may not realize the tax shelters that they themselves enjoy.

A protection from or reduction in taxes

A tax shelter, as the name implies, is a shelter or protection against taxes. This does not necessarily imply that an investor avoids taxes. Instead, a tax shelter may reduce taxes or defer them until a later date. Such reductions and deferments are available to everyone. An investor does not have to be wealthy to enjoy these benefits, and many investors probably use such shelters without recognizing them. For example, the first $100 of dividend income is excluded from taxable income. For a married couple, the dividend exclusion can be $200 provided that each spouse owns stock and receives $100 in dividend income.* Although there are some exceptions (e.g., dividends from foreign stocks), this is a general tax shelter that is available to all investors. However, the amount of the dividend exclusion is so small as to be almost trivial.

Dividend exclusion

Tax-exempt bonds

Another example of a tax shelter is the tax-exempt bond. As will be explained in Chapter 12, interest that is earned on state and local municipal debt is exempt from federal income taxation. (Correspondingly, interest on federal government debt is exempt from state and local government taxation.) This can be a significant tax shelter as one's income and marginal tax bracket rise. For example, an investor whose marginal tax rate is 40 per cent will find that the after-tax yields on a 10 per cent corporate bond that is subject to federal income tax are identical to those on a 6 per cent tax-exempt municipal bond.

Like the dividend exclusion this tax shelter is readily available to all investors. Although tax-exempt bonds are sold in minimum units of $5000, which excludes many individuals who do not have that sum to invest, there are mutual funds that invest in these bonds and subsequently sell their shares in smaller denominations. Dividends received from these shares are not subject to federal income tax. Since these mutual fund shares are sold in smaller denominations of less than $5000, this tax shelter is available to virtually all investors.

CAPITAL GAINS

Long-term capital gains

To the individual investor, perhaps the most important tax shelter is the reduction in taxes paid on long-term capital gains. The profits received through the purchase and subsequent sale of securities are considered to be capital gains. When the sales result in losses, these are capital losses. If the securities are held for less than one year, the gain or loss is "short-term" and is treated as if it were ordinary income. If securities are held for more than one year, the profit or loss is considered to be "long-term" and receives special tax treatment. Up to 40 per cent of the long-term gain or loss is considered ordinary income, which

---

*Eighty-five per cent of dividends received by a corporation are excluded from corporate income taxation.

EXHIBIT 5–1. How Long-Term Capital Gain Produces a Tax Shelter

Part I. Short-term Capital Gains and Losses:	
1. 100 Shares of XYZ Corporation	$ (500)
2. 50 Shares of EMEC Corporation	2200
3. Net short-term gain or (loss)	$1700
Part II. Long-term Capital Gains and Losses:	
4. 100 Shares of Cavalier Court	$2000
5. 100 Shares of MECHE Corporation	1200
6. Net long-term gain or (loss)	$3200
Part III. Taxable Income:	
7. 40 per cent of long-term capital gain	$1280
8. Taxable income from long-term and short-term capital gains	$2980

reduces the taxes on the profit. This reduction is an important tax shelter that is available to all investors. It applies not only to investments in securities but also to investments in other assets, such as a house.

How long-term capital gain produces a tax shelter is illustrated in Exhibit 5–1. This exhibit is based on Form 1040, Schedule D, which the taxpayer uses to report profits and losses on capital assets. In this example, the investor has made the following sales during the year:

	Date Acquired	Date Sold	Sale Price	Purchase Price	Profit or (Loss)
100 shares of					
Cavalier Court	1/3/72	1/4/79	$10,000	$8,000	$2,000
100 shares of					
MECHE Corporation	5/20/74	3/2/79	3,300	2,100	1,200
100 shares of					
XYZ Corporation	4/1/79	6/20/79	3,000	3,500	(500)
50 shares of					
EMEC Corporation	9/10/79	12/30/79*	9,500	7,300	2,200

Three of the transactions resulted in profits, and one sale produced a loss (XYZ Corporation). Some stock was sold before one year had elapsed, and therefore the profit is regarded as a short-term capital gain (EMEC Corporation). This profit will be taxed at the individual's tax rate on ordinary income. Other stock was sold after the investor had held the assets for more than one year (MECHE and Cavalier Court). These profits will be taxed as long-term capital gains in which classification only 40 per cent of the profits are considered to be ordinary income.

Part I of Exhibit 5–1 records the short-term profits and losses, while Part II records the long-term gains and losses. Part III summarizes the long-term and short-term capital gains, which are treated differently for tax purposes, and records their combined taxable income. Line 7 calculates 40 per cent of the net long-term capital gains ($1280). The amount on line 7 is then added to the amount on line 3 to determine what is to be reported as taxable income, which in this case is $2980 ($1700 + $1280).

The potential tax saving varies with the amount of long-term capital gains and the individual's marginal tax rate. In 1977 the maximum capital gains tax rate for many individuals was 25 per cent. Under the tax legislation of 1978, the maximum tax rate was reduced to 20 per cent. Thus, if the individual's marginal tax rate is 60 per cent, the tax advantage for long-term capital gains is even greater, since capital gains would be taxed at only 20 per cent. However, there are limits to this tax break. If an individual has capital gains totaling a certain amount in one year, that individual may have to report some of the gain as a

Preference items

special tax preference item. This will subject the gain to a special tax on preference items if it exceeds a specified amount. The tax laws pertaining to these preference items are very complex and are not discussed here. However, in accordance with these laws, some capital gains that are generated by the wealthier members of society do not receive the full benefit of the tax shelter.

Paper profits

Capital gains taxes may be deferred indefinitely. Profits are taxed only after the securities have been sold. Many profits from securities are only *paper profits*, for many investors do not sell the securities and *realize* the profits. The tax laws encourage such retention of securities by taxing the gains only when they are realized.

Holding an asset until death

The capital gains tax may be partially avoided if the individual holds the securities until he or she dies. The securities are then taxed as part of the deceased's estate. Any capital gain that occurred prior to January 1, 1977, is not subject to capital gains tax. Furthermore, if the securities are passed on as a gift and the recipients continue to hold them, they pick up the cost basis (the initial purchase price) and the capital gains continue to be deferred. These tax considerations thus encourage the retention of securities that have risen in price. Unfortunately, security prices that have risen may not continue to rise, and many investors who have retained securities have watched their paper profits dissolve when security prices subsequently declined.

PENSION PLANS

One tax shelter that may also ease the burden of retirement is the pension plan. Many firms contribute to these plans for their employees. The funds are invested in income-earning assets, such as stocks and bonds. In some cases the individual employee is required to make payments in addition to the employer's contributions. The amount of the employer's contribution is usually related to the earnings of the employee. These contributions are not included in taxable income. Thus, the worker does not have to pay taxes on the employer's payments to the pension plan. Instead, the funds are taxed when the worker retires and starts to use the money that has accumulated through the plan. At that time the taxes are usually less than those that would have been paid on the funds when they were contributed to the pension plan.

Prior to 1976, one criticism of these pension plans was that they were not available to all workers. However, Congress passed legislation in 1976 that enables all employees as well as the self-employed to set up their own pension plan; thus, the tax shelter that was previously provided only through employer-sponsored pension plans is now available to all. An employee who is not covered by a pension plan may set up an individual retirement account (IRA). Self-employed persons may establish a plan called a Keogh account, which is named after the congressman who sponsored the legislation.

IRA

Under an IRA, an individual may open an account with a financial institution, such as a commercial bank or a savings and loan association, and may deposit up to 15 per cent of his or her earned income, with a limit of $1500 per year. The amount invested is deducted from the individual's taxable income. Income earned by the account is also nontaxable until the individual withdraws the funds upon retirement. Then, as the funds are removed from the account, they are taxed as ordinary income. If the individual prematurely withdraws funds from the account, the money is taxed as ordinary income and a penalty tax is added.

Keogh plan

A Keogh plan is essentially the same as an IRA except that the amount that an individual may place in the account can be as much as $7500 per year (provided that the amount invested is not more than 15 per cent of the individual's earned income). The money placed in the account then earns income that will not be taxed until the funds are withdrawn at retirement. As in the case of the IRA, there is a penalty for premature withdrawal.

An example of savings that are possible with these tax shelters is presented in Exhibit 5–2. For illustrative purposes, it is assumed that the individual earns $20,000 and is not covered by a pension plan. The individual's personal income tax bracket is assumed to be 25 per cent, so for each dollar of additional income, the individual must pay $.25 in taxes. The example illustrates two cases. In the first, the individual pays the income tax and then saves $1500, which is placed in a savings account that pays 5 per cent annually. The interest income earned by the account is, of course, taxable. In the second case the individual places $1500 in an IRA, which also pays 5 per cent annually. However, the tax on this interest is deferred until the individual retires and withdraws the money.

In case A the saver starts with the $20,000 and pays the income tax ($5000), which leaves a disposable income of $15,000. Of this, $1500 is then placed in the savings account, leaving $13,500. In case B the saver initially contributes $1500 to an IRA which reduces taxable income by $1500 to $18,500. Taxes of $4625 are then paid, which leaves a dispos-

EXHIBIT 5–2. Potential Savings With A Tax Shelter

Variables	Case A	Case B
Present		
Taxable income	$20,000.00	$20,000.00
Contribution to IRA	0	1,500.00
Net taxable income	20,000.00	18,500.00
Taxes	5,000.00	4,625.00
Disposable income	15,000.00	13,875.00
Contribution to savings	1,500.00	0
Net disposable income	13,500.00	13,875.00
Tax savings	0	375.00
Year 1		
Amount invested	1,500.00	1,500.00
Interest earned	75.00	75.00
Taxes on interest	18.75	0
Net interest earned	56.25	75.00
Year 2		
Amount in account	1,556.25	1,575.00
Interest earned	77.81	78.75
Taxes on interest	19.45	0
Net interest earned	58.36	78.75
Year 3		
Amount in account	1,614.61	1,653.75
	•	•
	•	•
	•	•
Year 20		
Amount in account	3,132.23	3,979.95
Tax savings	0	847.72
Savings if $1,500 is deposited each year for 20 years	43,526.00	49,599.00

able income of $13,875. By placing $1500 in the IRA account and reducing taxable income, the saver reduces taxes by $375.

The initial tax saving, however, is only the first part of the potential savings. The $1500 placed in the savings account in case A now earns $75 in interest, but $18.75 of that is lost in taxes. Hence, the saver nets only $56.25 in interest. The 5 per cent interest rate generates a return after taxes of only 3.75 per cent. The $1500 in the IRA earns $75, but none of that interest is currently subject to tax.

Thus, after the first year (i.e., the beginning of the second year), there is $1556.25 in the account in case A, but in case B in which the saver placed funds in the IRA, the amount in the account is $1575.* The amounts in the accounts in case A and in case B grow to $1614.61 and $1653.75, respectively, at the beginning of the third year. After 20 years

---

*This example assumes that the tax on interest in case A is deducted from the interest and is not paid from net disposable income.

the initial $1500 that was placed in the account in case A will have grown to $3132.23 after taxes have been paid, but the proceeds in the IRA will have grown to $3979.95. The tax savings over 20 years will amount to almost $850.

This example assumes that the saver makes only one payment of $1500 in either a savings account or an IRA. However, savings plans usually imply that the investor periodically places funds in the account. If the investor were to place $1500 in either the savings account or the IRA every year for 20 years, the tax savings would be even greater. In that case the IRA would have $49,599, but the regular savings account would have only $43,526 after taxes. The difference then would exceed $6000. This difference is the result of the tax savings on the interest and does not include the $375 tax savings generated each year by depositing the $1500 in the account. In 20 years, $7500 would be saved in taxes, for a total tax savings of more than $13,000.

These tax savings would be even larger if the investor were to place a larger sum each year in the retirement plan account (as is possible under the Keogh plan) or if the individual's tax rate were higher. For the self-employed professional with a substantial amount of taxable income, such as a lawyer or a doctor, these retirement plans offer one of the best means available to shelter income from current taxation. However, the individual will still have to pay tax on this income when the funds are withdrawn from the plan, while the tax has already been paid on the funds in the savings account.

Potential savings increase with the amount and the marginal tax rate

TAXATION OF WEALTH

In addition to taxes on income, there are also taxes on wealth; these are in the form of estate, gift, and property taxes. Two types of taxes are exacted when a person dies: estate taxes and inheritance taxes. Estate taxes are imposed on the corpus or body of the deceased's estate. That includes not only the value of investments, such as stocks and bonds, but also the value of personal effects, such as automobiles and other personal property. Inheritance taxes are levied on the share of an estate received by an individual. Like the estate tax, it is imposed on the value of personal effects as well as on financial assets.

Estate taxes are primarily the domain of the federal government; however, 16 states also have such taxes. Inheritance taxes are levied by state governments. Like the personal income tax, estate and inheritance taxes are progressive. Selected rates from the federal estate tax are given in Exhibit 5–3.* As may be seen from this exhibit, the tax rates increase with the value of the estate.

Estate tax laws are extremely complex, and an investor who is planning the distribution of his or her estate should consult a lawyer. How-

Estate taxes

---

*These rates also apply to gifts.

EXHIBIT 5–3. Selected Federal Estate Tax Rates in Effect as of January, 1979

Taxable Value of the Estate	Tax		On Excess Over
	Base*	Plus Percentage†	
$ 0– 10,000	$ 0	18	$ 0
10,000– 20,000	1,800	20	10,000
20,000– 40,000	3,800	22	20,000
•	•	•	•
•	•	•	•
•	•	•	•
100,000– 150,000	23,800	30	100,000
150,000– 250,000	38,800	32	150,000
250,000– 500,000	70,800	34	250,000
•	•	•	•
•	•	•	•
•	•	•	•
1,000,000–1,250,000	345,800	41	1,000,000
1,250,000–1,500,000	448,800	43	1,250,000
•	•	•	•
•	•	•	•
•	•	•	•

*The base or minimum amount of tax is the tax paid on the amount shown in the left-hand column under the heading "Taxable Value of the Estate."
†The percentage applies to any amount in excess of that shown in the left-hand column and up to the amount shown in the right-hand column under the heading "Taxable Value of the Estate."

ever, the basic components of these taxes are as follows. First, a married individual may leave up to $250,000 or half of the estate (whichever is larger) to his or her spouse without the spouse's paying any tax on that part of the estate. Thus, a married individual with a net worth of $100,000 may leave the entire estate to a spouse and avoid estate taxes. This is really only a deferment of the tax liability, because this wealth is added to the wealth of the surviving spouse and is thus subject to estate tax when the spouse dies. Unless there are perceptible differences in the net worth of the individuals, leaving the maximum amount possible to a spouse may only defer some of the tax.

Second, the estate receives a tax credit, which reduces the amount of taxes due. As of 1981, the maximum credit will be $47,000. The effect of this credit is to exempt all estates the value of which is less than $175,625 from federal estate taxation. As a result of this tax credit and the ability to leave tax-free funds to one's spouse, modest estates will avoid federal taxation. For example, a husband with an estate the taxable value of which is $400,000 can leave $250,000 to his wife without her paying taxes. This reduces the taxable value of the estate to $150,000. Tax on $150,000 would be $38,800, which is reduced to nothing by the tax credit. However, larger estates may be taxed heavily even after the marital deduction and the tax credit are applied, since the rates rise rapidly for sums over the excluded amount.

Inheritance taxes   Inheritance taxes are levied by state governments on the distribution of estates of individuals living in the state. Even through the recipient of the inheritance may live in another state, that individual's inheritance is subject to tax by the state in which the deceased resided.

As with state income taxes, there are substantial differences in state inheritance taxes. There are also differences in the tax rates for recipients of an inheritance, depending on their relation to the deceased. The deceased's immediate family pays lower rates. Maximum rates apply to nonrelatives who receive a share of the estate.

Variations in tax rates

These differences are illustrated in Exhibit 5–4, which presents the maximum inheritance tax rates in effect in selected states. As may be seen from the exhibit, the maximum tax rates range from between 2 and 3 per cent for a spouse, a child, or a parent in Wyoming and Louisiana to 30 per cent in several states for nonrelatives.

The wide range of tax rates in different states may partly determine the choice of a retirement home. For example, the lack of inheritance taxes and the modest estate tax (as well as a variety of other factors, including the climate) encourage retirees to move to Florida.

In addition to estate and inheritance taxes, the investor must also be concerned with property taxes. These are primarily levied by counties, municipalities, and townships. Since there are thousands of such local governments, there is great diversity in property taxes.

Property taxes

Personal property taxes may be levied on tangible or intangible personal property. Tangible property is physical property, such as a house or an automobile. Intangible personal property includes nonphysical assets and financial assets such as stocks and bonds. Many localities tax only tangible property, with particular emphasis on real estate. However, some states, including Florida and Pennsylvania, permit the taxation of intangible personal property. In such states the individual's portfolio of stocks and bonds may be subject to property taxation.*

---

*For example, in Florida the tax rate is 1 per cent per $1000 valuation, with an exemption of $20,000 per person and $40,000 per couple. Thus, a portfolio of $500,000 after exemptions are deducted is taxed $500.

EXHIBIT 5–4. Selected Maximum State Inheritance Tax Rates as of September 1, 1977

State	Maximum Rate Applied to Inheritance of Spouse, Child, or Parent	Maximum Rate Applied to Inheritance Other Than a Relative
California	14%	24%
Connecticut	8	19
Illinois	14	30
Louisiana	3	10
Missouri	6	30
New Jersey	16	16
North Carolina	12	17
Pennsylvania	6	15
Virginia	5	15
Wyoming	2	6

Since there is considerable variation in this type of taxation, the investor would be wise to learn the specific tax laws that apply in his or her own state.

CORPORATE TAXATION

The tax schedule

Like individuals, firms are subject to taxation by the various levels of government. Income, capital gains, and property may all be subject to taxation. Although all of these taxes may affect the individual firm, this brief discussion is limited to the federal corporate income tax.

Like the federal personal income tax, the federal corporate income tax is progressive. However, as of January 1, 1979 the tax structure was made considerably simpler, as there are only three tax brackets:

Corporate Income ($)	Tax Rate (%)
0–25,000	20
25,000–50,000	22
over 50,000	46

Partially borne by stockholders

Under this tax schedule, the maximum rate applies to virtually all corporations of any significant size. Certainly for publicly held firms, the investor might as well view the amount of taxes owed as being about half of the firm's taxable income. Although it is extremely difficult to isolate the party that ultimately bears the tax, it is partially borne by the investors, since the tax reduces either the cash dividends or the capacity of the firm to reinvest its earnings and grow or both.

Depreciation

Like individual investors, corporate managements seek to reduce or at least to defer tax payments by taking advantage of certain deductions and tax credits. For example, the cost of long-term assets, such as plant and equipment, is deducted from income over the useful life of the assets, i.e., the asset is *depreciated* over its useful life. Under straight-line depreciation, the amount of the deduction is the same each year, but under accelerated depreciation this expense is increased during the early years of the asset's life. The effect of accelerated depreciation is to increase expenses in the present, which decreases current income and current taxes. The tax is deferred until after the period of accelerated depreciation has elapsed.

The tax credit

Another example of a means to alter the amount of taxes owed by a corporation is the investment tax credit. As the name implies, it is a credit to be applied against taxes for making certain investments. In an effort to stimulate spending on plant and equipment, the federal government permits corporations to reduce their taxes if they make certain investments. By channeling a firm's funds into these investments, management may be able to reduce significantly the amount of income tax that the firm must pay.

Accelerated depreciation and the investment tax credit are not the only means available to corporate management to maximize the firm's earnings and to minimize its income taxes. The potential impact of taxes influences management's decision making (just as it affects the individual investor's choice of assets). From the viewpoint of the individual investor, the corporate income tax laws increase the difficulty of analyzing and comparing companies. If a firm pays less than half of its earnings in taxes, that may be a clue to the investor to examine the firm more closely. Although management may be able to reduce taxes temporarily, this may also imply that current earnings are overstated.

REGULATION

Like many industries, the securities industry is subject to a substantial degree of regulation. This regulation comes from both the federal and state governments. Since the vast majority of securities are traded across state lines, most regulation is at the federal level.

The purpose of these laws is to protect the investor by insuring honest and fair practices. The laws require that the investor be provided with information upon which to base decisions. Hence, these acts are frequently referred to as the full disclosure laws, because publicly owned companies must inform the public of certain facts relating to the firm. The regulations also attempt to prevent fraud and the manipulation of stock prices. The laws, however, do not try to protect investors from their own folly and greed. The purpose of legislation governing the securities industry is not to insure that investors will profit from their investments; instead the laws try to provide fair market practices while allowing investors to make their own mistakes.

The purpose

Although current federal regulation developed during the 1930s as a direct result of the debacle in the security markets during the early part of that decade, state regulation started in 1911 with the pioneering legislation of the state of Kansas. These state laws are frequently called blue-sky laws because fraudulent securities were referred to as pieces of blue sky. Although there are differences among the state laws, they generally require that (1) security firms and brokers be licensed, (2) financial information concerning issues of new securities be filed with state regulatory bodies, (3) new securities meet specific standards before they may be sold, and (4) regulatory bodies be established to enforce the laws.

Laws passed in the 1930s

THE FEDERAL SECURITY LAWS

Security Act of 1933

The first modern federal legislation governing the securities industry is the Security Act of 1933. This act is primarily concerned with the issuing of new securities. It requires that new securities be "registered" with the Security and Exchange Commission (SEC). Registration consists of supplying the SEC with information concerning the firm, the nature of its business and competition, and its financial position. This information is then summarized in the prospectus (refer to Exhibit 2–3, p. 28–29), which makes the formal offer to sell the securities to the public.

The impact on the sale of new securities

Once the SEC has determined that all material facts that may affect the value of the firm have been disclosed, the securities are released for sale. When the securities are sold, the buyer must be given a copy of the prospectus. If the investor incurs a loss on an investment in a new issue of securities, a suit may be filed to recover the loss if the prospectus or the registration statement that was filed with the SEC contained false or misleading information. Liability for this loss may rest upon the firm, its executives and directors, the brokerage firm selling the securities, and any experts (e.g., accountants, appraisers) who were employed in preparing the documents. Owing to this legal accountability, those involved exercise caution and diligence in the preparation of the prospectus and the registration statement.

Security Exchange Act of 1934

Although the Security Act of 1933 applies only to new issues, the Security Exchange Act of 1934 (and subsequent amendments) extends the regulation to existing securities. This act forbids market manipulation, deception and misrepresentation of facts, and fraudulent practices. The SEC was also created by this act to enforce the laws pertaining to the securities industry.

Under the Security Exchange Act of 1934, publicly held companies are required to keep current the information on file with the SEC. This is achieved by having the firm file a report annually (called the 10-K report) with the SEC. The 10-K report contains a substantial amount of factual information concerning the firm, and this information is usually sent in summary form to the stockholders in the company's annual report. (Companies must upon request and without charge send a copy of the 10-K report to stockholders.)

Flow of information to the public

Firms are also required to release any information during the year that may materially affect the value of its securities. Information concerning new discoveries, lawsuits, or merger discussions must be disseminated to the general public. The SEC has the power to suspend trading in a company's securities for up to ten days if, in its opinion, the public interest and the protection of investors necessitate such a ban on trading. If a firm fails to keep investors informed, the SEC can suspend trading pending the release of the required information. Such a suspension is a drastic act and is seldom used, for most companies frequently issue news releases that inform the investing public of significant changes affecting the firm. Sometimes the company itself asks to have trading in its securities halted until a news release can be prepared and disseminated.

The disclosure laws do not require that the company tell everything about its operations. All firms have trade secrets that they do not want known by their competitors. The purpose of the full-disclosure laws is not to restrict the corporation but (1) to inform the investors so that they can make informed decisions and (2) to prevent a firm's employees from using privileged information for personal gain.

Inside information

It should be obvious that employees ranging from president of the company to those of lesser positions may have access to information before it reaches the general public. Such information (called inside information) may significantly enhance their ability to make profits by buying or selling the company's securities before the announcement is made. Such profiteering from inside information is illegal. Officers and directors of the company must report their holdings and any changes in their holdings of the firm's securities to the SEC. Thus, it is possible for the SEC to determine if transactions have been made prior to any public announcement that affected the value of the securities. If insiders do profit illegally from the use of such information, they may be prosecuted under criminal law and their gains may have to be surrendered to the firm.

OTHER REGULATIONS

Although the Security Act of 1933 and the Security Act of 1934 are the backbone of such regulations, subsequent laws have been passed. These include the Public Holding Company Act of 1935, which reorganized the utility industry by requiring better methods of financial accounting and more thorough reporting and by constraining the use of debt financing. The Investment Company Act of 1940 extended the regulations to include mutual funds and other investment companies. The most recent act of importance is the Securities Investors Protection Act of 1970, which is designed to protect investors from brokerage firm bankruptcies.

In addition to the state and federal securities laws, the industry itself regulates its members. The stock exchanges and the trade association, the National Association of Security Dealers, have established codes of behavior for their members. These include the relationships between brokers and customers, the auditing of members' accounts, and proficiency tests for brokers. While such rules may not have the force of law, they can have a significant impact on the quality and credibility of the industry and its representatives.

SUMMARY

Tax laws and security regulations have a significant impact on the environment of investing. These laws and regulations are issued by all levels of government. However, the most important laws in these areas have been passed by the federal government.

The federal government taxes income from investments, capital gains, and the individual's estate. Tax rates are progressive, which means that as the tax base increases, the tax rate increases. This taxation — especially the progressivity of the tax rates — causes individuals to seek means to reduce their tax liabilities. Investments that reduce or defer taxes are called tax shelters. Important tax shelters include long-term capital gains, tax-exempt bonds, and pension plans.

The federal laws governing the securities industry are enforced by the SEC. The purpose of these laws is to insure that individuals have access to information upon which to base investment decisions. Publicly owned firms must supply investors with financial statements and make timely disclosures of information pertaining to the firm and its financial condition.

Terms to Remember

Progressive tax	Paper profits	Tax credit
Regressive tax	IRA	Accelerated depreciation
Marginal tax rate	Keogh plan	Full-disclosure laws
Tax-exempt bond	Estate tax	
Capital gain	Inheritance tax	

Questions

1. Why are estate and personal income taxes called progressive?

2. Does a tax shelter necessarily mean that the investor avoids paying taxes?

3. What is a long-term capital gain? Why are these gains examples of a tax shelter?

4. What is the difference between an estate tax and an inheritance tax?

5. What are Keogh and IRA plans? What are their primary advantages to savers?

6. What is the role of the SEC?

7. Why are laws governing the securities industry frequently called "full-disclosure laws"?

SELECTED READINGS

Barnes, Leo, and Stephen Feldman (ed.): *Handbook of Wealth Management.* New York, McGraw-Hill Book Co., 1977, chapters 47–52 and 64–68.

Bloch, Ernest, and Arnold W. Sametz. *A Modest Proposal for a National Securities Market System and Its Governance,* bulletin 1977-1. New York University Graduate School of Business Administration, 1977.

Federal Tax Course. Englewood Cliffs, N.J., Prentice-Hall, Inc., published annually.

Lasser Institute: *J. K. Lasser's Your Income Tax.* New York, Simon & Schuster, Inc., published annually.

1979 U.S. Master Tax Guide. Chicago, Commerce Clearing House, Inc., 1978.

Securities Reform Act of 1975. Chicago, Commerce Clearing House, Inc., 1975.

Skousen, K. Fred: *An Introduction to the SEC.* Cincinnati, Ohio, South-Western Publishing Co., 1976.

The Tools of Investing

Once an understanding of the financial environment has been achieved, the investor needs several general tools with which to analyze specific assets. Like the material presented in Part One, the material presented in this section helps to lay the foundation for selecting securities and other assets.

Three tools are covered in Part Two. The first is a mathematical concept: the time value of money. A dollar received today and a dollar received tomorrow do not have the same value. Linking the future with the present is an extremely important concept for the valuation of assets, since investments are made in the present but the returns accrue in the future.

Financial statements are the next tool that is discussed in Part Two. A rudimentary ability to read financial statements is necessary to comprehend much of the analysis that is applied to firms in the evaluation of their securities.

The last chapter in Part Two discusses the sources of information that are available to the investor. Investing is certainly one area in which there is no dearth of facts, figures, reports, and analyses. The problem lies in converting this weatlh of information into usable knowledge.

Learning Objectives

After completing this chapter you should be able to

1. Explain why a dollar received tomorrow is not equal in value to a dollar received today.

2. Differentiate between compounding and discounting.

3. Distinguish between the present value of a dollar to be received in the future and the present value of an annuity.

4. Determine the compound value of a dollar and the present value of a dollar to be received in the future.

5. Apply present value (i.e., discounting) to security analysis.

6. Solve problems concerning the time value of money.

chapter 6

THE TIME
VALUE OF
MONEY

If $100 is deposited in a savings account today in a commercial bank, how much will the savings account be worth one year from now? If a certain stock pays $1 per share every year, is the stock worth $15 per share? If a stock that cost $50 is sold after one year for $60, what is the return on the investment? These questions illustrate a major concept in finance: the time value of money. A dollar in the future is not equivalent in value to a dollar in the present: That is the time value of money

The time value of money is one of the most crucial concepts in finance. An investment decision is made at a given time. For example, an investor buys stock or a firm decides to establish a pension plan today. The returns on these investment decisions will be received in the future. There has to be a means to compare the future results of these investments with their present cost. Such comparisons require an understanding of the time value of money, which is the subject of this chapter.

This chapter considers four concepts: (1) the compound value of a dollar, (2) the present value of a dollar, (3) the sum of an annuity, and (4) the present value of an annuity. After each has been explained, several examples apply these concepts to investments. The chapter closes with a brief introduction to valuation, for the valuation of securities depends upon the time value of money.

THE COMPOUND VALUE OF A DOLLAR

Funds in a savings account grow

If $100 is deposited in a savings account that pays 5 per cent annually, how much money will be in the account at the end of the year? The answer is easy to determine: $100 plus $5 interest, for a total of $105. This answer is derived by multiplying $100 by 5 per cent, which gives the interest earned during the year, and then by adding this interest to the initial principal. That is,

Initial principal + (interest rate × initial principal) =
principal after one year

This simple calculation is expressed in algebraic form in Equation 1, in which P represents the principal and i is the rate of interest. This equation employs subscripts to represent time. The subscript 0 indicates the present, and 1 means the end of the first year. (The second year, third year, and so on to any number of years will be represented by 2, 3, . . . n, respectively.)

(1) $$P_0 + iP_0 = P_1$$

If P_0 is the initial principal ($100) and i is the interest rate (5%), the principal after one year (P_1) will be

$$\$100 + .05(\$100) = \$105$$

The interest left on deposit earns interest

How much will be in the account after two years? This answer is obtained in the same manner by adding the interest earned during the second year to the principal at the beginning of the second year, i.e., $105 plus .05 times $105 equals $110.25, which may be expressed in algebraic terms:

(2) $$P_1 + iP_1 = P_2$$

After two years the initial deposit of $100 will have grown to $110.25; the savings account will have earned $10.25 in interest. This total interest is composed of $10 representing interest on the initial principal and $.25 representing interest that has accrued during the second year on the $5 in interest earned during the first year. This earning of interest on interest is called *compounding*. Money that is deposited in savings accounts is frequently referred to as being compounded, for interest is earned on both the principal and the previously earned interest.

The words *interest* and *compounded* are frequently used together. For example, banks may advertise that interest is compounded daily for savings accounts, or the cost of a loan may be expressed as 12 per cent compounded annually. In the previous example, interest was earned only once during the year; thus it is an example of interest that is compounded annually. In many cases interest is not compounded annually but quarterly, semiannually, or even daily. The more frequently it is compounded (i.e., the more frequently the interest is added to the principal), the more rapidly the interest is put to work to earn even more interest.

How much will be in the account at the end of three years? This answer can be determined by the same general formula that was previously used. The amount in the account at the end of the second year ($110.25) is added to the interest that is earned during the third year (5% × $110.25).
That is,

$$\$110.25 + \$5.5125 = \$115.76$$

or the formula may be expressed algebraically as

(3) $$P_2 + iP_2 = P_3$$

By continuing with this method, it is possible to determine the amount that will be in the account at the end of 20 or more years, but doing so is obviously a lot of work. Fortunately, there is a much easier way to ascertain how much will be in the account after any given number of years. This is done by the use of an interest table called the compound value of a dollar table.

Appendix A (p. 514) is an interest table that gives the compound value of a dollar. The interest rates at which a dollar is compounded annually are read horizontally at the top of the table. The number of years is read vertically along the left-hand margin. To determine the amount to which $100 will grow in three years at 5 per cent interest, find the interest factor (1.158) and multiply it by $100. That calculation yields $115.80, which is the answer that was derived previously by working out the equations (except for rounding off). To ascertain the amount to which $100 will grow after 25 years at 5 per cent interest compounded annually, multiply $100 by the interest factor, 3.386, to obtain the answer, $338.60. Thus, if $100 were placed in a savings account that paid 5 per cent interest annually, there would be $338.60 in the account after 25 years.

Interest tables for the compound value of a dollar are based on a general formulation of the simple equations that were previously used.

A compound interest table

**A general
formulation of the
compound value of
a dollar**

To determine the amount in the savings account at the end of year 1, the following equation was used:

(1) $$P_0 + iP_0 = P_1$$

which may be written as

$$P_0 (1 + i) = P_1$$

To calculate the amount after two years, the following equation was used:

(2) $$P_1 + iP_1 = P_2$$

which may be written as

$$P_1 (1 + i) = P_2$$

Since P_1 equals $P_0 (1 + i)$, the amount in the account at the end of year 2 may be expressed as

(3) $$P_0 (1 + i) (1 + i) = P_2$$

This equation uses the term $1 + i$ twice, for P_0 is being multiplied by $1 + i$ twice. Thus, it is possible to write Equation 3 as

(3) $$P_0 (1 + i)^2 = P_2$$

The amount to which a dollar will grow may always be expressed in terms of the initial dollar (i.e., P_0). The general formula for finding the amount to which a dollar will grow in n number of years, if it is compounded annually, is

(4) $$P_0 (1 + i)^n = P_n$$

Thus, the general formula for finding the compound value of a dollar for any number of years consists of (1) the initial dollar (P_0), (2) the interest factor $(1 + i)$, and (3) the number of years (n).

**The impact of time
and the interest rate**

As may be seen in Appendix A, the value of a dollar grows with increases in the length of time and in the rate of interest. These relationships are illustrated in Graph 6–1. If $1 is compounded at 5 per cent interest (*AB* in the graph), it will grow to $1.28 after five years and to $1.63 after ten years. However, if $1 is compounded at 10 per cent interest (*AC* on the graph), it will grow to $2.59 in ten years. These cases illustrate the basic nature of compounding: The longer the funds continue grow and the higher the interest rate is, the higher will be the ultimate value.

GRAPH 6-1. Compound Value of One Dollar

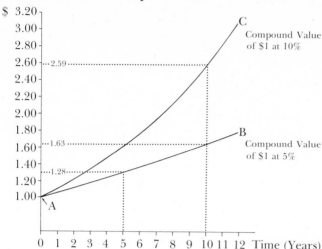

It should also be noted that doubling the interest rate does not double the amount of interest that is earned over a number of years. In the example just given, the interest rate doubled from 5 per cent to 10 per cent; however, the amount of interest that will have accumulated in ten years rises from $.63 at 5 per cent to $1.59 at 10 per cent. This is the result of the fact that compounding involves a geometric progression. The interest factor $(1 + i)$ has been raised to some power (n).

THE PRESENT VALUE OF A DOLLAR

In the preceding section, a dollar grew or compounded over time. In this section the reverse situation is considered. How much is a dollar that will be received in the future worth today? For example, how much will a payment of $1000 20 years hence be worth today if the funds earn 5 per cent annually? This question incorporates the time value of money, but instead of asking how much a dollar will be worth at some future date, it asks how much that future dollar is worth today. This is a question of *present value*. The process by which this question is answered is called *discounting*. Discounting determines the worth of funds that are to be received in the future in terms of their present value.

In the earlier section, the compound value of a dollar was calculated by Equation 4.

The opposite of compounding — discounting

(4)
$$P_0 (1 + i)^n = P_n$$

Discounting reverses this equation. The present value (P_0) is ascertained by dividing the future value (P_n) by the discount factor $(1 + i)^n$. This is expressed in Equation 5.

(5)
$$P_0 = \frac{P_n}{(1 + i)^n}$$

The future amount is discounted by the appropriate interest factor to determine the present value. For example, if the interest rate is 6 per cent, the present value of $100 to be received five years from today is

$$P_0 = \frac{\$100}{(1 + .06)^5}$$

$$P_0 = \frac{\$100}{1.339}$$

$$P_0 = \$74.68$$

A present value table

Working with discount factors that are raised to a large power (n) is difficult, but as with the compound value of a dollar, interest tables have been developed that ease the calculation of present values. Appendix B (p. 516) is a present value table. It gives the present value of a dollar for selected interest rates and years. The interest factors are read horizontally at the top, and the number of years is read vertically along the left-hand side. To determine the present value of $1 that will be received in five years if the current interest rate is 6 per cent, multiply $1 by the interest factor, which is found in the table under the vertical column for 6 per cent and in the horizontal column for five years. The present value of $1 is

$$\$1 \times .747 = \$.747$$

Thus, $100 that will be received after five years is currently worth only $74.70 if the interest rate is six per cent. This is the same answer that was determined with Equation 5 (except for rounding off).

The impact of time and the interest rate

As may be seen in Equation 5, the present value of a dollar depends upon (1) the length of time before it will be received and (2) the interest rate. The further into the future the dollar will be received and the higher the interest rate, the lower is the present value of the dollar. This is illustrated by Graph 6–2, which gives the relationship between the present value of a dollar and the length of time at various interest rates. Lines *AB* and *AC* give the present value of a dollar at 4 per cent and 7 per cent, respectively. As may be seen in this graph, a dollar to be received after 20 years is worth considerably less than a dollar to be received after five years when both are discounted at the same percentage. At 4 per cent (line *AB*) the current value of $1 to be received after 20 years is only $.456, whereas $1 to be received after five years is worth $.822. Also, the higher the interest rate (i.e., discount factor), the lower

GRAPH 6-2.   Present Value of One Dollar to Be Received in the Future

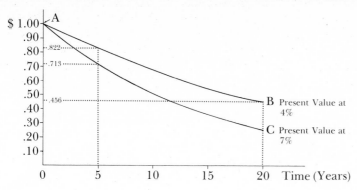

is the present value of a dollar. For example, the present value of $1 to be received after five years is $.822 at 4 per cent, but it is only $.713 at 10 per cent.

SUM OF AN ANNUITY

How much will be in a savings account after three years (i.e., at the beginning of the fourth year) if $100 is deposited annually in the account starting today? This question is no different conceptually from that of the compound value of a dollar, except that the payment is not one lump sum at the beginning but is a series of equal annual payments. An annuity is just that: a set of periodic payments of equal amount. In this example $100 is deposited annually into a savings account, and the question asks how much will be in the account at some future date. Of course, funds that are placed annually in the account will earn interest, and this interest will compound.

One means to ascertain how much will be in the account is to compound $100 at 5 per cent interest for three years, then to compound $100 at 5 per cent interest for two years, and finally to compound $100 at 5 per cent for one year. At the beginning of the fourth year (when the next $100 payment will be due), all of the deposits and the accrued interest will be added to obtain the amount in the account. This process is summarized in Exhibit 6–1. The left-hand column gives the date of each $100 deposit. Each vertical column gives the interest earned on the deposit as of a certain date. For example, the $100 that was deposited on January 1, 1978, earned $5 on January 1, 1979 and will have earned $5.25 on January 1, 1980 and $5.51 on January 1, 1981. The last entry in the last column gives the total deposits, interest, and the amount in the account ($431.01) on January 1, 1981, when the fourth $100 deposit will be made.

A series of equal payments

EXHIBIT 6–1. Compounding $100 at 5 Per Cent Interest

Deposit of $100	1/1/79	Interest Earned as of 1/1/80	1/1/81	Total in Account as of 1/1/81
Date of deposit				
1/1/78	$ 5.00	$ 5.25	$ 5.51	$115.76
1/1/79	. . .	5.00	5.25	110.25
1/1/80	. . .	. . .	5.00	105.00
1/1/81	. . .	. . .	. . .	100.00
Total annual interest earned	5.00	10.25	15.76	. . .
Amount in the account at end of each year	105.00	210.25	315.76	431.01

This procedure is formally stated in Equation 6. The compound sum (*CS*) of an annuity is

$$(6) \qquad CS = I(1 + i)^0 + I(1 + i)^1 + \ldots + I(1 + i)^{n-1}$$

This equation, applied to the aforementioned example in which $i = .05$ and $n = 4$, is

$$CS = \$100(1 + .05)^0 + \$100(1 + .05)^1 + \$100(1 + .05)^2 + \$100(1 + .05)^3$$

$$= \$100 + \$105 + \$110.25 + \$115.76$$

$$= \$431.01$$

An annuity table

Although it is possible to derive the sum of an annuity in this manner, it is very cumbersome. Fortunately, interest tables have been developed to facilitate these calculations. Appendix C (p. 518) is an example of such a table. It gives the sum of an annuity of one dollar for selected years and selected interest rates. The number of years is read vertically at the left, and the interest rates are read horizontally at the top. To ascertain the sum of the annuity in the previous example, this table is used as follows. The compound value of a $100 annuity at 5 per cent interest for four years (four annual $100 payments, with interest being earned for three years) is $100 times the interest factor that is found in Appendix C for four years at 5 per cent. This interest factor is 4.310, and therefore the compound value of the annuity is $100 times 4.310, which equals $431.00, this is the same answer that was derived by determining the compound value of each $100 deposit and totaling them. (The $.01 difference in the two answers is the result of rounding off.)

The impact of time and the interest rate

The value of an annuity of a dollar compounded annually depends upon the number of payments (i.e., the number of years over which deposits are made) and the interest rate. The longer the time period and the higher the interest rate, the greater will be the sum that will have accumulated in the future. This is illustrated by Graph 6–3. Lines *AB*

GRAPH 6–3. Compound Sum of an Annuity of One Dollar

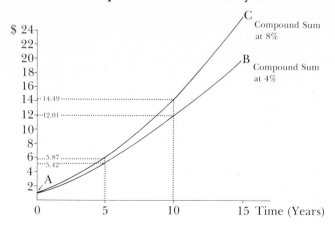

and *AC* show the value of the annuity at 4 and 8 per cent, respectively. After five years the value of the $1 annuity will grow to $5.87 at 8 per cent but to only $5.42 at 4 per cent. If these annuities are continued for another five years for a total duration of ten years, they will be worth $14.49 and $12.01, respectively. Thus, both the rate at which the annuity compounds and the length of the time affect the annuity's value.

THE PRESENT VALUE OF
AN ANNUITY

In investment analysis the investor is often not concerned with the compound value of an annuity but with its present value. The investor who receives periodic payments often wishes to know the current value of these payments. Of course, the present value of these future payments could be determined by obtaining the present value of each payment and summing these values. This approach is illustrated by the following simple example. The recipient expects to receive $100 at the end of each year for three years and wants to know how much this series of annual payments is currently worth if 6 per cent can be earned on alternative investments. One method to determine current worth is to calculate the present value of each of the $100 payments (find the appropriate interest factors in Appendix B and multiply them by $100) and to sum these individual present values, which in this case yields $267.30.

Future annuity payments have a present value

Payment	Year	Interest Factor	Present Value
$100	1	.943	$ 94.30
100	2	.890	89.00
100	3	.840	84.00
			$267.30

This process is expressed in more general terms by Equation 7. The present value *(PV)* of the annual payments *(I)* is then found by discounting these payments at the appropriate interest factor *(i)*.

(7)
$$PV = \frac{I}{(1+i)^1} + \ldots + \frac{I}{(1+i)^n}$$

$$PV = \sum_1^n \frac{I}{(1+i)^n}$$

When the values from the previous example are inserted into the equation, it reads

$$PV = \frac{\$100}{(1+.06)} + \frac{\$100}{(1+.06)^2} + \frac{\$100}{(1+.06)^3}$$

$$= \frac{\$100}{1.060} + \frac{\$100}{1.123} + \frac{\$100}{1.191}$$

$$= \$267.35$$

The present value of an annuity table

The calculation of the present value of an annuity can be a long and tedious process. To simplify this task, interest tables have been developed for the present value of an annuity. Appendix D (p. 520) is such a table. The interest factors for selected interest rates are read horizontally along the top, and the number of years is read vertically at the left. To determine the present value of an annuity of $100 that is to be received for three years when interest rates are 6 per cent, find the interest factor for three years at 6 per cent (2.673) and then multiply $100 by this interest factor. The present value of this annuity is $267.30, which is the same value (except for rounding off) that was derived by obtaining each of the individual present values and summing them. The price that one would be willing to pay at the present time in exchange for three future annual payments of $100 when the rate of return on alternative investments is 6 per cent is $267.30.

The impact of the interest rate and time

As with the present value of a dollar, the present value of an annuity is related to the interest rate and the length of time over which the annuity payments are made. The lower the interest rate and the longer the duration of the annuity, the greater is the current value of the annuity. Graph 6–4 illustrates the relationship between the duration of the annuity, the interest rate, and the present value of the annuity. As may be seen by comparing lines *AB* and *AC*, the lower the interest rate, the higher is the present dollar value. For example, if payments are to be made over five years, the present value of an annuity of $1 is $4.45 at 4 per cent but only $3.99 at 8 per cent. The longer the duration of the annuity the higher is the present value; hence the present value of $1 at 4 per cent is $4.45 for five years, whereas the present value is $8.11 for ten years.

GRAPH 6–4. **Present Value of an Annuity of One Dollar**

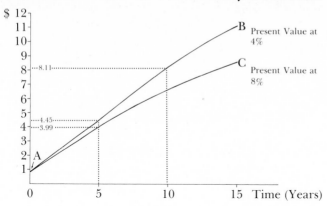

APPLICATIONS OF COMPOUNDING AND DISCOUNTING

The previous sections have explained the various computations involving time value, and this section will illustrate them in a series of problems that the investor may encounter. These illustrations are similar to examples that are used throughout the text. If one understands these examples, comprehending the rest of the text material should be much easier, because the emphasis can then be placed on the analysis of the value of specific assets instead of on the mechanics of the valuation.

(1) An investor buys a stock for $10 per share and expects to watch the value of the stock grow annually at 9 per cent for ten years, at which time the individual plans to sell it. What is the anticipated sale price? This is an example of the compound value of a dollar growing at 9 per cent for ten years. The future value is

$$P_n = P_0(1 + i)^n$$

$$P_{10} = \$10(1 + .09)^{10}$$

$$P_{10} = \$10(2.367) = \$23.67$$

where 2.367 is the interest factor for the compound sum of a dollar at 9 per cent for ten years. The investor anticipates selling the stock for $23.67.

(2) An investor sells a stock for $23.67 that was purchased ten years ago. A return of 9 per cent was earned. What was the original cost of the investment? This is an example of the present value of a dollar dis-

counted back at 9 per cent for ten years. The initial value ten years ago, or the former price, was

$$P_{-n} = \frac{P_0}{(1+i)^n}$$

$$P_{-10} = \frac{\$23.67}{(1+.09)^{10}}$$

$$P_{-10} = \$23.67\,(.4224) = \$10$$

where .4224 is the interest factor for the present value of a dollar discounted at 9 per cent for ten years. The investment cost $10 when it was purchased ten years ago.

The student should know that Questions 1 and 2 are two views of the same investment. In Question 1 the $10 investment grew to $23.67. In Question 2 the value at the time the stock was sold was brought back to the value of the initial investment. Another variation of this question would be as follows. If an investor bought stock for $10, held it for ten years, and then sold it for $23.67, what was the return on the investment? In this case the values of the stock at the time it was bought and sold are known, but the rate of growth (the interest factor) is unknown. The answer can be found by using *either* the compound value of a dollar table or the present value of a dollar table.

If the compound value table is used, the question is at what rate (x) will $10 grow in ten years to equal $23.67. The answer is

$$P_0(1+x)^n = P_n$$

$$\$10(1+x)^{10} = \$23.67$$

$$(1+x)^{10} = 2.367$$

The interest factor is 2.367, which, according to the compound value of a dollar table for ten years makes the interest rate 9 per cent. This interest factor is located under the vertical column for 9 per cent and in the horizontal column for ten years.

If the present value table is used, the question asks what discount factor (x) at ten years will bring $23.67 back to $10. The answer is

$$P_0 = \frac{P_n}{(1+x)^n}$$

$$\$10 = \frac{\$23.67}{(1+x)^{10}}$$

$$.4224 = \frac{1}{(1+x)^{10}}$$

The interest factor is .4224, which may be found in the present value of a dollar table for ten years in the 9 per cent column. Thus, this problem may be solved by the proper application of either the compound value or present value tables.

(3) An employer offers to start a pension plan for a 45-year-old employee. The plan is to place $1000 per year in a savings account that earns 6 per cent annually. The employee wants to know how much will have accumulated by retirement at age 65.

This is an example of the compound value of an annuity. The payment is $1000 annually, and it will grow at 6 per cent for 20 years. The fund will thus grow to

$$CS = I(1 + i)^0 + \ldots + I(1 + i)^{n-1}$$

$$CS = \$1000 \, (1 + .06)^0 + \ldots + \$1000 \, (1 + .06)^{19}$$

$$CS = \$1000 \, (36.786) = \$36,786$$

where 36.786 in the interest factor for the compound sum of an annuity of one dollar compounded annually at 6 per cent for 20 years.

(4) The same employer decides to place a lump sum in an account that earns 6 per cent and to draw on the account to make the annual payments of $1000. After 20 years all of the funds in the account will be depleted. How much must be deposited intially in the account?

This is an example of the present value of an annuity. The annuity is $1000 per year at 6 per cent for 20 years. Thus, the present value (i.e., the amount of the initial deposit) is

$$PV = \sum_{1}^{n} \frac{I_1}{(1 + i)} + \ldots + \frac{I}{(1 + i)^n}$$

$$PV = \frac{\$1000}{1 + .06} + \ldots + \frac{\$1000}{(1 + .06)^{20}}$$

$$PV = \$1000 \, (11.470) = \$11,470$$

where 11.470 is the interest factor for the present value of an annuity of a dollar at 6 per cent for 20 years. Thus, the employer need deposit only $11,470 in an account that earns 6 per cent to meet the $1000 pension payment for 20 years.

The student should notice the difference between the answers in Equations 3 and 4. In Equation 3 a set of payments earns interest, and thus the future value is larger than just the sum of the 20 payments of $1000. In Equation 4 a future set of payments is valued in present terms. Since future payments are worth less today, the current value is less than the sum of the 20 payments of $1000.

(5) An investment pays $50 per year for ten years, after which $1000 is returned to the investor. If the investor can earn 6 per cent, how

much should this investment cost? This question really contains two questions: What is the present value of an annuity of $50 at 6 per cent for ten years, and what is the present value of $1000 after ten years at 6 per cent? The answer is

$$PV = \sum_{1}^{n} \frac{I_1}{(1+i)^1} + \ldots + \frac{I_n}{(1+i)^n} + \frac{P_n}{(1+i)^n}$$

$$PV = \frac{\$50}{(1+.06)} + \ldots + \frac{\$50}{(1+.06)^{10}} + \frac{\$1000}{(1+.06)^{10}}$$

$$PV = \$50\,(7.360) + \$1000\,(.558) = \$926$$

where 7.360 and .558 are the interest factors for the present value of an annuity of a dollar and the present value of a dollar, respectively, both at 6 per cent for ten years.

This example illustrates that many investments may involve both a series of payments (the annuity component) and a lump sum payment. This particular investment is similar to a bond, the valuation of which is discussed in Chapter 10.

(6) AT&T's dividend has grown annually at the rate of 8 per cent. If this rate is maintained and the current dividend is $4.60, what will the dividend be after ten years? This is a simple compound value of a dollar problem. The dividend will grow to

$$P_n = P_0(1+i)^n$$
$$P_n = \$4.60\,(1+.08)^{10}$$
$$P_n = \$4.60\,(2.159) = \$9.93$$

where 2.159 is the compound value of $1 at 8 per cent for ten years. Although such a growth rate in AT&T's dividend may not be achieved, this problem illustrates how small annual increments can result in a substantial increase in an investor's dividend income over a number of years.

The importance of tables or electronic calculators

The previous examples illustrate the use of interest tables. These problems could be done without such tables, but the amount of calculation would be substantial. The use of interest tables is obviously expeditious in solving any problems that are somewhat involved. Students with access to pocket calculators will find these to be excellent substitutes for interest tables. Some models, such as the Texas Instruments MBA or the Hewlett Packard 38E, have been programmed to include interest tables.* Other calculators may be used to determine the appropriate interest factor.

---

*The Texas Instruments MBA can perform a host of business and financial calculations, including not only problems concerning the time value of money but also calculations involving forecasting, depreciation, cash management, and economic order quantities. See *Calculator Analysis for Business and Finance,* which is designed to accompany the MBA calculator and is published by Texas Instruments.

NONANNUAL COMPOUNDING

The student should have noticed that in the previous examples compounding occurred only once a year. Since compounding can and often does occur more frequently, e.g., semiannually, the equations that were earlier presented must be adjusted. This section extends the discussion of the compound value of a dollar to include compounding for time periods other than a year.

This discussion, however, is limited to the compound value of a dollar. Similar adjustments must be made in the present value of a dollar or present value of an annuity when the funds are compounded more frequently than annually. These adjustments are not explained here but may be found in specialized texts concerning the time value of money.*

Converting annual compounding to other time periods necessitates two adjustments in Equation 1. These adjustments are not particularly difficult. First, a year is divided into the same number of time periods that the funds are being compounded. For semiannual compounding a year consists of two time periods, whereas for quarterly compounding the year comprises four time periods.

Modifications necessitated by nonannual compounding

After adjusting for the number of time periods, the individual adjusts the interest rate to find the rate per time period. This is done by dividing the stated interest rate by the number of time periods. If the interest rate is 8 per cent compounded semiannually, then 8 per cent is divided by 2, giving an interest rate of 4 per cent earned in *each* time period. If the annual rate of interest is 8 per cent compounded quarterly, the interest rate is 2 per cent (8% ÷ 4) in each of the four time periods.

These adjustments may be expressed in more formal terms by modifying Equation 1 as follows:

$$P_0 \left(1 + \frac{i}{c}\right)^{n \times c} = P_1$$

The only new symbol is c, which represents the frequency of compounding. The interest rate (i) is divided by the frequency of compounding (c) to determine the interest rate in each period. The number of years (n) is multiplied by the frequency of compounding to determine the number of time periods.

The use of annual interest tables to solve nonannual compounding problems

The application of this equation may be illustrated in a simple example. An individual invests $100 in an asset that pays 8 per cent compounded quarterly. What will the future value of this asset be after five

---

*See, for instance, Gary Clayton and Christopher Spivey, *The Time Value of Money* (Philadelphia, W. B. Saunders Co., 1978).

years, i.e., $100 will grow to what amount after five years if it is compounded quarterly at 8 per cent? Algebraically, that is

$$P_5 = P_0 \left(1 + \frac{i}{c}\right)^{n \times c}$$

$$P_5 = \$100 \left(1 + \frac{.08}{4}\right)^{5 \times 4}$$

$$P_5 = \$100 \left(1 + .02\right)^{20}$$

In this formulation the investor is earning 2 per cent for 20 time periods. To solve this equation, the interest factor for the compound value of a dollar at 2 per cent for 20 years (1.486) is multiplied by $100. Thus, the future value is

$$P_5 = 100 \ (1.486) = \$148.60$$

The difference between compounding annually and compounding more frequently can be seen by comparing this problem with a problem in which the values are identical except that the interest is compounded annually. The question is then, $100 will grow to what amount after five years at 8 per cent compounded annually? The answer is

$$P_5 = \$100 \ (1 + .08)^5$$

$$P_5 = \$100 \ (1.469)$$

$$P_5 = \$146.90$$

This sum, $146.90, is less than the amount that was earned when the funds were compounded quarterly, which suggests the general conclusion that the more frequently interest is compounded, the greater will be the future amount.

The discussion throughout this text is generally limited to annual compounding. There is, however, one important exception: the valuation of bonds. Bonds pay interest semiannually and this affects their value. Therefore, semiannual compounding is incorporated in the bond valuation model that is presented in Chapter 10.

PRESENT VALUE AND SECURITY VALUATION

Valuation is an application of present value

The valuation of assets is a major theme of this text. Investors must be able to analyze securities to determine their value. This valuation requires forecasting future gains and discounting them back to the present. The present value of an investment, then, is related to future benefits, in the form of either future income or capital appreciation. For example, stocks are purchased for their *future* dividends and potential capital gains but *not* for their previous dividends and price performance. Bonds are purchased for future income. Real estate is bought for the future use of the land and for the potential price appreciation. The concept of discounting future earnings back to the present applies to all investments: It is the future and not the past that matters. The past is relevant only to the extent that it may be used to predict the future.

Some types of analysis (including the technical approach to selecting investments that is discussed in Chapter 15) use the past in the belief that it forecasts the future. Technical analysts employ such information as the past price movements of a stock to determine the most profitable times to buy and sell a security. However, most of the analytical methods that are discussed in this text use some form of discounting in the process of valuing the assets. Prices are the present value of future cash flows, such as dividends.

Subsequent chapters will discuss a variety of assets and the means for analyzing and valuing them. For debt, the current price is related to the series of interest payments and the repayment of the principal, both of which are discounted at the current market rate of interest. The current price of a stock is related to the firm's future earnings and its investment opportunities. Cash flows are discounted back to the present at the appropriate discount factor. For these reasons it is important that the reader start in this introductory chapter to view current prices as the present value of future cash flows. The various features of the different investments, including stocks and bonds, will be discussed, and their prices will be analyzed in terms of present value. If the reader does not understand the material on the time value of money presented in this chapter, the analytical sections of subsequent chapters may be incomprehensible.

Future earnings are discounted to the present

The student of investments should also realize that the markets in which investments are made are very efficient. Many individuals who make investment decisions are intelligent, well-trained professionals who are aware of the tools that will be discussed later in this text. Furthermore, they have the computers and other facilities to perform the necessary analysis for decision making. Information concerning particular investments is quickly disseminated among professional money managers. The novice investor, who does not usually have access to such information or facilities, should not expect to make investments that will yield abnormally high returns. Unless the investor has access to inside information that is not known by the investment community, is unusually lucky, or is a superior forecaster, he or she should not anticipate extraordinarily high returns. If the average stock portfolio earns an annual return of 9 per cent, then the typical investor's portfolio will probably also yield about 9 per cent.

The efficient market

The average return

If, however, someone has that extremely rare ability to forecast the future performance of securities with greater accuracy than the typical analyst, he or she may be able to outperform the market consistently, earning a return in excess of the average. Perhaps it is the conceit of the individual investor to believe that he or she can, in fact, outperform the majority of investors. However, be advised that few, if any, are able to achieve an outstanding return consistently. Efficient markets, which absorb new information and adjust prices accordingly, mean that most investors will achieve (as would be expected) only average results.

This discussion is not meant to discourage potential investors. Security markets are so efficient because of the elaborate system of communications and the training and expertise of many investors and professional money managers. Students are forewarned that if they know of what seems to be a particularly attractive investment, others will also be aware of it. The price that they pay for this investment will, in all probability, take into account their knowledge. It is unlikely that unusually high returns will be earned on the portfolio as a whole, even if a specific security performs particularly well.

This applies not only to the novice investor but also to the professional portfolio manager. As is explained in more detail in Chapters 22 and 25, security analysts and professional money managers do not consistently achieve superior investment results. Like the novice investor, these professionals must also compete in the efficient market.

SUMMARY

Money has time value. A dollar to be received in the future is worth less than a dollar received today. People will forgo current consumption only if future growth in their funds is possible. Such appreciation is called compounding. The longer the funds compound and the higher is the rate at which they compound, the greater will be the amount of funds in the future.

The opposite of compounding is discounting, which determines the present value of funds that are to be received in the future. The present value of a future sum depends both on how far in the future the funds are to be received and on the discount rate.

Compounding and discounting are applied both to single payments and to a series of payments. If the payments in a series are equal and are made annually, the series is called an annuity.

Security analysis involves the time value of money. Although an investment is made in the present, the returns are received in the future. These returns (e.g., the interest or dividends) must be discounted by the appropriate discount factor to determine the present value of the investment.

Terms to Remember

Compounding	Discounting	Semiannual compounding
Annuity	Present value	
Compound sum of an annuity	Present value of an annuity	

Problems

1. An investor bought a stock ten years ago for $20 and sold it today for $35. What is the rate of return on the investment?
2. A saver places $1000 in a certificate of deposit that matures after six years and pays 7 per cent interest, which is compounded annually until the certificate matures.
   a. How much interest will the saver earn if the interest is left to accumulate?
   b. How much interest will the saver earn if the interest is withdrawn each year?
3. A self-employed person deposits $1500 annually in a retirement account that earns 8 per cent.
   a. How much will be in the account when the individual retires at the age of 65 if the savings program starts when the person is age 45?
   b. How much additional money will be in the account if the saver defers retirement until age 70 and continues the annual contributions?
   c. How much additional money will be in the account if the saver discontinues the contributions but does not retire until the age of 70?
4. A saver wants $100,000 after ten years and believes that it is possible to earn 10 per cent on invested funds.
   a. What amount must be invested each year to earn $100,000?
   b. How much must be invested annually if the expected yield is only 7 per cent?
5. An investment offers $10,000 per year for 20 years. If an investor can earn 6 per cent on other investments, what is the current value of this investment? If its current price is $120,000, should the investor buy it?
6. The price of an excellent quality Oriental rug rose from $1500 to $5000 in just six years. What is the rate of increase in the price?
7. Graduating seniors currently earn $12,000. If the rate of inflation is 6 per cent annually, what must these graduates earn after 20 years to maintain their current purchasing power? If the rate of inflation rises to 12 per cent, will they be maintaining their standard of living if they earn $120,000 annually after 20 years?
8. A person who is retiring at the age of 65 and who has $200,000 wants to leave an estate of at least $30,000. How much can the individual draw annually on the $200,000 if the funds earn 7 per cent and the person's life expectancy is 85 years?

SELECTED READINGS

Calculator Analysis for Business and Finance. Texas Instruments Inc., 1977.

Cissell, Robert, and Helen Cissell: *Mathematics of Finance,* 4th ed. Boston, Houghton Mifflin Co., 1972.

Clayton, Gary, and Christopher B. Spivey: *The Time Value of Money.* Philadelphia, W. B. Saunders Co., 1978.

Smith, Jon M.: *Financial Analysis and Business Decisions on the Pocket Calculator.* New York, John Wiley & Sons, Inc., 1976.

Soldofsky, Robert M.: "Growth Yields." *Financial Analysts Journal, 17* (September-October 1961), pp. 43–48.

Learning Objectives

After completing this chapter you should be able to

1. Construct a list of current assets and current liabilities.

2. Distinguish between assets, liabilities, equity, book value, and net worth.

3. Differentiate the time periods covered by the income statement and the balance sheet.

4. Determine if receipts, income, profits, and cash are the same.

5. Define working capital.

6. Isolate the additional information that is learned from the statement of changes in financial position.

7. Identify the weaknesses of accounting data.

chapter 7

FINANCIAL STATEMENTS

The basic data for security analysis may be found in financial statements. Therefore, an understanding of accounting statements is crucial to the study of investment decision making. Unfortunately, it is not possible to explain in this text the subtleties and theories of accounting that are relevant to the construction of financial statements. This chapter does present the basic components of these financial statements and gives a foundation for understanding them, which is a minimum requirement for investors who wish to analyze securities.

The statements that are included here are the balance sheet, the income statement, the statement of retained earnings, and the statement of changes in financial position. This chapter is primarily descriptive and concentrates on the components of these financial statements. The application of this information will be discussed in subsequent chapters that analyze corporate debt and stock.

THE BALANCE SHEET

What is a business worth? One method of answering this question is to enumerate what a business owns and what it owes and to calculate the

The composition of the balance sheet

difference. This difference is called the *book value* or the *equity* that stockholders have in the firm. If the assets and the liabilities are correctly valued, the book value should give a true indication of the market value of the firm.

Exhibit 7–1 presents the balance sheet for CBS, Inc., that was reported in its 1977 annual report. This example combines the financial information for all of the subsidiaries of CBS and hence is called a *consolidated balance sheet*. The firm's assets are listed on the left-hand side of the balance sheet. These assets are divided into three groups: (1) current assets, which are expected to be used and converted into cash within a year, (2) long-term assets, the life span of which exceeds a year, and (3) investments. The liabilities and net worth (i.e., the stockholders' equity) are listed on the right-hand side. It is not necessary for a balance sheet to be arranged in this manner, with the assets listed on the left and the liabilities and equity

CONSOLIDATED BALANCE SHEETS

CBS Inc. and subsidiaries
(Dollars in thousands)

ASSETS

	December 31	
Current assets:	1977	1976
Cash and cash equivalents	$ 199,457	$ 335,086
Notes and accounts receivable, less allowances for doubtful accounts, returns and discounts:		
1977, $122,696; 1976, $73,608	510,024	387,727
Inventories	204,124	151,880
Program rights	121,328	94,214
Prepaid expenses	52,388	32,860
Total current assets	**1,087,321**	**1,001,767**
Investments	**27,838**	**20,990**
Property, plant and equipment:		
Land	26,045	25,226
Buildings	158,370	148,139
Machinery and equipment	269,113	235,969
Leasehold improvements	29,948	25,508
	483,476	434,842
Less accumulated depreciation	223,330	206,794
Net property, plant and equipment	**260,146**	**228,048**
Excess of cost over net assets of businesses acquired, less amortization	**62,619**	**53,376**
Other assets	**80,181**	**47,429**
	$1,518,105	**$1,351,610**

EXHIBIT 7–1. Balance sheets.

EXHIBIT 7–1 continued on page 121.

shown on the right. However, this is the form that is frequently used, for it clearly illustrates the assets, liabilities, and net worth of the firm.

Firms must have goods or services or both to sell. These are the firm's inventory. Not all inventory is ready for sale: Some of the goods may be unfinished (goods in process), and there may also be inventories of raw materials. According to the balance sheet for CBS, total inventory amounts to $204,124,000. The balance sheet does not subdivide the inventory into finished goods, work in process, and raw materials. The security analyst should remember that only finished items are available for sale. Considerable time and cost may be involved in processing raw materials into finished goods. Therefore, much of a firm's inventory may not be saleable and cannot be readily converted into cash. Since CBS does not report the breakdown of its inventory, it is not apparent if the goods are available for immediate sale or if they are in the form of raw materials or work in progress.

Current assets: Inventory

When the goods or services are sold, the firm receives either cash or a promise of payment in the future. A credit sale generates an account receivable, which represents money that is due to the firm. CBS has

Accounts receivable

LIABILITIES AND SHAREHOLDERS' EQUITY

	December 31 1977	December 31 1976
Current liabilities:		
Current maturities of long-term debt (note 5)	$ 3,962	$ 2,984
Accounts payable and accrued liabilities	461,034	348,023
Income taxes	53,838	63,165
Total current liabilities	**518,834**	**414,172**
Long-term debt (note 5)	**96,950**	**96,666**
Other liabilities	**70,788**	**64,619**
Deferred income taxes	**22,369**	**30,280**
Shareholders' equity:		
Preference stock (authorized 6,000,000 shares): $1.00 convertible Series A preference stock, par value $1.00 per share; authorized 3,300,000 shares; outstanding 303,982 shares in 1977 (aggregate liquidation value $13,223) and 543,519 shares in 1976 (note 6)	304	544
Common stock, par value $2.50 per share; authorized 100,000,000 shares in 1977 and 50,000,000 shares in 1976; issued 28,988,756 shares (notes 6 and 7)	72,472	72,472
Additional paid-in capital	209,681	219,651
Retained earnings	604,007	480,872
	886,464	773,539
Less common stock in treasury, at cost: 1,406,231 shares in 1977 and 579,191 shares in 1976 (note 6)	77,300	27,666
Total shareholders' equity	**809,164**	**745,873**
	$1,518,105	**$1,351,610**

See notes to consolidated financial statements

EXHIBIT 7–1.
Continued

$510,024,000 in receivables; this is a net figure obtained by subtracting the sum of doubtful accounts and discounts ($122,696) from the total amount of receivables. Since a firm does not always obtain payment from all of its accounts receivable, it is necessary to make an allowance for these "doubtful accounts." Thus, only the net realizable figure is included in the tabulation of the firm's assets.

Cash

A cash sale generates the asset cash for the firm. Since holding cash will earn nothing, some of it may be invested in short-term money instruments, such as treasury bills. Cash and short-term money instruments may be combined under a classification called cash and cash equivalents. For CBS, cash and marketable securities total $199,457,000. This money is available to meet the firm's immediate financial obligations.

Cash and cash equivalents, accounts receivable, and inventory are the major short-term assets. A firm, however, may have other short-term assets (as CBS does) including what is known as prepaid expense. CBS also includes in its short-term assets the rights to programs that it broadcasts.

The firm's current assets comprise cash and cash equivalents, accounts receivable, inventory, and other short-term assets. For CBS this amount is $1,087,321,000. These short-term assets will flow through the firm during its fiscal year and will be used to meet its financial obligations, which must be paid during the year. The total value and the nature of these assets are very important in determining the firm's ability to meet its current obligations.

Long-term assets: Property, plant, and equipment

Long-term assets include the firm's property, plant, and equipment, which are used for many years. The firm's employees utilize these long-term assets in conjunction with current assets to create the products or services that the company offers for sale. The type and the quantity of long-term assets that a company uses vary with the industry. Some industries, such as the utilities or transportation industries, require numerous plants and extensive equipment. Firms in these industries must have substantial investments in long-term assets in order to operate. Not all companies choose to own these long-term assets; instead, they may rent them, which is called leasing. Regardless of whether the firm leases or owns these assets, it is primarily the long-term assets that are utilized to produce the company's output.

CBS has $260,146,000 invested in long-term assets. The balance sheet indicates that the firm initially invested $457,431,000 in buildings, equipment, and leasehold improvements. These assets have depreciated by $223,330,000 and are currently being carried on the books at $234,101,000 ($260,146,000 minus the value of the land). Depreciation is important because it is the process of allocating the cost of the equipment over its useful life. Thus, the book value of long-term assets is reduced with time as the assets are used by the firm.

Hidden assets

CBS owns land that is worth $26,045,000. Land does not depreciate with use, and hence the book value of the land is usually the purchase price, unless the value of the land has been restated to indicate a price change. For example, the value of the land may rise as a result of inflation, in which case the accountants may increase the land's value on the books. However, because this revaluation rarely happens, many firms have "hidden assets," such as land whose market value is understated.

The remaining entries on the asset side of the balance sheet are miscellaneous and other assets, and investments. Miscellaneous and other assets include such things as rent and electricity deposits. Investments include securities such as stock in other companies. Even though such stock may be sold and converted into cash, it may be considered separately from the firm's current assets. For example, if the securities were purchased with the intention of holding them for several years as an investment, they would be placed in a separate category on the balance sheet. For CBS, $170,638,000 ($27,838,000 + $62,619,000 + $80,181,000) is tied up in such investments and other assets.

The total assets owned by CBS ($1,518,105,000) are the sum of the short-term assets ($1,087,321,000) the long-term assets ($260,146,000), and other assets ($170,638,000). These assets are financed by what the firm owes and owns — its liabilities and equity, which are on the other side of the balance sheet.

The firm's liabilities are divided into two groups: current liabilities, which must be paid during the fiscal year, and long-term liabilities, which are due after the fiscal year. Short-term liabilities are primarily accounts payable and short-term loans. Just as the firm may sell goods on credit, it may also purchase goods and raw materials on credit. This trade credit is short-term and is retired as the goods are produced and sold. In the balance sheet for CBS, accounts payable also include wages and salaries that have been earned but not paid.* In addition to accounts payable, the firm has other short-term debt that must be paid during the fiscal year. This includes short-term notes for funds that the company has borrowed from commercial banks or other lending institutions and that portion of its long-term debt that must be retired this year. CBS does not list separate entries for notes payable but includes all of these current liabilities in one entry ($461,034,000). The remaining current obligations are the interest owed (accrued interest), the taxes that must be paid during the year ($53,838,000), and that part of the long-term debt that matures during the year ($3,962,000). For CBS, the sum of all of these current liabilities is $518,834,000.

Long-term obligations are retired at some time after the current fiscal year. Such obligations may include bonds that are outstanding and mortgages on real property. These long-term debts represent part of the permanent financing because these funds are committed to financing the business for a long time. Short-term liabilities cannot be considered part of the firm's permanent financing because these liabilities must be paid within a relatively short period. For CBS, the long-term liabilities consist solely of long-term debt ($96,950,000). For a breakdown of the various debt issues,

Current liabilities: Accounts payable

Short-term notes

Long-term liabilities: mortgages and bonds

---

*Many balance sheets have a separate entry called accrued liabilities to cover these current liabilities.

the reader is referred to note 5, which is presented after the body of the financial statement in Exhibit 7–1.

In addition to short-term and long-term debt, CBS has other liabilities of $70,788,000 that have not been classified and deferred taxes of $22,369,000. Although these taxes may eventually be paid, such payments will not be made during the current fiscal year, and therefore they are not regarded as a current liability.*

Equity

In most balance sheets, the stockholders' equity is listed after the liabilities. There are three essential entries: the stock outstanding, the additional paid-in capital, and the earnings that have been retained. The stock outstanding shows the various types of stock that have been issued and their quantities. CBS has two issues — preference stock and common stock.† Many firms, however, have only common stock outstanding.

Must differentiate between preferred and common stock

When the term *book value* is used, it generally implies the net worth of the common stock only. This is because investors are primarily concerned with the value of the common stock, which, from an accounting point of view, is the sum of the common stock ($72,472,000), the additional paid-in capital ($209,681,000), and the retained earnings ($604,007,000). The retained earnings, like the common stock and the paid-in capital, represent an investment in the firm by stockholders. Since these stockholders would receive the earnings if they were distributed, retained earnings are part of the stockholders' contribution to the financing of the firm.

Net worth

The sum of the stock outstanding, the additional paid-in capital, and the retained earnings for CBS is $886,464,000, which is the net worth or book value of the firm. If the firm were to repurchase some of its outstanding shares, an adjustment would have to be made to account for the price that was paid for these shares. Such repurchases are partial liquidations that reduce the stockholders' investment in the firm. For CBS, such repurchases amount to $77,300,000. Total shareholders' equity is then $809,164,000, of which all but $304,000 (for the preference stock) represents the common stockholders' investment in the firm.

Book value per share

The individual investor is primarily concerned with the value of a share. To obtain the book value per share, the total equity available to the common stock is divided by the number of shares outstanding. For CBS, the per share book value is

$$\frac{\$809,164,000 - \$304,000}{28,988,756 - 1,406,231} = \$29.33$$

Notice that the total equity is reduced by the value of the shares of preference stock and that the number of shares outstanding (28,988,756) is reduced by the number of shares that have been repurchased and are being held by the firm. The book value per share ($29.33 for CBS) is the

---

*Deferred taxes arise from differences in various accounting methods for recognizing income and expenses. The procedure for allocating taxes that result from differences in the timing of revenues and expenses may lead to deferred taxes.

†Preference stock is a type of preferred stock and may be analyzed as if it were preferred stock.

accounting value of a share held by the firm's many common stockholders.

If CBS were to cease operations, sell its assets, and pay off its liabilities, the owners would receive their equity in the firm. If the assets and the liabilities are accurately measured by the dollar values on the balance sheet, then the book value is the amount that the owners will receive in the event of liquidation (i.e., $808,860,000 for common stockholders). From an accounting point of view, the net worth of the firm is the book value; however, for reasons that will be discussed subsequently, this value may be misleading.

A balance sheet gives the investor an indication of the firm's financial position. The balance sheet for CBS indicates that the firm owns assets valued at over $1.5 billion and has liabilities of $0.7 billion and equity of $0.8 billion. The sum of the liabilities and equity must equal the sum of all of the assets, for it is the liabilities and equity that finance the assets. The assets could not be acquired if creditors and owners did not provide the funds. Hence, the sum of the funds from the various sources (i.e., the liabilities and equity) must equal the sum of the assets. For CBS, the balance sheet indicates that liabilities finance 47 per cent ($0.7 billion ÷ $1.5 billion), and the equity finances 53 per cent ($0.8 billion ÷ $1.5 billion) of the total assets. Therefore, the balance sheet indicates the proportion of the assets that is financed with debt and the proportion that is financed with equity.

The balance sheet indicates a firm's financial position

Two additional points need to be made about balance sheets. First, a balance sheet is constructed at the end of a fiscal period (e.g., a year). It indicates the value of the assets, liabilities, and net worth at that time and only at that time. Since financial transactions occur continuously, the information contained in a balance sheet may become rapidly outdated. Second, the value assigned to the assets need not mirror their market value. Instead, the values of the assets may be overstated or understated. For example, the firm owns accounts receivable, not all of which will be paid. Therefore, the value of the firm's accounts receivable may be overstated. As was explained earlier, the firm does allow for these potential losses in an effort to make the balance sheet entries more accurate. However, the allowances may be insufficient, and thus the value of the assets will be overstated. Conversely, the value of other assets may be understated. For example, the land on which the plant is built may have increased in value but may continue to be carried on the company's books at its cost. This, of course, understates the value of the land if it has appreciated in price.

It is constructed at a given time

For the book value of the firm to be a true indication of its worth, all of the assets on the balance sheet should be valued at their market prices; however, this practice is not necessarily followed. Accountants suggest that assets be valued conservatively (1) at the cost of the asset or (2) at its market value depending on which is less. Such conservatism is prudent but may result in assets having hidden or understated value if their appreciation is not recognized. Because of these accounting methods, the equity or net worth of a firm may not be a good measure of its value.

Book value is not market value

THE INCOME STATEMENT

A summary of revenues

The income statement tells investors how much accounting income the company has earned during its fiscal year. It is a summary of revenues and expenses and hence indicates the firm's accounting profits or losses. It is not, however, a summary of cash receipts and disbursements.

Exhibit 7–2 is the income statement that was reported by CBS in its 1977 annual report. It gives earnings for both 1977 and 1976 to facilitate a year-to-year comparison. The statement starts with a summary of the firm's sources of revenue; for CBS, the sole source of revenue is sales ($2.776 billion). Next follows a summary of the cost of goods sold ($1.759 billion). (The difference between sales and the cost of goods sold is the gross profit, but CBS has chosen not to make a separate entry for it.) Then the selling and administrative expenses ($684,800,000) are subtracted to determine the operating income. If the firm has other sources of income (as CBS does), they are added to the operating income to give the company's total income before taxes. CBS has $7,940,000 in interest income and $22,043,000 in other income, so its total income before taxes is $361.65 million.

A summary of expenses

Earnings per share

Both federal and state governments levy corporate income taxes. To obtain the net income available to stockholders ($182,008,000), the corporate income tax ($179,642,000) is subtracted from the total income ($361,650,000). Stockholders are generally not concerned with total earnings but with *earnings per share*. The bottom line of the income statement show the total earnings divided by the number of shares outstanding, which yields the earnings per share (EPS = $6.50). This is the amount of earnings available to each share of common stock.

Profits are distributed or retained

When the firm earns profits, management must decide what to do with these earnings. There are two choices: (1) to pay out some or all of

CONSOLIDATED INCOME STATEMENTS
CBS Inc. and subsidiaries
(Dollars in thousands)

	Years ended December 31	
	1977	1976
Net sales	**$2,776,311**	**$2,230,576**
Cost of sales	1,759,844	1,386,610
Selling, general and administrative expenses	684,800	539,425
Operating income	**331,667**	**304,541**
Interest income, net (note 9)	7,940	8,039
Other income, net (note 9)	22,043	18,146
Income before income taxes	**361,650**	**330,726**
Income taxes (note 3)	179,642	166,731
Net income	**$ 182,008**	**$ 163,995**
Net income per share of common stock (note 4)	**$6.50**	**$5.75**

EXHIBIT 7–2. Income statements.

See notes to consolidated financial statements

these profits to stockholders in the form of cash dividends or (2) to retain the earnings. The retained earnings on the balance sheet are the sum of all of the firm's undistributed profits that have accumulated but that have not been paid out in dividends during the company's life. These retained earnings are used to finance the purchase of assets or to retire debt. How this year's earnings were used does not appear on the income statement. The income statement merely summarizes corporate revenues and expenses during the fiscal year and indicates whether the firm produced a net profit or loss. To learn how the earnings were employed and if there were changes in the firm's sources of financing during the fiscal year, it is necessary to consult the statement of retained earnings and the statement of changes in financial position.

THE STATEMENT OF RETAINED EARNINGS

The statement of retained earnings indicates the amount of the company's current earnings and adds them to its previously retained earnings. It shows the division of earnings between those distributed to the stockholders and those retained to finance additional assets or to retire debt. The statement of retained earnings for CBS is illustrated in Exhibit 7–3. This statement also includes changes (if any) in the additional paid-in

CONSOLIDATED STATEMENTS OF RETAINED EARNINGS AND ADDITIONAL PAID-IN CAPITAL

CBS Inc. and subsidiaries
(Dollars in thousands)

	Years ended December 31	
RETAINED EARNINGS	1977	1976
Balance at beginning of year	**$480,872**	**$367,152**
Net income	182,008	163,995
	662,880	531,147
Less cash dividends:		
Common stock: 1977, $2.10 per share;		
1976, $1.745 per share	58,526	49,612
Series A preference stock, $1.00 per share	347	663
Balance at end of year	**$604,007**	**$480,872**
ADDITIONAL PAID-IN CAPITAL		
Balance at beginning of year	**$219,651**	**$230,860**
Excess of cost of treasury stock over par value of preference stock exchanged on conversion	(8,807)	(10,937)
Miscellaneous, net...................................	(1,163)	(272)
Balance at end of year	**$209,681**	**$219,651**

See notes to consolidated financial statements

EXHIBIT 7–3. Statements of retained earnings.

capital. For CBS, these changes were minimal and will be omitted from this discussion.

The statement indicates that CBS had previously retained $480,872,000 of its earnings. In 1977, the corporation earned $182,008,000 and distributed cash dividends of $58,873,000. Thus, the firm retained over $123,135,000 of its earnings, entering its 1978 fiscal year with retained earnings of $604,007,000. This sum represents the accumulation of earnings over the life of CBS. These retained earnings are part of the stockholders' investment in the firm because they represent their claims on the firm's assets. Therefore, this amount must also appear in the equity section on the corporation's 1977 balance sheet. If the student reexamines Exhibit 7–1, the accumulated retained earnings of $604,007,000 are, in fact, given.

Retained earnings are not cash

There is a common misconception that if a company has retained earnings, it has cash and can pay cash dividends. Retained earnings are not cash. After the income has been earned, it is used to purchase income-earning assets or to retire outstanding debt. Thus, the income is used to increase the firm's future profitability and is not held in the form of cash. How these earnings and the company's other sources of finance were employed during the year is indicated in the statement of changes in financial position.

THE STATEMENT OF CHANGES IN FINANCIAL POSITION

A link between the income statement and the balance sheet

The balance sheet shows the book value of a firm's assets and liabilities at a given time. The income statement summarizes the revenues and expenses and shows the profits or losses for the accounting period. The statement of retained earnings reveals whether the earnings were distributed or retained. None of these statements indicates how the income was used or what other sources of finance the firm acquired during the accounting period. The statement of changes in financial position is the link between the income statement and the balance sheet because it identifies how funds were acquired and how they were used.

The importance of this statement is well recognized. Publicly held firms are required by the Securities and Exchange Commission to include it in their annual reports. The student should note that the statement is sometimes called by other names, such as the funds statement or the statement of sources and uses. However, the accounting profession recommends that it be called the statement of changes in financial position because it reveals the firm's sources of funds and their subsequent use in order to show changes in its financial position.

A company obtains funds from a variety of sources and puts them to use in a variety of ways. The term *funds* is not a synonym for *cash*. It is a broad term encompassing all of the sources available for financing a firm's assets. Some of these sources of funds are long–term, such as the sale of bonds and stocks, while others are short-term, such as accounts payable.* Correspondingly, some of the uses of these funds are long-term, including the purchase of plant and equipment, whereas others are short-term, including accounts receivable.† The statement of changes in financial position emphasizes the firm's current position (i.e., the management of short-term assets and liabilities).‡

This statement isolates changes in working capital. Working capital is the difference between the value of current assets and that of current liabilities. The bottom line of the statement indicates any change in the firm's working capital. Such changes can be very important in analyzing a firm's capacity to meet its financial obligations as they become due. An increase in the amount of working capital shows that the firm has increased its current assets relative to its current liabilities: It has more current assets flowing through the firm relative to its current liabilities. This should increase its capacity to meet these obligations as they become due.

Working capital

The statement of changes in financial position starts by listing all of the sources of working capital. These are the firm's income and the funds generated by the sale of long-term assets, long-term borrowing, and the sale of new securities. Next are listed all of the uses of working capital, including the distribution of cash dividends, the purchase of long-term assets, the repayment of long-term debt, and the repurchase of outstanding stock. The difference between the amount obtained from these sources and the amount spent on the uses of these funds, then, is the change in working capital.

Sources of working capital

The statement of changes in financial position for CBS is shown in Exhibit 7–4. At the top of the statement the firm's sources of working capital are given. The working capital that is provided by operations is listed first. This is income primarily from operations and depreciation. Although it is obvious that income is a source of capital, depreciation is not so obvious. Depreciation is a noncash expense that allocates the cost of an asset over its useful life. Since it is a noncash expense, the firm has those funds in its possession and management can use them as it sees fit. To adjust for this depreciation expense, accountants add the depreciation charges to the income from operations to obtain the total working capital from operations.

Operations provided $207.3 million in working capital for CBS. This consisted primarily of income ($182.0 million) and depreciation ($40.6 million). There were a few negative sources that reduced income from operations by $15.3 million.

---

*An account payable is a source of funds because the company has the use of an asset, such as cash, until the account is paid.
†An account receivable is a use of funds because someone must provide the money to cover the account until the money is collected.
‡Investors should analyze the appropriateness of the sources for particular uses. For example, short-term funds should not be used to acquire long-term assets.

**CONSOLIDATED STATEMENTS OF CHANGES
IN FINANCIAL POSITION**
CBS Inc. and subsidiaries
(Dollars in thousands)

	Years ended December 31	
Sources of working capital:	1977	1976
Income from operations	$182,008	$163,995
Items not affecting working capital:		
Depreciation and amortization	40,679	33,417
Deferred income taxes	(7,911)	7,537
Income from investments accounted for under		
the equity method	(7,438)	(4,154)
Working capital provided by operations	$207,338	$200,795
Issuance of treasury shares under employee benefit plans	$ 6,401	$ 8,124
Increase in other liabilities	6,169	1,645
Decrease in investments	590	2,345
Other, net	3,521	3,390
Total sources	**224,019**	**216,299**
Uses of working capital:		
Cash dividends	58,873	50,275
Purchase of property, plant and equipment	63,932	46,042
Purchase of treasury shares	66,247	20,606
Decrease (increase) in notes and mortgages payable	(284)	2,263
Increase in intangible and other assets	54,359	4,050
Total uses	**243,127**	**123,236**
Net increase (decrease) in working capital	**$ (19,108)**	**$ 93,063**
Changes in working capital:		
Increases (decreases) in current assets:		
Cash and cash equivalents	$(135,629)	$ 67,275
Notes and accounts receivable	122,297	47,808
Inventories	52,244	15,100
Program rights	27,114	15,343
Prepaid expenses	19,528	(2,115)
	85,554	143,411
(Increases) decreases in current liabilities:		
Current maturities of long-term debt	(978)	1,348
Accounts payable and accrued liabilities	(113,011)	(35,811)
Income taxes	9,327	(15,885)
	(104,662)	(50,348)
Net increase (decrease) in working capital	**$ (19,108)**	**$ 93,063**

EXHIBIT 7-4. Statements of changes in financial position.

See notes to consolidated financial statements

The sources of working capital other than operations are listed next. For CBS these include $6.4 million from the issuance of new stock to employees, $6.2 million in new debt, and $4.1 million from the sale of investment assets and from other sources. The total of these nonoperating sources of working capital is $16.7 million, which yields $224.0 million in working capital from all sources.

Working capital was used by CBS primarily to pay cash dividends ($58.9 million), to purchase property, plant, and equipment ($63.9 million), to repurchase stock ($66.2 million), and to increase other long-term assets, especially intangibles. (These intangibles include such assets as patents and goodwill, which CBS may acquire when it purchases another firm.) The summation of these uses of working capital is $243.1 million, giving a change in working capital of $−19.1 million ($224.0 million − $243.1 million). Such a change is perceptibly different from that of the preceding year, when working capital rose by $93.1 million. By comparing individual entries for changes in working capital for 1976 and 1977, it is obvious that the reduction in 1977 is not the result of changes in the sources or the amount of working capital. These were virtually the same for the two years ($224.0 million in 1977 versus $216.3 million in 1976). There was, however, considerable difference in the uses of working capital ($243.1 million in 1977 versus $123.3 million in 1976). Most of this difference can be attributed to the use of working capital to repurchase shares which are held in the firm's treasury ($66.2 million in 1977 versus $20.6 million in 1976), and to acquire intangible and other assets ($54.4 million in 1977 versus $4.1 million in 1976).

Uses of working capital

The final part of the statement of changes in financial position presents changes in specific current assets and current liabilities. The current assets of CBS increased by $85.6 million; this sum is composed of increases in receivables, inventory, program rights, and prepaid expenses. Part of this increase was offset by a decline in cash and cash equivalents, but there was a net increase in current assets.

Changes in specific currents assets and current liabilities

Current liabilities also rose by $104.7 million, reflecting primarily the increases in accounts payable and accrued liabilities. Current liabilities increased more than current assets, which again indicates that working capital declined (by $19.1 million). This is, of course, the same information that was presented earlier in the statement of changes in financial position. This last set of entries shows specifically which current assets and current liabilities changed and, in this case, which current liabilities caused the decline in working capital.

In 1977 CBS experienced a small decline in working capital, whereas in 1976 there was an increase. The decline indicates that CBS incurred more current liabilities than it acquired current assets and that some of the current liabilities were used to finance long-term assets. This violates a cardinal rule of finance: Never use short-term debt to purchase long-term assets. Short-term liabilities must be rolled over continually, i.e., the loans have to be repeatedly negotiated. Since the terms and cost of these loans may rise in the future, the use of short-term debt to acquire long-term assets will increase the element of financial risk. However, in this example, the decrease in working capital is minimal. CBS has demonstrated strong earnings growth and has very little long-term debt outstanding, so the decline in working capital cannot be interpreted as an indication of financial weakness.

Interpretation

THE ROLE OF THE AUTHOR
THE ROLE OF THE AUDITOR

Accounts must be examined

Accounting statements of publicly held firms must be audited by an independent certified public accountant (CPA). These audits, which are an official examination of accounts, must be held annually. After conducting the audit, the CPA issues an auditor's opinion that attests to the reasonableness of the financial statements and their conformity with generally accepted accounting principles. This auditor's opinion must be included in the firm's annual report.

The auditor's opinion

Exhibit 7–5 presents the auditor's opinion that was published in the 1978 CBS Annual Report. It is a brief document; the first paragraph covers the scope of the auditor's examination, and the second paragraph gives the opinion. On occasion, the evaluation may include a discussion of special factors that qualify the auditor's opinion concerning specific details of the financial statements.

Its importance to the investor

Since audits are held by independent accountants, investors can have confidence in the financial statements. The accountants' objectivity enhances their credibility. However, an auditor's opinion does not guarantee the accuracy of the statements. Responsibility for accuracy rests with the firm's management.

WEAKNESSES IN ACCOUNTING DATA

There are several weaknesses inherent in accounting statements, but this does not mean that financial analysis employing accounting data should be discounted. The financial analyst, however, needs to be aware of the limitations so that accounting statements may be interpreted in light of these weaknesses.

Nonmeasurable items

First, accounting data do not take into account nonmeasurable items,

---

Report of Independent Certified Public Accountants
To the Shareholders of CBS Inc.:
We have examined the consolidated balance sheets of CBS Inc. and subsidiaries as of December 31, 1977 and 1976, and the related consolidated statements of income, retained earnings, additional paid-in capital and changes in financial position for the years then ended. Our examinations were made in accordance with generally accepted auditing standards and, accordingly, included such tests of the accounting records and such other auditing procedures as we considered necessary in the circumstances.

In our opinion, the financial statements referred to above present fairly the consolidated financial position of CBS Inc. and subsidiaries at December 31, 1977 and 1976, and the results of their operations and the changes in their financial position for the years then ended, in conformity with generally accepted accounting principles applied on a consistent basis.

EXHIBIT 7–5. An auditor's opinion.

1251 Avenue of the Americas
New York, New York 10020
February 7, 1978

COOPERS & LYBRAND

such as the quality of the research department or the marketing performance of the firm. Performance is measured solely in terms of money, and the implication of accounting data is that if the firm consistently leads its industry (or is at least above average), its management and divisions are qualitatively superior to its competitors. There probably does exist a relationship between performance and superior financial statements. The strong financial statements of IBM mirror the quality of its management and of its research and marketing staffs. However, many firms may be able to improve their financial position temporarily and achieve short-term superior performance that cannot be maintained.

Second, accounting data may not be sufficiently challenged by auditors. Although accounting records are examined for reasonableness and conformity with accounting principles, the auditors may lack knowledge in specific areas pertinent to the firm's accounting statements. For example, the auditors may accept the estimates of the firm's engineers because the auditors lack the specialized knowledge necessary to challenge the estimates. This is not meant to suggest that the auditors are incompetent; they may, however, lack specific knowledge that is necessary to verify the authenticity of some of the data used by the corporation's accountants.

The auditors' insufficient knowledge

Third, accounting statements that are available to the public give aggregate data. Although the company's management has access to itemized data, individual investors or security analysts may not receive sufficiently detailed information to guide investment decisions. For example, a company may not give its sales figures according to product lines. Aggregate sales data do not inform the public as to which of the company's products are its primary sources of revenue. The use of aggregate numbers in the firm's income statements and balance sheets may hide important information that the investor or security analyst could use in the study of the company.

The problem of aggregate data

Fourth, accounting data may be biased. For example, the valuation of assets by the lower of either cost or market value may result in biased information if the dollar value of the assets has significantly risen (as may occur during periods of inflation). Such increases in value are hidden by the use of the historical cost, and thus using this method of valuation accounting statements do not give a true indication of the value of the firm's assets. If the value of the assets has risen and this is not recognized by the accounting data, then the rate of return earned by the company on its assets is slanted upward. If the true value of the assets were used to determine the rate of return that the firm earns on its assets, the rate would be lower. In this case the use of historical cost instead of market value results in inaccurate measures of the company's performance.

The inaccurate valuation of assets

Fifth, within the last decade inflation has caused a problem in interpreting accounting data. Inflation makes comparisons of accounting data since 1968 difficult. Items that were purchased in 1968 cannot currently be replaced at 1968 prices. As the firm's plant and equipment wear out, these assets will have to be replaced at higher prices. For the firm to maintain its current capacity, additional financing will be required to cover the higher

Inflation

costs. This decline in the purchasing power of money is not indicated by accounting data and poses one of the biggest problems for accountants to overcome.*

The preceding discussion illustrates some limitations and weaknesses in accounting data. Despite the problems that exist, financial analysis employing accounting data is a useful tool in evaluating a company's financial position. As long as the analyst is aware of the limitations of accounting data, financial statements may be interpreted in light of them.

SUMMARY

This chapter has briefly summarized the four major accounting statements that are published in the annual reports of publicly held firms. The balance sheet enumerates what a firm owns (its assets), what it owes (its liabilities), and the stockholders' investment or equity. The income statement summarizes the firm's revenues and other income, its expenses, and its profit or loss for the accounting period. The statement of retained earnings indicates the distribution or retention of earnings. Lastly, the statement of changes in financial position summarizes the sources of finance, their amounts, and how these funds were used. This statement emphasizes changes in the firm's working capital, which is the difference between its current assets and its current liabilities.

The data in accounting statements are used by security analysts and investors to indicate the firm's performance and financial condition. Although the investor does not need to have an accountant's understanding of these statements, a rudimentary understanding of security analysis will perhaps result in better communication with professionals, such as brokers and bankers, with whom the investor has contact.

Terms to Remember

Consolidated balance sheet	Hidden assets	Retained earnings
Current asset	Long-term debt	Earnings per share
Current liability	Stockholders' equity	Working capital
Long-term asset	Book value	Auditor's opinion

---

*This is also one of industry's major problems. Firms must replace aging plant and equipment at a higher cost, which requires greater capital investments than some firms are able to afford.

Questions

1. Specify which of the following are assets and which are liabilties: (a) cash, (b) accrued interest, (c) equipment, (d) accounts payable, (e) goods in process, and (f) additional paid-in capital.
2. Why may the market value of an asset be different from its book value?
3. What time period is covered by a balance sheet and by an income statement?
4. Are a firm's profits equal to its cash? What may a corporation do with its profits?
5. Why do retained earnings represent an investment in the firm by the stockholders?
6. What is depreciation?
7. Which of the following represent a use of funds and which represent a source of funds?
   a. an increase in inventory
   b. an increase in accounts payable
   c. a decrease in accounts receivable
   d. a reduction in long-term debt
   e. an increase in equipment
   f. an increase in depreciation
   g. an increase in cash
8. What is working capital? What effect does each of the following have on working capital?
   a. a new issue of stock
   b. an increase in accounts payable
   c. cash dividends paid by the firm
   d. a reduction in inventory
   e. a reduction in long-term debt
9. How does inflation affect the investor's interpretation of the accounting data used in statements?
10. From the investor's point of view, why is it important to have a firm's financial statements audited?

SELECTED READINGS

Bernstein, Leopold A.: *Financial Statement Analysis*, Revised ed. Homewood, Ill., Richard D. Irwin, Inc. 1978.

Bierman, Harold, Jr., and Alan R. Drebin: *Financial Accounting: An Introduction*, 3rd ed. Philadelphia, W. B. Saunders Co., 1978.

Briloff, Abraham: *Unaccountable Accounting*. New York, Harper & Row Publishers, Inc., 1972.

Davidson, S., J. S. Schindler, R. L. Weil, et al.: *Financial Accounting: An Introduction To Concepts, Methods, and Uses*. New York, Holt, Rinehart & Winston, Inc., 1976.

Hawkins, David F.: *Corporate Financial Reporting*. Homewood Il., Richard D. Irwin, Inc., 1977.

Meigs, Walter B., A. N. Mosich, and Charles E. Johnson: *Accounting – The Basis For Business Decisions*, 3rd ed. New York, McGraw-Hill Book Co., 1972.

Learning Objectives

After completing this chapter you should be able to

1. Name four categories of financial information that are generally available to investors.

2. List the publications concerning investments that are available in your library.

3. Distinguish between the contents of an annual report, a brokerage firm's research report, and an investment advisory report.

4. Identify inside information.

5. Explain the major drawback of the information that is available to investors.

6. Explain why many sources of information on investments are self-serving.

chapter 8

SOURCES OF INFORMATION

Investing requires knowledge. Savers who want to buy securities have a vast supply of information available to them. Their problems lie not in obtaining information but in determining which information is useful and then interpreting it. This chapter will describe and illustrate the variety of sources that are available to investors who are interested in purchasing stocks and bonds. Other types of investments, such as art, require specialized knowledge and specialized sources of information, which are not discussed in this chapter.

The major sources of information available to potential investors include corporate publications, brokerage firms' research reports, and investment advisory services. Some of this information, such as a firm's annual report, may be obtained at very little cost. Other information, such as the *Value Line Investment Survey*, can be purchased only at considerable expense. The costly sources of information, however, may be available in the public library or in a local college library.

CORPORATE SOURCES OF INFORMATION

Publicly held firms must inform stockholders

Publicly held firms are required by both federal and state laws, including the full-disclosure laws, to publish annual and quarterly reports, which are sent to stockholders. Furthermore, they require listed firms to publish news bulletins giving any pertinent changes in the firm's financial position and any other information that may alter the value of its securities.

Although this information is sent free of charge to all stockholders in whose name the securities are registered, other investors and potential investors may request that the firm place their names on its mailing list. Firms are not required to do this, but many will honor such requests.

THE ANNUAL REPORT

Perhaps the most important publication of the firm is its annual report. This covers a wide variety of topics, as may be seen in the table of contents of the 1977 CBS annual report (Exhibit 8–1).

Annual reports play a public relations role

Although the annual report includes a substantial amount of factual and financial information, it should be viewed as a public relations document. It is frequently printed on expensive paper and filled with colorful pictures of products and of smiling employees. One notable exception is the Coca-Cola Company, whose annual report is brief and designed to convey the impression of financial conservatism. In some years its annual report has even been printed on recycled paper to demonstrate the company's concern for the environment.

Firms use the annual report to explain, at least superficially, their achievements of the past year. These discussions are in general terms, but the firm's careful selection of words may allow the investor to read between the lines. Generally, the more substantive material is presented in the financial statements, particularly in the explanatory footnotes.

The typical annual report begins with a letter from the president of the company to the stockholders. The chairman of the board of directors also frequently signs this letter. The letter reviews the highlights of the year and points out certain noteworthy events, such as a dividend increase or a merger. It may also forecast events in the immediate future, such as next year's sales growth and earnings.

After the letter to the stockholders, the annual report may describe the various components of the business. For example, it may illustrate with words and pictures the various products that the firm makes, the type of research and development in which the company is engaged, the particular application of the firm's goods and services in different industries, and the outlook for the firm's products in the various industries in which it sells.

**1977
ANNUAL REPORT
TO THE
SHAREHOLDERS
OF CBS INC.**

Cover: The photographs on the cover represent activities of our four operating groups, from left to right: the craftsmanship of a worker in Gemeinhardt's flute manufacturing facility in Elkhart, Indiana, the production of the daytime broadcast *As the World Turns* on the CBS Television Network, Epic recording artist Ted Nugent in concert and high school students using a Holt, Rinehart and Winston textbook in the classroom.

EXHIBIT 8-1. Table of contents from the 1977 annual report of CBS.

After the descriptive material, there follows a set of financial statements. These statements include the balance sheet as of the end of the firm's fiscal year, its income statement for the fiscal year, and the statement of changes in financial position. (These statements were discussed and illustrated in Chapter 7.) A summary of financial information for the past several years may also be given. This summary permits the

Annual report includes financial statements

investor to view the firm's growth in sales, earnings, and dividends as well as the book value of the stock. Some of this information is frequently illustrated by graphs. Since the financial data have been audited, the investors may assume that the information is accurate and that the appropriate accounting principles have been applied consistently. Without this audit, year-by-year comparisons may be meaningless.

QUARTERLY REPORTS AND NEWS BULLETINS

Additional information made public

During the year, the firm publishes quarterly reports that summarize its performance during the preceding three months. They usually include a brief account of pertinent events as well as various financial statements. Although these statements are rarely as complete as the financial statements in the annual report, they do permit the investor to see the change in the firm's earnings and sales for the quarter and often for the last 12 months. Such quarterly statements are usually not audited and may subsequently be restated.

In addition to the annual report and quarterly reports, a firm typically issues news bulletins to the financial press concerning any major event that may alter the value of its shares. These reports include announcements of new products, merger activity, dividend payments, and new financing that the firm is in the process of obtaining. This information is readily accessible because the financial press efficiently disseminates it to the general public. In many cases the firm also sends copies of the news bulletins to its stockholders.

The 10–K report

Firms must file three documents with the Securities and Exchange Commission (SEC). These reports are available to investors. The first document is the 10–K report, which gives a much more detailed statement of the firm's fundamental financial position than is provided to stockholders in the annual report. The 10–K report also gives sales information by product line and a more detailed breakdown of expenses. Although the 10–K report is not automatically sent to stockholders, a company must supply stockholders with this document upon written request.

The 10–Q report

The second document is the 10–Q report, which the firm issues quarterly. This document must be sent to the SEC and is also available to stockholders. Like the 10–K, it is a detailed report of the firm's financial state. The quarterly report that the company sends to its stockholders is basically a summary of the 10–Q report.

The prospectus

The third document is the prospectus, which must accompany any new public issue of securities. Firms must file a 10–K report annually, but a prospectus is required only when new securities (either stocks or bonds) are issued. Both the 10–K report and the prospectus may be useful to the financial analyst.

INSIDE INFORMATION

In addition to the sources that have been previously discussed, there is the possibility of an investor's obtaining *inside information*. Inside information is not available to the general public, and it may be of great value in guiding investments in a particular firm. For example, news of a dividend cut or increment may affect a stock's price, Knowledge of such information before it is made public should increase the individual's ability to make profitable investment decisions. However, the use of such information for personal gain by employees of the firm or by brokers or investment managers is illegal.

This does not mean that employees cannot own securities issued by their firm; however, the SEC requires holdings by management to be made public and changes in these holdings to be disclosed. These changes are periodically reported in the financial press, and one publication, *The Insiders' Chronicle,* is devoted solely to reporting transactions by insiders.

The reasons for insiders' trading their shares are varied. For example, an individual may be using the proceeds of a sale to retire personal debt, or an executive may be exercising an option to buy the stock. Such transactions are legal and are done for reasonable, legitimate financial purposes. However, some financial analysts and investors believe that inside transactions offer a clue to management's perception of the future price performance of the stock. If many insiders sell their shares, this may be interpreted as a bearish sign indicating that the market price of the stock will decline in the future. Conversely, a large number of purchases by insiders implies that management expects the price of the stock to rise. Such purchases by insiders are interpreted as being bullish, which indicates that the price of the stock will subsequently rise. The reason for these interpretations is obvious: If management believes that the firm's earnings are growing, they will buy the stock. Insiders' purchases and sales may mirror management's view of the company's potential. This information may then be used by outside investors as a key to the direction of future stock prices.*

Insider activity as an indicator

BROKERAGE FIRMS' RESEARCH REPORTS

One service that some brokers offer to their customers is research on specific securities. Many brokerage firms have research staffs whose job it is to analyze firms and their securities; the purpose of such research is to identify undervalued securities that have the potential for price appreciation. In some cases these findings are published by the

---

*For a discussion of the use of inside information in selecting securities, see Chapter 17.

brokerage firm and are readily available to its customers. The cost of such research is included in the commission fee.

Brokerage firms' recommendations

Brokerage firms' recommendations take the form of "buy," "sell," or "hold."* The word *buy* means that the investor should purchase the security or add to existing holdings. *Sell* indicates the opposite, and existing shares should be sold. *Hold* signifies that the investor should not purchase the security but should not sell shares that are already owned. A hold recommendation should not be considered to be neutral, because the investor still holds securities even though no additional shares are purchased.

In most cases, brokerage firms' research reports tend to recommend purchasing the security. Rarely do such reports recommend the outright sale of shares. For this reason, the individual investor should probably use such reports in conjunction with other information. It should be remembered that brokerage firms and their salespeople profit from commissions; hence, there is a natural bias to encourage purchasing securities as opposed to holding money or placing it in a savings accounts.

Publications of brokerage firms

Some brokerage firms and commercial banks publish material that is purely informational and is available to the public without charge. The brokerage firm of Merrill Lynch Pierce Fenner and Smith Inc. is by far the largest supplier of this complimentary literature. These publications not only describe various securities and how they are acquired but also explain how they may be used as part of one's investment strategy. The investor may find some of this information extremely useful, especially in estate and portfolio planning. A selected bibliography of this material along with a list of the firms that publish it is given in Exhibit 8–2.

PURCHASED SOURCES OF INFORMATION

The investor may buy a variety of publications and services rendering information that is potentially useful in making investment decisions. This section will describe several of these sources of information.

NEWSPAPERS AND MAGAZINES

The Wall Street Journal

The foremost financial newspaper is *The Wall Street Journal*. This daily newspaper publishes not only daily stock prices and quotes but also bond prices and transactions, option transactions and prices,

---

*Some brokerage firms refine their buy and sell recommendations. For example, Merrill Lynch has five classes: buy, ok to buy, neutral, ok to sell, and sell.

EXHIBIT 8–2. Selected Bibliography of Publications Available From Brokerage Firms and Commercial Banks

How to Read a Financial Report	Merrill Lynch
How Over-the-Counter Securities Are Traded	Merrill Lynch
Investing for Tax-Free Income	Merrill Lynch
How to Buy and Sell Commodities	Merrill Lynch
What Is Margin	Merrill Lynch
Guide to Writing Options	Merrill Lynch
A Profile of Investment Banking	Securities Industry Association
The U.S. Government Securities Market	Harris Bank
Handbook of Securities of the United States Government and Federal Agencies	First Boston Corporation
Money Market Investments and Investment Vocabulary	Bank of America

quotes on treasury securities, and prices of commodities and foreign currencies. In addition to financial news, *The Wall Street Journal* includes news bulletins that are issued by firms and editorial comments on the national economic policy. Editorials tend to stress those policies that affect the investment community (e.g., the fiscal policy of the federal government, the monetary policy of the Federal Reserve Board, and proposed changes in federal tax laws).

The Wall Street Journal also publishes earnings reports and announcements of dividends that have been declared. These reports and dividends for CBS are illustrated in Exhibit 8–3. The right-hand side of the exhibit presents the earnings for CBS for the year ending December 31, 1978. These earnings are presented for both the last quarter and the entire year. The report also gives the earnings for 1977 and the last quarter of 1977. The left-hand side of Exhibit 8–3 illustrates the announcement of a cash dividend. The entry indicates the per share amount of the dividend ($.65) (if it is a quarterly dividend, it will be indicated by *Q*), the date of record (3/2/79), and the payment date (3/16/79). The date of record is the day on which the firm closes its books. All stockholders owning shares at that time receive the dividend. The date of payment is the day on which the investor is to receive the dividend.

In addition to *The Wall Street Journal*, there are several newspapers of interest to the investment community. These include *Barron's, Media General Financial Weekly*, the *Journal of Commerce, Over-the-Counter Weekly Review*, and *The Wall Street Transcript*. Particularly noteworthy is *Barron's*, which along with *The Wall Street Journal*, is published by Dow Jones. *Barron's* is a weekly newspaper that reports weekly security transactions and includes various feature articles of interest to the financial community as well as investment advisory reports. One particularly important piece of information is *Barron's* confidence index, which will be described in Chapter 17.

Other financial newspapers

A variety of magazines also report financial news. A selected list of these publications is given in Exhibit 8–4. The list is divided into three

Financial magazines

Dividend Announcement

for CBS

Earnings Announcement

for CBS

* * *

Dividends Reported February 14

Company	Period	Amt.	Payable date	Record date
REGULAR				
Albany International	Q	.25	4– 2–79	3– 9
Allied Capital Corp	Q	.12	3–30–79	3–16
Amer Medical Buildings ..	Q	.10	4–16–79	4– 2
Armstrong Rubber Co	Q	.30	4– 2–79	3– 2
Banister Cont'l	Q	b.10	4–16–79	3–23
Barnwell Industries	Q	.05	3–21–79	3– 7
Belding-Heminway Co	Q	.09	3–15–79	3– 1
Best Products	Q	.04	3– 9–79	2–26
Bowne & Co Inc	Q	.12	1–22–79	3– 9
Branch Industries Inc	Q	.05	3–15–79	2–28
CBS Inc	Q	.65	3–16–79	3– 2
Calgary Power	Q	b.60	4– 1–79	3– 2
Canadian Cablesystems ..	Q	b.12½	3–30–79	3–16
Chemineer Corp	Q	.06	3–15–79	3– 1
Chilton Corp	Q	.07	3–20–79	2–28
Clevetrust Corp	Q	.55	3–15–79	3– 1
Colt Industries pf A	Q	.40	3–31–79	3– 6
Colt Industries pf D	Q	1.06¼	3–31–79	3– 6
Consumers Water Co	Q	.40	5–25–79	5–10
Dayton Malleable Inc	Q	.25	3–29–79	3–15
First Nat'l Bancshares ...	Q	.35	3–30–79	3–16
First United Bancorp	Q	.29	3–30–79	3–16
Foremost Corp of Amer ..	Q	.10	3–26–79	3– 1
Gateway Industries	Q	.15	4– 2–79	3–15
Gov't Employees Ins pf ...	Q	.184	4– 1–79	3– 9
Guaranty Trust of Can ...	Q	b.04	3– 1–79	2–23
Gulf Energy & Develop ..	Q	.05	3–12–79	3– 1
House of Fabrics	Q	.09	6–15–79	5–15
International Tel&Tel	Q	.55	4– 1–79	2–22
Jaclyn Inc	Q	.10	5–15–79	4–13
Knudsen Corp	Q	.15	3–15–79	2–28
Louisiana Land & Explor ..	Q	.32	3–15–79	3– 1
Maremont Corp	Q	.25	3–31–79	2–26
Maryland Nat'l Corp	Q	.19	3–30–79	3–14
MassMutual Inco Inv	Q	.27	3–15–79	2–28
Mary Kay Cosmetics	Q	.12	3–30–79	3–16
McDermott (JRay) Co ...	Q	.25	4– 1–79	3–16
McDermott (JRay)pfA ...	Q	.55	1– 1–79	3–16
McDermott (JRay)pfB ...	Q	.65	4– 1–79	3–16
McGraw-Edison Co	Q	.45	3–12–79	2–26
Meenan Oil	Q	.06	3– 9–79	2–26

Amt. Credit ....
Amounts in Canadian dollars.

CBS INC. (N)		
Year Dec 31:	1978	1977
Revs	$3,290,052,000	$2,826,313,000
Net inco	198,079,000	182,008,000
Shr earns:		
Net inco	7.15	6.50
Quarter:		
Revenues	987,056,000	847,163,000
Net inco	56,496,000	50,366,000
Shr earns:		
Net inco	2.04	1.82

CERTIFIED CORP (A)

Quar Dec 31: 1978 1977

EXHIBIT 8–3. Earnings report and dividend announcement (Source: *The Wall Street Journal, February 15, 1979; reprinted with permission of Dow Jones & Company, Inc.*)

EXHIBIT 8–4. Selected Magazines of Potential Value to the Investment Community

Academic and professional:
Financial Analysts Journal
Harvard Business Review
Financial Management

General financial news:
Forbes
Business Week
Fortune
Financial World

Specialized:
Oil and Gas Journal
Realty Trust Review
Public Utilities Fortnightly

categories to designate the nature of the publication. General investors should be particularly interested in *Forbes, Business Week,* and *Fortune,* all of which publish articles concerning the general financial community. The academically and professionally oriented journals are more specialized, and their contents tend to be more difficult for the inexperienced investor to understand.

Specialized trade journals

The individual who is interested in a particular area of investment may also read specialized trade journals. For example, those who are considering investments in the oil and gas industry may find the *Oil and Gas Journal* a good source of information concerning discoveries of new oil fields and the amounts of reserves that have been determined to exist in these fields. Such trade publications will help the investor keep abreast of events in a particular industry.

INVESTMENT ADVISORY SERVICES

For the investor who wants additional information or advice, a variety of sources may be purchased, some of which are illustrated in this chapter. These sources include the corporate records that are published by Standard & Poor and by Moody. In addition, Standard & Poor publishes each month *Stock Guide* and a *Bond Guide*. Exhibit 8–5 reproduces a page from the *Stock Guide*. As may be seen in the exhibit, which highlights the stock of CBS, a considerable amount of information is given, including not only the price but also financial data such as dividends, earnings per share, and certain balance sheet items (current assets, current liabilities, long-term debt, and number of shares outstanding). Since this publication packs so much information into such a small space and is updated monthly, it is a widely used reference.

Standard & Poor's Stock Guide

In addition to *Corporation Records* and *Stock Guide,* Standard & Poor publishes *The Outlook,* an investment advisory service. A recent comment on CBS that appeared in the January 1, 1979, issue of *The Outlook* is presented in Exhibit 8–6. As may be seen in this exhibit, Standard & Poor is bullish on the stock of CBS. It should be noted that the comment is only a typical six-month follow-up and does not indicate how the conclusion was derived. In effect, the investor must take this recommendation on blind faith.

The Outlook

One important investor advisory service is the *Value Line Investment Survey*. Each week this publication includes new information on selected industries and specific firms within these industries and updates previously published information. During a three-month period, *Value Line* evaluates most of the important firms that trade their securities on the major exchanges or in the over-the-counter markets. In addition to evaluating individual firms, this service analyzes the industry and makes a recommendation for the price performance of specific stocks

Value Line Investment Survey

44 Car-Cen

STANDARD & POOR'S CORPORATION

INDEX	Ticker Symbol	STOCKS NAME OF ISSUE (Call Price of Pfd. Stocks)	Market	Com Rank. & Pfd. Rating	Par Val.	Inst. Hold Cos	Inst. Hold Shs. (000)	PRINCIPAL BUSINESS	PRICE RANGE 1960-76 High	1960-76 Low	1977 High	1977 Low	1978 High	1978 Low	Dec. Sales in 100s	December, 1978 Last Sale Or Bid High	Low	Last	% Div. Yield	P-E Ratio
1	CHH	Carter Hawley Hale	NYS,Bo,PS	A—	5	74	10623	Department store chain	45⅜	9⅞	22	16⅜	20⅞	1[illegible]¼	2454	17⅝	13¾	15⅝	6.4	6
2	Pr	$2 cm Cv Pfd ([52]46)	NYS,Bo,PS	BBB	5	15	647	chains of specialty stores	77	22	38	30⅞	36⅛	24¾	344	29	24¾	26⅛	7.7	..
3	CAR	Carter-Wallace	NYS,Bo,MW,Ph	B	1	7	14	Drug and toiletry products	35¼	4¾	10⅛	6¼	10	6¾	1433	7½	6¾	6⅞	5.8	9
4	CASC	Cascade Corp	OTC	B+	50¢	...	...	Comp for hvy mach & ind'l eq	24¾	5½	17¼	9¼	36½	15¾	154	32	28	32B	†2.7	4
5	CGC	Cascade Natural Gas	NYS	B	1	4	2	Dstr Wash, Ore: pipeline	16⅜	5	9⅛	7⅜	8½	6⅝	438	7	6⅝	6⅝	s7.5	19
6	CAS	Castle (A.M.) & Co.	ASE,MW	B	5	6	375	Dstr steel, alumin, other met	18½	4	14⅜	11⅛	18	12¼	34	15¼	14⅝	14⅞	6.7	7
7	CKE	Castle & Cooke	NYS,Ho,PS	A—	10	41	1598	Processed/fresh foods: R.E.	24	3½	16⅜	12	21⅜	14¾	1949	17¾	16⅜	17½	4.6	8
8	CVF	Castle Convertible Fund	ASE	...	1¢	1	.5	Closed end investment co	24⅞	10⅛	21⅜	17⅛	23⅞	19½	124	21	19⅝	19⅝	†8.8	..
9	CAT	Caterpillar Tractor	[1]NYS,Bo,Ci,De,MW,Ph	A	No	472	37805	Earthmoving mchy: diesel eng	62¼	8	59½	48¾	65	45⅜	9851	59¾	54⅜	58¾	3.6	9
10	CATO	Cato Corp	OTC	NR	1	3	15	Apparel shops:disc dept str	20	2½	6	3	8	4⅞	12	7½	7¼	7¼B	3.4	4
11	CAV	Cavitron Corp	ASE,Bo	B—	10¢	1	7	Dental/medic eq:ultrasonics	50⅞	4	19⅜	9¾	15⅞	6⅛	719	8⅞	7⅝	8⅛	...	d
12	CBTB	CB&T Bancshares	OTC	...	2½	2	19	Multi-bank hldg,Georgia	20¾	7½	16½	11	16½	11½	8	12	12	12B	4.3	8
13	CBS	CBS Inc	NYS,Bo,Ci,MW,Ph,PS	A	2½	238	9330	TV, radio network: station:	69⅛	12⅝	62¼	46⅜	64¾	43¼	5444	54¾	49¾	50¾	5.1	7
14	Pr	$1 cm Cv A Pref (43½)vtg	NYS,PS	A	1	4	1	records,instr,textbook,toy	42¾	15¼	42	32⅞	45	30	4	36⅞	34¾	34B	2.9	..
15	CBCT	CBT Corp	OTC	...	10	19	591	Bank hldg: Conn Bank & Tr	45½	15¾	26	21⅜	27¾	22¾	159	25¼	24¼	24¼B	8.2	5
16	CCI	CCI Corp	NYS,PS	B—	50¢	3	75	Constr/mtl hdlg eq:aerosp	27⅜	⅝	9½	3⅞	11⅝	4¾	3493	7⅛	5⅝	5⅞	...	5
17	CDI	CDI Corp	ASE	B—	10¢	...	...	Engr'g & technical services	35	¾	5	1¾	14⅞	3⅞	1041	8⅜	5¾	6⅝	...	4
18	CCP	Ceco Corp	NYS	B	No	12	214	Items for constr. industry	37	7	17⅝	9⅛	15¼	10⅝	226	12⅞	11⅛	11⅛	5.4	..
19	CEDR	Cedar Point	OTC	A—	1	7	551	Amusem't park, hotel, marina	25⅝	1⅞	18⅝	14⅛	31¼	18¼	373	30⅝	27⅜	28¾B	s3.8	10
20	CCL	Celanese Canada	TS,MS,VS	B—	No	12	598	Fibers,fabrics,carpets,chems	21¼	3	3⅞	2½	4⅛	2⅝	1077	3⅞	3½	3½	...	15
21	CZ	Celanese Corp	NYS,Bo,Ci,MW,Ph,PS	B+	No	91	4114	Fibers,chemicals,plastics	92	21	53	40	47⅛	35⅝	1868	42⅛	40	40⅛	7.5	6
22	Pr	4½% cm A Pfd (100)	NYS	BBB	100	7	20	paints/indust'l coatings	99	40	54	50	51	44¼	51	47	44¼	45	10.0	..
23	CELN.A	Celina Financial Cl A	OTC	...	50¢	3	79	Reinsurance:life:data proc	11¾	2¼	8¼	4¾	12⅛	8	1840	12⅛	11	11⅝B	3.1	6
24	CC	Cellu-Craft	ASE	B—	1	...	...	Flexible pkg:linen serv	27½	½	2½	1⅜	3¾	1⅝	435	2⅛	1¾	1¾	...	4
25	CNC	Cenco Inc	NYS,Ph,PS	B—	1	15	434	Scientific eq: other fields	32¼	1½	5½	2	8⅛	3	5158	4⅛	3½	3⅞	...	10
26	CNCRP	Cencor Inc $0.40 Pfd[64]	OTC	B—	1	4	28	Consum fin,temp help,school	17⅞	1⅝	3	2	6⅜	2⅛	576	3½	2⅞	3⅛B	...	6
27	CTX	Centex Corp	NYS	B+	25¢	35	1460	Real est dev, constr: cement	38¾	4	16⅜	10½	27	11⅜	2368	20¼	16½	17½	1.1	7
28	CBAN	Cent'l Bancorp Cin	OTC	...	5	17	1274	Multiple bank hldg:Cinn	22⅞	11⅛	27½	21½	27⅝	23⅜	183	26¼	25	26B	s6.7	7
29	CBSS	Cent'l Bancshrs South	OTC	...	2	13	279	Bank hldg: Alabama	30¾	7⅞	15¾	13⅛	15¾	11⅞	884	12½	11⅞	12B	6.7	5
30	CSYS	Central Banking Sys	OTC	...	2½	1	.1	Bank hldg: California	16¾	2½	10¼	8½	13¼	8¼	440	10⅝	9⅞	10⅝B	s3.8	6
31	CCBK	Cent Carolina Bk&Tr	OTC	...	5	...	...	Gen banking: No Carolina	40½	14	21¼	17¾	25½	20¾	53	23¼	21¼	21¼B	6.6	5
32	CNH	Central Hudson Gas&El	NYS	A—	No	13	158	Utility:elec & gas, NY State	42⅞	11	22½	19⅛	22⅛	19¾	228	20⅛	19¾	19⅞	9.9	6
33	CER	Central Illinois Lt	NYS,Bo,Ci,MW,Ph	B+	No	59	1663	Electric-gas utility	32	10	19¾	17⅝	18	15¼	945	16⅛	15¼	15½	10.3	8
34	Pr	4½% cm Pfd (110) vtg	NYS([10])	A	100	...	...	central part of Illinois	102¼	39½	56	50	52	44¾	13	47	45	46	9.8	..
35	Pr A	$2.875 Cl A cm Pfd([66]28.75)vtg	NYS([10])	A	No	1	9		31½	25	32¾	29¼	30½	26½	31	28½	27½	27¾	10.4	..
36	Pr B	$2.265 ClAcmPfd([67]27.62½)vtg	NYS([10])	A	No	...	...		29½	25	30½	28	28⅝	25	35	26½	25⅜	26¼	10.0	..
37	CIP	Central Ill. Pub Sv	NYS,Bo,Ci,MW,Ph	A—	No	81	2096	Electric & natural gas utility	30⅛	8½	16⅛	13⅞	14⅞	12¼	3557	13⅝	12½	12⅝	10.1	8
38	CJER	Central Jersey Bk&Tr	OTC	...	2½	...	...	Gen'l comm'l bank'g & trust	15¼	7⅞	9½	8⅜	11	9¼	138	10⅞	10⅜	10⅜B	‡7.5	6
39	CEL	Central Louisiana Energy	NYS	A	4	57	2256	Elec.,natural gas & water	28¼	10½	29⅛	20	26¾	18	1849	20⅞	19	19¾	7.7	6
40	CTP	Central Maine Power	NYS,Bo	B+	5	17	254	Utility supplies electricity	22¾	10⅛	17⅜	15½	16⅞	14⅜	887	15¾	14⅜	14⅞	10.2	7
41	Pr	3.50% cm Pfd (101)	ASE([10])	BBB	100	2	.3	central & southern Maine	77½	29½	41¾	38⅜	39¼	34¼	16	35⅛	34¼	34⅛B	10.3	..
42	CMRTS	Central Mtge & Rlty Tr	OTC	...	1	1	13	Real estate investment trust	20½	2	4⅝	3⅛	6⅞	3⅞	419	5⅛	5	5⅛B	...	6
43	CNBC	Central Natl Bancshrs	OTC	...	1	7	195	Multi-bank holding-Iowa	4	2	3½	2½	3⅞	3⅛	1078	3½	3⅛	3⅛B	7.7	9
44	CCHI	Central Nat'l Chic Corp	OTC	...	10	1	24	Bank hldg:Chicago, Ill	31⅞	6	8¼	6½	8½	5½	64	6¾	5½	5¾B	...	d

Uniform Footnote Explanations—See Page 1. Other: [1]PS. [51]®$2.16,'78. [52]To 3-31-79,scale to $45 in'80. [53]▲$0.44,'74. [54]△$0.11,'77. [55]△$0.05,'78. [56]®$0.86,'77. [57]®$1.86,'77. [58]©$0.63,'78. [59]®$4.99,'77. [60]®$1.43,'78. [61]■$1.32,'77. [62]®$4.56,'77. [63]®$0.30,'77. [64]Cv into com to Jan 18. [65]®$2.70,'77. [66]To 10-1-84,scale to $25.25 in'94. [67]To 10-1-80,scale to $25.25 in'95. [68]F.C. & Pfd divds, Times Earned. [69]®$1.39,'77.

COMMON AND PREFERRED STOCKS

Car—Cen 45

L I N D E X	Cash Divs. Ea. Yr. Since	DIVIDENDS							FINANCIAL POSITION			CAPITALIZATION					—$ Per Shr—EARNINGS—$ Per Shr—						Last 12 Mos.	INTERIM EARNINGS OR REMARKS		L I N D E X
		—Latest Payment—		Ex. Div.	So Far 1978	Total Ind. Rate	$ Paid 1977	Cash& Equiv.	Curr. Assets	Curr. Liabs.	Long Term Debt Mil-$	—Shs. 000—		E n d e d	Balance Sheet Date	Years—						Period	$—Per Share—		
		P f d $	Date									Pfd.	Com.			1974	1975	1976	1977	1978			1977	1978	
1	1941	Q0.25	11-30-78	11-9	1.00	0.92½	0.92½	15.8	640.	294.	306.	1962	p23814	Ja	10-28-78	1.71	2.11	1.97	1.96	E2.60	2.31	12 Mo Oct	1.96	▲2.31	1
2	1969	Q0.50	11-30-78	11-9	2.00	2.00	2.00					1962		Ja		16.42	21.18	21.36	512.37	2.31					2
3	1883	Q0.10	12-15-78	11-1	0.40	0.40	0.50	30.9	97.6	24.0	4.83		7669	53Mr	9-30-78	4.05	1.68	1.90	55△0.70	E0.75	0.80	6 Mo Sep	0.37	0.47	3
4	1965	Q0.40	12-15-78	11-24	0.80	0.85	0.40	1.56	33.1	12.7	11.4		6685	54△.51	9-30-78				4.64		7.54	9 Mo Oct	3.12	6.02	4
5	1964	Q0.25	2-15-79	1-15	0.477	0.50	s0.449	n/a	11.4	12.8	50.0	761	2419	Ja 0.07	9-30-78	1.44	1.44	0.76	56 0.94		0.34	12 Mo Sep	1.01	0.34	5
6◆	1934	Q0.25	11-22-78	11-1	0.916	0.80	0.833	1.85	69.7	33.8	18.3		1440	Dc	9-30-78	4.09	3.71	2.03	1.23		2.20	9 Mo Sep	1.38	2.35	6
7◆	1896	Q0.20	3-12-79	2-14	0.727	0.80	0.661	32.0	521.	278.	226.		23168	Dc	9-9-78	1.85	1.66	1.65	571.95	E25.95	2.13	36 Wk Sep	1.45	1.63	7
8◆	1972	Q0.40	1-15-79	12-22	51.64	@1.72	†1.18	Net Asset Val $23.19			992.	p166	994	Ja	12-22-78	816.93	818.61	822.32	571.95 824.68						8
9◆	1914	Q0.52½	11-20-78	10-18	1.87½	2.10	1.57½	237.	2598	1210	5.36		86263	Dc	12-27-78	2.67	4.64	4.45	595.16	E6.35	6.06	9 Mo Sep	4.65	6.06	9
10	1953	Q0.06¼	12-22-78	12-5	0.25	0.25	0.25	0.29	16.7	11.5			556	Ja	7-29-78	1.03	1.28	△1.65	1.15		1.80	9 Mo Oct	0.97	1.62	10
11	1930	Q0.13	2-15-77	1-17		Nil		0.78	12.7	4.79	1.80		1134	Sp	6-10-78	0.79	1.15	1.03	0.57	Pd0.14	d0.14	9 Mo Sep	△0.87	△1.21	11
12◆	1931	Q0.13	1-2-79	12-11	0.42	0.52	0.36	40.3	1169	578	4.65		2497	Dc	9-30-78	0.84	□0.96	1.20	△1.20		1.54		4.68	5.11	12
13◆	1967	Q0.65	12-8-78	11-17	2.45	2.60		Conv into 0.6886 shrs common			104.	258	2712	Dc	9-30-78	3.80	4.30	5.75	6.50	E7.10	6.93	9 Mo Sep	4.68	5.11	13
14	1924	Q0.50	12-29-78	11-17	1.00	1.00			Book Value $42.92			258		Dc		30.7	30.1	40.50							14
15		Q0.50	1-20-79	12-22	1.80	2.00	1.733				31.4		2651	Dc	9-30-78	△4.46	△3.24	3.00	3.66		4.45	9 Mo Sep	△2.58	□3.37	15
16		None Paid				Nil		3.77	83.9	55.5	37.8		6104	Ap	7-31-78	0.03	△d0.13	d0.21	0.77	1.18	1.19	9 Mo Sep	0.80	△0.81	16
17		Q0.17½	11-2-70	10-16		0.50		n/a	24.6	15.0	6.41		2081	Ap	10-31-78	△0.53	*0.30	d0.34	0.92	601 1.50	1.49	6 Mo Oct	0.75	0.74	17
18◆	1921	Q0.15	1-3-79	12-4	0.50	0.60	0.93½	2.14	113.	34.0	28.4	82	3291	Mr	9-30-78	3.18	2.54	1.25*	□0.97		0.03	9 Mo Sep	0.07	△1.07	18
19◆	1965	3% Stk	1-31-79	12-29	s0.849	1.10	s0.683	21.5	26.8	17.6	5.27	495	3200	Mr	9-30-78	1.58	1.64	2.38	2.47		2.85	6 Mo Sep	2.46	2.84	19
20		g0.10	6-30-76	6-3				14.0	112.	43.7	37.9		13372	Dc	9-30-78	0.90	0.51	0.83	0.02		0.23	9 Mo Sep	d0.02	*0.19	20
21	1939	Q0.75	12-15-78	11-27	2.85	3.00	2.80	195.	896.	467.	564.	964	14110	Dc	9-30-78	▲6.78	3.30	4.67	624.70	E6.50	5.95	9 Mo Sep	3.69	4.94	21
22	1951	Q1.12½	1-1-79	12-4	4.50	4.50	4.50					851		Dc		107.4	54.82	75.70	77.01						22
23◆	1970	Q0.09	12-4-78	11-17	0.34½	0.36	0.30	3.23	10.2	6.09	7.04	‡★1509	1509	Dc	7-31-78	0.72	0.74	1.38	1.75		1.91	9 Mo Sep	△1.40	△1.56	23
24		None Paid				Nil		10.6	78.6	32.1			1913	Dc		△0.16	*0.16	*0.30	*0.40		0.41	6 Mo Sep	*0.32	*△0.33	24
25		Q0.10	9-18-74	8-14		Nil					95.5	74	9973	Ap	7-31-78	0.52	d1.78	d4.57	*0.06	□0.52	0.37	6 Mo Oct	*0.36	*0.21	25
26		None Since Public				Nil		9.04	58.2	35.6	★35.2	p1634		Dc	9-30-78	0.01	0.13	0.40	0.42		0.49	9 Mo Sep	0.38	0.45	26
27	1973	Q0.18	1-4-79	12-1	0.18	0.20	0.14	Equity per shr $6.00			186.		11377	Dc	9-30-78	0.38	0.70	1.42	2.00	E2.50	2.14	9 Mo Sep	1.05	1.19	27
28◆	1937	Q0.437	1-5-79	12-11	s1.428	1.75	s1.233	Book Value $26.03			25.1		5033	Dc	9-30-78	2.44	△1.24	2.82	△3.16		3.58	9 Mo Sep	2.27	△2.69	28
29◆	1939	Q0.20	12-31-78	12-11	0.68	0.80	0.54	Book Value $11.85			20.9		6689	Dc	9-30-78	△1.52	△1.24	1.76	2.29		2.40	9 Mo Sep	△1.71	△1.82	29
30◆	1940	Q0.096	1-15-79	12-26	s0.380	0.40	s0.366	Book Value $11.24			2.89		2868	Dc	9-30-78	d0.15	△0.93	1.13	△1.42		1.68	9 Mo Sep	△1.03	*1.29	30
31	1934	Q0.35	1-25-79	12-22	1.11	1.40	0.90	Book Value $33.52			2.89	610	1038	Dc	9-30-78	△3.17	△3.20	△3.27	△3.85		4.57	9 Mo Sep	△2.77	□3.49	31
32	1903	Q0.49	2-1-79	1-4	1.94	1.96	1.80	3.16	39.7	46.0	168.	1918	5373	Dc	9-30-78	3.17	2.58	2.68	622.90		3.11	12 Mo Sep	2.93	3.11	32
33	1941	Q0.40	12-20-78	11-16	1.60	1.60	1.60	9.31	70.9	34.4	314.	111	10131	Dc	9-30-78	1.95	1.64	1.89	1.51		1.89	12 Mo Sep	1.57	1.89	33
34	1944	Q1.12½	1-2-79	12-4	4.50	4.50	4.50					1918		Dc		12.41	9.84	13.03	11.24						34
35	1975	Q0.71½	1-2-79	12-4	2.87½	2.87½	2.87½	Red restr to 10-1-79				672		Dc			9.84	13.03	11.24			SF 32,000 ea Oct 1,$25			35
36	1976	Q0.65¾	1-2-79	12-4	2.62½	2.62½	2.62½	Red restr (10½%)to 10-1-80			600.			Dc		881.53	881.44	881.54	881.47		1.62	12 Mo Nov	1.57	1.62	36
37	1947	Q0.32	1-2-79	11-9	1.28	1.28	1.28	Red restr $5.15			△435.	1200	823165	Dc		1.48	△1.67	△1.60	881.60		1.60	9 Mo Nov	1.62	1.62	37
38◆	1925	+Q0.25	1-2-79	12-11	†0.745	0.77	†0.647	Book Value $10.99			p5.36		3492	Dc	6-30-78	△1.35	△1.33	△1.32	△1.46		3.11	12 Mo Nov	2.71	□1.26	38
39	1925	Q0.38	11-15-78	10-26	1.52	1.52	1.40	Book Value $13.97			209.	362	9538	Dc	6-30-78	2.15	△1.58	1.28	2.80		3.11	9 Mo Nov	2.71	2.18	39
40	1943	Q0.38	12-29-78	12-4	1.46	1.52	1.41	0.96	61.1	81.3	216.	704	11705	Dc	9-30-78	1.48	1.48	1.75	1.87		2.18	12 Mo Sep	1.90	1.40	40
41	1946	Q0.87½	1-2-79	12-4	3.50	3.50	3.50	Equity per shr $12.82			0.47	220	775	Mr	9-30-78	27.96	29.89	36.99	29.82		0.87	6 Mo Sep	1.57	2.18	41
42		Q0.12	2-17-75	2-3		Nil		Book Value $3.97			19.6		10585	Dc	9-30-78	d0.01	d3.16	d1.58	d0.36		0.35	9 Mo Sep	d0.54	0.80	42
43◆◆	1934	Q0.06	1-9-79	12-22	0.24	0.24	0.244				14.9	60	1110	Dc	6-30-78	3.40	d10.82	d0.47	d0.94		d0.73	9 Mo Sep	d0.31	0.47	43
44◆◆	1958	Q0.05	2-15-78	1-30	0.05	Nil	0.20	Book Value $16.75						Dc				d0.37	d0.94			6 Mo Sep	△0.16	0.37	44

◆ Stock Splits & Divs By Line Reference Index ¹Adj to 3.22%,'78. ²2-for-1,'74-6-for-5,'78. ³Adj for 7%,'74-10%,'74,'75,'76,'77,'78. ³'3-for-2,'76. ¹²2-for-1,'76. ³3-for-2,'76. ¹³3-for-1,'77.
¹⁴Adj for 3%,'79(Ex⁷⁸). ²³2-for-1,'78. ²¹0%,'75;Adj to 5%,'79(ex'78). ³⁶Adj to 4%,'79(ex'78). ⁵³Adj for 7%. ⁵⁴10%,'78. ⁵⁶Adj to 4%,'78. ⁶⁰2-for-1,'75;2½-for-1,'77. ⁶¹10%,'74.

EXHIBIT 8–5. Page from *Standard & Poor's Stock Guide.*

Analyses of Issues

CBS continues to benefit from strong uptrends in its nonbroadcasting businesses—records, publishing, and consumer activities. However, the television network is being restricted by programming expenses and a battle for second place in prime time ratings. *The shares, at a P/E of less than seven based on estimated 1979 earnings of $7.65 and a yield of more than 5%, continue to be regarded as an above-average long-term holding.*

EXHIBIT 8–6. Typical six-month follow-up from *The Outlook* (January 1, 1979, p. 998).

relative to the price movements of the market for the immediate future. These recommendations consist of scores ranging from 5 (the lowest performance) to 1 (the highest performance.) A score of 1 does not mean that *Value Line* believes that the stock will earn a positive return; rather, it indicates that the stock should outperform the market, which in declining markets means that the investor will suffer milder losses.

Value Line asserts that the securities that it recommends will outperform the market. It maintains that the stocks ranked 1 and 2 by its analysts will do better than those ranked 4 and 5. For example, in January 1978, *Value Line* reported that the value of the securities that it had ranked 1 for 1977 had appreciated 15.8 per cent, while the value of the Dow Jones industrial average and Standard & Poor's 500 stock index had declined during the same period.

This conclusion is somewhat misleading. For the investor to have achieved this 15.8 per cent price appreciation, he or she would have had to purchase an equal amount of all 100 recommended stocks. Thus if only $1000 had been invested in each, a total outlay of $100,000 would have been required. Generally investors must select among the recommended stocks. The return would probably not have been 15.8 per cent because only some of the recommended securities would have outperformed the market, whereas others would have underperformed the averages.

SPECIALIZED INVESTMENT ADVISORY SERVICES

Other advisory services

In addition to the information published by publicly held firms, by Standard & Poor's and Moody's, and by advisory services like *Value Line,* there is a host of specialized investment advice that the investor may purchase. A casual survey of the advertisements in *The Wall Street Journal* or *Barron's* proves this. A representative list of this material and each publication's specialty is given in Exhibit 8–7. Since these publishers and authors earn their living by selling this service and not by investing, the purchaser should be somewhat cautious when acting on

EXHIBIT 8-7. Selected Investment Advisory Services

Commodity Trend Service
303 Northwest Tower
100 East Kimberly Road
Davenport, Iowa 52806

Dow Theory Forecasts
Box 4550, Grand Central Station
New York, N.Y. 10017

R.H.M. Survey of Warrants, Options, and Low-Priced Stocks
R.H.M. Associates, Department BW-92
Albertson, Long Island, N.Y. 11507

Trendline
345 Hudson Street
New York, N.Y. 10014

Value Line OTC Special Situations Service
c/o Arnold Bernhard & Co., Inc.
711 Third Avenue
New York, N.Y. 10017

The Zweig Forecast
Zweig Services
747 Third Avenue
New York, N.Y. 10017

any specific recommendations. Previous recommendations that proved successful do not guarantee future success.* Furthermore, past success must be judged relative to something. If the service makes several recommendations, some, according to the laws of probability, should be correct. The service's true performance may be reflected in the number of successes relative to the number of recommendations or in the returns earned on all of the recommendations relative to a measure of the market, such as the Dow Jones industrial average.

OTHER SOURCES OF INFORMATION

A variety of miscellaneous sources of investment help and advice is available. An investor may engage the services of a professional investment counselor. In addition, many banks offer investment services through trust departments. Investment counseling and trusts are expensive, particularly for small investors. Exhibit 8-8 illustrates the fees charged by the trust department of a commercial bank. The first column gives the market value of the portfolio, and the second column presents

Professional investment counselors and trust departments

---

*The SEC and state regulatory agencies forbid advisory services from providing illustrations or examples of previously successful recommendations.

EXHIBIT 8–8. Fee Schedule for Portfolio Management Charged by the Trust Department of a Commercial Bank*

Market Value of Portfolio	Fee per $1000 of Portfolio Value	Fee as a Percentage of the Portfolio's Total Value
$0–$500,000	$5 (Minimum charge, $600)	0.5
$500,001–1,000,000	4	0.5, declining to 0.45
Next $1,000,000	2	0.45, declining to 0.325
Over $2,000,000	Subject to analysis	

*Source: First National Bank of Princeton.

the trust department's fees. The last column expresses the fees as a percentage of the value of the portfolio. As is obvious from the exhibit, the percentage costs decline as the value of the portfolio increases.

The use of such services is generally limited to those few investors with substantially large portfolios. For those investors, the cost is moderate, and this expense is tax-deductible if the investor itemizes deductions. Presumably most investors with sizable portfolios do itemize, so the effective cost of professional portfolio management is considerably reduced.

Investment clubs

The investor may also join an investment club. Such clubs pool the funds of the members and invest them in securities. Most clubs invest only moderate sums. For example, members may pay $10 per month in dues, which are then invested in the club's name. Although such sums of money are trivial, the potential knowledge and experience that can be gained through membership in such clubs is not. Since members must agree on the club's investment goals, strategies, and choice of investments, the individual may learn a considerable amount concerning investments as the club formulates and executes policy. These clubs may have an additional advantage in that they may be able to obtain professional help at a fraction of the cost. For example, a salesperson from a brokerage firm may be willing to talk with members of the club and execute orders for them. The broker may do this not only for the potential commissions from the club but also for the potential commissions from individual members of the club who may become his clients. Unfortunately, the club may be dominated by one or a few outspoken individuals, and the club's goals may not coincide with the individual's goals or financial needs. Because of these factors, the individual should not rely solely on investment clubs to make personal investment decisions.

Adult education courses

Lastly, the individual investor should not exclude the possibility of taking courses in investments. Many adult education programs offer special courses in areas of investing such as portfolio planning and management. These classes usually have nominal tuition fees and may offer the individual investor an excellent source of information.

No shortage of information

There is no shortage of readily available information. The problem for the investor is separating the wheat from the chaff and processing it into a useful form from which to draw conclusions. Even if the investor relies solely on the advice of others, such as brokers or investment services, that individual must still select from the alternatives that are suggested. For example, the *Value Line Investment Survey* recommends 100 stocks that should, in its opinion, outperform the market. No investor is going to buy all of them. However, if an investor follows the advice of the publication and purchases several of its recommended stocks, he or she must still choose from the various recommended investment alternatives. Hence, the final investment decision rests with the individual investor, who earns the returns and bears the risk.

SUMMARY

This chapter has described some of the extensive literature that is available to investors. These publications range from the annual and quarterly reports of publicly held firms to specialized investment advisory services. Some of this information is readily available and may be obtained with little effort and at little cost. Other sources require that the investor pay a substantial sum for the material. Many brokerage firms carry some of the publications that have been described, and the investor may often find them at a local library.

Although none of the publications can consistently predict the future (and the investor should be skeptical of any publication claiming that the subscriber can make a fortune), investors do need to be well informed. Reading financial literature from diverse sources is an excellent means of keeping abreast of events in the financial markets. The investor should be aware of the many sources of potentially useful financial information. In addition to the material cited in this chapter, each chapter in this text ends with a list of readings on the material covered in the chapter.

Investment services, which are available from a professional counselor or a bank, are another source of financial information. Although such services may be costly for the small investor, the effective cost of professional counseling decreases as the value of the portfolio increases.

There is no shortage of information on financial markets and investing. Instead, the problems for the investor are processing this information and putting it into a usable form for making financial decisions. Ultimately it is the individual who reaps the returns earned by the investment and bears the risk of loss.

Terms to Remember

Annual report	10–Q report	Trust department
Quarterly report	Inside information	Investment club
10–K report	Buy, sell, or hold	

Questions

1. Describe the contents of an annual report.

2. What is a 10–K report. What is a prospectus?

3. Name several sources of information on investments that are available to individuals. In general, is there a shortage of available information?

4. Why may investment advisory research reports be self-serving?

5. The act of finding information is one of the best means to learn about the literature that is available to the investor. The student should try to locate the following and skim through each to become familiar with its contents. (a) *The Wall Street Journal* and *Barron's;* (b) *Value Line Investment Survey, The Outlook,* or some other advisory service publication; (c) *Forbes, Fortune,* or *Business Week;* and *Moody's Industrial Manual* or *Standard & Poor's Corporation Records.*

SELECTED READINGS

Engel, Louis: *How to Buy Stocks,* 5th ed., revised. Boston, Little, Brown and Co., 1971.
Levine, Sumner, N. (ed.): *Financial Analysts's Handbook.* Homewood, Ill., Dow Jones-Irwin, Inc., 1972.
New York Stock Exchange Fact Book, published annually.
Sarnoff, Paul: *The Wall Street Thesaurus.* New York, Ivan Obolensky, Inc., 1963.
Stock Market Encyclopedia New York, Standard & Poor's Corp., published annually.
Wyckoff, Peter: *The Language of Wall Street.* New York, Hopkinson and Blake, 1973.
Zarb, Frank G., and Gabriel T. Kerekes (eds.): *The Stock Market Handbook.* Homewood, Ill., Dow-Jones-Irwin, Inc., 1975.
Zweig, Martin E.: *Understanding Technical Forecasting: How To Use Barron's Market Laboratory Pages.* Princeton, N.J., Dow Jones & Company, Inc., 1978.

Investing in Fixed-Income Securities

Part Three considers investments in securities that pay a fixed annual income. The annual interest or dividend payments are the same each year. Since such investments consist primarily of long-term bonds that are issued by corporations and governments, most of Part Three is devoted to these bonds.

These securities produce a constant flow of income and are considered to be good investments for individuals who need additional income. They are also among the safest investments available. This combination of income and safety makes fixed-income securities particularly attractive to the conservative investor.

Learning Objectives

After completing this chapter you should be able to

1. Understand the features common to all bonds.

2. Explain the purpose of the indenture and the role of the trustee.

3. Differentiate between bearer bonds and registered bonds.

4. Ascertain the sources of risk to the bondholder.

5. Describe the procedure for buying a bond.

6. Differentiate among the types of corporate bonds.

7. Distinguish between the ways bonds are retired.

chapter 9

THE MARKET
FOR DEBT

Many corporations and governments have issued long-term debt to finance long-term investments, such as the expansion of plant and equipment or the construction of roads and schools. Internally generated funds (profits and depreciation for corporations and tax revenues for governments) may be insufficient to finance such investments on a pay-as-you-go basis. Long-term debt, which matures at a specified time longer than one year, permits firms and governments to acquire the assets now and pay for them over a period of years. The debt is then retired for corporations by the cash flow that is generated by plant and equipment and for governments by the fees or the tax revenues that are collected.

This chapter is concerned with long-term debt and covers (1) the characteristics common to all of these debt instruments, (2) the risks associated with investing in debt, (3) the mechanics of purchasing debt instruments, and (4) the retirement of debt. Chapter 10 covers the valuation of debt. Like stock, debt may be purchased initially either by financial institutions in a private placement or by individuals through a public offering. Once the securities have been issued, secondary markets develop. These debt instruments may be bought and sold on the organized security exchanges or in the over-the-counter markets. These securities are generally very marketable, since there is an active secondary market in corporate and government bonds.

GENERAL FEATURES OF DEBT INSTRUMENTS

INTEREST AND MATURITY

Principal

  All debt instruments have similar characteristics. They represent the indebtedness (liability) of their issuers in return for a specified sum, which is called the *principal.* Virtually all debt has a *maturity date,* which is the particular date by which it must be paid off. When debt is issued, the length of time to maturity is set, and it may range from one day to 20 or 30 years or more. If the maturity date falls within a year of the date of issuance, the debt is referred to as short-term debt. Long-term debt matures more than a year after it has been issued.* The owners of debt instruments receive a flow of payments which is called interest, in return for the use of their money. Interest should not be confused with other forms of income, such as the cash dividends that are paid by common and preferred stock. Dividends are distributions from earnings, whereas interest is an expense of borrowing.

**Maturity
interest**

  A bond is illustrated in Exhibit 9–1. This exhibit reproduces the face of the 8¾ per cent debenture of AT&T. If this bond were not a sample, the principal amount would have been stated immediately following the words "the principal sum of." This bond matures on May 15, 2000. A bond is also individually numbered for identification, and the name of the owner is recorded on the certificate's face. The certificates may be endorsed on the back by the owner, and the title may be readily changed from one owner to another by the transfer agent, which is usually the bank that countersigns the security and acts as the trustee for the bond issue.

Coupon rate

  When a debt instrument such as this bond is issued, the rate of interest to be paid by the borrower is established. This rate is frequently referred to as the bond's *coupon rate* (e.g., the 8¾ per cent in Exhibit 9–1). The amount of the coupon is usually fixed over the lifetime of the bond. (There are a few exceptions; for example, see the section on variable interest rate bonds later in this chapter and in Chapter 10.) The return earned by the investor, however, need not be equal to the coupon rate of interest because bond prices change. They may be purchased at a discount (i.e., a price below the face amount or principal) or at a premium (i.e., a price above the face amount of the bond). The

---

*Debt that matures in from one to five years is sometimes referred to as intermediate debt.

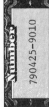

EXHIBIT 9-1. Example of the face of a corporate bond.

return actually earned, then, depends on the interest received, the purchase price, and what the investor receives upon selling the bond or redeeming it.

Yields: Current and to maturity

The potential return offered by a bond is referred to as the yield. Yield is frequently expressed in two ways: the *current yield* and the *yield to maturity*. Current yield refers only to the annual flow of interest or income. The yield to maturity refers to the yield that the investor will earn if the debt instrument is held from the moment of purchase until it is redeemed at par (face value) by the issuer. The difference between the current yield and the yield to maturity is discussed at length in the section on the pricing of bonds in Chapter 10.

Structure of yields

There is a relationship between yield and the length of time to maturity for debt instruments of the same level of risk. Generally, the longer the time to maturity, the higher is the rate of interest. This relationship is illustrated in Graph 9–1, which plots the yield on various United States government securities as of December 31, 1977. This graph, which is frequently referred to as a yield curve, shows that the bonds with the longest time to maturity have the highest interest rates. For example, bonds with one year to maturity yield 6.6 per cent, whereas bonds that mature after ten years offer more than 7.5 per cent.

One would expect such a relationship because the longer the time to maturity, the longer the investor will have his or her funds tied up. To induce investors to lend their money for lengthier periods, it is usually necessary to pay them more interest. Also, there is more risk involved in purchasing a bond with a longer period to maturity, since the fortunes of the issuer are more difficult to estimate for the longer term. This means that investors will ordinarily require additional compensation to bear the risk associated with long-term debt.

Although such a relationship between time and yield does usually exist, there have been periods when the opposite has occurred (i.e., when short-term interest rates exceeded long-term interest rates). This

GRAPH 9–1.   Positive-Sloped Yield Curve

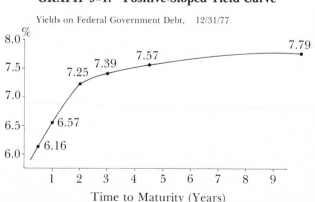

Yields on Federal Government Debt,   12/31/77

Time to Maturity (Years)

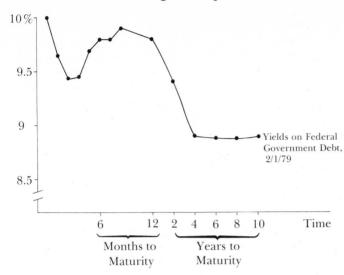

GRAPH 9–2. Negative-Sloped Yield Curve

happened from 1978 to 1979, when short-term interest rates were higher than long-term rates. The yields on treasury securities (securities issued by the Treasury Department) in February 1979 are illustrated in Graph 9–2. In this case the yield curve has a negative slope, which indicates that as the length of time to maturity increased, the interest rates declined. Thus, securities maturing in less than a year had a yield of greater than 9.5 per cent, while the long-term debt that matured after ten years yielded less than 9.0 per cent.

Negative-sloped yield curves

Such a yield curve can be explained by inflation, which exceeded 8 per cent in 1978. The Board of Governors of the Federal Reserve was pursuing a tight monetary policy in order to fight inflation. It sold short-term government securities (i.e., treasury bills) in an effort to reduce the capacity of commercial banks to lend. These sales depressed the prices of all fixed-income securities, which resulted in higher yields. (As is explained in detail in Chapter 10, yields on debt instruments rise as their prices fall.) The yields on short-term securities rose more than those on long-term securities, and this, coupled with other events in the money and capital markets, resulted in the negative-sloped yield curve. When the rate of inflation abates, the yield curve should return to the positive slope that it has maintained during most periods.

Interest rates fluctuate

Graphs 9–1 and 9–2 also illustrate that interest rates do change. (The student should remember that the interest rate is the current rate paid for the use of credit. This should not be confused with the coupon rate, which is fixed when the debt instrument is issued.) Although all interest rates fluctuate, short-term rates are more volatile than long-term interest rates. This is illustrated in Graph 9–3, which plots the yields on a six-month treasury bill and on a ten-year treasury bond. As may be

GRAPH 9–3. **Yields on Treasury Bonds and Treasury Bills**

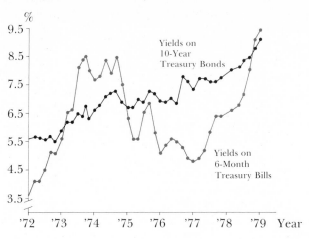

(Source: Federal Reserve Bulletins, Various Issues)

seen from the graph, the fluctuation in yields for the short-term treasury bill is greater than that for the long-term treasury bond. For example, the yield on a six-month treasury bill increased from 3.6 per cent per year in January 1972 to over 8.5 per cent in August 1973, while the yield on a ten-year treasury bond rose from 5.6 to only 6.8 per cent per year. This graph illustrates not only the greater fluctuation in short-term yields, but also how quickly changes can occur. For example, the annual short-term rate rose from 5.6 per cent to 8.6 per cent in only seven months (from January to August 1973) in response to changes in the demand for the supply of short-term credit.

THE INDENTURE

Terms are specified in the indenture

Each debt agreement has terms that the debtor must meet. These are stated in a legal document called the *indenture*.* These terms include the coupon rate, the date of maturity, and any other conditions required of the debtor. One of the more frequent of these requirements is the pledging of collateral, which is property that the borrower must offer to secure the loan. For example, the collateral for a mortgage loan is the building. Any other assets owned by the borrower, such as securities or inventory, may also be pledged to secure a loan. If the borrower defaults on the debt, the creditor may seize the collateral and sell it to recoup the principal. Default occurs when the borrower fails to

---

*For publicly held bond issues, the indenture is filed with the Securities and Exchange Commission.

meet not only the payment of interest but *any* of the terms of the indenture. The other conditions of the indenture are just as important as meeting the interest payments on time, and often they may be more difficult for the debtor to satisfy.

Examples of common loan restrictions include (1) limits on paying dividends, (2) limits on issuing additional debt, and (3) restrictions on merging or significantly changing the nature of the business without the prior consent of the creditors. In addition, loan agreements usually specify that if the firm defaults on any other outstanding debt issues, this debt issue is also in default, in which case the creditors may seek immediate repayment. Default on one issue, then, usually puts all outstanding debt in default.

These examples do not exhaust all the possible conditions of a given loan. Since each loan is separately negotiated, there is ample opportunity for differences among loan agreements. During periods of scarce credit, the terms of a loan agreement will be stricter, whereas during periods of lower interest rates and more readily available money, the restrictions will tend to be more lenient. The important point, however, is that if any part of the loan agreement is violated, the creditor may declare that the debt is in default and may seek a court order to enforce the terms of the indenture.

THE ROLE OF THE TRUSTEE

Many debt instruments are purchased by individual investors who may be unaware of all of the terms of the indenture. Even if individual investors are aware of the terms, they may be too geographically dispersed to take concerted action in case of default. To protect their interests, a *trustee* is appointed for each publicly held bond issue. It is the trustee's job to see that the terms of the indenture are upheld and to take remedial action if the company defaults on the terms of the loan. For performing these services, the trustee receives compensation from the issuer of the debt.

A trustee is appointed for publicly held bonds

Trustees are usually commercial banks that serve both the debtor and the bondholders. They act as transfer agents for the bonds when ownership is changed through sales in the secondary markets. The signature of a trustee on the bond is a guarantee of the authenticity of the bond. These banks also receive from the debtor the funds to pay the interest, and this money is then distributed to the individual bondholders. It is also the job of the trustee to inform the bondholders if the firm is no longer meeting the terms of the indenture. In case of default, the trustee may take the debtor to court to enforce the terms of the contract. If there is a subsequent reorganization or liquidation of the company, the trustee continues to act on behalf of the individual bondholders to protect their principal.

FORMS OF DEBT

Registered and bearer bonds

Debt instruments are issued in one of two forms: (1) *registered* bonds or (2) *bearer* bonds to which coupons are attached. Registered bonds are similar to stock certificates; the bonds are registered in the owner's name, and the interest payments are sent to the owner. When the bond is sold, it is registered in the name of the new owner by the transfer agent (i.e., the trustee). The AT&T bond in Exhibit 9–1 is an example of a registered bond. The names of both the owner (because this is a sample bond, the owner's name has been omitted) and the trustee (the Chemical Bank) are stated on the front of such bonds.

Bearer bonds are entirely different. Ownership is evidenced by mere possession of the bond and is transferred simply by passing the debt instrument from the seller to the buyer; no new certificates are issued. Thus, securities in this form are extremely easy to transfer. However, if they are lost, they are like currency. Therefore, the possibility of theft is a real concern that requires the owner to be extremely cautious when handling these bonds.

Coupons and coupon clippers

Since the debtor does not know the names of the owners of bearer securities, coupons for interest payments are attached to the bond. The owner must detach the coupon and send it to the paying agent (i.e., the trustee) to collect the interest. In the past, most bonds were of this type. Investors who relied on fixed interest income for their livelihood were frequently called coupon clippers.

Today some bonds are issued in both registered and coupon form. An investor who prefers a certain type can consult a bond publication, such as *Standard & Poor's Bond Guide,* to determine which are coupon bonds and which are registered bonds. If the bond issue has both forms, the investor may specify the type desired when the bond is purchased from the broker.

An example of a bearer bond with coupons attached is shown in Exhibit 9–2. The bond has 50 coupons (only the first ten are illustrated), and each represents a six-month interest payment. This particular bond is an income nonmortgage bond, which means that it is unsecured and among the riskiest of all debt instruments. It should be noted that the bond matured in 1951, but that all of the coupons are still attached, which illustrates how risky some bonds can be. The bond was never retired, and not one interest payment was ever made!

RISK

Another characteristic of all debt is risk: risk that the interest will not be paid, risk that the principal will not be repaid, risk that the price of the debt instrument may decline, and risk that inflation will continue, thereby reducing the purchasing power of the interest payments and of the principal when it is repaid. These risks vary significantly with different types of debt. For example, there is no risk of default on the interest payments and principal repayments of the debt of the federal government. The reason for this absolute safety is that the federal government has the power to create money. The government can always issue the money that is necessary to pay the interest and repay the principal.*

The safety of federal government debt

The procedure is more subtle than just printing new money. The federal government issues new debt and sells it to the Federal Reserve Board. With the proceeds of these sales, the federal government retires the old debt. The money supply increases because newly created money is used to pay for the debt. The effect of selling debt to the Federal Reserve Board and then using the proceeds to retire existing debt (or to finance a current deficit) is no different from printing and spending new money. The money supply expands in either case. Thus, the federal government can always pay its interest expense and retire its debt when it becomes due.

Risk from price fluctuations and inflation

Even though the federal government can refund its debt and hence is free of the risk of default, the prices of the federal government's bonds can and do fluctuate. In addition, the purchasing power of the dollar has declined as a result of inflation, and therefore the purchasing power of funds invested in debt has declined. Although the federal government can always repay the monetary amount of its debt obligations, inflation may have reduced the purchasing power of that money. Thus, investing in federal government securities is not entirely free of risk, since the investor may suffer losses from price fluctuations of the debt or from inflation.

The debt of firms, individuals, and state and local governments involves even greater risk, for all of these debtors may default on their obligations. To aid buyers of debt instruments, several companies have developed credit rating systems. The most important of these services are Moody, Dun and Bradstreet, and Standard & Poor. Although these firms do not rate all debt instruments, they do rate the degree of risk of a significant number.

Risk classifications and ratings

Exhibit 9–3 gives the risk classifications presented by Moody and Standard & Poor. The rating systems are quite similar, for each classification of debt involving little risk (high-quality debt) receives a rating of triple A, while debt involving greater risk (poorer quality debt) receives progressively lower ratings.

Since the rating firms are analyzing similar data, their ratings of specific debt issues should be reasonably consistent. This consistency is illustrated by Exhibit 9–4, which gives the ratings for several different bond issues. In most cases, both Moody and Standard & Poor assigned comparable ratings to certain debt instruments. Even when the ratings

---

*The decline in the value of the dollar in foreign countries may reduce the attractiveness of federal obligations. Fluctuations in the value of the dollar, then, do impose significant risk for foreigners who invest in these securities.

EXHIBIT 9-2. A coupon bond.

Exhibit continued on the opposite page

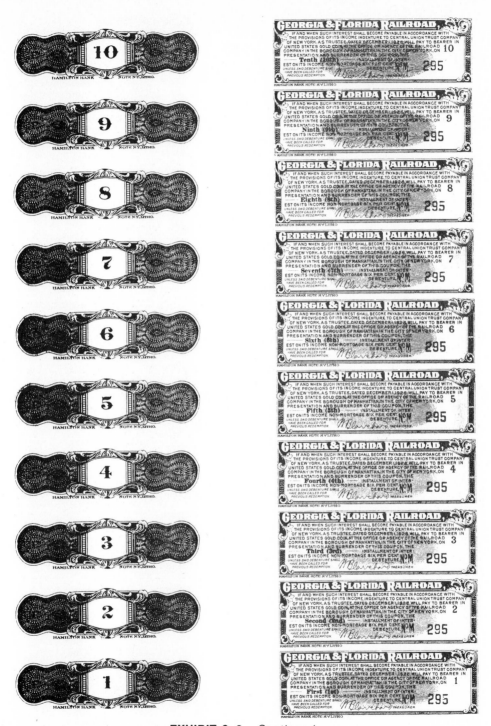

EXHIBIT 9-2. *Continued*

EXHIBIT 9–3. Bond Ratings*

Moody's Bond Ratings†

Aaa Bonds of highest quality

Aa   Bonds of high quality

A   Bonds whose security of principal and interest in considered adequate but may be impaired in the future

Baa Bonds of medium grade that are neither highly protected nor poorly secured

Ba   Bonds of speculative quality whose future cannot be considered well assured

B   Bonds that lack characteristics of a desirable investment

Caa Bonds in poor standing that may be defaulted

Ca   Speculative bonds that are often in default

C   Bonds with little probability of any investment value (lowest rating)

Standard & Poor's Bond Ratings‡

AAA Bonds of highest quality

AA   High-quality debt obligations

A   Bonds that have a strong capacity to pay interest and principal but may be susceptible to adverse effects

BBB Bonds that have an adequate capacity to pay interest and principal but are more vulnerable to adverse economic conditions or changing circumstances

BB   Bonds of lower medium grade with few desirable investment characteristics

B   }

CCC } Primarily speculative bonds with great uncertainties and major risk if exposed to adverse conditions

C   Income bonds on which no interest is being paid

D   Bonds in default

---

*Plus (+) and minus (−) are used to show relative strength within a rating category.

†Source: Adapted from *Moody's Bond Record*, April 1978.

‡Source: Adapted from *Standard & Poor's Bond Guide*, May 1978.

are different (e.g., the Gulf and Western 7 per cent bond that is due in 2003 or the Mobil Oil 7⅜ per cent bond that matures in 2001), the discrepancies are small.

These ratings play an important role in the marketing of debt obli-

EXHIBIT 9–4. Ratings for Selected Bonds as of May 1978*

Firm	Interest (Coupon), %	Year of Maturity	Moody's Rating	Standard & Poor's Rating
AT&T	7	2001	Aaa	AAA
Dow Chemical	8⁹/₁₀	2000	Aa	A+
Gulf and Western	7	2003	Ba	B
Mobil Oil	7³/₈	2001	Aaa	AA
Pennsylvania Railroad	4¹/₄	1981	Caa	D
Smith Corona Marchant	10	1996	Baa	BBB
Xerox	8⁵/₈	1999	Aa	AA

*Sources: *Moody's Bond Record*, April 1978, and *Standard & Poor's Bond Guide*, May 1978.

gations. Since the possibility of default may be substantial for poor-quality debt, some financial institutions and investors will not purchase debt with a low credit rating. Many financial institutions, especially commercial banks, are prohibited by law from purchasing bonds with a rating below Baa. Thus, if the rating of a bond issued by a firm or a municipality is low or declines from the original rating, the issuer may have difficulty selling its debt. Corporations and municipal governments try to maintain good credit ratings, since high ratings reduce the cost of borrowing and increase the marketability of the debt.

Besides the risk of default, creditors are also subject to the risk of price fluctuations. Once debt has been issued, the market price of the debt will rise or fall, depending on market conditions. If interest rates rise, the price of existing debt must fall so that its fixed interest payments relative to its price become competitive with the higher rates. In the event that interest rates decline, the opposite is true. The higher fixed interest payments of the bond make the debt more attractive than comparable newly issued bonds, and buyers will be willing to pay more for the debt issue. Why these fluctuations in the price of debt instruments occur is explained in more detail in Chapter 10, which discusses the valuation of debt instruments.

There is, however, one feature of debt that partially compensates for the risk of price fluctuations. The holder knows that the debt ultimately matures: The principal must be repaid. If the price of the bond decreases and the debt instrument sells for a discount (i.e., less than the face value), the value of the debt must appreciate as it approaches maturity because on the day of maturity, the full amount of the principal must be repaid.

The importance of maturity

The final risk that all creditors must endure is inflation, which reduces the purchasing power of money. During inflation the debtor repays the loan in money that purchases less. Creditors must receive a rate of interest that is at least equal to the rate of inflation to maintain their purchasing power. If lenders anticipate inflation, they will demand a higher rate of interest to help protect their purchasing power. For example, if the rate of inflation is 8 per cent, the creditors may demand 10 per cent, which nets them 2 per cent in real terms. Although inflation still causes the real value of the capital to decline, the higher interest rate partially offsets the effects of inflation.

The loss of purchasing power through inflation

If creditors do not anticipate inflation, the rate of interest may be insufficient to compensate for the loss in purchasing power. Inflation, then, hurts the creditors and helps the debtors, who are repaying the loans with money that purchases less.

The supposed inability of creditors to anticipate inflation has led to a belief that during inflation it is best to be a debtor. However, creditors invariably make an effort to protect their position by demanding higher interest rates. There is a transfer of purchasing power from creditors to debtors only if the creditors do not fully anticipate the inflation and do not demand sufficiently high interest rates. A transfer of pur-

The importance of anticipating the rate of inflation

chasing power from debtors to creditors will occur in the converse situation. If inflation is anticipated but does not occur, many debtors may pay artificially high rates of interest, which transfers purchasing power from them to their creditors. Hence, the transfer of purchasing power can go either way if one group inaccurately anticipates the future rate of inflation.*

THE MECHANICS OF PURCHASING BONDS

Bonds are purchased through brokers

Bonds may be purchased in much the same way as stocks. The investor can buy them through a brokerage firm, and some bonds (e.g., federal government securities) can be purchased through commercial banks. The various purchase orders that may be used to buy stock (e.g., the market order or the limit order with a specified price) also apply to the purchase of bonds. Bonds may be bought with cash or through the use of margin.

Listed bonds

The bonds of many companies are listed on the New York and American stock exchanges. In addition, there is a large volume of trading in bonds in the over-the-counter markets. Like listed stocks, transactions in bonds are reported by the financial press. Exhibit 9–5 is an example of an entry in *The Wall Street Journal* reporting the trading in an AT&T bond. This exhibit is a bit tricky to read. The entry is for a $1000 bond (though bonds generally trade in units greater than $1000); a price of $84⅜ means $843.75. The bond has a coupon rate of 7⅛ per cent and matures in the year 2003, which is reported as 7⅛ 03. The current yield is the annual interest payment divided by the price ($71.25 ÷ $843.75 = 8.4%). The number of bonds traded was 46, which means that, according to face value, $46,000 worth of these bonds changed ownership. The remaining entries are the same as those of stock transactions. These include the high (84⅜), low (84⅛), and closing (84⅜) prices and the net change (+ ⅛) from the previous day.

---

*See, for instance, Milton Friedman, "The Quantity Theory of Money — A Restatement," in Milton Friedman (ed.): *Studies in the Quantity Theory of Money* (Chicago, University of Chicago Press, 1956), pp. 3–21.

EXHIBIT 9–5. Illustration of an Entry for a $1000 Bond Traded on the New York Stock Exchange*

Bond	Current Yield	Volume	High	Low	Close	Net Change
AT&T 7⅛ 03	8.4%	46	84⅜	84⅛	84⅜	+⅛

*Source: *The Wall Street Journal*, June 5, 1978.

Scott & Stringfellow

MEMBERS
NEW YORK, AMERICAN (ASSOC.) AND RICHMOND STOCK EXCHANGES

909 EAST MAIN STREET, RICHMOND, VIRGINIA 23219, (703) 643-1811
29 EAST BEVERLEY STREET, STAUNTON, VIRGINIA 24401, (703) 886-2396
7 HOTEL STREET, WARRENTON, VIRGINIA 22186, (703) 347-2820
8 SOUTH BRADDOCK STREET, WINCHESTER, VIRGINIA 22601, (703) 667-3311

PLEASE RETAIN THIS COPY FOR YOUR INCOME TAX RECORDS

WE CONFIRM THE FOLLOWING TRANSACTION SUBJECT TO CONDITIONS ON REVERSE SIDE.

YOU BOUGHT	YOU SOLD	SECURITY DESCRIPTION	PRICE
2000		TESORO PETROLEUM 5 1/4 2/1/89RGD	77 7/8

TRADE DATE AND NUMBER		SECURITY NUMBER	PRINCIPAL	COMMISSION		STATE TAX OR INTEREST	S.E.C. FEE	POSTAGE MISCELLANEOUS
12/22/70	072	936492	1,557.50	10.00		43.46		

ACCOUNT NUMBER	TYPE	√	BRANCH	REG. REP.	CODES A	B	C	D
34295	1	1	01	03	2	1	2	

SEE REVERSE SIDE FOR EXPLANATION OF CODES.

	SETTLEMENT DATE	NET AMOUNT DUE *
8	12/30/70	1,610.96

Scott & Stringfellow Inc.

909 EAST MAIN STREET RICHMOND, VIRGINIA 23219
(804) 643-1811
MEMBERS
NEW YORK, AMERICAN (ASSOC.) AND RICHMOND STOCK EXCHANGES

OFFICES IN
BLUEFIELD, W. VIRGINIA 24701 (304) 325-3631
CULPEPER, VIRGINIA 22701 (703) 825-0783
STAUNTON, VIRGINIA 24401 (703) 886-2396
WARRENTON, VIRGINIA 22186 (703) 347-2820
WINCHESTER, VIRGINIA 22601 (703) 667-3311

PLEASE RETAIN THIS COPY FOR YOUR INCOME TAX RECORDS

WE CONFIRM THE FOLLOWING TRANSACTION SUBJECT TO CONDITIONS ON REVERSE SIDE.

YOU BOUGHT	YOU SOLD	SECURITY DESCRIPTION	PRICE
	2000	TESORO PETROLEUM 5 1/4 2/1/89RGD	77 3/4

TRADE DATE AND NUMBER		SECURITY NUMBER	PRINCIPAL	COMMISSION		STATE TAX OR INTEREST	S.E.C. FEE	POSTAGE MISCELLANEOUS
09/09/77	182	936492	1,555.00	20.00		13.13		

ACCOUNT NUMBER	TYPE	√	BRANCH	REG. REP.	CODES A	B	C	D
46078	1	8	01	19	1	1	8	

SEE REVERSE SIDE FOR EXPLANATION OF CODES.

	SETTLEMENT DATE	NET AMOUNT DUE *
8	09/16/77	1,548.13

223-54-4369

CUSIP 881609AA9

EXHIBIT 9–6. Confirmation statements for bond purchase and sale.

The confirmation statement

After the debt has been purchased, the broker sends a confirmation statement. Exhibit 9–6 presents the confirmation statements for the purchase and subsequent sale of $2000 in face value worth of Tesoro Petroleum bonds. In addition to a description of the securities, the confirmation statements include the price, the day of the transaction, the settlement day, the commission (note the increase in commission rates from $10 to $20 between the time of purchase and the time of sale), any fees, and accrued interest.

The handling of accrued interest

Bonds earn interest every day, but the firm distributes the interest payments only twice a year. Thus, when a bond is purchased, the buyer owes the previous owner accrued interest for the days that the owner held the bond. In the case of the first sale, the purchase was made several months after the last interest payment, so the accrued interest amounted to $43.46. This interest is added to the purchase price

EXHIBIT 9–7. Determination of Profit or Loss on the Sale of a Bond

Cost basis of the bond:	
Purchase price plus commissions	$1610.96
Less accrued interest	− 43.46
	$1567.50
Revenue from the sale:	
Proceeds of the sale less commissions	$1546.13
Less accrued interest	− 13.13
	$1533.00
Profit or (loss) on the investment:	
Return from the sale of the bond	$1533.00
Cost basis of the bond	−1567.50
Profit or (loss) on the investment	$ (34.50)

that the buyer must pay. When the bond is sold, the seller receives the accrued interest. The second sale occurred soon after the interest payment, and in this case the accrued interest was only $13.13, which was added to the proceeds of the sale.

The profit or loss from the investment cannot be figured as the difference between the proceeds of the sale and the amount that is due after the purchase (i.e., $1546.13 minus $1610.96 in Exhibit 9–7). Instead, an adjustment must be made for the accrued interest. This procedure is illustrated in Exhibit 9–7. First, the accrued interest must be subtracted from the amount due to obtain the cost of the bond. Thus, $1610.96 minus $43.46 is the cost ($1567.50) of this purchase. Second, the accrued interest must also be subtracted from the proceeds of the sale. Thus, $1546.13 minus $13.13 yields the revenues from the sale. To determine the profit or loss, the sale value is subtracted from the cost basis. In this particular instance, that is $1533 (the cost basis) minus $1567.50 (the sale value), which represents a loss of $34.50.

Bonds that trade flat   A few bonds do trade without accrued interest. These bonds are currently in default and are not paying interest. Such bonds are said to trade *flat,* and an F is placed next to them in the transactions reported by the financial press. These bonds are of little interest except to speculators. The risk in investing in them is substantial, but some do resume interest payments that can result in substantial returns. (See, for instance, the TWA bond illustrated in Exhibit 9–8, which is discussed later under income bonds.)

VARIETY OF CORPORATE BONDS

Corporations issue many types of bones: mortgage bonds, equipment trust certificates, debenture bonds and subordinated debentures, income bonds, convertible bonds, and variable interest rate bonds.

Each type has characteristics that differentiate it from the others. Investors should be aware of the differences among these bonds and of the risk and potential return associated with each type. This section will describe the various types of bonds, and the subsequent section will discuss several techniques for analyzing them.

MORTGAGE BONDS

Mortgage bonds are issued to purchase specific fixed assets, which are then pledged to secure the debt. This type of bond is frequently issued by utility companies. The proceeds that are raised by selling the debt are used to build power plants, and these plants secure the debt. As the plants generate revenues, the firm earns the cash flow that is necessary to service (pay interest on) and retire the debt. If the firm defaults on the interest or principal repayment, the creditors may take title to the pledged property. They may then choose to hold the asset and earn income from it (to operate the fixed asset) or to sell it. These options should give investors cause for thought: How many creditors could operate a power plant? If the investors choose to sell it, who would buy it?

Mortgage bonds are secured by real estate

These two questions illustrate an important point concerning investing in corporate debt. Although property that is pledged to secure the debt may decrease the lender's risk of loss, the creditor is not interested in taking possession of and operating the property. Lenders earn income through interest payments and not through the operation of the fixed assets. Such creditors are rarely qualified to operate the assets should they take possession of them. If they are forced to seize and sell the assets, they may find few buyers and may have to sell at distress prices. Despite the fact that pledging assets to secure debt increases the safety of the principal, the lenders prefer the prompt payment of interest and principal.

EQUIPMENT TRUST CERTIFICATES

Not all collateral has questionable resale potential. Unlike the mortgage bonds that are issued by utility companies, equipment trust certificates are secured by assets with substantial resale value. These certificates are issued to finance specific equipment, which is pledged as collateral. Equipment trust certificates are primarily issued by railroads and airlines to finance rolling stock (railroad cars) and airplanes. As the equipment is used to generate cash flow, the certificates are retired. The collateral supporting these certificates is considered to be of excellent quality, for, unlike some fixed assets (e.g., the aforementioned utility

Long-term debt is secured by equipment

plants), this equipment may be readily *moved* and sold to other railroads and airlines in the event that the firm defaults on the certificates.

DEBENTURES

Unsecured bonds   Debentures are unsecured promissory notes that are supported by
the general credit worthiness of the firm. This type of debt involves
more risk than bonds that are supported by collateral. In the case of
default or bankruptcy, the unsecured debt is redeemed only after all
secured debt has been paid off. Some debentures are subordinated, and
these involve even more risk, for they are redeemed after the other general debt of the firm has been redeemed. Even unsecured debt has a
superior position to the subordinated debenture. These bonds are
among the riskiest debt instruments issued by firms and usually have
higher interest rates or other attractive features, such as convertibility
into the stock of the company, to compensate the lenders for assuming
the increased risk.

Financial institutions, such as commercial banks or insurance companies, prefer a firm to sell debentures to the general public. Since the
debentures are general obligations of the company, they do not tie up
its specific assets. If the firm needs additional funds from a commercial
bank, it can use specific assets as collateral, in which case the bank will
be more willing to lend the funds. If the assets had been previously
pledged, the firm would lack this flexibility in financing.

Although the use of debentures may not decrease the ability of the
firm to issue additional debt, default on the debentures usually means
that all senior debt is in default as well. A common indenture clause
states that if any of the firm's debt is in default, all debt issues are also
in default. In this case the creditors may declare that all outstanding
debt is due. For this reason, a firm should not overextend itself through
excessive amounts of unsecured debt.

INCOME BONDS

Interest is paid only   Income bonds are the riskiest bonds issued by corporations. Interest
if earned   is paid only if the firm earns it. If the company is unable to cover its other
expenses, then it is not legally obligated to pay the interest on these
bonds. Owing to the great risk associated with them, income bonds are
rarely issued by corporations, but a few have existed. Exhibit 9–8 briefly chronicles the history of one of the most interesting examples of an
income bond: the TWA $6\frac{1}{2}$ per cent income bond that was due in 1978.
The interest payments were sporadic. For several years (1971, 1975, and
1976) the bond did not pay interest, but in 1977 interest payments were
resumed and the arrearage in payments was erased. This payment of
interest had a very positive effect on the price of the bonds, which had

EXHIBIT 9–8. Interest Payments Made by the TWA 6½ 78 Income Bond

Year	Payment
1970	$ 65.00
1971	0
1972	119.50
1973	86.00
1974	65.00
1975	0
1976	0
1977	162.50

reached a low of 46 in 1974 (i.e., a $1000 bond could be purchased for $460). In 1977, the bond traded near par. Those speculators who were willing to buy the bond in 1974 for less than half of its face value were well rewarded for taking the risk.

Although income bonds are rarely issued by firms, a similar type of security is often issued by state and municipal governments. These are revenue bonds, which are used to finance a particular capital improvement that is expected to generate revenues (e.g., a toll road or a municipal hospital). If the revenues are insufficient, then the interest is not paid.

Most projects have generated sufficient funds to service the debt, but there have been some notable exceptions: the West Virginia Turnpike and the Chesapeake Bay Bridge and Tunnel. Both issues are in default, and the amount of unpaid interest has been adding up for years. However, both bond issues may be of interest to speculators, for if use of these facilities increases, then the capacity to service the debt should also rise. Hence, the deferred interest may someday be paid.

CONVERTIBLE BONDS

Convertible bonds are a hybrid type of security. Technically they are debt: The bonds pay interest, which is a fixed obligation of the firm, and have a maturity date. But these bonds have a special feature: The investor has the option to convert the bond into a specified number of shares of common stock. The market price of these bonds depends on both the value of the stock and the interest that the bonds pay. If the price of the common stock rises, then the value of the bond must rise. The investor thus has the opportunity for capital gain should the price of the common stock rise. If, however, the price of the common stock does not appreciate, the investor still owns a debt obligation of the company and therefore has the security of an investment in a debt instrument.

Convertible bonds have been popular with both firms and investors. However, since they are a hybrid type of security, they are diffi-

Bonds that may be exchanged for stocks

cult to analyze. In addition, a convertible bond is, in part, an option (i.e., the option to convert the bond into stock). For these reasons, a detailed discussion is deferred until Chapter 20, which follows the material on options in Chapter 18.

VARIABLE INTEREST RATE BONDS

Interest coupons are not fixed

Prior to the mid 1970s the rate of interest that a bond paid was fixed at the date of issuance. With the advent of increased inflation in the 1970s, corporations started issuing bonds with variable interest rates. Citicorp was the first major American firm to offer bonds of variable interest rates to the general public. Two features of the Citicorp bond were unique at the time it was issued: (1) a variable interest rate that was tied to the interest rate on treasury bills and (2) the right of the holder to redeem the bond at its face value.

The interest rate to be paid by the Citicorp bond was set at 1 per cent above the average treasury bill rate during a specified period. This variability of the interest rate means that if short-term interest rates rise, the interest rate paid by the bond must increase. The bond's owner participates in any increase in short-term interest rates. Of course, if the short-term interest rates decline, the bond earns a lower rate of interest.

The second unique feature of the Citicorp bond was that two years after it was issued, the holder had the option to redeem the bond for its face value or principal. This option recurred every six months. If the owner needed the money more quickly, the bond could have been sold in the secondary market, for it was traded on the New York Bond Exchange. Therefore, the Citicorp bonds were very liquid debt instruments that offered the holder an opportunity to participate in higher short-term interest rates if they occurred.

The interest paid by this bond varied over time. When it was initially issued in 1974, it offered a current yield of 9.7 per cent. However, short-term interest rates subsequently declined. By 1977, the current annual yield was only 6.6 per cent, and many of the bondholders exercised their option to redeem the bonds. The decline in short-term interest rates resulted in a decline in investor fascination with variable interest rate bonds. However, with the return of high short-term interest rates in 1978 and 1979, these bonds are again attractive investments, and several firms have subsequently issued them.

RETIRING DEBT

Debt issues must ultimately be retired, and this retirement must occur on or before the maturity date of the debt. When the bond is issued, a method for periodic retirement is usually specified, for very few debt issues are retired in one lump payment at the maturity date. Instead, part of the issue is systematically retired each year. This systematic retirement may be achieved by issuing the bond in a series or by having a sinking fund.

SERIAL BONDS

In an issue of serial bonds, some bonds mature each year. This type of bond is usually issued by corporations to finance specific equipment, such as railroad cars, which is pledged as collateral. As the equipment depreciates, the cash flow that is generated by profits and depreciation expense is used to retire the bonds in a series as they mature.

The advertisement presented in Exhibit 9–9 for equipment trust certificates issued by St. Louis Southwestern Railway Company is an example of a serial bond. This issue of equipment trust certificates is designed so that one fifteenth of the bonds matures each year. Thus, the firm retires $1,440,000 of the certificates annually as each series within the issue matures. At the end of the 15th year, the entire issue of certificates will have been retired.

Bonds that are issued in a series

EXHIBIT 9–9. A serial bond.

New Issue   January 24, 1979

$21,600,000

St. Louis Southwestern Railway Company

Equipment Trust, Series G

9⅞% Equipment Trust Certificates
Non-Callable

Dividends to accrue from February 1, 1979. To mature in 15 annual installments of $1,440,000 on each February 1 from 1980 to 1994.

Issued under the Philadelphia Plan with 20% original cash equity.

MATURITIES AND YIELDS

1980	10.60%	1984	9.55%	1988	9.40%	1992	9.375%
1981	10.20	1985	9.50	1989	9.35	1993	9.375
1982	9.75	1986	9.50	1990	9.35	1994	9.375
1983	9.55	1987	9.40	1991	9.35		

These certificates are offered subject to prior sale, when, as and if issued and received by us, subject to approval of the Interstate Commerce Commission.

Salomon Brothers

Blyth Eastman Dillon & Co.
Incorporated

Drexel Burnham Lambert
Incorporated

Serial bonds are primarily issued by governments

Few corporations, however, issue serial bonds. They are primarily issued by state and local governments to finance capital improvements, such as new school buildings, or by ad hoc government bodies, such as the Port Authority of New York, to finance new facilities or other capital improvements. The bonds are then retired over a period of years by tax receipts or by revenues generated by the investment (e.g., toll roads).

SINKING FUNDS

Types of sinking funds

Sinking funds are generally employed to ease the retirement of long-term corporate debt. A sinking fund is a periodic payment to retire part of the debt issue. One type of sinking fund requires the firm to make payments to a trustee, who invests the money to earn interest. The periodic payments plus the accumulated interest retire the debt when it matures.

Another type of sinking fund requires the firm to set aside a stated sum of money and to select randomly the bonds that are to be retired. The selected bonds are called and redeemed, and the holder surrenders the bond because it ceases to earn interest once it has been called. This type of sinking fund is illustrated in Exhibit 9–10 by an advertisement taken from *The Wall Street Journal*. The principal amount of $224,000 in Atlantic Coast Railroad mortgage bonds is being retired through a sinking fund. The specific bonds being retired were selected by a lottery. Once they are chosen, these bonds are called. The owners must surrender the bonds to obtain their principal. If the bonds are not presented for redemption, they are still outstanding and are obligations of the company, but the debtor's obligation is limited to refunding the principal, since interest payments ceased at the call date.

Strong and weak sinking funds

Since each debt issue is different, there can be wide variations in sinking funds. A strong sinking fund retires a substantial proportion of the debt before the date of maturity. For example, if a bond issue is for $10 million and it matures in ten years, a strong sinking fund may require the firm to retire $1 million, or 10 per cent, of the issue each year. Thus, at maturity only $1 million is still outstanding. With a weak sinking fund, a substantial proportion of the debt is retired at maturity. For example, a sinking fund for a debt issue of $10 million that matures in ten years may require annual payments of $1 million commencing after five years. In this example, only $5 million is retired before maturity. The debtor must then make a lump sum payment to retire the remaining $5 million. Such a large final payment is called a *balloon* payment.

Several different types of sinking funds are illustrated in Exhibit 9–11, which presents the sinking fund requirements for selected debt issues. Some of these sinking funds are quite strong. For example, the Uniroyal bond requires that 6.67 per cent of the issue be retired each year. In this example, the entire issue is retired through the sinking

Atlantic Coast Line Railroad Company

General Mortgage 3⅝% Bonds, Series D
Due March 1, 1980

(Seaboard Coast Line Railroad Company
Successor by Merger to
Atlantic Coast Line Railroad Company)

← The Debt Issue

NOTICE IS HEREBY GIVEN that, pursuant to the provisions of Section 2.01 of the Fifth Supplemental Indenture, as modified, United States Trust Company of New York, as Corporate Trustee, has drawn by lot for redemption on March 1, 1979 at 100% of their principal amount out of moneys in the Series D Sinking Fund $224,000 principal amount of said General Mortgage 3⅝% Bonds, Series D due March 1, 1980 bearing the following distinctive numbers:

← Bonds Drawn by Lot

← $224,000—Principal Amount Being Retired

COUPON BONDS OF $1,000 BEARING DISTINGUISHING LETTERS DM

195	752	1487	1909	2380	2534	3472	3827
252	924	1744	1947	2405	2535	3639	3899
288	1330	1771	1951	2421	2557	3713	
509	1337	1828	1982	2455	2580	3725	
547	1349	1849	2080	2491	2612	3774	
587	1426	1863	2147	2518	2628	3786	

FULLY REGISTERED BONDS BEARING DISTINGUISHING LETTERS RDB

Bond Number	Amount Called	Bond Number	Amount Called	Bond Number	Amount Called
234	$ 9,000	276	$ 4,000	403	$ 1,000
259	12,000	277	2,000	411	1,000
260	9,000	278	12,000	413	2,000
261	5,000	286	1,000	414	1,000
262	9,000	295	3,000	417	1,000
263	8,000	308	2,000	421	1,000
269	1,000	358	1,000	425	10,000
274	82,000	383	1,000		
275	1,000	391	1,000		

Specific Bonds Being Called

Holders of coupon bonds called for redemption are required to present same at the office of United States Trust Company of New York, 130 John Street, New York, New York 10038, for payment of the redemption price. Coupons due March 1, 1979 should be detached and collected in the usual manner.

Holders of fully registered bonds, of which portions have been called for redemption, are required to present and surrender same at the aforesaid office of the Corporate Trustee for payment of the redemption price on the principal amount called for redemption and there will be issued new General Mortgage 3⅝% Bonds, Series D, of an aggregate principal amount equal to the unredeemed portions of such registered bonds surrendered. Interest payable March 1, 1979 on said fully registered bonds will be paid in the usual manner.

From and after March 1, 1979 interest on the bonds or portions thereof so called for redemption will cease to accrue.

← Interest Will Cease To Accrue

UNITED STATES TRUST COMPANY
OF NEW YORK, *Corporate Trustee*

Dated: January 30, 1979

EXHIBIT 9-10. Example of a sinking fund retiring debt.

EXHIBIT 9–11.   Selected Examples of Sinking Funds

Bond	Sinking Fund
General Telephone and Electronics 4 90	None
General Telephone and Electronics 5 92	5% to be retired annually starting in 1978 (75% of issue retired prior to maturity)
Uniroyal, Inc. 5½ 96	6⅔% to be retired annually starting in 1982 (100% of issue retired through the sinking fund)

fund. Other sinking funds are quite weak, and there is no sinking fund for the General Telephone and Electronics' 4 90 bond (i.e., the 4 per cent bond that matures in 1990).

The strength of a sinking fund affects the element of risk. A strong sinking fund requirement means that a substantial amount of the debt issue is retired during its lifetime, which makes the entire debt issue safer. The sinking fund feature of a debt issue, then, is an important factor in determining the amount of risk associated with investing in a particular debt instrument.

REPURCHASING DEBT

Debt may be repurchased

If bond prices decline and the debt is selling at a discount, the firm may try to retire the debt by purchasing it on the open market. The purchases may be made from time to time, in which case the sellers of the bonds need not know that the company is purchasing and retiring the debt. The company may also announce its intentions and offer to purchase a specified amount of the debt at a certain price within a particular period. Bondholders may then tender their bonds at the offer price; however, they are not required to sell their bonds and may continue to hold the debt.* The firm must then continue to meet the terms of the debt's indenture.

If debt is bought at a discount, it increases income

The advantage of repurchasing debt that is selling at a discount is the savings to the firm. If a firm issued $10 million in face value of debt and the bonds are currently selling for $.60 on the $1, the firm may reduce its debt by $1000 with a cash outlay of only $600, resulting in a $400 savings for each $1000 bond that is purchased. This savings is translated into income, because a reduction in debt at a discount is an extraordinary item that is treated in accounting as income. For example, in 1975 General Host purchased $12,504,000 in face value of debt for

---

*If more bonds are tendered than the company offered to buy, the firm prorates the amount of money that it had allocated for the purchase among the number of bonds being offered.

$7,205,000. This resulted in an extraordinary income gain after expenses of $4,607,000 which increased per-share earnings from $1.63 to $3.63.

On the surface, a firm's retiring debt at a discount may appear desirable. However, using money to repurchase debt is an investment decision, just like buying plant and equipment. If the company repurchases debt, it cannot use the funds for other purposes. Management must decide which is the better use of the money: purchasing other income-earning assets or retiring the debt. Unlike a sinking fund requirement (which management must meet), purchasing and retiring debt at a discount is a voluntary act. The lower the price of the debt, the greater is the potential benefit from the purchase, but management must still determine if it is the best use of the firm's scarce resource, cash. Many firms do not repurchase their debt, for the discount is not sufficient to justify such a use of funds. These corporations have better uses for their funds.

CALL FEATURE

Some bonds may be *called* for redemption prior to maturity. The issuer has the right to call and retire the bond. The bond is called for redemption as of a specific date. After that date, interest ceases to accrue, which forces the creditor to relinquish the debt instrument.

Some bonds may be called prior to maturity

Such premature retiring of debt through a call feature tends to occur after a period of high interest rates. If a bond has been issued during such a period and interest rates subsequently decline, it may be advantageous for the company to issue new bonds at the lower interest rate. The proceeds can then be used to retire the older bonds with the higher coupon rates. Such refunding reduces the firm's interest expense.

Of course, premature retirement of debt hurts the bondholders who lose the higher yield bonds. To protect these creditors, a call feature usually has a call penalty, such as the payment of one year's interest. If the initial issue had a 9 per cent interest rate, the company would have to pay $1090 to retire $1000 worth of debt. This call penalty usually declines over the lifetime of the debt. Exhibit 9–12 illustrates the call penalty associated with the 5¼ per cent convertible bond of Permaneer Corporation that matures in 1989. Initially the call penalty was 5¼ per cent, but this penalty declines to zero after 17 years. Such a call penalty does protect bondholders, and the debtor has the right to call the bond and to refinance debt if interest rates fall sufficiently to justify paying the call penalty.*

The call penalty is partial compensation for premature retirement

Several such refinancings occurred during 1977 and 1978, when interest rates fell below the levels of the mid 1970s. In particular utility companies that had issued debt with higher interest rates issued new

---

*How the call feature may affect the price of a bond is discussed in Chapter 10.

EXHIBIT 9–12. Schedule for the Call Penalty of a 5¹/₄ Per Cent Convertible Debenture of Permaneer Corporation Maturing in 1989

Year	Percentage of Face Value	Amount Required to Retire $1000 of Debt
1970	105¹/₄	$1052.50
1971	105	1050.00
1972	104⁵/₈	1046.25
⋮	⋮	⋮
1980	102¹/₈	1021.25
1981	101⁷/₈	1018.75
⋮	⋮	⋮
1986	100¹/₄	1002.50
1987	100	1000.00
1988	100	1000.00
1989	100	1000.00

bonds with lower yields, called the old debt, and paid the call penalty. For example, in 1977 Public Service Electric and Gas retired $84.3 million of its 12 per cent bonds that were due in 2004. It paid $1277.50 to retire $1000 in face value of debt (i.e., the premium penalty was $277.50 per $1000 bond). The refinancing, however, sufficiently reduced the company's interest expense to justify the refunding.

SUMMARY

This chapter discussed the general features of long-term debt. The terms of a debt issue include the coupon rate of interest and the maturity date. A trustee is appointed for each bond issue to protect the rights of the individual investors. The risks associated with investing in debt are attributable to price fluctuations and inflation as well as to the possibility of default on interest and principal repayment. To help investors, several firms have developed rating services that classify debt issues according to risk.

The mechanics of purchasing debt are very similar to those of buying stocks. However, while stocks are purchased through brokerage firms, some debt instruments (e.g., federal government securities) may be purchased through banks.

Debt may be retired in several ways. Some bonds are issued in a series, with a specified amount of debt maturing each year. Other debt issues have sinking funds that retire part of the bond issue prior to maturity. For some debt issues, the firm has the right to call the bonds prior to maturity. The debtor can also offer to buy the debt back from investors before it matures. Since creditors are as concerned with the return of their principal as they are with the payment of interest, the ability of the firm or government to retire its liabilities is one of the foremost factors in determining the risks associated with investing in debt.

Terms to Remember

Principal

Maturity date

Coupon rate

Yield curve

Indenture

Default

Trustee

Registered bond

Bearer bond

Rating systems

Accrued interest

Trading flat

Mortgage bond

Equipment trust certificate

Debenture

Income bond

Convertible bond

Variable interest rate bond

Serial bonds

Sinking fund

Balloon payment

Discount

Call feature

Refunding

Questions

1. What is the difference between bearer bonds and registered bonds? Which type is safer and why?

2. What is the relationship between the yield earned on bonds and the length of time to maturity? Does this relationship always hold?

3. Even though bonds are debt obligations, investing in them involves risk. What are the sources of risk? What service is available to aid the buyers of debt instruments in selecting a particular bond?

4. How may bonds be purchased?

5. What is the difference between a serial issue of bonds and term bonds with a specific maturity date and a sinking fund?

6. A call penalty protects whom from what? Why may firms choose to retire debt early after a period of high interest rates?

7. What advantages and disadvantages do bonds offer to investors?

8. What secures mortgage bonds and equipment trust certificates?

9. Why are many debentures and income bonds considered to be risky investments?

SELECTED READINGS

Bowlin, David D.: "The Refunding Decision: Another Special Case in Capital Budgeting." *Journal of Finance* (March 1966), pp. 55–68.

Pinches, George E., and Kent A. Mingo: "A Multivariate Analysis of Industrial Bond Ratings." *Journal of Finance* (March 1973), pp. 1–18.

Sherwood, Hugh C.: *How Corporate and Municipal Debt Is Rated.* New York, John Wiley & Sons, Inc., 1976.

Sherwood, Hugh: *How to Invest in Bonds.* New York, Walker & Co., 1974.

The Bond Book. New York, Merrill Lynch Pierce Fenner and Smith, Inc., 1974.

Learning Objectives

After completing this chapter you should be able to

1. Determine the price of a bond.

2. Isolate the factors that affect a bond's price.

3. Explain the relationship between changes in interest rates and bond prices.

4. Differentiate among current yield, yield to maturity, and yield to call.

5. Illustrate how discounted bonds may be used to help finance an individual's retirement.

chapter 10
THE VALUATION
OF DEBT

As was seen in Chapter 9, many bonds are sold to the general public and are traded like stocks. There is a very active secondary market in debt instruments. This chapter is concerned with how the market values debt instruments. Although there is a variety of debt instruments, each with its specific name, for the purpose of this chapter the term *bond* will be used to include all types of debt instruments.

Bond prices fluctuate daily. The price of a bond (in a given risk class) is primarily related to (1) the interest paid by the bond, (2) the interest that investors may earn on competitive bonds, and (3) the maturity date of the bond. This chapter will explore the effect of each. Initially only the first two factors are considered, and then the effect of maturity is added. Next follows a discussion of the various uses of the word *yield*. These include the current yield, the yield to maturity, and the yield to call. The chapter concludes with a brief discussion of yields and risk.

PERPETUAL DEBT

Some bonds never mature

A perpetual debt instrument is a bond that never matures. The issuer never has to retire the principal; it has only to meet the interest payments and the other terms of the indenture. Although such a bond may sound absurd, there are some in existence. For example, the British government issued perpetual bonds called consols to refinance the debt that was issued to support the Napoleonic Wars. These bonds will never mature, but they do pay interest, and there is an active secondary market in them.

Their value is related to (1) the amount of interest that they pay

How much can a perpetual bond be worth? The answer depends on the interest paid by the bond and what the investor can earn elsewhere. For example, a perpetual bond pays the following stream of interest income annually:

Year 1 ...	Year 2 ...	Year 20 ...	Year 100 ...	Year 1000 ...
$40 ...	$40 ...	$40 ...	$40 ...	$40 ...

How much are these interest payments worth? The question really is, what is the present value of each one of these $40 payments? In order to answer the question, the investor must know the rate of interest that may be earned on alternative investments. If the investor can earn 3 per cent elsewhere, the present value (*PV*) of the perpetual stream of $40 payments is

(2) What the investor may earn elsewhere

$$PV = \frac{\$40}{(1+.03)} + \frac{\$40}{(1+.03)^2} + \ldots + \frac{\$40}{(1+.03)^{20}} + \ldots + \frac{\$40}{(1+.03)^{100}} + \ldots + \frac{\$40}{(1+.03)^{1000}} + \ldots$$

$$PV = \$40(.971) + 40(.943) + \ldots + 40(.554) + \ldots + 40(.052) + \ldots + 40(.000) + \ldots$$

$$PV = \$38.84 + 37.72 + \ldots + 22.16 + \ldots + 2.08 + \ldots + 0 + \ldots$$

$$PV = \$1666.67$$

As may be seen in this example, the $40 interest payments received in the near future contribute most to the present value of the bond. Dollars received in the distant future have little value today. The sum of all of these present values is $1666.67, which means that if alternative investments yield 3 per cent, an investor would be willing to pay $1666.67 for a promise to receive $40 annually for the indefinite future.

The preceding may be stated in more formal terms. If *I* is the annual interest payment and *i* is the rate of return that is being earned on comparable investments, then the present value is

$$PV = \frac{I}{(1+i)} + \frac{I}{(1+i)^2} + \frac{I}{(1+i)^3} + \ldots$$

This is a geometric series, and its sum may be expressed as

(1)
$$PV = \frac{I}{i}$$

Equation 1 gives the current value of an infinite stream of interest payments. If this equation is applied to the previous example in which the annual interest payment is $40 and alternative investments can earn 3 per cent, then the present value of the bond is

$$PV = \frac{\$40}{.03} = \$1666.67$$

Their prices can fluctuate

If market interest rates of alternative investments were to increase (e.g., to 6 per cent), then the value of this perpetual stream of interest payments would decline; if market interest rates were to fall (e.g., to 2 per cent), then the value of the bond would rise. These changes occur because the bond pays a *fixed* flow of income, i.e., the dollar amount of interest paid by the bond is constant. Lower interest rates mean that more money is needed to purchase this fixed stream of interest payments, and with higher interest rates, less money is needed to buy this fixed flow of income.

If interest rates rise, bond prices fall

If interest rates fall, bond prices rise

The inverse relationship between interest rates and bond prices is illustrated in Table 10–1, which presents the value of the preceding perpetual bond at different interest rates. As may be seen from the table, as current market interest rates rise, the present value of the bond declines. Thus, if the present value is $1000 when interest rates are 4 per cent, the value of this bond declines to $200 when interest rates rise to 20 per cent.

Why this inverse relationship between bond prices and interest rates exists may be illustrated by a simple example. Suppose two investors offered to sell two different bond issues. The first is the perpetual bond that pays $40 per year in interest. The second is also a perpetual bond, but it pays $50 per year in interest. If the offer price in each case is $1000, which bond would be preferred? Obviously, if they are equal in every way except in the amount of interest, a buyer would prefer the second bond that pays $50. What could the seller of the first bond do to make the bond

TABLE 10–1. *Relationship Between Interest Rates and the Price of a Perpetual Bond*

CURRENT INTEREST RATE (i)	ANNUAL INTEREST PAID BY THE BOND (I)	PRESENT PRICE OF THE BOND $\left(PV = \frac{I}{i} \right)$
2%	$40	$2000
4	40	1000
6	40	667
8	40	500
10	40	400
15	40	267
20	40	200

more attractive to a buyer? The obvious answer is to lower the asking price so that the yield that the buyer receives is identical for both bonds. Thus, if the seller were to ask only $800 for the bond that pays $40 annually, the buyer should be indifferent as to which he or she chooses. Both bonds would then offer a yield of 5 per cent (i.e., $40 ÷ $800 for the first bond and $50 ÷ $1000 for the second bond).

BONDS WITH MATURITY DATES

The date of maturity affects value

The vast majority of bonds are not perpetual but have a finite life. They mature, and this fact must affect their valuation. A bond's price is related not only to the interest that it pays but also to its face amount (i.e., the principal). The current price of a bond equals the present value of the interest payments plus the present value of the principal to be received at maturity.

ANNUAL COMPOUNDING

A bond valuation model

The value of a bond is expressed algebraically in Equation 2 in terms of the present value formulas discussed in Chapter 5. A bond's value is

$$(2) \qquad P_B = \frac{I_1}{(1+i)^1} + \frac{I_2}{(1+i)^2} + \cdots + \frac{I_n}{(1+i)^n} + \frac{P}{(1+i)^n}$$

where P_B indicates the current price of the bond; I, the annual interest payment (with the subscripts indicating the year); n, the number of years to maturity; P, the principal; and i, the current interest rate.

Applications of the model

The calculation of a bond's price using Equation 2 may be illustrated by a simple example. A firm has a $1000 bond outstanding that matures in three years with a 6 per cent coupon rate ($60 annually). All that is needed to determine the price of the bond is the current interest rate, which is the interest rate that is being paid by newly issued, competitive bonds with the same length of time to maturity and the same degree of risk. If the competitive bonds yield 6 per cent, then the price of this bond will be par ($1000), for

$$P_B = \frac{\$60}{(1+.06)^1} + \frac{\$60}{(1+.06)^2} + \frac{\$60}{(1+.06)^3} + \frac{\$1000}{(1+.06)^3}$$

$$P_B = \$56.60 \quad + \quad \$53.40 \quad + \quad \$50.38 \quad + \quad \$839.62$$

$$P_B = \$1000.00$$

If competitive bonds are selling to yield 8 per cent, this bond will be unattractive to investors. They will not be willing to pay $1000 for a bond yielding 6 per cent when they could buy competing bonds at the same price that yield 8 per cent. In order for this bond to compete with the others, its price must decline sufficiently to yield 8 per cent. In terms of Equation 2, the price must be

$$P_B = \frac{\$60}{(1+.08)^1} + \frac{\$60}{(1+.08)^2} + \frac{\$60}{(1+.08)^3} + \frac{\$1000}{(1+.08)^3}$$

$$P_B = \$55.55 \quad + \$51.44 \quad + \$47.63 \quad + \$793.83$$

$$P_B = \$948.45$$

The price of the bond must decline to approximately $950, i.e., it must sell for a discount (i.e., a price less than the stated principal), in order to be competitive with comparable bonds. At that price investors will earn $60 per year in interest and approximately $50 in capital gains over the three years, for a total annual return of 8 per cent on their investment. The capital gain occurs because the bond is purchased for $948.45, but when it matures, the holder will receive $1000.

If comparable debt were to yield 4 per cent, the price of the bond in the previous example would have to rise. In this case the price of the bond would be

$$P_B = \frac{\$60}{(1+.04)^1} + \frac{\$60}{(1+.04)^2} + \frac{\$60}{(1+.04)^3} + \frac{\$1000 \text{ }^-}{(1+.04)^3}$$

$$P_B = \$60(.962) + \$60(.925) \quad + \$60(.889) \quad + \$1000(.889)$$

$$P_B = \$1055.56$$

The bond, therefore, must sell at a premium (i.e., a price greater than the stated principal). Although it may seem implausible for the bond to sell at a premium, this must occur if the market interest rate falls below the coupon rate of interest stated on the bond.

These price calculations are lengthy, but the number of computations can be reduced when one realizes that the valuation of a bond has two components: a flow of interest payments and a final repayment of principal. Since interest payments are fixed and are paid every year, they may be treated as an annuity. The principal repayment may be treated as a simple lump-sum payment. If a $1000 bond pays $60 per year in interest and matures after three years, its current value is the present value of the $60 annuity for three years and the present value of the $1000 that will be received after three years. If the interest rate is 8 per cent, the current value of the bond is

$$P_B = \$60\,(2.577) + \$1000\,(.794) = \$948.62$$

GRAPH 10–1.   Relationship Between Interest Rates and
a Bond's Price

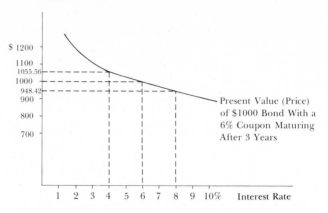

where 2.577 is the interest factor for the present value of a $1 annuity at 8 per cent for three years and .794 is the interest factor for the present value of $1 at 8 per cent after three years. This is approximately the same answer that was derived earlier, but the amount of arithmetic has been reduced. (The difference results from rounding off.)

The inverse relationship restated

These examples illustrate the same general conclusion that was reached earlier concerning bond prices and changes in market interest rates: They are inversely related. *When market interest rates rise, bond prices decline. When market interest rates fall, bond prices rise.* This relationship is illustrated in Graph 10–1, which plots the price of the aforementioned $1000 bond at various interest rates. As may be seen from the graph, higher interest rates depress the bond's current value. Thus, the bond's price declines from $1000 to $948.42 when interest rates rise from 6 to 8 per cent, but the price rises to $1055.56 when interest rates decline to 4 per cent.

Correct anticipation of direction of change produces profits

The inverse relationship between the price of a bond and the interest rate suggests a means to make profits in the bond market. All that the investor needs to know is the direction of future changes in the interest rate. If investors anticipate that interest rates will decline, then they are expecting the price of previously issued bonds with a given number of years to maturity and of a certain risk to rise. This price increase must occur in order for previously issued bonds to have the same yield as currently issued bonds. The reverse is also true, for if investors anticipate that interest rates will rise, then they are also anticipating that the price of currently available bonds will decline. This decline must occur for previously issued bonds to offer the same yield as currently issued bonds. Therefore, if investors can anticipate the direction of change in interest rates, they can also anticipate the direction of change in the price of bonds.

Investors, however, may anticipate incorrectly and thus suffer losses in the bond market. If they buy bonds and interest rates rise, then the market value of their bonds must decline and the investors suffer capital losses. These individuals, however, have something in their favor: The bonds must ultimately be retired. Since the principal must be redeemed, an investment error in the bond market may be corrected when the bond's price rises as the bond approaches maturity. The capital losses will eventually be erased. The correction of the error, however, may take years, during which time the investors have lost the higher yields that were available on bonds issued after their initial investments.

Incorrect anticipation of direction of change produces losses

SEMIANNUAL COMPOUNDING

The valuation of the bond with a finite life that was presented in Equation 2 is a bit misleading because bonds pay interest twice a year (i.e., semiannually). Equation 2 assumes that the interest payments are made only annually. However, Equation 2 may be readily modified to take into consideration semiannual (or even quarterly or weekly) compounding. This is done by adjusting the amount of each payment and the total number of these payments. In the previous example, each interest payment will be $30 if payments are semiannual, and instead of three annual payments, the bond will make a total of six $30 semiannual payments. Hence, the flow of payments that will be made by this bond is

Bonds pay interest semiannually

Year 1		Year 2		Year 3		
$30	$30	$30	$30	$30	$30	$1000

This flow of payments would then be discounted back to the present to determine the bond's current value. The question then becomes, what is the appropriate discount factor?

If comparable debt yields 8 per cent, the appropriate discount factor is not 8 per cent; it is 4 per cent. 4 per cent interest paid twice a year yields 8 per cent interest compounded semiannually. Thus, to determine the present value of this bond, the comparable interest rate is divided in half (just as the annual interest payment is divided in half.) However, the number of interest payments to which this 4 per cent is applied is doubled (just as the number of payments is doubled). Hence, the current value of this bond, which pays interest twice a year (i.e., is compounded semiannually) is

Modifying the valuation model for semiannual compounding

$$P_B = \frac{\$30}{(1+.04)^1} + \frac{\$30}{(1+.04)^2} + \frac{\$30}{(1+.04)^3} + \frac{\$30}{(1+.04)^4} + \frac{\$30}{(1+.04)^5} + \frac{\$30}{(1+.04)^6} + \frac{\$1000}{(1+.04)^6}$$

$P_B = \$30(.961) + \$30(.925) + \$30(.889) + \$30(.855) + \$30(.822) + \$30(.790) + \$1000(.790)$

$P_B = \$28.83 \quad + \$27.75 \quad + \$26.67 \quad + \$25.65 \quad + \$24.66 \quad + \$23.70 \quad + \$790.00$

$P_B = \$947.26$

With semiannual compounding, the current value of the bond is slightly lower (i.e., \$947.26 versus \$948.62). This is the result of the fact that the bond's price must decline more in order to compensate for the more frequent compounding. An investor would prefer a bond that pays \$30 twice per year to one that pays \$60 once per year, because the investor would have use of some of the funds more quickly. Thus, if interest rates rise, causing bond prices to fall, the decline will be greater if the interest on bonds is paid semiannually than if it is paid annually.

Equation 2 may be altered to include semiannual compounding. This is done in Equation 3. Only one new symbol, c, is added, which represents the frequency of compounding (i.e., the number of times each year that interest payments are made).

$$(3) \quad P_B = \frac{\frac{I}{c}}{\left(1+\frac{i}{c}\right)^1} + \frac{\frac{I}{c}}{\left(1+\frac{i}{c}\right)^2} + \ldots + \frac{\frac{I}{c}}{\left(1+\frac{i}{c}\right)^{n\times c}} + \frac{P}{\left(1+\frac{i}{c}\right)^{n\times c}}$$

When Equation 3 is applied to the earlier example, the price of the bond is

$$P_B = \frac{\frac{\$60}{2}}{\left(1+\frac{.08}{2}\right)^1} + \frac{\frac{\$60}{2}}{\left(1+\frac{.08}{2}\right)^2} + \ldots + \frac{\frac{\$60}{2}}{\left(1+\frac{.08}{2}\right)^{3\times2}} + \frac{\$1000}{\left(1+\frac{.08}{2}\right)^{3\times2}}$$

$$P_B = \$30(.961) + \$30(.925) + \ldots + \$30(.790) + \$1000(.790)$$

$$P_B = \$947.26$$

which, of course, is the same answer derived in the immediately preceding example.

Performing such calculations can obviously be quite tedious and time-consuming. However, several tools exist that will greatly reduce the labor. First, there are bond tables that present the value of a bond at various rates of interest. Exhibit 10–1 has been adapted from such a table. The bond's coupon rate, 8 per cent, is given in the title. The current rate of interest is read vertically at the left. The number of years to maturity is read horizontally at the top. If an investor wanted to know the price of an 8 per cent bond that would mature in ten years and that was priced to yield 7.5 per cent, he or she could consult the table to find the price. In this case it is \$103.47 (i.e., \$1034.70 for a \$1000 bond).

Bond tables

Although not all investors have bond tables at their disposal, the advent of the pocket calculator has put price calculations at the fingertips of virtually every investor. Sophisticated calculators (some of which are manufactured by Texas Instruments or Hewlett Packard) can be used to determine bond prices, and even the less sophisticated models can perform such computations. As was illustrated previously, all the investor needs to know to determine the bond's price are the interest factors for

EXHIBIT 10–1. Bond Table for a Bond With an 8 Per Cent Coupon*

	1	3	5	10	14
			Years to Maturity		
6.5%	$101.43	$104.03	$106.32	$110.90	$113.65
7.0	100.95	102.66	104.16	107.11	108.83
7.5	100.47	101.32	102.05	103.47	104.29
8.0	100.00	100.00	100.00	100.00	100.00
8.5	99.53	98.70	98.00	96.68	95.95
9.0	99.06	97.42	96.04	93.50	92.13
9.5	98.60	96.16	94.14	90.45	88.52
10.0	98.14	94.92	92.28	87.54	85.10

*Source: Adapted from Thorndike, David (ed.): *Thorndike Encyclopedia of Banking and Financial Tables*. Boston, Warren, Gorham, & Lamont, Inc., 1973.

Electronic calculators

the present value of an annuity and of a dollar for 8 per cent compounded semiannually. Such interest factors may be generated by using the less sophisticated pocket calculators. Thus, the individual investor does not need a computer, present value tables, or a bond table to price bonds. Pocket calculators have reduced both the tedium of the calculations and the reliance on sophisticated equipment or mathematical tables.

YIELDS

The word *yield* is frequently used with regard to investing in bonds. There are three important types of yield that the investor must be familiar with: the current yield, the yield to maturity, and the yield to call. This section will differentiate among these three yields.

THE CURRENT YIELD

The current yield is the percentage that the investor earns annually. It is simply

(4) $$\frac{\text{Annual interest payment}}{\text{Price of the bond}}$$

The bond used in the previous example has a coupon rate of 6 per cent. Thus, when the price of the bond is $947.26, the current yield is

$$\frac{\$60}{\$947.26} = 6.3\%$$

The current yield is important because it gives the investor an indication of the current return that will be earned on the investment. Investors who seek high current income prefer bonds that offer a high current yield.

The current yield does not consider price changes

The current yield, however, can be very misleading, for it fails to consider any change in the price of the bond that may occur if the bond is held to maturity. Obviously, if a bond is bought at a discount, its value must rise as it approaches maturity. The opposite occurs if the bond is purchased for a premium, for its price will decline as maturity approaches. For this reason it is desirable to know the bond's yield to maturity.

THE YIELD TO MATURITY

The yield to maturity includes any price change

The yield to maturity considers not only the current income that is generated by the bond but also any change in its value when it is held to maturity. If the bond referred to earlier is purchased for $947.26 and is held to maturity, after three years the investor will receive a return of 8 per cent. This is the yield to maturity, because this return considers not only the current interest return of 6.3 per cent but also the price appreciation of the bond from $947.26 at the time of purchase to $1000 at maturity. Since the yield to maturity considers both the flow of interest income and the price change, it is a more accurate measure of the return offered to investors by a particular bond issue.

The yield to maturity may be determined by using Equation 2.* That equation reads

$$P_B = \frac{I_1}{(1+i)} + \frac{I_2}{(1+i)^2} + \ldots + \frac{I_n}{(1+i)^n} + \frac{P}{(1+i)^n}$$

The i is the current rate of interest paid by newly issued bonds with the same term to maturity and the same degree of risk. If the investor buys a bond and holds it to maturity, the yield that is being paid by newly issued bonds (i) will also be the yield to maturity.

Determining the yield to maturity when the coupon rate of interest, the bond's price, and the maturity date are known is not easy, even with the use of an electronic calculator. For example, if the bond were selling for $947.26 and the investor wanted to know the yield to maturity, the calculation would be

$$\$947.26 = \frac{\$60}{(1+i)} + \frac{\$60}{(1+i)^2} + \frac{\$60}{(1+i)^3} + \frac{\$1000}{(1+i)^3}$$

Solving this equation can be a formidable task because there is no simple arithmetic computation to determine the value of i. Instead, the investor selects a value for i and plugs it into the equation. If this value equates the left-hand and right-hand sides of the equation, then that value of i is the

---

*Equation 3 is more correct, since bonds pay interest semiannually. However, Equation 2 is less formidable and still illustrates the point.

yield to maturity. If that value does not equate the two sides of the equation, then another value value must be selected. This process is repeated until a value for i is found that equates both sides of the equation. Obviously, that can be a long and tedious process.

A COMPARISON OF THE CURRENT YIELD AND THE YIELD TO MATURITY

The current yield and the yield to maturity are equal only if the bond sells for its principal amount or par. If the bond sells at a discount, then the yield to maturity exceeds the current yield. This may be illustrated by the bond in the previous example. When it sells at a discount (e.g., $947.26), the current yield is only 6.33 per cent. However, the yield to maturity is 8 per cent. Thus, the yield to maturity exceeds the current yield.

Effect on yield if bond sells for a premium or discount

If the bond sells at a premium, then the current yield exceeds the yield to maturity. For example, if the bond sells for $1055.50, then the current yield is 5.68 per cent ($60 ÷ $1055.50), and the yield to maturity is 4 per cent. The yield to maturity is less in this case because the loss that the investor must suffer when the price of the bond declines from $1055.50 to $1000 at maturity has been incorporated.

Table 10–2 presents the current yield and the yields to maturity at different prices for a bond with an 8 per cent coupon that matures in ten years. As may be seen in the table, the larger the discount (or the smaller the premium), the greater is both the current yield and the yield to maturity. For example, when the bond sells for $881.50, the yield to maturity is 9.9 per cent, but it rises to 11.5 per cent when the price declines to $795.10.

Discounted bonds offer conservative investors an attractive opportunity for financial planning. For example, a person who is currently 50 years old may purchase discounted bonds that mature after 15 years to help finance retirement. This investor may purchase several bonds that

Discounted bonds may be attractive investments

TABLE 10–2. *Current Yields and Yields to Maturity for a Ten-Year Bond With an 8 Per Cent Coupon*

PRICE OF BOND	CURRENT YIELD	YIELD TO MATURITY
$1109.00	7.2%	6.5%
1049.10	7.6	7.3
1000.00	8.0	8.0
966.80	8.3	8.5
910.50	8.8	9.4
881.50	9.1	9.9
831.30	9.6	10.8
795.10	10.1	11.5

TABLE 10–3. *Selected AT&T Bonds Selling at a Discount as of April 1978**

Coupon Rate	Maturity Year	Current Price (per $1000 in Face Value)	Yield to Maturity
$4^{3}/_{4}\%$	1992	$700	8.34%
$4^{1}/_{8}$†	1993	630	8.42
$4^{5}/_{8}$	1994	684	8.23
$5^{5}/_{8}$	1995	750	8.39
$4^{3}/_{8}$	1996	638	8.22

*Source: *Moody's Bond Record,* April 1978.
†This coupon rate is for a Chesapeake and Potomac Telephone Company bond (a subsidiary of AT&T).

mature 15, 16, 17, years and so on into the future. This portfolio will generate a continuous flow of funds during retirement as the bonds mature. Such a portfolio of AT&T bonds is illustrated in Table 10–3. The first column gives the coupon rate of interest, the second column gives the year of maturity, the third column presents the current discounted price for $1000 in face value worth of debt, and the last column gives the yield to maturity. By purchasing this portfolio for a total cost of $3402, the investor will own $5000 worth of bonds that mature between 1992 and 1996. Of course, by purchasing more discounted bonds that mature between 1992 and 1996, the investor will have an even greater flow of income during the particular time period to meet his or her financial goals (e.g., financing retirement or paying for children's college education).

THE YIELD TO CALL

Some bonds will never reach maturity but are retired before they become due. In some cases the issuer may call the bonds before maturity and redeem them. In other cases, the sinking fund will randomly call selected bonds from the issue and retire them. For these reasons the yield to call may be a more accurate estimate of the return that is actually earned on an investment in a bond that is held until redemption.

A call feature will affect a bond's value

The yield to call is calculated in the same way as the yield to maturity that was presented earlier, except that (1) the expected call date is substitured for the maturity date and (2) the principal plus the call penalty (if any) is substituted for the principal. Note that the anticipated call date is used. Unlike the maturity date, which is known, the date of a call can only be anticipated.

How the yield to call is calculated is illustrated by the following example. A bond that matures after ten years and pays 8 per cent interest annually is currently selling for $935.00. The yield to maturity is 9 per cent. However, if the investor believes that the company or government will call the bond after five years and will pay a penalty of $50 per $1000 bond to retire the debt prematurely, then the yield to call (i_c) is approximately

The valuation model can be adjusted for a call feature

$$\$935 = \frac{\$80}{(1 + i_c)^1} + \ldots + \frac{\$80}{(1 + i_c)^5} + \frac{\$1050}{(1 + i_c)^{55}}$$

$$i_c = 10.5\%$$

(This answer, like the yield to maturity, may be derived by using the present value tables. To do so, select an interest rate, find the appropriate interest factors, and substitute them for i_c. This process is continued until a value for i_c is found that equates both sides of the equation. This lengthy process may be avoided by the use of computers or calculators that are programmed to determine yields to maturity.)

In this example, the yield to call is higher than the yield to maturity because (1) the investor receives the call penalty and (2) the principal is redeemed early and hence the discount is erased sooner. Thus, in the case of a discounted bond, the actual return that the investor earns exceeds the yield to maturity if the bond is called and retired before maturity.

However, if this bond were selling for a premium (e.g., $1146.80 with a yield to maturity of 6 per cent) and the firm were to call the bond after five years, then the yield to call would become

$$\$1146.80 = \frac{\$80}{(1 + i_c)^1} + \ldots + \frac{\$80}{(1 + i_c)^5} + \frac{\$1050}{(1 + i_c)^5}$$

$$i_c = 5.5\%$$

This is less than the anticipated yield to maturity of 6 per cent. The early redemption produces a lower return for the investor because the premium is spread out over fewer years, which reduces the yield on the investment.

Which case is more likely to occur? If a firm wanted to retire debt that was selling at a discount before maturity, it would probably be to its advantage to purchase the bonds instead of calling them. By doing so, the firm would avoid the call penalty and might even be able to buy the bonds for less than par. If the firm wanted to retire debt that was selling at a premium, it would probably be advantageous to call the bonds and pay the penalty. If the bonds were selling for more than the call penalty, this would obviously be the chosen course of action.

An investor should not expect a firm to call prematurely a bond issue that is selling at a discount. However, if interest rates fall and bond prices rise, the firm may refinance the debt. It will then issue new debt at the lower (current) interest rate and use the proceeds to retire the old and more costly debt. In this case the yield to the anticipated call is probably a better indication of the potential return offered by the bonds than is the yield to maturity.

The preceding example also illustrates the importance of the call penalty. If an investor bought the bond in the anticipation that it would yield 6 per cent to maturity (i.e., paid $1146.80) and the bond is redeemed after five years for $1000, the return on the investment is only 4.6 per cent. Although the $50 call penalty does not restore the return to 6 per cent, the investor does receive a yield of 5.5 per cent, which is considerably better than 4.6 per cent.

RISK AND FLUCTUATIONS IN YIELDS

Investors will bear risk only if they anticipate a sufficient return to compensate for the risk. A higher anticipated return is necessary to induce investors to bear additional risk. This principle applies to investors who purchase bonds. Bonds involving greater risk must offer higher yields to attract investors. Therefore, the lowest yields are paid by bonds with the highest credit ratings, and low credit ratings are associated with high yields.

This relationship is illustrated by Exhibit 10–2, which presents Moody's ratings and the anticipated yields to maturity for four bonds issued by industrial firms that will mature in the year 2000. As may be seen in the exhibit, the bonds with the highest credit ratings have the lowest anticipated yield to maturity. An AT&T bond with an Aaa rating was selling to yield 8.48 per cent, but the Baa-rated bond of Georgia Power Company offered a yield to maturity of 9.4 per cent. The difference, or "spread," in the yields is partially due to the difference in risk between the two bonds. While the AT&T bond is considered to be quite safe (as judged by its rating), the Georgia Power Company bond is viewed as involving considerably more risk.

Because interest rates change over time, the anticipated yields on all debt vary. However, the yields on debt involving greater risk tend to fluctuate more. This is illustrated in Graph 10–2, which plots the yields on Moody's Baa-rated bonds in the top line and the yields on its Aaa-rated bonds in the bottom line. During this particular period there was con-

EXHIBIT 10–2. Credit Ratings and Yields to Maturity for Selected Bonds Maturing in the Year 2000*

Bond Issue	Moody's Bond Rating	Yield to Maturity
AT&T, 8¾ 00	Aaa	8.48%
Ford Motor Credit 9⁷⁄₁₀ 00	Aa	9.12
Tenneco Corp., 9⅞ 00	A	9.26
Georgia Power Co., 8⅞ 00	Baa	9.40

*Source: Moody's Bond Record, April 1978.

GRAPH 10–2. Fluctuations in Yield to Maturity for Moody's Aaa- and Baa-Rated Industrial Bonds

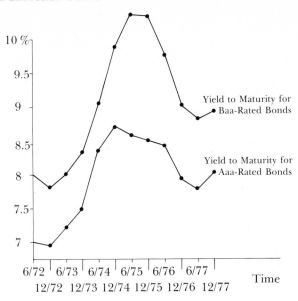

siderable change in the yields to maturity. During periods of higher interest rates, not only did the poorer quality debt offer a higher yield but also the spread between the yields was greater. For example, during 1974, when long-term interest rates were near their historic high, the yields to maturity on the Aaa- and Baa-rated bonds rose to 8.6 and 10.4 per cent. The spread, then, was 1.8 per cent. However, during 1977 the yields declined to 8.0 and 8.8 per cent, and the spread was 0.8 per cent.

These fluctuations in yields also imply that price fluctuations are greatest for bonds of poorer quality. As would be expected, all bond prices fall when interest rates rise, but the prices of the weaker (riskier) bonds tend to decline more. As the spread between yields rises, so too does the difference between the bond prices.

These differences in the fluctuations of bond prices and spreads are the market's way of adjusting for the relative risk of investing in debt instruments of different quality. During periods of high interest rates and relatively scarce credit, weaker firms find it more difficult to finance their assets. Issuing new debt either to finance new assets or to retire old debt is more costly. Lenders must allocate the scarce supply of available credit. This scarcity of credit means that its price (i.e., the interest rate) must rise. In addition, the possibility of default by the borrower is greater when interest rates are higher and the ability to borrow is reduced. The creditor must be compensated for assuming this increased risk of loss. Thus, despite the fact that all yields rise, the yields on the weakest debt instruments tend to rise the most. These bonds, then, sell for the largest discounts and experience greater price volatility than high-quality bonds.

SUMMARY

The price of a bond depends on the interest paid, the maturity date, and the return offered by comparable bonds. If interest rates rise, the price of existing bonds falls. The opposite is also true: If interest rates fall, the price of existing bonds rises.

The current yield considers only the flow of interest income relative to the price of the bond. The yield to maturity considers not only the flow of interest income but also any price change that may occur if the bond is held to maturity. The yield to call is similar to the yield to maturity, but it substitutes the call date and the call price for the maturity date and the principal.

Discounted bonds may be attractive to investors seeking current income, some capital appreciation, and the return of the principal at a specified date. Since most bonds mature, the investor knows exactly when the principal is to be received.

All bond prices fluctuate, but the price of bonds involving greater risk tends to fluctuate more. Thus, these bonds may sell for larger discounts and higher premiums than higher quality debt. Such bonds may be attractive investments for individuals who are seeking higher returns and who are willing to bear the additional risk.

SUMMARY OF BOND VALUATIONS

Perpetual Bond

(1)
$$PV = \frac{I}{i}$$

Finite Maturity—Annual Compounding

(2)
$$P_B = \frac{I_1}{(1+i)^1} + \frac{I_2}{(1+i)^2} + \ldots + \frac{I_n}{(1+i)^n} + \frac{P}{(1+i)^n}$$

Finite Maturity—Semiannual Compounding

(3)
$$P_B = \frac{\frac{I}{c}}{\left(1+\frac{i}{c}\right)^1} + \frac{\frac{I}{c}}{\left(1+\frac{i}{c}\right)^2} + \ldots + \frac{\frac{I}{c}}{\left(1+\frac{i}{c}\right)^{n \times c}} + \frac{P}{\left(1+\frac{i}{c}\right)^{n \times c}}$$

Terms to Remember

Perpetual bond	Yield to maturity	Discounted bond
Current yield	Yield to call	Premium

Questions

1. What causes bond prices to fluctuate?

2. Define the current yield and the yield to maturity. How are they different?

3. When is the yield to maturity greater than the current yield?

4. What advantages do discounted bonds offer to investors?

5. Why may a bond be called if it is selling at a premium?

6. Although all bond prices fluctuate, the price of which bonds tends to fluctuate more?

7. What is the yield to call? How does it differ from the yield to maturity?

Problems

1. A $1000 bond has the following features: a coupon rate of 8 per cent, interest that is paid semiannually (i.e., $40 every six months), and a maturity date of ten years.
   a. What is the bond's price if comparable debt yields 8 per cent? (Use both the bond table in Exhibit 10–1 and the present value tables. Are your answers different?)
   b. What is the bond's price if comparable debt yields 6 per cent?
   c. What is the current yield if the bond sells for the prices determined in questions a and b?
   d. Why are the prices different for questions a and b?

2. A $1000 bond has a coupon rate of 10 per cent and matures after eight years. Interest rates are currently 7 per cent.
   a. What will the price of this bond be if the interest is paid annually?
   b. What will the price be if investors expect that the bond will be called after two years?
   c. What will the price be if investors expect that the bond will be called after two years and there will be a call penalty of one year's interest?
   d. Why are your answers different for the questions a, b, and c?

3. A company has two bonds outstanding. The first matures after five years and has a coupon rate of 8 per cent. The second matures after ten years and has a coupon rate of 8 per cent. Interest rates are currently 10 per cent. What is the present price of each bond? Why are these prices different?

4. If a bond with a 9 per cent coupon (paid annually) and a maturity date of ten years is selling for $939, what is the current yield and the yield to maturity? (Hint: Try 8 per cent or 12 per cent.)

Learning Objectives

After completing this chapter you should be able to

1. Explain why the management of a firm's current assets is important to bondholders.

2. Identify the difference between the quick and the current ratio.

3. Differentiate inventory turnover from accounts receivable turnover.

4. Determine times-interest-earned.

5. Compare and contrast bonds and preferred stock.

6. Illustrate the pricing of preferred stock.

chapter 11
ANALYSIS OF CORPORATE DEBT AND PREFERRED STOCK

This chapter covers the fixed-income securities issued by corporations: bonds and preferred stock. The first part of the chapter presents a variety of financial ratios that may be used to measure the ability of the firm to service its debt. These include the liquidity ratios, which indicate the company's ability to meet its current obligations as they become due; the activity ratios, which indicate the rate at which assets flow through the firm; and the coverage ratios, which indicate the extent to which the company's operating income covers its current debt obligations.

The chapter ends with a discussion of preferred stock. Although preferred stock represents ownership, it is very similar to debt. Such stock pays a fixed dividend (like the fixed interest paid by bonds) and may be analyzed with the same tools that are used to analyze debt. The valuation of preferred stock is also discussed. As with debt, the price of preferred stock is related to its dividend and what investors can earn on comparable investments. The last section explains how several ratios may be used to analyze preferred stock.

RATIO ANALYSIS OF CORPORATE DEBT

Investors who acquire corporate debt are concerned with the firm's capacity to service that debt, i.e., to make the periodic interest payments and to redeem the principal at maturity. This depends upon the liquidity and quality of the firm's assets and the flow of income. Other factors that should be considered in the analysis of a bond are the extent to which the firm uses debt financing and the sinking fund requirements of the debt instruments. These last two considerations are discussed elsewhere. The extent to which a firm uses debt (i.e., financial leverage) and the debt ratio are covered in the section on the fundamental analysis of common stock in Chapter 16, and sinking funds were previously discussed in Chapter 9. This section is devoted to the financial ratios that may be used to analyze debt.

LIQUIDITY RATIOS

Liquidity is the "moneyness" of the asset

Liquidity is the ease with which assets may be quickly converted into cash without the firm's incurring a loss. If a firm has a high degree of liquidity, it will be able to meet its debt obligations as they become due. Therefore, liquidity ratios are a useful tool for the firm's creditors, who are concerned with being paid. Liquidity ratios are so called because they indicate the degree of liquidity or "moneyness" of the company's assets.

For purposes of illustration, the following balance sheet (Exhibit 11–1) and income statement (Exhibit 11–2) of CBS are employed. These are the same financial statements that were presented in Chapter 7 (Exhibits 7–1 and 7–2) and are reproduced here for convenience.

The Current Ratio

The current ratio is the ratio of current assets to current liabilities.

$$\text{Current ratio} = \frac{\text{current assets}}{\text{current liabilities}}$$

It indicates the extent to which the current liabilities, which must be paid within a year, are "covered" by current assets. For CBS the current ratio as of December 31, 1977, was

$$\frac{\$1,087,321}{\$518,834} = 2.1$$

which indicates that for every $1 that the firm had to pay within the year, there was $2.10 in the form of either cash or an asset that was to be converted into cash within the year.

For most industries, it is desirable to have more current assets than current liabilities. It is sometimes asserted that a firm should have at least $2 in current assets for every $1 in current liabilities or a current ratio of at least 2:1. If the current ratio is 2:1, then the firm's current assets could deteriorate in value by 50 per cent and the firm would still be able to meet its short-term liabilities.

It is desirable to have current assets exceed current liabilities

Although such rules of thumb are convenient, they need not apply to all industries. For example, electric utilities usually have current liabilities that *exceed* their current assets (i.e., a current ratio of less than 1:1). Does this worry short-term creditors? No, because the short-term assets are primarily accounts receivable from electricity users and are of high quality. Should a customer fail to pay an electricity bill, the company threatens to cut off service, and this threat is usually sufficient to induce payment. The higher the quality of the current assets (i.e., the greater the probability that these assets can be converted to cash at their stated value), the less vital it is for the current ratio to exceed 1:1. The reason, then, for selecting a rule of thumb such as a current ratio of at least 2:1 is for the protection of the creditors, who are aware that not all current assets will, in fact, be converted into cash.

Utilities may be an exception

Both creditors and investors want to know if the firm has sufficient liquid assets to meet its bills. Obviously, a low current ratio is undesirable because it indicates financial weakness, but a high current ratio may also be undesirable. A high current ratio may imply that the firm is not using its funds to best advantage. For example, the company may have issued long-term debt and used it to finance an excessive amount of inventory or accounts receivable. The high current ratio may also indicate that the firm is not taking advantage of available short-term financing or is mismanaging its current assets, which reduces its profitability. A high or low numerical value for the current ratio may be a signal to creditors and stockholders that the management of short-term assets and liabilities should be revised.

A high current ratio may also be undesirable

The Acid Test or Quick Ratio

The current ratio gives an indication of the company's ability to meet its current liabilities as they become due, but it has a major weakness. It

CONSOLIDATED BALANCE SHEETS
CBS Inc. and subsidiaries
(Dollars in thousands)

ASSETS

| | December 31 | |
Current assets:	1977	1976
Cash and cash equivalents	$ 199,457	$ 335,086
Notes and accounts receivable, less allowances for doubtful accounts, returns and discounts:		
1977, $122,696; 1976, $73,608	510,024	387,727
Inventories	204,124	151,880
Program rights	121,328	94,214
Prepaid expenses	52,388	32,860
Total current assets	**1,087,321**	**1,001,767**
Investments	**27,838**	**20,990**
Property, plant and equipment:		
Land	26,045	25,226
Buildings	158,370	148,139
Machinery and equipment	269,113	235,969
Leasehold improvements	29,948	25,508
	483,476	434,842
Less accumulated depreciation	223,330	206,794
Net property, plant and equipment	**260,146**	**228,048**
Excess of cost over net assets of businesses acquired, less amortization	**62,619**	**53,376**
Other assets	**80,181**	**47,429**
	$1,518,105	**$1,351,610**

EXHIBIT 11–1. Balance sheets.

Exhibit continued on the opposite page

The acid test excludes inventory

is an aggregate measure of liquidity that does not differentiate between the degrees of liquidity of the various types of current assets, which may be in the form of cash, accounts receivable, or inventory. Cash is a liquid asset, but it may take many months before inventory is sold and turned into cash. This failure of the current ratio to distinguish between the degrees of liquidity has led to the development of the quick ratio, which omits inventory from the calculation. The acid test or quick ratio (both names are used) is determined as follows:

$$\text{Acid test ratio} = \frac{\text{current assets} - \text{inventory}}{\text{current liabilities}}$$

LIABILITIES AND SHAREHOLDERS' EQUITY

	December 31 1977	December 31 1976
Current liabilities:		
Current maturities of long-term debt (note 5)	$ 3,962	$ 2,984
Accounts payable and accrued liabilities	461,034	348,023
Income taxes	53,838	63,165
Total current liabilities	**518,834**	**414,172**
Long-term debt (note 5)	**96,950**	**96,666**
Other liabilities	**70,788**	**64,619**
Deferred income taxes	**22,369**	**30,280**
Shareholders' equity:		
Preference stock (authorized 6,000,000 shares):		
$1.00 convertible Series A preference stock, par value $1.00 per share; authorized 3,300,000 shares; outstanding 303,982 shares in 1977 (aggregate liquidation value $13,223) and 543,519 shares in 1976 (note 6)	304	544
Common stock, par value $2.50 per share; authorized 100,000,000 shares in 1977 and 50,000,000 shares in 1976; issued 28,988,756 shares (notes 6 and 7)	72,472	72,472
Additional paid-in capital	209,681	219,651
Retained earnings	604,007	480,872
	886,464	773,539
Less common stock in treasury, at cost: 1,406,231 shares in 1977 and 579,191 shares in 1976 (note 6)	77,300	27,666
Total shareholders' equity	**809,164**	**745,873**
	$1,518,105	**$1,351,610**

See notes to consolidated financial statements

EXHIBIT 11-1 *Continued*

CONSOLIDATED INCOME STATEMENTS

CBS Inc. and subsidiaries
(Dollars in thousands)

	Years ended December 31 1977	Years ended December 31 1976
Net sales	**$2,776,311**	**$2,230,576**
Cost of sales	1,759,844	1,386,610
Selling, general and administrative expenses	684,800	539,425
Operating income	**331,667**	**304,541**
Interest income, net (note 9)	7,940	8,039
Other income, net (note 9)	22,043	18,146
Income before income taxes	**361,650**	**330,726**
Income taxes (note 3)	179,642	166,731
Net income	**$ 182,008**	**$ 163,995**
Net income per share of common stock (note 4)	**$6.50**	**$5.75**

See notes to consolidated financial statements

EXHIBIT 11-2. Income statements.

For CBS the acid test ratio is

$$\frac{\$1,087,321 - \$204,124}{\$518,834} = 1.7$$

which is lower than the current ratio of 2:1. The difference lies, of course, in the inventory that the company is carrying, which is excluded from the acid test.

The ability to pay is also affected by other factors

A low acid test ratio imples that the firm may have difficulty meeting its current liabilities as they become due if it must rely on converting inventory into cash. A low acid test value, however, does not indicate that the firm will fail to pay its bills. The ability to meet liabilities is influenced by such factors as (1) the rate at which cash flows into the firm, (2) the time at which bills become due, (3) the relationship between the company and its creditors and their willingness to roll over debt, and (4) the firm's ability to raise additional capital. The acid test merely indicates how well the current liabilities are covered by cash and by highly liquid assets that may be converted into cash relatively quickly. Because this test takes into account that not all current assets are equally liquid, it is a more precise measure of liquidity than is the current ratio.

The Components of Current Assets

Current assets may be ranked according to liquidity

Another approach to analyzing liquidity is to rank current assets with regard to their degree of liquidity and to determine the proportion of each asset in relation to total current assets. The most liquid current asset is cash, followed by marketable securities (i.e., cash equivalents), such as treasury bills or certificates of deposit, accounts receivable, and finally inventory. For CBS the proportion of each asset to total current assets is

Current Assets	Proportion of Total Current Assets
Cash and cash equivalents	18.3%
Accounts receivable	46.9
Inventory	18.8
Other current assets	16.0
	100.0%

Since this technique ranks current assets from the most liquid to the least liquid, it gives an indication of the degree of liquidity of the firm's current assets. If a large proportion of total current assets is inventory, the company is not very liquid. CBS appears to be quite liquid, as almost 70 per cent of its current assets are cash, cash equivalents, and accounts receivable.

This method of separating total current assets into their components and then ranking them according to their degree of liquidity, along with the acid test, gives management, creditors, and investors a better measure of the ability of the firm to meet its current liabilities as they become due than *does* the current ratio. These two measures, then, are basic supplements to the current ratio and should be used to analyze the liquidity of any firm that carries a significant amount of inventory in its operations.

ACTIVITY RATIOS

Activity ratios indicate at what rate the firm is turning its inventory and accounts receivable into cash. The more rapidly the firm turns over its inventory and receivables, the more quickly it acquires cash. High turnover indicates that the firm is rapidly receiving cash and is in a better position to pay its liabilities as they become due. Such high turnover, however, need not imply that the firm is maximizing profits. For example, high inventory turnover may indicate that the firm is selling items for too low a price in order to induce quicker sales. A high receivables turnover may be an indication that the firm is too stringent in extending credit to buyers, and this may reduce sales and result in lower profits.

Activity ratios measure the speed of conversion to cash

Inventory Turnover

Inventory turnover is defined as annual sales divided by average inventory. That is

$$\text{Inventory turnover} = \frac{\text{sales}}{\text{average inventory}}$$

This ratio uses average inventory instead of inventory as determined at the end of the fiscal year to reduce the impact of fluctuations in the level of inventory. If inventory is abnormally high at the end of the fiscal year, the turnover appears to be slower. Conversely, if inventory is lower than normal at the year's end, the turnover appears faster than in fact it is. Management may use any number of observations (e.g., monthly or weekly) to determine the average inventory. The information available to investors, however, may be limited to the level of inventory given in the firm's annual reports.

Two views of inventory turnover

For CBS the level of inventory was $201,124,000 in 1977 and $151,880,000 in 1976. The average for the two years was

$$\frac{\$201,124,000 + \$151,880,000}{2} = \$176,502,000$$

Thus, for CBS inventory turnover was

$$\frac{\text{Sales}}{\text{Average inventory}} = \frac{\$2,776,311,000}{\$176,502,000} = 15.7$$

This indicates that annual sales are 15.7 times the level of inventory. Inventory thus turns over 15.7 times a year or about once every three weeks.

Inventory turnover may also be defined as the cost of goods sold divided by the inventory. That is,

$$\text{Inventory turnover} = \frac{\text{cost of goods sold}}{\text{average inventory}}$$

If this definition is used, CBS's inventory turnover is

$$\frac{\$1,759,844,000}{\$176,502,000} = 10.0$$

This definition places more emphasis on recouping the cost of the goods. However, creditors may prefer to use sales, since sales produce the funds to service the debt. Dun and Bradstreet uses sales in its industry averages, and any creditors or bondholders who use Dun and Bradstreet data as a source of comparison must remember to use sales instead of cost of goods sold in order to be consistent.

Receivables Turnover: The Average Collection Period

How long it takes to collect receivables

The average collection period measures how long it takes a firm to collect its accounts receivable. The faster the company collects its receivables, the more rapidly it receives cash and hence can pay its obligations, such as its interest expense. The average collection period (ACP) is determined as follows:

$$\text{ACP} = \frac{\text{receivables}}{\text{sales per day}}$$

Sales per day are total sales divided by 360 (or 365) days. For CBS the average collection period is

$$\frac{\$510,024}{\$2,776,111 \div 360} = 66.1$$

This indicates that the firm takes 66.1 days to convert its receivables into money.

Alternative definitions of receivables turnover

Receivables turnover, which is another way of viewing the average collection period, may be defined as annual credit sales divided by receivables.* By this definition,

$$\text{Receivables turnover} = \frac{\text{annual credit sales}}{\text{accounts receivable}}$$

---

*Some analysts may prefer to average the accounts receivable in the same way that inventory was averaged for the inventory turnover ratio.

An alternative definition of receivables turnover substitutes annual sales for annual credit sales. That is,

$$\text{Receivables turnover} = \frac{\text{annual sales}}{\text{accounts receivable}}$$

Either definition is acceptable as long as it is applied consistently. Although management has access to the information used in both formulas, investors may be limited to the data provided by the firm. If annual credit sales are not reported by the firm, the investor will have no choice but to use annual sales.

Since the CBS income statement does not give annual credit sales, the first definition cannot be used; hence, for CBS

$$\text{Receivables turnover} = \frac{\$2,776,311}{\$510,024} = 5.4$$

This indicates that annual sales are 5.4 times the amount of receivables. The larger the ratio, the more rapidly the firm turns its credit sales into cash. A turnover of 5.4 times per year indicates that receivables are paid off on the average of every 2.2 months. This is the same information that was derived by computing the average collection period, since 66.1 days is approximately 2.2 months.

Both of the previously mentioned turnover ratios need to be interpreted with much caution. These ratios are static, for they use information derived at a given time (i.e., the year-end figures on the balance sheet). The ratios, however, are dealing with dynamic events, for they are concerned with the length of time it takes for an event to occur. Because of this problem with time, these turnover ratios, which are based on year-end figures, may be misleading if the firm has (1) seasonal sales, (2) sporadic sales during the fiscal year, or (3) any growth in inventory and sales during the fiscal year. Creditors and bondholders need to be aware of these potential problems, since they can lead to incorrect conclusions concerning the firm's capacity to service its debt.

There is a need for caution in interpreting the results

THE TIMES-INTEREST-EARNED RATIO

The ratios that were discussed previously are used to analyze a firm's general capacity to meet any of its liabilities. There are also ratios that specifically measure the ability of a firm to service its long-term debt, i.e., to pay the interest and retire the principal. One such ratio indicates by how many times the earnings of the company exceed the interest expense, and hence this ratio is called times-interest-earned. Times-interest-earned

Times-interest-earned indicates the safety of interest payments

is the ratio of earnings that are available to pay the interest divided by the amount of interest. That is,

$$\text{Times-interest-earned} = \frac{\text{earnings before interest and taxes}}{\text{annual interest charges}}$$

A ratio of 2 indicates that the firm has $2 after meeting other expenses to pay $1 of interest charges. The larger the times-interest-earned ratio, the more likely it is that the firm will be able to meet its interest payments. The times-interest-earned ratio cannot be computed for CBS because it earned more in interest on its cash equivalents than it paid on its debt, (i.e., it had a net interest income of $7.9 million).

The ability to cover the interest expense is important, for failure to meet interest payments as they become due may throw the firm into bankruptcy. A decline in the times-interest-earned ratio may serve as an early warning to creditors and investors as well as to management of a deteriorating financial position and of the increased probability of default on interest payments.

In the previous equation, the times-interest-earned ratio is an aggregate value that lumps together all interest payments. Some debt issues may be subordinated to other debt issues and are paid only after senior debt issues are redeemed. Thus, it is possible to pay the senior debt issues in full and to have no funds left with which to pay the interest on the subordinate debt. When this subordination exists, the times-interest-earned statistic may be altered to acknowledge this subordination. For example, consider a company with $1000 in earnings before interest and taxes and $10,000 in debt consisting of two issues. Issue A has a principal amount of $8000 and carries an interest rate of 5 per cent. Issue B has a principal amount of $2000 and carries an interest rate of 7 per cent. Issue B is subordinate to issue A. The subordination may explain why the second issue has the higher interest rate, for creditors usually demand higher rates in return for debt issues involving greater risk.

The times-interest-earned ratio for each debt issue is computed as follows. The firm has two debt issues (A and B) and $1000 in earnings before interest and taxes. The interest on issue A is $400 and on issue B is $140. For issue A there is $1000 available to pay the $400 in interest expense and thus the coverage ratio is

There is a need to adjust for subordination

$$\frac{\$1000}{\$400} = 2.50$$

For issue B there is $1000 to cover the interest on A and B. Thus, for issue B the coverage ratio is

$$\frac{\$1000}{\$400 + \$140} = 1.85$$

It would be misleading to suggest that the coverage for issue B is the amount available after issue A was paid. In such a case that would indicate a coverage of

$$\frac{\$600}{\$140} = 4.29$$

which is incorrect. Issue B would then have the higher coverage ratio and would appear to be safer than the senior debt. The proper way to adjust for subordination is to add the interest charges to the denominator and *not* to subtract the interest paid to the senior debt issue from the numerator. For successive issues of subordinated debt, the interest payments would be added to the denominator. Since the total amount of earnings available before taxes to pay the interest is spread out over ever-increasing interest payments, the coverage ratio declines and hence gives the true indication of the actual coverage of the subordinated debt.

Coverage ratios have also been developed to include the repayment of principal, lease payments, and other rental payments. However, such ratios are beyond the scope of this text. The preceding discussion indicates the desirability of computing the coverage ratio (times-interest-earned) and its possible interpretations. This ratio is a measure of the safety of interest payments, for it indicates the firm's ability to cover this expense.

PROBLEMS WITH INTERPRETATION

Interpreting the results of ratio analysis is not easy. First, firms change over time. For example, CBS has diversified into industries other than broadcasting. Today it manufactures toys (Creative Playthings) and publishes books as well as operates one of the three major television networks. A comparison of ratios computed for different years may not be indicative of the financial condition of the firm, because the composition of the firm has changed.

Second, although a comparison may be made with other firms in the industry, defining the appropriate industry may be difficult. For example, RCA and CBS are both operators of television networks, but the two firms are quite different. While CBS has diversified into toy manufacturing and publishing, RCA has expanded into electronics and defense products. The two firms are not really comparable even though they compete in the field of broadcasting.

This problem of defining the industry may be illustrated by comparing the current ratio, the inventory turnover, and the average collection period for CBS with the averages computed by Dun and Bradstreet for book publishing. The values for each ratio are as follows:

Method of Analysis	*CBS*	*Dun and Bradstreet Average*
Current ratio	2.1:1	2.6:1
Inventory turnover	15.8×	4.4×
Average collection period	66.1 days	58 days

The current ratio and average collection period for CBS are comparable to the industry averages, but the inventory turnover is much faster. However, one should not conclude that CBS is turning over its inventory at a very rapid rate. Since the field in which CBS is primarily involved is broadcasting (which requires little inventory), the amount of inventory relative to sales is small. This gives the impression of a rapid turnover. A true comparison could be made only if the analyst isolates the sales and inventory associated with the publishing subsidiaries of CBS and determines their turnover.

PREFERRED STOCK

Preferred stock represents ownership

Preferred stock is similar to common stock in that it represents ownership in a corporation, but it is in a sense superior to common stock. Preferred stockholders are paid dividends before common stockholders, and in the case of liquidation, preferred stock is redeemed before the common stockholders receive any proceeds from the liquidation. Preferred stock is therefore said to be senior to common stock. Although there is no obligation on the part of the firm to pay a dividend for preferred stock, it is generally understood that if the firm earns sufficent profit, it will do so. Even if the firm operates at a loss, it may still pay this dividend if it has available funds.

It stands before common stock

It pays a fixed dividend

Preferred stock is also similar to debt in that it pays a fixed dividend just as bonds pay a fixed amount of interest. Since preferred stock represents ownership, it does not entail the legal obligations of debt (e.g., the terms of a bond's indenture). Thus, preferred stock is a hybrid type of security that combines some elements of debt and some of equity. Accountants treat it as equity, but since it pays a fixed dividend that cannot grow, investors should analyze it as if it were debt. Preferred stock, then, is viewed in the same way as long-term debt.

Some companies have also issued a "preference" stock (see the CBS balance sheet). This stock is subordinate to preferred stock but has preference over common stock in the payment of dividends. Such stock is another form of preferred stock, and in this text no distinction is made between the two.

A COMPARISON OF PREFERRED STOCK AND DEBT

Both generally lack voting rights

Bondholders and preferred stockholders usually do not have the right to vote at stockholders' meetings, although occasionally preferred stockholders have this right. A lack of voting power, however, does not mean that bondholders and preferred stockholders lack representation. Major creditors may demand representation on the board of directors of the firm as a condition for granting the credit, and if the preferred stock is held by a financial institution (such as an insurance company), the preferred stockholders may also be represented on the board. Such representation may be considerably more substantive than that of the common stockholders who vote their shares at annual meetings. Despite the fact that bondholders and preferred stockholders may not have the right to vote, it cannot be concluded that they have no voice in the operation of the company.

Although preferred stock and long-term bonds are similar in some ways, their differences are significant. First, if the firm fails to pay the interest, the bondholders may take the firm to court to force payment or to seek liquidation of the corporation in order to protect their principal. Preferred stockholders do not have that power, for the firm is not obligated to pay the dividend. If the corporation does not pay, the dividend is said to be in *arrears,* but the firm does not have to remove this arrearage. In most cases, however, any preferred stock dividends that are in arrears have to be paid before any dividends can be paid to the holders of the common stock. In this case the preferred stock dividends accumulate, and the stock is referred to as *cumulative preferred.* Most preferred stock is cumulative, but there are examples of preferred stocks that are not; accordingly, these are called *noncumulative.*

Preferred dividends are not a legal obligation

The meaning of "cumulative"

For firms in financial difficulty, the difference between cumulative and noncumulative stock may be immaterial. Forcing the company to pay dividends to erase the arrearage may further weaken the firm, which would be more disadvantageous to the owners of the preferred stock than forgoing the dividend. Once the corporation has regained its profitability, erasing the arrearage may become important not only to the holders of the preferred stock but also to the company, which is anxious to demonstrate its improved financial condition. For example, Avco suspended dividends on its preferred stock in September 1974. The dividends accumulated until 1976, when Avco resumed payments to the preferred stockholders, and in 1978 it erased the arrearage. Obviously, any speculator who purchased the shares in 1974 when they were selling for about $10 per share was well rewarded for taking the risk, for these investors collected the previously missed dividends.

Second, the most important difference between debt and preferred stock is that interest on debt is a tax-deductible expense for the firm, while the dividend on preferred stock is not. Preferred dividends are distributions of income. If the corporate income tax rate is 46 per cent, then the firm must earn $1.85 before taxes in order to pay $1 in preferred dividends. Thus, preferred stock is much more expensive to the firm than debt because of the tax laws. The fact that the interest on debt is treated as a tax-deductible expense strongly argues in favor of the firm's issuing debt instead of preferred stock. For this reason, many companies have not issued preferred stock, and those that have usually issue convertible preferred stock. Since convertible preferred stock is similar to convertible bonds, it is discussed in Chapter 18.

Dividends are not a tax-deductible expense

The third difference between debt and preferred stock is the retire-

Preferred stock may be perpetual

ment of the issue. Debt eventually must be retired, while preferred stock may be perpetual. Although some preferred stocks do have required sinking funds, many do not. Once these preferred stocks have been issued, the firm may never have to concern itself with retiring them. This may be both an advantage and a disadvantage. If the firm never has to retire its preferred stock, it does not have to generate the money to do so. Instead, the corporation may use its funds elsewhere (e.g., to purchase plant and equipment). However, should the company ever want to change its capital structural and substitute less expensive debt financing for the preferred stock, it may have difficulty retiring the issue. The firm may have to purchase the preferred stock on the open market, and in order to induce the holders to sell their shares, the company will probably have to bid up the price. If the firm does not want to pay cash for the preferred stock, it may offer these stockholders the opportunity to trade their shares for some other security, such as common stock or debt. This will also probably require generous terms to induce the preferred stockholders to trade their shares.

Some preferred stock has a call feature

A company, in order to exercise some control over the preferred stock, may add a call feature to the issue. This gives the firm the option to call and redeem the shares. Although the actual terms of the call feature vary with each preferred stock issue, the general features are similar: (1) The call is at the option of the firm; (2) the call price is specified; (3) the firm may have to pay a call penalty (e.g., a year's dividends); and (4) after the issue is called, future dividend payments will cease. This last feature, of course, forces any stockholders who are still retaining their shares to surrender them. Such a feature gives the firm the option to retire the preferred stock in the future should financial conditions warrant such action.

THE VALUATION OF PREFERRED STOCK

Valuation is similar to that used for perpetual debt

The process of evaluating preferred stock is essentially the same as that used to evaluate debt. Even though preferred stock is technically equity and represents ownership, it is viewed in finance as an alternative to debt financing. This is because of the fixed dividend paid by the preferred stock. Since the holders of preferred stock do not participate in the firm's earnings except for the fixed dividend, any earnings in excess of this dividend requirement accrue to the common stockholder.

The method used to value a preferred stock depends on whether it is perpetual or finite. If the preferred stock does not have a required sinking fund or a call feature, it may be viewed as a perpetual debt instrument. The flow of dividends (D) will continue indefinitely. These dividends must then be discounted at the appropriate discount rate (k) in order to determine the present value (P) of the flow of dividend income over time. This process is illustrated in Equation 1:

(1)
$$P = \frac{D}{(1+k)} + \frac{D}{(1+k)^2} + \frac{D}{(1+k)^3} + \cdots$$

As in the case of the perpetual bond, this equation is reduced to

(2)
$$P = \frac{D}{k}$$

Thus, if a preferred stock pays an annual dividend of $4 and the appropriate discount rate is 8 per cent, the present value of the preferred stock is

$$P = \frac{\$4}{(1+.08)} + \frac{\$4}{(1+.08)^2} + \frac{\$4}{(1+.08)^3} + \cdots$$

$$P = \frac{\$4}{.08} = \$50$$

If an investor buys this preferred stock for $50, he or she can expect to earn 8 per cent (i.e., $50 × .08 = $4) on the investment. Of course, the realized rate of return on the investment will not be known until the investor sells the stock and adjusts this 8 per cent return for any capital gain or loss. However, at the current price, the preferred stock is selling for a 8 per cent dividend yield.

    If the preferred stock has a finite life, this fact must be considered in determining its value. As with the valuation of long-term debt, the amount that is repaid when the preferred stock is retired must be discounted back to the present value. Thus, when preferred stock has a finite life, the valuation equation becomes

The impact of finite life on valuation

(3)
$$P = \frac{D}{(1+k)} + \frac{D}{(1+k)^2} + \cdots + \frac{D}{(1+k)^n} + \frac{S}{(1+k)^n}$$

where S represents the amount that is returned to the stockholder when the preferred stock is retired after n number of years. If the preferred stock in the previous example is retired after 30 years for $100 per share, its current value would be

$$P = \frac{\$4}{(1+.08)} + \cdots + \frac{\$4}{(1+.08)^{30}} + \frac{\$100}{(1+.08)^{30}}$$

$$P = \$4(11.258) + \$100(.099)$$

$$P = \$54.93$$

where 11.258 is the interest factor for the present value of an annuity of $1 for 30 years at 8 per cent and .099 is the present value of $1 to be received after 30 years when yields are 8 per cent. Instead of selling the stock for $50, in which case the investor would realize 8 per cent, the preferred stock would sell for $54.93. The yield is still 8 per cent, but the return in this case consists of a current dividend yield of 7.28 per cent ($4 ÷ 54.93) and a capital gain as the price of the stock rises from $54.93 to $100 when it is retired 30 years hence.

The inverse relationship between price and yield

Since preferred stock pays a fixed dividend and is priced like a debt instrument, its price rises and declines with changes in the interest rate. If the interest rate rises, the rate at which preferred stock is discounted also rises, causing the price of preferred stock to decline. Conversely, when the interest rate falls, the rate at which preferred stock is discounted falls, causing its price to rise. Like bond prices, the price of preferred stock moves inversely with changes in the interest rate. Any investor who knows the direction of change of future interest rates knows the direction of price changes in preferred stock.

Individuals who desire income from their investments may find preferred stock attractive. However, these investors should realize that the firm is not bound to pay dividends on preferred stock. Unlike debt, which imposes legal obligations on the firm, preferred stock imposes only moral obligations. Therefore, from the firm's point of view, preferred stock involves less risk than debt.

Stock is riskier than debt for the stockholder

From the investor's point of view, preferred stock is riskier than debt, since the dividends are not legal obligations. Income-seeking investors would probably prefer to own long-term debt instead of preferred stock, unless the stock has certain features that make it more attractive. For this reason, most preferred stock that is issued by industrial firms is convertible into the firm's common stock. Convertible preferred stock is perceptibly different from nonconvertible preferred stock because its price rises and declines with the price of the stock into which it may be converted. Whereas nonconvertible stock is analyzed as if it were debt, convertible preferred stock is analyzed as both debt and equity.

ANALYSIS OF PREFERRED STOCK

Analysis is similar to that of debt

Since preferred stock is similar to debt, the tools used to analyze it are similar to those used to analyze debt. Because preferred stock is an income-producing investment, the analysis is primarily concerned with the capacity of the firm to meet the dividend payments. Therefore, the degree of liquidity, the turnover rate of inventory and accounts receivable, and the dividend coverage are important factors to consider—possibly more important than the firm's earnings. Although dividends must ultimately be related to current earnings and the firm's future earning capacity, preferred dividends are paid from cash. Even if the firm is temporarily running a deficit (i.e., experiencing an accounting loss), it may still be able to pay dividends to the preferred stockholders if it has sufficient cash. In fact, cash dividends may be paid despite the deficit to indicate that the losses are expected to be temporary and that the firm is financially strong.

The analyses of liquidity and turnover are no different for preferred stock than for debt. The times-interest-earned ratio, however, must be altered. For debt this ratio uses earnings before interest and taxes. However, the cash dividends for preferred stock are paid after taxes, and therefore their coverage ratio must use earnings after taxes. The coverage ratio of preferred stock dividends, then, equals

$$\frac{\text{Earnings after taxes}}{\text{Dividends on preferred stock}}$$

The larger this ratio, the safer should be the preferred stock's dividend. Notice that the numerator consists of *total* earnings. Although the preferred stock dividends are subtracted from the total earnings to derive the earnings that are available to the common stockholders, all of the firm's earnings are available to pay the preferred stock dividend.

A variation on this coverage ratio is earnings per preferred share. This ratio is

$$\frac{\text{Earnings after taxes}}{\text{Number of preferred shares outstanding}}$$

The larger the preferred earnings per share, the safer is the dividend payment. However, neither of these ratios indicates whether the firm has sufficient cash to pay the dividends. They can only indicate the extent to which earnings cover the dividend requirements of the preferred stock.

How each ratio is computed can be illustrated by the following simple example. A firm has earnings of $6,000,000 and is in the 40 per cent tax bracket. It has 100,000 shares of preferred stock outstanding, and each share pays a dividend of $5. The coverage ratio of the dividends is

$$\frac{\$6,000,000 - \$2,400,000}{\$500,000} = 7.2$$

and the earnings per preferred share are

$$\frac{\$6,000,000 - \$2,400,000}{100,000} = \$36$$

Both ratios, in effect, show the same thing. In the first, the preferred dividend is covered by a multiple of 7.2:1. The second ratio yields an earnings per preferred share of $36, which is 7.2 times the $5 dividend paid by each share.

SUMMARY

This chapter has discussed the analysis of corporate bonds and preferred stock. This analysis stresses the capacity of the firm to service its debt, i.e., the firm's ability to pay the interest and retire the principal. This capacity is related to the management of the firm's current assets and especially the rate at which inventory and accounts receivable are converted into cash. Analysis of the firm's current position (including the turnover of inventory, the average collection period, the current and quick ratios, and the coverage ratios) indicates its capacity to generate internally the funds necessary to service its debt.

Preferred stock is similar to debt because it pays a fixed dividend. Although the use of debt financing results in legal obligations for the firm, the use of preferred stock does not. The payment of dividends is only a moral obligation. For this reason, the analysis of preferred stock emphasizes the earnings available to pay the dividends.

The value of preferred stock depends upon the fixed dividend and the return that investors can earn on comparable investments. Preferred stock may be valued as if it were a perpetual bond. If the preferred stock has a sinking fund or a call feature, a modification in the valuation model is required. In this case the preferred stock is no longer perpetual but will eventually be retired by the firm. This return of the investor's capital affects the current price of the preferred stock.

Terms to Remember

Liquidity ratio	Average collection period	Arrearage
Current ratio	Times-interest-earned	Earnings per preferred
Acid test	Preferred stock	share
Inventory turnover	Cumulative preferred stock	

Questions

1. What is the difference between the current ratio and the acid test?

2. If accounts receivable increase, what effect will this have on the average collection period?

3. What is the difference between the liquidity ratio and the activity ratio?

4. What is times-interest-earned, and what does it add to the analyst's knowledge of the firm?

5. Why is preferred stock, which represents ownership, analyzed as if it were a debt instrument?

6. Does preferred stock mature? If preferred stock has a call feature, what role does it play?

7. Why is preferred stock less risky than debt from the firm's point of view, but more risky than debt from the investor's point of view?

Problems

1. If a preferred stock pays a $4 per year dividend and the investor can earn 10 per cent on alternative investments, what is the maximum price that the investor should pay for this stock?

2. If the preferred stock in Problem 1 has a call feature and the investor expects it to be called for $100 after ten years, what is the maximum price that he or she should pay for the stock?

3. If investors can earn 12 per cent on comparable investments, what should the price of the preferred stock in Problem 1 be?

SELECTED READINGS

Altman, Edward I.: "Financial Ratios, Discriminant Analysis, and the Prediction of Corporate Bankruptcy." *Journal of Finance* (September 1968), pp. 589–610.

Atamian, Elliott L.: "Negotiating the Restrictive Covenants of Loan Agreements Associated With the Private Placement of Corporate Debt Securities." Reprinted in W. Serraino, S. Singhvi, and R. Soldofsky: *Frontiers of Financial Management.* Cincinnati, South-Western Publishing Co., 1971, pp. 210–225.

Bloch, Ernest: "Pricing a Corporate Bond Issue: A Look Behind the Scenes." Reprinted in E. F. Brigham: *Readings in Managerial Finance.* New York, Holt, Rinehart and Winston, Inc., 1971, pp. 280–287.

Donaldson, Gordan: *Corporate Debt Capacity.* Boston, Harvard University Press, 1961.

Donaldson, Gordan: "In Defense of Preferred Stock." *Harvard Business Review* (July-August 1962), pp. 123–136.

Graham, Benjamin, David L. Dodd, Sidney Cottle, et al.: *Security Analysis: Principles and Techniques,* 4th ed. New York, McGraw-Hill Book Co., Inc., 1962, Part 3.

Graham, Benjamin: *The Intelligent Investor,* 4th ed. New York, Harper & Row Publishers, Inc., 1973.

Murray, Roger: "Lessons for Financial Analysis." *Journal of Finance* (May 1971), pp. 327–332.

Norgaard, Richard L.: "An Examination of the Yields of Corporate Bonds and Stocks." *Journal of Finance,* (September 1974), pp. 1275–1286.

Learning Objectives

After completing this chapter you should be able to

1. Distinguish among the types of federal government debt.

2. Identify the sources of risk from investing in federal government securities.

3. Distinguish between the federal government's moral obligation and its full-faith and credit obligations to its agencies' debt.

4. Name the primary advantage of state and local government bonds.

5. Illustrate how to equalize yields on corporate bonds and state and local government bonds.

6. Differentiate revenue bonds from general obligation bonds.

7. Compare the ratios used to analyze corporate and state and local government debt.

chapter 12

GOVERNMENT SECURITIES

Fiscal policy encompasses the taxation, expenditures, and debt management of the federal government. It is used to pursue national economic goals: full employment, price stability, and economic growth. When government expenditures exceed revenues, this deficit must be financed. In order to do so, the federal government issues a variety of securities. This variety helps the government tap the different sources of funds that are available in the money and capital markets.

This chapter is concerned with government securities. The first section discusses the various types of debt issued by the federal government, which range from short-term treasury bills to long-term treasury bonds. The second section briefly considers the debt issued by the various agencies of the federal government, and the last section discusses the debt issued by state and local governments. Special emphasis is placed on the feature that distinguishes state and local government debt from other securities: The interest paid to bondholders is exempt from federal income taxation.

THE VARIETY OF FEDERAL GOVERNMENT DEBT

In 1977 the federal government made interest payments of $38.1 billion on its debt. This sum was substantial and amounted to about 10 per cent of the total expenditures made by the federal government in that year. This debt was financed by a variety of investors, including individuals, corporations, and financial institutions. To induce this diverse group of investors to purchase its debt, the federal government issued different types of debt instruments that appealed to the various potential buyers.

The safety of the principal and interest

For investors, the unique advantage offered by the federal government's debt is its safety. These debt instruments are the safest of all possible investments, for there is no question that the United States Treasury is able to pay the interest and repay the principal. The source of this safety is the federal government's constitutional right to print money. Because there is no legal limitation on the federal government's capacity to create money, there is no restriction on its ability to pay interest and retire (or at least refinance) its debt.

The emphasis is on the use of short-term debt

The various types of federal government debt and the amount outstanding of each are illustrated in Exhibit 12–1. As may be seen in the exhibit, there has been an emphasis on the use of short- and intermediate-term financing by the Treasury. This emphasis is partially explained by interest costs. Interest rates on short-term debt are usually lower than those on long-term debt. Hence, the use of short-term financing reduces the Treasury's interest expense. Furthermore, Congress restricts the interest rate that the Treasury may pay on long-term debt, but it does not restrict the interest rate on short-term securities. Thus, during periods of high interest rates, the Treasury may not be permitted to sell long-term securities even if it desires to do so.

NONMARKETABLE FEDERAL GOVERNMENT DEBT

Series E bonds

Perhaps the most widely held federal government debt is the series E bonds. This bond was designed to encourage saving by people of modest means, as it was sold in small denominations (e.g., $25, $100, $500, and up to $10,000). Although virtually every person should have been able to place modest amounts of savings in these bonds, an individual was allowed to purchase no more than $10,000 worth of series E bonds in a calendar year.

Series E bonds are purchased at a discount

Series E bonds pay no interest but are purchased at a discount (i.e., below their face value). For example, if a saver purchases a $25 series E bond for $18.75 and holds it until maturity five years and five months later, he or she will receive $25 and will have earned 6 per cent annually on the investment. If the bonds are cashed in prior to maturity, the holder re-

EXHIBIT 12-1. The Variety of Federal Government Debt as of October 1978*

	Length of Time to Maturity	Value (in Billions of Dollars)	Percentage of Total Debt
Treasury bills	Less than 1 year	161.2	26.1
Intermediate-term notes	One to 5 years	272.6	44.2
Long-term bonds	Over 5 years	57.8	9.4
Savings bonds	Various maturities	80.5	13.1
Other debt	Various maturities	44.6	7.2
			100.0%

*Source: *Federal Reserve Bulletin*, November 1978, p. A32. Debt held by United States government agencies and trust funds is excluded.

ceives less than $25 and earns a yield of less than 6 per cent. (The yield starts at 4 per cent and rises over the lifetime of the bond until it reaches 6 per cent at the bond's maturity. This ascending structure of yields is an incentive to hold the bonds until maturity).

Series E bonds were initially issued in 1941 to help finance World War II expenditures. At that time the bonds had a maturity of ten years and a yield of 2.9 per cent. As interest rates have risen, the length of time to maturity has been reduced, which has had the effect of increasing the yield on the bonds.

These bonds have been extremely popular with many investors. During 1978, over $8 billion worth of bonds were sold, which brought the total amount outstanding to over $70 billion. More than 16 million people buy savings bonds each year.

Although series E bonds do mature, the Treasury has not required that the bonds be redeemed. Instead, the maturities have been extended and interest has continued to accrue. The rate earned on these older bonds has been increased to 6 per cent, so the yield is comparable to that earned by the series E bond that is currently being sold. Thus, if an investor bought a $100 savings bond in May 1941 and still owns it, that individual is earning 6 per cent on the funds he or she lent to the government. As of May 1978, this bond had a redemption value of $299.80. Of this amount, only $75 is principal and $224.80 is accrued interest. However, after 1981 the Treasury will no longer extend the maturity of bonds that were issued between 1941 and 1952. At that time these series E bonds will cease to earn interest, and holders will have to redeem or exchange them for other bonds.

The extension of maturity

On January 2, 1980, the Treasury started to issue a new bond, series EE, to replace the series E bonds. Like the E bonds, the new bonds are issued at a discount. In this case the smallest denomination is $50; the cost is $25, and after 11 years and 9 months the investor will receive $50. This time to maturity results in an annual yield of 6 per cent. As with series E bonds, the new bonds may be redeemed prior to maturity. However, they must be held at least six months before redemption.

Series EE bonds

There are several major differences between the series E and EE bonds and most other investments, such as savings accounts. The interest earned on series E or EE bonds is not subject to federal income taxation until the bonds are redeemed. The interest earned on other investments, including savings accounts, is subject to federal income taxation during the year in which it is earned. Although the federal income tax on the E or EE series may be deferred until the bonds are redeemed, are disposed of, or mature (whichever comes first), the owner does have the option to have the interest taxed each year. Even though the funds are not received until the bond is redeemed, the owner may report the interest to the Internal Revenue Service on an accrual basis. However, most holders of series E bonds have preferred to defer the tax payment. Presumably owners of series EE bonds will follow the same strategy.

Tax deferment

The deferment of interest income until the bonds are redeemed can be advantageous in that the saver can cash in series E and EE bonds in those years when income from other sources is lower. For example, these bonds are potentially good investments to be redeemed during retirement or times of temporary unemployment. It is likely that the individual's taxable income will be lower during these periods, and thus the taxes paid on the accrued interest earned by the bonds will be lower. By allowing investors to determine when the interest will be subject to taxation, series E and now series EE bonds offer the investor an opportunity to reduce the amount of taxes paid on the interest. Since they are sold in small units, these bonds offer a means that is available to virtually every investor to shelter income from taxes. Such tax sheltering of interest income is not available through other savings instruments, such as accounts in commercial banks or savings and loan associations.

No secondary market

Another important difference between series E and EE bonds and other bonds is that there is no secondary market in the former. If the owner wants immediate cash, the bonds cannot be sold. Instead, the investor redeems them at a commercial bank. Nor can the bonds be transferred as a gift, although they can be transferred through an estate. The Treasury also forbids the use of series E and EE bonds as collateral. Thus, while corporate debt may be used to secure a personal loan, these bonds cannot.

Series H and HH bonds

The investor may exchange series E for series H bonds, and as of 1980 they may exchange them for HH bonds. The HH series (like the EE bonds) is a new series that is designed to replace the series H bonds. Series H and HH bonds are different from E and EE bonds in several ways. They are sold at par in larger denominations, with $500 being the minimum investment. The bonds mature in ten years and pay 6 per cent interest if held to maturity. The interest is paid every year and does not accumulate as it does with the series E and EE bonds. Thus, interest is subject to federal income taxation each year, while taxation on series E and EE bonds may be deferred until the bonds are redeemed. Series HH bonds are more attractive to investors who need safe sources of current income while series EE bonds are attractive to conservative investors who wish to build up capital but who do not need current income.

MARKETABLE SECURITIES

Treasury Bills

Short-term federal government debt is in the form of treasury bills. **Short-term debt**
These bills are sold in denominations of $10,000 to $1,000,000 and mature
in 3 to 12 months. Treasury bills pay no set amount of interest. Like series
E bonds, they are sold at a discount; however, unlike series E bonds, the
discounted price is not set. Instead, the Treasury continually auctions off
the bills, which go to the highest bidders. For example, if an investor bids
$9700 and obtains the bill, he or she will receive $10,000 when the bill
matures, which is a yield of 3.1 per cent ($300 ÷ $9700). If it is a six-month
bill, the annual rate of interest is 6.2 per cent. If the bid price had been
higher, the interest cost to the Treasury (and the yield to the buyer) would
have been lower.

Once treasury bills have been auctioned, they may be bought and **Treasury bills have**
sold in the secondary market. They are issued in bearer form, which **a secondary market**
makes them highly negotiable and easily marketed. There is an active
secondary market in these bills, and they are quoted daily in the financial
press and many city newspapers. These quotes are reported in the following form:

	Bid	Ask
Maturity	Discount	
10/17	6.83	6.77

These quotes indicate that for a treasury bill maturing on October 17 (i.e.,
10/17), buyers were willing to bid a price that yielded 6.83 per cent. Sellers,
however, were willing to sell (i.e., offer) the bills at a smaller discount
(i.e., a higher price) that yielded only 6.77 per cent.

Treasury bills may be purchased through brokerage firms, commer- **How they are**
cial banks, and any Federal Reserve Bank. These purchases may be new **purchased**
issues or bills that are being traded secondarily. Bills with one year to
maturity are auctioned once a month. Shorter term bills are auctioned
weekly. If the buyer purchases the bills directly through the Federal
Reserve Bank, there are no commission fees. Brokers and commercial
banks do charge commissions, but the fees are modest (e.g., $25 for
$15,000 worth of bills) compared with those charged for other investment
transactions, such as the purchase of stock.

Treasury bills are among the best short-term debt instruments available to investors who desire liquidity and safety.* The bills mature quickly, and there are many issues from which the investor may choose. Thus,
the investor may purchase a bill that matures when the principal is

---

*Treasury bills are issued in bearer form and thus are easily transferred if *stolen*. In that sense,
 they lack some element of safety.

needed. For example, an individual who has ready cash today but who must make a payment after three months may purchase a bill that matures at the appropriate time. In doing so, the investor puts the cash to work for three months.

Like all treasury debt, the bills are safe, for there is no question that the federal government has the capacity to refund or retire the bills. Although companies with excess cash or commercial banks with an unused lending capacity are the principal buyers of treasury bills, individual savers may also purchase them. However, the large minimum denomination of $10,000 virtually excludes most savers. Individual investors who desire such safe short-term investments may purchase shares in mutual funds that specialize in buying short-term securities including treasury bills. For a discussion of these investments, see the section on mutual funds in Chapter 21.

Treasury Notes and Bonds

Intermediate- and long-term debt

Intermediate-term federal government debt is in the form of Treasury notes. These notes are issued in denominations of $1000 to more than $100,000 and mature in one to seven years. Treasury bonds, the government's debt instrument for long-term debt, are issued in denominations of $1000 to $1,000,000, and these bonds mature in more than five years from the date of issue. Notes and bonds are issued in both bearer and registered forms. These issues are the safest intermediate- and long-term investments available and are purchased by pension funds, financial institutions, or savers who are primarily concerned with moderate income and safety. Since these debt instruments are so safe, their yields are generally lower than that which may be obtained with high quality corporate debt, such as AT&T bonds. For example, in early 1978, AT&T bonds that were rated triple A yielded about 8.5 per cent, while Treasury bonds with approximately the same time to maturity yielded 8 per cent. Although the difference is less than a percentage point, the market still placed a higher return on the AT&T bonds.

How treasury bonds are purchased

Like treasury bills, new issues of treasury bonds may be purchased through commercial banks and brokerage firms. These firms will charge commissions ranging from $10 to $25. The individual may avoid such fees by purchasing the securities from any of the Federal Reserve banks or their branches. Payment, however, must precede purchase, except when the individual pays cash. Unless the individual investor submits a competitive bid, the purchase price is the average price that is charged institutions that buy the bonds through competitive bidding. By accepting this noncompetitive bid, the individual assures matching the average yield earned by financial institutions, which try to buy the securities at the lowest price (highest yield) possible.

Although there is no question that the federal government can pay the interest and refund its debt, there are ways in which the holder of treasury notes and bonds can suffer losses. These debt instruments pay a fixed amount of interest, which is determined when the notes and bonds are issued. If interest rates subsequently rise, existing issues will not be as attractive, and their market prices will decline. If an investor must sell the debt instrument before it matures, the price will be lower than the principal amount and the investor will suffer a capital loss.

Interest rates paid by treasury debt have varied over time. The extent of this variation is illustrated by Graph 9–3 in Chapter 9, which shows the yields on treasury bills and treasury bonds from 1972 to 1978. Yields not only change over time but also can fluctuate rapidly. For example, yields on three-month treasury bills fluctuated from a high of 8.4 per cent in August 1974 to 5.2 per cent only ten months later. These fluctuations in yields are due to variations in the supply of and demand for credit in the money and bond markets. As the demand and supply vary, so will the market prices and the yields on all debt instruments, including the debt of the federal government. When demand becomes strong and exceeds supply at the old prices, bond prices will rise and yields will decline. The reverse occurs when supply exceeds demand: bond prices decline and yields rise.

Yields have varied

An investor may also lose through investments in treasury debt when the rate of inflation exceeds the interest rate earned on the bonds. For example, during 1974 the yields on government bonds rose to 7.3 per cent, but the rate of inflation for consumer goods exceeded 10 per cent. The investor then suffered a loss in purchasing power, for interest payments were insufficient to compensate for the inflation.

The impact of inflation

These two factors, fluctuating yields and inflation, illustrate that investing in federal government debt, like all types of investing, subjects the investor to risk. Therefore, although federal government debt is among the safest of all investments with regard to the certainty of payment of interest and principal, some element of risk still exists.

FEDERAL AGENCIES' DEBT

In addition to the debt issued by the federal government, certain agencies of the federal government and federally sponsored corporations issue debt. These debt instruments encompass the entire spectrum of maturities, ranging from short-term securities to long-term bonds. Like many United States Treasury debt issues, there is an active secondary market in some of the debt issues of these agencies, and price quotations for many of the bonds are given daily in the financial press.

Several federal agencies have come into existence to fulfill specific financial needs. For example, the Banks for Cooperatives were organized under the Farm Credit Act. These banks provide farm business services and make loans to farm cooperatives to help purchase supplies. The Federal Home Loan Mortgage Corporation was established to strengthen the secondary market in residential mortgages insured by the Federal Housing Administration. This federal corporation buys and sells home mortgages to give marketability to these mortgages and thus increase their attractiveness to private investors. The Student Loan Marketing Association was created to provide liquidity to the insured student loans made under the Guaranteed Student Loan Program by commercial banks, savings and loan associations, and schools that participate in the program. This liquidity should expand the funds available to students from private sources.

Agency bonds have higher yields than treasury debt

Agency bonds are not issued by the federal government and are not the debt of the federal government. Hence, they tend to offer higher yields than those available on United States Treasury debt. However, the bonds are extremely safe because they have the backing of the federal government. In some cases this backing is only moral, which means that in case of default the federal government does not have to support the debt (i.e., to pay the interest and meet the terms of the indenture). Some of the debt issues, however, are supported by the full faith and credit of the federal government. These bonds, then, are secured by the United States Treasury. Should these issues go into default, the federal government is legally bound to assume the obligations of the debt's indenture.

These bonds are excellent credit risks

The matter of whether the bonds have the legal or the moral backing of the federal government is probably academic. All of these debt issues are excellent credit risks. Since they tend to sell for slightly higher yields than those that are available on United States Treasury debt, the bonds of the federal agencies have become very attractive investments for conservative investors seeking higher yields. This applies not only to individual investors who wish to protect their capital but also to financial institutions, such as commercial banks, insurance companies, or credit unions, which must be particularly concerned with the safety of the principal in making investment decisions.

Federal agency debt can be purchased by individuals, but few individual investors do own these bonds, except indirectly through pension plans, mutual funds, and other institutions that own the debt. Many individual investors are probably not even aware of the existence of this debt and the potential advantages that it offers. Any investor who wants to construct a portfolio with an emphasis on income and the relative safety of the principal should consider these debt instruments.

STATE AND LOCAL GOVERNMENT DEBT

State and local governments also issue debt to finance capital expenditures, such as schools or roads. The government then retires the debt as the facilities are used. The funds used to retire the debt may be raised through taxes (e.g., property taxes) or through revenues generated by the facilities themselves.

Variations in the quality

Unlike the federal government, state and local governments do not have the power to create money. These governments must raise the funds necessary to pay the interest and retire the debt, but the ability to do so varies with the financial status of each government. Municipalities with wealthy residents or valuable property within their boundaries are able to issue debt more readily and at lower interest rates because the debt is safer. The tax base in these communities is larger and can support the debt.

THE TAX EXEMPTION

The primary factor that differentiates state and local government debt from other forms of debt is the tax advantage that it offers to investors. The interest earned on state and municipal government debt is exempt from federal income taxation. Hence, these bonds are frequently referred to as tax exempts. Although state and local governments may tax the interest, the federal government may not.* The rationale for this tax exemption is legal and not financial. The Supreme Court ruled that the federal government does not have the power to tax the interest paid by the debt of state and municipal governments. Since the interest paid by all other debt, including corporate bonds, is subject to federal income taxation, this exemption is advantageous to state and local governments, for they are able to issue debt with substantially lower interest rates.

Investors are willing to accept a lower return on state and local government debt because the after-tax return is equivalent to higher yields on corporate debt. For example, if an investor is in the 40 per cent income tax bracket, the return after taxes is the same for a corporate bond that pays 10 per cent as for a state or municipal government bond that pays 6 per cent: The after-tax return is 6 per cent in either case.

The after-tax return is competitive

The willingness of investors to purchase state and local government debt instead of corporate and United States Treasury debt is related to their income tax bracket. If an investor's federal income tax rate is 60 per cent, a 5 per cent nontaxable municipal bond gives the investor the same yield after taxes as a 12.5 per cent corporate bond the interest of which is subject to federal income taxation. The individual investor may determine the equivalent yields on tax-exempt bonds and nonexempt bonds by using the following equation:

The importance of the individual's tax bracket

(1) $$i_c\,(1-t) = i_m$$

where i_c is the interest rate paid on corporate debt, i_m is the interest rate paid on municipal debt, and t is the individual's tax bracket (i.e., the marginal tax rate). This equation is used as follows. If an investor's tax

---

*Conversely, state and local governments may not tax the interest paid by federal government securities.

bracket is 60 per cent and tax-exempt bonds offer 5 per cent, then the equivalent corporate yield is

$$i_c(1 - 0.6) = 0.05$$

$$i_c = \frac{0.05}{0.4} = 12.5\%$$

A table of equivalent yields

The equivalent yields on taxable and nontaxable bonds for selected taxable incomes are given in Table 12–1. As the individual's income rises, the marginal tax rate also increases because the federal income tax rates are progressive. This means that the before-tax interest rate paid by a nonexempt bond must rise to compensate for the additional tax. If one's taxable income rises from the 42 per cent to the 48 per cent bracket, a taxable bond must pay 9.6 per cent to have the same after-tax yield that is earned by a tax-exempt bond paying 5 per cent. If the tax bracket is 62 per cent and tax-exempt bonds pay 7 per cent, that is equivalent to a yield of 18.4 per cent on the taxable bonds. Thus, it is not surprising that the primary buyers of these nontaxable bonds are people with high incomes who are in high tax brackets.

A tax shelter

Exempting the interest on these bonds from federal income taxation has been frequently criticized because it is an apparent means for the rich to avoid federal income taxation. The exemption does, however, reduce the interest cost for the state and municipal governments that issue debt, which in effect is a subsidy to those governments. From an economic point of view, the important question is whether the exemption is the best means to aid or subsidize state and local governments. Other means, such as federal revenue sharing, could be used for this purpose.

The interest exemption is primarily a political question. Changes in the legal structure may alter the tax exemption in the future. Until that time, however, the interest on state and municipal debt is exempt from federal income taxation, with the effects being that (1) state and local governments can issue debt with interest rates that are lower than individuals and corporations must pay and (2) these bonds offer the wealthier members of our society a means to obtain tax-sheltered income.

TABLE 12–1. *Equivalent Yields for Taxable and Nontaxable Bonds at Selected Levels of Taxable Income*

SELECTED TAXABLE INCOMES (JOINT RETURN)	TAX BRACKET (MARGINAL TAX RATE FOR 1978)	A TAX-EXEMPT YIELD OF 5% IS EQUAL TO A TAXABLE YIELD OF	7%
$ 20,000–24,000	32%	7.3%	10.3%
32,000–36,000	42	8.6	12.1
40,000–44,000	48	9.6	13.5
52,000–64,000	53	10.6	14.9
100,000–120,000	62	13.2	18.4

YIELDS AND PRICES OF STATE AND LOCAL GOVERNMENT BONDS

Like yields on other securities, yields on tax-exempt bonds have varied over time. Graph 12–1 shows the average yields on Aaa- and Baa-rated bonds over several years. During this period there was considerable fluctuation in the interest rates paid by tax-exempt bonds. For example, in 1971 the yields to maturity were only 4.8 per cent for the Aaa-rated bonds, but these yields rose to 6.7 per cent in 1975. The fluctuation in the yields of the Baa-rated bonds was even greater, for they rose from 5.4 per cent to 8 per cent during the same period. A yield of 8 per cent is comparable to a yield of 20 per cent on a corporate bond for an individual in the 60 per cent income tax bracket. Even for individuals in the 20 per cent tax bracket, the comparable yield on taxable bonds is 10 per cent.

In addition to showing the fluctuation in yields, the graph shows the difference in yields. As would be expected, the yields on the Baa-rated bonds exceed those on the Aaa-rated bonds, and the spread in yields between the Aaa- and Baa-rated bonds varies. During periods of higher interest rates, the spread widens. For example, the spread rose to over 1.9 per cent during 1976. However, when interest rates declined, the spread between the yields on the Aaa- and Baa-rated bonds declined to 0.7 per cent in 1978.

Like the price of the debt of corporations and the federal government, the price of state and local government bonds depends on the supply of credit relative to the demand. The equations used to determine the value of bonds in Chapter 10 also apply to the valuation of municipal bonds.

Fluctuations and differences in yields

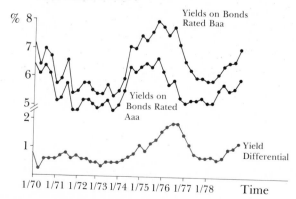

GRAPH 12–1. **Average Yields and the Spread Between Aaa- and Baa-Rated Municipal Bonds From 1970 to 1977**

(Source: Adapted From *Moody's Bond Record,* February 1979.

Their yields are inversely related to their prices. When a state or municipal government bond's price rises, its yield declines. When the bond's price falls, the yield rises. Thus, these bonds can sell at a discount or at a premium, depending on the direction of change in interest rates.

TYPES OF TAX-EXEMPT SECURITIES

General obligation and revenue bonds

State and local governments issue a variety of debt instruments; these can be classified either according to the means by which the security is supported or according to the length of time to maturity. State and municipal debt is supported by either the taxing power of the issuing government or the revenues generated by the facilities that are financed by the debt. If the bonds are secured by the taxing power, the debt is a general obligation of the government. The majority of tax-exempt bonds are of this type.

Bonds supported by the revenue generated by the project being financed with the debt are called revenue bonds. These are issued to finance particular capital improvements, such as a toll road that generates its own money. As these revenues are collected, they are used to pay the interest and retire the principal.

The registered and coupon forms

Tax-exempt bonds are issued in both registered and coupon form. The minimum denomination is $5000 in face value. There is an active secondary market in this debt; however, the bonds are traded only in the over-the-counter market, and only a handful are quoted in the financial press. Small denominations (e.g., $5000) tend to lack marketability, but that does not mean that an investor trying to sell one $5000 bond issued by a small municipality cannot sell it. It does imply, however, that the market is extremely thin and that the spread between the bid and ask prices may be substantial.

Bonds that are currently offered for sale are listed in a specialized publication, the *Blue List*, which is published daily by Standard & Poor. An investor who is looking for securities issued by a particular municipality or for bonds that mature at a particular time may consult this publication, which is carried by many brokerage firms. Brokerage firms also have lists of bonds that they have in inventory and offer for sale.

Serial bonds

Although most corporate bonds are issued with a particular term to maturity and a sinking fund requirement, many tax-exempt bonds are issued in a series. With a serial issue, a specific amount of the debt falls due each year. Such an issue is illustrated in Exhibit 12–2, which reproduces a tombstone advertisement for bonds sold by Dade County, Florida. (These advertisements are placed by the underwriting syndicate to describe a public offering. They are frequently referred to as tombstones because they resemble an epitapth on a tombstone.) Over $50 million of this $65 million issue is in serial bonds. A portion of the issue

New Issue

$65,000,000

Dade County, Florida

Guaranteed Entitlement Revenue Bonds, Series A

Dated: February 1, 1978   Due: February 1 and August 1, as shown below

The Series A Bonds are subject to redemption prior to maturity as more fully described in the Official Statement.

In the opinion of Bond Counsel interest on the Series A Bonds is exempt from all present Federal income taxes.

$50,670,000 Serial Bonds

Amount February 1	Amount August 1	Due	Coupon Rate	Price or Yield	Amount February 1	Amount August 1	Due	Coupon Rate	Yield or Price
$1,185,000	$1,210,000	1988	4.90%	100%	$2,070,000	$2,130,000	1998	5.60%	5.65%
1,260,000	1,295,000	1989	5	100	1,610,000	625,000	1999	5.70	100
1,340,000	1,375,000	1990	5.10	100	645,000	665,000	2000	5¾	100
1,415,000	1,455,000	1991	5.20	100	685,000	705,000	2001	5¾	100
1,490,000	1,530,000	1992	5.30	100	725,000	745,000	2002	5.80	100
1,565,000	1,605,000	1993	5.40	100	770,000	790,000	2003	5.80	100
1,660,000	1,705,000	1994	5.40	5.45	815,000	840,000	2004	5.80	5.85
1,750,000	1,790,000	1995	5½	100	865,000	890,000	2005	5.80	5.85
1,830,000	1,875,000	1996	5½	5.55	915,000	940,000	2006	5.80	5.90
1,940,000	1,995,000	1997	5.60	100	970,000	1,000,000	2007	5.80	5.90

$14,330,000   5.80% Term Bonds due February 1, 2008

Yield 5.85%

(Plus accrued interest)

Smith Barney, Harris Upham & Co.
Incorporated

Bache Halsey Stuart Shields
Incorporated

John Nuveen & Co.
Incorporated

Kidder, Peabody & Co.
Incorporated

EXHIBIT 12–2. Tombstone for a serial bond (Source: *The Wall Street Journal*).

matures each year. For example, $1,340,000 worth of the bonds matures on February 1, 1980, and another $1,375,000 matures on August 1, 1980. Serial bonds offer advantages to both the issuer and the buyer. In contrast to corporate debt, in which a random selection of the bonds is retired each year through the sinking fund, the buyer knows when each bond will mature. The investor can then purchase bonds that mature at the desired time, which helps in portfolio planning. Because a portion of the issue is retired periodically with serial bonds, the issuing government does not have to make a large, lump-sum payment. Since these bonds are scheduled to be retired, there is no call penalty. If the government wants to retire additional debt, it can call some of the remaining bonds. For example, if Dade County, Florida, wanted to retire prematurely some of these bonds, it would call the term bonds that are due in 2008. (Most issues like the Dade County bonds shown in Exhibit 12–2 require that any debt retired before maturity be called in reverse order. Thus, the term bonds with the longest time to maturity are redeemed first.)

Anticipation notes

Although most of the debt sold to the general public by state and local governments is long-term, there are two notable exceptions: tax or revenue anticipation notes and project notes. Tax or revenue anticipation notes are what their name implies. The issuing government anticipates certain receipts in the future and issues a debt instrument against these receipts. When the taxes or other revenues are received, the notes are retired. The maturity date is set to coincide with the timing of the anticipated receipts so that the notes may be easily retired.

Project notes

Project notes are short-term debt issued to finance urban renewal. States have formed local public agencies to plan and carry out urban renewal projects. Before low-rent housing can be built or slum neighborhoods can be redeveloped, the agencies need short-term financing for land acquisition, site improvement, construction, and working capital. After the projects are completed, the agencies issue long-term bonds that provide the projects with more permanent financing. However, during the initial stages of development, the agencies need a major source of short-term financing, and this has led to the development of project notes.

Each agency does not market its own project notes. Instead, the United States Department of Housing and Urban Development (HUD) combines the various issues into one large issue of notes. In effect, HUD is the conduit through which the various notes are initially sold to the public. The notes are auctioned twice a month and are issued in bearer form, with denominations ranging from $1000 to $100,000. Interest is payable at maturity, which ranges from 3 to 12 months.

Although project notes are sold through HUD, they are the obligations of the issuing state and local housing and urban renewal agencies. Since the notes represent the obligations of state and local agencies, the interest they pay is exempt from federal income taxation and may also be exempt from income taxes in the state of issue.

In addition to the tax exemption, project notes are guaranteed by HUD. Thus, they are backed by the full faith and credit of the United States Government. Since the notes are fully secured by the federal government, they are as safe as treasury bills. Project notes and treasury bills, then, have strong similarities, and one may be preferred to the other on the basis of any difference in yields.

ANALYSIS OF STATE AND
LOCAL GOVERNMENT DEBT

Finding information on particular bond issues can be fairly difficult for the individual investor. Municipal bonds are not registered with the Securities and Exchange Commission (SEC) prior to their sale to the general public, and state and local governments do not publish annual reports and send them to bondholders. Instead, investors may consult the latest issues of Moody's *Municipal and Government Manual* or *Standard & Poor's Bond Guide*. At least one of these advisory services can usually be found in many local libraries. Fortunately for investors, both of these firms rate a considerable number of the tax-exempt bonds that are sold to the general public. These ratings are based on a substantial amount of data, for the rating services require the municipal and state governments to provide them with financial and economic information. Since failure of the bond issue to receive a favorable rating will dissuade many potential buyers, the state and local governments supply the rating services with the required information.

Municipal debt is not registered with the SEC

The importance of rating services

The analysis of state and local government debt is similar to that of corporate debt because in both cases the analyst is trying to determine the same thing: the ability of the borrower to service the debt. In particular, the creditor is concerned with the capacity of the borrower to pay the interest and retire the principal. In Chapter 11 several ratios were used to determine the borrower's liquidity and ability to cover the interest payments. Similar ratios may be developed for analyzing state and local government debt.

Although individual investors rarely perform ratio analysis for municipal debt, the rating services do use this type of analysis.* Standard & Poor computes the following ratios for any government that desires to have its general obligations rated:

Ratio analysis applied to tax-exempt bonds

$$\frac{\text{Total debt}}{\text{Population}}$$

$$\frac{\text{Per capita debt}}{\text{Per capita income}}$$

$$\frac{\text{Total debt}}{\text{Total market value of taxable property}}$$

These ratios are similar to the debt ratios used to analyze a firm. The lower the numerical value for each, the safer the debt should be. Be-

---

*This section draws heavily on Hugh L. Sherwood's *How Corporate and Municipal Debt Is Rated*. New York, John Wiley & Sons, Inc., 1976, Chapter 13.

cause these ratios do not show the flow of funds available to service the debt, the following coverage ratio is also computed:

$$\frac{\text{interest plus principal repayments}}{\text{gross revenues}}$$

If the amount that a government pays in interest and principal is only 10 per cent of its gross revenues (i.e., if its debt service is covered by a factor of 10), then the debt should be quite safe. If, however, the coverage declines so debt service consumes 20 of 25 per cent of revenues, then the debt is considered to be fairly risky.

For revenue bonds, the variables used by Standard & Poor are somewhat different. Since these bonds are not supported by the government's power to tax, ratios such as debt service to tax revenues have no meaning. Instead, Standard & Poor considers debt service relative to the revenues generated by the facilities, the stability of these revenues, and basic security provisions, such as the pledging of assets as stated in the bond's indenture. Poor coverage of debt service or fluctuating revenues mean that the debt involves greater risk and therefore will receive a lower rating.

SUMMARY

When the federal government spends more than it receives in tax revenues, this deficit must be financed. In order to tap funds from many sources, the federal government issues a variety of debt instruments. These include series EE and HH bonds, which are sold in small denominations, and treasury bills and bonds, which are sold in large denominations.

Federal government debt is the safest of all possible investments, as there is no possibility of default. However, the investor still bears the risk of loss through fluctuations in the price of the marketable debt and through inflation. If the rate of inflation exceeds the yield on the debt instruments, then the investor experiences a loss of purchasing power.

In addition to the debt issued by the federal government itself, bonds are issued by its agencies. These bonds tend to offer a slightly higher yields, but they are virtually as safe as the direct debt of the federal government. In some cases the agency's debt is even secured by the full faith and credit of the United States Treasury.

State and local governments also issue debt to finance capital improvements. This debt is retired as revenues are received during the lifetime of the facilities.

State and municipal debt is distinguished from other investments because the interest is exempt from federal income taxation. These bonds pay lower rates of interest than those paid by taxable securities (e.g., corporate bonds). However, the after-tax yields on the tax-exempt bonds may be equal to or even greater than the yields on taxable bonds. The nontaxable bonds are particularly attractive to investors in high income tax brackets because they provide a means to shelter some income from taxation.

Tax-exempt bonds can be risky investments, as the capacity of state and local governments to service the debt varies. Moody's and Standard & Poor's rating services analyze this debt based on the government's ability to pay the interest and retire the principal. These ratings give the investor an indication of the risk associated with investing in a particular debt issue.

Terms to Remember

Series E and EE bonds

Series H and HH bonds

Treasury bills

Treasury notes

Treasury bonds

Federal agency bonds

Moral backing

Tax-exempt bond

Serial bond

Anticipation note

Project note

General obligation bond

Revenue bond

Questions

1. Why is the debt of the federal government considered to be the safest of all possible investments?

2. What distinguishes series EE bonds from Treasury bills?

3. When interest rates rise, what happens to the price of federal government bonds? What happens to the price of state and local government bonds?

4. What is the difference between the following:
   a. a bond secured by a moral obligation and a bond secured by full faith and credit?
   b. a revenue bond and a general obligation bond?
   Are there any similarities between a bond secured by a moral obligation and a revenue bond?

5. What are the sources of risk of investing in
   a. federal government debt?
   b. municipal debt?

6. What is the difference between a term bond issue and a serial bond issue?

Why are many capital improvements that are made by state and local governments financed through serial bonds?

7. Why do rating services analyze such ratios as debt to population, debt to value of property, and interest expense to revenues when they rate state and local government debt?

8. If a three-month treasury bill is purchased for $.98 on a dollar (i.e., $98,000 for a $100,000 bill), what is the approximate annual rate of interest?

9. An investor is in the 40 per cent income tax bracket and can earn 8.3 per cent on corporate bonds. What is the comparable yield on a nontaxable bond?

SELECTED READINGS

Barnes, Leo, and Stephen Feldman: *Handbook of Wealth Management*. New York, McGraw-Hill Book Co., Inc., 1977, Chapters 26–28.

First Boston Corporation: *Handbook of Securities of the United States Government and Federal Agencies*. Boston, published biennially.

Hawk, William A.: *The U. S. Government Securities Market*. Chicago, Harris Trust and Savings Bank, 1976.

Polakoff, Murray E., et al.: *Financial Institutions and Markets*. Boston, Houghton-Mifflin Co., 1970.

Scott, Ira O. Jr.: *Government Securities Market*. New York, McGraw-Hill Book Co., Inc., 1965.

Sherwood, Hugh C.: *How Corporate and Municipal Debt is Rated*. New York, John Wiley & Sons, Inc., 1976.

Part Four

Investing in Common Stock

For many individuals the word *investing* is synonymous with buying and selling common stocks. Although alternatives are certainly available, common stocks are the primary instrument of investing for many people. Perhaps this is the result of the considerable exposure individuals have to common stocks. Newspapers report stock transactions, market averages are quoted on the nightly television news, and brokerage firms advertise the attractiveness of such investments.

This section discusses investing in common stocks. To identify the stocks with the greatest earnings potential, various techniques are used to analyze the issuing firms. In addition, Part Four considers the return earned in the past on investments in common stock.

Unlike bonds, which pay a fixed amount of interest, the dividends paid by common stocks vary. As the economy prospers and corporate earnings grow, dividends and the value of common stocks may also increase. For this reason, common stocks are a good investment for individuals who have less need for current income but desire capital appreciation.

Learning Objectives

After completing this chapter you should be able to

1. Differentiate between a simple price average and a value-weighted average.

2. Illustrate how aggregate measures of stock prices adjust for stock splits.

3. Contrast the Dow Jones averages with other indices of stock prices.

4. Explain the difference between an average rate of return and the true rate of return.

5. Compare the results of various studies concerning the rates of return earned on investments in common stock.

6. Identify the advantage of "averaging down."

chapter 13

MEASURES OF SECURITY PRICES

Security prices fluctuate daily and over years may appear to follow cycles. Such price fluctuations are one of the sources of risk with which the investor must contend. This market risk cannot be avoided by any investor who purchases securities.

A potential investor may wish to know how investments in stock have performed in view of this fluctuation in prices. The answer to this question depends partially on the measure of stock prices used. The first section of this chapter discusses several of these aggregate measures of price performance. These include the Dow Jones averages, Standard & Poor's 500 stock index, and the New York Stock Exchange (NYSE) composite index. Each is different from the others in its composition and in its method of computation.

The second section is devoted to the returns earned on securities. It includes an explanation of the methods used to compute the rate of return and the various types of graphs that may be used to plot these values along with a discussion of the academic studies of the returns earned by investors. These returns are then compared to the rate of inflation as measured by an index of the general price level.

The chapter concludes with a discussion of one strategy that may reduce the impact of price fluctuations. This strategy is to buy stock systematically which smoothes out the price fluctuations and reduces the average cost of the position (the commitment in a particular stock).

MEASURES OF STOCK PERFORMANCE: AVERAGES AND INDICES

CONSTRUCTION OF MEASURES OF SECURITY PRICES

Which securities to include

Constructing a measure of security prices may appear to be easy, but there are several possible problems. The first concerns the choice of which securities to include. Although this certainly was a problem before the advent of computers, it is not a major concern today, for a measure may include any number of securities (e.g., all stocks listed on the NYSE may be included).

The problem of weights

A more important problem concerns the weight that should be given to each security. For example, suppose there are two stocks: A sells for $10 and has 1 million shares outstanding, and B sells for $20 and has 10 million shares outstanding. The total market value of A is $10 million, and the total market value of B is $200 million. How should these two securities be weighted? There are basically two choices: to treat each stock's price equally or to adjust for B's larger number of shares.

The first choice is a simple average of the prices of both stocks. In this case, the two prices are treated equally, giving an average price per share of

$$\begin{array}{r} \$\ 10 \\ +20 \\ \hline 30 \end{array} \qquad \frac{\$30}{2} = \$15$$

An average gives equal weight to each stock and does not recognize differences in the number of shares outstanding.

If this technique is used, a problem immediately arises concerning the handling of stock splits. The subject of stock splits is treated in greater detail in Chapter 15. However, since stock splits affect the construction of price measures, let us consider a simple example. The price of a stock adjusts for a split. For example, a two-for-one stock split reduces the price of the stock by half. Since the total value of the stock has not changed, such splits do not affect the value of the firm and should not affect the measure of security prices.

Consider what would happen to the average that was determined earlier if stock B were to split two for one. Its price would become $10, and the number of shares outstanding would increase to 20 million. If the measure of security prices is simply the average of the stock prices, the average price per share is reduced to $10 (i.e., [$10 + $10] ÷ 2). Even though there has been no change in the stockholders' wealth by the two-for-one stock split, there has been a significant decline in the average of stock prices. This decline is misleading; thus, the method of computing the average must be modified.

This problem can be avoided for the simple average by adjusting the denominator for the stock split. This adjustment is best demonstrated by an illustration. Before the stock split, the average was

$$\begin{array}{r} \$\ 20 \\ +10 \\ \hline \$30 \end{array} \qquad \frac{\$30}{2} = \$15$$

The problem now is to determine what new divisor (or denominator) will yield $15 when the price of A's stock changes as the result of the split. That is,

$$\begin{array}{r} \$\ 10 \\ +10 \\ \hline \$20 \end{array} \qquad \frac{\$20}{X} = \$15$$

Solving this simple equation for X yields 1.333. If the divisor is reduced from 2 to 1.333, the value of the average is not affected (i.e., $20 ÷ 1.33 = $15). Such an adjustment, then, erases the problem caused by stock splits and stock dividends.

An alternative way of measuring stock performance is to construct an average that allows for the different number of shares each firm has outstanding. If the preceding example is used, the total value of A and B is

$$\begin{array}{lll} \text{Price} \times \text{number of shares} & = & \text{total value} \\ \$10 \times\ \ 1{,}000{,}000 & = & \$10{,}000{,}000 \\ \$20 \times 10{,}000{,}000 & = & \underline{+\$200{,}000{,}000} \\ & & \$210{,}000{,}000 \end{array}$$

244 INVESTING IN COMMON STOCK
The average value of a share of stock is then $19.09 ($210,000,000 ÷
11,000,000). This method obviously places more emphasis on stock B. Its
higher price and greater number of shares result in an increase in the
The total value of the two stocks can be used without constructing
an average value of a share. Instead, all values may be expressed in
terms of this initial total value. For example, suppose the prices of A
and B rise to $18 and $22, respectively. The total value is
$$\$18 \times 1,000,000 = \$ 18,000,000$$
$$\$22 \times 10,000,000 = \$220,000,000$$
$$\$238,000,000$$
This value then may be expressed relative to the first year, which is
$$\frac{\$238,000,000}{\$210,000,000} = 1.13$$
This answer indicated that the current value is 1.13 times the value in
A value-weighted index is an index that is weighted for the
number of shares that a firm has outstanding. Such an index automatically adjusts for stock splits. For example, if stock B splits the shares
$$\$18 \times 1,000,000 = \$ 18,000,000$$
$$\$11 \times 20,000,000 = \$220,000,000$$
$$\$238,000,000$$
Thus, there has been no change in the total value. The price has been
cut in half, but the number of shares has doubled. Therefore, the index
$$\frac{\$238,000,000}{\$210,000,000} = 1.13$$
Thus, the value-weighted index is not affected by stock splits. This fact
along with the emphasis that is placed on the total value of all stocks
included in the index argues strongly for the use of this type of meas-
THE DOW JONES AVERAGES
One of the first measures of stock prices was the average developed
by Charles Dow.* Initially the average consisted of the stock from only
*In 1882 Edward Jones joined Charles Dow to form a partnership that grew into Dow,
Jones and Company.

11 companies but was later expanded to include more firms. Today this average is called the Dow Jones industrial average, and it is probably the best known and most widely quoted average of stock prices.

The industrials

The Dow Jones industrial average is a simple average. It is computed by summing the prices of the stocks of 30 companies and then dividing that total by an adjusted value. The divisor is not the number of stocks (30) but a value that has been adjusted over the years so that the index is not affected by stock splits and stock dividends. No adjustment is made for cash dividends; hence, the index declines when stocks like AT&T or Exxon go ex-div (pay a dividend) and their prices decline. (The reason a stock's price declines when the firm pays a dividend is explained in Chapter 15.)

The Dow Jones industrial average for the period from 1939 to 1977 is presented in Graph 13–1, which plots the high and low values of the average for each year. As may be seen in the graph, there was a pronounced increase in the average during the 1950s, when the annual high rose from less than 300 to almost 700. Although the average has risen since 1959, it has not experienced a similar steady increase during the 1960s and 1970s. The average has even dropped below its high of 1959, for in both 1970 and 1974 it dipped below 650.

Other Dow Jones averages

In addition to the industrial average, Dow Jones computes an average for transportation stocks, utility stocks, and a composite average of all of the stocks included in the three separate averages. All three averages are composed of a relatively small number of companies. Thirty stocks are included in the industrial average, 20 stocks compose the

GRAPH 13–1. High and Low Values of the Dow Jones Industrial Average from 1939 to 1977

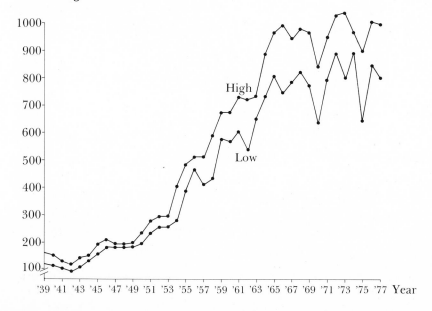

EXHIBIT 13–1. Stocks Included in the Dow Jones Averages

The Dow Jones Industrials

Allied Chemical	International Harvester
Aluminum Co. of America	International Paper
American Brands	Johns-Manville
American Can	Merck
American Telephone and Telegraph	Minnesota Mining and Manufacturing
Bethlehem Steel	Owens-Illinois
Du Pont	Procter & Gamble
Eastman Kodak	Sears, Roebuck & Co.
Exxon	Standard Oil of California
General Electric	Texaco
General Foods	Union Carbide
General Motors	United Technologies
Goodyear	United States Steel
IBM	Westinghouse Electric
Inco	Woolworth

The Dow Jones Transportation Stocks

American Airlines	Pan American World Airways
Burlington Northern	St. Louis-San Francisco
Canadian Pacific	Santa Fe Industries
Chessie System	Seaboard Coastline
Consolidated Freight	Southern Pacific
Eastern Airlines	Southern Railway
McLean Trucking	Transway International
Missouri-Pacific	Trans World Corp.
Norfolk and Western	UAL, Inc.
Northwest Airlines	Union Pacific

The Dow Jones Public Utility Stocks

American Electric Power	Niagara Mohawk Power
Cleveland Electric	Pacific Gas and Electric
Columbia Gas System	Panhandle Electric Power and Light
Commonwealth Edison	Peoples Gas
Consolidated Edison	Philadelphia Electric
Consolidated Natural Gas	Public Service Electric and Gas
Detroit Edison	Southern California Edison
Houston Industries	

transportation average, and 15 stocks make up the utilities average. The firms included are among the largest and best known in the nation, as may be seen in Exhibit 13–1. Many firms that have grown into prominence since World War II (e.g., Xerox and Johnson & Johnson), however, are excluded from these averages.*

Criticism of these averages

This small number of firms is one source of criticism of the Dow Jones averages. It is argued that the small sample is not indicative of

---

*Effective July 1, 1979, IBM and Merck replaced Chrysler and Esmark. This may increase the volatility of the average and make it more responsive to changes in stock prices.

the market as a whole. For this reason, other measures of stock prices that have broader bases, such as the NYSE index or Standard & Poor's 500 stock index, may be better indicators of the general market's performance.

OTHER INDICES OF STOCK PRICES

Unlike the Dow Jones industrial average, Standard & Poor's 500 stock index is a value-weighted index. The base year, 1943, is the time at which the index was 10. Thus, if the index is currently 100, the value of these stocks is ten times their value in 1943.

S&P's 500

In addition to Standard & Poor's indices, there is the New York Stock Exchange composite index, which includes all common stocks listed on the NYSE. Like Standard & Poor's averages, the NYSE index is a value-weighted index with a base of 50 as of December 31, 1965.

NYSE index

In addition, there are indices of the American Stock Exchange (Amex) and over-the-counter (OTC) securities. The Amex index is a value-weighted index that encompasses all of the common stocks on that exchange. The National Quotation Bureau compiles an index of 35 over-the-counter stocks. It would be a virtual impossibility to include all OTC stocks, since there are thousands of them, many of which sell for mere pennies. The exclusion of such penny stocks does not reduce the comprehensiveness of the index. The index, however, is not widely quoted. Investors who are primarily concerned with these securities had best keep their own record of this index.

Amex index

Index of OTC prices

The National Association of Security Dealers (NASD) also publishes an index of more than 1600 OTC stocks. This NASDAQ (National Association of Security Dealers Automatic Quotation System) industrial index was started in 1971 and thus cannot be used to show long-term trends. The NASD also publishes broad-based indices of nonindustrial OTC stocks (e.g., banking, utilities, insurance, and transportation).

PRICE FLUCTUATIONS

The fluctuations in security prices are illustrated in Graph 13–2, which plots the Dow Jones industrial average, Standard & Poor's 500 stock index, and the NYSE index from January 1973 to January 1978. All three aggregate measures document the decline in stock prices that started in January 1973. In two years, the Dow Jones industrial average fell from above 1000 to just above 600, which is a 40 per cent decline. Standard & Poor's 500 stock index fell from 117 to under 70 (a 40 per cent decline), and the NYSE index declined from 68 to 35, representing a 49 per cent fall in prices.

Indices show price fluctuations

GRAPH 13–2.   Indices of Stock Prices from January 1973 to 1978

These graphs indicate, as would be expected, that all three measures of stock prices move together. The amount of movement, however, differs. From 1973 to 1975 the percentage decline in the Dow Jones industrial average and in Standard & Poor's index was 40 per cent, but the NYSE index declined by almost 50 per cent. In 1976 the Dow Jones industrial average almost reached its former high, while the other two indices were considerably below their levels of January 1975.

Fluctuations shown by price indices may differ

This divergence in the three measures does give some credibility to the argument that the Dow Jones industrial average may not be typical of the market as a whole. However, Standard & Poor's stock index more closely followed the Dow Jones industrials during 1973 and 1974 and then performed more in line with the NYSE index in 1976 and 1977.

The question of which measure is the best indicator of performance will probably remain unanswered. However, the answer is important, because the performance of an individual's portfolio depends on what it is measured against. Since investment advisory fees (e.g., management

fees charged by mutual funds) may be related to performance, the index
by which this performance is measured affects the cost of such service.

SECURITY PRICES AND INVESTORS' PURCHASING POWER

Another means to measure security price performance is to compare one of the market indices with a general price index. This gives an
indication of the losses inflicted on the investing public by inflation. If
the general price index rises more rapidly than an index of security
prices, the implication is that stock holders suffer a loss of purchasing
power. This occurs even if stock prices increase but at a slower rate
than consumer prices.

This loss of purchasing power is illustrated in Graph 13–3, which
plots the Dow Jones industrials from 1965 to 1977 and the Dow Jones
average deflated (i.e., divided by the general price level). Although the
Dow Jones average of security prices fluctuated, its year-end value for

**Inflation reduces
investors' real
return**

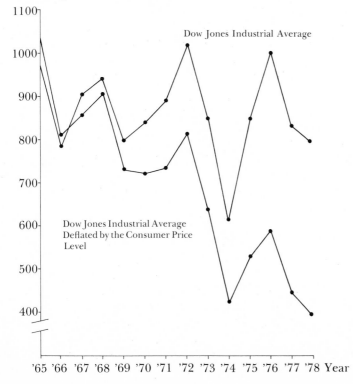

**GRAPH 13–3. Purchasing Power of the Dow Jones Industrial
Average from 1965 to 1978**

1977 was approximately the same as its value at the end of 1966. However, during the same period the consumer price level almost doubled, reducing the purchasing power of the stocks in the Dow Jones industrials by half. Thus, an investor's real return as measured by the Dow Jones industrial average and deflated by the Consumer Price Index was negative.

RATES OF RETURN ON INVESTMENTS IN COMMON STOCK

COMPUTING RATES OF RETURN

What returns have been earned on investments in securities? One method of answering this question is to consider the purchase price of the security (or group of securities) and the sale price. The difference between the two prices indicates the profit or the loss on the security. However, certain factors must be taken into consideration to avoid arriving at a misleading conclusion.

Misleading ways to compute returns

Consider the following example. An investor buys a stock for $10 per share and sells it after ten years to $20. What is the return on the investment? This simple question can produce several misleading answers. The individual may respond by answering "I doubled my money!" or "I made 100 per cent!" That certainly sounds impressive, but it completely disregards the length of time needed to double the individual's money. The investor may assert that he or she made 10 per cent annually (100% ÷ 10 years). This figure is less impressive than the claim that the return is 100 per cent, but it is also misleading because it fails to consider compounding. Some of the return earned during the first year earned a return, which was not taken into consideration when the investor averaged the return over the ten years.

Rates of return are another example of the time value of money

The correct way to determine what return was earned is to phrase the question as follows: "At what rate does $10 grow to $20 after ten years?" The student should recognize this as another example of the time value of money. The equation used to answer this question is

$$P_o\,(1+g)^n = P_n$$

where P_0 is the cost of the security, g is the rate of return, n is the number of years, and P_n is the price at which the security is sold.

When the proper values are substituted, the equation becomes

$$\$10(1 + g)^{10} = \$20$$

which asks at what rate $10 will grow for ten years to become $20. To answer this question, the student solves the equation to determine the interest factor.

$$(1 + g)^{10} = \$20 \div \$10 = 2$$

Thus, 2 is the interest factor for the compound value of $1 for ten years. If the student locates this factor in the compound value of a dollar table, (Appendix A, p. 514) he or she will find that the value of g is approximately 7 per cent. Thus, $10 compounded annually at 7 per cent grows to $20 dollars at the end of ten years. The correct rate of return on the investment (excluding any dividend income) is 7 per cent, which is considerably less impressive than "I doubled my money!" or "I averaged 10 per cent each year."

Averaging positive and negative rates of return

The investor may be tempted to avoid this problem of compounding by determining the rate of return each year. For example, if the price of the stock were to rise from $20 to $22, the annual rate of return would be 10 per cent ($2 ÷ $20). If the stock were to fall in price from $20 to $15, the annual rate of return would be −25 per cent (−$5 ÷ $20).

There is nothing wrong with this technique until the investor averages the resulting annual percentage changes. Like the average of the ten-year total return, this procedure can be misleading. Consider the following example. An investor buys a stock for $20. At the end of the year it is selling for $25, but the investor holds the stock for a second year and then sells it at cost (i.e., $20). What is the rate of return? Obviously the investor earned nothing and the rate of return should indicate this fact.

If, however, the investor computes the annual rate of return each year, and then averages these annual rates, the investment will have a positive rate of return. In the first year the stock's price rose from $20 to $25, indicating a 25 per cent gain ($5 ÷ $20). During the second year the stock declined from $25 to $20, for a 20 per cent loss (−$5 ÷ $25). What is the average rate of return? The answer is

$$\begin{array}{c} 25\% \\ \underline{-20\%} \\ 5\% \end{array} \qquad \frac{5\%}{2} = 2.5\%$$

Owing to the magic of numbers, the investor has earned a 2.5 per cent annual return, even though the investment produced neither a gain nor a loss. This example illustrates how averaging positive and negative numbers can lead to misleading results. The correct means to determine the annual rate of return is to use the compound (or present value) calculations presented previously.

THE INCLUSION OF DIVIDEND
AND INTEREST INCOME

Dividends and interest must be included

Many investments earn income as well as appreciate in price. This income is also part of the total return earned by the investor. Therefore, to determine the rate of return earned on an investment, any income such as interest or dividends must be included in the calculation. For example, if an individual buys a stock for $50, collects a $2.00 dividend in the first year, $2.10 in the second year, and $2.25 in the third year, and then sells the stock for $60, the return consists of the dividend payments and the capital gain.

To determine the rate of return earned on the investment, the investor could find the growth rate that equates the discounted value of the dividends and the sale price with the cost of the investment. The equation is

$$P_o = \frac{D_1}{(1+g)^1} + \ldots + \frac{D_n}{(1+g)^n} + \frac{P_n}{(1+g)^n}$$

where P_o is the cost of the security, g is the rate of return, $D_1 \ldots D_n$ is the flow of income, such as the payment of dividends during the years the investor held the security, and P_n is the price at which the security is sold. When this equation is applied to the preceding example, the rate of return on the investment may be determined.

$$\$50 = \frac{\$2}{(1+g)^1} + \frac{\$2.10}{(1+g)^2} + \frac{\$2.25}{(1+g)^3} + \frac{\$60}{(1+g)^3}$$

These calculations can be rather tedious, but computers can solve the equation with relative ease. The annual rate of return on the investment is 10.25 per cent, which considers both the flow of dividend income and the capital appreciation.

RATES OF RETURN AND
GRAPHIC ILLUSTRATIONS

Use of semilogarithmic graphs

The investor who reads certain financial publications, such as the *Media General Financial Weekly* or the *Value Line Investment Survey*, will find charts constructed on semilogarithmic paper. This type of graph is used because it gives a truer picture of the *change* in the price of the stock.

This fact may be illustrated by the following monthly range of stock prices and percentage increases:

Month	Price of Stock	Percentage Change in Monthly Highs
January	$10–5	. . .
February	15–10	50
March	20–15	33
April	25–20	25

GRAPH 13–4. Use of Semilogarithmic Paper to Illustrate Stock Price Movements

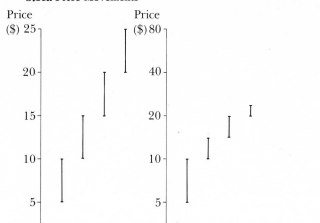

Even though the monthly price increases are equal ($5), the percentage increments decline. The investor who bought the stock at $10 and sold it for $15 made $5 and earned a return of 50 per cent. The investor who bought it at $20 and sold for $25 also made $5, but the return was only 25 per cent.

These monthly prices may be plotted on graph paper that uses absolute dollar units for the vertical axis. This is done on the left-hand side of Graph 13–4. Such a graph gives the appearance that equal price movements yield equal returns. However, this is not so, as the preceding illustration demonstrates.

To avoid this problem, semilogarithmic paper can be used. This is done in Graph 13–4, and the prices are plotted on the right-hand side. Equal units on the vertical axis are in terms of percentage change. Thus, a price movement from $10 to $15 appears to be a greater price movement than one from $20 to $25, because in percentage terms it *is* greater.

Some financial services use this type of graph to give a more accurate view of the change in the security's price. Because absolute price changes are reduced to percentage price changes, these graphs are better indicators of rates of return. Such returns are more important than simply a security's absolute price change.

STUDIES OF INVESTMENT RETURNS

Several studies have been conducted by academicians on the returns earned by investments in common stocks; hence, these reports should not contain any bias. Unfortunately, research done by brokerage firms, investment advisory services, or the trust department of commercial banks may involve a conflict of interest. Although the results may seem valid, one may still be hesitant to accept them as honest appraisals of the returns earned by investors.

Fisher and Lorie's study

Perhaps the most famous (or at least most frequently cited) study on the rates of return earned by investments in common stocks was done by Fisher and Lorie. They studied the annual rates of return from investments in all common stocks listed on the NYSE from 1926 through 1965 and found that the average annual rate of return was 9.3 per cent. The rates of return, of course, varied from year to year and depended on the assumptions made.

Table 13–1 is adapted from Fisher and Lorie's study. Although this table uses only six selected years, the researchers presented the results for the inclusive years of the study. Table 13–1, however, does illustrate the annual rates of return under Fisher and Lorie's three different sets of

TABLE 13–1. *Selected Annual Rates of Return (Per Cent) on Investments in Common Stocks Listed on the NYSE*

	DIVIDENDS REINVESTED				
From	1/1926	12/1935	12/1945	12/1955	12/1964
To					
12/1926	−1.6	. . .	. . .	. . .	. . .
12/1936	6.6	63.9	. . .	. . .	. . .
12/1946	5.5	10.2	−9.9	. . .	. . .
12/1956	8.5	12.6	13.3	6.5	. . .
12/1965	9.3	12.6	12.6	12.5	28.3

	DIVIDENDS NOT REINVESTED				
From	1/1926	12/1935	12/1945	12/1955	12/1964
To					
12/1926	−1.8	. . .	. . .	. . .	. . .
12/1936	6.3	64.2	. . .	. . .	. . .
12/1946	4.2	9.1	−9.8	. . .	. . .
12/1956	6.5	11.0	11.7	6.6	. . .
12/1965	7.3	11.2	11.7	12.2	28.3

	DIVIDENDS IGNORED				
From	1/1926	12/1935	12/1945	12/1955	12/1964
To					
12/1926	−5.7	. . .	. . .	. . .	. . .
12/1936	3.1	59.7	. . .	. . .	. . .
12/1946	0.7	5.4	−13.6	. . .	. . .
12/1956	3.4	7.0	7.0	2.0	. . .
12/1965	4.6	7.5	7.5	8.6	24.7

Source: Adapted from Lawrence Fisher and James H. Lorie, "Rates of Return on Investments in Common Stock—The Year-by-Year Record, 1926–1965," *The Journal of Business* 40(July 1968), pp. 1–26.

assumptions. In the first section it is assumed that dividends are reinvested in common stocks. In the second section it is assumed that dividends are not reinvested (i.e., that the investor pockets any dividends that are received), and in the last section the dividends are ignored. In all three cases, the impact of taxes is not taken into consideration (i.e., these are before-tax rates of return).

As would be expected, the failure to include dividends reduces the rates of return and hence is not indicative of the total return earned on the investment (i.e., the figures in the third section are simply the rates of return generated by any price changes). In the other two cases, the rates of return are very similar. For example, the rates of return earned on an investment held from December 1935 until December 1965 yielded 12.6 per cent when the dividends were reinvested and 11.2 per cent when they were not. When the price change alone was considered, the rate of return was 7.5 per cent, which indicates that the dividend return during that particular time was in excess of 3 per cent.

According to Fisher and Lorie's study, investments in common stocks listed on the NYSE during the period studied earned an excellent return. (The student should remember that an annual return of 9.3 per cent means $1000 will grow to more than $2000 in eight years.) The rates of return were even higher during the 1950s and early 1960s when the country and the stock market experienced prosperity and rapid growth. During this time the annual rates of return on stocks averaged as high as 15 per cent.

These results are impressive, but the student should remember that although this study encompassed all of the common stocks listed on the big board, no investor could have duplicated these results. The individual investor owns a portfolio of selected securities and not all stocks. Thus, an aggregate measure of the rate of return does not necessarily apply to a particular individual's portfolio. In fact, one study found that securities selected by individual investors (i.e., nonprofessional money managers) tended to outperform the market (before considering transaction costs).*

Studies of the stock market by Holmes and by Brigham and Pappas corroborated the results of Fisher and Lorie.** Holmes's study covered the period between 1871 and 1971. The annual rate of return earned for the 100-year period was 7.8 per cent. For the years that overlapped with Fisher and Lorie's study, the rate of return was 9.7 per cent. This small difference (9.7 versus 9.3 per cent) could be attributed to commission costs. Fisher and Lorie included a commission cost for

Other studies of market returns

*See Gary G. Schlarbaum, Wilbur G. Lewellen, and Ronald C. Lease, "Realized Returns on Common Stock Investments: The Experience of Individual Investors," *Journal of Business* 51(April 1978), pp. 299–325.

**See John Russel Holmes, "100 Years of Common Stock Investing," *Financial Analysts Journal*, 30(November–December 1974), pp. 38–45, and Eugene F. Brigham and James L. Pappas, "Rates of Return on Common Stock," *Journal of Business* 42(July 1969), pp. 302–316.

stock purchases, while Holmes's study did not. Hence, one would expect Fisher and Lorie's rates of return to be less.

Brigham and Pappas's study covered the period from 1946 to 1965. They concluded that the average rate of return was about 15 per cent. Although this figure is considerably higher than the overall averages in Fisher and Lorie's and in Holmes' studies, it is similar to their returns for the comparable time period.

Rates of return have also been computed for OTC stocks. A study by Jessup and Upson found that for short periods, such as a year, these rates of return were inferior to those earned on stocks listed on the NYSE.* However, as the length of time increased to five years, the rates of return were similar for listed and OTC stocks.

OTC stocks may have been inferior investments

These results suggest that OTC stocks are inferior investments. Since the rates of return on listed stocks and OTC stocks are similar, these investments should involve equal risk. However, the study also found that the OTC stocks are more volatile. Since their prices tend to fluctuate more, these stocks are riskier. Presumably, if an investment involves greater risk, it should offer a higher return. If it does not, then the investment is inferior, because, given a choice of two portfolios with the same rate of return, the investor will always prefer the portfolio with less risk. For this reason, Jessup and Upson concluded that investments in OTC stocks have resulted in inferior returns.

Past returns may not be indicative of future returns

Before jumping to conclusions as to what an investor in the stock market can earn, the student should realize that studies of investment returns must have a beginning and a closing date. The choice of these dates may influence the results. Unfortunately, all of the aforementioned studies concluded before the severe market decline that occurred between 1973 and 1975 (which is illustrated in Graph 13–1). Many of the positive returns earned during the prosperous 1960s seem to have vanished during the ensuing decade. Hence, it is quite possible that the rates of return from investments in common stocks during the 1970s have not generated Fisher and Lorie's annual rate of return of 9.3 per cent. In fact, a more recent study by these authors suggests that the average return has declined.**

The return that investors can expect is obviously difficult to determine. Historical rates of return cannot be taken as indicative of future stock price performance. If this were so, the investor could select a portfolio at random and expect it to earn 9.3 per cent annually according to Fisher and Lorie's earlier study or 15 per cent according to Brigham and Pappas's study. Obviously, there is a contradiction, because the investor cannot earn both rates of return. A return of 9.3 per cent is obviously greater than the return earned on savings accounts, time depos-

---

*See Paul F. Jessup and Roger B. Upson, *Returns in Over-the-Counter Stock Markets.* Minneapolis, University of Minnesota Press, 1973.

**See Lawrence Fisher and James H. Lorie, *A Half Century of Returns on Stocks and Bonds: Rates of Return on Investments in Common Stocks and on U.S. Treasury Securities, 1926–1976.* Chicago, University of Chicago Press, 1977.

its, and many other investments. If an investor could randomly buy a portfolio of stocks and earn 9.3 per cent, there would be no need for analysis and the investment decisions. Unfortunately, this is not the case.

Not all securities meet the investor's specific goals. For example, individuals who are in need of income should select securities whose return consists primarily of dividends. Other investors may desire capital appreciation and therefore should choose stocks whose price is expected to increase. A randomly selected portfolio would not meet either of these specific goals. Thus, even if a 9.3 per cent rate of return is anticipated, these investors with different needs would still have to make investment decisions in order to construct a portfolio that meets their financial goals.

A portfolio should meet the investor's goals

REDUCING THE IMPACT OF PRICE FLUCTUATIONS: AVERAGING

One strategy for accumulating shares and reducing the impact of security price fluctuations is to "average" the position. By buying shares at different times, the investor accumulates the shares at different prices. Such a policy may be achieved through the dividend reinvestment plans that are discussed in Chapter 15. An alternative is for the investor to systematically purchase shares of stock through a broker. There are two basic methods for achieving this averaging: the periodic purchase of shares and the purchase of additional shares if the stock's price falls (i.e., to "average down").

The systematic purchase of securities

PERIODIC PURCHASES

Under the periodic purchase plan, the investor decides to buy additional shares of a stock at regular intervals. For example, the investor may elect to buy $2000 worth of a stock every quarter or every month. This purchase is made at the appropriate interval, no matter what the price of the stock is. The aim of such purchases is to acquire more shares of the stock when its price is down and fewer when its price is up.

The effect of such a program is illustrated in Table 13–2, which shows the number of shares of EMEC stock purchased at various prices when $2000 is invested each quarter. The first column gives the dates of purchase, and the second column presents the various prices of the stock; the third and fourth columns list the number of shares purchased and the total number of shares held in the position. The last column presents the average price of the stock held in the position. The student

Periodic purchases

TABLE 13–2.   *Average Position in EMEC Stock When $2000 Worth Is Purchased Each Quarter*

DATE	PRICE OF STOCK	NUMBER OF SHARES OWNED	CUMULATIVE NUMBER OF SHARES OWNED	AVERAGE COST OF POSITION
1/1/80	$25	80	80	$25.00
4/1/80	28	71	151	26.50
7/1/80	33	60	211	28.44
10/1/80	27	74	285	28.07
1/1/81	21	95	380	26.32
4/1/81	18	111	491	24.44
7/1/81	20	100	591	23.69
10/1/81	25	80	671	23.85

should notice that when the price of the stock rises, $2000 buys fewer shares. For, example, at $33 per share, $2000 buys only 60 shares, but at $18 per share the investor receives 111 shares. Because more shares are acquired when the price of the stock falls, this has the effect of pulling down the average price of a share. In this example, after two years the average cost of the stock had fallen to $23.85 and the investor had accumulated 671 shares. If the price of the stock rises subsequently, the investor will earn more profits on the lower priced shares and thus will increase the return on the entire position.

AVERAGING DOWN

Purchases after price declines

Some investors find it difficult to purchase stock periodically, especially if the price of the stock has increased. Instead, they prefer to purchase additional shares of the stock only if the price declines. Such investors are following a policy of averaging down. Averaging down is a means by which the investor reduces the cost basis of an investment in a particular security by buying more shares as the price declines so that the average cost of the entire position in the security is reduced. This may be particularly rewarding if the price rises subsequently, because the investor has accumulated shares at decreased prices and earns a gain when the price increases.

There are several methods for averaging down. The investor may "dollar average," which means that the same dollar amount is spent on shares each time a purchase is made. Or the investor may average down by purchasing the same number of shares (i.e., "share average") every time a purchase is made.

Table 13–3 illustrates these averaging down strategies. The price of the stock is given in column 1. Column 2 uses the dollar averaging method; the investor purchases $1000 worth of stock every time the price declines by $5. As is readily seen in column 2, the number of shares in each successive purchase is larger. The last entry in the column gives the total amount that the investor has spent ($5000), the total number of shares that have been purchased (289), and the average cost of the shares ($17.30). The average cost of the total position has declined perceptibly below the $30 price of the initial commitment. However, if the price of the stock were to increase to $30, the entire position would be worth $8470. The investor would have made a profit of $3470 and earned a gain of 69 per cent on the entire position.*

Column 3 illustrates the share averaging methods, which means that the same number of shares are bought every time the investor makes a purchase. When the price declines by $5, the investor buys 100 shares. If the price of the stock were to fall to $10, the investor would have accumulated 500 shares under share averaging, for a total cost of $10,000. If the price of the stock were to return to $30, the entire position would be worth $15,000, and the investor's profit would be $5000, for a gain of 50 per cent.

There is a greater reduction in the average cost of the entire position with dollar averaging than with share averaging. When the investor dollar averages, the amount spent is held constant and the number of shares purchased varies. When the investor share averages, the number of shares purchased is held constant and the dollar amount varies. Because the investor purchases a fixed number of shares with share averaging regardless of how low their price falls, the average cost of a share in the position is not reduced to the extent that it is with dollar averaging.

The preceding discussion and examples explain the essentials of averaging. The investor may choose any number of variations on this basic concept. For example, the investor may choose to average down on declines of any dollar amount in the price of the stock or may select any dollar amount to invest for periodic purchases or for averaging

Average cost of the position is reduced

---

*Of course, the annual rate of return will be different if it takes more or less than a year for this profit to be made.

TABLE 13–3. *Averaging Down Strategies*

PRICE OF THE STOCK	NUMBER OF SHARES PURCHASED ($1000 EACH PURCHASE)	COST OF 100 SHARES
$30	33	$ 3000
25	40	2500
20	50	2000
15	66	1500
10	100	1000
	289 shares	$10,000
	(for a cost of $5000 and an average cost of $17.30 per share)	(500 shares, for a cost of $10,000 and an average cost of $20 per share)

Depressed stocks may remain depressed

down. The effect is the same, i.e., to reduce the average cost basis of the position in that particular security.

The investor, however, should not assume that such a strategy will lead to a positive return on the investments. Stocks that have a downward price trend may not change course, or many years may pass before the price of the security rises to its previous level. The individual should view the funds spent on the initial investment as a fixed or sunk cost that should not influence the decision to buy additional shares. This type of reasoning is difficult to put into practice. Most individuals will not readily admit that they have made a poor investment. Unfortunately, they then follow a program of averaging down in the belief that it will vindicate their initial investment decision.

The investor should reanalyze the firm

The investor should not automatically follow a policy of averaging down. Before additional purchases are made, the stock should be reanalyzed. If the potential of the company has deteriorated (which may be why the price of the stock has fallen), the investor would be wiser to discontinue the policy of averaging down, to sell the stock, and to take a tax loss. If the stock lacks potential, it makes no sense to throw good money (the money used to buy the additional shares) after bad (the money previously invested in the stock). Some questions that the investor should ask are "Does the firm still have potential?" or "Is there a substantive reason for maintaining the current position in the stock?" If the answer is yes, then averaging down and periodic purchase are two means of accumulating shares while reducing their cost basis. Such a strategy reduces the impact of security price fluctuations and may produce greater profits if the price of the stock rises subsequently.

SUMMARY

Security prices fluctuate daily. Several measures have been developed to show these price movements. These include the Dow Jones averages, Standard & Poor's indices of stock prices, and the NYSE index. Although the composition of each measure differs, the indices show the same movements in security prices.

Studies have shown that during a certain period investors in common stock have earned a return in excess of 9 per cent annually. However, the returns earned during the 1970s have been smaller, and the real rate of return is even less when the rate of inflation is considered. These poor results explain in part why investors have sought alternative investments to common stocks.

One strategy designed to reduce the impact of price fluctuations is averaging. The investor either makes periodic purchases or buys additional shares of stock after their price has declined. Such purchases reduce the average cost of the position in the stock and may result in larger gains if the price of the stock rises.

Terms to Remember

Dow Jones industrial
  average
Standard & Poor's 500
  stock index

NYSE index
Semilogarithmic paper

Rate of return
Dollar averaging

Questions

1. What is a value-weighted average? Why does such an average place more emphasis on such firms as General Motors or Exxon than on other companies?

2. How does the Dow Jones industrial average differ from Standard & Poor's 500 stock index and the NYSE index?

3. During the last decade what has happened to the real return (i.e., the return adjusted for price level changes) earned by investors in common stock?

4. Why may averaging rates of return yield an inaccurate measure of the true rate of return?

5. Historically, what rates of return have investors earned on investments in common stocks?

6. What is the advantage of using semilogarithmic paper to construct graphs of security prices?

7. What is averaging down? What is dollar averaging? Why may this strategy result in poor investment decisions?

SELECTED READINGS

Brealey, Richard A.: *An Introduction to Risk and Return From Common Stocks.* Cambridge, Mass., M.I.T. Press, 1969.

Brigham, Eugene F., and James L. Pappas: "Rates of Return on Common Stock." *Journal of Business 42* (July 1969), pp. 302–316.

Fisher, Lawrence, and James H. Lorie: *A Half Century of Returns on Stocks and Bonds.* Chicago, University of Chicago Press, 1977.

Fisher, Lawrence, and James H. Lorie: "Rates of Return on Investments in Common Stock — The Year-by-Year Record, 1926–1965." *The Journal of Business 40*(July 1968), pp. 1–27.

Holmes, John Russel: "100 Years of Common Stock Investing." *Financial Analysts Journal, 30*(November–December 1974), pp. 38–45.

"Is the Market Doing Better Than We Think, or Worse?" *Forbes* (April 3, 1978), pp. 40–41.

Jessup, Paul F., and Roger B. Upson: *Returns in Over-the-Counter Stock Markets.* Minneapolis, University of Minnesota Press, 1973.

Lorie, James H., and Mary T. Hamilton: "Stock Market Indexes," in *Modern Developments in Investment Management.* Lorie, J. H., and Brealey, R. A. (eds.): New York, Praeger Publishers, Inc., 1972.

Schlarbaum, Gary G., Wilbur G. Lewellen, and Ronald C. Lease: "The Common-Stock-Portfolio Performance Record of Individual Investors: 1964–1970." *The Journal of Finance 33*(May 1978), pp. 429–441.

Sharpe, William F., and H. B. Sosin: "Risk, Return and Yield on Common Stocks." *Financial Analysts Journal, 32*(March–April 1976), pp. 33–43.

Learning Objectives

After completing this chapter you should be able to

1. Name the advantages of the corporate form of business.

2. Identify the components of an investor's required rate of return.

3. Examine the determinants of a stock's price.

4. Calculate the value of a stock using a simple present value model.

5. Explain why debt financing may increase a firm's per share earnings.

6. Understand how the use of financial leverage may increase risk.

chapter 14

THE VALUATION OF COMMON STOCK

The valuation of common stock is one of the most important and elusive topics covered in this text. The current value of a share of common stock depends on properly discounting its future earnings and dividends back to the present. This is no different than the valuation of a bond. However, a bond pays a fixed amount of interest and matures at a specified date. Common stock does not pay a fixed dividend nor does it mature. These two facts considerably increase the difficulty of valuing stock.

Common stock is described initially in this chapter, followed by a simple model of common stock valuation in which discounting future dividends and their growth back to the present is emphasized. The chapter ends with a discussion of the use of debt financing to increase a firm's per share earnings. Such increases in earnings, however, may not cause the price of the stock to rise, since the use of debt financing may also increase the element of risk.

THE CORPORATE FORM OF BUSINESS

Establishing a corporation

A corporation is an artificial, legal, economic unit. Every corporation must be established by a state. Since there is great variation in the laws that establish corporations, some states are more popular than others for the formation of corporations. Under state laws, the firm is issued a *certificate of incorporation* that indicates the name of the corporation, the location of its principal office, its purpose, and the number of shares of stock (shares of ownership) that are authorized (i.e., the number of shares that the firm may issue). Stock, then, represents ownership or equity in a corporation. In addition to the certificate of incorporation, the firm receives a *charter* that specifies the relationship between the corporation and the state. At the initial meeting of stockholders, *bylaws* are established that set the rules by which the firm is governed, including such issues as the voting rights of the stockholders.

Stock certificates

The firm issues stock certificates to its owners. These certificates are evidence of ownership in the corporation. An example of a stock certificate is presented in Exhibit 14–1. The face of the certificate identifies the name of the owner, the number of shares, and the bank that serves as the transfer agent. It is the transfer agent that keeps the firm's record of stockholders and transfers the certificates as they are bought and sold.

EXHIBIT 14–1. CBS stock certificate (reproduced with the permission of CBS, Inc.).

THE ADVANTAGES

In the eyes of the law, a corporation is a legal entity that is separate from its owners. It may enter into contracts and is legally responsible for its obligations. This significantly differentiates corporations from sole proprietorships and partnerships. Once a firm is incorporated, the owners of the corporation are liable only for the amount of their investment in the company. This *limited liability* is a major advantage of incorporation. Creditors may sue the corporation for payment if it defaults on its obligations, but the creditors cannot sue the stockholders.

For many small, privately held corporations, limited liability may not exist. Creditors may ask the stockholders to pledge their personal assets to secure loans. If the corporation defaults, the creditors may seize the assets that the shareholders have pledged. In this event, the liability of the shareholders is not limited to their initial investment.

Limited liability does apply to investments in publicly held firms. Therefore, an investor knows that if he or she purchases stock in a company such as General Motors, the maximum amount that can be lost is the amount of the investment. If the firm were to go bankrupt, the creditors could not seize the assets of the stockholders. Such limited liability is a major advantage of investing in publicly held firms.* Occasionally, a large corporation (e.g., Penn Central) does go bankrupt, but owing to the stockholders' limited liability, they cannot be sued by the firm's creditors.

A second advantage of the corporate form of business is the ease with which a title of ownership may be transferred from one investor to another. All that is necessary for such transfer is for the investor to sell the shares of stock, endorse the certificates, and have the name of the new owner(s) recorded on the corporation's record of stockholders. Such transfers occur daily through organized security exchanges, such as the New York Stock Exchange (NYSE). The transfer of ownership may be considerably more difficult for small corporations or corporations that are owned by just a few stockholders. Since there is no ready market in the stock of small, privately held corporations, finding a buyer may be very difficult. Although the ease of transferring ownership is an advantage of incorporating, it does not apply equally to all corporations.

A third advantage of the corporate form of business is permanence. Since the corporation is established by the laws of the state, it is permanent until dissolved by the state. Proprietorships and partnerships cease when one of the owners dies or goes bankrupt. In order to continue to operate, the proprietorship or partnership must be reconstitut-

Limited liability

Ease of transfer of title

Permanence

---

*Investors in proprietorships and many partnerships do not have this privilege. Their assets may be seized (with court approval) to meet the firm's liabilities.

ed. Corporations, however, continue to exist when one of the owners dies. The stock becomes part of the deceased owner's estate and is transferred to the heirs. The company continues to operate independently of the change in ownership.

Disadvantage of incorporation

There is one major disadvantage of incorporating: the double taxation of earnings that are distributed as cash dividends. As was discussed in Chapter 5, corporate profits are taxed. These earnings are taxed again when they are distributed to stockholders as cash dividends. The earnings of proprietorships and partnerships are taxed only once through the individual owner's share of the firm's profits. The disadvantage, the double taxation of distributed corporate earnings, is sufficient to keep many proprietorships and partnerships from incorporating.

THE RIGHTS OF STOCKHOLDERS

Voting rights

Since stock represents ownership in a corporation, investors who purchase it obtain all of the rights of ownership. These rights include the option to vote the shares. The stockholders elect a board of directors that selects the firm's management. Management is then responsible to the board of directors, which, in turn, is responsible to the firm's stockholders. If the stockholders do not think that the board is doing a competent job, they may elect another board to represent them.

For publicly held corporations, such democracy rarely works. Stockholders are usually widely dispersed, while the firm's management and board of directors generally form a cohesive unit. Rarely does the individual investor's vote mean much. However, there is always the possibility that if the firm does poorly, another firm may offer to buy the outstanding stock held by the public. Once such purchases are made, the new owners of the stock may remove the board of directors and establish new management. To some extent this possibility encourages a corporation's board of directors and management to pursue the goal of increasing the value of the firm's stock.

Cumulative voting

A stockholder generally has one vote for each share owned, but there are two ways to distribute this vote. One system, called *cumulative voting*, gives minority stockholders a means to obtain representation on the firm's board of directors.

How cumulative voting works is best explained by an example. Suppose a firm has a board of directors composed of five members. With the traditional *voting*, each share gives the stockholder the right to vote for one individual for each seat on the board. Since the individual share represents one vote for each seat, that totals five votes. Under cumulative voting, the individual may cast one vote for each seat or as many as five votes for one individual running for one seat. (Of course, then the stockholder cannot vote for anyone running for the remaining four seats.)

A minority group of stockholders can use the cumulative method of voting to elect a representative to the firm's board of directors. By banding together and casting all of their votes for a specific candidate, the minority may be able to win a seat. Although this technique cannot be used to win a majority, it does offer the opportunity for representation that is not possible through the traditional method of distributing votes (i.e., one vote for each elected position). As would be expected, management rarely supports the cumulative voting system.

Since stockholders are owners, they are entitled to the firm's earnings. These earnings may be distributed in the form of cash dividends, or they may be retained by the corporation. If they are retained, the individual's investment in the firm is increased (i.e., the stockholder's equity increases). However, for every class of stock, the individual investor's relative position is not altered. Some owners of common stock cannot receive cash dividends, whereas others have their earnings reinvested. For a given class of stock, the distribution or retention of earnings applies equally to all stockholders.*

Earnings are either distributed or retained

This equity in the firm is sometimes referred to as the firm's *book value*. Book value is the difference between the corporation's assets and its liabilities and thus represents the investors' equity. The total equity divided by the number of shares outstanding gives the *per share book value*, which is each share's investment in the firm. As profits are earned and retained, the book value rises. This is another means to express the growing investment in the firm by its stockholders.

Book value

Although the advantages of investing in publicly held corporations include limited liability, stock ownership does involve risk. As long as the firm prospers, it may be able to pay dividends and grow. However, if earnings fluctuate, dividends and growth may also fluctuate. It is the owners — the stockholders — who bear the risk of these fluctuations. If the firm should default on its debt, it can be taken to court by its creditors to enforce its obligations. If the firm should fail or become bankrupt, the stockholders have the last claim on its assets. Only after all of the creditors have been paid will the stockholders receive any funds. In many cases of bankruptcy, this amounts to nothing. Even if the corporation survives bankruptcy proceedings, the amount received by the stockholders is uncertain.

Risk

---

*Some corporations have different classes of stock, which permit some stockholders to receive dividends while other stockholders do not. For example, Winn-Dixie Stores, Inc., has two classes of common stock. The A stock receives cash dividends, but the B stock does not. The B stock may be converted into the A stock, and the number of shares into which it may be converted increases each year. Thus, the value of the B stock should rise more than the value of the A stock in compensation for the owners' forgoing the cash dividend.

PREEMPTIVE RIGHTS

**The right to
maintain
proportionate
ownership**

Some stockholders have preemptive rights, which are their prerogative to maintain their proportionate ownership in the firm. If the firm wants to sell additional shares to the general public, these new shares must be offered initially to the existing stockholders. This sale is called a *rights offering*. If the stockholders wish to maintain their proportionate ownership in the firm, they can exercise their rights by purchasing the new shares. However, if they do not want to take advantage of this offering, they may sell their privilege to whoever wants to purchase the new shares. (The value of a right is discussed in the appendix to chapter 18.)

Preemptive rights may be illustrated by a simple example. If a firm has 1000 shares outstanding and an individual has 100 shares, that individual owns 10 per cent of the firm's stock. If the firm wants to sell 400 new shares and the stockholders have preemptive rights, these new shares must be offered to the existing stockholders before they are sold to the general public. The individual who owns 100 shares would have the right to purchase 40 or 10 per cent of the new shares. If the purchase is made, then that stockholder's relative position is maintained, for the stockholder owns 10 per cent of the firm both before and after the sale of the new stock.

**A decline in the
importance of
preemptive rights**

Although preemptive rights are required in some states for incorporation, their importance has diminished and the number of rights offerings has declined. In 1969 there were 118 public rights offerings, but the number declined to only 20 in 1976. Some firms have tried to have their bylaws changed in order to eliminate preemptive rights. For example, in 1975 AT&T asked its stockholders to relinquish these rights. The rationale for this request was that issuing new shares through rights offerings was more expensive than selling the shares to the general public through an underwriting. Investors who desired to maintain their relative position could still purchase the new shares, and all stockholders would benefit through the cost savings and the flexibility given to the firm's management. Most stockholders accepted the management's request and voted to relinquish their preemptive rights. Now AT&T does not have to offer any new shares to its current stockholders before it offers them publicly.

INVESTORS' REQUIRED
RATE OF RETURN

**Investors anticipate
a total return of
dividends and price
appreciation**

Investors purchase stock with the anticipation of a *total return* consisting of a dividend yield and a capital gain. The dividend yield is the flow of dividend income paid by the stock. The capital gain is the increase in the value of the stock, which is related to the growth in the firm's earnings. If the corporation is consistently able to achieve growth in earnings, then dividends can be increased and the price of the shares will rise. This increase in the value of the shares produces a capital gain for the stockholders.

An investor's required rate of return (*r*) is expressed algebraically in Equation 1.

(1)
$$r = \frac{D}{P} + g$$

The dividend yield is the cash dividend (*D*) divided by the price of the stock (*P*). The growth rate in earnings and dividends is expressed by the symbol *g*. In this form the model assumes that the firm's earnings and dividends are both growing at the same rate. According to this assumption, the firm's dividend policy does not change over time (i.e., the proportion of earnings distributed by the firm remains constant).

Equation 1 is applied in the following example. A firm's earnings are growing annually at the rate of 7 per cent, the common stock is expected to pay a dividend of $1 per share during the year, and the stock is currently selling for $25 per share. Thus, the anticipated return on an investment in this stock consists of a 4 per cent dividend yield and a 7 per cent growth rate.

$$r = \frac{\$1}{\$25} + .07$$
$$r = .11 = 11\%$$

If an individual requires an 11 per cent return on investments in common stock of comparable risk, then this stock is meeting that investor's requirement. If, however, the investor's required rate of return is in excess of 11 per cent, the anticipated yield on this stock is inferior, and the investor will not purchase the shares. Conversely, if the required rate of return on comparable investments in common stock is 10 per cent, this particular stock is an excellent purchase because the anticipated return exceeds the required rate of return.

In a world of no taxes or commission fees, investors should be indifferent to the composition of their return. An investor seeking an 11 per cent return should be willing to accept a dividend yield of zero if the capital gain is 11 per cent. Conversely, a capital growth rate of zero should be acceptable if the dividend yield is 11 per cent. Of course, any combination of growth rate and dividend yield with an 11 per cent return should be acceptable.

Effect of taxes and commissions

Because of taxes, commissions, and risk, however, the investor is concerned with the composition of the return. Since tax rates on long-term capital gains are lower than those on ordinary income (which includes dividend income), the investor may prefer a growth in the value of the shares to dividends. But to realize the growth in the value of the shares, the investor must sell the security and pay commission fees. This cost suggests a preference for dividend yield. In addition, capital gains occur in the future and may be less certain than the flow of current dividends. The uncertainty of future capital gains versus the likelihood of current dividends also favors dividends over capital appreciation.

Investors have different goals

Since each investor's situation and financial goals are different, it is not surprising that the required rate of return for various investors is different. Retired people may prefer a dividend yield for the income it provides. Investors with other sources of income who are in high income tax brackets may prefer growth and capital gains. And any investor who wishes to minimize risk may prefer dividends to capital growth.

Since the required rates of return differ among investors and since the individual's financial needs and goals change, it is not surprising to find investors making changes in their portfolios. It is the role of security markets to bring these buyers and sellers together so that their portfolio changes can be consummated.

VALUATION AS THE PRESENT VALUE OF DIVIDENDS AND THE GROWTH OF EARNINGS

The appropriate discount rate

As with the valuation of debt, the valuation of stock involves bringing its future value back to the present at the appropriate discount factor. For the individual investor, that discount factor is the required rate of return. For the investment to be attractive, the anticipated return must equal or exceed the investor's required rate of return. Thus, the valuation of stock is basically the discounting of future cash flows (i.e., dividends) and the future price of the stock back to the present value at the investor's required rate of return. This present value is then compared with the present price to see if the stock is a good purchase.

Discounting future cash flows

This process is readily illustrated by the simple case in which the stock pays a fixed dividend (D) that is not expected to grow. If the investor's required rate of return is r, then the stock's valuation (V) is

(2)
$$V = \frac{D}{(1 + r)^1} + \frac{D}{(1 + r)^2} + \ldots + \frac{D}{(1 + r)^\infty}$$

which simplifies to

(3)
$$V = \frac{D}{r}$$

If a stock pays a dividend of $1 and the investor's required rate of return is 12 per cent, then the valuation is

$$\frac{\$1}{.12} = \$8.33$$

Any price greater than $8.33 will result in a yield that is less than 12 per cent. Therefore, for this investor to achieve the required rate of return of 12 per cent, the price of the stock must not exceed $8.33.

Valuation with fixed dividends

The student has probably recognized that the preceding valuation is identical to the valuation of perpetual debt and preferred stock presented in Chapter 10. If the common stock's dividend were fixed and expected to be paid indefinitely, then common stock would be the same as preferred stock for the purpose of valuation. Its value would be related only to the dividend and the required rate of return. If the dividend were fixed, the value of the stock would change with fluctuations in the required rate of return (i.e., the rate earned on comparable investments).

However, the dividend for common stock is not fixed. It is the potential for growth, both in value and in dividends, that differentiates common from preferred stock. If the investor expects the dividend to grow at some fixed rate (g) for an indefinite period, the valuation model becomes

The valuation model when dividends grow

$$(4) \qquad V = \frac{D\,(1+g)^1}{(1+r)^1} + \frac{D\,(1+g)^2}{(1+r)^2} + \frac{D\,(1+g)^3}{(1+r)^3} + \ldots + \frac{D\,(1+g)^\infty}{(1+r)^\infty}$$

which simplies to

$$(5) \qquad V = \frac{D\,(1+g)}{r-g}$$

The stock's intrinsic value is thus related to (1) the current dividend, (2) the growth in earnings and dividends, and (3) the required rate of return. The application of this model may be illustrated by a simple example. If the investor's required rate of return is 12 per cent and the stock is currently paying a $1 per share dividend and is growing at 6 per cent annually, its value is

$$V = \frac{\$1\,(1+.06)}{.12 - .06} = \$17.67$$

Any price greater than $17.67 will result in a total yield of less than 12 per cent. Conversely, a price of less than $17.67 will produce a return in excess of 12 per cent. For example, if the price is. $20, according to Equation 1 the return is

Overvaluation

$$r = \frac{\$1\,(1+.06)}{\$20} + .06$$

$$r = 11.3\%$$

Undervaluation   Since this return is less than the 12 per cent required by the investor, it is inferior. Therefore, this investor would not buy the stock and would sell it if he or she owned it.

If the price is $15, the return is

$$r = \frac{\$1\ (1 + .06)}{\$15} + .06$$

$$r = 13.1\%$$

This return is greater than the 12 per cent required by the investor. Since the security offers a superior return, it is undervalued. This investor then would try to buy it.

Only at a price of $17.67 does the stock offer a return of 12 per cent. At that price it equals the rate of return available on alternative investments of the same risk. The investment will yield 12 per cent because the dividend yield during the year is 6 per cent and the earnings and dividends are growing annually at the rate of 6 per cent. These relationships are illustrated in Graph 14–1, which shows the growth in dividends and prices of the stock that will produce a constant yield of 12 per cent. After 12 years the dividend will have grown to $2.02, and the price of the stock will be $35.55. The total return on this investment will still be 12 per cent. During that year the dividend will grow to $2.14, giving a 6 per cent dividend yield, and the price will continue to appreciate annually at the 6 per cent growth rate in earnings and dividends.

The student should note that in Graph 14–1 the lines representing the dividend and the price of the stock are not straight. The earnings and the price of the stock are growing at the same rate, but they are not growing by the same amount each year. This is another illustration of the time value of money, as the earnings, dividends, and prices of the stock are all compounding annually at 6 per cent.

GRAPH 14–1.   Earnings, Dividends, and Price of Stock Over Time Yielding 12 Per Cent Annually

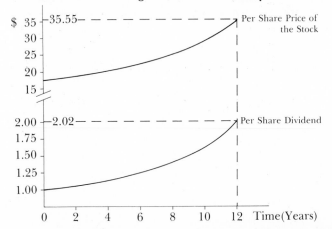

GRAPH 14–2. Earnings Growth Averaging 6 Per Cent Annually

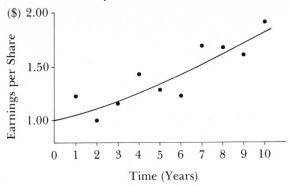

A firm's earnings need not grow steadily at this rate. Graph 14–2 illustrates a case in which the firm's earnings grow annually at an average of 6 per cent, but the year-to-year changes stray considerably from 6 per cent. These fluctuations are not in themselves necessarily reason for concern. The firm does exist within the economic environment, which fluctuates over time. Exogenous factors, such as a strike or an energy curtailment, may also affect earnings during a particular year. If these factors continue to plague the firm, they will obviously play an important role in the valuation of the shares. However, the emphasis in valuation is on the flow of dividends and the growth in earnings over a period of years. This longer time dimension smooths out temporary fluctuations in earnings and dividends.

Earnings may fluctuate

Although the previous model assumes that the firm's earnings will grow indefinitely and that the dividend policy will be maintained, such need not be the case. The model may be modified to encompass a period of increasing or declining growth or one of stable earnings. Many possible variations in growth patterns can be built into the model. Although these variations change the equation and make it appear far more complex, the fundamentals of valuation remain unaltered. Valuation is still the process of discounting future dividends and growth in earnings and dividends back to the present at the appropriate rate of discount.

Modifications in the dividend growth model

To illustrate such a variation, consider the following pattern of earnings and dividends.

Year	Earnings	Yearly Dividends	Change in Earnings and Dividends
1	$1.00	$.40	. . .
2	1.60	.64	60%
3	1.94	.77	21
4	2.20	.87	12
5	2.29	.91	4
6	2.38	.95	4
7	2.47	.98	4

After the initial period of rapid growth, the firm matures and is expected to grow annually at the rate of 4 per cent. Each year the firm pays dividends, which contribute to its current value. However, the simple model summarized in Equation 5 cannot be used because the earnings and dividends are not growing at a constant rate. Equation 4 can be used, and when these values along with a required rate of return of 12 per cent are inserted into the equation, the value of the stock is

$$V = \frac{\$.40}{(1+.12)} + \frac{\$.64}{(1+.12)^2} + \frac{\$.77}{(1+.12)^3} + \frac{\$.87}{(1+.12)^4} + \frac{\$.91}{(1+.12)^5} +$$

$$\frac{\$.95}{(1+.12)^6} + \frac{\$.98}{(1+.12)^7} + \dots$$

$$V = \$9.16$$

This answer is derived by dividing the flow of dividends into two periods: a period of super growth (years 1 through 4) and a period of normal growth (from year 5 on). The present value of the dividends in the first four years is

$$V_{1-4} = \frac{\$.40}{(1+.12)} + \frac{\$.64}{(1+.12)^2} + \frac{\$.77}{(1+.12)^3} + \frac{\$.87}{(1+.12)^4}$$

$$= \$.36 + \$.51 + \$.55 + \$.55$$
$$+ \$1.97$$

The dividend growth model is applied to the dividends from year 5 on:

$$V_{5-\infty} = \frac{\$.87(1+.04)}{.12-.04} = \$11.31$$

This $11.31 is the value at the end of year 4, so it must be discounted back to the present:

$$\frac{\$11.31}{(1+.12)^4} = \$11.31\,(.6355) = \$7.19$$

The total value of the stock, then, is the sum of the two parts:

$$\begin{array}{r} \$1.97 \\ + 7.19 \\ \hline \$9.16 \end{array}$$

Assumptions concerning risk

As this example illustrates, modifications can be made in this valuation model to account for the different periods of growth and dividends. Adjustments can also be made for differences in risk. The student should realize that the model does not by itself adjust for different degrees of risk. If a security analyst applies the model to several firms in one industry, e.g., utilities, to determine which stocks are underpriced, there is the implication that investing in all of the firms involves equal risk. If the analyst uses the same required rate of return for each firm, then no risk adjustment has been made. The element of risk is assumed to be the same for each company.

In addition to assuming that risk is the same for all securities, the dividend-growth model summarized in Equation 5 assumes that the firm does not use financial leverage. Many firms, however, do use debt financing to increase their earnings and growth. How financial leverage increases the per share earnings is explained in the next section.

Assumptions concerning financial leverage

THE IMPACT OF FINANCIAL LEVERAGE ON EARNINGS

Financial leverage is the use of another person's money in return for a fixed payment. If a firm borrows funds, it issues debt and must make a fixed interest payment for the use of the money. A company may also obtain financial leverage by paying a fixed dividend on stock. This type of stock is given preference or prior claim on the earnings of the company (i.e., it is preferred stock). Since preferred stock has a fixed dividend, it is similar to debt and is a source of financial leverage.

The use of debt financing

A firm agrees to make fixed interest and dividend payments because it *anticipates* being able to earn more with the borrowed funds than it has to pay. This will increase the return on the common stockholders' investment. The creditors are willing to lend the money in return for the fixed payments. The creditors receive a relatively assured flow of income from the loans but do not bear the risk of owning and operating the business. If the creditors had the skills and desired to do so, they would enter the business themselves. There are, however, many people who lack either the skills or the desire to enter a particular business and are satisfied to let a corporation use their money for the promised fixed return. They are, of course, aware that the firm anticipates earning more with their money than it has agreed to pay.

Management wants to increase the value of the firm's stock. Since the use of financial leverage may increase the return to the common stockholders, management may decide to use financial leverage. Its use, however, may also increase the level of risk. Thus, management must try to determine the optimal amount of financial leverage, for the use of insufficient leverage will decrease the stockholders' return but the use of excessive leverage will subject the stockholders to excessive risk.

Management wants to increase the value of the stock

HOW FINANCIAL LEVERAGE INCREASES THE RATE OF RETURN ON EQUITY

How financial leverage works may be shown by a simple illustration. Firm A needs $100 in capital to operate and may acquire the

The firm with leverage

money from the stockholders (owners) of the firm. Alternatively, it may acquire part of the money from stockholders and part from creditors. If management acquires the total amount from the owners, the firm uses no debt financing (financial leverage) and would have the following simple balance sheet.

ASSETS	LIABILITIES AND EQUITY
Cash $100	Debt $0
	Equity $100

Once in business, the firm generates the following simplified income statement:

Sales	$100
Expenses	−80
Gross profit	$ 20
Taxes (40%)	− 8
Net profit	$ 12

What is the return that the firm has earned on the owners' investment? The answer is 12 per cent, for the investors contributed $100 and the firm earned $12 after taxes. The firm may pay the $12 to the investors in cash dividends or may retain the money to help finance future growth. Either way, however, the stockholders' rate of return on their investment is 12 per cent.

The firm without leverage

By the use of financial leverage, management may be able to increase the owners' rate of return on their investment. What happens to their rate of return if management is able to borrow part of the capital needed to operate the firm? The answer to this question depends upon (1) the proportion of total capital that is borrowed and (2) the interest rate that must be paid to the creditors. If management is able to borrow 50 per cent ($50) of the firm's capital needs at an interest cost of 6 per cent, the balance becomes

ASSETS	LIABILITIES AND EQUITY
Cash $100	Debt $50
	Equity $50

Since the firm borrowed $50, it is now obligated to pay interest. Thus, the firm has a new expense that must be paid before any earnings are available for the common stockholders. The simple income statement becomes

Sales	$100.00
Expenses	− 80.00
Gross profit	$ 20.00
Interest expense	− 3.00
Taxable income	$ 17.00
Taxes	− 6.80
Net Profit	$ 10.20

The use of debt causes the total net profit to decline from $12 to $10.20, but the owners' rate of return increases from 12 per cent to 20.4 per cent. Since the owners invested only $50 and earned $10.20 on that amount, they made 20.4 per cent on their investment, whereas without the use of leverage they earned only 12 per cent on their $100 investment.

There are two sources of this additional return. First, the firm borrowed money and agreed to pay a fixed return of 6 per cent. The firm, however, was able to earn more than 6 per cent with the money, and this additional earning accrued to the owners of the firm. Second, the entire burden of the interest cost was not borne by the firm. The federal tax laws permit the deduction of interest as an expense before taxable income is determined, and thus this interest expense is shared with the government. The greater the corporate income tax rate, the greater is the portion of interest expense borne by the government. In this case 40 per cent, or $1.20 of the $3.00 interest expense, was borne by the federal government in lost tax revenues. If the corporate income tax rate were 60 per cent, the government would lose $1.80 in taxes by permitting the deduction of the interest expense.

The impact of taxes

As was seen in the preceding example, a firm's management may increase the owners' rate of return through the use of debt financing, i.e., the use of financial leverage. By increasing the proportion of the firm's assets that are financed by debt (by increasing the debt ratio), management is able to increase the rate of return on the owners' equity. Table 14–1 shows various combinations of debt and equity financing along with the resultant earnings for the firm and the rate of return on the investors' equity. The table is constructed on the assumption that the interest rate is 6 per cent regardless of the proportion of the firm's assets financed by debt. As may be seen from Table 14–1, as the proportion of debt financing rises, the rate of return on the owners' equity not only rises but does so at an increasing rate. This indicates dramatically how the use of financial leverage may significantly increase the rate of return on a firm's equity.

FINANCIAL LEVERAGE AND RISK

Since the use of financial leverage increases the owners' rate of return, why not use ever-increasing amounts of debt financing? The answer is that as the proportion of financial leverage rises, the element of risk increases. This amplication of risk increases (1) the potential for fluctuations in the owners' returns and (2) the interest rate that the creditors charge for the use of their money.

The use of financial leverage increases risk

How the use of financial leverage increases the potential risk to the owners is illustrated by employing the simple example presented in the

TABLE 14–1. *Relationship Between Debt Financing and the Rate of Return on Equity*

Proportion of assets financed by debt (%)	0	20	50	70	90
Amount of debt outstanding ($)	0	20	50	70	90
Equity ($)	100	80	50	30	10
Sales ($)	100	100	100	100	100
Expense ($)	−80	−80	−80	−80	−80
Gross profit ($)	20	20	20	20	20
Interest expense ($) (6% interest rate)	0	1.20	3.00	4.20	5.40
Taxable income ($)	20	18.80	17.00	15.80	14.60
Income tax ($) (40% tax rate)	−8	−7.52	−6.80	−6.32	−5.84
Net profit ($)	12	11.28	10.20	9.48	8.76
Rate of return on equity (%)	12	14.1	20.4	31.6	87.6

previous section. What happens to the rate of return on the equity if sales decline by 10 per cent from $100 to $90, but expenses remain the same? The income statements for a firm with and a firm without financial leverage become

	Firm Without Leverage (0% Debt)	Firm With Leverage (50% Debt)
Sales	$90.00	$90.00
Expenses	−80.00	−80.00
Gross profit	$10.00	$10.00
Interest	− 0	− 3.00
Taxable Income	$10.00	$ 7.00
Taxes	− 4.00	− 2.80
Net profit	$ 6.00	$ 4.20

Earnings may decline more rapidly

The 10 per cent decline in sales produces a substantial decline in the earnings and the rate of return on the owners' investment in both cases. For the firm without debt financing the rate of return declines to 6 per cent ($6 ÷ $100); for the firm with financial leverage the rate of return plummets from the 20.4 per cent in the previous example to 8.4 per cent. The decline is greater when financial leverage is used than when it is not.

The return decreased more for the firm with financial leverage because of the interest payment. When the firm borrowed the capital, it agreed to make a *fixed* interest payment. This fixed interest payment was the source of the increase in the owners' rate of return in the second example when sales were $100 and is the cause of the larger decline in the owners' rate of return when the firm's sales declined from $100 to $90. If the firm had used leverage to a greater extent (i.e., if it had borrowed more), the decline in the rate of return on the owners' investment would have been even greater. As the proportion of a firm's assets that are financed by fixed obligations increases, the potential fluctuation in the owners' rate of return also increases. Small changes in revenue or costs will produce greater fluctuations in the earnings of a firm with a considerable amount of financial leverage.

Firms that use large amounts of financial leverage are viewed by investors (both creditors and stockholders) as being risky. Creditors may refuse to lend to a firm that uses debt financing extensively, or they may do so only at higher rates of interest or under more stringent loan conditions. Equity investors will also require a higher rate of return to justify bearing the risk. As is explained in the next section, this increase in the required rate of return may result in a decline in the value of the stock.

An increase in risk may cause the price of the stock to fall

FINANCIAL LEVERAGE AND VALUATION

Since financial leverage may increase earnings, investors may be willing to pay more for the stock. For example, for a particular required rate of return on an investment, an increase in earnings from $1 to $1.20 per share should increase the value of the stock. Because the investor desires a set return and the firm earns more, the investor should be willing to pay more for the stock.

This concept can be illustrated by the use of Equation 5. If the firm earns $1 before using financial leverage, distributes $.60, and retains the remaining $.40 so that it can grow, the value of the stock is

$$P = \frac{\$.60}{.12 - .05}$$

$$P = \$8.57$$

when the required rate of return is 12 per cent and the firm is able to grow annually at the rate of 5 per cent.

If the firm now uses financial leverage successfully to increase earnings, it can increase its dividend without reducing its ability to grow, or it can increase its growth rate without decreasing its cash dividend. If the firm's earnings rise to $1.20 and the additional $.20 is distributed as cash dividends (i.e., cash dividends rise to $.80), the value of the stock is

$$P = \frac{\$.80}{.12 - .05}$$

$$P = \$11.43$$

**The potential
impact on the
required rate of
return**

Thus, the successful use of financial leverage results in an increase in
the value of the stock.

The use of financial leverage, however, may increase the element of
risk. Therefore, to induce investors to bear this additional risk, the return must be larger. The required return, then, is increased as a result
of the additional risk, which is attributable to the use of an increased
amount of financial leverage.

The potential impact of this increase in the required rate of return
may be illustrated by the preceding example. The cash dividends have
increased to $.80 as a result of the use of financial leverage, and the
required rate of return has increased from 12 per cent to 14 per cent. In
this case the value of the stock becomes

$$P = \frac{\$.80}{.14 - .05}$$

$$P = \$8.89$$

Although the value of the stock does rise (from $8.57 to $8.89), the
amount of the increase is small. The increase in the required rate of
return that occurred when the firm used more financial leverage almost
completely offset the increase in value from the higher earnings and
cash dividends.

The use of financial leverage may not result in an increase in the
value of stock. Although it may result in higher earnings, it may also
cause investors' required rate of return to rise. This increase in the required rate of return will certainly offset part, if not all, of the effect of
the increase in earnings. It is even possible that the value of the stock
will decline if the required rate of return increases sufficiently.

**Management should
strive for the
optimal
combination of debt
and equity
financing**

Management, then, must be concerned with the extent to which the
firm uses debt financing. The goal of management is to maximize the
value of the shares, but the extensive use of financial leverage may have
the opposite effect and cause the value of the firm's stock to decline.
Therefore, management must determine that combination of debt and
equity financing that offers the benefits of financial leverage without
unduly increasing the element of risk. Such a capital structure should
help to maximize the value of the firm's stock.

DIFFERENCES IN THE
AMOUNT OF FINANCIAL
LEVERAGE USED BY FIRMS

**Some industries
inherently use a
substantial amount
of financial leverage**

Although virtually every firm uses financial leverage, there are differences in the degree to which it is used. For some firms, the nature of
the business enterprise necessitates the extensive use of financial leverage, and this influences the behavior of the firms in the industry. For

TABLE 14–2. *Earnings per Share (EPS) and Usage of Debt Financing by Selected Airlines**

YEAR	AMERICAN AIRLINES		EASTERN AIRLINES		TWA	
	EPS†	Debt as a Proportion of Total Assets	EPS†	Debt as a Proportion of Total Assets	EPS†	Debt as a Proportion of Total Assets
1977	$2.54	61.2%	$1.73	69.1%	$3.83	67.5%
1976	1.97	64.3	2.32	77.1	2.51	80.1
1975	(.78)	73.3	(2.65)	79.5	(6.68)	81.8
1974	.72	61.3	.37	70.0	(2.01)	77.9
1973	(1.69)	62.4	(2.73)	68.5	3.25	75.6
1972	.20	64.1	1.02	76.3	3.01	75.6
1971	.13	61.7	.32	75.2	.11	74.4
1970	(1.30)	64.5	.39	77.2	(6.39)	77.7

*Source: *Standard & Poor's Corporation Records* and annual reports.
†The numbers in parentheses represent a loss.

example, commercial banks use a large amount of financial leverage because most of their assets are financed by their deposit liabilities. Slight changes in the revenues of a commercial bank may produce greater fluctuations in the earnings. Bankers are well aware of this effect of financial leverage and are usually not willing to take inordinate risks. The nature of a bank's operations and the high degree of financial leverage require that bankers be conservative.

Other firms need large amounts of fixed equipment to operate and may use leverage extensively if this equipment is financed through the issuance of debt. The airlines are an excellent example of an industry that has a large investment in equipment that is frequently financed by debt. This high degree of financial leverage explains, in part, the large fluctuations in the earnings of airline companies. Table 14–2 presents the earnings per share (EPS) for selected airlines and the proportion of their assets financed by debt. The information in this table indicates that there have been large and sudden fluctuations in the earnings per share of these airlines. Although these fluctuations are the result of changes in the demand for and in the cost to provide the service, they are magnified by the use of debt financing. For example, TWA finances three fourths of its assets with debt and has experienced severe fluctuations in earnings that have ranged from a loss of over $6.60 per share in 1975 to profits of $2.51 in 1976.

Management may choose to use a substantial amount of financial leverage

SUMMARY

A corporation is created by a state. Ownership in the corporation is represented by stock. Stock certificates may be readily transferred from one individual to another. In addition, investors in publicly held corporations have limited liability.

Investors in common stock anticipate a return in the form of cash dividends or capital appreciation. Capital gains taxation laws favor price appreciation over dividends.

A simple model of stock valuation suggests that this value depends upon the firm's earnings, its dividend policy, and the investors' required rate of return. According to this model, future earnings and dividends should be discounted back to the present in order to determine a stock's value. The emphasis is placed on future earnings and dividends. Since these are not known with certainty, application of the model may be difficult.

A firm may increase the return earned by its owners through the successful use of financial leverage. By borrowing funds and agreeing to pay a fixed rate of interest, the firm may be able to earn more on the funds than it must pay for them. The difference, then, accrues to the firm's owners. Although the use of debt financing may increase the return on the owners' investment in the firm, it may also increase risk. This increase in risk may offset the increment in earnings so the value of the stock is not enhanced.

Terms to Remember

Bylaws	Total return	Required rate of return
Charter	Dividend-growth	Financial leverage
Preemptive rights	model	

Questions

1. What does it mean to say that investors who buy stock in such firms as IBM have limited liability?

2. What are preemptive rights?

3. What are the sources of return to an investor in stock? How do taxes on income and capital gains affect the total return?

4. What variables affect a stock's price according to the constant growth model? What role do past earnings play in this model?

5. What is financial leverage? Why may it increase a firm's per share earnings?

6. Why may the use of financial leverage increase the element of risk?

7. Higher earnings per share may be obtained through the successful use of financial leverage. Why do the increased earnings not necessarily result in a higher stock price?

Problems

1. Given the following data, what should the price of the stock be

required rate of return	10%
present dividend	$1
growth rate	5%

   a. If the growth rate increases to 6 per cent and the dividend remains $1, what should the stock's price be?

   b. If the required rate of return declines to 9 per cent and the dividend remains $1, what should the price of the stock be? If the stock is selling for $20, what does that imply?

2. If an investor requires a rate of return of 12 per cent and a stock sells for $25, pays a dividend of $1, and the earnings compound annually at 7 per cent, will this investor find the stock attractive? What is the maximum amount that this investor should pay for the stock?

3. A firm's stock earns $2 per share, and the firm distributes 40 per cent of its earnings as cash dividends. Its earnings grow annually at 7 per cent. What is the stock's price if the required rate of return is 10 per cent?

   a. The aforementioned firm borrows funds and, as a result, its earnings and dividends increase by 20 per cent. What happens to the stock's price if the growth rate and the required rate of return are unaffected? What will the stock's price be if after using financial leverage and increasing the dividend to $1, the required rate of return rises to 12 per cent? What may cause this required rate of return to rise?

SELECTED READINGS

Brigham, Eugene F., and James L. Pappas: "Duration of Growth, Changes in Growth Rates, and Corporate Share Prices." *Financial Analysts Journal* (May–June 1966), pp. 157–162.

Durand, David: "Growth Stocks and the Petersburg Paradox." *The Journal of Finance* 12 (September 1957), pp. 348–363.

Gordon, Myron: *The Investment, Financing, and Valuation of the Corporation.* Homewood, Ill., Richard D. Irwin, Inc., 1962.

Wendt, Paul F.: "Current Growth Stock Valuation Methods: General Motors — An Illustration." *Financial Analysts Journal* (March–April 1965), pp. 91–101.

Learning Objectives

After completing this chapter you should be able to

1. List the important dates for dividend payments.

2. Explain why changes in dividends generally follow changes in earnings.

3. Determine the impact of stock dividends and stock splits on the earning capacity of the firm.

4. Explain the effect of stock splits and stock dividends on the price of a stock.

5. Identify the advantages of dividend reinvestment plans.

6. Analyze the tax implications of stock repurchases and liquidations.

chapter 15

THE ROLE OF DIVIDENDS

After a corporation has earned profits, it must decide what to do with the funds: They may be either retained or distributed as cash dividends. If the firm retains its earnings, it will put the funds to work by investing in income-earning assets or by retiring debt. Such retained earnings should result in higher earnings and dividends in the future. The retention of earnings also increases the stockholders' equity in the firm and causes the degree of financial leverage to fall (unless the firm simultaneously increases its borrowings). This decrease in the use of financial leverage may be desirable, for it may reduce the risk associated with the firm and result in a rise in the price of the firm's stock.

This chapter is concerned with dividends. Initially the various forms of dividends, which range from the regular quarterly cash dividends to irregular and stock dividends, are described. Then follows a discussion of dividend reinvestment plans, which permit investors to have their cash dividends reinvested in the firm's stock. Earnings retention and growth are then considered along with the impact of taxes on income and capital gains. The chapter concludes with a discussion of the repurchase of stock and partial liquidations as an alternative to cash dividends.

CASH DIVIDENDS

THE VARIETY OF CASH DIVIDENDS

A dividend policy

Many companies pay cash dividends and have a dividend policy that is known to the investment community. Even if the policy is not explicitly stated by management, the continuation of such practices as paying a quarterly cash dividend implies a specific policy.

Quarterly cash distributions

Most American companies that distribute cash dividends pay a regular dividend on a quarterly basis. A few companies make monthly distributions (e.g., Winn-Dixie Stores and Wrigley), and some make the distribution semiannually or annually. Frequently in the case of semiannual and annual payments, the dollar amount is small. Instead of paying $.025 per share quarterly, the company pays $.10 per share annually, which reduces the expense of distributing the dividend.

Extras

Although most companies with cash dividend policies pay regular quarterly dividends, there are other types of dividend policies. Some companies pay quarterly dividends plus an additional sum (extras). General Motors pays a quarterly dividend but distributes extras twice a year if the company has had a profitable year. Such a policy is appropriate for a firm in a cyclical industry because earnings fluctuate over time and the firm may be hard pressed to maintain a higher level of regular quarterly dividends. By having a set cash payment that is supplemented with extras in good years, the firm is able not only to maintain a fixed payment that is relatively assured but also to supplement the cash dividend when the extra is warranted by the earnings.

The payout ratio

Management may view the dividend policy as the distribution of a certain proportion of the firm's earnings. The ratio of dividends to earnings is the payout ratio, which is the proportion of the earnings that the firm is distributing. For some firms this ratio has remained rather stable for a period, indicating that management views the best dividend policy in terms of a particular payout ratio.

Irregular dividends

Other firms pay cash dividends that are irregular: There is no set dividend payment. For example, real estate investment trusts (frequently referred to as REITs) are required by law to distribute their earnings to maintain their favorable tax status. These trusts pay no corporate income tax; instead, their earnings are distributed and the stockholders pay the tax. To ensure this favorable tax treatment, REITs must distribute at least 90 per cent of their earnings. Since the earnings of such trusts fluctuate, the cash dividends also fluctuate. The special tax laws pertaining to REITs cause them to have irregular dividend payments.

While American firms tend to follow a policy of quarterly dividend distributions, firms in other countries do not. Instead, dividend payments are irregular. Even when the cash payments occur at regular intervals, the dollar amount tends to vary. Of course, part of this variation is the result of fluctuations in the dollar value of each currency. Hence, if the value of

EXHIBIT 15–1. Sample Dividend Payments in 1977*

Company	Quarter				Indicated Annual Rate
	1	2	3	4	
	Regular Dividend Payments				
AT&T	$.95	$1.05	$1.05	$1.05	$4.20
	Irregular Dividend Payments				
General Motors	.85	1.85	.85	3.25	4.00
Realty Refund	.56	.60	.59	.55	. . .

*Source: Standard & Poor's stock reports, April 1978.

the dollar falls relative to the German mark, then any dividends that are distributed in marks translate into more dollars when the marks are converted. The converse is also true. If the dollar value of the mark should fall, then the dividend buys fewer dollars when the currency is converted. Americans seeking predictable flows of dividend income are usually advised to purchase American stocks and to avoid foreign securities.

The various dividend policies are illustrated in Exhibit 15–1. The top of the exhibit presents the regular dividend payments of AT&T. The bottom section illustrates the irregular payments distributed by General Motors and Realty Refund, which is a REIT. The exhibit is constructed to show quarterly payments and the indicated annual payments. The indicated annual rate need not equal the sum of previous payments if the dividend amount has been changed. Thus, total dividends for AT&T in 1977 were $4.10, while the anticipated annual rate was $4.20 ($1.05 quarterly). However, General Motors paid $6.80 in 1977, but the anticipated annual rate was only $4.00 ($1.00 per quarter). Realty Refund's dividend varied each quarter, and there was no indicated annual rate. However, if the 1977 dividends are maintained, the total should be almost $2.20 (or $.55 per quarter).*

EARNINGS, GROWTH, AND DIVIDEND INCREMENTS

As the earnings of a company grow, it is able to increase its cash dividend. Managements, however, may be reluctant to increase the cash dividend immediately when earnings increase. They want to be certain that the higher level of earnings will be maintained. Therefore, dividend increments tend to lag behind increases in earnings. This pattern is illustrated in Graph 15–1, which presents the quarterly per share earnings and the quarterly cash dividends that were paid by Emhart from 1974

A lag in dividends

---

*Past dividends may not be indicative of future dividends, as Realty Refund's dividend declined to $1.91 in 1978.

GRAPH 15–1. Earnings per Share and Cash Dividends of Emhart from 1974 to 1978

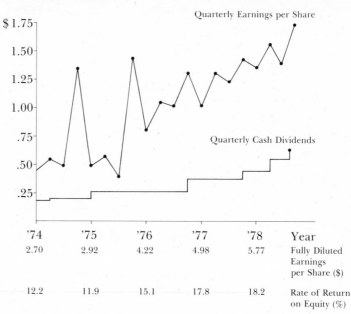

Year	'74	'75	'76	'77	'78	
	2.70	2.92	4.22	4.98	5.77	Fully Diluted Earnings per Share ($)
	12.2	11.9	15.1	17.8	18.2	Rate of Return on Equity (%)

A reluctance to cut dividends

through 1978. Although there is a consistent pattern of increased quarterly earnings, the dividend rises only intermittently.

The cause of this lag in dividend increments is management's reluctance to reduce dividends if earnings decline. Thus, the large year-end earnings that Emhart reported in 1974 and 1975 did not lead to dividend increments, but the subsequent declines in earnings did not result in dividend cuts. Instead, a pattern of growing earnings over many quarters leads to dividend increments.

Dividend reductions may be interpreted as a sign of financial weakness. However, a decrease in earnings may not mean the firm's capacity to pay cash dividends is reduced. For example, an increased depreciation expense may result in lower earnings but a higher cash flow, which maintains the firm's capacity to pay the dividend.*

The dividend policy is often stated

Most companies announce their dividend policy. Many areas of a firm's operation are unknown to investors and perhaps would not be understood even if they were known. The dividend policy is readily understood and may be a deciding factor in purchasing stock in the firm. Some stockholders need income from their investments and prefer stocks that pay generous cash dividends. These investors will purchase the stock of companies that distribute a large proportion of their earnings in divi-

---

*At least one empirical study has shown that dividends are more highly correlated with cash flow (i.e., earnings plus depreciation) than with earnings. See John A. Brittain, *Corporate Dividend Policy*, Washington, D.C., The Brookings Institute, 1966, pp. 10–12.

dends. Other investors prefer capital gains and purchase the stock of companies that retain their earnings to finance future growth. Because investors need to know the dividend policy, it is advisable that firms make this knowledge public, and most companies do so.

THE DISTRIBUTION OF DIVIDENDS

The process by which dividends are distributed is time-consuming. The first step is the meeting of the firm's directors. If they declare a dividend, two important dates are established. The first date determines who is to receive the dividend. On a particular day, the *date of record*, the ownership books of the corporation are closed, and everyone who owns stock in the company at the end of that day receives the dividend.

The time dimension of dividend payments

If the stock is purchased after the date of record, the purchaser does not receive the dividend. The stock is traded *ex dividend,* for the price of the stock does not include the dividend payment. This *ex dividend day* is four trading days prior to the date of record, because the settlement date for a stock purchase is five working days after the transaction.

The ex dividend day

In the financial press, transactions in the stock on the ex dividend day are indicated by an X before the volume of transactions. The following entry, derived from *The Wall Street Journal,* indicates the stock of CBS traded on that day exclusive of the dividend.

CBS   2.40   X131 $61\frac{3}{4}$ $61\frac{1}{8}$ $61\frac{1}{2}$ $+$ $\frac{1}{4}$

The $.60 (i.e., $2.40 ÷ 4) quarterly dividend will be paid to whomever bought the stock on the previous day and will not be paid investors who purchased the stock on the ex dividend day.

The investor should realize that buying or selling stock on the ex dividend date will not result in a windfall gain or a substantial loss. Generally, the price of the stock falls by the amount of the dividend. If a stock that pays a $.60 dividend is worth $62 on the day before it goes ex dividend, it cannot be worth $62 on the ex dividend date. If it were worth $62 on both days, investors would purchase the stock for $62 the day before the ex dividend day, sell it for $62 on the ex dividend day, and collect the $.60 dividend. If investors could do this, the price would exceed $62 on the day preceding the ex dividend date and would be less than $62 on the ex dividend date. In effect, this price pattern does occur because this stock would sell for $62 and then be worth $62 minus $.60 on the ex dividend date.

The price adjusts for the dividend

This price change is illustrated in the previous example from *The Wall Street Journal.* There was a net change of 1/4 point in the price of CBS stock for the ex dividend day. This indicates that the closing price on the previous day was $61⅞ and not $61¼ as might be expected from the increase of ¼ point for the day. Since the current buyers will not receive the $.60 dividend, the net change in the price of the stock is reduced for the dividend. The net change is figured from the adjusted price (i.e., 61⅞ minus the $.60 dividend).

The distributiion date

The second important date established when a dividend is declared is the day on which the dividend is paid, or the *distribution date*. The distribution date may be several weeks after the date of record, as the company must determine who the owners were as of the date of record and process the dividend checks. The company may not perform this task itself; instead, it may use the services of its commercial bank, for which the bank charges a fee. The day that the dividend is received by the stockholder is thus likely to be many weeks after the board of directors announces the dividend payment.

Many firms try to maintain consistency in their dividend payment dates. For example, AT&T makes payments on the first business day of January, April, July, and October. Public Service Electric & Gas pays its dividends on the last day of March, June, September, and December. Such consistency in payments is beneficial to investors and the firm, as both can plan for this receipt and disbursement.

STOCK DIVIDENDS

Some firms make a practice of paying stock dividends in addition to or in lieu of cash dividends. Stock dividends are a form of *recapitalization* and do *not* affect the assets or liabilities of the firm. Since the assets and their management produce income for the firm, a stock dividend does not by itself increase the potential earning power of the company. Some investors, however, may believe that stock dividends will enhance the earning capacity of the firm and consequently the value of the stock. They mistakenly believe that the stock dividend increases the firm's assets.

The following balance sheet demonstrates the transactions that occur when a firm issues a stock dividend:

ASSETS		LIABILITIES AND EQUITY	
Total assets	$10,000,000	Total liabilities	$2,500,000
		Equity: $2 par common stock (2,000,000 shares authorized; 1,000,000 outstanding)	2,000,000
		Additional paid-in capital	500,000
		Retained earnings	5,000,000

Since a stock dividend is only a recapitalization, the assets and the liabilities are not affected by the declaration and payment of the stock dividend. However, the entries in the equity section of the balance sheet are affected. The stock dividend transfers amounts from retained earnings to common stock and additional paid-in capital. The amount transferred depends on (1) the number of new shares issued through the stock dividend and (2) the market price of the stock.

Assets and liabilities are not affected

If the company in the preceding example issued a 10 per cent stock dividend when the price of the common stock was $20 per share, 100,000 shares would be issued with a market value of $2,000,000. This amount is subtracted from retained earnings and transferred to common stock and additional paid-in capital. The amount transferred to common stock will be 100,000 times the par value of the stock ($2 × 100,000 = $200,000). The remaining amount ($1,800,000) is transferred to additional paid-in capital. The balance sheet then becomes

ASSETS		LIABILITIES AND EQUITY	
Total assets	$10,000,000	Total liabilities	$2,500,000
		Equity: $2 par	2,200,000
		common stock	
		(2,000,000 shares	
		authorized; 1,100,000	
		outstanding)	
		Additional paid-in	
		capital	2,300,000
		Retained earnings	3,000,000

The student should note that no funds (or money) have been transferred. While there has been an increase in the number of shares outstanding, there has been no increase in cash and no increase in assets that may be used to earn profits. All that has happened is a recapitalization: The equity entries have been altered.

The number of shares is increased

The major misconception concerning the stock dividend is that it increases the ability of the firm to grow. If the stock dividend is a substitute for a cash dividend, then this belief may be partially true because the firm still has the asset cash that would have been paid to stockholders if a cash dividend had been declared. The firm, however, will still have the cash even if it does not pay the stock dividend because a firm may retain its earnings. Hence, the decision to pay the stock dividend does not increase the amount of cash; it is the decision *not to pay* the cash dividend that conserves the money. When a stock dividend is paid in lieu of cash, it may even be interpreted as a screen: The stock dividend is hiding the firm's reluctance to pay cash dividends.

A firm's earning capacity is not increased

Although the stock dividend does not increase the wealth of the stockholder, it does increase the number of shares owned. In the previous example, a stockholder who owned 100 shares before the stock dividend

The wealth of the stockholder is not increased

had $2000 worth of stock. After the stock dividend is distributed, this stockholder owns 110 shares that are also worth $2,000, for the price of the stock falls from $20 to $18.18. The price of the stock declines because there are 10 per cent more shares outstanding, but there has been no increase in the firm's assets and earning power. The old shares have been *diluted*, and hence the price of the stock must decline to indicate this dilution.

If the price of the stock did not fall to adjust for the stock dividend, all companies could make their stockholders wealthier by declaring stock dividends. However, because the stock dividend does not increase the assets or earning power of the firm, investors are not willing to pay the former price for a larger number of shares; hence, the market price must fall to adjust for the dilution of the old shares.

Disadvantages of stock dividends

There are some significant disadvantages associated with stock dividends. The primary disadvantage is the expense. The costs associated with these dividends include the expense of issuing new certificates, payments for any fractional shares, any taxes or listing fees on the new shares, and the revision of the firm's record of stockholders. These costs are indirectly borne by the stockholders. There are also costs that fall directly on the stockholders, including increased transfer fees and commissions (if the new securities are sold), additional odd lot differentials, and the cost of storage.*

Perhaps the primary advantage of the stock dividend is that it brings to the current stockholders' attention the fact that the firm is retaining its cash in order to grow. The stockholders may subsequently be rewarded through the firm's retention of assets and its increased earning capacity. By retaining its assets, the firm may be able to earn more than the stockholders could if the funds were distributed. This should increase the price of the stock in the future. However, this same result may be achieved without the expenses associated with the stock dividend.

THE STOCK SPLIT

After the price of a stock has risen substantially, management may decide to split the stock. The rationale for the split is that it lowers the price of the stock and makes it more accessible to investors. Implicit in this reasoning are the beliefs that investors prefer lower priced shares and that reducing the price of the stock benefits the current stockholders by widening the market for their stock.

Like the stock dividend, the stock split is a recapitalization. It does not affect the assets or liabilities of the firm, nor does it increase its earning power. The wealth of the stockholder is increased only if investors prefer lower priced stocks, which will increase the demand for this stock.

---

*See Stephen H. Sosnick, "Stock Dividends Are Lemons, Not Melons," *California Management Review*, III (Winter 1961), pp. 61–70.

The balance sheet used previously for illustrating the stock dividend may also be used to illustrate a two-for-one stock split. In a two-for-one stock split, one old share becomes two new shares, and the par value of the old stock is halved. There are no changes in the additional paid-in capital or retained earnings. The new balance sheet becomes

ASSETS		LIABILITIES AND EQUITY	
Total assets	$10,000,000	Total liabilities	$2,500,000
		Equity: $1 par common stock (2,000,000 shares authorized; 2,000,000 shares outstanding)	$2,000,000
		Additional paid-in capital	500,000
		Retained earnings	5,000,000

There are now twice as many shares outstanding, and each new share is worth half as much as one old share. If the stock had sold for $80 before the split, each share becomes worth $40. The stockholder with 100 old shares worth $8000 now owns 200 shares worth $8000 (i.e., $40 × 200).

No change in assets or liabilities

An easy way to find the price of the stock after the split is to multiply the stock's price before the split by the reciprocal of the terms of the split. For example, if a stock is selling for $54 per share and is split three for two, then the price of the stock after the split will be $54 × 2/3 = $36. Such price adjustments must occur because the old shares are diluted and the earning capacity of the firm is not increased.

The price adjusts for the split

Stock splits may be any combination of terms. Exhibit 15–2 illustrates the terms of several stock splits in 1978. Although two-for-one splits are the most common, there can be unusual terms, such as the

EXHIBIT 15–2. Selected Stock Splits Declared or Distributed in 1978

Company	Terms of the Split
Getty Oil	4 for 1
Nabisco	2 for 1
Continental	2 for 1
Girard	2 for 1
Lukens Steel	2 for 1
Morrison–Knudsen	3 for 2
Seafirst	3 for 2
Morse Shoe	4 for 3
Nucor	7 for 5
Palm Beach	5 for 4
Wyly	1 for 4

five-for-four split of Palm Beach Corporation. There is no obvious explanation for such terms except that management wanted to reduce the stock's price to a particular level and selected the terms that would achieve the desired price.

The reverse split

Occasionally there is a *reverse split,* such as Wyly Corporation's one-for-four split. A reverse split reduces the number of shares and raises the price of the stock. The purpose of such a split is to add respectability to the stock (i.e., to raise the price above the level of the "cats and dogs"). Since some investors will not buy low-priced stock and since commissions on such purchases are higher, it may be in the best interest of all stockholders to raise the stock's price through a reverse split.

Stock splits, like stock dividends, do not by themselves increase the wealth of the stockholder, for the split does not increase the assets or earning capacity of the firm. The split does decrease the price of the stock and thereby may increase its marketability. Thus, the split stock may be more widely distributed, which increases investor interest in the company. This wider distribution may increase the wealth of the current stockholders over time.

Academic studies, however have not been able to demonstrate that stock splits or stock dividends increase the value of stock.* Instead, these studies consistently show that other factors, such as increased earnings, increased cash dividends, or a rise in the general market, result in higher prices for individual stocks. The stock dividends and stock splits do not by themselves affect the value of the stock. In fact, stock splits generally occur after the price of the stock has risen. Instead of being a harbinger of good news, they mirror an increase in the firm's earnings and growth.

Splits do not increase the wealth of the stockholder

From the investor's point of view, there is little difference between a stock split and a stock dividend. In both cases the stockholders receive additional shares, but their proportionate ownership in the firm is unaltered. In addition, the price of the stock adjusts for the dilution of per share earnings caused by the new shares.

Accountants, however, do differentiate between stock splits and stock dividends. Stock dividends are generally less than 20 to 25 per cent. A stock dividend of 50 per cent would be treated as a three-for-two stock split. Only the par value and the number of shares that the firm has outstanding would be affected. There would be no change in the firm's retained earnings. A stock split of 11 for 10 would be treated as a 10 per cent stock dividend. In this case, retained earrings would be reduced, and the amount would be transferred to the other accounts (i.e., common stock and paid-in capital accounts). Total equity, however, would not be affected.

---

*See, for instance, W. H. Hausman, R. R. West, and J. A. Largay, "Stock Splits, Price Changes, and Trading Profits: A Synthesis," *Journal of Business,* 44 (January 1971), pp. 69–77.

DIVIDEND REINVESTMENT PLANS

Many corporations that pay cash dividends also have dividend reinvestment programs in which the cash dividends are used to purchase additional shares of stock. Dividend reinvestment programs started in the 1960s, but the expansion of the programs occurred in the early 1970s. By the late 1970s more than 600 companies offered some version of the dividend reinvestment plan.*

TYPES OF DIVIDEND REINVESTMENT PLANS

There are two general types of dividend reinvestment programs. In most plans a bank acts on behalf of the corporation and its stockholders. The bank collects the cash dividends for the stockholders and in some plans offers the stockholders the option of making additional cash contributions. The bank pools all of the funds and purchases the stock on the open market. Since the bank is able to purchase a larger block of shares, it receives a substantial reduction in the per share commission cost of the purchase. This reduced brokerage fee applies to all of the shares purchased by the bank. Thus, all investors, ranging from the smallest to the largest, receive this advantage. The bank does charge a fee for its service, but this fee is usually modest and does not offset the savings in brokerage fees.

Funds are pooled and existing shares are purchased

In the second type of reinvestment plan, the company issues new shares of stock for the cash dividend, and the money is directly rechanneled to the company. The investor may also have the option of making additional cash contributions. This type of plan offers the investor an additional advantage in that the brokerage fees are entirely circumvented. The entire amount of the cash dividend is used to purchase shares, with the cost of issuing the new shares being paid by the company. This type of reinvestment plan is offered primarily by utilities, such as telephone and electric and gas companies. Utilities need continual sources of new equity funds, and dividend reinvestment plans are one means of raising this capital.

New shares of stock are issued

ADVANTAGES OF DIVIDEND REINVESTMENT PLANS

Dividend reinvestment plans offer advantages to both firms and investors. For stockholders the advantages include the purchase of shares

A reduction in commission

---

*In 1979 Standard & Poor's published a list of firms that had dividend reinvestment plans. See *The Outlook* (March 12, 1979), pp. 880–881. In addition, several firms sell the new shares at a discount of 5 per cent less than the market price. See "Everybody Wins but the Brokers," *Forbes* (August 7, 1978), p. 74.

at a substantial reduction in commissions. Even reinvestment plans in which the fees are paid by the stockholder offer this savings. Both types of plan are particularly attractive to the small investor, for few brokerage firms are interested or willing to buy $100 worth of stock, and substantial commissions are charged on such small transactions.

Forced savings

Perhaps the most important advantage to investors is that the plans are automatic. The investor does not receive the dividends, for the proceeds are automatically reinvested. The plans are a means to force the individual to save.* For any investor who lacks the discipline to save, such forced saving may be a means to systematically accumulate shares.

An incentive not to cut dividends

There may also be an advantage to income-oriented stockholders if these plans encourage the company to distribute cash dividends. A dividend reinvestment plan, especially one that results in the issue of new shares, may be an incentive for the company to maintain cash dividends. Even if the company desires to cut dividends in order to build its equity base, such a move reduces the funds that are available through reinvested dividends. If the company's reinvestment plan involves the issue of new shares, the increase in the equity base that is achieved through cutting the dividend is partially offset by the reduction in reinvested dividends and cash contributions. Hence, the reinvestment plans may result in fewer dividend cuts and perhaps more dividend increments.†

Goodwill

For the firm the primary advantages are the goodwill that is achieved by providing another service for its stockholders and some cost savings in the delivery of dividend checks. The plans that involve the issue of new shares also raise new equity capital. Firms that frequently must raise large amounts of externally generated funds may find the dividend reinvestment plan to be a major source of new capital. For example, AT&T stated in its 1977 annual report that its plan resulted in the issue of 9.4 million shares, which raised over $566 million in equity capital. This automatic flow of new equity reduced the need for the sale of shares through underwriters.

The dividends are still subject to income tax

Currently the Internal Revenue Service considers dividends that are reinvested to be no different from cash dividends that are received. Such dividends are subject to federal income taxation (after the $100 dividend exclusion). The exclusion of dividend income that is reinvested from federal income taxation has been considered as one possible change in the tax code. The purpose of this alteration would be to increase equity capital; however, no Congressional action has been taken to alter the current tax treatment of reinvested dividend income.

---

*See K. Larry Hasties's Comment on "Automatic Dividend Reinvestment Plans of Nonfinancial Corporations," *Financial Management,* 3(Spring 1974), p. 26.

†At present there is no evidence that such plans do affect firms' dividend policies. See Richard H. Pettway and R. Phil Malone, "Automatic Dividend Reinvestment Plans of Nonfinancial Corporations," *Financial Management,* 2(Winter 1973), pp. 11–17.

EARNINGS RETENTION AND GROWTH

Since management seeks to maximize the wealth of the stockholders, the dividend decision should depend upon who can put the funds to better use, the stockholders or the firm. Management, however, probably does not know the stockholders' alternative uses for the funds and thus pursues a policy that it believes is in the stockholders' best interests. Stockholders who do not like the dividend policy of the firm may sell their shares. If sellers exceed buyers, the price of the stock will be depressed, and management will be made aware of the investors' attitude toward the dividend policy. Certainly Consolidated Edison's stockholders indicated their dissatisfaction when management discontinued cash dividends in 1974. Angry stockholders not only voiced their opinions at the annual stockholders' meeting but also offered their stock for sale. This selling caused the stock's price to decline drastically, from $18 to $7 ⅝ per share, within a period of only three weeks.

Alternative uses of funds

THE EFFECT OF TAXATION

As was discussed in Chapter 5, an institutional factor, federal income taxes, argues strongly for the retention of earnings over cash dividends. A stockholder's dividend income is treated as ordinary income and is taxed at income tax rates. Long-term capital gains are given special tax treatment, and for most individuals these gains are taxed at forty per cent of the tax rate on ordinary income. If a company is able to reinvest its earnings and grow, then the investor should be able to sell the shares at a higher price that reflects the growth. The profits from the sale are then taxed at the lower long-term capital gains tax rates.

Taxes encourage retention

The tax treatment of long-term capital gains favors the retention of earnings over their distribution in the form of cash dividends. If an investor is in the 40 per cent tax bracket, he or she loses 40 per cent of any cash dividends to income taxes. However, only 20 per cent of any long-term capital gains is lost to federal income taxes. Under such circumstances, $1000 in dividends and $1000 in capital gains net $600 and $800, respectively, after taxes. This investor then has to earn considerably more on the $600 in order to compensate for the additional tax. Thus, cash dividends are preferable to capital gains only if the stockholder has excellent uses for the money and can earn a return that will offset the difference in the tax rates.

Many investors may not have such excellent uses for their money. Therefore, the retention of earnings is frequently considered to be consistent with management's goal to maximize the wealth of the stockholders. After the firm retains earnings and achieves growth, investors may be able to sell their shares and realize long-term capital gains, which will be taxed at the more favorable rates.

EARNINGS RETENTION AND SECURITY PRICES

Retained earnings may produce growth

In the 1960s dividend policy was not a major concern of management. During this period the emphasis was on growth and the retention of earnings to finance that growth. Management retained as much of the earnings as it believed necessary to finance growth, and any residual was paid to stockholders. It was a period of spectacular growth by major firms, such as I.B.M., Xerox, and Johnson & Johnson. For example, during the years between 1964 and 1972, IBM's earnings and stock price increased at an annual rate of 14 per cent. Investors in these growth-oriented companies were rewarded as the price of the stocks rose. Obviously, the best use of corporate funds was to finance growth, for few investors could have earned a comparable return through alternative uses of the money. These stockholders were well rewarded for forgoing current dividend income.

With the onset of inflation in the 1970s and the increase in interest rates, dividend policy became more important. Investors had several potential uses for funds, such as the purchase of material goods the price of which investors anticipated would continue to rise. Bonds, which were yielding historically high interest rates, were an attractive investment. Investors had more obvious alternative uses for the money earned by companies. Failure on the part of corporations to pay cash dividends or to increase the dividends in response to increased earnings played a role in the decline of security prices that occurred from 1973 to 1974. The dividend policy of the firm became more important to investors as they viewed the return on their investments as including not only the growth in the value of the shares but also the dividend return.

EXHIBIT 15–3 Teledyne's Earnings per Share and High-Low Stock Prices

Year	Earnings per Share	High–Low Stock Prices
1978	$19.13	$119.7–52.0
1977	14.42	67.5–43.1
1976	9.29	62.2–18.4
1975	5.22	21.0– 7.9
1974	1.11	12.2– 6.2
1973	2.04	16.1– 7.5
1972	1.31	21.3–12.2
1971	1.24	24.7–10.9
1970	1.46	27.9– 9.4

Even in the 1970s earnings and dividend growth were rewarded by higher security prices. The companies that experienced growth tended to be smaller, and the growth in their earnings and stock prices were both less spectacular and less well publicized than the success stories of the 1960s. Such a case is Teledyne, whose growth in earnings per share and stock price are illustrated in Exhibit 15–3. While Teledyne has not achieved the publicity of IBM or Johnson & Johnson, its earnings grew annually in excess of 28 per cent from 1970 through 1977, and the price of the stock rose perceptibly during that period.

Higher earnings should lead to higher stock prices

REPURCHASES OF STOCK AND LIQUIDATIONS

A firm with excess cash may choose to repurchase some of its outstanding shares of stock or to liquidate the corporation. This section briefly covers repurchases and liquidations. A repurchase is in effect a partial liquidation, as it decreases the number of shares outstanding. This reduction should increase the earnings per share because the earnings are spread over fewer shares.

While the repurchase of shares is a partial liquidation, it may also be viewed as an alternative to the payment of cash dividends. Instead of distributing the money as cash dividends, the firm offers to purchase shares from stockholders. This offer has several advantages for stockholders. First, they have the option to sell or to retain their shares. If the stockholders believe that the firm's potential is sufficient to warrant the retention of the shares, they do not have to sell them. Second, if the shares are sold back to the company, any resulting profits will be taxed as capital gains. This will provide favorable tax treatment if the stockholder has owned the shares for the required length of time. If the company had distributed the earnings as cash dividends, they would have been taxed as ordinary income of the recipient. Since the tax rates on income exceed those on long-term capital gains, the repurchase of shares instead of the distribution of cash dividends produces a tax savings for stockholders who do sell their shares.

Repurchase as an alternative to cash dividends

One company that has followed a policy of retiring shares is Teledyne. The corporation does not pay cash dividends but either has offered stockholders the option to exchange their shares for debt issued by the company or has repurchased the stock. In 1975 it repurchased 3.6 million shares at $18 per share, and in 1976 it repurchased 2.5 million shares at $40 per share.

Favorable tax treatment

The result of this recapitalization has been to reduce the number of shares outstanding from 34.4 million in 1972 to 11.4 million in 1976. This reduced number of shares plus an excellent growth in earnings has resulted in a substantial increase in Teledyne's per share earnings. These earnings and the stock's high and low prices are illustrated in Exhibit 15–3. Since the repurchases were made in 1975 and 1976 the

Recapitalization reduces the number of shares outstanding

price of the stock has risen, which has certainly benefited the remaining stockholders. Even those stockholders who sold their shares cannot complain, because they were not forced to sell. These investors sold their shares presumably because they thought that selling was better than continuing to hold the shares.

Occasionally a firm is liquidated. The final distribution of the firm's assets is called a liquidating dividend. The use of the term *dividend* is a bit misleading, because the distribution is not really a dividend. It is treated for tax purposes as a distribution of capital and is taxed at the appropriate capital gains tax rate. Thus, liquidating dividends are treated in the same manner as realized sales for federal income tax purposes.

A liquidation dividend in cash

How such a dividend works may be illustrated by a simple example. A firm decides to liquidate and sells all of its assets for cash. The stockholders then receive the cash. If the sales raise $25 in cash per share, then the stockholder surrenders the stock certificate and receives $25 in cash. The capital gain is then determined by subtracting the stockholder's cost basis of the share from the $25. If the stockholder paid $10 for the share, the capital gain is $15. The stockholder then pays the appropriate capital gains tax. If the cost basis were $40, the investor would suffer a capital loss of $15, which may be used for tax purposes to offset other capital gains or income. In either case this is no different than if the stockholder had sold the shares. However, in a sale the stockholder does have the option to refuse to sell and thus may postpone any capital gains tax. In a liquidation the stockholder must realize the gain or loss. Once the firm has adopted a plan of liquidation, it must execute it or face penalties. When a firm liquidates, the stockholder cannot postpone the capital gains tax.

A liquidation dividend in property

In the preceding example, the liquidating dividend was cash. However, the dividend need not be cash but may be property. For example, a real estate holding company could distribute the property it owns. Or a company that has accumulated stock in other companies could distribute the stock instead of selling it. Such distributions may be desirable if the stockholders want the particular assets being distributed. However, if the stockholders want or need cash (perhaps to pay the capital gains tax), then the burden of liquidating the assets is passed onto them.

An example of a firm that did liquidate is Tishman Realty. In November 1977 the stockholders adopted a plan of liquidation. The firm then sold most of its assets for $200 million to Equitable Life Assurance. In December the company paid an initial $11 per share liquidating dividend. In 1978 further cash distributions were made. After all of the cash dividends were distributed, a partnership was established to hold the remaining assets, which consisted primarily of mortgages on properties sold. These partnership shares were then distributed to stockholders to complete the liquidation.

SUMMARY

After a firm has earned profits, it may either retain them or distribute them in the form of cash dividends. Many publicly held corporations follow a stated dividend policy and distribute quarterly cash dividends. A few firms supplement this dividend with extra dividends if earnings warrant the additional distribution. Some firms pay irregular dividends that vary in amount from quarter to quarter.

Dividends are related to the firm's capacity to pay them. As earnings rise, dividends also tend to increase, but there is usually a lag between higher earnings and increased dividends. Most managements are reluctant to cut dividends and thus do not raise the dividend until they believe that the higher level of earnings can be sustained.

In addition to cash dividends, some firms distribute stock dividends. These dividends and stock splits do not increase the earning capacity of the firm. Instead, they are recapitalizations that alter the number of shares that the firm has outstanding. Since stock dividends and stock splits do not alter the earning capacity of the firm, they do not increase the wealth of the stockholders. The price of the stock adjusts for the change in the number of shares that results from stock dividends and stock splits.

The retention or distribution of earnings should be a question of who can put the funds to better use — the firm or its stockholders. If a firm retains earnings, it should grow and the value of the shares should increase. When this occurs, the stockholders may be able to sell their shares for a profit and thereby receive favorable capital gains tax treatment. Since the income tax laws favor capital gains over dividend income, this encourages the retention of earnings instead of their distribution.

Many firms offer their stockholders the option of having their dividends reinvested in the firm's stock. This is achieved through either the firm's issuing new shares or purchasing existing shares. Dividend reinvestment plans offer the stockholders the advantages of forced savings and a reduction in brokerage fees.

Instead of paying cash dividends, a firm may offer to repurchase some of its existing shares. Such repurchases reduce the number of shares outstanding and may enhance the growth in the firm's per share earnings because there will be fewer shares outstanding. Any profits earned on such repurchases receive the favorable capital gains tax treatment, as do liquidating dividends that occur when a corporation is disbanded and its assets are distributed to the stockholders.

Terms to Remember

Regular dividends	Date of record	Stock split
Irregular dividends	Ex dividend day	Recapitalization
Payout ratio	Distribution date	Dilution
Extra dividend	Stock dividend	Dividend reinvestment plan

Questions

1. Why may a firm distribute dividends even though earnings decline?

2. Why may a dividend increment lag after an increase in earnings?

3. Define *ex dividend day, date of record,* and *distribution date.*

4. Explain the differences between the following dividend policies: (a) regular quarterly dividends; (b) regular quarterly dividends plus extras; and (c) irregular dividends.

5. How are stock dividends and stock splits similar?

6. What are the advantages to stockholders of dividend reinvestment plans?

7. What tax advantages apply to stock repurchases that do not apply to cash dividend distributions?

8. Why should dividend policy be a question of who can put the funds to better use, the firm or its stockholders?

SELECTED READINGS

Brittain, John A.: *Corporate Dividend Policy*. Washington, D.C., The Brookings Institute, 1966.

Eisemann, Peter C., and Edward A. Moses: "Stock Dividends: Management's View." *Financial Analysis Journal*, (July–August, 1978), pp. 77–80.

Finnerty, Joseph E.: "Corporate Stock Issue and Repurchase." *Financial Management*, 4(Autumn 1975), pp. 62–71.

Mayo, Herbert B.: "Savings From Dividend Reinvestment Plans." *Public Utilities Fortnightly*, (September 12, 1974), pp. 36–40.

Millar, James A., and Bruce D. Fielitz: "Stock-Split and Stock-Dividend Decisions." *Financial Management*, 2(Winter 1973), pp. 35–45.

Pettway, Richard M., and R. Phil Malone: "Automatic Dividend Reinvestment Plans of Nonfinancial Corporations." *Financial Management*, 2(Winter 1973), pp. 11–17.

Sosnick, Stephen H.: "Stock Dividends Are Lemons, Not Melons." *California Management Review*, III(Winter 1961), pp. 61–70.

Walsh, Francis J., and Patrick J. Davey: "Automatic Dividend Reinvestment Programs." *The Conference Board Record*, X(February 1973), pp. 45–46.

West, R. R., and A. B. Brouilette: "Reverse Stock Splits — Harbinger of Bad Times or Valid Management Technique?" *Financial Executive*, (January 1970), pp. 12–17.

Learning Objectives

After completing this chapter you should be able to

1. Explain the impact of monetary policy on security prices.

2. Describe the mechanics of open market operations.

3. Explain the relationship between economic activity and security prices.

4. Identify cyclical companies.

5. Differentiate time-series from cross-sectional analysis.

6. Distinguish among the measures of profitability.

7. Contrast the two measures of debt financing.

chapter 16

THE FUNDAMENTAL APPROACH TO THE SELECTION OF STOCK

Two methods other than random choice or "hot tips" are used by investors to select securities: the fundamental approach and the technical approach. The fundamental approach stresses economic conditions, such as the level of employment and economic growth, and financial conditions, such as the level and direction of change in interest rates. This approach also examines a firm's earning capacity, its growth potential, and its sources of finance. Financial analysts who use this method compare firms within an industry to identify those with the greatest potential and strongest financial position. Emphasis is placed on a firm's economic performance and the potential to improve its relative position within its industry. Ratios, financial data, and astute observation are the primary tools of fundamental analysis.

The technical approach is based on the past market performance of a firm's securities. It attempts to identify superior investments by analyzing the price performance and the volume of transactions in the firm's stock. This type of analysis emphasizes price trends and deviations from these trends. For example, stocks that are rising in price will usually continue to do so. When the technical analyst perceives that this trend is coming to a halt, it is time to liquidate the position in that security, even if the firm has superior management, excellent growth potential, and a strong balance sheet.

Although both methods attempt to identify superior securities for purchase, the two approaches are significantly different. Fundamental analysis is based on the premise that real factors, such as the firm's productivity and profitability, will ultimately govern the stock's price. Technical analysis, however, stresses market factors and suggests that future stock prices are related to past market behavior.

This and the following chapter will explore these techniques. Chapter 16 focuses on fundamental analysis. The first section discusses the general economic environment. The impact of the Federal Reserve's monetary policy on interest rates is explained next. The bulk of the chapter is devoted to fundamental analysis of the firm. Particular emphasis is placed on the various ratios used in this type of analysis. Chapter 17 discusses technical analysis and illustrates several techniques that are used by advocates of this approach. The student should realize that these two chapters cannot cover these important topics in depth; entire books have been written on each topic alone. This text includes only basic methods used in fundamental and technical analysis.

THE ECONOMIC ENVIRONMENT

All firms work within the economic environment. Their survival may depend on how the economy as a whole is faring. During periods of economic prosperity, the demand for the goods and services of firms may result in increased sales and higher profits. Even financially weak or incompetently managed firms may experience increased sales and earnings if they are swept up in the general economic prosperity.

Recession may cause earnings to decline

Hard times or periods of recession (i.e., periods of rising unemployment) may have the opposite impact. Financially weak firms may fail, and even the financially strong may feel the effects of poor economic conditions. Recession leads to a general decline in economic activity, which in turn results in a lessening of demand for the output of virtually all firms. Sales become sluggish or even decline, and earnings tend to diminish

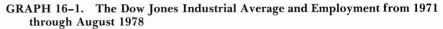

GRAPH 16–1. The Dow Jones Industrial Average and Employment from 1971 through August 1978

even more rapidly because certain fixed costs (such as interest and depreciation) must still be met, which may severely reduce profit margins.

During periods of prosperity, security prices as a whole tend to rise. Thus, even poor investment decisions may produce acceptable or even superior results. Conversely, during periods of economic downturn, even excellent investment analysis and the proper decisions may not protect the investor from declining security prices. For these reasons, the ability to forecast the future economic environment may be even more important than the purchase of specific securities.*

During prosperity security prices may rise

This relationship between economic activity and security prices is illustrated in Graph 16–1, which plots the level of employment and the Dow Jones industrial average. As was explained in Chapter 13, this average is an aggregate measure of the market's performance, and the employment rate is one indicator of the state of the economy. While other measures of the stock market and the economy could be used, these two illustrate the relationship between stock prices and the aggregate economy. During periods of rising employment, security prices tend to rise. Although the relationship between the two variables is not fixed, there is a tendency for them to move together.

An ability to anticipate changes in the economy should aid in investment decision making. Such forecasting, however, is virtually impossible for the individual investor. Even access to sophisticated techniques, com-

A need to forecast

---

*Frank K. Reilly, "The Misdirected Emphasis in Security Valuation," *Financial Analysts Journal*, (January–February, 1973).

puters, and more complete data does not guarantee accurate forecasts. Certainly, if various economic groups, such as the Council of Economic Advisors (to the President), have difficulty predicting the economy, the individual investor cannot expect to do what those trained analysts are unable to do.

The individual investor, however, has access to the predictions of the various forecasting services, which are reported in the financial press. For example, *Fortune* and *Financial World* publish annual forecasts at the beginning of the calendar year. These predictions include the growth in gross national product, which measures the nation's final output of goods and services for the year; the level of unemployment; and the rate of inflation, i.e., the rate of increase in the level of prices. Although the various forecasts are different, they vary only in degree, since all analysts are working with essentially the same information.

The importance of direction of change

The importance of these forecasts to investors is not so much the actual predicted numbers but the direction and amount of change. Since profits are related to economic activity, forecasts of such activity may be helpful in predicting the level of a firm's earnings. However, the investor should realize that stock prices frequently precede changes in economic activity (as is seen in Graph 16–1). Thus, estimates of economic growth may be too late to help investors if stock prices have already risen. The investor should also realize that not all companies benefit from periods of economic growth. Analysis of the financial condition and the growth potential of the individual firm is still warranted.

THE FEDERAL RESERVE

The central bank

In addition to forecasts of aggregate economic activity, the investor should be concerned with the monetary policy of the Federal Reserve. The Federal Reserve is the country's central bank. Although in many countries the treasury and the central bank are one and the same, in the United States they are independent of each other. Such independence is an example of the checks and balances of the country's political system. However, both the United States Treasury and the Federal Reserve have the same general economic goals of full employment, stable prices, and economic growth.

Economic goals

The Federal Reserve pursues these economic goals through the regulation of the supply of credit and money. Monetary policy refers to changes in the supply of money and credit. When the Federal Reserve wants to increase the supply of money and credit to help expand the level of income and employment, it follows an "easy" monetary policy. When it desires to contract the supply of money and credit to help fight inflation, it pursues a "tight" monetary policy.

The Federal Reserve has several tools by which it may affect the supply of money and the availability of other credit. These tools work primarily by altering the ability of commercial banks to grant loans, thereby expanding the money supply (creating money). Commercial banks must hold reserves against their deposit liabilities. Any reserves in excess of those required may be lent. By increasing the excess reserves of commercial banks, the Federal Reserve increases the ability of banks to lend and thereby expands the supply of money. By reducing the excess reserves of commercial banks, the Federal Reserve decreases the capacity of these banks to lend and may even cause them to contract their outstanding loans, which further reduces the supply of money.

Of the major tools of monetary policy, by far the most important is open market operations. Open market operations refer to the purchase or sale of government securities by the Federal Reserve. By buying and selling these securities, the Federal Reserve is able to alter both the supply of money in circulation and the reserves of the commercial banking system. The Federal Reserve may buy and sell securities at any time and in any volume and thus is able to affect the supply of money and credit whenever it chooses to do so.

Open market operations

When the Federal Reserve wants to increase the supply of money and the reserves of the banking system, it purchases securities. Ownership of the securities is transferred to the Federal Reserve, and the Federal Reserve pays for the securities by writing a check drawn on itself, which the seller deposits in a commercial bank. The bank clears the check and receives reserves from the Federal Reserve.

Increasing the supply of money

These transactions have the following effect on each participant's balance sheet.

FEDERAL RESERVE		COMMERCIAL BANK		GENERAL PUBLIC	
Government Securities ↑	Reserves of Commercial Banks ↑	Reserves ↑	Demand Deposits ↑	Government Securities ↓ Demand Deposits ↑	

The general public has sold securities and received payment. In effect, it traded one asset (the government securities) for another (the demand deposit). The bank, however, has received a new liability (the new checking account) and a new asset (the reserves). The Federal Reserve acquired a new asset (the government securities) and paid for the securities by issuing a new liability on itself (the reserves of the commercial bank).

The total effect of the transaction has been (1) to increase the supply of money by increasing demand deposits and (2) to increase the reserves of the banking system. The required reserves of the bank rise, for the deposit liabilities of the commercial bank have risen. However, only a fraction of the increase in reserves will be required reserves. Thus, the excess reserves of the commercial bank will have also risen. This increase in excess reserves means that the capacity of the commercial banking system to expand the supply of money and to issue more credit has risen. The purchase of government securities by the Federal Reserve from the general public brings about not only an increase in the supply of money but also

**Contracting the
supply of money**

the potential for additional increases through an increase in the excess reserves of commercial banks.

When the Federal Reserve desires to contract the money supply, it sells government securities. Once again it is the payment for the purchased securities that alters the money supply and the capacity of commercial banks to lend. If the public buys the securities, demand deposits decrease along with the money supply and the reserves of commercial banks. The sale of securities by the Federal Reserve affects the balance sheets of the Federal Reserve, commercial banks, and the public as follows:

FEDERAL RESERVE		COMMERCIAL BANKS		GENERAL PUBLIC	
Government Securities ↓	Reserves of Commercial Banks ↓	Reserves ↓	Demand Deposits ↓	Demand Deposits ↓ Government Securities ↑	

The general public has traded one asset (the demand deposit) for another (the government securities). Commercial banks lose demand deposits, and when the check clears and payment is made to the Federal Reserve, the reserves of commercial banks on deposit at the Federal Reserve are reduced. The Federal Reserve loses an asset (the government securities) and a liability (the reserves). It has, in effect, retired a liability by giving up an asset.

The total effect of this transaction is (1) a decrease in the money supply because demand deposits have decreased and (2) a decrease in the total reserves of the banking system because commercial banks have fewer reserves on deposit at the Federal Reserve. Since only a percentage of these reserves is required against deposit liabilities, the excess reserves of the bank also decrease. Thus, by selling securities in the open market, the Federal Reserve decreases the supply of money and decreases the excess reserves of commercial banks. The decrease in excess reserves reduces the ability of the commercial banking system to lend and to issue credit.

THE IMPACT OF MONETARY POLICY ON SECURITY PRICES

**Open market
operations affect
security prices**

The importance of open market operations for investment analysis is twofold. First, the buying and selling of government securities have an immediate impact on interest rates and bond prices. Second, there is an indirect effect on security prices that results from the impact of monetary policy on a firm's earning capacity.

When the Federal Reserve buys treasury securities, it bids up their prices and causes yields to decline. The rate differential between treasury debt and corporate debt widens, and as a result investors purchase corporate bonds. This causes their prices to rise and their yields to decline, and the effect of the open market purchases by the Federal Reserve is transferred to other debt instruments.

The converse happens when the Federal Reserve sells government securities. This depresses their prices and increases interest rates. The rate differential between corporate and federal government debt is reduced, and investors move from corporate to government securities. This reduces the price of corporate bonds and increases their yield. Thus, the effect of the sale of government securities by the Federal Reserve is transferred to corporate and all other forms of debt.

The second source of the impact of monetary policy is the effect of changes in monetary conditions on the earning capacity of a firm. Since all assets must be financed, any change in monetary policy affects the cost of a firm's financing. Tightening credit will increase the cost of financing which by itself will result in lower earnings. The increased cost of credit will be reflected in the prices charged by the firm, which should dampen the demand for the company's output. Its buyers will find their credit more expensive, which may result in individuals', governments', and firms' buying fewer goods and services. This reduction in demand will reinforce the increased cost of finance and cause earnings to decline.

The cost of credit is altered

In addition to the impact on earnings, the tighter monetary policy will probably result in individuals' increasing their required rate of return on equity investments. If investors can earn more on debt instruments than was possible before the increase in interest rates, then they will require higher returns on equity investments. Higher returns are possible only if stock prices fall. Thus, there is pressure from two sources on stock prices to fall. The higher interest rates will probably result in lower earnings and in higher required rates of return. Both of these will depress stock prices.

Investors' required rate of return may increase

This argument can be expressed in more formal terms by using the dividend growth valuation model that was presented in Chapter 14. That model is

Impact of monetary policy on stock prices

$$V = \frac{D}{k-g}$$

where V is the value of the stock; D, the dividend that is paid during the year; k, the investors' required rate of return on stock; and g, the firm's growth rate in earnings and dividends. A tightening of credit by the Federal Reserve may reduce the firm's growth rate and its capacity to pay dividends. Therefore the value of D or g or both will decline, which will cause the price of the stock to decline. In addition, the required rate of return (k) will rise. This increases the denominator and causes the price of the stock to fall. Thus, tighter credit and higher interest rates generally indicate that the value of stock will decline. In terms of the constant growth valuation model, tight money reduces the numerator and increases the denominator, which puts downward pressure on the value of the stock.

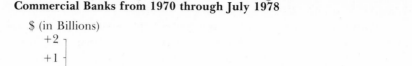

GRAPH 16–2. The Dow Jones Industrial Average and the Free Reserves of Commercial Banks from 1970 through July 1978

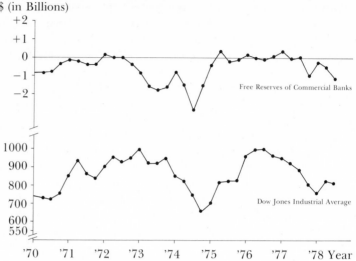

This impact of monetary policy on security prices is illustrated in Graph 16–2. The graph relates the lending capacity of commercial banks to security prices. The capacity of commercial banks to lend is measured by their free reserves, which are the excess reserves of commercial banks minus their borrowings from the Federal Reserve. These reserves increase when credit is easy but decline and become negative when credit is tight. As may be seen from the graph, there is a definite relationship between commercial banks' capacity to lend and the level of stock prices. This graph strongly suggests that if the investor can anticipate changes in monetary policy, he or she should adopt a strategy of converting securities into cash or short-term assets as money gets tighter to produce positive investment results. The reverse strategy should be implemented when credit becomes easier.

The problem, of course, lies in determining which monetary policy is currently being followed by the Federal Reserve. This is best perceived through changes in the nation's stock of money and the reserves of commercial banks and through the policy statements of the leaders of the Federal Reserve (i.e., the Board of Governors).* The first two factors are reported in the monthly *Federal Reserve Bulletin*, which may be readily obtained by subscription or in libraries. Policy statements are published in the financial press but are not neatly collected in one volume or publication for easy access. However, if the investor follows the monetary statistics on the money supply and the capacity of commercial banks to lend, he or she should have a reasonable idea of the direction of monetary policy.

---

*See, for instance, Beryl W. Sprinkel, *Money and Stock Prices,* Homewood, Ill., Richard D. Irwin, Inc., 1964.

INDUSTRY ANALYSIS

Firms are not unique unto themselves but exist within the framework of a specific industry. Some industries tend to be very cyclical and move with the economy. Examples of cyclical industries include the automobile and building industries. Since consumers can defer such high-priced items from one year to the next, sales in these industries tend to be exaggerated by economic fluctuations. Car sales and housing starts can vary significantly from year to year and, as would be expected, earnings of firms in these industries also tend to fluctuate.

Cyclical industries

The fluctuations in sales and earnings for two cyclical firms are illustrated in Graph 16–3. For Chrysler, annual sales and earnings per share declined in 1973, but in 1975 sales rose slightly while earnings continued to fall. Masonite also experienced a significant decline in earnings during 1973, but both sales and earnings rose during 1975 and 1976.

The investor should note that earnings tend to fluctuate more than sales, as firms have some fixed costs that cannot be deferred. Although some costs vary with the level of sales, fixed costs do not. Even when sales decline, these costs still exist and must be met, which causes greater variations in earnings than in sales.

While some industries are cyclical, others are not. Some are quite

Stable industries

GRAPH 16–3. Cyclical Sales and Earnings

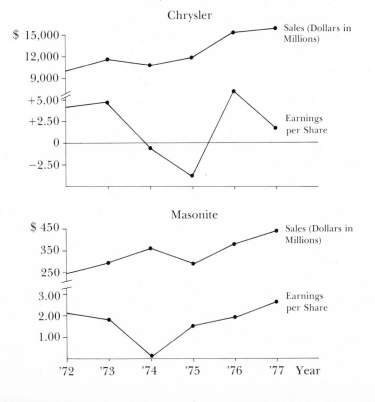

stable even though the economy may be in a recession. These industries include food processing and retailing. Such purchases must be made on a continual basis by consumers. People have to eat, and such purchases cannot be deferred. Graph 16–4 illustrates two firms that are representative of these industries. The sales and earnings per share of Allied Stores and Campbell Soups did not fluctuate as much as the sales and earnings of Chrysler and Masonite, as shown in Graph 16–3. The earnings rose almost consistently during the same period.

The fact that some firms are in cyclical industries while others are in more stable industries does not imply that investors should purchase securities in the latter to the exclusion of those in the former. Security markets tend to smooth out the fluctuations in earnings so the firm's value is related to its performance over a period of time. As the valuation models presented in the previous chapter indicated, the flow of dividend income and the growth in the firm's earnings over many years (all properly discounted back to the present) ultimately determine the value of the shares. The fact that a firm is in a cyclical industry does not by itself imply that the firm's securities are inferior investments. Nor does the fact that a firm is in a more stable industry mean that the firm's securities are superior investments.

Growth industries   Perhaps the ideal investment is in a firm in a growing industry. Demand for the firm's output can be anticipated to grow, and even if more companies enter the market the expansion of the market itself will permit the firm to maintain its profits in the face of increased competition.

GRAPH 16–4. Noncyclical Sales and Earnings

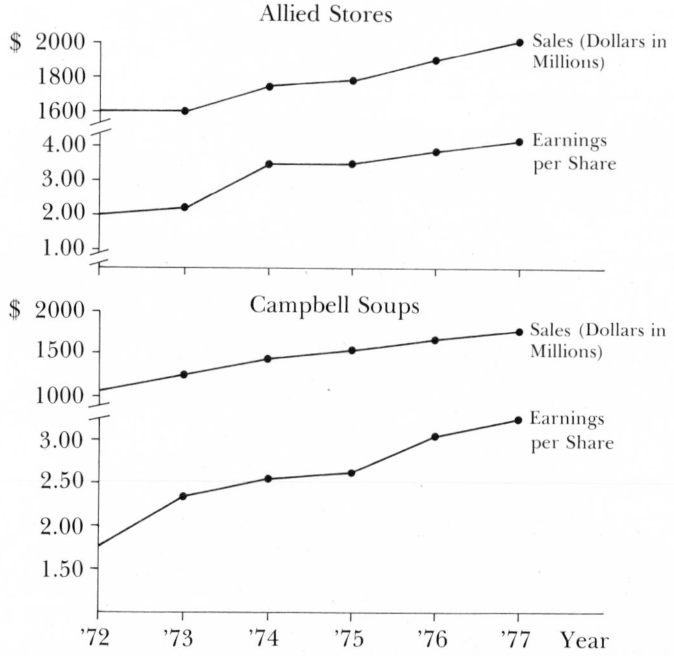

Identifying such industries is not easy. Airlines were considered a growth industry in the 1960s but fell on hard times in the 1970s. Other technologically oriented industries, such as those that produce copiers, semiconductors, and computers, have provided excellent examples of past growth. Perhaps solar energy will be tomorrow's growth industry. Even industries that were once considered mature may regain their former growth. Coal may be such an industry if the use of oil and natural gas is sufficiently reduced and other forms of energy are not developed.

While many previous growth industries were based on technological change, future growth need not necessarily be built on technology. Consumer tastes change, and as incomes increase, consumers may buy different types of products. More income may be spent on services, travel, or fine quality consumer durable goods, such as crystal instead of glass. Companies in these industries may become the next generation of growth firms. The best investments, then, should prove to be in the securities of firms that are able either to capitalize on technological change or to expand and take advantage of shifts in demand.

While a specific market may enhance the performance of a company for a period of time, ultimately the firm is judged on its own capabilities. For this reason firms in the same industries are generally compared with one other to ascertain which ones are the best performers, i.e., which firms earn the most and outperform their competitors. A substantial effort is devoted to comparison of firms within an industry, and these comparisons are the backbone of fundamental analysis.

A need to analyze the specific firm

RATIO ANALYSIS

Ratios are probably the most frequently used tool to analyze a company. Ratios are popular because they are readily understood and can be computed with ease. In addition, the information used in ratio analysis is easy to obtain, for many ratios employ data available in a firm's annual and quarterly reports. Ratios are used not only by investors but also by a firm's management and creditors. Management may use ratio analysis to plan, to control, and to identify weaknesses within the firm. As was illustrated in Chapter 11, ratio analysis may be used by creditors to establish the ability of the borrower to pay interest and to retire debt.

Ratios may be computed and interpreted from two positions. They may be compiled for a number of years to perceive trends. This is called *time-series analysis.* An alternative is to compute ratios at a given time for several firms within an industry. This is called *cross-sectional analysis.* Time-series and cross-sectional analysis may be used together, but rarely will all of the ratios indicate the same general tendency. When they are taken as a group, the ratios give the investigator an indication of the direction in which the firm is moving and its financial position in comparison with other firms in its industry.

Comparisons are made over time or with other firms

A need to select appropriate ratios

Although a variety of people use ratio analysis, they do not necessarily compute the same ratios. Since a large number of ratios may be calculated, the individual should select those that are best suited to his or her specific purpose. For example, a bondholder is concerned primarily with the firm's ability to pay the interest and repay the principal and is less concerned with the rate at which the firm's inventory is sold. While the rate at which inventory turns over may affect the ability of the company to pay the interest and the principal, the typical bondholder is more concerned with an aggregate picture of the firm's financial position.

The investor may find that a specific industry requires addditional ratios or more sophisticated versions of a particular ratio. For example, the ratios used to analyze public utilities are considerably different from those used to analyze railroads. Although both are highly regulated and have many similarities, such as large investments in plant and equipment, the nature of the industries is quite different, including such factors as the labor requirements, the element of competition, and the demand for each service. Emphasis, then, is placed on different factors, such as miles traveled per ton of freight for railroads versus the peak load requirements relative to the average demand for electricity for an electric utility.

Several ratios will be discussed and illustrated. The examples used draw on the income and balance sheets for CBS that were presented in Chapters 8 and 11. The ratios presented here do not exhaust all of the possible ratios, and many have been previously illustrated (e.g., the ratios in Chapter 11). At the conclusion of this chapter there is a summary of ratios used in this text to analyze a firm's securities.

THE PRICE-TO-EARNINGS RATIO

Price to earnings

One particularly important ratio that is used in fundamental analysis is the ratio of a stock's price to the firm's per share earnings. This ratio is commonly referred to as the price-to-earnings, or PE, ratio. By expressing each firm's stock price relative to its earnings, this ratio facilitates the comparison of firms. The PE ratio indicates the amount that the market is willing to pay for each dollar of earnings. A PE ratio of 12 means that the stock is selling for 12 times the firm's earnings and that the market believes that $1 of earnings is currently worth $12. There is also the implication that if earnings increase by $1, the price of the stock will rise by $12.

A PE ratio is affected by many variables. Those directly related to the firm include the growth and stability of its earnings over a period of years, its profitability, its financial strength, and the quality of its management. Factors outside the firm include the nature and prospects of the industry in which it operates and the general economic environment.

The industry's average PE ratio

Firms in the same industry tend to have similar PE ratios. This is illustrated in Exhibit 16–1, which gives the earnings, the price of the stock,

EXHIBIT 16-1. Per Share Earnings, Stock Price, and PE Ratio for Selected Chemical Companies as of December 31, 1978*

Company	Per Share Earnings for the Preceding 12 Months	Price of the Stock	PE Ratio
Allied Chemical	$ 4.60	$ 28¼	6
Celanese	5.95	40⅛	6
Dow Chemical	2.98	24⅞	8
duPont	14.07	126	8
Ethyl	4.15	21½	5
Grow Chemical	1.52	9½	6
Monsanto	7.66	47	6
Pennwalt	4.63	32⅝	7
Rohm and Haas	4.31	31⅝	7
Union Carbide	5.79	34	6
	Average PE: 6.5		

*Source: *Standard & Poor's Stock Guide,* year's end, 1978.

and the PE ratio for ten chemical companies. The average PE ratio for the industry (i.e., 6.5 in Exhibit 16–1) may be indicative of the appropriate PE ratio for an individual firm's stock. If the company's ratio is higher than the industry's average, the stock may be overpriced. Conversely, if the PE ratio is lower than the industry's average, it may indicate that the stock is undervalued.

Unfortunately, security analysis and selection are not that simple. If a firm has an excellent record of earnings growth and the security market anticipates that this growth will continue, the PE ratio tends to be higher than the industry's average. This higher growth has value. These earnings may achieve a higher price, in which case the stock sells for a higher PE ratio (e.g., Dow Chemical in Exhibit 16–1). If a firm is considered to be riskier than is typical of firms in its industry, the PE ratio tends to be lower. The earnings of a firm involving greater risk are worth less. Thus, the stock's price and the PE ratio are lower than industry's average. For example, the PE ratio of Ethyl Corporation tends to be low relative to the industry's average (5 for Ethyl versus the 6.5 industry average). Although Ethyl has achieved substantial growth in sales and earnings, the market views the firm as involving greater risk because its primary product is lead for gasoline. (Lead is a primary source of pollutants, and all new American-made cars must now use lead-free gas.) This foreseeable reduction in demand for lead and the very nature of the product have decreased the market's valuation of Ethyl's earnings.

Why PEs may differ

While the PE ratio is frequently used, it does not tell the investor much about the firm. Of course, it does permit easy comparison of firms (as was illustrated in Exhibit 16–1), but it considers only the earnings and the price of the stock. It tells nothing of how the earnings were achieved or why the market may view one firm's earnings as inferior or superior to the earnings of another firm. Other ratios give a better indication of the firm's performance and earning capacity.

PROFITABILITY RATIOS

Earnings to sales

The amount that a firm earns is particularly important to investors. Earnings accrue to stockholders and either are distributed to them as dividends or are retained. Retained earnings represent an additional investment in the corporation by stockholders. Obviously a firm's performance is a crucial element in fundamental analysis.

Profitability ratios are measures of performance that indicate the amount that the firm is earning relative to some base, such as sales, assets, or equity. The gross profit margin is operating income divided by sales, and the net profit margin is the ratio of profits after taxes to sales. That is,

$$\text{Gross profit margin} = \frac{\text{operating income}}{\text{sales}}$$

$$\text{Net profit margin} = \frac{\text{profits after taxes}}{\text{sales}}$$

For CBS, the gross profit margin for 1977 was

$$\text{Gross profit margin} = \frac{\$331,667}{\$2,776,311} = .119$$

and the net profit margin was

$$\text{Net profit margin} = \frac{\$182,008}{\$2,776,311} = .065$$

These ratios indicate that the company earned $.12 before interest and taxes on every $1 of sales and $.065 after interest and taxes on every $1 of sales.

The impact of taxes

The computation of both these ratios may seem unnecessary, but, as the preceding equations indicate, interest (either earned or an expense) and taxes do have an impact on a firm's profitability. For example, if the investor computes only the net profit margin, an increase in tax rates will decrease the profit margin even though there has been no internal deterioration in the profitability of the company.

Earnings on assets

Other profitability ratios measure the return on assets and the return on equity. The return on assets is earnings divided by assets. That is,

$$\text{Return on assets} = \frac{\text{profits after taxes}}{\text{total assets}}$$

For CBS, the return on assets was

$$\frac{\$182,008}{\$1,518,105} = 11.9\%$$

Thus, CBS earned $.12 on every $1 of assets. This ratio measures the return on the firm's resources (i.e., its assets). It is an all-encompassing measure of performance that indicates the total that management is able to achieve on all of the firm's assets. This return on assets takes into account the profit margins and the rate at which the assets are turned over (e.g., the rate at which the firm collects its accounts receivable and sells its inventory).

Although return on assets gives an aggregate measure of the firm's performance, it does not tell how the management is performing for the stockholders. This is indicated by the return on equity, which is earnings available to common stockholders divided by the equity or the net worth of the firm. That is,

Earnings on equity

$$\text{Return on equity} = \frac{\text{profit after taxes}}{\text{equity}}$$

Equity is the sum of common stock, additional paid-in capital (if any), and retained earnings (if any). The return on equity measures the amount that the firm is earning on the common stockholders' investment.

If the company has any preferred stock, this ratio must be adjusted by subtracting the dividends paid to preferred stockholders from the earnings. This gives the earnings available to the common stockholders. In addition, the contribution of the preferred stock to the firm's equity must be subtracted to obtain the investment of the common stockholders. Common stockholders are interested in the return on their investment or their equity in the firm. Thus, preferred stock should not be included in determining the return on equity attributable to common stock.

Adjustments for preferred stock

For CBS, the return on equity for 1977 was

$$\text{Return on equity} = \frac{\$182,008}{\$809,164} = 22.5\%$$

(This calculation includes both common stock and preference stock. Since this issue of preference stock may be converted into common stock, it may be treated as if it were common stock.) The ratio indicates that CBS earned a return of $.225 for every $1 invested by stockholders. Thus, while CBS achieved only 11.9 per cent on its total assets, it was able to earn 22.5 per cent on the shockholders' investment.

CAPITALIZATION RATIOS

How can a firm magnify the return on the stockholders' investment? One method, which was discussed in Chapter 14, is the use of financial leverage. By successfully using debt financing instead of equity financing, management is able to increase the return to the residual: the common stockholder. This use of financial leverage may be measured by capitaliza-

Debt ratios

tion ratios, which indicate the extent to which the firm finances its assets by the use of debt or preferred stock. These ratios are also referred to as debt ratios.

Since the use of debt financing can have such impact on the firm, each of these ratios is extremely valuable in analyzing the financial position of the firm. The most commonly used capitalization ratios are (1) the debt-to-equity ratio and (2) the debt-to-total assets ratio. These ratios are

$$\frac{\text{Debt}}{\text{Common equity}} \qquad \frac{\text{Debt}}{\text{Total assets}}$$

For CBS, the values for these ratios for 1977 were as follows:

$$\frac{\text{Debt}}{\text{Equity}} = \frac{\$708,941}{\$809,164} = .876$$

$$\frac{\text{Debt}}{\text{Total assets}} = \frac{\$708,941}{\$1,518,105} = .467$$

For CBS, the debt-to-equity ratio indicates that there was $.876 in debt for every $1 of common stock. The ratio of debt to total assets indicates that debt was used to finance 46.7 per cent of the firm's assets.

Since these ratios measure the same thing (i.e., the use of debt financing), the student may wonder which is preferred. Actually, either is acceptable, and preference is a matter of choice. The debt-to-equity ratio expresses debt in terms of equity, while the debt-to-total assets ratio gives the proportion of the firm's total assets that are financed by debt. Financial analysts or students should choose the one that they feel most comfortable working with.

Debt ratios are aggregates

These capitalization ratios are aggregate measures. They both use *total* debt and hence do not differentiate between short-term and long-term debt. The debt-to-equity ratio uses total equity and therefore does not differentiate between the financing provided by preferred and common stock. The debt-to-total assets ratio uses total assets and hence does not differentiate between current and long-term assets.

Financial leverage and declines in the value of assets

The fact that these ratios are aggregate measures does not present a problem, for they measure the extent to which total assets (both short-term and long-term) are financed by creditors. The smaller the proportion of total assets financed by creditors, the larger is the decline in the value of assets that may occur without threatening the creditors' position. Capitalization ratios thus give an indication of risk. Firms that have small equity capital are considered to involve greater risk because there is less cushion to protect creditors if the value of the assets deteriorates. For example, the ratio of debt to total assets for CBS was 46.7 per cent. This indicates that the value of the assets may decline by 53.3 per cent (100% − 46.7%) before the equity is destroyed and only enough assets remain to pay off the debt. If the debt ratio had been 70 per cent, then a decline of

TABLE 16–1. *The Ratio of Debt to Total Assets for Selected Industrial Firms**

FIRM	RATIO
LTV	81.4%
Gulf & Western	70.3
Reynolds Metals	62.3
Greyhound	56.6
Exxon	49.1
Georgia Pacific	47.8
St. Joe Minerals	39.7
Coca-Cola	28.7
Freeport Minerals	24.1

*Source: 1977 annual reports.

only 30 per cent in the value of the assets would endanger the creditors' position.

Capitalization ratios are an indication of risk as much to investors as they are to creditors, for firms with a high degree of financial leverage are riskier investments. If the value of the assets declines or if the firm experiences declining sales and losses, the equity deteriorates more quickly for firms that use financial leverage than for those that do not use debt financing. Hence, the degree of financial leverage is an important measure of risk for investors as well as for creditors.

Capitalization ratios differ significantly among firms. In Table 16–1 the debt ratios for several large industrial firms are presented. Several of these firms use a substantial amount of debt financing. For example, LTV has acquired over 80 per cent of its assets through debt financing. Freeport Mineral, however, has financed more than 75 per cent of its assets through equity.

Table 16–2 presents the debt ratio for the four largest telephone utilities. This table is arranged in descending order from the firm that uses the greatest amount of debt financing to the firm that uses the least. As may be seen from Tables 16–1 and 16–2, the proportion of a firm's total assets financed by debt varies not only from industry to industry but also within an industry. The debt ratios of the telephone companies do, however, have less variation than those of the selected industrial firms.

Financial theory suggests that there is an optimal combination of debt to total assets. This optimal combination of debt and equity financing is

Risk

Debt ratios differ among firms

TABLE 16–2. *Debt Ratios for Four Telephone Utilities as of December 1977**

UTILITY	RATIO
United Telecommunications	68.8%
Continental Telephone	67.6
General Telephone and Electronics	67.3
American Telephone and Telegraph	56.8

*Source: 1977 annual reports.

The optimal combination of debt to equity

important to maximize the value of a firm. The optimal use of financial leverage may significantly benefit the common stockholder by increasing the per share earnings of the company and by permitting faster growth and larger dividends. If, however, the firm uses too much financial leverage or is *undercapitalized,* creditors may require a higher interest rate to compensate them for the increased risk. Investors may also be willing to invest their funds in a corporation with a high degree of financial leverage only if the anticipated return is higher. Thus, the debt ratio, which measures the extent to which a firm uses financial leverage, is one of the most important ratios that managers, creditors, and investors may calculate.

SUMMARY

Fundamental analysis selects stocks by identifying the strongest firms. Emphasis is placed on economic performance as measured by a variety of ratios. These include profit margins, which calculate the return earned on the firm's sales, assets, and equity, and capitalizaton ratios, which measure the extent to which a firm uses debt financing.

The analyst also considers the industry in which the firm operates. Even if the firm is financially strong, it must still compete and grow in order to prosper. A growth in demand or competition as well as technological change will have an impact on the firm and its earnings. The fundamentalist seeks those firms that are able to satisfy an increased demand and to enlarge their share of the market.

In addition to analyzing the firm and its industry, the fundamentalist considers the direction in which the aggregate economy is moving. Security prices respond to economic activity. During periods of prosperity, stock prices tend to rise. Conversely, when recession occurs and unemployment increases, stock prices tend to fall.

The aggregate economy is affected by many factors, but it is particularly important to consider the monetary policy of the Federal Reserve in selecting securities. The Federal Reserve buys and sells government securities in order to affect the nation's supply of money and credit. These open market operations affect security prices by altering both interest rates and the earnings of firms.

SUMMARY OF RATIOS

Current Ratio

$$\frac{\text{Current assets}}{\text{Current liabilities}}$$

Acid Test or Quick Ratio

$$\frac{\text{Current assets minus inventory}}{\text{Current liabilities}}$$

Inventory Turnover

1. $$\frac{\text{Sales}}{\text{Average inventory}}$$

2. $$\frac{\text{Cost of goods sold}}{\text{Average inventory}}$$

Average Collection Period

$$\frac{\text{Receivables}}{\text{Sales per day}}$$

Receivables Turnover

1. $$\frac{\text{Annual credit sales}}{\text{Accounts receivable}}$$

2. $$\frac{\text{Annual sales}}{\text{Accounts receivable}}$$

Times-Interest-Earned Ratio

$$\frac{\text{Earnings before interest and taxes}}{\text{Annual interest charges}}$$

Coverage of Preferred Stock Dividends

$$\frac{\text{Earnings after taxes}}{\text{Dividends on preferred stock}}$$

Price-to-Earnings Ratio

$$\frac{\text{Price of stock}}{\text{Per share earnings}}$$

Gross Profit Margin

$$\frac{\text{Operating income}}{\text{Sales}}$$

Net Profit Margin

$$\frac{\text{Profits after taxes}}{\text{Sales}}$$

Return on Assets

$$\frac{\text{Profits after taxes}}{\text{Total assets}}$$

Return on Equity

$$\frac{\text{Profits after taxes}}{\text{Equity}}$$

Debt Ratio

1. $$\frac{\text{Debt}}{\text{Common equity}}$$

2. $$\frac{\text{Debt}}{\text{Total assets}}$$

Terms to Remember

Recession	Reserves	Gross profit margin
Forecasting	Cyclical industry	Net profit margin
Federal Reserve	Time-series analysis	Return on assets
Open market operations	Cross-sectional analysis	Return on equity
Supply of money	PE ratio	Debt ratio

Questions

1. Where can the investor find economic forecasts?

2. What is the Federal Reserve? What are its economic goals?

3. What are open market operations? How may they affect stock prices?

4. What is a "cyclical" industry? Is it desirable to invest in firms in these industries?

5. What is a PE ratio? What may a low PE ratio imply?

6. What is the difference between the gross and net profit margins?

7. What is a capitalization ratio? Do all firms within an industry use the same amount of debt financing?

8. Why may the return on equity exceed the return on a firm's total assets?

SELECTED READINGS

"A Conversation With Benjamin Graham." *Financial Analysts Journal,* (September–October 1976), pp. 20–23.
Benishay, Haskell: "Economic Information in Financial Ratio Analysis." *Accounting and Business Research, 2* (Spring 1971), pp. 174–179.
Burns, Arthur F.: *The Business Cycle in a Changing World.* New York, National Bureau of Economic Research, 1969.
Graham, Benjamin, David L. Dodd, Sidney Cottle, and Charles Tatham: *Security Analysis — Principles and Techniques,* 4th ed. New York, McGraw-Hill Book Co., 1962.
Henning, Charles N., William Pigott, and Robert Haney Scott: *Financial Markets and the Economy.* Englewood Cliffs, N.J., Prentice-Hall, Inc., 1975.
Horrigan, James C.: "A Short History of Financial Ratio Analysis." *Accounting Review,* 43 (April 1968), pp. 284–294.
Kaufman, George G.: *Money, the Financial System, and the Economy,* 2nd ed. Chicago, Rand McNally & Co., 1977.

Murray, Roger: "Lessons for Financial Analysis." *Journal of Finance*, 26 (May 1971), pp. 327–332.

Ritter, Lawrence, and William L. Silber: *Money*, 2nd ed. New York, Basic Books, Inc., 1973.

Sprinkel, Beryl W.: *Money and Stock Prices*. Homewood, Ill., Richard D. Irwin, Inc., 1964.

The Federal Reserve System — Purposes and Functions. Washington, D.C., Board of Governors, 1974.

Learning Objectives

After completing this chapter you should be able to

1. State the purpose of technical analysis.
2. Differentiate between the various technical approaches to security selection.
3. Construct X–O charts and bar graphs.
4. Calculate a moving average.
5. Explain why studying insider activity may result in the selection of superior securities.
6. Explain why the technical approach has little support from many investors.

chapter 17

TECHNICAL ANALYSIS

Technical analysis is a very broad topic because there are so many different varieties of this type of analysis. However, they all have the same thing in common: the use of past data to forecast future stock prices. These data are accumulated and tabulated in a variety of charts and graphs. For this reason, investors who use these techniques are often referred to as chartists.

This chapter covers several of the popular technical approaches to the market and security selection. These include the Dow theory, point-and-figure charts, and moving averages. The discussion is primarily descriptive and explains how these measures are constructed and used. The chapter ends with a brief discussion of empirical studies on the validity of technical analysis. The results of these studies strongly suggest that the various technical approaches do not lead to superior investment results. However, while many academicians who teach investment courses do not believe that the technical approaches result in superior gains, those who use technical analysis obviously do.

THE PURPOSE OF THE TECHNICAL APPROACH

The importance of the past

The technical approach attempts to predict future stock prices by analyzing past stock prices. In effect, it asserts that tomorrow's stock price is influenced by today's price. That is a very appealing assertion, because it eliminates the need to perform the fundamental analysis discussed in Chapter 16. No longer does the investor have to be concerned with ratios, financial leverage, and appropriate discount rates. Instead, he or she keeps a record of specific market factors, such as who is buying and selling the stock, and of specific information on individual stocks, such as the closing price and the volume of transactions. This information is then summarized in a variety of forms, such as charts and graphs, which in turn tell the investor when to buy and sell the securities.

Market indicators

There are many different technical approaches to the selection of securities. Only a few will be discussed in this chapter. These are classified into two groups. The first techniques are designed to indicate the general direction of the market. Since security prices move together, the direction of the market is the overriding factor in the decision to buy and sell securities. In fact, it is the single most important factor in these technical approaches. This first group of techniques includes the Dow theory (which is perhaps the oldest of all the technical approaches to the market), Barron's confidence index, and odd lot purchases versus odd lot sales. These three approaches may be constructed from information reported in the financial press. For practical purposes, the investor may consider these sources of information as virtually free.

Specific security indicators

The second group of technical approaches discussed in this chapter is designed not only to discern the direction of the market but also to decide when to buy or sell specific securities. These include point-and-figure charts, bar graphs, moving averages of stock prices, and insider transactions. The information necessary to perform this analysis is also readily available in the financial press. Thus, the investor may either perform the analysis or purchase advisory services that perform the analysis.

A warning

Before reading further, the student should be forewarned that the presentations of the various approaches make their application appear to be easy. Also, the examples have been selected to illustrate the techniques. In actual practice the buy and sell signals indicated by technical analysis may frequently be less obvious than the illustrations used in the text.

A need to practice

The student should probably practice the techniques and be familiar with the subtle differences between them before actually using technical analysis to make investment decisions. Furthermore, there are other technical approaches that are not covered in this chapter along with variations on the methods discussed. The individual should learn more about these techniques before applying any of them. For additional reading concerning technical analysis, the student should consult some of the suggested publications listed at the end of the chapter.

MARKET INDICATORS

THE DOW THEORY

The Dow theory is one of the oldest technical methods for analyzing security prices. It is an aggregate measure of security prices and hence does not predict the direction of change in individual stock prices. What it purports to show is the direction that the market will take. Thus, it is a method that identifies the top of a bull market and the bottom of a bear market.

The Dow theory developed from the work of Charles Dow, who founded Dow Jones and Company and was the first editor of *The Wall Street Journal.** Dow identified three movements in security prices: primary, secondary, and tertiary. Primary price movements are related to the security's intrinsic value. Such values depend upon the earning capacity of the firm and the distribution of dividends. Secondary price movements, or "swings," are governed by current events that temporarily affect value and by the manipulation of stock prices. These price swings may persist for several weeks and even months. Tertiary price movements are daily price fluctuations to which Dow attributed no significance.

Price movements

Although Charles Dow believed in fundamental analysis, the Dow theory has evolved into a primarily technical approach to the stock market. It asserts that stock prices demonstrate patterns over four to five years and that these patterns are mirrored by indices of stock prices. The Dow theory employs two of the Dow Jones averages, the industrial average and the transportation average. The utility average is generally ignored.

Dow theory evolved into a technical approach

Indices of stock prices were discussed in greater detail in Chapter 13. For the purpose of this chapter all the student needs to remember is that the Dow Jones averages are measures of aggregate stock market activity. When an average is rising, then the market as a whole is rising. While a specific stock may move against the average, the majority of them cannot because they compose the average. Hence, if the majority of stocks are rising in price the index also rises.

The Dow theory is built upon the assertion that measures of stock prices tend to move together. If the Dow Jones industrial average is rising, then the transportation average should also be rising. Such simultaneous price movements suggest a strong bull market. Conversely, a decline in both the industrial and transportation averages suggests a strong bear market. However, if the averages are moving in opposite directions, the market is uncertain as to the direction of future stock prices.

Stock prices move together

If one of the averages starts to decline after a period of rising stock prices, then the two are at odds. For example, the industrial average may be rising while the transportation average is falling. This suggests that the industrials may not continue to rise but may soon start to fall. Hence, the smart investor will use this signal to sell securities and convert to cash.

When averages move in opposite directions, that is a buy or sell signal

---

*See George W. Bishop, Jr., *Charles H. Dow and the Dow Theory*, New York, Appleton–Century–Crofts, 1960, pp. 225–228.

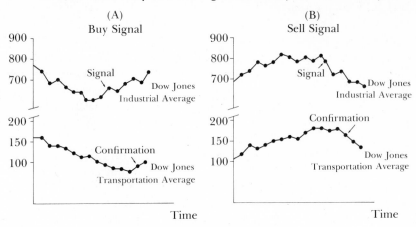

GRAPH 17–1.   Buy and Sell Signals Given by the Dow Theory

The converse occurs when, after a period of falling security prices one of the averages starts to rise while the other continues to fall. According to the Dow theory, this divergence suggests that the bear market is over and that security prices in general will soon start to rise. The astute investor will then purchase securities in anticipation of the price increase.

These signals are illustrated in Graph 17–1. Part A illustrates a buy signal. Both the industrial and transportation averages have been declining when the industrials start to rise. Although the transportation index is still declining, the increase in the industrial average suggests that the declining market is over. This change is then confirmed when the transportation average also starts to rise.

Part B illustrates the opposite case in which both the industrial and transportation averages have been rising. Then the industrial average starts to decline while the transportation average continues to rise. This suggests that the market is going through an unsettled period and, until they start moving together again, there is uncertainty as to the future direction of stock prices. However, in the case illustrated in Graph 17–1, part B, the transportation average also starts to fall, which confirms the direction of the industrial average and indicates that a bear market is underway. Of course, this implies that investors should try to liquidate security holdings.

Signals may be self-fulfilling prophecies

If investors believe this theory, they will try to liquidate when a sell signal becomes apparent, which in turn will drive down prices. Buy signals have the opposite effect. Investors will try to purchase securities, which will drive up their prices. This points out an interesting phenomenon concerning technical analysis in general. If investors believe the signals and act accordingly, the signals will become self-fulfilling prophecies. Unfortunately, by the time many investors perceive the signal and act, the price change will have already occurred, and much of the potential profit from the alterations in the portfolio will have evaporated.

There are several problems with the Dow theory. The first is that it is not a theory but an interpretation of known data. It does not explain why the two averages should be able to forecast future stock prices. In addition, there may be a considerable lag between actual turning points and those indicated by the forecast. It may be months before the two averages confirm each other, during which time individual stocks may show substantial price changes.

The Dow theory does not explain why prices move

The accuracy of the Dow theory and its predictive power have been the subject of much criticism. Greiner and Whitcomb assert that "the Dow Theory provides a time tested method of reading the stock market barometer."[*] However, between 1929 and 1960 the Dow theory made only 9 correct predictions out of 24 buy or sell signals.[†] Such results are less accurate than the investor may obtain by flipping a coin and have considerably diminished support for the technique.

The Dow theory may not be accurate

BARRON'S CONFIDENCE INDEX

Barron's confidence index is based on the belief that the differential between the returns on quality bonds and bonds of lesser quality will forecast future price movements. During periods of optimism, investors (especially professionals) will be more willing to bear risk and thus will move from investments in higher quality debt to more speculative but higher yielding, lower quality debt. This selling of higher quality debt will depress its price and raise its yield. Simultaneously, the purchase of poor quality debt should drive up its price and lower the yield. Thus, the difference between the two yields will diminish.

It compares yields on poor and high quality debt

The opposite occurs when sentiment turns bearish. The investors and especially those who "know" what the market will do in the future will sell poor quality debt and purchase higher quality debt. This will have the effect of increasing the spread between the yields, as the price of poor quality debt falls relative to that of the higher quality debt.

Barron's confidence index is constructed by using Barron's index of yields on high and lower quality bonds. These yields and the confidence index are illustrated in Graph 17–2. When the yield differential is small (i.e., when the yields on high quality debt approach those that can be earned on poor quality debt), the ratio rises. This is interpreted as showing investor confidence. Such confidence means that security prices will tend to rise. Thus, when the index rose to over 95 in August 1974, the implication was that security prices would subsequently rise and hence stocks should be purchased.

---

[*]Perry P. Greiner and Hale C. Whitcomb, *The Dow Theory and the Seventy-Year Record*, Larchmont, N.Y., Investors Intelligence, Inc., 1969, p. 130.
[†]See Leonard T. Wright, *Principles of Investments — Text and Cases*, 2nd ed., Columbus, Ohio, Grid, Inc., 1977, pp. 312–317.

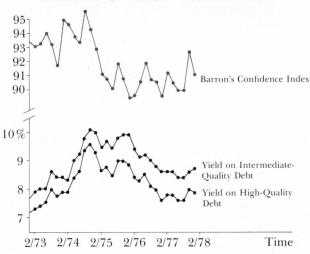

GRAPH 17–2.   Barron's Confidence Index

(Source: Adapted From Data in *The Dow Jones
Investor's Handbook 1978*)

Conversely a declining index is interpreted to mean that security prices will fall. When the index was below 90 during 1976, the implication was that security prices would fall. Investors who had faith in the index should have acted accordingly.

Like the other technical approaches, Barron's confidence index has been subjected to scrutiny. Although it may indicate a tendency, it does not give conclusive market signals. For example, the purchase signal in the summer of 1974 was followed by lower rates and higher security prices. However, if purchases had been made only a year earlier when the index was also above 90, the investor would have experienced losses because interest rates subsequently rose, causing security prices to fall.

**Problems of
ambiguity and lags**

In addition to the ambiguity of the signals, there is a time lag between a signal and the subsequent change in the direction of the market. The time of the lag varies. When the index rises, an investor will want to know if security prices will start to fall immediately or after months of continuing rising prices. The index cannot answer this question. Owing to these problems, the index is an unreliable predictor of future stock prices.

PURCHASES AND SALES OF ODD LOTS

Another technical indicator of the market is the purchase and sale of securities by small investors. These investors buy in small quantities (i.e., odd lots of less than 100 shares). The volume of such odd lot purchases and sales is reported in the financial press along with other financial data. The ratio of these odd lot purchases to odd lot sales is taken by some technicians as an indicator of the direction of future prices.

The rationale behind the use of the ratio of odd lot purchases to sales is that small investors are frequently wrong. Such investors will get caught up in the enthusiasm of a bull market and expand their purchases just as the market is reaching the top. The converse occurs at the market bottom. During declining markets, small investors become depressed about the market. After experiencing losses, they sell out as the market reaches its bottom. Such sales are frequently referred to as the passing of securities from "weak" hands to "strong" hands. The weak hands are, of course, the small investors who are misjudging the market, and the strong hands are the large investors who are more informed and capable of making correct investment decisions.

Empirical work has not been able to verify that odd lot purchases and sales are a good predictor of future prices.* These studies indicate that during rising markets, purchases do tend to exceed sales. Conversely, during periods of declining markets the odd lot sales increase. Like the Dow theory and Barron's confidence index, the odd lot theory illustrates a tendency, but there is also little concrete evidence of its ability to forecast accurately when the market will change. It assumes that purchasers of odd lots make inferior investment decisions, but it should be remembered that many large investors are also sellers at the market bottom and buyers at the market top. Incorrect investment decisions are not the monopoly of small investors!

Small investors may be wrong

The weak and strong hands

The prediction of future prices has not been verified

SPECIFIC STOCK INDICATORS

The preceding section discussed several technical approaches to the market as a whole. This section considers several techniques that may be applied to either the market or individual securities. When applied to the market, their purpose is to identify the general trend. When applied to individual securities, these techniques attempt to inform the investor when to buy, when to sell, or when to maintain current positions in a specific security.

POINT-AND-FIGURE CHARTS (THE X–O CHART)

An X–O chart is constructed by placing an X on the chart when the price of the stock rises by some amount, such as $1 or $2, and an O on

---

*See Richard A. Brealey, *An Introduction to Risk and Return From Common Stocks*, Cambridge, Mass., M.I.T. Press, 1969, pp. 129–140.

GRAPH 17–3.   The Construction of an *X-O* Chart

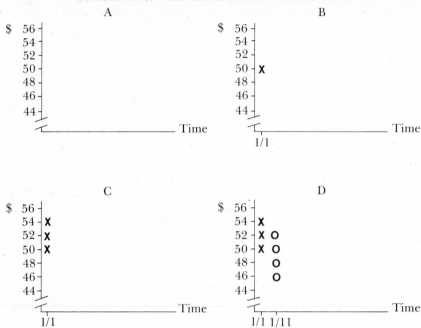

the chart when it declines by that amount. Such a chart requires following the stock on a daily basis and noting the price at the end of the day. If the price has changed by the specified amount, then an entry is made on the chart.

This procedure is best explained by an illustration. Suppose the price of a stock had the following day-to-day price changes and the investor wanted to construct an *X–O* chart for price movements of $2. The procedure is illustrated in Graph 17–3.

Daily Closing Prices for January

Date	Prices				
1/1–1/5	$50⅛	51⅜	51¾	52⅛	54½
1/8–1/12	$53½	53⅛	52½	51⅞	51⅛
1/15–1/19	$49½	49¾	47⅛	48¾	47⅞
1/22–1/26	$49¾	46⅞	46⅛	45⅞	44⅞

Graph 17–3 is divided into four quadrants, which illustrate the four steps necessary to create the chart.

Construction of the graph

The first quadrant (A) sets up the axes: time on the horizontal axis and dollars on the vertical axis. The dollar unit that is selected depends on the price of the stock. For lower priced stocks the units should be $1, but for higher priced stocks the units may be larger, such as $2 or

$3. Since a movement from $40 to $42 is the same percentage increase as a price movement from $20 to $21, the use of the large increments for higher priced stocks does not reduce the quality of the X–O chart. In addition, the use of larger units will reduce the amount of entries necessary to create the chart. Since the price of the stock in question is in the $50 range, a $2 interval is selected, and the vertical axis shows the increments in $2 units.

The second quadrant (B) plots the price of the stock on the first day of observation. Since the price of the stock is rising, the chartist enters an X at $50 on the graph. Additional Xs are entered only after the price of the stock rises by $2 (e.g., $50 to $52). All small movements in price both up and down are ignored, and only after the price has risen by $2 is a second X entered on the graph. Thus, although the price of the stock rose during the first three days, no entry is made. The effect of such omissions is both to reduce the work required to construct the chart and to minimize the effect of small daily price fluctuations.

The third quadrant (C) plots the price increases that occurred on days 4 and 5. The price closed above $52 on day 4, so an X is placed on the chart. The same applies to day 5, when the stock closed above $54.

After reaching a high of $54½, the price of the stock starts to fall. The chartist now uses only Os instead of Xs to indicate the declining price. Once again the price must fall by $2 before an entry is made (i.e., the stock must sell for $52 or less, since $54 was the highest X entry). The date on which Os began to be recorded on the chart is noted on the horizontal axis. The analyst will continue to place Os on the chart until the present downward trend is reversed and the price of the stock rises by the necessary $2. Then the analyst will start a new column and enter an X to indicate an increase in the stock's price.

The fourth quadrant (D) illustrates the decline in the stock's price. After the initial price rise illustrated in quadrant C, the price falls. Once it reaches $52, an O is placed on the chart. This occurs on January 11. The price of the stock now appears to be declining. Should the price fall to $50 or below, another O will be placed on the chart. If, however, the price again reaches $54 an X will be placed in the next column and the date will be recorded to indicate the change in the direction of the price.

In this case the price of the stock continues to decline. Each time the stock breaks the two-point barrier, another O is placed on the chart. If the price continues to decline, the column will fill up with Os. If the stock's price stabilizes, then no entries will be made until a two-point movement occurs.

Signals of future prices

After a period of stable prices, a deviation signals the direction of future price changes. Such signals are illustrated in Graph 17–4. On the left-hand side (A), after a period of trading between $52 and $58, the price of the stock rises to a new high of $60. This suggests that a new upward price trend is being established, which is a buy signal. On the right-hand side (B), the opposite case is illustrated. The price declines below $52,

GRAPH 17–4.   Buy and Sell Signals

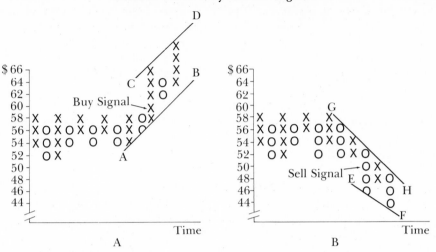

A

B

which suggests that a new downward price trend is being established. If the investor owns the stock, the shares should be sold.

It is interesting to note that in both cases illustrated in Graph 17–4, the purchases and sales appear to be made at the wrong time. In the case of the purchase, it is made after the stock has already increased in price. Conversely, the sale is made after the stock has declined in price. Thus, purchases are not made at the lows, and sales are not made at the highs. Instead, the purchases appear to be made when the stock is reaching new highs, and the sales are made when the stock is reaching new lows. The rationale for this behavior rests primarily on the belief that the charts indicate new trends. Despite the fact that the investor missed the high prices for the sale and the low prices for the purchase, if the price change that is being forecasted proves accurate, then the investor will have made the correct investment decision even though the purchases and sales were not made at the exact turning points.

Signals for possible trading strategies

Besides indicating the buy or sell signals when trends are being established, these charts suggest possible trading strategies during the trends, which are also illustrated in Graph 17–4. While the left-hand side shows a price that is obviously rising, the price is still fluctuating. The right-hand side illustrates a downward trend, but the price is also fluctuating. During the upward trend, which is illustrated in Graph 17–4, part A, each high is higher than the preceding high price, and each low is higher than the preceding low price. Obviously, if an investor buys this stock and holds it, the return will be positive over this period. However, the return may be increased by judiciously buying at each low, selling at each high, and repeating the process when the cycle within the trend is repeated.

In order to isolate these opportunities, a set of lines have been drawn in Graph 17–4 connecting the high and the low prices that the stock is achieving. These lines are believed to have special significance because they indicate when to make the buy and sell decisions. The bottom lines (*AB* and *EF*), which connect the lowest prices, suggest a price level that generates "support" for the stock. Technical analysis asserts that when the price of the stock approaches a support line, the number of purchases will increase, which will stop further price declines. Hence, the approach of a stock's price toward a support line suggests that a buying opportunity is developing. Should the price reach the line and start back up, then the investor should buy the stock.

The opposite occurs at the top line (*CD* and *GH* in Graph 17–4, parts A and B), which represents "resistance." Since the price of the stock has risen to that level, more investors will want to sell their stock, which will thwart further price advances. Accordingly, the investor should sell the stock when the price reaches a line of resistance. After the stock has been sold, the investor then waits for the price to decline to the level of price support.

Although a discussion of the efficiency or validity of the various technical approaches is deferred until the end of the chapter, it should be obvious to the student at this time that the *X–O* chart has a major flaw. If the investor follows all of the signals and makes many transactions, much of the potential profit will be consumed by brokerage fees. Thus, even if the *X–O* chart is an accurate predictor of price fluctuations, it still may not result in superior returns if the investor must continuously buy and sell. This generates a substantial amount of commissions for the broker and reduces the profits from the transactions.

"Support"

"Resistance"

BAR CHARTS

Bar charts are similar to point-and-figure charts. Like the *X–O* charts, they require a day-to-day compilation of data, and they use essentially the same information as the *X–O* chart. Preference for one over the other is a matter of choice, and while the investor could construct both, such work would seem redundant.

A bar chart is constructed by using three price observations: the high, the low, and the closing price for the day. If the prices were

Construction of bar charts

Price	Monday	Tuesday	Wednesday	Thursday	Friday
high	$10	$9½	$9⅞	$10½	$12
low	9	9	9¼	9⅞	10⅛
close	9	9⅜	9⅞	10	11½

the bar charts for each day would be

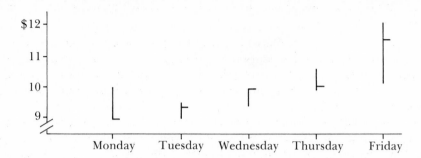

The vertical lines represent the range of the stock's price (i.e., the high and the low prices), and the horizontal lines represent the closing price.

It is obvious that such a chart is easy to construct, but it does require a substantial amount of work to keep several of these charts up to date on a daily basis. Each stock requires 15 price observations per week, which means 150 observations for just ten stocks per week. Since an entry is made on an *X–O* chart only if the price of the stock has moved to the next interval, less work is required to construct such a chart, and it may be preferred to the bar chart for this reason alone.

Patterns of stock prices

As with the *X–O* chart, the bar graph is supposed to indicate future price movements in the stock by the pattern that emerges. There are several possible patterns. For example, one brief paperback book on charting identifies at least ten patterns, each with a descriptive name such as head and shoulder, wedge, flag, or pennant.* Space limits this discussion to only one pattern: the head and shoulder. The student who is interested in the variety of patterns should consult a book that explains the different patterns and how they are used to predict future stock prices.

The head-and-shoulder pattern

A head-and-shoulder pattern does just what its name implies: The chart forms a pattern that resembles a head and shoulders. Such a pattern is illustrated in Graph 17–5. Initially, the price of the stock rises. Then it levels off before rising to a new high, after which the price declines, levels off, and then starts to fall. To illustrate the head-and-shoulder pattern, several lines have been imposed on the graph. These lines are similar to the lines of resistance and support found on the *X–O* charts. Line *AB* shows the left shoulder and also represents a line of resistance. However, once it is penetrated, the price of the stock rises to a new high, where it meets new resistance (line *CD*).

When the stock is unable to penetrate this new resistance, the price starts to decline and forms the head. However, after this initial decline in price the stock reaches a new level of support, which forms the right shoulder (line *EF*). When the price falls below line *EF*, the head-and-

---

*See Anthony J. Lerro and Charles B. Swayne, Jr., *Selection of Securities: Technical Analysis of Stock Market Prices*, Morristown, N.J., General Learning Corporation, 1976.

shoulder pattern is completed. This is interpreted to mean that the stock's price will continue to fall and is taken as a very bearish sign by followers of this type of analysis.

While the head-and-shoulder pattern in Graph 17–5 indicates that the price of the stock will subsequently fall, the same pattern upside down implies the exact opposite. In this case, penetration of the right shoulder indicates that the price of the stock will rise and is taken as a very bullish sign by those who use bar graphs.

MOVING AVERAGES

A moving average is an average computed over time. For example, in 1977 the closing monthly values for the Dow Jones industrial average were as follows:

Averages over time

January	954.4	April	926.9	July	890.1	October	813.4
February	936.4	May	898.7	August	861.5	November	829.8
March	919.1	June	916.5	September	847.1	December	831.2

A six-month moving average of the Dow Jones industrials would be computed as follows. The average for the first six months is computed first.

How the Dow Jones industrial average is computed

$$\frac{954.4 + 936.4 + 919.1 + 926.9 + 898.7 + 916.3}{6} = \frac{5551.8}{6} = 925.3$$

Then the average is computed again, but the entry for July (890.1) is added in and the entry for January (954.4) is deleted:

$$\frac{936.4 + 919.1 + 926.9 + 898.7 + 916.3 + 890.1}{6} = \frac{5487.5}{6} = 914.6$$

The average is thus 914.6, which is less than the average for the preceding six months (925.3).

GRAPH 17–5. Head-and-Shoulder Pattern

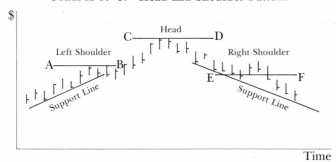

GRAPH 17–6.   Dow Jones Industrials and a Six-Month Moving Average of the Dow Jones Industrials

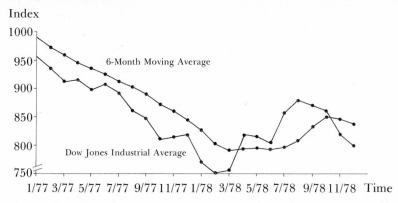

To obtain the next entry, the average is computed again, with August being added and February being dropped. The average in this case becomes 902.1. By continuing this method of adding the most recent entry and dropping the oldest entry, the averages move through time.

The moving average for the Dow Jones industrials

Graph 17–6 presents both the Dow Jones industrial average for 1977 through 1978 and the six-month moving average. As may be seen from the graph, the moving average follows the Dow Jones industrials. However, when the Dow Jones industrials are declining, the moving average is greater than the industrial average. The converse is true when the Dow Jones industrial average is rising: the moving average is less than the industrial average. At one point the two are equal (i.e., where the two lines cross). In this example, the Dow Jones industrial averages and the six-month moving average are equal to 790 toward the end of March 1978. Technicians place emphasis on such a crossover, for they believe that it is indicative of a change in the direction of the market. (It may also indicate a change in a specific security's price when the moving average is computed for particular stock.) In this case, there appears to be some validity to the claim, because the market did rise in the summer of 1978.

200-Day moving average

The average that is most frequently used is a 200-day moving average. Thus, for a specific stock, the investor must keep a daily tabulation of 200 stock prices and recompute the average daily! Such a calculation is obviously tedious if a significant number of stocks are included. However, brokers may have access to these averages, or the investor may purchase an advisory service that computes them.

INSIDER TRANSACTIONS

Insider purchases and sales

In Chapter 5 we learned that insiders, such as officers, directors, and very large stockholders, can not legally use inside information for personal gain. However, they can and often do purchase and sell the stock of the firm in which they have access to privileged information. Such transactions are legal if they are reported to the SEC.* Since insiders may have the best picture of how the firm is faring, some believers of technical analysis feel that these inside transactions offer a clue to future earnings, dividends, and stock price performance. A greater number of purchases than sales is believed to be a bullish indicator, and more sales transactions than purchases imply that the stock will fall.

The hypothesis that insider activity may be indicative of future stock prices has received some support in the academic literature. As is discussed in the following section on the verification of technical analysis, very little support has been found for the various technical approaches to security selection. However, several reports do suggest that the study of insider activity may indeed lead to the selection of superior securities. For example, Martin Zweig reported that from June 1974 to April 1976 more than 60 per cent of stocks with significant insider purchases outperformed the market, but only 37 per cent of stocks with significant insider sales outperformed the market.† This study and others reported in the academic literature give some credence to this particular method of technical analysis that is lacking in the other techniques previously discussed.‡ This suggests that the individual investor would be well advised to keep track of insider activity in those securities of particular interest.

Insider activity may predict future price behavior

THE VERIFICATION OF TECHNICAL ANALYSIS

At first glance technical analysis seems so very appealing. One needs only to construct a set of charts or compute some simple ratios and then follow the signals given by the analysis. Such simple rules for investing literally beg for verification to ascertain if they are, in fact, good predictors.

Several studies have sought to answer that question. The use of computers not only eases calculations but also makes it possible to test several variations of each technical approach. For example, the investigator may have the computer calculate various moving averages (e.g., 200-day, 100-day, or 50-day averages) to determine if one is the best predictor. Thus, the computer greatly eases the burden of calculations

---

*The *Insiders Chronicle* reports these transactions weekly. This publication is devoted almost exclusively to reporting transactions by insiders.

†See Martin E. Zweig, "Canny Insiders" *Barron's,* (June 21, 1976), p. 5.

‡These studies include Jeffrey F. Jaffe, "Special Information and Insider Trading," *Journal of Business,* (July 1974), and James H. Lorie and Victor Niederhoffer, "Predictive and Statistical Properties of Insider Trading," *Journal of Law and Economics,* 11(April 1968), pp. 35–53.

and makes it possible to test the various technical approaches to the market.

There is little empirical evidence to support the technical approach

The majority of this research has failed to verify the various technical approaches to investing.* These results suggest that the technical approach does not lead to superior investment performance and that the investor would do just as well to buy a randomly selected portfolio and hold it. When commissions are included, the return from following the technical approach may be even less than earned on a randomly selected portfolio. These conclusions have resulted in a general rejection of technical analysis by academically trained teachers of finance.

The primary cause for the inability of the technical approach to result in the selection of securities that outperform the market is that the market is very efficient. (This efficient market hypothesis is discussed in detail in Chapter 25.) Information is readily disseminated among the investing public, and prices adjust accordingly. Thus, if an investor were to develop an approach that outperformed the market, it would be a matter of time before the technique would be learned by others. The method would no longer achieve the initial results as the mass of investors applied it. A system that works (if one can be found) can succeed only if it is not known by the majority of investors. Thus, it is naive for an investor to believe that he or she can use a known technical approach to beat the market. A new and unknown system is needed. However, when one realizes that many investors are looking for and testing various approaches, it is hard to believe that the individual investor will find a technical approach that can beat the market.

Although the technical approach lacks verification, it is still used by investors, and one frequently sees in the financial press advertisements for advisory services that employ various technical approaches. Perhaps the investor should ask why the service is being sold and not being applied exclusively by those who know the "secret." Certainly, if one knows how to beat the market, one should be able to earn a substantial return on investments and should not need to sell the secret for monetary gain.

SUMMARY

Technical analysis seeks to identify superior investments by examining the past behavior of the market and of individual securities.

---

*For example, see Michael C. Jensen and George A. Bennington, "Random Walks and Technical Theories: Some Additional Evidence," *The Journal of Finance,* 25(May 1970), pp. 469–482; Eugene Fama, "The Behavior of Stock-Market Prices," *Journal of Business,* 37(January 1965), pp. 34–105; F. E. James, Jr., "Monthly Moving Averages — An Effective Investment Tool?" *Journal of Financial and Quantitative Analysis,* (September 1968), pp. 315–326; and J. C. VanHorne and G. G. C. Parker, "The Random Walk Theory: An Empirical Test," *Financial Analysts Journal,* (November–December 1967), pp. 87–92. (The student should be warned that most of this material may be difficult to comprehend.)

These analysts, or "chartists," stress the past as a means to predict the future. This approach is diametrically opposed to the fundamental approach, which stresses future earnings and dividends appropriately discounted back to the present.

Several technical approaches (the Dow theory, Barron's confidence index, and odd lot purchases versus odd lot sales) attempt to identify changes in the direction of the market. Since individual security prices move together, the determination of a change in the direction of the market should identify the future movement of individual security prices.

Other technical approaches (X–O charts, bar graphs, moving averages, and analysis of insider activity) may be applied to individual securities. By constructing various charts and graphs, the technical analyst determines when specific securities should be bought or sold.

Whether the technical approach leads to superior investment results is open to debate. However, with the exception of insider activity, little support has been found to verify technical analysis. The results of these studies imply that the investor may achieve similar results by purchasing a random selection of securities.

Terms to Remember

Dow theory	X–O chart	Head-and-shoulder pattern
Barron's confidence index	Moving average	Insider transactions
Odd lot theory	Bar graph	Technical analysis

Questions

1. What is the purpose of technical analysis?

2. Why are those who use technical analysis sometimes referred to as chartists?

3. What changes represent a sell signal in the Dow theory, Barron's confidence index, and the odd lot theory?

4. What is a moving average? What is the significance when a stock's price equals a moving average of that price?

5. Why may technical analysis produce self-fulfilling predictions?

6. Why may the construction of some charts or graphs used in technical analysis be tedious and time-consuming?

7. What is the problem with time lags in technical analysis?

8. Why does technical analysis receive little support from academically oriented students of investment?

9. Which technical approach may be the best?

SELECTED READINGS

Bishop, George W., Jr.: *Charles Dow and the Dow Theory*. New York, Appleton-Century-Crofts, Inc., 1960.
Brealey, Richard A.: *An Introduction to Risk and Return From Common Stocks*. Cambridge, Mass., M.I.T. Press, 1969.
Cohen, A. W.: *Point and Future Stock Market Trading*. Larchmont, N.Y., Chartcraft, Inc., 1968.
Ehrbar, A. F.: "Technical Analysis Refuses to Die." *Fortune, 92*(August 1975), p. 99.
Fama, Eugene F., and Marshall E. Blume: "Filter Rules and Stock Market Trading." *Journal of Business,* (January 1966), pp. 226–241.
Greiner, Perry P., and Hale C. Whitcomb: *The Dow Theory and the Seventy-Year Record*. Larchmont, N.Y., Investors Intelligence, Inc., 1969.
Lerro, Anthony J., and Charles B. Swayne, Jr.: *Selection of Securities: Technical Analysis of Stock Market Prices*. Morristown, N.J., General Learning Press, 1971.
Lorie, James H., and Mary T. Hamilton: *The Stock Market: Theories and Evidence*. Homewood, Ill., Richard D. Irwin, Inc., 1973.
Malkiel, Burton, G.: *A Random Walk Down Wall Street*. New York, W. W. Norton & Co., Inc., 1973.
Rhea, Robert: *The Dow Theory*. New York, Barron's Publishing Co., 1932.
"Vindication for the Technical Analysts," *Business Week,* (June 9, 1975), pp. 66–67.
Zahorchak, Michael G.: *The Art of Low Risk Investing*. New York, Van Nostrand Reinhold Co., 1972.
Zweig, Martin E.: *Understanding Technical Forecasting—How To Use Barron's Laboratory Pages*. Princeton, N.J., Dow Jones & Co., Inc., 1978.

Investing in Options

Parts Five and Six are devoted to the less traditional investments. Although some of these are very speculative, others, such as home ownership, are conservative forms of investment.

Part Five is devoted to options. An option is a right, and in security markets it implies the right to buy or sell a security at a specified price.

Many options are speculative investments. Only those investors who are willing and able to bear substantial risk should consider them. However, puts, calls, and warrants do offer the possibility of a large return. Those investors who are willing to bear the risk for the potential return may find the next two chapters to be the most fascinating in the text.

Chapter 20 is devoted to the convertible bond, which is a hybrid type of security that combines features of both debt and stock. Since the bondholder has the option to convert the bond into stock, this type of bond is included in this section on options. A convertible bond is, however, a considerably safer investment than the other securities discussed in Part Five.

Learning Objectives

After completing this chapter you should be able
to

1. Define the word *option* as it applies to securi-
    ties.

2. Explain short-selling.

3. Determine the source of profit in a short sale.

4. Differentiate between an option's market value
    and its theoretical value.

5. Understand how options offer leverage.

6. Examine the sources of risk from investing in
    options.

chapter 18

INTRODUCTION TO OPTIONS*

An option is the right to do something. In the security markets an option is the right to buy or sell stock at a specified price within a specified time period. Options take various forms, including warrants, calls, puts, convertible bonds, and convertible preferred stock. Part Five is devoted to these securities. This chapter serves as a general introduction to investing in options. It covers features that apply to all types of options: their intrinsic value, the leverage they offer, and the premium paid for an option.

The next chapter discusses the speculative options: puts, calls, and warrants. Owners of these securities do not receive the benefits offered by common stock. But some investors buy these options instead of a firm's stock because the anticipated return on the option is greater. These inves-

---

*This and the subsequent chapter borrow heavily from Herbert B. Mayo, *"Using the Leverage in Warrants and Calls to Build a Successful Investment Program,* Larchmont, N.Y., Investors Intelligence, 1974. Permission to use this material has been graciously given by the publisher.

tors expect the price of the speculative option to rise more rapidly than the price of the stock that the option represents the right to buy. This rapid growth in the value of the option relative to the value of the stock is another illustration of the use of leverage. Without the possibility of such leverage, investors would not buy speculative options.

The last chapter in Part Five covers convertible bonds and convertible preferred stock. These securities do not offer investors potential leverage. However, they do offer modest returns with some potential for growth in value. In addition, convertible bonds and convertible preferred stocks are less risky investments than common stock, but they are more risky than investments in nonconvertible bonds (i.e., straight debt).

This chapter commences with a discussion of the short sale. Before one can discuss options, it is necessary to understand the short sale, because it plays an important role in the pricing of an option. Hence, the mechanics of short selling are covered, followed by an explanation of an option's intrinsic value and the potential leverage available through options. Lastly, the premium paid for an option is discussed.

THE SHORT SALE

How does an investor make money in the security markets? The obvious answer is to buy at low prices and to sell at high prices. For most people this implies that the investor first buy the security and then sell it at some later date. This is called the *long position* and was discussed in Chapter 3. Can the investor sell the security first and buy it back later at a lower price? The answer is yes, for a *short sale* reverses the order. The investor sells the security first with the intention of purchasing it in the future at a lower price.

Selling what one does not own

Since the sale precedes the purchase, the investor does not own the securities that are being sold short. Selling something that a person does not own may sound illegal, but there are many examples of such short selling in normal business relationships. A magazine publisher who sells a subscription, a professional such as a lawyer, engineer, or teacher who signs a contract for future services, and a manufacturer who signs a contract for future delivery are all making short sales.* If the cost of fulfilling the contract increases, the short seller loses. If the cost declines, the short seller profits. Selling securities short is essentially no different: It is a current sale with a contract for future delivery. If the securities are subsequently purchased at a lower price, the short seller will profit. However, if the cost of the securities rises in the future, the short seller will suffer a loss.

An illustration of the short sale

The mechanics of the short sale can be illustrated by a simple example employing the stock of CBS, Inc. Although most short sales involve commission fees and the use of margin, these factors are omitted in this illustration to simplify the explanation.

---

*See Mark Weaver, *The Technique of Short Selling.* Palisades Park, N.J., Investors' Press, 1963, p. 2.

If the current price of stock in CBS is $50 per share, the investor may buy 100 shares at $50 per share for a total cost of $5000. Such a purchase represents taking a long position in the stock. If the price subsequently rises to $75 per share and the stock is sold, the investor will earn a profit of $2500 ($7500 − $5000).

The short position reverses this procedure: The investor sells the stock first and buys it back at some time in the future. The investor sells 100 shares of CBS short at $50 ($5000). Such a sale is made because the investor believes that the stock is *overpriced* and that the price of the stock will *fall*. In a short sale the investor does not own the 100 shares sold. The buyer of the shares, however, certainly expects delivery of the stock certificate. (Actually, the buyer does not know if the shares come from an investor who is selling short or an investor who is liquidating a position in the security.) The short seller has to borrow 100 shares of CBS to deliver to the buyer. The shares are usually borrowed from the broker, who in turn probably borrows them from clients who have left their securities with the broker. (Shares held in a margin account may be used by the broker, and one such possible use is to lend the shares to a short seller. However, shares left with the broker in a cash account cannot be lent to a short seller.)

Sell short when anticipating a price decline

Although the investor has sold the securities, the proceeds of the sale are not delivered to the seller but are held by the broker. These proceeds will be subsequently used to repurchase the shares. (In the jargon of security markets such repurchases are referred to as covering the short sale.) In addition, the short seller must deposit with the broker an amount of money equal to the value of the sale. This money protects the broker (i.e., it is the short seller's collateral) and is returned to the short seller plus any profits or minus any losses when he or she buys the shares and returns them to the broker. This flow of certificates and money is illustrated in Exhibit 18–1. The broker receives money from the short seller (the $5000 collateral) and from the buyer of the stock (the $5000 in proceeds from the sale). The investor who sells the stock short receives nothing, but the borrowed securities flow through this investor's account en route to the buyer. The buyer then receives the securities and remits the funds to pay for them.

The proceeds of sale are held by the broker

The short seller must put up collateral

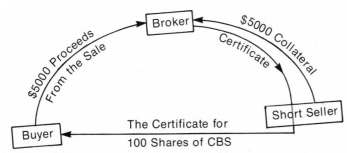

EXHIBIT 18–1.   The flow of money and certificates in a short sale.

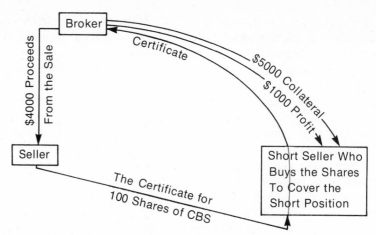

EXHIBIT 18–2. The flow of money and certificates when covering a profitable short sale.

What occurs if the price of the stock falls

If the price of a share declines to $40, the short seller can buy the stock for $4000. This purchase is no different from any purchase made on an exchange or in the over-the-counter market. The stock is then returned to the broker, and the loan of the stock is repaid. The short seller will have made a profit of $1000 because the shares were purchased for $4000 and sold for $5000. The investor's collateral is then returned by the broker plus the $1000 profit. These events are illustrated in Exhibit 18–2. The 100 shares of CBS stock are purchased for $4000 by the short seller. When the certificate for the 100 shares is received, it is returned by the short seller to the broker (who, in turn, returns the shares to whomever they were borrowed from). The broker returns the investor's $5000 that was put up for collateral. Since the investor uses only $4000 of the $5000 in proceeds from the short sale to purchase the stock, the broker sends the investor the remainder of the proceeds (the $1000 profit).

What occurs if the price of the stock rises

If the price of the stock had risen to $60 per share and the short seller had purchased the shares and returned them to the broker, the short position would have resulted in a $1000 loss. The proceeds from the short sale would have been insufficient to purchase the shares. One thousand dollars of the collateral would have had to be used in addition to the proceeds to buy the stock and cover the short position. The broker would owe the short seller only what was left of the collateral ($4000) after the transactions had been completed.

Although the previous transactions may sound complicated, they really are not. All that has occurred is that an investor has bought and sold a security. Instead of the investor's first purchasing the security and then selling it, the investor initially sold the security and subsequently purchased the shares to cover the short position. Because the sale occurred first, there is additional bookkeeping to account for the borrowed securities, but the transaction itself is not complicated.

Unfortunately, there is a belief among many investors that short selling is gambling. They believe that if investors sell short and the price of the stock rises substantially, the losses could result in financial ruin. However, short sellers can protect themselves by placing stop-loss purchase orders to cover the short position if the stock's price rises to a particular level.* Furthermore, if these investors fail to place stop-loss orders, the brokers will cover the position for them once their collateral has shrunk and can no longer support the short position. Thus the amount that an investor can lose is limited to the collateral. Short selling really involves no greater risk than purchasing securities, for when investors buy securities, they can lose all of their funds invested.

Short selling is not gambling

Actually, short selling is consistent with a rational approach to the selection of securities. If the investor analyzes a company and finds that its securities are overpriced, he or she will certainly not buy the securities. Instead, any that are currently owned should be sold. In addition, if the individual has confidence in the analysis and believes that the price will decline, the investor may sell short. The short sale, then, is the logical strategy given the basic analysis. Securities that are overpriced should be considered for short sales, just as securities that the investor believes are undervalued are the logical choice for purchase.

Sell short when securities are overpriced

Short selling is not limited to individual investors, as market makers may also sell short. If there is an influx of orders to buy, the market makers may partially satisfy this demand by selling short. They will then repurchase the shares in the future to cover the short position after the influx of orders has subsided. Frequently this transaction can be profitable. After the speculative increase in price that results from the increased demand, the price of the security may decline. When this occurs, the market makers profit because they sell short when the price rises but cover their positions after the price subsequently falls.**

Market makers may also sell short

THE THEORETICAL VALUE OF AN OPTION

The minimum price that an investor may pay for an option is its intrinsic value *as an option*. The intrinsic value is sometimes referred to as the option's theoretical value. This value is the difference between the price of the stock and the per share exercise price of the option (the price at which the owner has a right to buy the stock).†

Value as an option

If the stock is selling for a price greater than the per share exercise price, the option has positive theoretical value. This may be referred to as an option's being "in the money." If the common stock is selling for a price that is less than the per share exercise price, then the option has no

---

*For a discussion of a stop-loss order, see Chapter 3.
**For a stinging criticism of market makers' capacity to profit from short sales, see Richard Ney, *The Wall Street Jungle*, New York, Grove Press, Inc., 1970.
†If an option is the right to buy stock at $30 per share and the stock is selling for $40, then the intrinsic value of the option is $10 (i.e., $40 − $30 = $10).

TABLE 18–1. *The Price of a Stock and the Theoretical Value of an Option to Buy the Stock at $50 per Share*

PRICE OF THE STOCK	PER SHARE EXERCISE PRICE OF THE OPTION	THEORETICAL VALUE OF THE OPTION
$ 0	$50	$–50
10	50	–40
20	50	–30
30	50	–20
40	50	–10
50	50	0
60	50	10
70	50	20
80	50	30
90	50	40

intrinsic value. No one would purchase *and* exercise an option (trade it for stock) when the stock could be purchased for a price that is less than the exercise price of the option. However, as is explained subsequently, such options may still trade.

The relationship between the price of a stock and the theoretical value of the option

These relationships among the price of a stock, the exercise price of an option, and the option's theoretical price are illustrated in Table 18–1 and Graph 18–1. In this example, the option is the right to buy the stock at $50 per share. The first column of the table (the horizontal axis on the graph) gives various prices of the stock. The second column presents the exercise price of the option ($50), and the last column gives the intrinsic value of the option (i.e., the difference between the values in the first and second columns). The values in this third column are illustrated in the graph by line *AB*, which shows the relationship between the price of the stock and

GRAPH 18–1. **The Relationship Between the Price of a Stock and the Theoretical Value of an Option to Buy the Stock**

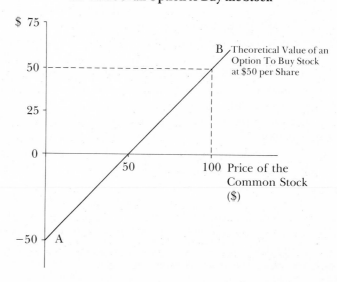

the option's theoretical value. It is evident from both the table and the graph that as the price of the stock rises, the theoretical value of the option also rises. However, for all stock prices below $50, the theoretical value is negative (or zero since security prices are never negative). Only after the stock's price has risen above $50 does the option's theoretical value become positive.

The theoretical value is one of the most important aspects of analyzing options. First, the market price of an option must approach its theoretical value as the option approaches its expiration date. On the day that the option is to expire, the market price can be only what the option is worth as stock. It can be worth only the difference between the market price of the stock and the exercise price of the option. This fact means that the investor may use the theoretical value of an option as an indication of the option's future price, for the investor knows that the market price of the option must approach its theoretical value as the option approaches expiration.

The importance of the theoretical value

Second, because of arbitrage, the theoretical value of an option sets the minimum price that the security will command. Arbitrage is the act of simultaneously buying and selling a commodity or security in two different markets in order to make a profit from the different prices offered by the markets. In the case of an option, the two markets are the market for the stock and the market for the option. The essence of the arbitrage position is a short sale of the stock and a long position (i.e., a purchase) in the option. After these transactions are effected, the arbitrager will exercise the option. Then the shares acquired by exercising the option will be used to cover the short position in the stock.

Arbitrage

This act of arbitrage may be clarified by using the simple example presented in Table 18–1. If the price of the stock is $60 and the exercise price of the option is $50, the option's theoretical value is $10. If the current market price of the option is $6, an investor can buy the option and exercise it to acquire the stock. By doing so the investor saves $4, for the total cost of the stock is $56 (i.e., $6 for the option and $50 to exercise the option). The investor then will own stock that has a market value of $60.

An illustration of arbitrage

The investor, however, cannot immediately realize that $4 profit, for it will take time for the option to be delivered and subsequently exercised. It may be several weeks before the investor will receive the stock certificate and thus be able to sell the stock. During those weeks the market price of the common stock will fluctuate and could decline. If the market price were to fall to $56 or less, the investor would no longer realize a profit. The gain would have evaporated during the time it took to exercise the option and to receive the stock certificate.

There is, however, a means to avoid this problem concerning time. If the investor simultaneously were to buy the option and sell the stock short, the $4 profit would be guaranteed. In other worlds, the investor arbitrages, the required steps for which are presented in Exhibit 18–3. The investor sells the stock short at $60 and purchases the option for $6 (step

EXHIBIT 18–3. The Steps Required for Arbitrage

Givens
Price of the stock	$60
Per share exercise price of the option	50
Price of the option	6

Step 1
Buy the option for $6
Sell the stock short for $60

Step 2
Exercise the option, thereby acquiring the stock for $50

Step 3
After acquiring the stock, cover the short position

Determination of profit or loss
Proceeds from the sale of the stock		$60
Cost of the stock		
Cost of the option	$ 6	
Cost to exercise the option	50	
Total cost		56
Net profit		$ 4

1). The stock certificate is borrowed from the broker and delivered to the buyer. Then the investor exercises the option (step 2). Several weeks later after receiving the stock certificate acquired by exercising the option, the investor covers the short position by giving the certificate to the broker (step 3). This set of transactions locks in the $4 profit, because the investor sold the stock short at $60 per share and simultaneously purchased and exercised the option for a combined cost of $56 per share. By selling the stock short and purchasing the option at the same time, the investor insures that he or she will gain the difference between the theoretical value of the option and its price. Through arbitrage the investor guarantees the profit.

Arbitrage causes prices to change

Of course, the act of buying the option and selling the stock short will drive up the option's price and put pressure on the price of the stock to fall. Thus, the opportunity to arbitrage will disappear, because arbitragers will bid up the price of the option to at least its theoretical value. Once the price of the option has risen to its intrinsic value, the opportunity for a profitable arbitrage disappears. However, if the price of the option were to fall again below its theoretical value, the opportunity for arbitrage would reappear, and the process would be repeated. Thus, the theoretical value of an option becomes the minimum price that the option must command, for arbitragers will enter the market as soon as the price of the option falls below its intrinsic value as an option.

If the price of the option were to exceed its theoretical value, arbitrage would offer no profit, nor would an investor exercise the option. If the option to buy the stock in the previous examples were to sell for $5 when the price of the common stock was $50, no one would exercise the option.

The cost of the stock acquired by exercising the option would be $55 (i.e., $50 + $5). The investor would be better off buying the stock outright than purchasing the option and exercising it. The opportunity for arbitrage thus occurs only when the price of the option is less than the option's theoretical value. The option would not be purchased or exercised when its price exceeded its theoretical value.

Actually, the opportunity for the typical investor to execute a profitable arbitrage is rare. Market makers are cognizant of the possible gains from arbitrage and are in the best possible position to take advantage of any profitable opportunities that may emerge. Hence, if the opportunity to purchase the option for a price less than its theoretical value existed, the purchases would be made by the market makers, and the opportunity to arbitrage would not become available to the general public. For the general investor the importance of arbitrage is not the opportunity for profit that it offers but the fact that it sets a *floor* on the price of an option, and that floor is the theoretical or intrinsic value.

The opportunity to execute arbitrage is rare

LEVERAGE

The advantage that some options (i.e., speculative options) offer investors is *leverage*. The potential return on an investment in a speculative option may exceed the potential return on an investment in the underlying stock (i.e., the stock that the option represents the right to purchase). Like the use of margin, this magnification of the potential gain is an example of leverage. Other options (i.e., the conservative options discussed in Chapter 20) may offer investors more safety than is possible from an investment in common stock. This section illustrates the potential leverage offered by speculative options. Unless these options offer investors this leverage, there is no reason to purchase them in preference to the stock.

Options offer leverage

This potential leverage offered by an option may be seen by referring to Table 18–1. This table, which illustrates the relationship between the price of a stock and an option's theoretical value, also demonstrates the potential leverage that options offer. For example, if the price of the stock rose from $60 to $70, the theoretical value of the option would rise from $10 to $20. The percentage increase in the price of the stock is 16.67 per cent ([$70 − $60] ÷ $60) whereas the percentage increase in the theoretical value of the option is 100 per cent ([$20 − $10] ÷ $10). The percentage increase in the theoretical value of the option exceeds the percentage increase in the price of the stock. If the investor could purchase the option for its theoretical value and the price of the stock then rose, the return on the investment in the option would exceed the return on the investment in the stock.

An illustration of the potential leverage

The leverage, however, works in both directions. Although it may increase the investor's potential return, it may also increase the potential for loss if the price of the stock declines. For example, if the price of the stock in Table 18–1 fell from $70 to $60 for a 14.2 per cent decline, the theoretical value of the option would fall from $20 to $10 for a 50 per cent decline. Thus, an investor increases not only the potential profit by purchasing speculative options but also the potential loss. As with any investment, the investor must decide if the increase in the potential return offered by the leverage is worth the increased risk.

THE PREMIUM PAID FOR AN OPTION

A premium over the theoretical value

If a speculative option offers a greater potential return than does the stock, investors may prefer to buy the option. In an effort to purchase the option, investors will bid up its price, in which case the market price will exceed its theoretical value. A speculative option tends to sell for a premium above its theoretical value, because investors are willing to pay for the potential leverage that it offers. This premium, in turn, reduces the potential profit and increases the potential loss.

An illustration of this premium

The premium is illustrated in Table 18–2, which adds to Table 18–1 a hypothetical set of option prices in column 4. The hypothetical market prices are greater than the theoretical values of the option because investors have bid up the prices. To purchase the option, an investor must pay the market price and not the theoretical value. Thus, in this example when the market price of the stock is $60 and the theoretical value of the option is $10, the market price of the option is $22. The investor must pay $22 to purchase the option, which is a premium of $12 over the option's theoretical value.

The relationships in Table 18–2 among the price of the stock, the theoretical value of the option, and the hypothetical price of the option are illustrated in Graph 18–2. The premium paid for the option over its theoretical value is easily seen in the graph, for it is the difference between the line representing the hypothetical market price of the option (line *CD*) and the line representing its theoretical value (line *AB*).

TABLE 18–2. *The Relationship Between the Price of Stock, the Theoretical Value of an Option, and the Hypothetical Market Price of the Option*

PRICE OF THE COMMON STOCK	Per Share Exercise Price	OPTION Theoretical Value	Hypothetical Market Price
$ 10	$50	$ 0	$ 1
20	50	0	5
30	50	0	9
40	50	0	13
50	50	0	18
60	50	10	22
70	50	20	27
80	50	30	34
90	50	40	42
100	50	50	51

GRAPH 18–2. **The Relationship Between the Price of the Stock, the Theoretical Value of the Option, and the Hypothetical Price of the Option**

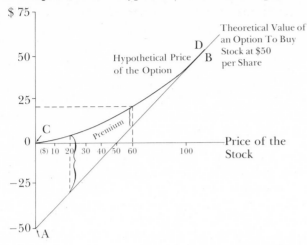

As may be seen in the graph, the amount of the premium tends to vary at the different price levels of the stock. At low stock prices, the premium is usually substantial. However, the amount of the premium declines as the price of the stock rises. Once the price of the stock has risen considerably the option may command virtually no premium over its theoretical value. At $100 per share, the option is selling at approximately its intrinsic value of $50. The primary reason for this decline in the premium is that as the price of the stock and the intrinsic value of the option rise, the potential leverage is reduced. In addition, at higher prices the potential price decline in the option is greater if the price of the stock falls. For these reasons investors become less willing to bid up the price of the option as the price of the stock rises, and hence the amount of the premium diminishes.

The premium varies

The effect of the premium is to decrease the potential leverage and return from investing in options. If, for example, the price of this stock rose from $60 to $70 for a 16.7 per cent gain, the option's price would rise from $22 to $27 for a 22.7 per cent gain. The percentage increase in the price of the option still exceeds the percentage increase in the price of the stock; however, the difference between the two percentage increases is smaller, since the option is selling for a premium over its theoretical value. The premium has substantially reduced the potential leverage that the option offers investors.

The premium reduces the potential leverage

Investors who are considering purchasing options should ask themselves what price increase they can expect in the option if the price of the underlying stock should rise. For the option to be attractive, its anticipated percentage increase in price must exceed the anticipated percentage increase in the price of the stock. The option must offer the investor leverage to justify the additional risk. Obviously an investor should not purchase the option if the price of the stock is expected to appreciate in value more rapidly than the price of the option. The previous example illustrates that the premium paid for an option may substantially decrease the potential leverage. Thus, recognition of the premium that an option commands is one of the most important considerations in the selection of an option for investment.

SUMMARY

This chapter covered the features common to all options: their intrinsic value as an option, the potential leverage they offer investors, and the premium that investors must pay to purchase them. The short sale was also discussed in order to explain why the theoretical value of an option sets its minimum price. If an option were to sell for a price below its theoretical value, arbitragers would seize the opportunity to make a profit. By simultaneously purchasing the option and selling the stock short, they would bid up the price of the option so that it would sell for at least its theoretical value (i.e., its intrinsic value as an option).

There are a variety of options, and the next two chapters are devoted to them. Chapter 19 considers the more speculative options: warrants, puts, and calls. Chapter 20 discusses the more conservative options — convertible bonds and convertible preferred stock. In both of these chapters the terms that were introduced in this chapter (i.e., theoretical value, leverage, and premium) are used extensively as they are applied to the specific option being discussed.

Terms to Remember

Short sale	Intrinsic or theoretical	Leverage
Covering a short	value	Premium
position	Arbitrage	

Questions

1. When should an investor sell short? How can an investor sell something he or she does not own? What is the source of profit in a short sale?

2. What is an option? How is an option's theoretical (or intrinsic) value determined?

3. How does arbitrage assure that the price of an option will not be less than the option's intrinsic value?

4. What advantage do options offer investors? Why are options considered to be speculative investments?

5. What does it mean to say that an option sells for a premium? What effect does this premium have on the potential leverage offered by an option?

6. If you saw that the price of a share of stock was selling for $20, the exercise price of an option to buy the share was $10, and the price of the option was $5, what would you do?

SELECTED READINGS

Gastineau, Gary L.: *The Stock Options Manual.* New York, McGraw-Hill Book Co., 1975.
Meeker, J. Edward: *Short Selling.* New York, Harper and Brothers, 1932. Reprinted by Arno Press, New York, 1975.
Noddings, Thomas C.: *The Dow Jones-Irwin Guide to Convertible Securities.* Homewood, Ill., Dow Jones-Irwin, Inc., 1973.
Weaver, Mark: *The Technique of Selling Short.* Palisades Park, N.J., Investors' Press, Inc., 1963.

APPENDIX: Rights Offerings

As was explained in Chapter 14, some stockholders have preemptive rights that enable them to maintain their proportionate ownership in the corporation. If the firm wants to raise additional equity capital by issuing more shares of stock, it must first offer these shares to its current stockholders. The stockholders are not required to buy the new shares, but they do have the privilege of purchasing or refusing them. If the stockholders do purchase the new shares to which they are entitled, they maintain their proportional ownership in the firm.

Preemptive rights

Firms that have granted preemptive rights present a *rights offering* when they issue new stock. This offering gives the stockholder the option to purchase the additional shares at a predetermined price. Evidence of this option is called a *right*, and one right is issued for every existing share of stock. This right specifies the exercise price of the right, the expiration date, and the number of shares that the right is an option to buy.

The sale of securities to existing stockholders

For example, suppose a company has 1,000,000 shares outstanding and wants to raise $12,500,000. The price of its stock is currently $60, and management believes that it can sell additional shares to its current stockholders at $50. The firm then will have to issue 250,000 new shares at $50 each to raise the $12,500,000. These 250,000 new shares will increase the number of shares outstanding by 25 per cent. The firm offers its current stockholders the right to buy additional shares. Each existing share receives a right to buy one quarter of a new share at $50 per share. Thus, it takes four rights to buy an additional share. If the stockholder has 100 shares, he or she may purchase 25 additional shares for $1250 (25 × $50). If the stockholder does buy the new shares, the individual's proportional ownership in the firm is unaltered. The stockholder then owns 125 shares of the 1,250,000 shares outstanding, whereas before the

An illustration of a rights offering

A rights offering occurs over time

rights offering that stockholder owned 100 of the 1,000,000 shares outstanding.

The issuing of rights, like the declaration and distribution of dividends, occurs over time. The following series of dates illustrate the time frame of a rights offering. On January 1 stockholders have no knowledge of a rights offering. On January 10 the firm announces that a rights offering will be made and that stockholders owning shares at the close of the business day on January 31 will receive the rights to purchase the new shares. From January 10 through January 31 the stock continues to trade on the open market, and anyone who purchases the stock during that period and holds the stock until February will receive the rights to purchase the new shares. During this time the price of the stock includes the value of the right. The stock trades with the *rights on* (i.e., the stock still confers the rights).

Ex rights

On February 1 purchasers of the stock no longer receive the rights, and the stock trades exclusive of the rights, or *ex rights*. Purchasing the stock after January 31 means the purchaser may not participate in the rights offering. However, the price paid for the stock will be lower because the existing shares have been diluted. As with the distribution of cash dividends, stock dividends, or stock splits, the price of the stock must decline on February 1 to account for the dilution of the existing shares.

The stockholders who owned the shares on January 31 receive their rights from the company. These stockholders may exercise the rights or sell them in the open market. The rights now trade independently of the common stock. The only constraint on these stockholders is that they act (i.e., exercise or sell the rights) by the expiration date of the right, which is usually about four weeks after the rights are issued (in this case March 1). The market price of the right may rise or fall. If speculators anticipate that the price of the stock will rise, they will seek to buy the right and may even bid up the price so that it sells for a premium over its value as stock. If the stock's price does subsequently rise, these speculators will realize a profit because the value of the rights must also increase.

The value of a right

The value of a right, like the value of any option, is related to the market price of the stock, the exercise (or subscription) price of the right, and the number of rights necessary to purchase a new share. When the firm offers the rights to stockholders it must fix (1) the number of rights necessary to purchase a new share and (2) the exercise price of the rights. The market price of the stock, however, may continue to fluctuate, which will cause the value of the right to fluctuate.

How is the value of a right determined? The answer depends on whether the individual wants the value of the right when it is still affixed to the stock (i.e., when the stock is trading rights on) or after the right has been issued and is trading independently of the stock. There is a simple formula for determining the value of the right as an option in either case. If the stockholder wants the rights-on value of the option (i.e., the value of the rights before they trade independently of the stock), the simple formula is

Rights-on value

(1)
$$V = \frac{M - E}{n + 1}$$

where V indicates the value of the right; M, the current market price of the stock; E, the exercise price of the right (which is also referred to as the subscription price); and n, the number of rights necessary to purchase one share. If the investor applies this formula to the example presented previously, the value of the right is

$$V = \frac{\$60 - \$50}{4 + 1}$$

$$V = \frac{\$10}{5}$$

$$V = \$2$$

This formula helps to illustrate the dilution that occurs when additional shares are issued. The "$n + 1$" in the denominator adjusts for the dilution that will occur when the stock trades ex rights. The "$+ 1$" represents the new share that will come into existence for every n number of shares the firm currently has. In this case the firm issues one new share for every four shares currently outstanding.

The effect of dilution

After the stock goes ex rights, its price declines by the value of the right. Thus, in this case the market price of stock declines by $2 from $60 to $58. The rights are now traded independently of the stock (i.e., traded "rights off"). The formula for the value of a right after the stock trades ex rights is

Rights-off value

(2)
$$V = \frac{M - E}{n}$$

The only difference between the two formulas is the "$+ 1$." Since the price of the stock has already been adjusted for the dilution, the "$+ 1$" is no longer necessary. Now the value of the right is

$$V = \frac{\$58 - \$50}{4}$$

$$V = \$2$$

Notice that the market price of the stock is lower as a result of the dilution, but the value of the right is unaltered. The terms of the option have not been changed, but the increase in the total number of shares that will occur when the new shares are issued has caused a dilution of the old shares, and this dilution caused the price of the stock to decline by the value of the right.

These rights are an example of an option and as such may attract speculative interest. Should the price of the stock rise, the value of the right will tend to rise more rapidly because the rights offer potential leverage. If this occurs, speculators may be rewarded for purchasing the right from those stockholders who did not wish to exercise the option. For example, consider the impact of a four-point increase in the price of the preceding stock from $58 to $62. What effect does that have on the value of the right? The answer is

These rights may attract speculators

$$V = \frac{\$62 - \$50}{4}$$

$$V = \$3$$

The small increase in the price of the stock causes the value of the right to rise by 50 per cent ([$3 − $2] ÷ $2).

Such potential leverage may attract speculators who anticipate an increase in the price of the stock. Of course, if the price of the stock declines, then the value of the right will decline. Leverage works both ways, and speculators who purchase rights for the potential increase in value must also bear the risk of loss that will occur if the price of the stock falls.

Learning Objectives

After completing this chapter you should be able to

1. Identify the factors affecting the premium paid for a warrant.

2. Demonstrate how hedging with warrants may yield a profit regardless of whether the price of the stock rises or falls.

3. Explain the difference between a call and a warrant.

4. Demonstrate the potential profit from writing covered and uncovered calls.

5. Explain the difference between a put and a call.

6. Identify the source of risk from buying put and call options.

7. Compare buying a put with selling short.

chapter 19
WARRANTS, PUTS, AND CALLS

During the 1960s firms increasingly used warrants as a means to obtain money from the capital market. This increased use of warrants culminated when AT&T floated a huge bond issue in excess of $1.5 billion with warrants attached. These bonds had a generous yield (8¾ per cent) and were purchased by a large cross section of the investing public. The purchasers received both the bonds and the warrants, although it is probably safe to assume that a majority of the buyers did not know much about the warrant component of their purchase.

In the spring of 1973 a new type of option was introduced that has become the "hottest game in town." This is a call option and is traded on the Chicago Board Options Exchange (CBOE), which was created solely for this purpose. Because of the initial success of the CBOE, call options can now be traded on other exchanges.

This chapter is devoted to these speculative options: warrants, puts, and calls, which are traded on the CBOE and other exchanges. Their respective features and the possible rewards for investing in these speculative options are explained. Since investing in speculative options frequently results in losses, the potential risks are continuously stressed. Finally, a method for using these options to reduce risk (i.e., hedging with options) is discussed in some detail.

WARRANTS

Warrant defined

A warrant is the option to buy the stock of a company at a specified price within a specified time period. This definition includes the essential elements of all warrants.* An example of such an option is the AT&T warrant mentioned earlier. It was an option to buy one share of AT&T common stock at a price of $52 per share through May 15, 1975. Anyone who owned the warrant could buy one share of common stock by surrendering the warrant and paying $52. After May 15, 1975, the warrant ceased to exist, as the options expired.

An example of a current warrant is the one issued by American Airlines, which is the option to buy the common stock at $14 per share through April 1, 1984. If this option is not exercised by April 1, 1984, it will expire and become worthless. Thus, unlike stock, which is perpetual (i.e., continues in existence until the company is liquidated or is merged into another company), most warrants have a finite life. Very few are perpetual.

Conversion to per share

Most warrants, such as the AT&T and American Airlines warrants, are an option, or right, to buy one share of common stock. Some warrants, however, are the option to buy more or less than one share. Such terms may be the result of stock dividends, stock splits, or a merger. For example, a warrant that is the option to buy 0.4 share may have evolved through a merger. The warrant initially represented the option to purchase one share of the company. However, the company subsequently merged into another firm, and the terms of the merger were 0.4 share of the acquiring firm (i.e., the surviving company) for each share of the company being acquired. The warrant then became an option to buy one share that had been converted into 0.4 share of the surviving company.

If a warrant is an option to buy more or less than one share, the exercise price and the market price of the warrant can be readily converted to a per share basis. Such conversion is desirable to facilitate comparisons among warrants. For example, an option gives the right to buy 0.4 share at $10 and is currently selling for $4. The exercise price and the market price

---

*While this definition covers the essential nature of all warrants, there can be subtle differences among warrants. For example, the specified exercise price of a warrant may rise at predetermined intervals (e.g., every five years).

of the warrant are divided by the number of shares that the warrant is an option to buy. Thus, the per share exercise price is $25 ($10 ÷ 10.4), and the per share market price of the warrant is $10 ($4 ÷ 0.4). Stated differently, 2.5 warrants are necessary to buy one share for $25.

Warrants are sweeteners

Warrants are usually issued by firms in conjunction with other financing. They are attached to other securities, such as debentures or preferred stock, and are a sweetener to induce investors to purchase the securities. For example, in July 1978, Chrysler Corporation issued preferred stock with warrants attached. The warrants were an added inducement to purchase the stock.

The impact of finite life

When a warrant is exercised, the firm issues new stock and receives the proceeds. For this reason, most warrants usually have a finite life. The expiration date ultimately forces the holder to exercise the option if the exercise price is less than the current market price of the stock. However, if the exercise price exceeds the stock's price at expiration (i.e., if the warrant has no intrinsic value), the warrant will not be exercised and will expire. After the expiration date, the warrant is worthless. This was the case with the Gulf and Western warrant that expired on January 31, 1978: The warrant was not exercised because it had no intrinsic value as an option. On that day the price of the stock was $11, but the exercise price of the warrant was $19.37. No one would exercise the warrant at $19.37 when the stock could be purchased for $11 on the New York Stock Exchange.

The premium

Table 19–1 presents selected warrants, their exercise price, market price, and theoretical value, along with the market price of the stock and the expiration date of the warrants. The last column gives the difference between the warrant's theoretical value and its price (i.e., the premium). As may be seen in the table, all of the warrants sell for a premium (i.e., the market price exceeds the theoretical value). Most of these warrants have exercise prices that exceed the price of the stock. These warrants have no

TABLE 19–1. *Terms and Premiums Paid for Selected Warrants as of December 30, 1977**

COMPANY	PRICE OF THE STOCK	WARRANT				
		Per Share Exercise Price	*Expiration Date*	*Market Price*	*Theoretical Value†*	*Premium Paid‡*
American Airlines	$10⅝	$14.00	4/ 1/84	$3⅞	($3.375)	$ 7.25
Braniff International	9⅝	22.94	12/ 1/86	6¾	(13.315)	20.07
Commonwealth Edison	28⅞	30.00	4/30/81	9¼	(1.125)	10.38
Textron	26½	11.25§	5/ 1/84	16⅛	15.25	.88

*Source: *Standard & Poor's Stock Guide,* Year End, 1977.
†The theoretical value is the price of the stock minus the per share exercise price of the warrant.
‡The premium paid for the warrant is the market price minus the theoretical value.
§This exercise price was effective May 1, 1979.

positive theoretical value and sell for a substantial premium.* As is evident in the last column, there can be considerable variation in the premiums, which range from only $.88 for the Textron warrant to $26.82 for the Braniff International warrant.

The premium is affected by many factors

What accounts for this variation in the premiums? Cash dividends paid on the common stock, the expiration date of the warrant, and the volatility of the price of the common stock as well as the absolute price of the warrant and the potential dilution of the common stock from exercising the warrant are all factors that explain the observed differences in the premiums.

Dividends affect the premium

Warrants of companies that pay cash dividends tend to sell for lower premiums. There may be two explanations for this relationship between the payment of cash dividends and lower premiums. Companies that do not distribute earnings but retain them will have more funds available for investments. By retaining and reinvesting their earnings, the companies may grow more rapidly. This growth may be reflected in the price of their stock, and hence the potential gain in the price of the warrant may be greater if the firm retains its earnings and does not pay a dividend. A second explanation is that if the company pays a cash dividend, the holder of the warrant does not receive the cash payment. The warrant will be less attractive relative to the common stock, for the owner of the warrant must forgo the dividend. Therefore, investors will not be as willing to pay as much for the warrant, and it will sell for a lower premium.

The time to expiration affects the premium

A second reason for the differences in the premiums paid for warrants is the proximity of the expiration date. As the warrant approaches expiration, its market price must approach its theoretical value. On the expiration date, the warrant cannot command a price greater than its true value as an option. Thus, as the warrant nears expiration, it will sell for a lower premium.

The price volatility of the stock affects the premium

A third factor that may influence the premium paid for a warrant is the volatility of the price of the common stock. If the price of the stock fluctuates substantially, the warrant may be more attractive and hence may command a higher premium. When the price of the common stock is volatile, the chance of earning a profit with the warrant may be greater Since the price of the warrant follows the price of the common stock, fluctuations in the price of the stock will be reflected in the price of the warrant. The more volatile the price of the stock, the more opportunity the warrant offers speculators. Thus, the warrants of volatile common stocks may be more attractive (especially to speculators), and hence the premium commanded by these warrants will tend to be greater than the premium commanded by warrants of less volatile stocks.

Low-priced warrants affect the premium

There also appears to be a negative relationship between the premium and the per share price of the warrant. As the price of the warrant

---

*Notice that in calculating the premium the negative theoretical value is, in effect, added to the price of the warrant. For example, the premium for the American Airline warrant is $3.875 − (−$7.25), which equals $11.13.

declines, the premium rises. This is particularly true for very low-priced warrants. There are two possible explanations for this inverse relationship between the premium and the price of the warrant: (1) The potential leverage is greater for low-priced warrants, and (2) the potential dollar loss on low-priced warrants is small.

The last factor that may affect the premium paid for a warrant is the dilution that may result from exercising the warrant. When the warrant is exercised, the company receives cash and issues new stock. This increases the number of shares that the company has outstanding, which may cause the price of the common stock to fall. If investors anticipate considerable dilution, they may be less willing to bid up the price of the warrant, and thus it may sell for a lower premium.

Dilution affects the premium

Dilution may not be a particularly significant determinant of the premium paid for warrants for two reasons. First, firms report per share earnings on both a diluted and an undiluted basis. If the warrants threaten to dilute the existing shares, this potential dilution is known before it occurs. Second, a company must have money to maintain operations and grow. Investors are aware that firms need outside sources of funds, and warrants are one source. When the warrants are exercised, the firm receives funds that it may use profitably to enhance its earnings in the future. Thus, although warrants may dilute current earnings, they may be a means to future growth. If investors realize that the warrants represent the potential future earnings of the company, any current dilution caused by the warrants may be considered insignificant. Potential dilution, then, may have no effect on the prices of the common stock and the warrant or on the premium that warrants command in the security market.

HEDGING WITH WARRANTS

Although warrants are speculative investments, they can be used in hedge positions to reduce risk. A hedge position offers the investor a modest gain in return for this reduction in risk. Before executing a hedge position, the investor must determine whether the reduction in risk is worth the loss in potential profit.

Hedging can be used to reduce risk

Hedging with warrants means that the investor simultaneously takes a long position and a short position. In the usual hedge position, the investor sells the warrant short and purchases the stock that the warrant is an option to buy. The investor may also reverse this traditional hedge and sell the stock short and purchase the warrant. The conditions under which such a reverse hedge would be profitable are rarer. Thus, the main concern of this section will be the usual hedge: a short position in the warrant and a long position in the stock.

Sell the warrant short and buy the stock

To determine if a hedge will be profitable, the investor needs an indication of the potential gain or loss from the position. The current market price of the warrant, the current market price of the stock, and the per share exercise price of the warrant are known. The investor also knows when the warrant will expire and that as the warrant approaches expiration, its market price must approach its theoretical value. No one will pay more than the intrinsic value of the warrant on the option's expiration date. Thus, on the expiration date the warrant must be worth its theoretical value, which is the difference between the market price of the stock and the per share exercise price of the warrant. This information permits the investor to calculate the possible gain from a hedge position at various prices of the stock.

An illustration of the potential profit

The possible gain from a hedge position may be seen in Table 19–2. In this example the current market price of the stock and of the warrant are $30 and $20, respectively. The warrant is an option to buy the common stock at $15 per share and expires after one year. Its theoretical value is $15 (i.e., $30−$15), and thus the warrant is selling at a premium of $15 over its theoretical value. This premium must diminish until it is zero on the expiration date of the warrant, for on that day no one would be willing to pay more than the value of the warrant as an option.

Column 1 in Table 19–2 gives various prices of the stock on the expiration date of the warrant. Column 2 gives the profit or loss on the long position in the stock (i.e., the profit or loss from purchasing the stock now at $30 and holding it until the warrant expires a year from now). Column 3 gives the theoretical value of the warrant on the expiration date at various stock prices. Since the price of the warrant approaches its theoretical value as the expiration date nears, this value estimates the price of the warrant as it approaches expiration.

The profit or loss on a short position in the warrant at different hypothetical prices of the stock is presented in column 4. This profit or loss is the difference between the purchase and sales prices. The warrant would be sold short today for $20 and would be purchased to cover the short position near its expiration date. The theoretical value of the warrant

TABLE 19–2. *Net Profit on a Hypothetical Hedge Position When the Current Price of Stock is $30, the Current Price of the Warrant is $20, and the Exercise Price of the Warrant is $15*

PRICE OF THE COMMON STOCK	PROFIT OR LOSS ON THE COMMON STOCK BOUGHT LONG	THEORETICAL VALUE OF THE WARRANT AT EXPIRATION	PROFIT OR LOSS ON THE WARRANT SOLD SHORT	NET PROFIT*
5	−25	0	20	−5
10	−20	0	20	0
15	−15	0	20	5
20	−10	5	15	5
25	−5	10	10	5
30	0	15	5	5
35	5	20	0	5
40	10	25	− 5	5
45	15	30	−10	5
50	20	35	−15	5

*The net profit is determined by adding the profit or loss on the common stock bought long and the profit or loss on the warrant sold short.

GRAPH 19–1.   **Relationship Between the Price of the Common Stock and the Profit on a Hypothetical Hedge Position**

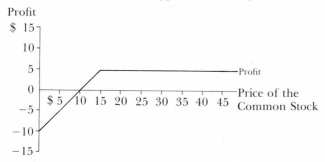

in column 3 indicates the price that the investor will pay when the warrant is purchased in the future to cover the short position.

The net profit or loss on the entire hedge position is presented in column 5. This profit is the sum of the profits (or losses) on the long position in the stock (column 2) and on the short position in the warrant (column 4). The information given in column 5 is plotted in Graph 19–1. As can be seen from either Table 19–2 or Graph 19–1, a hedge position established at a price of $30 for the stock and $20 for the warrant yields a profit for all prices of the stock above $10 per share. The hedge position would be profitable even if the price of the common stock were to *fall* from $30 to $10 a share. Such a hedge position substantially reduces the risk of loss, for the investor earns a profit even if the price of the common stock declines. The investor need not be concerned with the direction of change in the price of the stock. A fall in the price of the stock guarantees a profit on the short position in the warrant. A rise in the price of the common stock guarantees a profit on the long position in the common stock. As long as the price of the common stock stays within the profitable range (in this case above $10 per share), the investor cannot lose money. However, it should also be noted that the potential profit is modest. In this example, the maximum possible profit before commissions is only $5 for each warrant sold short and each share purchased.

A hedge position need not be limited to a ratio of one share purchased to one warrant sold short. Any ratio of shares to warrants is possible. Altering the mix, however, alters (1) the range of stock prices that yields a profit on the hedge position and (2) the potential return on the hedge position. Table 19–3 illustrates the possible gains from two other hedge positions of different combinations of the warrants and stock that were presented in Table 19–2. The top section gives the potential profit from a hedge of one share purchased to two warrants sold short. The bottom section gives the potential profit from one share purchased to three warrants sold short. The profit potential of these hedges is summarized in Graph 19–2, which reproduces Graph 19–1 and adds the relationship between the price of the stock and the profit from these additional hedge positions.

The net profit or loss

TABLE 19–3. *Profit and Loss on Hedge Positions With Various Ratios of Warrants Sold Short to Common Shares Purchased Long*

PRICE OF THE STOCK	PROFIT ON THE STOCK	THEORETICAL VALUE OF THE WARRANTS	PROFIT ON THE WARRANTS	NET PROFIT
One Share Of Stock Purchased at $30; Two Warrants Sold Short at $20 Each (Exercise Price = $15)				
$ 0	$–30	$ 0	$ 40	$ 10
5	–25	0	40	15
10	–20	0	40	20
15	–15	0	40	25
20	–10	10	30	20
25	– 5	20	20	15
30	0	30	10	10
35	5	40	0	5
40	10	50	–10	0
45	15	60	–20	– 5
One Share of Stock Purchased at $30; Three Warrants Sold Short at $20 Each (Exercise Price = $15)				
$ 0	$–30	$ 0	$ 60	$ 30
5	–25	0	60	35
10	–20	0	60	40
15	–15	0	60	45
20	–10	15	45	35
25	– 5	30	30	25
30	0	45	15	15
35	5	60	0	5
40	10	75	–15	– 5
45	15	90	–30	–15

More warrants sold short place emphasis on a decline in the price of the stock

Both of these hedge positions offer a range of stock prices that yield a net profit on the entire position. For example, a hedge position of three warrants sold short to one share of stock purchased will yield a profit for all prices of the stock below $37.50 per share. As can be seen from Table 19–3 and Graph 19–2, as the proportion of warrants sold short to shares of common stock purchased long is increased, (1) the range of prices of the stock that yield a profit is narrowed and (2) the potential gain on the hedge position is increased. Thus, the net profit will be larger if the price of the common stock falls, and the loss will be greater if the price of the stock rises. As the investor sells more warrants short, more emphasis is placed on the price of the stock remaining stable or falling. The investor has weighted the hedge position on the short side in the warrant. The potential gain is realized if the price of the common stock and hence the theoretical value of the warrant do not rise. The investor is also increasing the potential risk of loss, for the emphasis is now on a decline in the price of the stock.

The ratio of warrants sold short to shares purchased is a major consideration in establishing a hedge position. This ratio depends upon the investor's view of the potential for the stock. The more pessimistic or bearish the investor is with regard to the stock's potential, the larger should be the proportion of warrants sold short to shares purchased. If the investor is relatively bullish or optimistic about the company, the proportion of shares purchased to warrants sold short should be greater. Of course, the investor may decide to dispense with the hedge entirely and buy either the stock or the warrant. The investor then bears the risk of loss that will occur if the security's price falls.

An investor who is contemplating a hedge position must consider not only what ratio of warrants to common stock should be selected but also when the position should be established. An investor does not want a hedge position for the life of the warrant. The profit from the hedge position arises from the warrant's premium ceasing to exist when the warrant expires. Thus, the investor establishes the hedge position as the warrant approaches expiration and only if the warrant sells for a premium over its theoretical value. If the position is established many years before the warrant expires, the long wait to realize the gain will substantially reduce the annual percentage return. The yield on a hedge position may be respectable, but it is not large. If this yield is spread over many years, the rate of return will be insufficient to such a justify use of the money. Other investments offer a superior return without an increase in risk.

Conversely, if an investor chooses to wait until a few months before the expiration date of the warrant, he or she may not be able to establish a hedge position. The Board of Governors of the SEC, which regulates trading on the exchanges, will ban short sales in the warrant as it approaches expiration. The purpose of this ban is to reduce undue speculation during the last few months of the warrant's existence. Such a ban

The hedge position is established as the warrant approaches expiration

GRAPH 19–2. Profit Potential of Various Hedge Positions

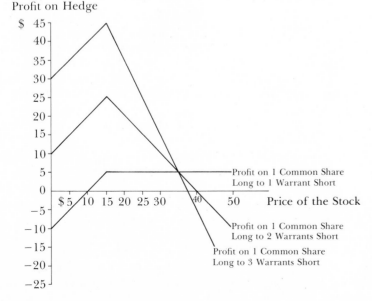

means that investors will be unable to establish a hedge position. Thus, the establishment of a hedge position will require action on the part of the investor before the ban on short sales. Such action may be necessary one year before the expiration date of the warrant.

A need to reevaluate the position

Even after a hedge position has been established and time has elapsed, the investor should reevaluate and perhaps alter the position. For example, if the price of the stock has fallen along with the price of the warrant, the investor may decide to increase the ratio of warrants sold short to shares purchased. The decline in the price of the stock and the lapse of time may indicate that the warrant's potential for a price increase has been reduced. The investor may take advantage of this additional information and alter the proportion of warrants sold short. Hedge positions, like all investments, need to be reevaluated periodically so that changes that are consistent with the investor's goals can be made.

CALLS

Although warrants were the popular speculative option during the 1960s, they were displaced in popularity in the 1970s by the call. A call is an option to buy a specified number of shares (usually 100) of stock at a specified price within a specified time period.* The owner of a call has the right *to call forth* the shares of stock and to purchase the shares at the specified price. (There is also the opposite type of option, which is called a put. A put is an option to sell a specified number of shares [usually 100] at a specified price within a specified time period. A put, then, is an option *to place or put* with someone else shares owned by the holder of the option. Puts are discussed later in this chapter.)

Calls differ from warrants

Calls are issued by individuals

Calls are very similar to warrants (i.e., their definitions are essentially identical), but they have several distinguishing features. Warrants are issued by companies. Calls are issued by individuals and are sold to other individuals. This ability of the individual investor to write calls is a very important difference between calls and warrants, for the investor may be either a buyer *or* an issuer of call options. By enabling the individual to write options, calls offer investors an opportunity for profit that is not available with warrants.

Calls are of short duration

A second distinction between warrants and calls is the duration of the option. When warrants are issued their expiration date is set. It is generally several years into the future (e.g., five years), and some warrants may be perpetual. Calls are of relatively short duration: three, six, or nine months.

No new stock is issued with calls

The third distinguishing feature of calls becomes evident when they are exercised. When a warrant is exercised, the firm issues new stock and

---

*Actually, call options are not new. They existed as early as the 1630s, when options on tulip bulbs played a role in the speculative tulip bulb craze that swept Holland.

receives the proceeds. The seller of a call, however, cannot issue new stock when the call is exercised. Instead, the seller must either purchase the stock on the open market or surrender the stock from personal holdings. When the stock is supplied for the exercised call option, the option writer and not the firm receives the proceeds.

THE CHICAGO BOARD OPTIONS EXCHANGE

Prior to the formation of the Chicago Board Options Exchange (CBOE), calls were purchased only in the over-the-counter market. If an investor wanted to purchase a call option, the call was purchased from an options dealer. Each option that was sold was different, because the exercise price and the expiration date of the option were negotiated with each sale. Once the option was purchased, the investor who desired to sell it had difficulty, because there was no secondary market in options.

OTC trading

With the advent of the CBOE, an organized market in call options on selected securities was created. For the first time investors could buy and sell call options through an organized exchange. In addition, a secondary market in these options came into being. An investor who purchases a call on the CBOE knows that there will be a market for that option in the future. This ability to sell options that had been previously purchased gave a degree of marketability to call options that had not existed earlier.

CBOE provided a secondary market

There are several features of the CBOE that are conducive to the development of secondary markets for the calls. First, transactions are continuously reported, and daily summaries of transactions appear in leading newspapers. Exhibit 19–1 presents the call options of CBS that were traded on the CBOE on June 9, 1978, as reported in *The Wall Street Journal*. For CBS there were six options. Three had an exercise price of $50 and expired at the end of August 1978, November 1978, and February 1979. The other three options had an exercise price of $60 and also expired at the end of August 1978, November 1978, and February 1979.

Transactions are reported in the financial press

For the 50's of August (i.e., the $50 option that expired in August 1978), the volume of trading was 57 (i.e., 57 contracts each to buy 100 shares) and the price of the last trade was $8¼, which is considerably

EXHIBIT 19–1. Summary of CBS Calls Traded on the CBOE on June 9, 1978*

Option and Price	August Expiration		November Expiration		February Expiration		Close†
	Volume	Last Trade	Volume	Last Trade	Volume	Last Trade	
CBS $50	57	8¼	11	9¼	3	10	58½
CBS $60	144	1¾	130	$^{15}/_{16}$	2	3½	58½

*Source: Adapted from *The Wall Street Journal*, June 9, 1978.
†*Close* indicates the last price for the stock on the New York Stock Exchange.

higher than the $1¾ paid for the August 60's. This difference in prices is the result of the higher exercise price of the August 60's option (i.e., $60 versus $50).

The clearing house

Second, a clearing house was established for the CBOE that maintains a daily record of options issued in the accounts of its members. The members are required to keep a continuous record of their respective customers' positions in options. No actual options certificates are issued; only the bookkeeping is maintained by the clearing house. A centralized clearing house greatly facilitates trading in the options, for it serves as the intermediary through which purchases and sales of the calls are recorded.

The CBOE is self-regulated

Third, the CBOE is self-regulated. It has the power to impose requirements that must be met before calls may be traded on the exchange, and options on only a selected number of securities have been accepted for trading on the exchange. Investors must be approved before they can purchase and sell through the CBOE, and there is a limit to the number of options on a single stock that an investor may own. Brokers on the floor of the exchange must have a minimum amount of capital. Although such self-regulation does not guarantee the absence of illegal transactions, it is conducive to the development of organized security markets.

Other secondary markets

The initial success of the CBOE exceeded expectations. Soon after its formation other exchanges started to list call options. Currently, call options are traded not only on the CBOE but also on the American, Pacific, Philadelphia, and Midwest exchanges. While all companies do not meet the criteria for having options listed, several hundred firms are eligible to have the call options traded on their stock listed.*

THE PRICING OF CALLS

The price that the investor pays for a call traded on the CBOE or any other exchange is determined by the demand for and the supply of the option. This price of a call is frequently referred to as the premium. To some extent this term is a misnomer, for the price of a call may include some intrinsic value as an option. For consistency with the rest of this text, the term *price* will be used to denote the market price. The term *premium* will be used to denote the extent to which the price of the call exceeds its theoretical or intrinsic value as an option.

The minimum price of a call

The minimum price of a call, like the minimum price of any option, is set by the option's intrinsic value as stock. The price of a call cannot fall below (for any significant length of time) the difference between the price of the common stock and the per share exercise price of the call. If the price of the call were to fall below its true value as an option, arbitragers would purchase calls and simultaneously sell the stock short. These actions

*The criteria for having call options listed on an exchange include the following: The firm must have at least 8,000,000 shares outstanding, 10,000 shareholders, and an annual turnover of 2,000,000 shares for the last two years.

would bid up the price of the call and put downward pressure on the price of the stock until the price of the option equaled or exceeded its theoretical value.

The actual price that investors pay for a call traded on the CBOE or on other exchange depends on their willingness to bid for the options and the willingness of other investors to supply the options. Through supply and demand a single price is determined for each option. Several of the variables that influence the demand for options include (1) the potential leverage that the option offers, (2) the duration of the option, and (3) the potential for an increase in the price of the common stock in the immediate future. The long-term potential growth of the company may be of little significance in the decision to purchase a CBOE call, for the growth may occur too far in the future. Since the call has a short life span, the emphasis is primarily on short-term increases in the market price of the stock and not on the long-term growth potential of the company.

The price of a call

THE ADVANTAGE OF PURCHASING CALLS: LEVERAGE

Warrants and calls are similar in many ways. Both represent the right to buy stock at a specified price within a specified time period. The reason for purchasing either warrants or calls is the potential leverage that they offer the investor. Calls, however, tend to offer greater leverage than warrants, since they sell for a smaller premium above their theoretical value. Because of the short duration of the call option, the premium paid is less than that paid for a warrant, which is of longer duration.

The considerable potential leverage offered by a call to buy CBS stock at $60 is shown in Table 19–4. This table presents the price of the CBS stock (column 1); the exercise price of the call (column 2); the theoretical value of the call, i.e., the difference between the price of the common stock and the per share exercise price of the call (column 3); and some hypothetical market prices of the call (column 4). The table also includes the percent-

The potential leverage

TABLE 19–4.   *Potential Leverage Offered by CBOE Call to Buy CBS Stock at $60*

Price Of CBS Stock	Exercise Price Of The Call	Theoretical (Or Intrinsic) Value Of The Call	Hypothetical Price Of The Call	Percentage Change In The Price Of The Stock	Percentage Change In The Price Of The Call
$50	$60	$ 0	$ ¼	. . .	. . .
55	60	0	1	10%	300%
60	60	0	3	9.1	200
65	60	5	6	8.3	100
70	60	10	10½	7.7	75

age change in the price of the common stock for successive increments of $5 (column 5) and the percentage change in the hypothetical price of the call (column 6). As may be seen in the table, if the price of the common stock of CBS rose from $60 to $65 (an 8.3 per cent increase), the hypothetical price of this call would rise from $3 to $6 (a 100 per cent increase). If equal amounts were invested in the common stock and the call, the call would have the potential to yield much more profit.

A high degree of risk

Although the potential leverage that calls offer to investors is the primary reason for purchasing them, the investor does accept substantial risk. On its expiration date the call can be worth only its theoretical value. The call will be worthless if the price of CBS stock is less than the per share exercise price of the call (i.e., below $60). This call will prove to be a profitable investment only if the price of the common stock rises. Thus, for a call to be profitable, the price of the common stock must increase during the call's relatively short life span.

THE ADVANTAGE OF ISSUING CALLS: INCOME

Issuing calls is a source of income

The preceding section considered the reason for purchasing calls; this section will consider the advantages of issuing them. Calls give the investor an opportunity to profit not only from the leverage that options offer but also from the revenue that is obtained through the sale of options. Issuing options, however, precludes the investor's taking advantage of the leverage that is available from purchasing options. Nonetheless, the issue of options offers the investor an opportunity to make a respectable return on the amount invested and to reduce the risk of loss. Issuing options, then, is similar to hedging with warrants. Both offer modest returns and a reduction in risk.

Covered options

There are two ways to write (i.e., sell) options. The first is the more conservative method, which is called covered option writing. The investor buys the stock and then sells an option to buy that stock. If the option is exercised, the investor supplies the stock that was previously purchased (i.e., "covers" the option with the stock). The second method entails selling the call without owning the stock. This is referred to as naked

Naked options

option writing, for the investor is exposed to considerable risk. If the price of the stock rises and the call is exercised, then the option writer must buy the stock at the higher market price in order to supply it to the buyer. With naked option writing the potential for loss is considerably greater than with covered option writing in which the investor owns the stock before he or she sells the option.

The potential profit

The primary reason for writing options is the income to be gained from their sale. The potential profit from writing a covered option may be seen in Table 19–5. In this example the investor purchases the common stock of CBS at the current market price of $50 per share and simultaneous-

TABLE 19–5. *Profit on a Hedge Position Consisting of the Purchase of 100 Shares of CBS Stock and the Sale of One Call to Buy 100 Shares of CBS at $50 a Share*

PRICE OF CBS STOCK	NET PROFIT ON THE STOCK	THEORETICAL VALUE OF THE CALL	NET PROFIT ON THE SALE OF THE CALL	NET PROFIT ON THE POSITION
$42	$−800	$ 0	$ 500	$−300
44	−600	0	500	−100
46	−400	0	500	100
48	−200	0	500	300
50	0	0	500	500
52	200	200	300	500
54	400	400	100	500
56	600	600	−100	500
58	800	800	−300	500
60	1000	1000	−500	500

ly sells for $5 a call to buy the shares at an exercise price of $50. Thus, the investor sells the call for $500 (i.e., $5 × 100 shares). The possible future prices for CBS stock are given in column 1. Column 2 presents the net profit to the investor from the purchase of the stock. Column 3 gives the theoretical value of the call, and column 4 presents the profit to the investor from the sale of the call. As may be seen in column 4, the sale of the call is profitable to the investor as long as the price of the common stock remains below $55 per share. The last column gives the net profit on the entire position. As long as the price of the common stock stays above $45 per share, the entire position will yield a profit before commission fees. The maximum amount of this profit, however, is limited to $500. Thus, by selling the call the investor forgoes the possibility of large gains. For example, if the price of the stock were to rise to $70 per share, the holder of the call would exercise it and purchase the 100 shares from the investor at $50 per share. The investor would then make only the $500 that was received from the sale of the call.

If the price of the stock were to fall below $45, then the entire position would result in a loss to the investor. For example, if the price of the common stock were to fall to $40, the investor would lose $1000 on the purchase of the stock. However, $500 has been received from the sale of the call. Thus, the net loss is only $500. The investor still owns the stock and may now write another call on that stock. As long as the investor owns the stock, the same 100 shares may be used over and over to cover the writing of options. Thus, even if the price of the stock does fall, the investor may continue to use it to write more options. The more options that can be written, the more profitable the shares become. For individuals who write options, the best possible situation would be for the price of the stock to remain stable. In that case the investors would receive the income from writing the options and never suffer a capital loss from a decline in the price of the stock on which the option is being written.

The potential loss

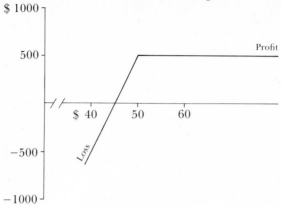

GRAPH 19-3.   Profit or Loss on Selling a Covered Call

The relationship between the price of the stock and the profit or loss on writing a covered call option is illustrated in Graph 19–3, which plots the first and fifth columns of Table 19–5. As may be seen from the graph, the sale of the covered option produces a profit (before commissions) for all prices of the stock above $45. However, the maximum profit (before commissions) is only $500.

The potential profit from naked calls

Option writers do not have to own the common stock on which they write calls. Although such naked or uncovered option writing exposes the investor to a large amount of risk, the returns may be considerable. If the writer of the CBS option given in Table 19–5 had not owned the stock and had sold the option for $500, the position would have been profitable as long as the price of the common stock remained below $55 per share. The investor would have earned the profit *without* tying up $5000 to buy the stock. The potential loss, however, is theoretically infinite, for the naked option loses $100 for every $1 increase in the price of the stock above the call's exercise price. For example, if the price of the stock were to rise to $70 per share, the call would be worth $2000. The owner of the call would exercise it and purchase the 100 shares for $5000. The writer of the call would then have to purchase the shares on the open market for $7000. Since the writer received only $500 when the call was sold and $5000 when the call was exercised, the loss would be $1500. Therefore, uncovered option writing exposes the writer to considerable risk if the price of the stock rises.*

The relationship between the price of the stock and the profit or loss on writing an uncovered or naked call option is illustrated in Graph 19–4. In this case the option writer earns a profit (before commissions) as long as

---

*This risk may be reduced by a stop-loss order to purchase the stock at $55. If the price of the stock rises, the stop-loss order is executed so that the option writer buys the stock.

GRAPH 19–4. Profit or Loss on Selling a Naked Call

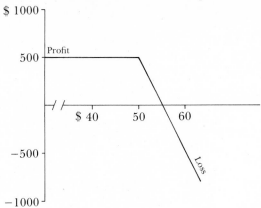

the price of the call does not exceed $55. Notice that the investor earns the entire $500 if the stock's price falls below $50. However, the potential for loss is considerable if the price of the stock increases.

Investors should write uncovered call options only if they anticipate a decline (or at least no increase in) the price of the stock. These investors may write covered call options if they believe that the price of the stock may rise but are not certain of the price increase. And they may purchase the stock and not write options if they believe that there is substantial potential for a price increase.

A COMPARISON OF SELLING CALLS AND HEDGING WITH WARRANTS

There is much similarity between selling covered options and hedging with warrants. Selling a covered call option is like buying stock and selling the warrant short. In both cases the potential profit from an increase in the price is limited. However, if the price of the stock declines, the sale price of the call and the premium commanded by the warrant protect the investor from loss.

This similarity may be seen by comparing Graphs 19–1 and 19–3. In both cases the profit is limited, and in both cases the investor gains even if the price of the stock declines. Thus, there exists potential profit if the price of the stock rises or falls, but the gain is small. This is exactly the reason for hedging: to reduce the risk of loss from price movements. Hedging with warrants or selling covered options does just that. For accepting a smaller return, the investor reduces the risk of loss from fluctuations in the price of the stock.

Selling covered call options is like hedging with warrants

PUTS

Puts — the option to sell

  Initially, only call options were traded on the CBOE and other exchanges, but as of May 31, 1977, a limited number of put options were admitted for trading. A put is an option to *sell* stock (usually 100 shares) at a specified price within a specified time period. As with calls, the time period is short — three, six, or nine months. Like all options, a put has a theoretical value, which is the difference between the exercise price of the put and the price of the stock. The relationship between the price of a stock and the intrinsic value of a put is illustrated in Table 19–6. This put is an option to sell 100 shares at $30 per share. The first column gives various hypothetical prices of the stock, the second column gives the exercise price of the put, and the third column gives the theoretical value of the put (i.e, the exercise price minus the price of the stock).

The value of a put rises as the price of the stock declines

  As may be seen in the example, as the price of the stock declines the theoretical value of the put rises. Since the owner of the put may sell the stock at the price specified in the option agreement, the value of the option rises as the price of the stock falls. Thus, if the price of the stock is $15 and the exercise price of the put is $30, the put's intrinsic value as an option must be $1500 (for 100 shares). The investor can purchase the 100 shares of stock for $1500 on the stock market and sell them for $3000 to the person who issued the put. The put, then, must be worth the $1500 difference between the purchase and sale prices.

The potential leverage

  Why should an investor purchase a put? The reason is the same for puts as it is for other speculative options: The put offers potential leverage to the investor. The potential leverage may be seen in the example presented in Table 19–6. When the price of the stock declines from $25 to $20 (a 20 per cent decrease), the theoretical value of the put rises from $500 to $1000 (a 100 per cent increase). In this example a 20 per cent decline in the price of the stock produces a fivefold percentage increase in the intrinsic value of the put. It is this potential leverage that makes put options attractive to investors.

  As with other speculative options, investors are willing to pay a price that is greater than the put's theoretical value: The put commands a premium above its intrinsic value as an option. As with warrants and calls, the amount of this premium depends on such factors as the volatility

TABLE 19–6.   *The Relationship Between the Price of a Stock and the Intrinsic Value of a Put*

PRICE OF THE STOCK	EXERCISE PRICE	THEORETICAL VALUE OF THE PUT
$40	$30	$−10
35	30	− 5
30	30	0
25	30	5
20	30	10
15	30	15

TABLE 19–7. *Relationship Between the Price of the Stock, the Exercise Price of the Put, and the Hypothetical Price of the Put*

PRICE OF THE STOCK	EXERCISE PRICE OF THE PUT	THEORETICAL VALUE OF THE PUT	HYPOTHETICAL PRICE OF THE PUT
$15	$30	$ 15	$15
20	30	10	11
25	30	5	7
30	30	0	3
35	30	− 5	1
40	30	−10	0

of the stock's price, the duration of the put, and the potential for *decline* in the price of the stock.

The relationships among the price of the stock, the exercise price of the put, and the hypothetical prices for the put are illustrated in Table 19–7. The first three columns are identical to those in Table 19–6. The first column gives the market price of the stock, the second column gives the exercise price of the put, and the third column gives the put's intrinsic value as an option. The fourth column presents hypothetical prices for the put. As may be seen in Table 19–7, the hypothetical price of the put exceeds the theoretical value of the put, for it commands a premium over its intrinsic value as an option.

Graph 19–5 illustrates the relationships among the price of the common stock (P_s), the intrinsic value of the put (P_i), and the hypothetical market value of the put (P_m) that were presented in Table 19–7. This graph shows the inverse relationship between the price of the stock and the put's

GRAPH 19–5. Premium Paid for a Put Option

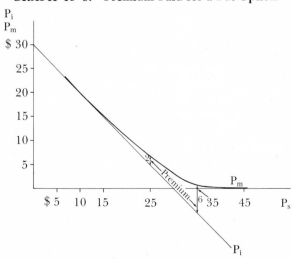

theoretical value. As the price of the stock declines, the value of the put increases (e.g., from $5 to $10 when the stock's price declines from $25 to $20). The graph also readily shows the premium paid for the option, for the line representing the market price of the put is above the line representing the put's intrinsic value. When the price of the stock is $35, the premium is $6. When the price of the stock is $25, the premium is $2.

As may be seen in both Table 19–7 and Graph 19–5, the hypothetical market price of the put converges with the put's theoretical value as the price of the stock declines. If the price of the stock is sufficiently high (e.g., $40 in Table 19–7), the put will not have any value because the price of the stock must decline substantially in order for the put to have any intrinsic value. At the other extreme, when the price of the stock is low (e.g., $15), the price of the put is equal to the put's intrinsic value as an option. There are two reasons for this convergence of the price of the put and its theoretical value. First, if the price of the stock rises, the investor may lose the funds invested in the put. As the price of the stock declines below the exercise price of the put, the greater is the potential risk to the investor if the price of the stock rises. Thus, investors are less willing to pay a premium above the put's theoretical value. Second, as the theoretical value of a put rises when the price of the put declines, the investor must spend more to buy the put and therefore the potential return on the investment is less. As the potential return declines, the willingness to pay a premium diminishes.

PUTS COMPARED WITH SHORT SALES

Investors purchase put options when they believe that the price of the stock is going to decline. Purchasing puts, however, is not the only method investors can use to profit from falling security prices. As was explained in Chapter 18, an investor who believes that the price of a stock is going to fall may profit from such a decline by selling short. The put option offers the investor two major advantages over selling short. First, the amount of potential loss is less; second, puts may offer a greater return on the investor's capital because of their leverage.

Puts are an alternative to selling short

In order to execute a short position, the investor must sell the stock, deliver the borrowed stock, and later purchase the stock to cover the position. The profit or loss is the difference between the price at which the borrowed stock was sold and the price at which the stock is purchased to repay the loan. If the price of the stock declines, the investor reaps a profit, but if the price of the stock rises, the investor suffers a loss. This loss may be substantial if the price of the stock rises significantly. For example, if 100 shares are sold short at $30 and later purchased at $50, the investor loses $2000 plus commissions on the investment. The higher the price of the stock rises, the greater is the loss that the short position inflicts on the investor.*

Purchasing a put option does not subject the investor to a large potential capital loss. If the investor purchases for $300 a put that is the option to sell 100 shares at $30, then the maximum amount that the investor can lose is $300. If the price of the common stock rises from $30 to $50, the maximum that can be lost with the put is still only $300. However, the loss on the short position is $2000 when the price of the stock rises from $30 to $50. Puts reduce the absolute amount that the investor may lose.

Besides subjecting the investor to potentially large losses, the short sale ties up a substantial amount of capital. When the investor sells short, the broker will require that he or she put up funds as collateral. The minimum amount that the investor must remit is the margin requirement set by the Federal Reserve, and individual brokers may require that the investor supply more collateral than this minimum. Selling short thus requires the investor to tie up capital, and the larger the amount that the investor must remit, the smaller is the potential return on the short position.

Less capital is required to invest in a put. While the amount of margin varies at different time periods, it certainly will never be as low as the price of the put. Thus, purchasing the put instead of establishing the short position ties up a smaller amount of the investor's funds. The potential return is greater if the price of the stock declines sufficiently to cover the cost of the put, because the amount invested is smaller. Puts thus offer the investor more leverage than does the short position.

Short sales, however, offer one important advantage over puts. Puts expire, but a short position can be maintained indefinitely. If an investor anticipates a price decline, it must occur during the put's short life in order for the investment to be profitable. With a short sale, the investor does not have this time constraint and may maintain the position indefinitely.

Buying a put requires less capital

The short position may be maintained indefinitely

SUMMARY

Warrants, calls, and puts are all speculative options. The first two are options to buy stock at a specified price by a specified date. A put is an option to sell stock at a specified price by a specified date. All three offer investors who are willing to bear a substantial amount of risk the potential for a large return.

Warrants are issued by firms, whereas puts and calls are issued and sold by individuals. When a warrant is exercised, the firm issues new

---

*Once again the investor may limit this potential loss by establishing a stop-loss order to purchase the stock should the price rise to some predetermined level.

stock and receives the proceeds. When a call is exercised, the individual who sold the call must supply the stock and in turn receives the proceeds from the sale. This stock comes either from the individual's holdings or from shares purchased to cover the option.

Puts and calls that are traded on organized exchanges have become very popular with many investors. Individuals seeking to supplement their income may write puts and calls against their portfolio holdings. Speculators buy these options because they offer potential leverage and substantial gains.

Options are very risky securities, and investments in them frequently result in losses. However, these options may be used in hedge positions to reduce risk. The investor may purchase stock and sell warrants short or sell covered call options. Such hedge positions reduce the risk of loss because the investor may earn a profit independently of movements in the price of the stock. Even if the stock's price declines, a hedge position may be profitable.

Terms to Remember

Warrant	Put	Premium
Expiration date	CBOE	Covered option
Hedging	Leverage	Naked option
Call		

Questions

1. What factors affect the premium paid for a warrant?

2. In what ways are warrants and calls similar? How are they different?

3. Why does hedging with warrants reduce risk?

4. What is the difference between covered and naked call option writing?

5. Why do some investors buy calls? Why do some investors write calls?

6. If an investor anticipates a decline in security prices, why may selling short or purchasing puts be a desirable strategy?

7. Why does the theoretical value of a call rise with the price of the stock, whereas the theoretical value of a put declines as the price of the stock rises?

Problems

1. A warrant has the following terms: It gives the option to buy stock at $10 per share, expires after two years, and is currently selling for $8. The stock that it is an option to buy is selling for $15. Construct a hedge position showing the potential profit for (1) one warrant sold short to one share purchased and (2) three warrants sold short to one share purchased. Compare the risks and potential profits from these two hedges.

2. What are the theoretical values and premiums paid for the following options?

Option		Price of the Option	Price of the Stock
Calls:	XYZ, Inc., 30	$7	$34
	XYZ, Inc., 35	$2^{1}/_{2}$	34
Puts:	XYZ, Inc., 30	$1^{1}/_{4}$	34
	XYZ, Inc., 35	$4^{1}/_{4}$	34

If the stock sells for $31 at the expiration date of the preceding options, what are the profits or losses for the writers and the buyers of these options?

3. A warrant is the option to buy stock at $20 per share and expires in one year. Currently the price of the stock is $25, and the price of the warrant is $9. Determine the range of stock prices that will produce a profit for the following hedge positions:

   a. One warrant sold short for every share purchased.
   b. Three warrants sold short for every share purchased.
   c. One warrant purchased for every share sold short.

4. A particular call is the option to buy stock at $25. It expires in six months and currently sells for $4 when the price of the stock sells for $26.

    a. What is the theoretical or intrinsic value of the call? What is the premium paid for the call?
    b. What will the value of this call be after six months if the price of the stock is $20? $25? $30? $40?
    c. If the price of the stock rises to $40 at the expiration date of the call, what is the percentage increase in the value of the call? Does this example illustrate favorable leverage?
    d. If an individual buys the stock and sells this call, what will the profit on the position be after six months if the price of the stock is $20? $26? $40?
    e. If an individual sells this call naked, what will the profit or loss be on the position after six months if the price of the stock is $20? $26? $40?

5. A particular put is the option to sell the stock at $40. It expires after three months and currently sells for $2 when the price of the stock is $42.

    a. If an investor buys this put, what will the profit be after three months if the price of the stock is $45? $40? $35?
    b. What will the profit from selling this put be after three months if the price of the stock is $45? $40? $35?

SELECTED READINGS

Black, Fischer, and Myron Scholes: "The Pricing of Options and Corporate Liabilities." *The Journal of Political Economy* (May–June 1973), pp. 637–654.

Black, Fischer: "Fact and Fantasy in the Use of Options." *Financial Analysts Journal, 31* (July–August 1975), pp. 36–41.

Fried, Sidney: *Speculating With Warrants.* New York, RHM Associates, 1971.

Gastineau, Gary L.: *The Stock Options Manual.* New York, McGraw-Hill Book Co., 1975.

Hayes, S. L. III, and H. B. Reiling: "Sophisticated Financing Tool: The Warrant." *Harvard Business Review, 47*(January 1969), pp. 137–150.

Hettenhouse, G. W., and D. J. Puglisi: "Investor Experience with Options." *Financial Analysts Journal, 31*(July–August 1975), pp. 53–72.

Reback, Robert: "Risk and Return in Option Trading." *Financial Analysts Journal, 31*(July–August 1975), pp. 42–52.

Rosen, Lawrence R.: *How To Trade Put and Call Options.* Homewood, Ill., Dow Jones-Irwin, Inc., 1974.

Shelton, J. P.: "Relation of the Price of a Warrant to the Price of its Associated Stock." *Financial Analysts Journal, 23*(May 1967), pp. 143–151, and 24(July 1967), pp. 88–99.

Thorp, Edward O., and Sheen T. Kassouf: *Beat the Market.* New York, Random House, Inc., 1967.

Turov, Daniel: "Stock or Warrant? Figuring Out Which to Buy Can be Important." *Barrons 50*(March 9, 1970), p. 9.

Wellemeyer, Marilyn (ed.): "The Value in Options." *Fortune* (November 1973), pp. 89–96.

Yeasting, K. L.: "CD Warrants." *Financial Analysts Journal, 26*(March 1970), pp. 44–47.

Learning Objectives

After completing this chapter you should be able to

1. Describe the feature common to all convertible bonds.

2. Determine the "floor" or minimum price of a convertible bond.

3. List the factors that affect the price of a convertible bond.

4. Identify the two premiums paid for a convertible bond.

5. Explain why the two premiums are inversely related.

6. Compare convertible bonds with convertible preferred stock.

chapter 20
CONVERTIBLE BONDS AND CONVERTIBLE PREFERRED STOCK

Convertible bonds and convertible preferred stock may be converted at the holder's option into the stock of the issuing company. Unlike warrants, puts, and calls, these securities offer the investor a conservative alternative to the stock of the company. They tend to have both higher flows of income (i.e., interest or dividends) and smaller price fluctuations than the stock into which they may be converted.

This chapter covers the various facets of convertible securities. Initially, the features and terms of convertible bonds are described, followed by a discussion of their pricing. This includes the premiums paid for convertible bonds, and the relationship between their price and the price of the stock into which they may be converted. The element of safety of convertible bonds is emphasized. The third section is devoted to convertible preferred stock. These shares are similar to convertible bonds but lack the safety implied by the debt element of convertible bonds. The chapter ends with the brief histories of two convertible bonds that illustrate the potential profits and risk associated with investing in them.

FEATURES OF CONVERTIBLE BONDS

Convertible into stock

Convertible bonds are debt instruments that may be converted at the holder's option into the stock of the issuing company. As was seen in Chapter 11, firms issue a variety of debt instruments to tap funds in the capital markets. Convertible bonds are one means to do so: The conversion feature is granted to bondholders to induce them to buy the debt.

Usually subordinated

Since the firm has granted the holder the right to convert the bonds, these bonds are usually subordinate to the firm's other debt. They also tend to offer a lower rate of interest (i.e., coupon rate) than is available on nonconvertible debt. Thus, the conversion feature means that the firm can issue lower quality debt at a lower interest cost. Investors are willing to accept this reduced quality and interest income because the market value of the bond will appreciate *if* the price of the stock rises. These investors are thus trading quality and interest for possible capital gains.

An important source of funds

Convertible bonds have been a popular means for firms to raise funds in the capital markets. A sample of firms and their convertible bonds is presented in Exhibit 20–1. As may be seen in the exhibit, the bonds are not just issued by lower quality firms with poor credit ratings. Some of the country's most prestigious firms, including Xerox and Georgia Pacific, have convertible bonds outstanding.

Debt features

Since convertible bonds are long-term debt instruments, they have

EXHIBIT 20–1.   Selected Convertible Bonds*

Firm	Coupon Rate Of Interest	Year Of Maturity	Moody's Rating
American Airlines	4¼%	1992	Ba
Ashland Oil	4¾	1993	Baa
Black and Decker	4	1992	Baa
Eastern Airlines	10	2002	B
Fedders	5	1996	B
Georgia Pacific	5¼	1996	A
Greyhound	6½	1990	Baa
Pan American World Airways	4½	1984	B
Xerox	6	1995	A

*Source: *Moody's Bond Record*, April 1978.

features that are common to all bonds. They are usually issued in $1000 denominations, pay interest semiannually, and have a fixed maturity date. However, if the bonds are converted into stock, the maturity date is irrelevant because the bonds are retired when they are converted. Convertible bonds frequently have a sinking fund requirement, which, like the maturity date, is meaningless once the bonds are converted.

The call feature

A noteworthy feature of convertible bonds is that they may be called by the issuing firm. The firm uses the call to force the holders to convert the bonds. Once the bond is called, the owner must convert, or any appreciation in price that has resulted from an increase in the stock's value will be lost. Such forced conversion is extremely important to the issuing firm, because it no longer has to repay the debt.

Attractive to conservative investors

Convertible bonds are attractive to conservative investors because they offer some of the safety features of debt. The firm must meet the terms of the indenture, and the bonds must be retired if they are not converted. The flow of interest income usually exceeds the dividend yield that may be earned on the firm's stock. In addition, since the bonds may be converted into stock, the holder will share in the growth of the company. If the price of the stock rises in response to the firm's growth, then the value of the convertible bond must also rise. It is this combination of the safety of debt and the potential for capital gain that makes convertible bonds an attractive investment, particularly to conservative investors who desire income and some capital appreciation.

Default risk

Like all investments, convertible bonds subject the holder to risk. If the company fails, the holder of a bond stands to lose the funds invested in the debt. This is particularly true with regard to convertible bonds, because they are usually subordinate to the firm's other debt. Thus, convertible bonds are considerably less safe than senior debt or debt that is secured by specific collateral. In case of default or bankruptcy, holders of convertible bonds may at best realize only a fraction of the principal amount invested. However, their position is still superior to that of the stockholders.

Price fluctuations

Default is not the only potential source of risk to investors. Convertible bonds are actively traded, and their prices can and do fluctuate. As is explained in detail in the next section, their price is partially related to the value of the stock into which they may be converted. Fluctuations in the value of the stock produce fluctuations in the price of the bond. These price changes are *in addition* to price movements caused by variations in interest rates.

During periods of higher interest rates and lower stock prices, convertible bonds are doubly cursed. Their lower coupon rates of interest cause their prices to decline more than those of nonconvertible debt. This, in addition to the decline in the value of the stock into which they may be converted, results in considerable price declines for convertible bonds. Such declines are illustrated in Exhibit 20–2, which gives the high and low prices of several convertible bonds during 1974. During this time period,

EXHIBIT 20–2. The High and Low Prices of Selected Convertible Bonds in 1974 Compared With 1978's Year End Price

Bond	Prices		December 31, 1978
	1974 High	1974 Low	
Ampex 5½ 94	48½	34	61
Gulf and Western 5½ 93	70	48	78
Pan American World Airways 4½ 86	42½	13	59
Seatrain 6 95	38	20½	56
TWA 4 92	46⅞	22	47½

the Dow Jones industrial average fell from 850 in January 1973 to 607 in September 1974. During the same time period, interest rates on Baa-rated bonds rose from 8.5 per cent to 9.8 per cent. Thus, the prices of convertible bonds fell sharply, which is illustrated in Exhibit 20–2. Each bond selected for this exhibit sold for less than half its principal value, and in the case of the Pan American World Airways 4½ 86 the $1000 bond sold for as little as $130.

The exhibit also includes the prices of the bonds at the end of 1978. As may be seen in the last column, each bond's price had risen considerably from the 1974 lows. If these bonds had been purchased in 1974, their rates of return would have been substantial, because they not only paid interest when due but also appreciated in price.

THE VALUATION OF CONVERTIBLE BONDS

This section considers the valuation of convertible bonds. The value of a convertible bond is related to (1) the value of the stock into which it may be converted and (2) the value of the bond as a debt instrument. Although each of these factors affects the market price of the bond, the importance of each element varies with changing conditions in the security markets. In the final analysis, the valuation of a convertible bond is extremely difficult, because it is a hybrid security that combines debt and equity.

This section has three subdivisions. The first considers the value of the bond solely as stock. The second covers the bond's value only as a debt instrument, and the last section combines these values to show the hybrid nature of convertible bonds. In order to differentiate the value of the bond as stock from its value as debt, subscripts are added to the symbols used. S will represent stock, and D will represent debt. Although this may make the equations appear more complex, it will clearly distinguish the value of the bond as stock from the value as debt.

THE CONVERTIBLE BOND AS STOCK

The value of a convertible bond in terms of the stock into which it may be converted (C_s) depends upon (1) the face or principal amount of the bond (F), (2) the conversion (or exercise) price of the bond (P_e), and (3) the market price of the common stock (P_s). The face value divided by the conversion price of the bond gives the number of shares into which the bond may be converted. For example, if a $1000 bond may be converted at $20 per share, then the bond may be converted into 50 shares ($1000 ÷ $20). The number of shares times the market price of a share gives the value of the bond in terms of stock. If the bond is convertible into 50 shares and the stock sells for $15 per share, then the bond is worth $750 in terms of stock ($15 × 50).

This theoretical value of the bond as stock is expressed in Equation 1:

The value of the bond as stock

$$(1) \qquad C_s = \frac{F}{P_e} \times P_s$$

and is illustrated in Table 20–1. In this example a $1000 bond is convertible into 50 shares (i.e., a conversion price of $20 per share). The first column gives various prices of the stock. The second column presents the number of shares into which the bond is convertible (i.e., 50 shares). The third column gives the value of the bond in terms of stock (i.e., the product of the values in the first two columns). As may be seen in the table, the value of the bond in terms of stock rises as the price of the stock increases.

This theoretical relationship between the price of the convertible bond and the conversion value of the bond is illustrated in Graph 20–1. The price of the stock (P_s) is given on the horizontal axis, and the conversion value of the bond (C_s) is shown on the vertical axis. As the price of

A graphic illustration

TABLE 20–1. *The Relationship Between the Price of a Stock and the Value of a Convertible Bond*

PRICE OF THE STOCK	SHARES INTO WHICH THE BOND IS CONVERTIBLE	VALUE OF THE BOND IN TERMS OF STOCK
$ 0	50	$ 0
5	50	250
10	50	500
15	50	750
20	50	1000
25	50	1250
30	50	1500

GRAPH 20–1. The Relationship Between the
Price of a Convertible Bond and the Conversion
Value of the Bond

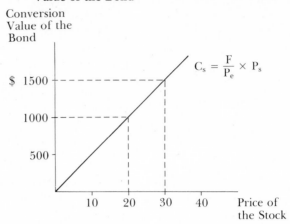

the stock rises, the conversion value of the bond increases. This is shown
in the graph by cline C_s, which represents the theoretical value of the bond
in terms of stock. Line C_s is a straight line running through the origin. If
the stock has no value, the value of the bond in terms of stock is also worthless. If the exercise price of the bond and the market price of the stock are
equal (i.e., $P_s = P_e$, which in this case is $20), then the bond's value as
stock is equal to the principal amount (i.e., the bond's face value). As the
price of the stock rises above the exercise price of the bond, the value of
the bond in terms of stock increases to more than the principal amount of
the debt.

The theoretical value sets the minimum price

As with speculative options, which were discussed in the previous
chapter, the market price of a convertible bond cannot be less than the
bond's theoretical value as stock. If the price of the bond were less than its
value as stock, an opportunity to arbitrage would exist. Arbitragers would
sell the stock short, purchase the convertible bond, exercise the conversion feature, and use the shares acquired through the conversion to cover
the short sale. The arbitragers would then make a profit equal to the
difference between the price of the convertible bond and the conversion
value of the bond. For example, if in the preceding example the bond were
selling for $800 when the stock sold for $20 per share, arbitragers would
enter the market. At $20 per share, the bond is worth $1000 in terms of the
stock (i.e., $20 × 50). Arbitragers would then sell 50 shares short for $1000.

Arbitrage

At the same time they would buy the bond for $800 and exercise the
option. After the shares have been acquired through the conversion of the
bond, the arbitragers would cover the short position and earn $200 in
profit (before commissions).

As arbitragers seek to purchase the bonds, they will drive up their
price. The price increase will continue until there is no opportunity for

profit. This occurs when the price is equal to or greater than the bond's value as stock. Thus, the theoretical value of the bond in terms of stock sets the minimum price of the bond. Because of arbitrage, the market price of a convertible bond will be at least equal to its conversion value.

However, the market price of the convertible bond is rarely equal to the conversion value of the bond. The bond frequently sells for a premium over its conversion value, because the convertible bond may also have value as a debt instrument. As a pure (i.e., nonconvertible) bond, it competes with other nonconvertible debt. Like the conversion feature, this element of debt may affect the bond's price. Its impact is important, for it also has the effect of putting a minimum price on the convertible bond. It is this price floor that gives investors in convertible bonds an element of safety that stock lacks.

The premium paid for convertible bonds

THE BOND AS DEBT

The value of the convertible bond as debt (C_D) is related to (1) the annual interest or coupon rate that the bond pays (I), (2) the current interest rate that is paid on comparable nonconvertible debt (i), and (3) the requirement that the principal or face value (F) be retired at maturity (after n number of years) if the bond is not converted. In terms of present value calculations, the value of a convertible bond as nonconvertible debt is given in Equation 2:

The value of the bond as debt

(2)
$$C_D = \frac{I}{(1+i)^1} + \frac{I}{(1+i)^2} + \ldots + \frac{I}{(1+i)^n} + \frac{F}{(1+i)^n}$$

Equation 2 is simply the current price of any bond. (The derivation of the Equation was discussed in Chapter 10.)

Equation 2 may be illustrated by the following example. Assume that the convertible bond in Table 20–1 matures in ten years and pays 5 per cent annually. Nonconvertible debt of the same risk class currently yields 8 per cent. When these values are inserted into Equation 2, the value of the bond as nonconvertible debt is $798.50.

A bond valuation model

$$C_D = \frac{\$50}{(1+.08)} + \frac{\$50}{(1+.08)^2} + \ldots + \frac{\$50}{(1+.08)^9} + \frac{\$50}{(1+.08)^{10}} + \frac{\$1000}{(1+.08)^{10}}$$

$$C_D = \$50(6.710) + \$1000(0.463) = \$798.50$$

This equation may be solved by the use of present value tables or a bond table. The 6.710 is the interest factor for the present value of an annuity of $1 for ten years at 8 per cent, and 0.463 is the interest factor for the present value of $1 to be received ten years in the future when it is

GRAPH 20–2. The Relationship Between the Price of Common Stock and the Value of the Bond as Nonconvertible Debt

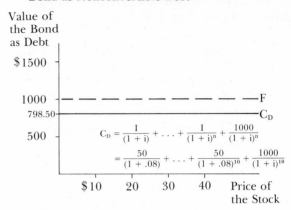

discounted at 8 per cent. To be competitive with nonconvertible debt, this bond would have to sell for $798.50.

The relationship between the price of the common stock and the value of this bond as nonconvertible debt is illustrated in Graph 20–2. This graph consists of a horizontal line (C_D) that shows what the price ($798.50) of the bond would be if it were not convertible into stock, in which case the price is independent of the value of the stock. The principal amount of the bond is also shown in Graph 20–2 by the broken line F, which is above the line C_D. The principal amount exceeds the value of the bond as pure debt because this bond must sell at a discount to be competitive with nonconvertible debt.

The value fluctuates with changes in the interest rate

The value of the convertible bond as debt varies with market interest rates. Since the interest paid by the bond is fixed, the value of the bond as debt varies inversely with interest rates. An increase in interest rates causes this value to fall; a decline in interest rates causes the value to rise.

The relationship between the value of the preceding convertible bond as debt and various interest rates is presented in Table 20–2. The first

TABLE 20–2.   *The Relationship Between Interest Rates and the Value of a Bond*

INTEREST RATE	COUPON RATE	VALUE OF A TEN-YEAR BOND
3%	5%	$1170.50
4	5	1081.55
5	5	1000.00
6	5	926.00
7	5	864.20
8	5	798.50

column gives various interest rates; the second column gives the nominal (i.e., coupon) rate of interest; and the last column gives the value of the bond as nonconvertible debt. The inverse relationship is readily apparent, for as the interest rate rises from 3 per cent to 8 per cent the value of the bond declines from $1170.50 to $798.50.

    The value of the bond as nonconvertible debt is important because this value sets another minimum price that the bond will command in the market. At that price the convertible bond is competitive with nonconvertible debt of the same maturity and degree of risk. If the bond were to sell below this price, it would offer a yield that is more attractive (i.e., higher) than that of nonconvertible debt. Investors would seek to buy the bond to attain this higher yield. They would bid up the bond's price until its yield were comparable to that of nonconvertible debt. Thus, the bond's value as nonconvertible debt becomes a floor on the price of the convertible bond. Even if the value of the stock into which the bond may be converted were to fall, this floor would halt the decline in the price of the convertible bond.

Its value as debt sets a price floor

    The actual minimum price of a convertible bond combines its value as stock and its value as debt. This is illustrated in Graph 20–3, which combines the preceding graphs for the value of the bond in terms of stock and the value of the bond as nonconvertible debt. These values set a minimum price for the bond, because its price cannot be lower than either of these two values. If the price of the convertible bond were below its value as common stock, arbitragers would bid up its price. If the bond sold for a price below its value as debt, investors in debt instruments would bid up the price.

The impact of the bond's value as debt and as stock

    The minimum price of the convertible bond is either its value in terms of stock or its value as nonconvertible debt, but the importance of these determinants varies. For low stock prices (i.e., stock prices less than P_{s1} in

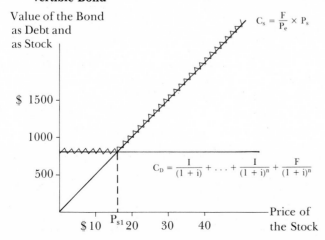

GRAPH 20–3. **The Actual Minimum Price of a Convertible Bond**

Value of the Bond as Debt and as Stock

$C_s = \frac{F}{P_e} \times P_s$

$$C_D = \frac{I}{(1 + i)} + \dots + \frac{I}{(1 + i)^n} + \frac{F}{(1 + i)^n}$$

Price of the Stock

$10 P_{s1} 20   30   40

Graph 20–3), the minimum price is set by the bond's value as debt. However, for stock prices greater than P_{s1}, it is the bond's value as stock that determines the minimum price.

THE BOND'S VALUE AS A HYBRID SECURITY

The extreme values

The market price (P_m) of the convertible bond combines both the conversion value of the bond and its value as nonconvertible debt. If the price of the stock were to decline significantly below the exercise price of the bond, the market price of the convertible bond would be influenced primarily by the bond's value as nonconvertible debt. In effect, the bond would be priced as if it were a pure debt instrument. As the price of the stock rises, the conversion value of the bond rises and plays an increasingly important role in the determination of the market price of the convertible bond. At sufficiently high stock prices, the market price of the bond is identical with its conversion value.

These relationships are illustrated in Graph 20–4, which reproduces Graph 20–3 and adds to it the market price of the convertible bond (P_m). For prices of the common stock below P_{s1}, the market price is identical to the bond's value as nonconvertible debt. For prices of the common stock above P_{s2}, the price of the bond is identical to its value as common stock.

Prices between the extremes

At these extreme stock prices, the bond may be analyzed as if it were either pure debt or stock. For all prices between these two extremes, the market price of the convertible bond is influenced by the bond's value both as nonconvertible debt and as stock. This dual influence makes the analysis of convertible bonds difficult, since the investor pays a premium over the bond's value as stock and as debt.

GRAPH 20–4. Determining the Market Price of a Convertible Bond

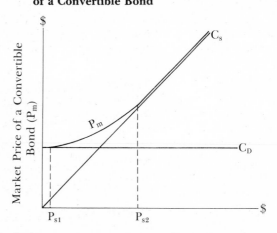

PREMIUMS PAID FOR
CONVERTIBLE DEBT

One way to analyze a convertible bond is to measure the premium over the bond's value as debt or as stock. For example, if a particular convertible bond is commanding a higher premium than is paid for similar convertible securities, perhaps this bond should be sold. Conversely, if the premium is relatively low, the bond may be a good investment.

The premiums paid for a convertible bond are illustrated in Table 20–3, which reproduces Table 20–1 and adds the value of the bond as nonconvertible debt (column 4) along with hypothetical market prices for the bond (column 5). The premium that an investor pays for a convertible bond may be viewed in either of two ways: the premium over the bond's value as stock or the premium over the bond's value as debt. Column 6 gives the premium in terms of stock. This is the difference between the bond's market price and its value as stock (i.e., the value in column 5 minus the value in column 3). This premium declines as the price of the stock rises and plays a more important role in the determination of the bond's price. Column 7 gives the premium in terms of nonconvertible debt. This is the difference between the bond's market price and its value as debt (i.e., the value in column 5 minus the value in column 4). This premium rises as the price of the stock rises, because the debt element of the bond is less important.

The inverse relationship between the two premiums is also illustrated in Graph 20–5. The premiums are shown by the difference between the line representing the market price (P_m) and the lines representing the value of the bond in terms of stock (C_s) and the value of the bond as nonconvertible debt (C_D).

When the price of the stock is low and the bond is selling close to its value as debt, the premium above the bond's intrinsic value as stock is substantial, but the premium above the bond's value as debt is small. For example, at P_{s1} the price of the stock is $10, the bond's value in terms of stock is $500 (Line *AB* in Graph 20–5), and the premium is $298.50 (Line *BC*). However, the bond is selling for its value as nonconvertible debt ($798.50), and there is no premium over its value as debt. When the price of the stock is $25 and the bond is selling for $1300, the premium in terms of stock is only $50 (Line *EF*). However, the bond's premium over its value as nonconvertible debt is $401.50 (Line *DF*).

As these examples illustrate, the premium paid for the bond over its theoretical value as stock declines as the price of the stock rises. This decline in the premium is the result of the increasing importance of the conversion value of the bond's market price and the decreasing importance of the debt element of the bond's price.

As the price of the stock rises, the safety feature of the debt diminishes. If the price of the common stock ceased to rise and started to fall, then the price of the convertible bond could decline considerably before

Margin notes

The premiums

The price over the bond's value as stock

This premium declines as the price of the stock rises

The premium over the bond's value as debt rises as the price of the stock rises

TABLE 20–3. Premiums Paid for Convertible Debt

Price Of The Stock	Shares Into Which The Bond May Be Converted	Value Of The Bond In Terms Of Stock	Value Of The Bond As Non-convertible Debt	Hypothetical Price Of The Convertible Bond	Premium In Terms Of Stock*	Premium In Terms Of Non-convertible Debt†
$ 0	50	$ 0	$798.50	$ 798.50	$798.50	$ .00
5	50	250	798.50	798.50	548.50	.00
10	50	500	798.50	798.50	298.50	.00
15	50	750	798.50	900.00	150.00	101.50
20	50	1000	798.50	1100.00	100.00	301.50
25	50	1250	798.50	1300.00	50.00	501.50
30	50	1500	798.50	1500.00	.00	701.50

*The premium in terms of stock is equal to the hypothetical price of the convertible bond minus the value of the bond in terms of stock.
†The premium in terms of nonconvertible debt is equal to the hypothetical price of the convertible bond minus the value of the bond as nonconvertible debt.

GRAPH 20–5. Premiums Paid for a Convertible Bond

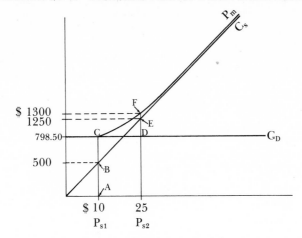

it reached the floor price set by the nonconvertible debt. The safety feature diminishes as the price of the stock rises. For example, if the price of the stock declined from $30 to $15 (a 50 per cent decline), the price of the convertible bond could fall from $1500 to $798.50 (a 46.8 per cent decline). Such a price decline would indicate that the floor value of $798.50 had little impact on the decline in the price of the bond.

In addition, as the price of the stock (and hence the price of the convertible bond) rises, the probability that the bond will be called rises. When the bond is called, it can only be worth its value as stock. The call forces the holder to convert the bond into stock. For example, when the price of the stock is $30, the bond is worth $1500 in terms of stock. Should the company call the bond and offer to retire it for its face value ($1000), no one would accept the offer. Instead they would convert the bond into $1500 worth of stock. If the investor paid a premium over this conversion value (such as $1600) and the bond were called, then the investor would suffer a loss. Thus, as the probability of a call increases, the willingness to pay a premium over the bond's value as stock declines, and the price of the convertible bond ultimately converges with its value as stock.

The probability of a call

This decline in the premium also means that the price of the stock will rise more rapidly than the price of the bond. While speculative options offer investors potential leverage, convertible bonds do not. As may be seen in both Table 20–3 and Graph 20–5, the market price of the convertible bond rises and falls with the price of the stock, because the conversion value of the bond rises and falls. However, the market price of the convertible bond does not rise as rapidly as the conversion value of the bond. For example, when the stock's price increased from $20 to $25 (a 25 per cent increase), the convertible bond's price rose from $1100 to $1300 (an 18.2 per cent increase). The reason for this difference

The price of the stock fluctuates more than the price of the bond

in the rate of increase is the declining premium paid for the convertible bond. Since the premium declines as the price of the stock rises, the rate of increase in the price of the stock must exceed the rate of increase in the price of the bond. In summary, convertible bonds offer investors the opportunity for some capital growth with less risk.

A common misconception

Because of these advantages, some investors may have the misconception that convertible bonds offer the best of both worlds: high return plus safety. In many cases a convertible bond may prove to be an inferior investment. For example, if the price of the stock rises rapidly, then the stock is a superior investment because it will produce a larger capital gain. The stock outperforms the bond because the investor paid a premium for the convertible bond. In the opposite case when the price of the stock does not rise, a nonconvertible bond will outperform the convertible bond because it earns more interest. Thus, the very sources of a convertible bond's attractiveness (i.e., the potential capital growth plus the safety of debt) are also the sources of its lack of appeal (i.e., the inferior growth relative to the stock and the inferior interest income relative to nonconvertible debt).

The advantages

For investors, the advantages offered by convertible bonds do not include (1) the potential leverage of options, (2) the potential growth of stock, or (3) the safety and interest income of debt. The advantage is some combination of capital gain, interest income, and the safety of debt. As the previous example illustrated, the investor does receive interest income, and if the price of the stock rises, then the price of the bond must also rise. If the stock's price does not rise, the convertible bond must eventually be retired because it is a debt obligation of the firm. Hence, the bond does offer some element of safety that is not available through investments in common stocks in addition to some growth potential that is not available through nonconvertible debt.

CONVERTIBLE PREFERRED STOCK

Convertible preferred stock is similar to convertible debt

In addition to convertible bonds, many firms have issued convertible preferred stock. As its name implies, this stock may be converted into the common stock of the issuing corporation. A sampling of convertible preferred stock is presented in Exhibit 20–3. This exhibit illustrates the diversity of companies that have this security outstanding, including telephone, chemical, financial, oil, and retailing firms. Thus, while nonconvertible preferred stock is primarily issued by utilities, the entire spectrum of firms issues convertible preferred stock.

It may be issued in mergers

Several of these issues of convertible preferred stock came into existence through mergers. The tax laws permit firms to combine through an exchange of stock, which is not taxable (i.e., it is a tax-free exchange). If one firm purchases another firm for cash, the stockholders

EXHIBIT 20–3. Terms of Selected Convertible
Preferred Stocks as of April 1978*

Firm	Dividend Rate	Shares of Common Stock Into Which Preferred Stock May Be Converted
AT&T	$4.00	1.05
Atlantic Richfield	3.00	3.40
Green Giant	1.76	1.40
Household Finance	2.375	2.25
Monsanto	2.75	1.12
Sperry and Hutchinson	3.00	1.42

*Source: *Standard & Poor's Stock Guide,* May 1978.

who sell their shares have an obvious realized sale. Profits and losses from the sale are then subject to capital gains taxation. However, the Internal Revenue Service has ruled that an exchange of "like securities" is not a realized sale and thus is not subject to capital gains taxation until the investor sells the new shares.

The impact of tax laws

This tax ruling has encouraged mergers through the exchange of stock. In many cases the firm that is taking over (the surviving firm) offers to the stockholders of the firm that is being taken over an opportunity to trade their shares for a new convertible preferred stock. Since the stock is convertible into the common stock of the surviving firm, it is a "like security." Thus, the transaction is not subject to capital gains taxation. To encourage the stockholders to tender their shares, the surviving firm may offer a generous dividend yield on the convertible preferred stock. For this reason many convertible preferred stocks have considerably more generous dividend yields than that which is available through investing in the firm's common stock.

It is equity

Convertible preferred stock is similar to convertible debt; however, there are some important differences. The differences are primarily the same as those between nonconvertible preferred stock and nonconvertible debt. Preferred stock is treated as an equity instrument. Thus, the firm is not under any legal obligation to pay the dividends. In addition, the preferred stock is a perpetual security and does not have to be retired as debt must be. However, many convertible preferred stocks do have a required sinking fund, which forces the firm to retire the preferred stock over a period of years.

Its valuation

The value of convertible preferred stock (like convertible bonds) is related to the price of the stock into which it may be converted and to the value of competitive nonconvertible preferred stock. As with convertible bonds, these values set floors on the price of the convertible preferred stock. It cannot sell for any significant length of time below its theoretical value as stock. If it did, arbitragers would enter the market and buy the preferred stock, which would increase its price. Thus, the minimum value of the convertible preferred stock (like the minimum value of the convertible bond) must be equal to the conversion of the stock (P_c). In equation form that is

$$(3) \qquad\qquad P_c = P_s \times N$$

where P_s is the market price of the stock into which the convertible bond may be converted, and N is the number of shares an investor obtains through conversion. Equation 3 is similar to Equation 1 which gave the theoretical value of the convertible bond as stock.

The impact of dividends and their appropriate discount factor

The convertible preferred stock's value as nonconvertible preferred stock (P_{pfd}) is related to the dividend it pays (D_{pfd}) and to the appropriate discount factor (k_{pfd}), which is the yield earned on competitive nonconvertible debt. In equation form that is

$$(4) \qquad\qquad P_{pfd} = \frac{D_{pfd}}{k_{pfd}}$$

which is essentially the same as the convertible bond's value as debt, except that the preferred stock has no definite maturity date. (Equation 4 was derived in Chapter 10.) However, this value does set a floor on the price of a convertible preferred stock because at that price it is competitive with nonconvertible preferred stock.

As with convertible bonds, the convertible preferred stock is a hybrid security whose value combines its worth both as stock and as nonconvertible preferred stock. Except for its extreme values, the convertible preferred stock tends to sell for a premium over its value as stock and its value as straight preferred stock. Thus, Graphs 20–4 and 20–5, which illustrated the value of the convertible bond at various prices of the stock into which it may be converted, also apply to convertible preferred stock. The only difference is the premium that the preferred stock commands over the value as common stock. This premium tends to be smaller. The reason for this reduced premium is that the preferred stock does not have the element of debt. Its features are more similar to common stock than are the features of the convertible bond. Thus, its price usually commands less of a premium over its value as stock.

THE HISTORY OF TWO CONVERTIBLE BONDS

Illustrations of convertible bonds

Perhaps the best way to understand investing in convertible bonds is to examine the history of two such bonds. The first is a success story in that the price of the common stock rose, and therefore the value of the bond also rose. The second is a not-so-successful story, for the price of the stock declined and so did the value of the bond. However, the story of this bond has not ended, for it is still a debt obligation of the company and must be retired at maturity even if it is not converted into stock.

THE AMERICAN QUASAR 7¼ 91

American Quasar is a firm devoted to exploring and drilling for oil and gas. It not only develops known reserves but also drills wells in search of new discoveries. Such wells (called wildcats) can prove to be highly lucrative; however, the majority of such drilling leads only to dry holes (i.e., no oil or gas is found). Because of the nature of its operations, American Quasar is a speculative firm at best. Speculative firms, however, need funds to operate, so in July 1976 the firm issued $17,500,000 in face value of convertible bonds. The coupon rate was set at 7¼ per cent, which is quite generous for a convertible bond. The high coupon rate was indicative of the element of risk involved in investing in the security. The exercise price of the bond was $21 (i.e., it was convertible into 47.6 shares), which was a premium of 17 per cent over the approximate price of the stock ($18) at the date of issue.

After the bond was issued, American Quasar's stock did particularly well. Perhaps the discovery of some sizable wells in the Midwest and the problems associated with energy in general helped bolster the firm's stock. Of course, the value of the convertible bond rose as the price of the stock rose. The prices of the bond and the stock moved closely together until the bond was called in October 1977, which forced conversion of the bond into the stock. The bond's life was short, as it was called less than two years after it was issued.

A success

What was the return earned by investors in these securities? Obviously an investment in either the stock or the bond was quite profitable, since the price of the stock rose so rapidly. The bond's price rose from $1000 to $1500 during the time it was outstanding. The bond paid $145 in interest. The return earned over the 15 months on an investment in the bond was

$$\frac{\text{Price appreciation} + \text{interest earned}}{\text{cost}} = \frac{\$1500 - \$1000 + \$145}{\$1000} = \frac{\$645}{\$1000} = 64.5\%$$

For the stock the return was

$$\frac{\text{Price appreciation} + \text{dividends}}{\text{cost}} = \frac{\$32 - \$18 + \$0}{\$18} = \frac{\$14}{\$18} = 77.7\%$$

(It should be noted that the stock did not pay any cash dividends while the bond was outstanding.) As may be seen by these calculations, the returns are both positive. The stock did better because the bond was initially sold for a premium over its value as stock. However, an investor who purchased this convertible bond certainly has little cause for complaint.

THE PAN AMERICAN WORLD AIRWAYS 4½ 86

A poor investment

While the previous example illustrated how the price of a convertible bond may rise as the price of the stock rises, the Pan American World Airways 4½ 86 demonstrates the opposite. When the price of the stock declined, the price of the convertible bond followed it. This bond was issued in 1966, when Pan Am was riding the crest of popularity (which may partially explain why the coupon rate of interest was low on the bond).

Unfortunately for investors purchasing either the stock or the bond, Pan Am's popularity vanished, and with years of continued deficits the price of the stock declined drastically. The decline and its effect on the price of the convertible bond are illustrated in Graph 20–6, which plots the high and low stock and bond prices for 1967 through 1978. Both the stock and the bond fell to "bargain basement" prices in 1974. The mar-

GRAPH 20–6.   The Annual Price Range for Pan Am's Stock and 4½ 86 Convertible Bond

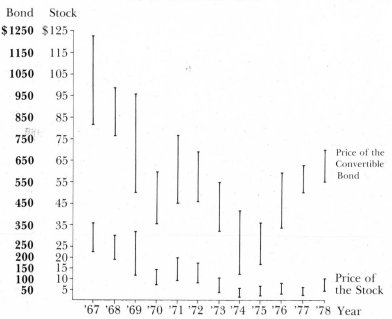

ket seemed to think that the firm would certainly default on the debt and enter bankruptcy. At that time the bond reached a low of $130 for a $1000 bond!

After this nadir, the price of both the bond and the stock recovered somewhat so that in June 1978 the stock was selling for $7 per share and the bond was selling for $620. However, both prices were still below the prices of 1966 when the bond was initially issued.

This example certainly illustrates the risk associated with investing in convertible bonds. If the firm becomes financially weak, the price of the convertible bond can fall drastically. The price of the stock fell from a high of $36¾ in 1966 to a low of $1¾ in 1974, and the price of the bond fell from $1221 to $130. However, the bond is still an obligation of Pan Am that they must retire by 1986. Thus, if Pan Am does redeem the bond, investors who purchased it initially for $1000 will get this principal back. However, during the many years that the bond has been outstanding, there have certainly been many periods when it appeared that the bond would become worthless.

This bond illustrates the risk

SUMMARY

A convertible bond is a debt instrument that may be converted into stock. The value of this bond depends on the value of the stock into which the bond may be converted and on the value of the bond as a debt instrument.

As the value of the stock rises, so does the value of the convertible bond. If the price of the stock declines, the value of the bond will also fall. However, the stock's price will decline faster, because the convertible bond's value as debt will halt the fall in the bond's price.

Since a convertible bond's price rises with the price of the stock, the bond offers the investor an opportunity for appreciation as the value of the firm increases. In addition, the bond's value as debt sets a floor on the bond's price, which reduces the risk of loss to the investor. Should the stock decline in value, the debt element reduces the risk of loss to the bondholder.

Convertible bonds, like other options, may sell for a premium. For these bonds the premium may be viewed relative to the bond's value as stock or relative to its value as debt. These two premiums are inversely related. When the price of the stock rises, the premium that the bond commands over its value as stock diminishes, but the premium over its value as debt rises. When the price of the stock falls, the premium over the bond's value as stock rises, but the premium relative to the bond's value as debt declines.

Convertible preferred stock is similar to convertible debt, except that it lacks the safety implied by a debt instrument. Its price is related to its conversion value, the flow of dividend income, and the rate that investors may earn on nonconvertible preferred stock.

Terms to Remember

Convertible bond	Call feature	Theoretical value as debt
Convertible preferred stock	Theoretical value as stock	Premium

Questions

1. What differentiates convertible bonds from other bonds?

2. How is the value of convertible bond in terms of stock determined? What effect does this value have on the price of the bond?

3. How is the value of a convertible bond in terms of debt determined? What effect does this value have on the price of the bond?

4. Why may convertible bonds be called by the firm? When are these bonds most likely to be called?

5. Why are convertible bonds less risky than stock but usually more risky than nonconvertible bonds?

6. Why does the premium over the bond's theoretical value as stock decline as the value of the stock rises?

7. How are convertible preferred stocks different from convertible bonds?

8. What advantages do convertible securities offer investors? What are the risks associated with these investments?

Problems

1. Given the following information concerning a convertible bond

principal	$1000
coupon	5%
maturity	15 years
call price	$1050
conversion price	$37 (i.e., 27 shares)
market price of the common stock	$32
market price of the bond	$1040

answer the following questions:
a. What is the current yield of this bond?
b. What is the value of the bond based on the market price of the common stock?
c. What is the value of the common stock based on the market price of the bond?
d. What is the premium in terms of stock that the investor pays when he or she purchases the convertible bond instead of the stock?
e. Nonconvertible bonds are selling with a yield to maturity of 7 per cent. If this bond lacked the conversion feature, what would the approximate price of the bond be?
f. What is the premium in terms of debt that the investor pays when he or she purchases the convertible bond instead of a nonconvertible bond?
g. If the price of the common stock should double, would the price of the convertible bond double? Briefly explain your answer.
h. If the price of the common stock should decline by 50 per cent, would the price of the convertible bond decline by the same percentage? Briefly explain your answer.
i. What is the probability that the corporation will call this bond?
j. Why are investors willing to pay the premiums mentioned in Problems d and f?

SELECTED READINGS

Baumol, William J., Burton G. Malkiel, and Richard E. Quandt: "The Valuation of Convertible Securities." *Quarterly Journal of Economics, 80* (February 1966), pp. 48–59.

Brigham, Eugene: "An Analysis of Convertible Debentures: Theory and Some Empirical Evidence." *Journal of Finance, 21* (March 1966), pp. 35–54.

Dawson, Steven M.: "Timing Interest Payments for Convertible Bonds." *Financial Management, 3*(Summer 1974), pp. 14–16.

Fried, Sidney: *Investing and Speculating With Convertibles.* New York, R.H.M. Associates, Inc., 1968.

Liebowitz, Martin L.: "Understanding Convertible Securities." *Financial Analysis Journal,* (November-December 1974), pp. 57–67.

Miller, Alexander B.: "How To Call Your Convertible." *Harvard Business Review, 49* (May-June 1971), pp. 66–70.

Pinches, George E.: "Financing with Convertible Preferred Stocks, 1960–1967. *Journal of Finance, 25* (March 1970), pp. 53–64.

Part Six

Miscellaneous Investments

The last part of the text considers a variety of assets that an individual may acquire as alternatives to stocks and bonds. These include futures contracts, shares in investment companies, collectibles, and real estate. The recent poor performance of common stocks and the continuing impact of inflation have increased investors' interest in these assets, especially in collectibles and real estate.

Unfortunately, the novice investor may not recognize the special risks or have the necessary information to invest successfully in these assets. While there are reports of spectacular returns earned on the purchase of a home or a painting, these results do not apply in all cases.

All investors compete against one another, and it simply is not possible for everyone to achieve abnormally large returns. In light of this, the text ends with a reminder that the environment of investing is very efficient. Information is disseminated very rapidly and prices adjust accordingly. The individual cannot realistically expect to outperform the market consistently. Instead, the investor should seek to acquire those assets that fulfill his or her requirements. Although such a strategy may not produce a spectacular return, it should help the individual to achieve his or her investment goals.

Learning Objectives

After completing this chapter you should be able to

1. Differentiate between closed-end and open-end investment companies.

2. Define *net asset value.*

3. Identify the costs of investing in mutual funds and closed-end investment companies.

4. List the advantages offered by investment companies.

5. Distinguish among the types of mutual funds.

6. Evaluate the return earned on investment company shares.

chapter 21

INVESTMENT COMPANIES

Because many investors find managing their own portfolios to be difficult or time consuming or both, they purchase shares in investment companies. The managements of these companies then invest the funds primarily in stocks and bonds. Investment companies have been popular vehicles for savers and play a significant role in security markets.

There are two general types of investment companies: closed-end and open-end. The open-end investment company is commonly referred to as a mutual fund. This chapter discusses these two types of investment companies, the mechanics of investing in them, the costs, and the potential sources of profit. Also included are the various specialized investment companies that have recently developed, which offer investors a broad spectrum of investment alternatives to the direct purchase of stocks and bonds. The chapter concludes with a general discussion of the return that investment companies have earned for investors.

INVESTMENT COMPANIES:
ORIGINS AND TERMINOLOGY

Investment companies started over a century ago

Investment companies are not a recent development but were established in Britain during the 1860s. Initially, these investment companies were referred to as trusts because the securities were held in trust for the firm's stockholders. These firms issued a specified number of shares and used the funds that were obtained through the sale of the stock certificates to acquire shares of other firms. Today the descendents of these companies are referred to as closed-end investment companies because the number of shares is fixed.

Mutual funds

While the first trusts offered a specified number of shares, the most common type of investment company today does not. Instead, the number of shares varies as investors buy more shares from the trust or sell them back to the trust. This "open-end" type of investment company is commonly called a mutual fund. Such funds started in 1924 when Massachusetts Investor Trust offered new shares and redeemed (i.e., bought) existing shares upon demand by stockholders.

The rationale for investment companies

The rationale for investment companies is very simple and appealing. The firms receive the funds from many investors, pool them, and purchase securities. The individual investors receive (1) the advantage of professional management of their money, (2) the benefit of ownership in a diversified portfolio, (3) the potential savings in commissions, as the investment company buys and sells in large blocks, and (4) custodial services (e.g., the storing of certificates and the collecting and disbursing of funds).

These advantages and services help to explain why both the number of mutual funds and the dollar value of their shares have grown very rapidly since 1940. This growth is illustrated in Graph 21–1, which presents the number of funds and the net sales in new shares from 1945 to 1975. (Net sales are gross sales minus redemptions, which are shares sold back to the mutual funds.) The graph dramatically illustrates not only the growth after World War II but also the decline in the popularity of mutual funds in the 1970s. During the 1970s redemptions started to exceed sales of mutual fund shares, so net sales were negative. One possible cause of this decline in the popularity of the funds was the poor return earned on the stockholders' investment. This return is discussed later in this chapter.

Closed-end investment companies have demonstrated a similar growth pattern. The value of their assets grew from $613 million in 1940 to over $6,637 million in 1976.* However, the total value of their assets is only one tenth of the value of the assets held by mutual funds. In terms of total dollars, mutual funds as a group are worth considerably more than closed-end investment companies.

Special tax treatment

Investment companies receive special tax treatment. Their earnings (i.e., dividend and interest income) and capital gains are exempt from

---

Investment Companies, New York, Wiesenberg Services, Inc., 1977, p. 12.

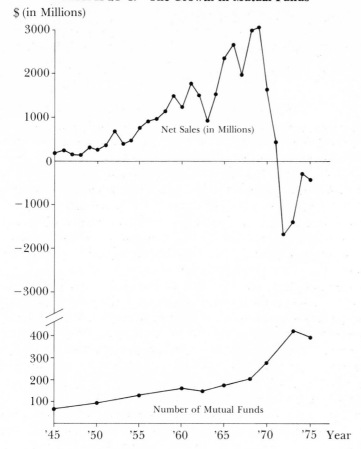

GRAPH 21-1.   The Growth in Mutual Funds

taxation at the corporate level. Instead, these profits are taxed through their stockholders' income tax returns. Dividends, interest income, and capital gains realized (whether they are distributed or not) by the investment companies must be reported by their shareholders, and they must pay the appropriate taxes.

For this reason, income that is received by investment companies and capital gains that are realized are usually distributed. The companies, however, offer their stockholders the option of having the firm retain and reinvest these distributions. While such reinvestments do not erase the stockholders' tax liabilities, they are an easy, convenient means to accumulate shares. The advantages offered by the dividend reinvestment plans of individual firms that were discussed in Chapter 15 also apply to the dividend reinvestment plans offered by investment companies. Certainly, the most important of these advantages is the element of forced savings. Since the stockholder does not receive the money, there is no

Their income and gains are distributed

The net asset value

temptation to spend it. Rather, the funds are immediately channeled back into additional income-earning assets.

One term frequently encountered in a discussion of an investment company is its *net asset value*. The net asset value of an investment company is the total value of its stocks, bonds, cash, and other assets minus any liabilities. The net value of any share of stock in the investment company is the total net asset value of the fund divided by the number of shares outstanding. Thus net asset value may be obtained as follows:

Value of stock owned	$1,000,000
Value of debt owned	+1,500,000
Value of total assets	$2,500,000
Debt outstanding	− 100,000
Net worth	$2,400,000
Number of shares outstanding	1,000,000
Net asset value per share	$2.40

The net asset value is extremely important for the valuation of an investment company, for it gives the value of the shares should the company be liquidated. Changes in the net asset value, then, alter the value of the investment company's shares. Thus, if the value of the firm's assets appreciate, the net asset value will increase, which may also cause the price of the investment company's stock to increase.

CLOSED-END INVESTMENT COMPANIES

The fixed capital structure

As was explained in the previous section, the difference between the open-end and closed-end investment companies is the nature of their capital structure. The closed-end investment company has a set capital structure that may be composed of all stock or a combination of stock and debt. The number of shares and the dollar amount of debts that the company may issue are specified. In an open-end investment company (i.e., a mutual fund), the number of shares outstanding varies as investors purchase and redeem them. Since the closed-end investment company has a specified number of shares, an individual who wants to invest in a particular company must purchase existing shares from current stockholders. Conversely, any investor who owns shares and wishes to liquidate the position must sell the shares. Thus, the shares in closed-end investment companies are bought and sold in the open market, just as the stock of IBM is traded. Shares of these companies are traded on the New York Stock Exchange (e.g., Adams Express), on the American Stock Exchange (e.g., Value Line Development Capital), and in the over-the-counter markets (e.g., Precious Metal Holdings). Sales and prices of these shares are reported in the financial press along with the shares of other firms.

The market value of these shares is related to the potential return on the investment. The market price of stock in a closed-end company, however, need not be the net asset value per share; it may be above or below this value, depending on the demand and the supply of stock in the secondary market. If the market price is below the net asset value of the shares, the shares are selling for a discount. If the market price is above the net asset value, the shares are selling for a premium.

The premium and the discount

These differences between the investment company's net asset value per share and the stock price are illustrated in Exhibit 21–1, which gives the price, the net asset value, and the discount or the premium for selected closed-end investment companies.* Most of the shares sell for a discount, and in several cases the discount exceeds 20 per cent of the net asset value of the shares. For example, shares of General American Investors had a net asset value of $13.06 but were selling for only $10.25, which is a discount of 18 per cent.

The shares of virtually all closed-end investment companies tend to sell below their net asset values. The cause of this discount is not really known, but it is believed to be the result of taxation. The potential impact of capital gains taxation on the price of the shares is illustrated in the following example.

The cause of the discount

A closed-end investment company initially sells stock for $10 per share and uses the proceeds to buy the stock of other companies. If costs are ignored, the net asset value of a share is $10, and the shares may trade in the secondary market for $10. The value of the firm's portfolio subsequently rises to $16 (i.e., the net asset value is $16). The firm has a potential capital gain of $6 per share. If it is realized and these profits are distributed, the net asset value will return to $10 and each stockholder will receive $6 in capital gains, for which they will pay the appropriate capital gains tax.

Suppose, however, that the capital gains are not realized (i.e., the net asset value remains $16). What will the market price of the stock be? This is difficult to determine, but it will probably be below $16. Why? Suppose an investor bought a share for $16 and then the firm realized and distributed the $6 capital gain. After the distribution of the $6, the investor would be responsible for any capital gains tax, but the net asset value of the share would decrease to $10.

Obviously this is not advantageous to the buyer. Individuals may be willing to purchase the shares only at a discount that reduces the potential impact of realized capital gains and the subsequent capital gains taxes. Suppose the share had cost $14 (i.e., it sold for a discount of $2 from the net asset value), and the firm realized and distributed the gain. The buyer who paid $14 now owns a share with a net asset value of $10 and receives a capital gain of $6. Although this investor will have to pay the appropriate capital gains tax, the impact is reduced because the investor paid only $14

---

*The investor may readily find the current discount or premium every Monday in *The Wall Street Journal*.

EXHIBIT 21–1. Net Asset Value and Market Price of Selected Closed-End Investment Companies

Company	December 31, 1977			December 31, 1978		
	Price	Net Asset Value	Discount or (Premium) as a Percentage of Net Asset Value	Price	Net Asset Value	Discount or (Premium) as a Percentage of Net Asset Value
Adams Express	$12¼	$14.51	16%	$11⅜	$14.49	21%
American General Bond	24⅞	24.33	(+2)	19⅝	22.16	11
Chase Convertible Fund	8⅞	11.39	22	7¾	11.38	32
Drexel Bond– Debenture Trust	16¼	19.60	17	15⅛	19.05	21
General American Investors	10¼	13.06	18	10½	14.40	27
National Aviation	18	24.08	25	27¾	31.65	12

to purchase the share whose total value is $16 (i.e., the $10 net asset value plus the $6 capital gain).

Since the shares may sell for a discount or a premium relative to their net asset value, it is possible for the market price of a closed-end investment company to fluctuate even if the net asset value is stable. For example, the net asset value of Chase Convertible Fund (presented in Exhibit 21–1) was virtually the same at the end of 1977 and 1978. But the market price declined, and the discount rose from 22 to 32 per cent. Since the market price can change relative to the net asset value, an investor is subject to an additional source of risk. The value of the investment may decline not only because the net asset value may decrease but also because the shares may sell for a larger discount from their net asset value.

The discount or the premium may change

Some investors view the market price relative to the net asset value as a guide to buying and selling the shares of a closed-end investment company. If the shares are selling for a sufficient discount, they are considered for purchase. If the shares are selling for a small discount or at a premium, they are considered for sale. Of course, determining the premium that will justify the sale or the discount that will justify the purchase is not simple.

The essence of this technique is illustrated in Graph 21–2. The year-end discount or premium for Niagara Share Corporation and the average discount are given. As may be seen from the graph, the discount reached a high of 14 per cent, but the stock sold for a premium in 1970 and 1974. The

GRAPH 21–2. The Discount or Premium Paid for Shares of Niagara Share Corporation

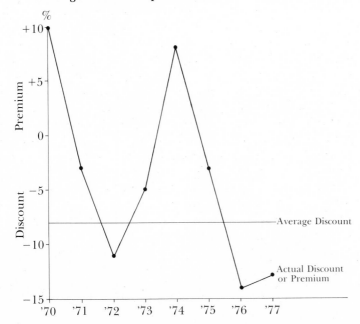

discount averaged about 8 per cent. This implies that if the discount rises above 8 per cent, the stock of Niagara Share Corporation may be considered a good purchase. Conversely, when the shares sell near their net asset value, the stock should be sold.

Sources of Profit From Investing in Closed-End Investment Companies

Profits are the difference between costs and revenues. Investing in closed-end investment companies involves several costs. First, since the shares are purchased on the open market, there is the brokerage commission for the purchase and for any subsequent sale. Second, the investment company charges a fee to operate the assets. This fee is subtracted from any income that the firm's assets earn. These management fees range from 1 to 2 per cent of the net asset value. Third, when the investment company purchases or sells securities, it also has to pay brokerage fees, which are passed on to the investor.

Other investments may not involve these costs

The purchase of shares in closed-end investment companies thus involves three costs that the investor must bear. Some alternative investments, such as savings accounts in commercial banks, do not involve these costs. Although commission fees are incurred when stock is purchased through a broker, the other expenses associated with a closed-end investment company are avoided. However, the investment company does relieve the individual of some of the cost of storing securities and keeping the records necessary for the preparation of tax papers.

The sources of profit

Investors in closed-end investment companies may earn profits in a variety of ways. If the investment company collects dividends and interest on its portfolio of assets, this income is distributed to the stockholders in the form of dividends. Second, if the value of the firm's assets increases, the company may sell the assets and realize profits. These profits are then distributed as capital gains to the stockholders. Third, the net asset value of the portfolio may increase, which will cause the market price of the company's stock to rise. In this case the investor may sell the shares in the market and realize a capital gain. Fourth, the market price of the shares may rise relative to the net asset value (i.e., the premium may increase or the discount may decrease); the investor may then earn a profit through the sale of the shares.

These sources of profit are illustrated in Exhibit 21–2, which presents the distributions and price changes for Lehman Corporation from December 31, 1975, through December 31, 1977. As may be seen from this exhibit, the firm distributed cash dividends of $.245 and capital gains of $.81 in 1977. The net asset value rose from $13.16 in 1975 to $14.72 in 1976, and the price of the stock likewise rose (from 10½ in 1975 to 12⅜ in 1976). An investor who bought these shares in December 1975 and sold them in December 1976 earned a return of 20 per cent on the investment.

EXHIBIT 21–2. Return on an Investment in Lehman Corporation

Distributions and Price Changes	1976	1977
Income distributions (per share)	$ .225	$ .245
Capital gain distributions (per share)	$ .00	$ .81
Year-end market price ($10½ on 12/31/75)	$12⅜	$10½
Year-end net asset value ($13.16 on 12/31/75)	$14.72	$13.06
Annual return from dividends and capital gain distributions	2.1%	8.5%
Percentage appreciation (depreciation) in the price of the stock	17.9%	(17.9%)
Total return	20.0%	(9.4%)

The potential for loss is also illustrated in Exhibit 21–2. If an investor bought the shares on December 31, 1976, he or she suffered a loss during 1977. While the firm distributed $.245 in income and $.81 in capital gains, the net asset value and the price of the stock declined, which more than offset the income and capital gains distributions.

The potential for loss

Dual-Purpose Funds

In the 1960s a special type of closed-end investment company was formed — the dual-purpose investment company. This type of firm issued two classes of stock: a preferred stock and a common stock. These are sometimes referred to as income shares and capital shares, respectively. All of the firm's investment income (after expenses) is distributed to the preferred stockholders. Thus, the preferred stockholders receive the income that is earned on the funds that they invested and on the funds that the common stockholders invested. This magnifies the potential income return to the preferred stock.

Why would the common stockholders agree to this distribution of investment income? The answer is that the funds will be liquidated at some future date. At that time the preferred stockholders will receive a specified amount, and the remaining assets will be distributed to the common stockholders. This increases the potential capital appreciation of the common stock.

The investor buys the common stock of a dual-purpose fund solely in the belief that the value of the shares will appreciate. However, like the shares of any other closed-end investment company, the current market price may be below or above the net asset value of the stock. Any discount or premium must disappear when the firm is liquidated, for the investor will receive the net asset value of each share. For this reason the common stock of a dual-purpose investment company that is bought at a discount may be an attractive investment.

MUTUAL FUNDS

Open-end investment companies

Open-end investment companies, which are commonly called mutual funds, are similar to closed-end investment companies. However, there are some important differences. The first concerns their capital structure. Shares in mutual funds are not traded like other stocks and bonds. Instead, an investor who wants a position in a particular mutual fund purchases shares directly from the company. After receiving the money, the mutual fund issues new shares and purchases assets with these newly acquired funds. If an investor owns shares in the fund and wants to liquidate the position, the shares are sold back to the company. The shares are redeemed, and the fund pays the investor from its cash holdings. If the fund lacks sufficient cash, it will sell some of the securities it owns to obtain the money to redeem the shares. The fund cannot suspend this redemption feature except in an emergency, and then it may be done only with the permission of the Securities and Exchange Commission (SEC).

Loading fees

A second important difference between open-end and closed-end investment companies pertains to the cost of investing. Mutual funds continuously offer to sell new shares, and these shares are sold at their net asset value plus a sales fee, which is commonly called a loading charge. When the investor liquidates the position, the shares are redeemed at their net asset value. For most funds no additional fees are charged for the sale.

The loading fee may range from zero for "no-load" mutual funds to between 5 and 9.3 per cent for "load funds." Exhibit 21–3 presents the loading fees for ten mutual funds. Although these fees vary, 8.5 per cent is the most common figure.

If the individual makes a substantial investment, the loading fee is

EXHIBIT 21–3. Loading Charges for Selected Mutual Funds

Company	Fee
Aetna Fund	8.5%
American Balanced Fund	8.5
American General Income	8.5
Bond Fund of America	8.5
Century Shares	7.25
Chemical Fund	8.5
Composite Fund	7.0
Fidelity Fund	8.5
John Hancock Funds	8.0
Pilgrim Fund	5.0

usually reduced. For example, the Aetna Fund offers the following schedule of fees:

Investment	Fee
$25,000	6%
50,000	5
100,000	4
250,000	3

The fees may vary with the amount invested

The investor should be warned that mutual funds state the loading charge as a percentage of the *offer* price. The effect of the fee being a percentage of the offer price and not a percentage of the net asset value is an increase in the effective percentage charged. If the loading charge is 8 per cent and the offer price is $10, then the loading fee is $.80. However, the net asset value is $9.20 ($10 minus $.80). In this example, the loading charge as a percentage of the net asset value is 8.7 per cent ($80 ÷ $9.20), which is higher than the stated 8 per cent loading charge.

Which funds are no-load funds is immediately apparent by the way in which mutual fund prices are quoted. Exhibit 21–4, which reproduces a quotation of mutual fund prices from *The Wall Street Journal*, illustrates this difference. The publication reports the net asset value (NAV), the offer price, and any change in the asset value from the previous day. If the offer price and net asset value are the same (i.e., if the fund has no loading

No-load funds

Mutual Funds

Thursday, February 22, 1979
Price ranges for investment companies, as quoted by the National Association of Securities Dealers. NAV stands for net asset value per share; the offering includes net asset value plus maximum sales charge, if any.

	Offer NAV	NAV Price Chg.
Acorn Fnd	18.16	N.L. − .03
Afuture Fd	12.37	N.L. − .06
AGE Fund	4.60	4.69 + .01
Allstate	9.01	N.L. − .06
Alpha Fnd	11.70	N.L. − .04
Am Birthrt	9.90	10.82 − .04
American Funds Group:		
Am Bal	x8.08	8.83 − .15
Amcap F	8.56	9.36 − .02
Am Mutl	10.10	11.04 − .02
An Gwth	6.90	7.54 − .04
Bnd FdA	13.84	15.13 − .02
Cash Mt	1.00	N.L. ...
Fund Inv	6.77	7.40 − .04
Gth FdA	7.41	8.10 − .05
Inc FdA	7.87	8.60 − .02
I C A	15.07	16.47 − .10
Nw Prsp	6.16	6.73 − .03
Wash Mt	6.74	7.37 − .03
American General Group:		
A GnCBd	8.33	9.10 ...
A GC Gr	4.34	4.74 − .02
AG Entp	6.21	6.79 − .03
High Yld	11.71	12.56 ...

	Offer NAV	NAV Price Chg.
M M M	1.00	N.L. ...
Mon Mkt	1.00	N.L. ...
Optn Inc	13.15	14.06 − .03
Tax Free	12.13	N.L. ...
US Gvt S	9.00	N.L. − .39
Fidelity Group Funds:		
Aggr Inc	9.66	N.L. + .01
Bd Corp	8.06	N.L. − .01
Capital	8.10	8.85 − .04
Contra	10.31	N.L. − .04
Daily Inc	1.00	N.L. ...
Destiny	9.79	(z) − .05
Eq Incm	17.18	N.L. − .10
Fidel Fd	15.39	16.82 − .09
High Yld	14.27	N.L. ...
Ltd Muni	9.26	N.L. ...
Mageln	35.86	(z) − .31
Muncpl	9.51	N.L. ...
Puritan	10.12	11.06 − .03
Salem	5.11	5.58 − .03
Thrift Tr	9.79	N.L. − .01
Trend	22.95	25.08 − .17
Financial Programs:		
Dynam	5.60	N.L. + .01

	Offer NAV	NAV Price Chg.
Lutheran Brotherhood:		
Broth Fd	10.17	11.11 − .04
Bro Inc	8.74	9.55 − .03
Bro MBd	9.48	10.36 ...
Broth US	9.26	10.12 − .01
Massachusetts Co:		
Freedm	7.94	8.68 − .04
Indep Fd	8.82	9.64 − .03
Mass Fd	10.82	11.83 − .03
Income	14.13	15.44 − .01
Mass Financial Services:		
MIT	9.84	10.61 − .07
MIG	8.85	9.54 − .08
MID	13.62	14.68 − .06
MCD	9.27	9.99 − .07
MFD	13.83	14.91 − .11
MFB	14.37	15.49 − .03
MMB	9.31	9.77 ...
MCM	1.00	N.L. ...
MFH	7.37	7.95 − .01
Mather Fd	14.52	N.L. − .06
Merrill Lynch:		
Basc Val	9.83	10.24 − .08
Captl Fd	14.17	14.76 − .08
EquiBd 1	9.60	10.00 − .03
Hi Incm	9.66	10.06 − .02
Muni Bd	9.16	9.35 − .01
Rdy Asst	1.00	N.L. ...
Sp'l Valu	9.16	9.54 − .04
Mid Amer	5.31	5.80 − .03

	Offer NAV	NAV Price Chg.
Scudder Stevens Funds:		
Commn	10.14	N.L. − .09
Income	13.15	N.L. − .02
Intl Fnd	15.38	N.L. ...
Man Res	10.00	N.L. ...
Muni Bd	9.71	N.L. − .01
Specl Fd	31.17	N.L. − .18
Security Funds:		
Bond Fd	9.27	9.53 ...
Equity	4.43	4.84 − .03
Invest	7.23	7.90 − .01
Ultra Fd	11.08	12.11 − .05
Selected Funds:		
Select Am	6.79	N.L. − .04
Selct Spl	12.23	N.L. − .06
Sentinel Group Funds:		
Apex Fd	3.62	3.96 − .02
Bal Fund	7.09	7.75 − .02
Com Stk	11.18	12.22 − .04
Growth	8.84	9.66 − .07
Sentry Fd	14.39	15.64 − .07
Sequoia	22.95	N.L. − .02
Shearson Funds:		
Apprec	20.33	22.22 − .06
Income	17.24	18.84 − .12
Invest	10.48	11.45 − .02
Shrm Dean	24.15	N.L. + .50
Sierra Gro	10.05	N.L. − .09
Sigma Funds:		
Captl Sh	10.02	10.95 − .04

EXHIBIT 21–4. Offer price and net asset value (NAV) for selected mutual funds (Source: *The Wall Street Journal*, February 23, 1979; reproduced with permission of Dow Jones & Company, Inc.)

charge), "N.L." is printed in the offer price column. For example, the Alpha Fund has a net asset value of $11.70, and "N.L." appears in the offer column. Thus, these shares may be bought and sold from the company at their net asset value.

The quotation of funds with loading fees includes the net asset value and the offer price. For example, American Balanced Fund has a net asset value of $8.08 per share and an offer price of $8.83. It is a load fund. The buyer pays $.75 ($8.83 − $8.08) to purchase a share worth $8.08. Such a charge is 8.5 per cent of the asking price and 9.3 per cent of the net asset value.

In addition to loading charges, investors in mutual funds have to pay management fees, which are deducted from the income earned by the fund's portfolio. The fund also pays brokerage commissions when it buys and sells securities. The total cost of investing in mutual funds may be substantial when all of the costs (the loading charge and management and brokerage fees) are considered. Of course, the cost of investing is substantially reduced when the individual buys shares in no-load funds. The investor, however, must still pay the management fees and commission costs.

Sources of profit

The third difference between closed-end and open-end investment companies is the source of profits to the investor. As with closed-end investment companies, individuals may profit from investments in mutual funds from several sources. Any income that is earned from the fund's assets in excess of expenses is distributed as dividends. If the fund's assets appreciate in value and the fund realizes these profits, the gains are distributed as capital gains. If the net asset value of the shares appreciates, the investor may redeem them at the appreciated price. Thus, in general the open-end mutual fund offers investors the same means of earning profits as does the closed-end investment company, with one exception. In the case of closed-end investment companies, the price of the stock may rise relative to the net asset value of the shares. The possibility of a decreased discount or an increased premium is a potential source of profit that is available only through closed-end investment companies. It does not exist for mutual funds because their shares never sell at a discount.* Hence, changes in the discount or premium are a source of profit or loss to investors in closed-end but not in open-end investment companies.

THE PORTFOLIOS OF INVESTMENT COMPANIES

The portfolios of investment companies may be diversified or very specialized, but most may be classified into one of four types: income, growth, special situations, and balanced. The names of the classes are descriptive of the assets owned by the companies.

---

*Load funds are actually sold at a premium (i.e., the loading fee).

Income funds stress assets that produce income; they buy stocks and bonds that pay generous dividends or interest income. The Value Line Income Fund is an example of a fund whose objective is high income. Virtually all of its assets are income stocks, such as those of utilities (e.g., General Telephone and Electronics and Continental Telephone). These firms pay generous dividends and periodically increase them as their earnings grow.

Growth funds stress appreciation in the value of the assets, and little emphasis is given to current income. The portfolio of the Value Line Fund is an example of a growth fund. The majority of the assets are the common stocks of companies with potential for growth. These growth stocks include not only the shares of very well known firms (e.g., Polaroid, Avon, and Aetna) but also those of smaller firms that may offer superior growth potential.

Special situation investment companies specialize in more speculative securities that, given the "special situation," may yield large returns. These investment companies are perhaps the riskiest of all the mutual funds. The portfolio of Value Line Special Situation Fund illustrates this element of risk. The stocks in this portfolio tend to be in small companies or in companies that have fallen on bad times but whose course may be changing (e.g., Levitz Furniture or Pan Am). Investments in special situation securities can be very rewarding (e.g., Pan Am rose from $3\frac{5}{8}$ in 1977 to $10\frac{3}{4}$ in 1978), but many do not fulfill this potential return.

Balanced funds own a mixture of securities that sample the attributes of the assets of other mutual funds. A balanced fund, such as the Sentinel Group Balanced Fund, owns a variety of stocks, some of which offer potential growth, while others are primarily income producers. A balanced portfolio may include short-term debt, such as U.S. treasury bills, long-term debt, and preferred stock. Such a portfolio seeks a balance of income from dividends and interest and capital appreciation.

THE PORTFOLIOS OF SPECIALIZED INVESTMENT COMPANIES

Investment trusts initially sought to pool the funds of many savers and to invest these funds in a diversified portfolio of assets. Such diversification spread the risk of investing and reduced the risk of loss to the individual investor. While a particular investment company had a specified goal, such as growth or income, the portfolio was still sufficiently diversified so that the element of risk was reduced.

Diversification and the distribution of risk

Today, however, a variety of funds have developed that have moved away from this concept of diversification and the distribution of risk. Instead of offering investors a cross section of American business, many funds have been created to offer investors specialized investments. For

Special investment companies

example, an investment company may be limited to investments in the securities of a particular industry, such as the airlines (e.g., National Aviation) or gold (e.g., ASA, Limited) industries. There are also funds that specialize in a particular type of security, such as bonds (e.g., American General Bond Fund).

During the 1970s the scope of some investment companies became even narrower. For example, the Dreyfus Mergers and Acquisition Fund, which originated in 1978, seeks to identify firms that are potential candidates for merger or for take-over by other firms. Such mergers and take-overs often result in substantial profits for the stockholders of the target firms. These profits can be even larger if two firms seek to take over a third company and a bidding war erupts. The management of the Dreyfus Merger and Acquisition Fund seeks to identify the stocks of companies that appear to be underpriced and that may be bought out at substantial premiums over their current prices. Obviously, this is a very specialized fund, and its investors bear two considerable risks not borne by investors in the traditional mutual fund. These risks involve (1) the ability of the fund's management to identify take-over candidates and (2) the possibility that the mergers and take-overs will not actually occur. If a stock is underpriced but no one seeks to take over the firm, then the stock may remain underpriced for a long period of time!

Perhaps the extreme in specialized funds arose in October 1978, when the shares of Gaming Funds Incorporated were registered with the SEC. This fund specializes in gaming and sports investments. The securities it purchases may even include stocks for which there is no secondary market. Furthermore, the fund employs speculative techniques, such as short selling and the use of financial leverage. Obviously such a fund does not offer the advantages of diversification and the reduction of risk that are offered by traditional mutual funds.

In addition to these speculative funds, several specialized investment companies have been established that offer real alternatives to the traditional types of investments. These include the index funds, tax-exempt funds, money market instrument funds, and funds that specialize in foreign securities.

Index funds

The purpose of an index fund is almost diametrically opposed to the traditional purpose of a mutual fund. Instead of identifying specific securities for purchase, the managements of these funds seek to duplicate the composition of an index such as Standard & Poor's 500 stock index. Such funds should then perform in tandem with the market as a whole. Although they cannot generally outperform the market, neither can they underperform the market. In a sense, these funds have a defeatist attitude: because they cannot beat the market, they try to avoid earning a return less than that of the market as a whole. Part of the popularity of such funds has been attributed to the poor performance of mutual funds in general in the past. (The returns earned by mutual funds will be discussed later in this chapter.) While these funds cannot overcome any risk associated with price fluctuations in the market as a whole, they do eliminate the risk associated with the selection of specific securities.

Another recently introduced specialized mutual fund is the investment company whose portfolio is devoted to tax-exempt bonds. Until 1976, open-end mutual funds were legally barred from this market. However, with the passage of legislation, mutual funds were permitted to own tax-exempt bonds. Several funds were immediately started that specialize in tax-exempt securities. These funds offer investors, especially those with modest funds to invest, an opportunity to earn tax-free income and maintain a diversified portfolio. Since municipal bonds are sold in minimum units of $5000, a sizable sum is required for an individual investor to obtain a diversified portfolio. Ten bonds of ten different state and local governments would cost about $50,000. The advantages of tax-free income and a reduction in risk virtually were impossible for most investors.

Tax-exempt funds

Mutual funds that specialize in tax-exempt bonds, however, offer small investors both of these advantages. The funds are sold in smaller denominations. For example, $1000 may be the minimum initial investment, and additional investments may be made for as little as $100. The ability to buy in small denominations means that modest investors may buy shares in these funds. Since the firms pool the funds of many investors, small investors also obtain the advantage of diversification.

Money market funds invest in short-term securities (i.e., money market instruments). These include United States Government treasury bills, the commercial paper (unsecured, short-term promissory notes) of corporations, and negotiable certificates of deposit of commercial banks. Individual investors are not excluded from buying these securities. However, the minimum unit is $10,000 for treasury bills, and commercial paper and negotiable certificates of deposit sell for $100,000. In effect, the vast majority of investors are excluded from these markets.

Money market funds

Money market funds pool the money of many investors and purchase these short-term securities. These funds make available an investment alternative that many individuals could not purchase for themselves. In addition, short-term money market instruments may offer yields that are superior to the yields earned on savings accounts in commercial banks.

Investment companies may also specialize in foreign securities. Stock exchanges are not unique to the United States. There are many foreign companies whose securities are actively traded, and these may offer excellent investment opportunities. Conceptually, the decision to invest in the securities of a foreign company is no different from the decision to buy stocks and bonds issued by AT&T or Exxon. However, foreign investments subject the investor to special risks. Such risks include political instability, fluctuations in the exchange rate, and the possibility of fraud.

Foreign investments

While the political climate in the United States does change, it is generally quite stable. Such stability may not exist in other countries, or even if it does exist, the political climate can change. Many Americans with investments abroad have experienced the nationalization and expropria-

Political risks

tion of firms in which they had invested. Governments may also default on debt obligations. Such acts tend to occur when there are sudden and often violent changes in governments. For example, after Castro seized power in Cuba, many American firms with operations in Cuba lost their investments to nationalization. The new government also refused to accept the debt obligations of the previous government and defaulted on interest and principal repayments. These experiences are similar to events that occurred after World War II when communist governments took control of Eastern Europe.*

The risk from exchange rates

There is also a risk from fluctuations in exchange rates. The prices of foreign moneys (i.e., foreign exchange rates) vary daily in relation to the demand and supply of each currency. Such exchange rate fluctuations can have a severe impact on investments abroad. Since exchange rates change daily, the investor continuously runs the risk of loss through a decline in a currency's value. Of course, if the currency should rise in value, the investor will gain from the revaluation.

These losses or profits occur because foreign securities are denominated in another country's currency. For example, Volkswagen is a German company. If the value of the German mark rises, then the mark can buy more dollars. A share of Volkswagen stock will be worth more in terms of dollars even if its price in terms of marks is constant. Conversely, if the value of the German mark declines, the value of stock denominated in marks declines. Thus, foreign investments may yield profits or losses from fluctuations in the value of foreign currencies that are independent of changes in the value of the securities themselves.

The risk from fraud

Last, there is the risk of fraud. For example, suppose an American investor buys a Japanese stock and takes delivery of a certificate written in Japanese. There is certainly a high probability that the investor cannot read the certificate. Such a situation makes this investor easy prey for fraudulent dealers.

ADRs

This problem of fraud can be avoided by buying through reputable security dealers. Instead of getting certificates written in foreign languages, the investor receives receipts (called American Depository Receipts, or ADRs) for the securities. These ADRs are created by financial institutions that deal in foreign securities, and they guarantee the authenticity of the certificate.

Perhaps the easiest way to invest in foreign securities is through investment companies. While some of these firms buy foreign securities as part of their portfolios, others specialize in securities of a particular

---

*To this day many debt issues of such countries as Cuba, Poland, and Hungary are still outstanding. Perhaps even more surprising is that some of these bonds are still traded. For example, an issue of Cuban bond that was due in 1977 was trading in 1978 for .16 on the dollar (i.e., $160 for a $1000 bond). Even though the bond is past maturity and has not paid interest for years, there is still a market for it. Presumably, investors who purchase this bond are gambling on an improvement in political relations between the United States and Cuba that might result in repayment of some of the debt.

country. For example, the Japan Fund, as its name implies, holds Japanese securities. From 1967 through 1976 the net asset value of its shares rose by more than 700 per cent. How the individual investor fared depended upon the price paid for the shares, the discount from the net asset value at the time of purchase, and whether the investor accepted the distributions in cash or additional shares.

Although investing in these specialized funds does not eliminate the risks associated with investing in foreign securities, it does reduce them. Since the investment company owns a diversified portfolio, the effect of nationalization of a particular firm is reduced. Also, the problem of fraud is probably eliminated. However, the impact of fluctuations in exchange rates still exists, and that is one source of risk that the investor in foreign securities cannot avoid.

THE RETURNS EARNED ON INVESTMENTS IN MUTUAL FUNDS

As was previously explained, investment companies offer individuals several advantages. First, the investor receives the advantages of a diversified portfolio, which reduces risk. Some investors may lack the resources to construct a diversified portfolio, and the purchase of shares in an investment company permits these investors to own a portion of a diversified portfolio. Second, the portfolio is professionally managed and under continuous supervision. Many investors may not have the time and the expertise to manage their own portfolios and, except in the case of large portfolios, may lack the funds to obtain professional management. By purchasing shares in an investment company, individuals buy the services of professional management, which may increase the investor's return. Third, the administrative detail and the custodial aspects of the portfolio (e.g., the physical handling of securities) are taken care of by the management of the company.

The advantages of investment companies

Although investment companies offer advantages, there are also disadvantages. The services offered by an investment company are not unique but may be obtained elsewhere. For example, the trust department of a commercial bank offers custodial services, and leaving the securities with the broker and registering them in his or her name relieves the investor of storing the securities and keeping some of the records. In addition, the investor may acquire a diversified portfolio with only a modest amount of capital. Diversification does not require 100 different stocks. Five to ten securities may be sufficient. If the investor has $10,000, a diversified portfolio may be produced by investing in the stock of eight companies in different industries. One does not have to purchase shares in an investment company to obtain the advantage of diversification.

The disadvantages

Investment companies, however, do offer the advantage of professional management. Despite this service, they cannot guarantee to outperform the market. A particular firm may do well in any given year, but it may do very poorly in subsequent years. Several studies have been undertaken to determine if professional management results in superior performance for mutual funds.

The returns earned

The first study, conducted for the SEC, covered the period from 1952 through 1958.* This study found that the performance of mutual funds was not significantly different from that of an unmanaged portfolio of similar assets. About half the funds outperformed Standard & Poor's indices, but the other half underperformed these aggregate measures of the market. In addition, there was no evidence of superior performance by a particular fund over a number of years.

These results were confirmed by later studies.† When the loading charges are included in the analysis, the return earned by investors tends to be less than that which would be achieved through a random selection of securities.

Managements are not incompetent

These results are easy to misinterpret. They do not imply that the managements of mutual funds are incompetent. The findings do give strong support for the efficient market hypothesis that is discussed in Chapter 25. In an efficient market, only competent managers would be able to match the market over a period of years. The incompetent would be forced out by their inferior results.

A means to match the market

What these findings do imply is that mutual funds and other investment companies may offer investors a means to match the performance of the market and still obtain the advantages of diversification and custodial services. For some, these are sufficient reasons to invest in the shares of investment companies instead of directly in stocks and bonds. These investors do not have to concern themselves with the selection of individual securities.

The problem of selection

However, they must still be concerned with the selection of an investment company. There exist over 400 mutual funds. Obviously the investor does not buy shares in all of them but must choose among them. Thus, while investment companies may relieve individuals from selecting particular stocks and bonds, they do not relieve them from selecting among the funds that meet their goals (e.g., growth or income).

This choice is, of course, not easy. The individual investor may obtain a fund's prospectus, which states the company's goals, current portfolio, and recent performance. The services and fees are also specified. Funds with loading charges have sales staffs to market their shares. Although

---

*See Irwin Friend et al, *A Study of Mutual Funds*, Washington, D.C., U.S. Government Printing Office, 1962.

†See, for instance, William F. Sharpe, "Mutual Fund Performance," *Journal of Business*, special supplement, 39(January 1966), pp. 119–38, and Michael C. Jensen, "The Performance of Mutual Funds in the Period 1945–64," *Journal of Finance*, 23(May 1968), pp. 389–416.

these staffs are a source of information concerning the fund, the investor will be subjected to a certain degree of sales pressure. No-load funds do not have these salespersons, which is the primary reason why there is no loading fee. Information concerning these companies may be obtained by writing directly to the firm.

The investor can obtain addresses and a substantial amount of information concerning all investment companies by reading the publications of Wiesenberg Services, Inc. This firm annually publishes a summary of investment company performance. It is the standard reference on investment companies and should be readily available in local libraries. Forbes also publishes an annual summary of investment company results. The investor, however, should remember that past performance need not be indicative of future performance. While investment companies offer a viable alternative to selecting one's own portfolio, they are not a cure-all that will produce a superior return on the investor's funds.

The sources of information

SUMMARY

Instead of directly investing in securities, individuals may buy shares in investment companies. These firms, in turn, invest the funds in various assets, such as stocks and bonds.

There are two types of investment companies. A closed-end investment company has a specified number of shares that are bought and sold in the same manner as the stock of firms such as AT&T. An open-end investment company (i.e., a mutual fund) has a variable number of shares that are sold directly to investors. Investors who desire to liquidate their holdings sell them back to the company.

Investment companies offer several advantages, including professional management, diversification, and custodial services. Dividends and the interest earned on the firm's assets are distributed to stockholders. In addition, if the value of the company's assets rises, then the stockholders profit as capital gains are realized and distributed.

Investment companies may also be classified by the types of assets they own. Some stress income-producing assets, while others seek capital appreciation. There are also investment companies that specialize in tax-exempt securities, money market instruments, special situations, and foreign securities.

Although investment companies are professionally managed, the returns on the assets they own have not been superior. Instead, these companies as a whole have earned a return that is consistent with price changes in the security markets. While investment companies do not beat the market, they relieve investors of the need for security selection and various custodial aspects of investing.

Terms to Remember

Open-end investment
   company

Closed-end investment
   company

Mutual fund

Net asset value

Premium and discount
   from net asset value

Loading charge

No-load fund

Index fund

Tax-exempt fund

Money market fund

ADRs

Foreign exchange

Questions

1. What is the difference between a closed-end and an open-end investment company?

2. Are mutual funds subject to federal income taxation?

3. What custodial services do investment companies provide?

4. What is a loading charge? Do all investment companies charge this fee?

5. Why may the small investor prefer mutual funds to other investments?

6. What is a specialized mutual fund? How is it different from a special situation fund?

7. Should an investor expect a mutual fund to outperform the market? If not, why should the investor buy the shares?

SELECTED READINGS

Friend, Irwin, et al: *A Study of Mutual Funds*. Washington, D.C., U.S. Government Printing Office, 1962.

Investment Companies. New York, Wiesenberg Services, Inc., published annually.

Jensen, Michael C.: "The Performance of Mutual Funds in the Period 1945–64." *Journal of Finance*, 23(May 1968), pp. 389–416.

Mead, Stuart B.: *Mutual Funds*. Braintree, Mass., D. H. Mark Publishing, 1971.

Sharpe, William F.: "Mutual Fund Performance." *Journal of Business*, special supplement, 39 (January 1966), pp. 119–138.

Treynor, Jack L.: "How To Rate Management of Investment Funds." *Harvard Business Review*, 43(January–February 1965), pp. 63–76.

Learning Objectives

After completing this chapter you should be able to

1. Define *commodity contract*.

2. Differentiate between the long and short positions in a commodity.

3. Contrast the role of margin in the stock market with its role in the commodity markets.

4. Identify the sources of leverage in commodity futures.

5. Distinguish speculators from hedgers and describe the role played by each in the commodity markets.

6. Identify the forces that determine the price of a commodity.

chapter 22
COMMODITIES

Commodities are among the riskiest investment alternatives. Prices change rapidly and produce sudden losses or profits. This chapter briefly covers commodities and their risks and rewards.

The chapter begins with a definition of commodity contracts and a description of the mechanics of investing in commodities. This includes the way in which the contracts are purchased and sold and the difference between the long and short positions in commodities.

Leverage is the name of the game in commodities. The sources of leverage and the important role played by margin are discussed. The potential profits and losses are illustrated.

An important facet of commodity markets is the role played by growers, producers, and other users of commodities. They seek to protect themselves from price flucutations and hedge their positions. By hedging they pass the risk of loss to the speculators who purchase commodity contracts.

The price of a commodity ultimately depends on demand and supply. The chapter ends with a brief discussion of these forces and the use of technical or fundamental analysis to forecast future changes in supply or demand.

WHAT IS INVESTING IN COMMODITIES

A futures contract

A commodity may be purchased for current delivery or for future delivery. Investing in commodities refers to the buying or the selling of a contract to deliver a commodity in the future. For this reason these investments are sometimes referred to as "futures." A futures contract is a formal agreement between a buyer or seller and a commodity exchange. In the case of a purchase contract, the buyer agrees to accept a specific commodity that meets a specified quality in a specified month. In the case of a sale, the seller agrees to deliver the specified commodity during the designated month.

Commodities are very speculative

Investing in commodities is considered to be very speculative. For that reason investors should participate in this market only after their financial obligations and goals have been met. There is a large probability that the investor will suffer a loss on any particular purchase or sale. Individuals who buy and sell commodity contracts are generally referred to as speculators, which differentiates them from the growers, processors, warehousers, and other dealers who also buy and sell commodity futures.

The potential leverage

The primary appeal of commodity contracts to speculators is the potential for a large return on the investment. The large return is the result of the leverage inherent in commodity trading. This leverage exists because (1) a commodity contract controls a substantial amount of the commodity and (2) the investor must make only a small payment to buy or sell a contract (i.e., there is a small margin requirement). These two points are discussed in some detail later in this chapter.

THE MECHANICS OF INVESTING IN COMMODITIES

THE ROLE OF BROKERS

How they are purchased

Like stocks and bonds, commodity futures may be purchased in several markets. The most important individual market is the Chicago Board of Trade, which executes contracts in agricultural commodities such as wheat, soybeans, and livestock. Other commodities are traded in various cities throughout the country. Over 50 commodities are traded on 10 exchanges in the United States and Canada. As may be expected, the markets for some commodities are close to the area where they are produced. Thus, the markets for wheat are located not only in Chicago but also in Kansas City and Minneapolis. The market for several commodities is in New York. Cocoa, coffee, sugar, potatoes, and orange juice are bought and sold there. This geographical diversity does not hamper commodity traders, who may buy and sell commodity contracts in any market through their brokers.

Commodity contracts are purchased through brokers just as stocks and bonds are. The broker owns a seat on the commodity exchange. Membership on each exchange is limited, and only members are allowed to buy and sell the commodity contracts. If the investor's broker lacks a seat, then that broker must have a correspondent relationship with another broker who does own a seat.

The role of brokers

The broker acts on behalf of the investor by purchasing and selling contracts through the exchange. Each commodity exchange has a clearing house that watches the various buy and sell orders. The investor opens an account by signing an agreement that requires the contracts to be guaranteed. Since trading commodity contracts is considered to be speculative, some brokers will open accounts only after the investor has proved the capacity both to finance the account and to withstand the losses. For example, Merrill Lynch Pierce Fenner and Smith, Inc., requires that the investor have a net worth of $75,000 over and above the value of such assets as a home and a car before the firm will execute commodity orders.

Once the account has been opened, the investor may trade commodity contracts. These are bought and sold in much the same way as stocks and bonds. A commodity order specifies whether the contract is a buy or a sell (i.e., whether the investor will take delivery or make delivery), the commodity and the number of units, and the delivery date (i.e., the month in which the commodity is to be delivered). The speculator can request a market order and have the contract executed at the current market price. Or the speculator may place orders at specified prices. Such orders may be for a day or until the investor cancels them (i.e., the order is good till canceled). Once the order is executed, the broker will provide the speculator with a confirmation statement of the purchase or sale and statements of the investor's positions in the various commodities.

A commodity order

The broker will also charge a fee or commission for executing the orders. This fee tends to be modest, such as $30 per contract, and it covers both the purchase *and* subsequent sale of the contract. Perhaps the reduction in paperwork partially explains the modest fees. An investment in commodities relieves the broker and the investor of handling dividend checks, the certificates from stock splits and stock dividends, proxies and votes, and other custodial matters associated with an investment in stocks and bonds.

Fees

COMMODITY POSITIONS

The investor may purchase a contract for future delivery. This is the "long" position in which the investor will profit if the price of the commodity and hence the value of the contract rise. The investor may also sell

The long position

The short position a contract for future delivery. This is the "short" position in which the seller agrees to make good the contract (i.e., to deliver the goods) sometime in the future. This investor will profit if the price of the commodity and hence the value of the contract decline. These long and short positions are analogous to the long and short positions that the investor takes in the security market. Long positions generate profits when the value of the security rises, whereas short positions result in profits when the value of the security declines.

The source of profits The way in which each position generates a profit can be seen in a simple example. Assume that wheat is $3.50 per bushel. If a contract is purchased for delivery in six months at $3.50 per bushel, the buyer will profit from this long position if the price of wheat *rises*. If the price increases to $4.00 per bushel, the buyer can exercise the contract by taking delivery and paying $3.50 per bushel. The speculator then sells the wheat for $4 per bushel, which produces a profit of $.50 per bushel.

The opposite occurs when the price of wheat declines. If the price of wheat falls to $3.00 per bushel, the individual who bought the contract for delivery at $3.50 suffers a loss. But the speculator who sold the contract for the delivery of wheat (i.e., who took the short position) earns a profit from the price decline. The speculator can now buy wheat at the spot price of $3.00, deliver it for the contract price of $3.50, and earn a $.50 profit per bushel.

If the price rises, the short position will produce a loss. If the price increases from $3.50 to $4.00 per bushel, the speculator suffers a loss of $.50 per bushel, because he or she must pay $4.00 to obtain the wheat that will be delivered for $3.50 per bushel.

The delivery need not occur Actually, the preceding losses and profits are generated without the goods being delivered. Of course, when a speculator buys a contract for future delivery, there is always the possibility that this individual will receive the goods. Conversely, if the speculator sells a contract for future delivery, there is the possibility that the goods will have to be supplied. However, such deliveries occur infrequently, because the speculator can cancel the contract before the delivery date. This is achieved by buying or selling the opposite type of contract than the one that the speculator owns.

The process of canceling a contract This process of canceling existing contracts is illustrated in the following example. Suppose a speculator has a contract to buy wheat in January. If the individual wants to close the position, he or she can sell a contract for the delivery of wheat in January. The two contracts cancel each other, as one is a purchase and the other is a sale. If the speculator actually received the wheat by executing the purchase agreement, he or she could pass on the wheat by executing the sell agreement. However, since the two contracts cancel each other, the actual delivery and subsequent sale are not necessary. Instead, the speculator's position in wheat is closed, and the actual physical transfers do not occur.

Correspondingly, if the speculator has a contract for the sale of wheat in January, it can be canceled by buying a contract for the purchase of wheat in January. If the speculator were called upon to deliver wheat as the result of the contract to sell, the individual would exercise the contract to purchase wheat. The buy and sell contracts then cancel each other, and no physical transfers of wheat occur. Once again the speculator has closed the initial position by taking the opposite position (i.e., the sales contract is canceled by a purchase contract).

Because these contracts are canceled and actual deliveries do not take place, it should not be assumed that profits or losses do not occur. The two contracts need not be executed at the same price. For example, the speculator may have purchased a contract for the future sale of wheat at $3.50 per bushel. Any contract for the future delivery of comparable wheat can cancel the contract for the sale. But the cost of the wheat for future delivery could be $3.60 or $3.40 (or any conceivable price). If the price of wheat rises (e.g., from $3.50 to $3.60 per bushel), then the speculator suffers a loss. If the price declines (e.g., from $3.50 to $3.40 per bushel), then the speculator earns a profit.

THE UNITS OF COMMODITY CONTRACTS

To facilitate trading, contracts must be uniform. For a particular commodity the contracts must be identical. Besides specifying the delivery month, the contract must specify the grade and type of the commodity (e.g., a particular type of wheat) and the units of the commodity (e.g., 5000 bushels). Thus, when an individual buys or sells a contract, there can be no doubt as to the nature of the obligation. For example, if the investor buys wheat for January delivery, there can be no confusion with a contract for the purchase of wheat for February delivery. These are two different commodities in the same way that AT&T common stock, AT&T preferred stock, and AT&T bonds are all different securities. Without such standardization of contracts there would be chaos in the commodity (or any) markets.

The uniformity of contracts

The units of trading vary with each commodity. For example, if the investor buys a contract for corn, the unit of trading is 5000 bushels. If the investor buys a contract for eggs, the unit of trading is 22,500 dozen. A list of selected commodities, the markets in which they are traded, and the units of each contract is given in Exhibit 22–1. While the novice investor may not remember the units for a contract, the experienced investor is certainly aware of them. As will be explained later, because of the large units of many commodity contracts, a small change in the price of the commodity produces a considerable change in the value of the contract and in the investor's profits or losses.

The units of trading

EXHIBIT 22–1. Selected Commodities, Their Markets, and Their
Units of Trading

Commodity	Market	Unit of One Contract
Corn	Chicago Board of Trade	5000 bushels
Soybeans	Chicago Board of Trade	5000 bushels
Barley	Winnipeg Commodity Exchange	20 metric tons
Cattle	Chicago Mercantile Exchange	30,000 tons
Coffee	New York Coffee and Sugar Exchange	37,500 pounds
Copper	Commodity Exchange, Inc., of New York	25,000 pounds
Platinum	New York Mercantile Exchange	50 troy ounces
Silver	Commodity Exchange, Inc., of New York	5000 troy ounces
Lumber	Chicago Mercantile Exchange	100,000 board feet
Cotton	New York Cotton Exchange	50,000 pounds

REPORTS OF FUTURES TRADING

**Reports in the
financial press**

Commodity prices and contracts are reported in the financial press in much the same way as stock and bond transactions are. This is illustrated in Exhibit 22–2, which was taken from *The Wall Street Journal*. As may be seen in the exhibit, corn is traded on the Chicago Board of Trade (CBT). The unit for trading is 5000 bushels, and prices are quoted in cents per bushel. The opening price for December delivery was 264½¢ ($2.645) per bushel, while the high, low, and closing (i.e., the "settle") prices were 266¢, 264¢, and 264¼¢, respectively. This closing price was ¾¢ higher than the closing price on the previous day. The high and low prices (prior to the previous day of trading) for the lifetime of the contract were 264¼¢ and 244¢, respectively. The open interest, which is the number of contracts in existence, was 22,760.

THE REGULATION OF COMMODITY MARKETS

Regulation

The commodity exchanges, like the stock exchanges, are subject to regulation. Federal laws pertaining to commodity exchanges and commodity transaction laws are enforced by the Commodity Exchange Authority, which is a division of the Department of Agriculture. As with the regulation of security transactions, the regulations do not protect investors or speculators from their own folly. Instead, the regulations establish uniform standards for each commodity. The regulatory authority also has control over trading procedures, the hours of trading, and the maximum allowable daily price movements.

Commodity profits, like all investment profits, are subject to income tax. Unless the individual's business involves a particular commodity, these contracts are considered by the Internal Revenue Service to be capital assets and are therefore subject to capital gains taxation. Unfortunately, since most of the transactions (i.e., the purchase and the sub-

Taxes

EXHIBIT 22–2. Commodity prices (Source: *The Wall Street Journal*, February 23, 1979, p. 28). Reprinted with permission of Dow Jones, Inc.

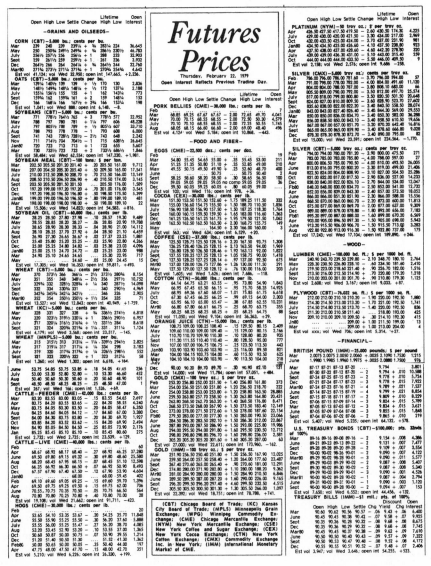

sequent sale) occur within a year, commodity profits and losses are short-term capital gains or losses. Thus, commodity transactions generally do not receive the benefits of the lower tax rates that are associated with long-term capital gains.

LEVERAGE

Margin

Commodities are paid for when they are delivered. Thus, a contract for future delivery means that the goods do not have to be paid for when the contract is executed. Instead, the investor (either a buyer or a seller) provides an amount of money, which is called margin, to protect the broker and to guarantee the contract. This margin is not to be confused with the margin that is used in the purchase of stocks and bonds. In the trading of stocks and bonds, margin represents the investor's equity in the position, whereas margin for a commodity contract is a deposit to show the investor's good faith and to protect the broker against an adverse change in the price of the commodity.

In the stock market, the amount of margin that is required varies with the price of the security, but in the commodity markets the amount of margin does not vary with the dollar value of the transaction. Instead, each contract has a fixed minimum margin requirement. This amount is established by the exchange, but individual brokers may require more. The minimum margin requirement tends to be only 5 to 10 per cent of the value of the contract. In Exhibit 22–2 that would amount to between $.10 and $.15 per bushel of corn. This small amount of margin is one reason why commodities offer so much potential leverage.

A major source of leverage

The potential leverage from speculating in commodities may be illustrated in a simple example. Consider a contract to buy wheat at $3.50 per bushel. Such a contract controls 5000 bushels of wheat worth a total of $17,500 (5000 × $3.50). If the investor buys this contract and the margin requirement is 5 per cent, the investor must remit $875 (i.e., .05 × $17,500). An increase of only $.20 per bushel in the price of the commodity produces an increase of $1000 in the value of the contract. This $1000 is simply the product of the price change ($.20) and the number of units in the contract (5000). The investor then earns a profit of $125 (i.e., $1000 − $875). Since the margin requirement is only $875 (i.e., 5 per cent of the value of the contract), a small price increase of $.20 produces a profit on the investment.

What is the rate of return on the investment? With a margin of $875, the return is 14.3 per cent (i.e., $125 ÷ $875). An increase of less than 6 per cent in the price of wheat produces a return on the speculator's money of 14.3 per cent. Such a return is the result of leverage that comes from the small margin requirement and the large amount of the commodity controlled by the contract.

Leverage works both ways

Leverage, of course, works both ways. In the previous example if the price of the commodity declines by $.10, then the contract will be worth

$17,000. A decline of only 2.9 per cent in the price reduces the investor's margin from $875 to $375. To maintain the position, the investor must deposit additional margin with the broker. The broker's request for additional funds is referred to as a margin call. Failure to meet the margin call will result in the broker's closing the position. Since the contract is supported only by the initial margin, further price declines will mean that there is less collateral to support the contract. Should the investor default on the contract, then the broker becomes responsible for the execution of the contract. The margin call thus protects the broker.

Actually, there are two margin requirements. The first is the minimum initial deposit, and the second is the maintenance margin. The maintenance margin specifies how far the investor's collateral can decline before the broker makes a margin call. Thus, a margin call will occur before the price of the commodity changes sufficiently to wipe out the initial deposit. For example, a minimum maintenance of 25 per cent means a margin call will be made when the speculator's initial deposit has been reduced by 75 per cent through changes in the price of the commodity.

The maintenance margin

Margin requirements are set by the commodity exchanges, but they cannot be below the minimums established by the Commodity Exchange Authority. These requirements are designed to protect brokers from the losses incurred by speculators. Individual brokers may further protect themselves from price fluctuations by requiring larger amounts of margin for commodity contracts.

While commodity prices can and do fluctuate, limits are imposed by the markets on the amount of price change per day. There are two types of limits. One is the daily limit, and the other is the daily range. The daily limit establishes the maximum permissible price increase or decrease from the previous day. The daily range establishes the maximum permissible range in the commodity's price for the day. These limits may be the same, or the daily range may be twice as large as the daily limit. In this latter case the price can rise and fall by the amount of the daily limit. However, if the daily limit and the daily range are the same, then the price of the commodity can rise but cannot fall (or vice versa) by the amount of the limit.

Price limits

These limits are illustrated in the following example. Suppose a commodity's price is $4.00, and the daily limit is $.10. Accordingly, the price could increase to $4.10 or decline to $3.90. However, if the maximum daily range is also $.10, then the price could rise to $4.10 but could not fall below $4.00. Or the price could fall to $3.90 but could not rise above $4.00. The price could range from $4.10 to $3.90 only if the daily range is twice the daily limit (i.e., a daily range of $.20 in this example).

The daily limit and the daily range

Once the price of the commodity rises by the permissible daily limit, further price increases are not allowed. This does not mean that trading ceases, because transactions can still occur at the maximum price or below should the price of the commodity weaken. The same applies to declining prices. Once the daily limit has been met, then the price cannot continue to fall, but transactions can still occur at the lowest price and above should the price of the commodity strengthen. These limits help to maintain orderly markets and to reduce the potentially disruptive effects from large daily swings in the price of the commodity.

HEDGING

Hedging reduces the risk of loss

One of the prime reasons for the development of commodity markets was the desire of producers to reduce the risk of loss through price fluctuations. The procedure for this reduction in risk is called hedging, which consists of taking opposite positions at the same time.* In effect, a hedger simultaneously takes the long and the short position in a particular commodity.

Hedging is best explained by illustrations. In the first example, a wheat farmer expects to harvest a crop at a specified time. Since the costs of production are determined, the farmer knows the price that is necessary to earn a profit. Although the price that will be paid for wheat at harvest time is unknown, the current price of a contract for the future delivery of wheat is known. The farmer can then sell a contract for future delivery. Such a contract is a hedged position, because the farmer takes a long position (the wheat in the ground) and a short position (the contract for future delivery).

The risk from price declines

Such a position reduces the farmer's risk of loss from a price decline. Suppose the cost to produce the wheat is $2.50 per bushel and September wheat is selling in June for $2.75. If the farmer sells wheat for September delivery, a $.25 per bushel profit is assured, because the buyer of the contract agrees to pay $2.75 per bushel upon delivery in September. If the price of wheat declines to $2.50, the farmer is still assured of $2.75. However, if the price of wheat rises to $3.10 in September, the farmer still gets only $2.75. The additional $.35 gain goes to the owner of the contract who bought the wheat for $2.75 but can now sell it for $3.10.

Is this transaction unfair? Remember that the farmer wanted protection against a decline in the price of wheat. If the price had declined to $2.40 and the farmer had not hedged, the farmer would have suffered a loss of $.10 (the $2.40 price minus the $2.50 cost) per bushel. To obtain protection from this risk of loss, the farmer accepted the modest profit of $.25 per bushel and relinquished the possibility of a larger profit. The speculator who bought the contract bore the risk of loss from a price decline and received the reward from a price increase.

The risk from price increases

Users of wheat hedge in the opposite direction. A flour producer desires to know the future cost of wheat in order to plan production levels and the prices that will be charged to distributors. However, the spot price

---

*Hedging cannot erase risk and may even increase it. For a discussion of how such an increase may occur see Richard J. Teweles, Charles V. Harlow, and Herbert L. Stone, *The Commodity Futures Game — Who Wins, Who Loses? Why?* New York, McGraw-Hill Book Co., 1974, pp. 35–43.

of wheat need not hold into the future. This producer then buys a contract for future delivery and thereby hedges the position. This is hedging because the producer has a long position (the contract for the future delivery of wheat) and a short position (the future production of flour, which requires the future delivery of wheat).

If the producer buys a contract in June for the delivery of wheat in September at $2.75 per bushel, the future cost of the grain becomes known. The producer cannot be hurt by a price increase in wheat from $2.75 to $3.10, because the contract is for delivery at $2.75. However, the producer has forgone the chance of profit from a decline in the price of wheat from $2.75 to $2.40 per bushel.

Instead, the possibility of profit from a decline in the price of wheat rests with the speculator who sold the contract. If the price of wheat were to decline, the speculator could buy the wheat in September at the lower price, deliver it, and collect the $2.75 that is specified in the contract. However, this speculator would suffer a loss if the price of September wheat rose over $2.75. Then the cost would exceed the delivery price specified in the contract.

These two examples illustrate why growers and producers hedge. They often take the opposite side of hedge positions. If all growers and producers agree on prices for future delivery, there would be no need for speculators; but this is not the case. Speculators buy or sell contracts when there is an excess or an insufficient supply. If the farmer in the preceding example could not find a producer, a speculator would buy the contract and accept the risk of a price decline. If the producer could not find a farmer to supply a contract, the speculator would sell the contract and accept the risk of a price increase.

Speculators take opposite positions

Of course, farmers, producers, and speculators are simultaneously buying and selling contracts. No one knows who buys and who sells at a specific moment. However, if there is an excess or a shortage of one type of contract, then the future price of the commodity changes, which induces a certain behavior. For example, if September wheat is quoted at $2.75 per bushel, but no one is willing to buy at that price, the price declines. This induces some potential sellers to withdraw from the market and some potential buyers to enter the market. By this process, an imbalance of supply and demand contracts for a particular delivery date is erased. It is this interaction of the hedgers and the speculators that establishes the price of each contract.

THE SELECTION OF COMMODITIES

As with the selection of securities, there are two basic methods for the selection of commodities: the technical approach and the fundamental approach. The technical approach uses the same methods that are applied.

The technical approach

to the selection of securities. Various averages, point-and-figure charts, and bar graphs and their patterns are constructed for various commodities and are used to identify current price movements and to predict future price movements. Since this material was covered previously in Chapter 17, it is not repeated here.*

The fundamental approach

The fundamental approach is primarily concerned with those factors that affect the demand for and the supply of the various commodities. While the approach is similar to the selection of securities in that it uses economic data and analyzes accounting data, the specifics are different. The price of a commodity depends upon the supply of that commodity relative to the demand. Since the commodities are produced (e.g., wheat) or mined (e.g., silver), there are identifiable sources of supply. Correspondingly, there are identifiable sources of demand. However, there are also a variety of exogenous factors that may affect the supply of or the demand for a particular commodity, and these factors can have a powerful impact on the price of a specific commodity.

To illustrate these points, consider a basic commodity such as wheat. It takes several months for wheat to be produced. It has to be planted, grown, and then harvested. The amount of wheat that is planted is known because statistics are kept by the Commerce Department of the United States government. Such statistics are necessary for government forecasts of the economy, and this information is certainly available to those firms and individuals concerned with the size of the wheat crop.

The size of the crop that is planted and the size that is harvested, however, may be considerably different. The actual harvest depends not only on the amount planted but also on other factors. Particularly important is the weather, which can increase or decrease the yield. Good weather at the appropriate time can result in a bountiful harvest. A larger than anticipated supply of wheat should depress its price. On the other hand, bad weather, be it drought or excess rain, will have the opposite effect and will significantly reduce the anticipated supply. A reduction in supply should increase the price of wheat.

Demand, like supply, depends on both predictable and unpredictable forces. The demand for wheat depends on the needs of the firms that use the grain in their products. The producers of flour and cereals are obvious potential customers for wheat. However, the total demand also includes exports. If a foreign government enters the market and buys a substantial amount of wheat, this may cause a significant increase in its price.

Government intervention

Such government intervention in the market is not limited to foreign governments. The United States federal government also buys and sells commodities. Sometimes it buys in order to absorb excess supplies of a commodity and thus supports the commodity's price. In other cases the

---

*The investor who is interested in the application of technical analysis to commodity selection should consult Richard J. Teweles, Charles V. Harlow, and Herbert L. Stone, *The Commodity Futures Game — Who Wins? Who Loses? Why?* New York, McGraw-Hill Book Co., 1974, Chapter 7.

federal government may sell from its surplus stocks of a given commodity. This, of course, has the opposite impact on the price of the commodity. The increased supply tends to decrease the price or at least to reduce a tendency for the price to rise. These exogenous forces in the commodity markets are just another source of risk with which the speculator must contend.

Obviously the speculator seeks to identify shifts in demand or supply before they occur in order to take the appropriate position. Anticipation of a price increase indicates the purchase of a futures contract, whereas an anticipated price decline indicates the sale of a futures contract. Unfortunately, the ability to predict accurately changes in demand and supply is very rare. This should be obvious! If an individual could predict the future, he or she would certainly make fortune not just in the commodity markets but in any market. Mortals, however, lack such clairvoyance, which leaves them with fundamental and technical analysis as a means to select commodities for purchase.

Whether an investor uses technical or fundamental analysis, there is an important strategy for trading commodities. The speculator should seek to limit losses and permit profits to run. Successful commodity trading requires the ability of the speculator to recognize bad positions and to close them before they generate large losses. Many speculators, especially novices, do the exact opposite by taking small profits as they occur but maintaining positions that sustain losses. Then, when price changes produce margin calls, the speculator is forced either to close the position at a loss or to put up additional funds. If the speculator meets the margin call by committing additional funds, that individual is violating the strategy. Instead of taking the small loss, this investor is risking additional funds on the hope that the commodity price will recover. Such action may truly be an example of sending good money after bad!

The need to limit losses

SUMMARY

Investing in commodities is the buying or selling of contracts for future delivery. The speculator may take a long position, which is the purchase of a contract for future delivery, or a short position, which is the sale of a contract for future delivery. The long position generates profits if the commodity's price rises, while the short position results in a gain if the commodity's price falls.

Commodity contracts are purchased through brokers who own seats on commodity exchanges. The contracts are supported by deposits, which are called margin, that signify the investor's good faith. The margin requirement is only a small fraction of the value of the contract, and this produces considerable potential for leverage. A small change in the price of the commodity produces a large profit or loss relative to the small amount of margin. For this reason, commodity contracts are considered very speculative.

Heding plays an important role in commodity markets. Growers, miners, and other users of commodities often desire to reduce their risk of loss from price fluctuations and thus hedge their positions. Growers sell contracts for future delivery, and producers buy contracts for future delivery. Frequently it is the speculators who are buying and offering the contracts sought by the hedgers. In this way the risks that the hedgers seek to reduce are passed on to the speculators.

The price of a commodity and thus the value of a futures contract are related to the supply of and the demand for the commodity. Speculators may use technical or fundamental analysis to help forecast supply, demand, and price movements. Unfortunately, many exogenous factors, such as the weather or government intervention, make accurate forecasting difficult. These forces also contribute to the price fluctuations experienced in the commodity markets and are a major source of the risk associated with investing in commodities.

Terms to Remember

Futures contract	Futures price	Margin call
Long position	Daily limit	Hedging
Short position	Daily range	Fundamental approach
Delivery	Margin	Technical approach
Spot price		

Questions

1. What is a futures contract? What is the spot price of a commodity?

2. Why is investing in commodity futures considered to be speculative?

3. What is the difference between a long and a short position in a commodity?

4. What is margin and why is it a source of leverage? What is a margin call?

5. Why do farmers and other users of commodities hedge their positions?

6. If an investor anticipates a decline in a commodity's price, which position should he or she take?

7. How may government intervention affect commodity prices? Are commodity markets subject to government regulation?

SELECTED READINGS

Gould, Bruce G.: *Dow Jones-Irwin Guide to Commodities Trading.* Homewood, Ill., Dow Jones-Irwin, Inc., 1973.

Hieronymus, Thomas A.: *Economics of Futures Trading.* New York, Commodity Research Bureau, Inc., 1971.

Teweles, Richard J., Charles V. Harlow, and Herbert L. Stone: *The Commodity Futures Game — Who Wins? Who Loses? Why?* New York, McGraw-Hill Book Co., 1974.

Learning Objectives

After completing this chapter you should be able to

1. Compare the sources of risk from investing in collectibles and other physical assets with the sources of risk from investing in financial assets.

2. Define *income-in-kind* and illustrate how it applies to investments in some physical assets.

3. Describe the market for art.

4. Explain the role of auctions in investing in collectibles.

5. Explain why the valuation of art is exceedingly subjective.

6. List the possible mediums for investing in gold.

7. Explain why an investment in gold may result in a loss.

chapter 23

INVESTING IN COLLECTIBLES

Investing in collectibles is essentially no different from investing in financial assets. The investments are made now and the returns are earned in the future. The returns consist of income or services generated by the physical asset plus any capital gains. In order to realize capital gains, the asset must be sold. Hence, there must exist a market for the asset. Realized gains are subject to capital gains taxation. And, as with any investment, there is the element of risk.

While investing in physical assets is similar to investing in financial assets, there are important differences. Physical assets have their own markets, and investing in them requires specialized knowledge, which is considerably different from the knowledge used in the selection of financial assets. An entire lifetime may be spent learning the fine points that make an individual an expert in a particular type of asset, such as art or real estate.

This chapter briefly covers investing in collectibles including art, Oriental rugs, antiques, and gold. It can be only a cursory survey of the field. The emphasis will be placed on the elements most similar to those associated with investing in financial assets: the potential returns, an asset's marketability, and the risks involved. Implicit throughout the discussion is the assumption that the individual needs specialized information in order to know and understand these specialized investments. Such information can best be obtained through careful and extensive study of the particular physical assets of interest to an individual.

While the chapter primarily uses art and gold to illustrate investments in collectibles, these do not exhaust the possibilities. Many physical assets that people accumulate have the characteristics of an investment. Old baseball cards, antique furniture, bisque dolls, stamps, and autographs can serve as potential stores of value. They may prove to be excellent investments that yield substantial returns for individuals who take the time to learn what differentiates the wheat from the chaff and who judiciously acquire quality representations of these collectibles.

RETURNS, MARKETS, AND RISK

Investing in physical assets requires that the investor have a broad definition of markets, returns, and risk. A market brings together buyers and sellers in order to transact the exchange of goods and services. When a mutually acceptable price is determined, the goods are transferred from the seller to the buyer. This is obviously what occurs in the organized security markets such as the New York Stock Exchange (NYSE). Sellers and buyers of securities are brought together, and they trade securities for money.

The market is informal

Many securities, however, are bought and sold in that informal market called the over-the-counter market. There is no centralized place where transactions in the over-the-counter market are consummated. It exists wherever a buyer and a seller can trade cash for securities.

The market for art and other collectibles is also an informal market that is similar to the over-the-counter market for securities. There is no organized center such as the NYSE for the transfer of these physical assets. While there may be certain centers, such as the diamond district in New York, the market is geographically dispersed and not formally organized.

Because there is no formal market, there are none of the advantages offered by such formality. For example, price quotations (i.e., bid and ask prices) are not readily available. The volume of transactions is generally not recorded, and when it is, this information is not widely disseminated as are reports of security trades, which are published in the financial press. Specialized publications may report some of this information, but these are frequently not well known to the investor and may not be readily available.

Furthermore, there is little or no regulation of these informal markets.

While the Securities and Exchange Commission may work to reduce fraud and to assure the timely disclosure of pertinent financial information that may affect the value of a firm's securities, no such government organization exists to protect the buyers of many physical assets. It is a case of "let the buyer beware," and the unsuspecting investor is certainly an easy target for the forger or any other shady dealer who can prey on the individual's desire to find an asset that will offer an exceptional return. **There is less regulation**

The return offered by an investment in a physical asset such as gold comes from the same sources as the gain from an investment in a financial asset: the potential for price appreciation and the flow of income. The return earned through price appreciation is the difference between the net sale price and the purchase price. The net sale price is the realized price minus any commissions or fees necessary to make the sale. While the commissions for buying and selling stock may be only 2 or 3 per cent of the price, the commissions for buying and selling physical investments may be considerably more. These fees vary with the different types of assets, but they can consume a substantial portion of any profit earned through price appreciation. **The return**

The potential impact of commissions can be seen in a very simple numerical example. Suppose an investor buys a painting for $1000 and after holding it for ten years is able to sell it for $2500. What is the rate of return on this investment if the commissions are 30 per cent of the sale price? This question is a simple example of the compound value of a dollar: $1000 grows at what rate for ten years to 70 per cent of $2500? The answer is **The impact of fees**

$$\$1000(1 + x)^{10} = \$2500 - .3(\$2500)$$
$$x = \$1750 \div \$1000$$
$$x = 1.750$$

The interest factor of 1.750 for the compound value of a dollar for ten years yields an annual return of approximately 6 per cent. If there had been no commissions, the interest factor would have been 2.50 and the annual return would have been approximately 10 per cent. The large commission thus reduced the annual return to only 6 per cent, which is about the rate that an investor would have earned on a regular savings account.

In addition to commissions, other expenses may be incurred with an investment in physical assets that are not incurred with financial assets. The investor may take out special insurance to cover insurable risks. For example, insurance may be desirable for investments in art, which are subject to theft and fire. Or the investor may rent space (e.g., a safe deposit box) to store the assets. This certainly would apply to valuable stamps, coins, and gold. These additional expenses reduce the return earned by the investment. **Other expenses**

Besides the return earned through price appreciation, the investor may receive a return through income received. Many physical assets that **Income-in-kind** are held as investments offer income-in-kind (i.e., a nonmonetary form of income). Oriental rugs may be functional; art works are decorative, and housing provides shelter and space. These flows of income-in-kind may not be considered income by the typical investor, but they should be because they are part of the return earned by the investment. Actually, the potential flow of services offered by some physical assets should be the prime reason for buying them. It is not so much the potential for price appreciation but the flow of income-in-kind that makes some investments attractive. This concept will be developed further when it is applied to several specific investments that are subsequently discussed.

Sources of risk   Investing in art and collectibles subjects the investor to the same basic risks associated with investing in financial assets. There may be elements of risk attributable to the market (i.e., the risk associated with price changes) or attributable to the business (i.e., the risk associated with a particular company or asset). In addition, the investor must face the risk of loss from inflation and the problems associated with theft and fraud.

Price fluctuations   The markets for physical assets vary over time. Prices do fluctuate and not always upward. Presumably, if prices in general move in a particular direction, then the value of specific assets will move accordingly. Hence, if the price of gold rises, then the value of gold coins will rise. Conversely, if the price of gold declines, the value of gold coins will fall. The investor who buys gold and gold coins cannot avoid this market risk, which applies to all physical assets.

The investor must bear the risk associated with the specific investment. This is analogous to the business risk associated with investing in financial assets. Changes in taste alter the public's demand for specific goods. For example, if the demand for Oriental rugs increases, then the value of most Oriental rugs will appreciate. However, even within this group some will appreciate more than others. The rugs that are popular today will not necessarily be those that are popular tomorrow. Thus, the investor may experience losses on specific investments even though the market as a whole moves upward in price.

Inflation   One of the reasons for puchasing physical assets is that they help the investor to beat inflation. While the value of financial assets such as stock often declines when the rate of inflation increases, the price of physical assets may keep pace. But even if inflation occurs, it is, of course, not necessarily true that the price of all physical assets will rise. Their prices can rise, fall, or remain the same. Inflation inflicts a loss of puchasing power on any investor if that individual's particular portfolio does not keep pace with the rate of inflation. While some physical assets have appreciated in price (e.g., housing), this is not true for all physical assets. For example, the price of gold declined between January 1975 and July 1976, but the rate of inflation during the same period was approximately 11 per cent. Obviously, the rate of inflation exceeded the rate of return on an investment in gold during that particular period.

Theft and fraud   The last sources of risk are theft and fraud. Although financial assets such as stocks and bonds can be left with custodians (e.g., brokers), that is not necessarily the case with physical assets. One's house is not left with the real estate broker. The investor in Oriental rugs or art will probably want to use these items or at least display them in order to enjoy them. The coin and stamp collector probably enjoys looking at the collection and does not leave it with coin and stamp dealers. While coins, gold, stamps, art, and Oriental rugs may be stored with a dealer or in a safe deposit box when the investor cannot care for them, most of the time these items are kept at home, where they are subject to theft and fire. Although the individual may seek to protect these investments with insurance, such insurance will require detailed records to verify the asset's value in order to obtain adequate protection.

Last, the investor must bear the risk of fraud. Fakes and misrepresentations are frequently sold to unsuspecting buyers who lack the knowledge to appraise them properly. This applies not only to novices but also to sophisticated professionals who, on occasion, have been completely deceived. The possibility of fraud, or at least of excessive pricing, truly makes the art and collectibles markets areas in which the novice should move with caution.

This suggests several practical steps for investing in these assets. First, investors should buy only after doing their homework. They should know what they are looking at and what to look for. Second, investors should seek to specialize in those particular physical assets that appeal to them. For example, one should not buy Oriental rugs because they are Oriental rugs but should collect them because they can be enjoyed and are very functional. Third, one should invest in art and collectibles only after sufficient financial assets have been accumulated to meet financial emergencies and contingencies. Physical assets offer little, if any, liquidity. Fourth, the investor should be willing to lose the entire investment in the art object or other collectible. This implies that the asset should have sufficient use in itself to justify its purchase. Under these circumstances the investor will not be deluded into thinking that the asset will offer extraordinary gains. Such gains rarely, if ever, accrue to the novice, and investors in art and other collectibles are competing with professionals who have a lifetime of experience upon which to base decisions.

Some practical advice

ART, ORIENTAL RUGS, AND ANTIQUES

Perhaps over the last decade no investments have done better than those in art (i.e., paintings, sculpture, and graphics). One art expert, Willi Bongard (who is also an economist), has estimated that the value of the works of leading modern artists has increased 18 per cent compounded annually in the period from 1965 to 1975.* That is the equivalent of $1.00

Past returns

---

*D. McConathy, "Art as Investment," *Artscanada*. (Autumn 1975), p. 46.

growing to $5.25 after ten years. Such a return compares very favorably with the Dow Jones industrial average or Standard & Poor's 500 stock index. During the same period, the stock market declined according to these two price indices! Such comparisons, however, can be misleading because stocks are homogeneous and their values are easily measured. Art works are very difficult to compare (i.e., each is unique), and their values can only be approximated.

THE MARKET FOR COLLECTIBLES

How to buy collectibles

Art objects may be purchased in a variety of ways. The primary means is through dealers, many of whom make a market in the items. Such dealers not only sell but also buy. Why do they do both? The art and security markets are very similar in that they are primarily secondhand markets. Since van Gogh and Rembrandt are no longer producing, sales of their work can only be secondary transactions. The same applies to many Oriental rugs and to antiques. Any exchanges after the initial sale are in the secondary markets. In order for dealers to have these items for sale (i.e., inventory), many either acquire them or hold them on consignment. Dealers who purchase art, antiques, and Oriental rugs hold them in inventory for future sale. They could not continue to operate solely on new output, especially since the most valuable works of art and Oriental rugs and all antiques are those already in existence.

Market makers

Since some dealers make markets, they, in effect, establish bid and ask prices. While such prices may not be readily known to the investor, any dealer who is willing to buy used rugs, antiques, or art is offering a bid. Of course, the offer to sell establishes an asking price.

Since the volume of transactions is low and the number of dealers in these specialized areas is relatively small, the spread between the bid and the ask will be substantial. For example, a dealer in Oriental rugs may be willing to repurchase a rug (in acceptable condition) at the original sale price. If the rug has appreciated in value and the dealer can subsequently sell it at the appreciated price, then the spread will be substantial.

Instead of repurchasing the rug, the dealer may offer to hold the rug on consignment. The title remains with the owner while the dealer tries to sell the rug. If a sale occurs, then the dealer receives a set percentage of the price. This commission can be as high as 30 or 40 per cent of the sale price. Obviously, the price of collectibles must rise substantially for the owner to recoup the cost, pay the commission, and still net a profit.

Auctions

The second major market for valuable art, Oriental rugs, and antiques is the auction. While the word *auction* may imply the Saturday afternoon sale of an estate, many major works are sold through auctions. The important auction houses of the world (e.g., Sotheby Parke-Bernet or Christie's, both of which have offices in New York and London) hold auctions that handle many valuable art treasures.

EXHIBIT 23–1. Sotheby Parke-Bernet's Standard Commission for the Sale of Paintings*

Realized Price	Commission Rate
First $1000	25.0%
$1000–$5000	20.0
$5000–$15,000	15.0
Over $15,000	12.5

*Source: Richard H. Rush, "Art as an Investment," in L. Barnes and S. Feldman, *Handbook of Wealth Management,* New York, McGraw-Hill Book Co., 1977, p. 37–15.

Fees

Such auction houses permit the owners of valuable art, antiques, and Oriental rugs to offer them for sale, but the sale price that will be realized is unknown in advance. Although the auction house places an estimated value on the item, the realized price can be higher or lower than the estimate. After the sale, the auction house takes its fee or commission from the realized price. This fee can be as high as one third of the sale price for small dollar amounts. The percentage charged often declines as the realized value increases. An illustration of such a sliding scale is given in Exhibit 23–1, which presents the commissions charged by Sotheby Parke-Bernet.

Although the fees for selling art, antiques, and Oriental rugs are substantial, there is a secondary market for these goods. The investor can seek to avoid the costs by directly marketing the items. However, the dealers and auction houses may be able to realize a better price than the individual could. These specialists have a better idea of the value of a specific item and hence may price it more realistically than, and perhaps more profitably, for, the seller.

THE RETURN ON COLLECTIBLES

Sources of return

The return on investments in art, antiques, or Oriental rugs comes from two sources: price appreciation and the flow of services generated by the investment (i.e., income-in-kind). How price appreciation generates a return is obvious, since it is the difference between the net proceeds of the sale (i.e., the sale price minus the commissions) and the purchase price. As has already been discussed, the commissions may consume a substantial portion of any gross profits.

Income-in-kind

The second source of the return, the income-in-kind, is also obvious, since art, many antiques, and Oriental rugs are functional. Many individuals may not view these services as a flow of income, but they are. The services of Oriental rugs and antiques and the aesthetic pleasure of art generate nonmonetary income.

The flow of services

An Oriental rug, antique, or painting may offer a superior total return when both the flow of services and price appreciation are considered. For example, if the investor compares the cost of wall-to-wall carpeting with the cost of an Oriental rug, the return offered by the Oriental rug will probably be superior. The wall-to-wall carpeting depreciates and cannot be moved if the investor changes homes. The Oriental rug performs the same service, may not depreciate and may even appreciate in value, and is easily moved. No wonder such rugs are viewed by some individuals as excellent investments, because these rugs generate many years of service and offer the potential for price appreciation.

The same applies to art works and many antiques. Paintings, lithographs, and sculpture all generate a flow of service. The owner derives pleasure from them, which is part of the total return on the investment. Of course, calculating this flow of income is probably impossible. So the true return on an investment in these items cannot be determined.

THE VALUATION OF COLLECTIBLES

Value is related to scarcity

What gives art, antiques, or Oriental rugs their value? The answer to this question is both simple and complex. The obvious answer is scarcity relative to demand. There are only so many paintings by a master, and certainly this scarcity enhances their value.

Although there is a paucity of works by major artists, there is an abundance of what passes for art. This abundance (or an abundance relative to the demand) has resulted in very low prices for the vast majority of paintings, graphics, and poor quality Oriental rugs. But scarcity alone does not explain value.

The work's creator and quality

The valuation of art objects actually depends on many factors.* Value is affected not only by the reputation of the artist and quality of the work but also by many other factors, including attributes of the work itself and exogenous factors.

The creator of the work and its quality are the easiest attributes to isolate. The paintings of old and modern masters are readily identified, and the quality of their work is well known. However, the cost of their works frequently exceeds $100,000 and may reach into millions of dollars. Such prices virtually exclude all but a handful of collectors and museums.

Even many lesser name artists are readily identifiable, and an investor may determine the quality of their work through reading, studying, and viewing the art firsthand. A minor name in art history is usually minor for a reason. Investments in this type of art may appreciate (especially if art

---

*This section draws heavily on Richard H. Rush, "Art as an Investment," in L. Barnes and S. Feldman, *Handbook of Wealth Management*, New York, McGraw-Hill Book Co. 1977, pp. 37–1 through 37–16.

prices rise in general), but the probability of a large increase in value is small.

In addition to the artist and the quality of the work, value depends on several factors that are both inherent in and external to the specific piece. Factors indigenous to the work itself include the medium and the subject matter. For example, oil paintings tend to cost more than watercolors by the same artist. Landscapes command higher prices than portraits. Dark or somber scenes may be less valuable than brightly colored and cheerful ones.

Additional factors that affect value

Factors affecting value that are independent of the piece itself include the condition of the work, the former owners, the museums or shows in which the work was previously exhibited, and the seller.

Condition obviously affects value. As one would expect, a damaged painting or antique or a badly worn Oriental rug commands a lower price. However, the owner may be able to have damaged works restored (for a price). Such restoration should help increase the value of the work. Just the cleaning of an old painting or an Oriental rug will bring out the colors and perhaps make the piece both more attractive and marketable.

Who has previously owned the work, where it has been exhibited, and who is selling it may also affect the value of an art object. If a painting has passed through the collection of an important museum or major collector, its value is enhanced. In a sense, previous owners and exhibitions are like a pedigree. They establish authenticity and credibility that can enhance the value of a particular art object.

As the preceding discussion suggests, the valuation of art is very subjective. Professionals (e.g., art dealers and museum curators) know this and are capable of making reasonably accurate valuations. When a piece is offered at an auction, these professionals know approximately how much the work should bring. If it appears that such a price will not be obtained, these professionals may enter the bidding and purchase the piece for their own galleries or collections. For this reason the novice investor should not expect to acquire quality art, antiques, or Oriental rugs at bargain prices. Those in the know will outbid such a naive investor.

The valuation is subjective

THE SELECTION OF COLLECTIBLES

How does the investor tackle the problem of selecting among the works of art or other collectibles that are available? Essentially the choice is either to buy the works of known artists or to try to identify the artists that will gain acceptance in the future. In a sense, this is similar to buying stock issued by IBM or AT&T, which are known firms in excellent financial condition, versus buying stock in the over-the-counter market that is issued by some small company that offers promise for the future. The works of the known artists, of course, will cost more. However, even the

The problem of choice

works of minor names in art may command high prices, and the investor, in essence, must decide whether to bite the bullet and pay the price or to select the works of the unknown artists.

Unknown versus known artist

The works of an unknown artist will, of course, tend to be inexpensive, and if the artist subsequently acquires a "name," his or her works will appreciate in value. However, the probability of this occurring is small, in which case the investor will probably be lucky to recoup even the meager cost of the investment.

Quality and reputable dealers

There are, however, several things that the investor can do to help increase the chance of earning a positive return on an investment in a painting or an Oriental rug. First, the investor should buy from reputable dealers. Although prices from dealers will tend to be higher, their reputation increases the authenticity of the work. This is illustrated in Exhibit 23–2, which presents the confirmation statement from a dealer for the sale of a painting. In addition to the title of the work and the medium (oil), the statement presents the year of the painting's execution (1974) and the work's identifying number (58). Such a statement not only is proof of purchase but also serves to authenticate the work.

Buying from known dealers or through major auction houses will also aid in any subsequent sale. Dealers often specialize in the work of particular artists and are thus aware of the market for these artists. Should the investor want to sell the piece, the dealer may be a primary source of information regarding the market and may even be able to execute the sale.

Avoid copies

Second, the investor should avoid buying prints and other objects that masquerade as potential investments. Unsigned prints and reproductions may be an excellent means to decorate a room and to learn about art, but they are not originals. Nor are they unique. Generally, unsigned prints and reproductions are not investments, and the individual should realize this fact and not be deluded into believing that such items will appreciate in value.*

Develop a specialty

Third, the investor should develop a specialty. Just as one cannot learn about all possible firms and their securities, the individual cannot know everything concerning all forms of art. The best strategy, then, is to develop a specialty that will permit the investor to learn which factors affect the value of particular art objects. In this way the investor can accumulate a collection that is decorative and that serves as a store of value.

GOLD

Gold as a medium of exchange

Gold has held a specific fascination for centuries. It has been minted into coins and used as a medium of exchange. Its color and durability have

---

*In the past, print makers (e.g., Dürer) did not sign their works, but these unsigned, original prints are potential investments. However, prints and reproductions of these originals should not be considered to be investments.

EXHIBIT 23–2. Confirmation for the sale of a painting.

princeton gallery of fine art
9 SPRING STREET • PRINCETON, N.J. 08540 • 609/921-8123

NAME *M. Herbet Mayo*

ADDRESS *29 Dunbar St.*

Trenton N.J.

TELEPHONE _____

DATE *May 13 1975*

DESCRIPTION	INV. NO.	AMOUNT
Wolf Kahn – Oil Painting	$	1100.00
"Barn with open door"		
#58 - 1974		
Pd in full		
May 13, 1975		
	TAX	55.00
	TOTAL	1155.00

SIGNATURE

CUSTOMER COPY

made it a popular metal for jewelry. Gold is also a very popular store of value. Some investors, who are frequently referred to as gold bugs, consider it to be among the best investments available. A few investment advisory services even recommend that investors hold a substantial proportion of their portfolios in some form of gold.

Its universal acceptability

The prime reason for investing in gold is a belief that it is the best insurance against inflation. The universal acceptability of gold makes it the one commodity to own during a period of rapid inflation. The price of gold tends to mirror fears of inflation. If the rate of inflation rises, purchases of gold will increase along with its price. Conversely, during periods of declining inflation, the price of gold tends to decrease. This is illustrated in Graph 23–1, which plots the price of an ounce of gold and the rate of inflation. As may be seen in the graph, the price of gold does seem to respond to the rate of inflation.

The profit is not assured

Graph 23–1 also points out another fact: Investors can lose money by buying gold. As with any other investment, there is always the risk of loss. Holders of gold not only forgo income, such as dividends and interest, but also have to store the metal and bear the risk of fraud and capital loss from declining prices. From February 1975 through August 1976, the price of an ounce of gold declined by nearly one half — from $180 to $110. Obviously, investors who purchased gold in January 1975 (when it was first legal for Americans to own gold bullion) learned an

GRAPH 23–1. The Price of Gold and the Change in
the Consumer Price Index

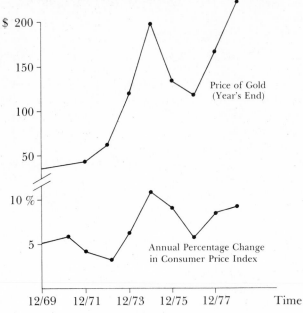

essential lesson: There is no risk-free investment. However, those who bought gold in August 1976 earned a substantial return, as the price rose to over $400 an ounce in October 1979.

The variety of potential investments

There are several mediums for investing in gold: jewelry, coins, bullion, which is usually in the form of gold bars, stocks of mining companies, and futures contracts. As an investment, gold jewelry is a poor choice because the cost of the jewelry includes not only the cost of the gold but also the cost of the copper that is used to strengthen the gold and the wages of the craftspeople who design and construct the jewelry. There may be excellent reasons for buying gold jewelry, but it is not a good choice as an investment. (Jewelry, especially rare gems, may prove to be an acceptable investment. However, such investments are very illiquid and produce no monetary income.)

GOLD COINS

Coins

Gold coins are a better vehicle than jewelry for investing in gold. These coins initially came into existence as currency, but in the United States they no longer serve as a medium of exchange. Many coins still exist from the past and may be purchased through coin dealers and at auctions.

Like jewelry, gold coins have a serious weakness as an investment. Their price is related to two things: the bullion content and the coin's numismatic value. The bullion value of a coin depends on the gold content and the price of gold. This price, in turn, depends upon the market's demand for and supply of gold. Gold is used in various products (e.g., jewelry) and is continually being mined. The demand for gold in its various uses (including investments) relative to the supply that is offered determines the market price of gold bullion.

The value of gold coins depends not only on the value of bullion but also on the numismatic value of the coin. Some coins are much scarcer than others and hence are more valuable as collector's items. For example, the value of an uncirculated ten dollar gold piece minted in the United States in 1861 rose from $37.50 in 1946 to $200 in 1974, but an uncirculated three dollar piece minted in 1889 rose in value from $25 to $1100 during the same period.* The difference, of course, is the result of the scarcity of three dollar gold pieces. This gives it great numismatic value in addition to its value as gold.

If the investor is concerned only with accumulating gold, then numismatic rarities may be of little interest because the investor pays more for the same amount of gold. The premium paid over the bullion value can be substantial; the investor, therefore, is really gambling on the coin as a collector's item and not on its gold content.

Investors who seek both coin collections as well as gold bullion may prefer such rarities. These will probably increase in value more rapidly than the more common gold coins. In general, it is the rarer items that appreciate the fastest. Collectors of gold coins (and stamps, antiques, and other collectibles) may find that the best strategy is to buy a few expensive high quality representations instead of trying to amass large collections of the less rare and cheaper specimens.

One coin of particular interest to gold collectors is the Krugerrand, which is issued by the Union of South Africa. That country is the world's primary producer of gold, and it mints the Krugerrand to sell to gold collectors. While this coin may be used as money in the Union of South Africa, it is not generally circulated. Such use would scar the coins and reduce their value. Instead, the coins are sold in plastic packages designed to protect their mint condition.

The primary attractiveness of the Krugerrand is that the coin is issued in exactly one troy ounce of fine gold. This uniformity of metal content increases its marketability in the secondary markets. In addition, the South African government sells the Krugerrand for only a 3 to 5 per cent premium over the value of the gold bullion in the coin. Other gold coins, especially commemorative coins or limited edition foreign coins, are frequently sold (at least initially) at a considerable premium over their value as bullion. The investor runs a substantial risk in that the price of these

The numismatic value

Coin rarities

Krugerrands

---

*See Q. David Bowers, *Collecting Rare Coins for Profit*, New York, Harper & Row Publishers, Inc., pp. 303–304.

commemorative coins may decline to the value of the gold bullion in the secondary markets. This potential price decline, however, does not apply to Krugerrands.

GOLD BULLION

Gold bars

Until January 1, 1975, gold coins and jewelry offered Americans the only legal means to own gold. However, Americans can now own gold bullion in the form of gold bars. These may be bought through gold dealers and brokerage firms. Once the investor purchases the gold, he or she may take possession of it or leave it with the dealer or the broker. Leaving the gold with the broker involves storage and insurance costs, which increases the price of the investment.

The investor may take delivery

The investor may take delivery and store the gold in a presumably safe place. The gold ingots should be stamped and numbered by the refiner, who also supplies correspondingly numbered certificates. These must be delivered with the gold should the investor ever sell the ingots. If the certificates are lost, the ingots will have to be assayed to prove their gold content. This expense must be paid by the investor to insure the marketability of the gold bars. Even if the documentation is not lost, the investor may have to have the gold assayed because taking possession results in a loss of the guarantee of the gold's quality, and this guarantee can only be restored by having the gold assayed.

The problem of fraud

The need to assay the metal points out a major problem with investing in gold: fraud. Coins and bars can be passed off as gold with fake numbers and fake documentation. By purchasing gold bullion from a reputable dealer or through a brokerage firm, the investor can substantially reduce the possibility of fraud. Certainly, no investor should buy unassayed gold that is offered at a discount from the price of gold bullion. Such a purchase will certainly prove to be a bad investment.

GOLD MINING STOCKS

Mining companies

The investor may also buy the shares of gold mining companies. This, of course, is not owning gold. Instead, the firm may own gold mines and mining equipment. Presumably, the value of the shares is related to the value of the gold, but it is possible for the price of gold to rise while the price of the mining company's stock declines. Various factors, such as a strike or a fire, can affect the value of the mining firm and its securities, but such events may have no impact on the price of gold.

Political forces

These exogenous factors (especially political forces) are particularly important in the valuation of gold mining stocks. The primary producers of gold are the Union of South Africa and the Soviet Union. The Union of South Africa alone accounts for about two thirds of the world's output of newly mined gold. The political climate in the Union of South Africa is somewhat unstable, and this instability can have a large impact on the value of gold mining shares in South African companies.

U.S. and Canadian gold stocks

The investor may avoid these political problems by limiting purchases to shares in gold mining companies in the United States and Canada. From 1977 to 1979, the value of these shares tended to follow closely the price of bullion. Their value is not affected by the risks associated with the South African gold mining stocks. This is illustrated in Graph 23–2, which shows the price performance of shares of Dome Mines (an American firm) and the price of gold. As may be seen in the graph, the price of these shares moved in tandem with the price of gold. Thus, shares of American and Canadian gold mining companies may offer the investor a viable alternative to owning gold bars. Such shares not only avoid the costs of storage, insurance, and assaying but also may pay dividend income, which is not possible from any other form of investment in gold.

GOLD FUTURES

Gold as a commodity

In addition to gold coins, gold bullion, and gold mining shares, the investor may speculate in gold futures. Like many other commodities, there exists an active market in contracts for the future delivery of gold. This market is a recent development; it came into existence only after it became legal for Americans to own gold bullion. The principal markets for these gold futures are the Chicago International Monetary Market and the New York Commodity Exchange.

Considerable leverage

As with other commodity contracts, the appeal of gold futures is in the great leverage that they offer investors. A contract for the future

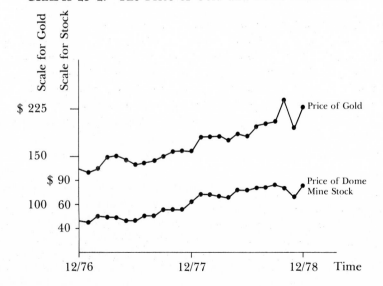

GRAPH 23–2. The Price of Gold and Dome Mine Stock

delivery of gold is for 100 troy ounces. At $225 per ounce, the contract has a face value of $22,500. The margin requirement may be as small as $2000; thus, for an investment of $2000, the speculator has a claim on $22,500 worth of gold. If the price were to rise by only $10 per ounce, the value of the contract would rise by $1000 to $23,500. The speculator would then make $1000 on an investment of only $2000. Of course, if the price of gold were to fall by only $10 per ounce, then the speculator would lose $1000. Since gold prices can and do fluctuate rapidly, there exists considerable potential for large profits and losses, which is a primary reason for the attractiveness of gold futures to speculators.

The special risks   While all forms of investing in gold involve several sources of risk, gold futures involve a special source of risk. Government and international agencies participate in the market for gold. For example, the United States Treasury periodically sells gold, and this additional supply tends to reduce its price. In addition, the International Monetary Fund of the United Nations sells gold to raise currency for its international transactions. This also tends to reduce the price of gold. These sales make investing in gold futures more risky, as they alter the demand and supply of the metal.

SUMMARY

The poor performance of stocks during the 1970s and the continuation of inflation have increased investor interest in various collectibles and other physical assets. Art objects, Oriental rugs, antiques, stamps, coins, gold, and silver have attracted the attention of some investors as alternatives to the more traditional investments (i.e., stocks and bonds).

These physical assets offer investors potential price appreciation and, in some cases, income from services. They may be purchased from dealers or at auctions, and while these assets are not purchased on organized exchanges, secondhand markets exist in which the investor can sell the assets.

Investors who acquire physical assets, like investors who acquire financial assets, bear the risk of loss. This risk is due to fluctuations in the prices of the assets in general and of the specific asset, inflation, theft, and fraud. To help overcome these risks, the investor needs to be well informed and to specialize in a particular type of physical asset.

Art and gold were used in this chapter to illustrate two types of possible investments in physical assets. The valuation of art objects is extremely subjective, because it depends not only on the work and its creator but also on several intangibles. However, art objects can be very decorative, and they do suggest to others the taste of the investor.

Gold may be acquired in a variety of forms, including jewelry, coins, and bullion. The investor can also buy the stock of gold mining companies and futures contracts. Gold jewelry is the poorest means to invest in gold, and a futures contract is the riskiest. Most investors prefer gold coins and bullion as their vehicle for an investment in gold.

Like any investment, acquiring gold subjects the investor to risk. The price of gold, like the price of other assets, can fall and has done so in the past. This, plus the fact that gold must be stored, insured, and assayed, reduces the potential return on the investment. A positive return on gold, as on all other investments, cannot be assured.

Terms to Remember

Income-in-kind	Krugerrand	To assay

Questions

1. How are collectibles and gold bought and sold?
2. Why is it important to have specialized knowledge when investing in physical assets, such as art or gold?
3. What are the sources of risk from investing in collectibles and gold?
4. What is income-in-kind and how does it apply to investments in art and Oriental rugs?
5. Why have the prices of selected art objects risen? Is there a secondary market for art objects? What are the special costs associated with investing in art?
6. What are the sources of return from an investment in art and other collectibles?
7. What are the mediums for investing in gold? What are the special costs associated with these investments?
8. Why may gold bullion have to be assayed? Why may individuals who desire to invest in gold prefer bullion to gold coins?
9. What is the relationship between the rate of inflation and the price of gold?

SELECTED READINGS

Bongard, Willi: "Wall Stocks." *Across the Board*, 14(November 1977), pp. 42–57.

Bowers, Q. David: *Collecting Rare Coins for Profit*. New York, Harper & Row, Publishers, Inc., 1975.

Hoppe, Donald J.: *How to Invest in Gold Stocks and Avoid the Pitfalls*. New Rochelle, N.Y., Arlington House, 1972.

Jacobsen, Charles W.: *Oriental Rugs – A Complete Guide*. Rutland, Vt., Charles E. Tuttle Co., Inc., 1962.

"Magic Carpets?" *Forbes*, (October 1, 1975), p. 54.

McConathy, D.: "Art as Investment." *Artscanada*, 32(Autumn 1975), p. 46.

O'Hanlon, James: "Limited Edition Lithography: Buyer Beware!" *Forbes*, (July 10, 1978), pp. 65–67.

Patterson, Jerry E.: "The High-Flying Oriental Carpets." *Art News*, 75(April 1976), pp. 96–99.

Porter, Sylvia: "The Boom Is in Oriental Rugs." Syndicated Column, June 10, 1978.

Shapiro, Cecile, and Lauris Mason: *Fine Prints: Collecting, Buying, and Selling*. New York, Harper & Row, Publishers, Inc., 1976.

Learning Objectives

After completing this chapter you should be able to

1. Explain how income-in-kind applies to investments in real estate.

2. Name the tax advantages of home ownership as an investment.

3. Explain why home ownership may be the best hedge against inflation.

4. Compare the sources of risk from investing in homes with those from investing in financial assets.

5. Differentiate among the ways an individual may invest in land.

6. Explain how financial leverage and tax deductions may increase the return on an investment in land.

7. Distinguish among the types of real estate investment trusts.

8. Apply the stock valuation model to the shares of real estate investment trusts.

chapter 24
INVESTING IN REAL ESTATE

There are several means to invest in real estate. This chapter is devoted to three of them: home ownership, land, and the shares of real estate investment trusts. These investments are essentially no different from any of the investments previously discussed in this text. They offer a potential return but require the acceptance of risk.

The initial section is devoted to home ownership. This section explores the advantages of home ownership as an alternative to renting, including the returns on investments in homes. Next follows a discussion of investments in both unimproved and improved land. Since improved land is primarily a business venture, the bulk of the discussion is related to unimproved land.

The chapter ends with a discussion of real estate investment trusts. These are a type of investment company that specializes in real estate. The types of trusts, their methods of financing, and the potential returns and risks associated with this particular type of investment are covered. The chapter ends with a discussion of how the stock valuation model presented in Chapter 14 may be applied to the shares of these trusts.

HOME OWNERSHIP

People must secure living space

Every person must live somewhere. This obvious fact differentiates home ownership from all other investments. People must secure living space. Their choices are either to rent it or to own the property and, in effect, rent the space to themselves. If they rent, individuals are consuming space. If they own, they are simultaneously consuming space and making an investment.

There are many reasons for owning a home instead of renting. These include the psychic income that comes with the pride of owning a place that can be called one's home. Home ownership also offers a very pragmatic advantage over renting: It is a means to force saving. Every payment on a mortgage represents interest and principal. The amount that the individual has invested in the home increases with each mortgage payment. These payments become a convenient means to force oneself to save. In addition, any repairs and improvements made in the property accrue to the owner and not to the landlord.

The tax benefits and the potential return

There are two major financial reasons for home ownership. The first pertains to the tax benefits, and the second is the potential return on the investment. Of course, this return depends partially on the tax shelters generated by home ownership. These tax breaks are rarely referred to as tax shelters, but they are because they either reduce taxable income or defer tax payments. The tax shelters or tax advantages of home ownership are (1) the deductions from income that the homeowner who itemizes expenses in his income tax report is able to take, (2) the possible deferment or even avoidance of capital gains taxes when the property is sold, and (3) the tax-free income generated by the living space.

INCOME TAX DEDUCTIONS

Mortgage financing

The vast majority of homes are purchased through the use of mortgages. The interest paid is a tax-deductible expense. If the homeowner itemizes deductions, the deduction of interest reduces taxable income and thus results in a tax savings. This savings can be substantial. If the homeowner is carrying a $30,000 mortgage at 9 per cent, the interest charge is $2700 in the first year of the mortgage. Itemization of this interest expense reduces taxable income by $2700.

Tax savings

The potential tax savings for different taxable incomes is given in Table 24–1. Columns 1 and 2 give the taxable income for a married couple before and after the deduction. The federal tax liability without and with the deduction is presented in columns 3 and 4. The net savings in taxes is given in column 5. As may be seen in the table, the tax savings rise as the level of taxable income increases because the marginal tax rate rises with an increase in taxable income.

The effective interest cost

The effect of this deduction is a reduction in the true or effective cost of a mortgage loan. The individual's true cost of a mortgage is related to (1)

TABLE 24–1. *Potential Tax Savings From Deducting the Interest Expenses ($2700) From Selected Taxable Incomes**

Taxable Income	Taxable Income After Deducting Interest	Taxes Paid Without the Deduction	Taxes Paid After the Deduction	Reduction in Taxes
$13,900	$11,200	$ 1,974	$ 1,380	$ 594
25,900	23,200	4,016	3,280	736
41,900	39,200	11,555	10,340	1,215
69,900	67,200	25,905	24,420	1,485

*The rates apply to income earned in 1978.

the interest rate and (2) his or her marginal income tax rate. If an investor borrows funds and pays 8 per cent, then the *before-tax* interest rate is 8 per cent. Since the tax laws permit the deduction of interest before the computation of taxable income, the interest expense is shared with the federal government. As was illustrated in Table 24–1, the amount of this sharing depends on the investor's marginal income tax rate. Thus, the marginal tax rate must be used to determine the impact of the deduction on the true cost of the mortgage.

A simple example illustrates how the deduction reduces the effective cost of the debt. If an investor has a marginal tax rate of 40 per cent and borrows funds at 8 per cent interest, then the effective cost of the mortgage is 4.8 per cent. The effective cost of debt is

Cost of debt = before-tax interest rate (1 − marginal tax rate)

For this individual the calculation is

$$.048 = .08 \ (1 - .40)$$

This effective cost of debt (i_e) is expressed in symbolic form in Equation 1

(1) $$i_e = i(1 - t)$$

The effective cost of debt (i_e) is simply the product of the stated interest rate (i) and the tax deduction ($1 - t$), where t represents the investor's marginal income bracket. Obviously, the higher the individual's marginal tax rate, the lower is the true cost of borrowing.

The homeowner is also permitted to deduct from taxable income the property taxes that are paid on the home. As with the interest deduction, the homeowner must itemize expenses in order to receive the benefit of the deduction. The effect of itemizing property taxes is a reduction in the individual's taxable income and therefore a reduction in federal income

The deduction of property taxes

tax liability. Since the property tax charged by some local governments amounts to over $1000 on even moderately valued homes (e.g., $40,000 to $50,000 homes), the property tax deduction can result in substantial savings on income taxes for middle-income homeowners.

Renters cannot take advantage of these deductions

Owing to these deductions, several important expenditures or cash outlays associated with home ownership come from *before*-tax dollars. Most expenditures made by individuals come from *after*-tax dollars. Renters, who cannot take advantage of these deductions, pay rent with after-tax dollars. If an individual is in the 25 per cent tax bracket, that person must earn $1000 to make $750 in rental payments. However, that same individual could reduce taxes by $25 for every $100 paid in interest or property taxes on a house. The differences are even greater as the individual's taxable income, and therefore marginal tax rate, increases. If the tax bracket is 50 per cent, then $1500 in income is necessary to pay $750 in rent, but taxes are reduced by $50 for every $100 in deductible expenses. Home ownership certainly becomes more attractive as the individual's income and tax bracket rise.

CAPITAL GAINS DEFERMENT

Realized capital gains may be deferred

In addition to the previous deductions, a homeowner may receive a tax break when the home is sold. If the owner sells for a profit and reinvests the funds in another home within 18 months, any realized capital gains may be deferred. Thus, if a homeowner bought a house for $20,000 in 1960 and sold it for $45,000 in 1978, the $25,000 capital gain is not realized for federal income tax purposes as long as the homeowner buys a new house that costs at least $45,000. Instead of a capital gain, the cost basis of the initial house is transferred to the new home.

If the price of the new house were $50,000, its cost basis would be $25,000, which is the $20,000 cost of the original house plus the $5000 difference between the purchase price of the new house and the sale price of the old house. If the price of the new house were $40,000, then the cost would be less than the proceeds of the sale by $5000 ($45,000 − $40,000). This $5000 must be reported to the Internal Revenue Service as a capital gain. However, the tax on the remaining $20,000 in profit is deferred, and the cost basis of the new house becomes $20,000 (i.e., the cost basis of the original house).

A special exemption

Legislation was passed in 1978 that gives some homeowners an even larger tax break. This legislation exempts a capital gain of up to $100,000 from taxation provided the individual is over 55 years old. The investor is allowed this tax break only once. Under this legislation, a homeowner who bought a house for $20,000 in 1945 and upon retirement in 1980 at the age of 65 sold it for $85,000 could completely avoid taxation on the capital gain. In fact, the sale price would have to exceed $120,000 before the capital gain would be subject to capital gains tax.

INCOME-IN-KIND

Individuals either rent space or own it and "rent" it to themselves. **The flow of services**
The money that homeowners do not pay to a landlord may be viewed as
rent that they pay to themselves. The homeowner receives income-in-kind
(just as the owner of an Oriental rug or an art work does). Such income is
not subject to federal income tax. While home ownership generates a
tax-free flow of services, renting does not. Tax-free services, like deductions that reduce taxable income, increase the attractiveness of investing
in a house or a condominium. While the importance of this tax-free
income varies with the financial situation and income level of the investor,
it generally is more advantageous to own than to rent as the individual's
income and tax bracket rise.

In light of these tax advantages, it is not surprising to find that many
individuals are investing in homes. The ability to reduce taxable income
by certain deductions, the capital gains deferment, and the tax-free
income-in-kind all favor investments in residential homes. In addition,
the individual can generally obtain mortgage money at an effective cost
that is less than the rate of inflation. Since the tax laws favor the homeowner, investments in houses and condominiums may offer the individual one of the best possible investments.

These reasons for home ownership also apply to condominiums. A **Condominiums**
condominium is similar to an apartment, but instead of renting, the
individual owns the "apartment." The grounds and general facilities
belong to all of the owners of the condominiums, who pay a fee for their
maintenance.* The portion of the building that the individual owns may
be subsequently sold, and the seller may earn a capital gain if the property
is sold for a profit. In addition, since the individual owns and does not
rent the space, the tax advantages of home ownership apply. Thus, in
some ways ownership of a condominium is no different from ownership
of a home; a condominium may be treated as an investment just as a home
is.

The condominium is particularly attractive to people who have little
need or desire for lawns and shrubs. The maintenance of a home and the
grounds can be expensive in terms of both time and money. While the
condominium owner does not avoid the monetary cost of this maintenance, he or she does not have to expend the effort. If the individual lacks
the time or the inclination for home maintenance, the condominium may
offer the best of both worlds: the convenience of renting and the advantages of home ownership.

---

*The investor should read carefully the agreement that specifies what is covered by the
    maintenance fee. Some managements do not fulfill their part of the contracts and leave
    condominium owners with additional obligations that must be met to comply with local
    health and fire regulations.

RISKS AND RETURNS

A hedge against inflation

Many people believe that residential homes are among the best investments. The appreciation in the value of the home acts as a hedge against inflation, and at the same time the investor receives the services of the home.

The rate of price appreciation in residential homes is presented in Graph 24–1. The graph also presents the Dow Jones industrial average for the same time period. As is obvious from the graph, the prices of residential homes have appreciated while the Dow Jones industrial average has fluctuated but has shown no pattern of steady growth. This tends to confirm the belief that during the last decade home ownership has been a superior investment to the purchase of common stocks.

The increased cost of construction

Part of the explanation for the increase in home values is the increased cost of construction. The rising building costs of new homes translate into increased values for old homes. Old and new homes are substitutes for each other. If the cost of one rises relative to the cost of the other, buyers will seek to purchase the cheaper home. As the cost of new homes rises, some individuals will seek to purchase existing homes. This, in turn, will drive up the prices of older homes to keep them in line with the prices of newly constructed homes.

The increased demand

Another explanation for the increased value of homes is the continued increase in demand for them. Conventional wisdom suggests that home ownership is a good investment. This belief encourages individuals to buy homes even though they may have to take on more financial obliga-

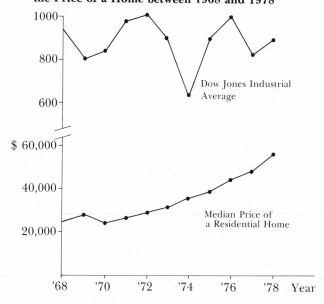

GRAPH 24–1. The Dow Jones Industrial Average and the Price of a Home between 1968 and 1978

tions than is prudent for their capacity to service the debt. As is subsequently discussed, the tendency on the part of some homeowners to use excessive amounts of debt financing (i.e., excessive financial leverage) is a major source of risk of investing in homes. However, to the extent that these individuals are willing and able to obtain this mortgage money, they increase the demand for homes and hence help to increase their prices.

The realized returns

Is an investment in a home really one of the best hedges against inflation? One recent study found that *only* private residential real estate offered complete protection against inflation.* Other investments, such as debt instruments, were a successful hedge against anticipated inflation, because their yields adjusted for the rate of inflation. However, these assets did not protect against unanticipated inflation. Only private residential real estate provided a safeguard against both expected and unexpected inflation. This study thus supports the conventional wisdom that home ownership is one of the best investments available, especially during inflationary times.

There are risks

Although in the aggregate home ownership has been a successful hedge against inflation, it does not follow that there are no risks or that home ownership is desirable for everyone. Home ownership can produce many headaches for the individual. Owners are responsible for maintenance, which (even if the cost is recouped when the home is sold) still requires a current outlay of cash and may require considerable effort. In addition, the cost of running a home rises with the rate of inflation. The increased costs of insurance, energy, and various other expenses (which are not deductible from taxable income) may strain the individual's budget if personal income does not rise as rapidly. Even though the resale value of the house may be increasing, that is not cash currently received. But it is current cash that is necessary to meet the expenses associated with running the home.

The excessive use of financial leverage

Another source of risk is the use of debt financing to acquire the home. Carrying the mortgage is a fixed monthly expense that must be met, or the holder of the mortgage may seize the home (through a court proceeding) and sell it to recoup the funds lent to the homeowner. Investors thus run considerable risk of loss should they be unable to maintain mortgage payments. Some individuals purchase expensive homes and anticipate that home values and their salaries will rise while mortgage payments remain constant, only to find that the mortgage payment becomes a real burden when adversity strikes (e.g., the loss of a job or an extended illness).

The different rates of price appreciation

The last source of risk is due to the fact that not all real estate values increase at the same rate. During the 1970s suburban homes appreciated in value more rapidly than city properties. However, pockets within some cities have appreciated very rapidly since 1975. If the individual had the

---

*Eugene F. Fama and G. William Schwert, "Asset Returns and Inflation," *Journal of Financial Economics*, 5 (November 1978), pp. 115–146.

foresight to buy in an area where home values subsequently appreciated, then the home has also served as a hedge against inflation. But many individuals do not have this foresight (or are not so lucky), and while their homes may have appreciated in value, the return need not have kept pace with the rate of inflation.

LAND

Unimproved land

An alternative means to invest in real estate is to purchase land, i.e., to acquire nonresidential land. Land is either unimproved or improved. Unimproved land is raw land, whereas improved land has curbs and sewers, has buildings constructed on it, or has been cleared for farming or other agricultural uses. Unimproved land is a passive investment that may require little action on the part of the investor. However, improved land may require considerable attention from the investor.

LEVERAGE AND TAX WRITE-OFFS

The potential return

The primary appeal of investing in nonresidential real estate is, of course, the potential return on the investment. This potential return is enhanced by the ability to use substantial amounts of financial leverage and to obtain advantageous tax write-offs. This use of leverage and tax write-offs may be seen in the following simple example. A piece of land costs $100,000. It may be purchased with a 20 per cent down payment, with the balance being financed through a mortgage loan at 9 per cent annual interest rate. The individual's investment out of pocket is only $20,000.

The tax write-offs

Land cost	$100,000
Loan	80,000
Equity	20,000

Several of the costs of carrying this investment (e.g., interest and property taxes) are tax deductible. If property tax rate is 3 per cent, then the deductible expenses are

Interest	$7200
Property tax	+3000
	$10,200

If the individual is in the 40 per cent tax bracket, the effective cost of carrying the land is reduced to

$$\$10,200 \ (1 - .4) = \$6120$$

There is a tax savings of $4080 ($10,200 − $6120). For an initial cash outlay of $20,000 and an annual cash outlay (after adjusting for taxes) of $6120, the individual has control of over $100,000 worth of land.

If the land were to appreciate in one year by 10 per cent, the investor would realize a $10,000 gross profit (excluding commissions). This gross profit is reduced to $3880 by the after-tax cash outlays for property taxes and interest ($10,000 − $6120). But this net profit still means that the investor earned a return of 19.4 per cent ($3,880 ÷ $20,000). It should be noted that in this example, even though the total cash outlay exceeded the gross profit ($10,200 outlay versus $10,000 profit); the tax savings of $4080 resulted in the investment being profitable and yielding a return of almost 20 per cent. The small down payment plus the deduction of interest and property taxes from taxable income significantly increased the return on the investor's funds.

The ability to use a large amount of borrowed funds and the capacity to write off certain (and important) expenses against taxable income increase the attractiveness of speculating in nonresidential real estate. Although the use of debt financing is not limited to investments in real estate, the ability to apply leverage is greater. The investor's capacity to use leverage in investments in stocks and bonds is subject to the margin requirements set by the Federal Reserve. And these requirements are considerably higher than the down payments required to purchase real estate.

A substantial amount of financial leverage

Of course, the use of a substantial amount of leverage does increase the element of risk. However, many investors believe that the continuation of inflation will tend to increase real estate values. The potential for loss is viewed as being smaller than the potential for profits, which justifies the bearing of risk that results from the use of a large amount of financial leverage.

Risk

UNIMPROVED LAND

Unimproved land by itself produces nothing and hence cannot generate a flow of income. Any income generated is the result of using the land for some activity, such as farming or mining. Even cutting down trees for sale as firewood requires expenditures on labor and tools. Since unimproved land cannot by itself generate income, the primary source of the return on such an investment is the potential for price appreciation.

No flow of income

For land to appreciate in value, it must have some potential for use in the future, such as lots for building, acreage for farming, or rights for mining. For the investment to earn a return commensurate with the risk, the investor must acquire land with potential for future value. Such future value may be difficult to foresee, as it depends on location, zoning requirements, road frontage or access to roads, and proximity to population centers. These factors can and do vary. Zoning laws may change, or the owner may be able to obtain a variance. New roads are built and the

Land must have some potential for use

population moves. All of these factors affect the value of land and in some cases even cause its value to decline.

Factors that reduce the return

The potential return on an investment in unimproved land may be reduced by several other factors. First, many state and local governments tax land as well as other real estate investments. Second, land may be difficult to sell. Although the title can be readily transferred, finding a buyer may take several months or even years. Third, real estate commissions on the sale of land may be as high as 10 per cent of the sale price. Therefore, the price of the land must appreciate sufficiently to recoup these commissions plus any other fees that may be associated with the sale (e.g., lawyer's fees) and still earn a profit.

To be a good investment, land must have the traits of other investments: marketability, income, and the potential for capital appreciation. Land offers little income, may be very difficult to sell, and has varying potential for future use. The investor should not be swayed by ads claiming "Buy land; they aren't making it any more!" There are still many acres of undeveloped land, but only that land which has the potential for future use will prove to be a desirable investment today. For example, there are undeveloped acres in the middle of Maine that could be very valuable for timber. However, if there is no access to the land and the trees, they are of little value.

The valuation

The valuation of land, then, is essentially no different from the valuation of any investment. The estimated future cash flow is discounted back to the present at the appropriate discount rate. Therein lies the clue to the problem of investing in unimproved land. The future cash flows are very uncertain, and the discount factor is quite subjective. For most investors, raw, undeveloped land is a poor investment. However, for those individuals who are willing to wait, forgo current income, and even pay out cash to carry the land, the return may be considerable if economic trends alter the unimproved land's potential.

IMPROVED LAND

A business venture

The investor may buy improved land, which includes land on which buildings are constructed, such as apartments, or land with other improvements, such as curbs and sewers. Such purchases are alternatives to investments in financial assets, but they may also be viewed as business ventures. As with any business venture, the management of improved land requires special knowledge that differs markedly from the knowledge employed in the selection of financial assets. The necessity to know such things as zoning and other land use laws, the laws regulating the relationship between landlord and tenant, and the management of accounts receivable (i.e., rent owed) make an investment in improved real estate more of a business venture than an investment in a financial asset, such as stocks or bonds.

This does not mean that the individual should avoid improved land as a viable investment. Obviously the investor must select among options that include both financial assets and business ventures. Investing in improved real estate is a possible alternative, but so are many other business ventures that may range from becoming a dealer in collectibles to the raising of champion dogs or publishing books. Ultimately, each individual must decide how to allocate his or her savings among the many possible alternatives, which include business ventures. These investments may offer superior returns if the investor has the specialized knowledge and capacity to manage them. However, many individuals lack either the knowledge or the inclination to risk their savings on a business venture and thus select financial assets. While business ventures are beyond the scope of this book, the individual should realize that such ventures offer alternatives to investments in financial assets.

An investor must select among alternatives

REAL ESTATE INVESTMENT TRUSTS

One means to invest indirectly in real estate is to buy shares in real estate investment trusts (commonly called REITs). These real estate trusts are another type of closed-end investment company. They receive the special tax treatment granted other investment companies (e.g., mutual funds). As long as a REIT derives 70 per cent of its income from real estate (e.g., interest on mortgage loans and rents) and distributes at least 90 per cent of the income as cash dividends, the trust is exempt from federal income tax. Thus, REITs, like mutual funds and other closed-end investment companies, are conduits through which earnings pass to the shareholders.

REIT — a type of investment company

Shares of REITs are bought and sold like the stocks of other companies. Some are traded on the New York Stock Exchange (e.g., Hubbard Real Estate Investment Trust), while others are traded on the American Stock Exchange (e.g., Washington REIT) and in the over-the-counter markets (e.g., Atlanta National REIT). The existence of these markets means that the shares of REITs may be readily sold. This ease of marketability certainly differentiates shares of REITs from other types of real estate investments.

Shares are traded like other stocks

Real estate investment trusts are also different from some forms of investments in real estate because they offer the potential for monetary income. Since REITs must distribute most of their income in order to maintain their tax status, most trusts distribute virtually all of their earned income. This often results in significant divided yields on investments in these shares. Selected dividend yields are illustrated in Exhibit 24–1, which presents the prices of the stock of five REITs, their dividends for the previous year, and the dividend yield (i.e., the dividend divided by the price of the stock). In many cases this yield exceeds 8.5 per cent annually.

The income is distributed

EXHIBIT 24–1. Selected REITs and Their Dividend Yields

Firm	Price of the Stock as of 1/8/79	Dividend Paid During the Previous 12 Months	Dividend Yield
Continental Illinois Properties	$15⅜	$1.30	8.5%
Hubbard REIT	16¾	1.52	9.1
Pennsylvania REIT	16½	1.45	8.8
Realty Income Trust	11¼	1.40	12.4
Washington REIT	21¾	1.88	8.6

*Source: *Barrons,* January 9, 1979.

The dividends fluctuate

Unlike the dividends of many firms (e.g., industrial firms or utilities), the dividends of REITS tend to fluctuate. Whereas other firms may seek to maintain stable dividends and increase them only after there has been an increase in earnings that management anticipates will continue, the dividends of REITs often fluctuate from year to year. This is the result of the tax regulations that require the distribution of earnings in order to maintain the trust's tax status. Thus, as earnings fluctuate, so do the dividends that are distributed. This fluctuation in earnings and hence in dividends is illustrated in Exhibit 24–2, which presents the earnings and dividends per quarter for Mass Mutual Mortgage and Realty Investors. As may be seen in the exhibit, the earnings and the

EXHIBIT 24–2. Quarterly Earnings and Dividends of
Mass Mutual Mortgage and Realty Investors*

Quarter Ending	Earnings per Share	Cash Dividends per Share
9/30/78	$.37	$.34
6/30/78	.35	.34
3/31/78	.32	.32
12/31/77	.31	.31
9/30/77	.31	.31
6/30/77	.30	.30
3/31/77	.29	.29
12/31/76	.27	.27
9/30/76	.27	.27
6/30/76	(.10)	.28
3/31/76	.27	.28
12/31/75	.26	.28
9/30/75	.33	.31
6/30/75	.30	.30
3/30/75	.28	.28

*Source: *Value Line Investment Survey.*

dividends vary almost each quarter. Shares of REITs, therefore, may not be desirable investments for individuals who need steady and stable sources of income. These investors may find such fluctuations in dividends undesirable and probably would prefer other stocks that offer high yields, such as those of utilities.

CLASSIFICATION OF REITs

REITs may be grouped according to either the types of assets they acquire or their capital structure. Equity trusts own property and rent it to other firms (i.e., they lease their property to others). Mortgage trusts make loans to develop property and finance buildings. There is a considerable difference between these two approaches to investing in real estate. Loans to help finance real estate, especially developmental loans, can earn high interest rates, but some of these loans can be very risky. Contractors may be unable to sell or lease the completed buildings, which may consequently cause them to default on their loans. In addition, any inflation in the value of the property cannot be enjoyed by the lender, who owns a fixed obligation.

Mortgage trusts

In an equity trust the REIT owns the property and rents space. This can also be risky because the properties may remain vacant. Unleased property, of course, does not generate any revenue, but the owner still has expenses, such as insurance, maintenance, and depreciation. Like any operation with few variable costs and many fixed expenses, there can be large fluctuations in the earnings of equity trusts. However, should there be an increase in property values, the trust may experience capital appreciation.

Equity trusts

The second method for differentiating REITs is according to their capital structure or the extent to which they use debt financing. Some trusts use virtually no debt financing, while others use a large amount of leverage. The latter can be very risky investments because the trusts borrow from one group either to lend or to invest directly in real estate. If their loans turn sour and the borrowers default or if the properties remain unrented, these trusts that employ extensive financial leverage will have difficulty meeting their own debt obligations.

The varying use of debt financing

These differences among REITs are illustrated in Exhibit 24–3, which lists ten trusts that were earning profits as of December 1977. The exhibit is constructed in two parts. The top half shows equity trusts whose primary assets are real estate. The second half presents trusts whose primary assets are mortgages. The entries in each section are listed in descending order according to their debt ratios (column 3). Thus, Hubbard REIT is an equity trust with virtually no debt, but General Growth Properties uses a great deal of leverage because over 85 per cent of its assets are financed by debt.

EXHIBIT 24–3. Selected REITs by Types of Assets and Capital Structure

Firm	Real Estate Owned as a Percentage of Real Estate Investments	Debt Ratio (Debt to Total Assets)
General Growth Properties	100%	85.1%
GREIT	98	69.7
First Fidelity Investors	92	68.8
Continental Illinois Properties	85	47.4
Hubbard REIT	95	9.1

Firm	Mortgages as a Percentage of Real Estate Investments	Debt Ratio (Debt to Total Assets)
M&T Mortgage	100%	65.5%
Realty ReFund	100	56.5
First Continental REIT	93	56.5
Lomas and Nettleton Mortgage	75	54.5
Hospital Mortgage Group	69	33.3

RETURNS EARNED BY INVESTMENTS IN REITs

REITs were popular

Initially, REITs were very popular, and several hundred came into existence. Many were financed with substantial amounts of debt. Commercial banks were only too happy to lend them funds because the loans were very profitable for the banks. Not only did the banks lend money to REITs, but they also formed advisory services and received management fees from the trusts.

REITs fell on hard times

While interest was being received and properties were leased, the extensive use of financial leverage posed no problems. However, when short-term interest rates rose to record heights in 1973 and 1974, many trusts found that they were unable to collect the interest owed them. Partially completed buildings were left unfinished, as there was virtually no demand for the properties. Those properties that did sell often went for prices that produced losses for the builders, who in turn defaulted on loans from the trusts. The trusts were then unable to meet their own interest payments. A substantial number defaulted on their debt. Some creditors seized properties, and a long period of reorganization for the trusts followed.

Today REITs are considerably different. Those that weathered the storm are much healthier firms today than the industry as a whole was in 1973 and 1974. Several of these stocks are now selling near their historic highs. However, many of the trusts (e.g., BT Mortgage, Chase Manhattan, and Cousins Mortgage and Equity) are still unprofitable and investments in them must be considered to be speculative. Such stocks should be considered only by investors who are willing to accept a substantial amount of risk.

THE VALUATION OF SHARES IN REITs

The valuation of shares in REITs is essentially no different from the valuation of any other security. The valuation model for common stocks that was presented in Chapter 14 also applies to the shares of REITs. According to that model, the value of stock depends upon the dividends that the firm will pay in the future brought back to their present value at the appropriate discount rate. However, the application of this model is particularly difficult with regard to the shares of REITs.

First, there is the problem of estimating future earnings and dividends. Although many firms grow and their dividends follow a steady pattern of growth in response to higher earnings, the dividends of REITs fluctuate from quarter to quarter. In many cases the dividend cannot grow because the earnings are not retained but are distributed.

Estimating future earnings and dividends

Earnings and dividends may be increased if the firm successfully increases its use of financial leverage. But this may also increase the element of risk, which may offset the value of the increased dividends. This suggests a second important problem in the valuation of the shares of REITs: the determination of the appropriate discount factor. Many REITs are very risky firms. Some have issued a substantial amount of debt, and others own real estate that may lie unrented. Risk is inherent in both sides of a REIT's balance sheet. For many of these firms, the type of assets they own and the sources from which they obtain financing may result in a substantial amount of both business risk and financial risk.

Accounting for risk

If the investor can account for these risks and estimate future dividends, the valuation of the stock becomes straightforward. This is illustrated in the following example, which uses the model of security valuation that was presented in Chapter 14. In this example the investor expects the following pattern of dividend payments:

Year	1	2	3	4	5
Dividend	$2.50	1.80	1.50	2.25	2.70

At the end of five years, the investor anticipates selling the shares for $30. If the anticipated dividend in the fifth year is $2.70, a sale price of $30 gives a dividend yield of 9 per cent ($2.70 ÷ $30), which this investor believes to be appropriate. However, this individual requires a 12 per cent return for bearing the risk. In order to earn a 12 per cent return in five years the present value (V) of the shares should be

An illustration

$$V = \frac{\$2.50}{(1+12)^1} + \frac{\$1.80}{(1+.12)^2} + \frac{\$1.50}{(1+.12)^3} + \frac{\$2.25}{(1+.12)^4} + \frac{\$2.70}{(1+.12)^5} + \frac{\$30}{(1+.12)^5}$$

$$V = \$2.50(.893) + \$1.80(.797) + \$1.50(.712) + \$2.25(.636) + \$2.70(.567)$$
$$+ 30(.567)$$

$$V = \$2.23 + \$1.43 + \$1.07 + \$1.43 + \$1.53 + \$17.01$$

$$V = \$24.70$$

If the current market price exceeds \$24.70, then this investor believes that the shares are overpriced and should be avoided. However, if the current market price is less than \$24.70, the shares are underpriced according to the investor and should be purchased.

The need for accurate forecasts

It must be emphasized that the value that any investor places on the shares through the use of this model is simply the result of the dividends that have been forecast and the application of the appropriate discount rate. This valuation model can only be as good as its inputs. Forecasting the future dividends of a REIT and determining the appropriate discount may be extremely difficult. However (as is discussed in detail in the next chapter), there is reason to believe that the current price of a share in a REIT does appropriately discount the future prospects of the firm.

SUMMARY

The poor performance of stocks during the 1970s and the increase in the rate of inflation have resulted in investors broadening their portfolios to include physical assets such as real estate. This chapter has been devoted to three types of real estate investments: home ownership, land ownership, and real estate investment trusts (REITs).

In recent years home ownership has been a particularly attractive investment. Since the individual must live somewhere, it may be more advantageous to own than to rent, especially if the cost of housing continues to rise. The federal income tax laws encourage investments in homes. In addition to untaxed income-in-kind, several expenses (e.g., interest and property taxes) are allowed as deductions in the determination of the individual's taxable income. Under some circumstances, capital gains taxes on the sale of a home may be deferred or even avoided.

Investors may also buy land. The potential return on such investments is also enhanced by the income tax laws, which permit the deduction of several expenses from taxable income. Unimproved land may appreciate in value if there is potential use for the land in the future. An investment in improved land is essentially a business venture and may earn a return from the cash flow generated by the improvements and the potential for capital appreciation.

Real estate investment trusts (REITs) offer investors an alternative means to invest in real estate. These trusts are a type of investment company, and stockholders enjoy the same tax benefits given to the stock-holders of other closed- and open-end investment companies. Real estate investment trusts either make loans to firms that develop and manage real estate or own properties and lease them.

The valuation of the shares of REITs is essentially no different from the valuation of any stock: Future dividend payments are brought back to the present value at the appropriate discount rate. However, estimating future dividends and determining the appropriate discount rate may be extremely difficult.

Terms to Remember

Effective cost of debt	Financial leverage	REIT
Long-term capital gains	Unimproved land	Equity trust
Income-in-kind	Improved land	Mortgage trust
Condominium		

Questions

1. What are the sources of risk from investing in real estate?

2. What is income-in-kind and how does it apply to an investment in a home?

3. What are the special tax advantages associated with investing in real estate?

4. What does it mean to say that a home is a hedge against inflation?

5. What is the difference between improved and unimproved land?

6. Why do investors use financial leverage when they purchase real estate?

7. What is the source of the return from an investment in land?

8. What is a REIT? What types of investments do such firms make? Define *financial leverage* and explain its effects on REITs. Why did many REITs fail in 1973 and 1974?

SELECTED READINGS

Beaton, William R.: *Real Estate Finance*. Englewood Cliffs, N.J.: Prentice-Hall, Inc., 1975.

Dasso, Jerome, Alfred A. Ring, and Douglas McFall: *Fundamentals of Real Estate*. Englewood Cliffs, N.J., Prentice-Hall, Inc., 1977.

Hall, John T. (ed.): *REITs: The First Decade*. Mequon, Wis., John T. Hall, Inc., 1974.

Mader, Chris: *The Dow Jones-Irwin Guide to Real Estate Investing*. Homewood, Ill., Dow Jones-Irwin, Inc., 1975.

Rudnitsky, Howard: "Speculating in White Elephants." *Forbes* (December 1, 1977), pp. 79–86.

Seldin, Maury: *Land Investment*. Homewood, Ill., Dow Jones-Irwin, Inc., 1975.

Learning Objectives

After completing this chapter you should be able to

1. Differentiate the strong from the weak form of the efficient market hypothesis.

2. State the implication of the efficient market hypothesis for the individual investor.

3. Describe the importance of financial goals.

4. Match types of assets with individual financial goals.

5. Construct a balance sheet of your assets and liabilities.

6. Construct a cash budget for your receipts and disbursements.

7. Explain the role of an individual's financial plan.

chapter 25

EFFICIENT MARKETS AND PORTFOLIO CONSTRUCTION

The investor should know the various investments that are available. The investor should also understand both the efficient market in which investments in securities are made and the need to construct a portfolio designed to satisfy specific goals. This chapter adds these two elements to the investment alternatives and analytical techniques that have been previously discussed.

The chapter begins with a brief reminder that the current value of an asset is primarily related to the future benefits it offers to the buyer. This is followed by a discussion of the efficient market hypothesis. This hypothesis suggests that security markets are very competitive and that it is very unlikely the individual investor will be able to outperform the market.

The chapter and book end with a discussion of matching the portfolio with the investor's goals. There are many reasons for saving and accumulating assets. Not all assets, however, will meet specific goals. Investors must specify investment goals and analyze their resources in order to construct portfolios with a purpose. Only then can financial planning aid in the construction of the best portfolio to meet an individual's needs and financial goals.

VALUATION REVIEWED

Forecasting

Conceptually, the pricing of the various assets discussed in the text is easy. The future benefits that the asset offers are brought back to their present value by the appropriate discount rate. Unfortunately, the execution of this procedure can often be very difficult because of problems in estimating the future benefits of an asset and in determining the appropriate discount rate.

Income and price appreciation

The future benefits include the income generated by the asset, such as interest or dividends, and price appreciation. For example, a stock may pay dividends and may appreciate in value; a bond may pay interest and the principal may be redeemed. A house offers income-in-kind and may appreciate in value, and the value of collectibles may rise. None of these events is certain, as they all involve risk.

The valuation of debt

Debt instruments tend to be the safest investments. The amount of interest is usually fixed, and the date of maturity is known. This greatly facilitates their valuation. All that is needed is the appropriate discount factor to bring the future interest payments and principal back to their present values. The determination of the discount factor is relatively easy, as rating services rank bonds according to risk classes, and the risk associated with other debt instruments, such as federal government debt or savings accounts, is small. The valuation of debt, then, has few of the substantive problems associated with the valuation of other assets.

The valuation of stock

The valuation of stock requires forecasts of what the future earnings will be, whether the company will distribute them as cash dividends or retain them, and how the market will value the earnings in the future. Even after estimating these variables, the investor still must determine the appropriate discount factor. Obviously, none of this is easy from a pragmatic point of view. However, as is discussed in the subsequent section, the individual investor is partially relieved of making these estimates. The efficient market tends to value securities in accordance with the general principle of appropriately discounting future dividends, growth, and possible price appreciation.

The valuation of other assets

The valuation of assets other than securities is even more difficult. The estimation of income-in-kind from a house or a collectible is very subjective. The future price of the asset is unknown, and in some instances there may not even be a market for a particular item, in which case it has virtually no value.

In addition, although securities are purchased in an efficient market, the investor may not buy and sell other assets in such a market. This means that the price need not reflect the intrinsic value of the asset, i.e., the price may not reflect the asset's potential flow of income or price appreciation. Since the markets for assets other than securities are dispersed, and all transactions are, in effect, over-the-counter, the dissemination of information and prices is limited. This tends to reduce the efficiency of markets and to result in prices that can be too high or too low. While such a situation may offer excellent opportunities for the astute and the knowledgeable, it can also spell disaster for the novice.

THE EFFICIENT MARKET HYPOTHESIS

It is perhaps the conceit of some individuals to think that they can outperform the market. But the efficient market hypothesis suggests that they cannot. This hypothesis asserts that the security markets are so efficient that the current price of a stock properly values its future dividends and earnings, which are appropriately discounted back to the present. Today's price, then, is a true measure of the security's worth. For the individual investor, security analysis that is designed to determine if the stock is overpriced or underpriced is futile, because the stock is neither.

Current prices are correct valuations

The second facet of the efficient market hypothesis concerns the speed with which security prices adjust to new information. The hypothesis asserts that the market adjusts prices extremely rapidly as new information is disseminated. In the modern world of advanced communication, information is rapidly disbursed in the investment community. The market then adjusts security prices in accordance with the impact of the news on the firm's future earnings and dividends. By the time that the individual investor has learned the information, security prices probably will have already changed. Thus, the investor will not be able to profit from acting on the information.

Prices adjust rapidly

The important implication of this theory is that the individual investor cannot consistently beat the market but will tend to earn a return that is consistent with the market. While this statement will subsequently be slightly modified, the student should realize that the probability of outperforming the market over any extended period is very small. That does not mean that an investor cannot outperform (or underperform) the market during a short period of time. During a brief period, such as a year, some investors will earn returns that are different from the return earned by the market. However, there is very little chance that those investors will be able to achieve such results for a period of several years. Before discussing this implication further and its effect on the individual investor's strategy, let us proceed to the two forms of the efficient market hypothesis.

An investor cannot consistently outperform the market

THE WEAK FORM

**The price reflects
public information**

The weak form of the efficient market hypothesis asserts that the current price of a stock reflects the public's knowledge of the company. This knowledge includes both the firm's past history and its potential for the future. One individual's analysis of this information cannot be expected to produce superior investment results. Notice that the hypothesis does not state that the analysis cannot produce superior results. It just asserts that superior results should not be expected. However, there is the implication that while the analysis of information may produce superior results in some cases, it will not produce superior results over many investment decisions.

This conclusion should not be surprising to anyone who thinks about the investment process. Many investors and analysts study the same information. Their thought processes and training are similar, and they are in competition with one another. Certainly, if one perceives a fundamental change in a particular firm, this information will be readily transferred to other investors, and the price of the security will change. The competition among the potential buyers and among the potential sellers will result in the security's price reflecting the firm's intrinsic worth. Only if one is able to perceive *and* act before the crowd will one beat the crowd. And even if the individual achieves this once, there is no reason to believe that he or she will continuously be able to achieve such superior investment results.

Inside information

There is, however, one major exception to this conclusion of the weak form of the efficient market hypothesis. If the investor has access to inside information, that individual may consistently achieve superior results. In effect, this individual has information that is not known by the general investing public. Such information as dividend cuts or increments, new discoveries, or potential take-overs may have significant impact on the value of the firm and its securities. If the investor has advance knowledge of such events and has the time to act, that individual should be able to achieve superior investment returns.

Of course, most investors do not have access to inside information or at least do not have access to information concerning a number of firms. An individual may have access to privileged information concerning a firm for whom he or she works. But as was previously pointed out, the use of such information for personal gain is illegal. To achieve continuous superior results the individual would have to have a continuous supply of correct inside information. Probably few, if any, investors have this continuous supply. This lack of inside information probably explains why both fundamentalists and technical analysts watch sales and purchases by insiders as a means to glean a clue as to the true future potential of the firm as seen by its management.*

---

*The student should review the section on inside information and its usefulness to investors that was presented in Chapter 17.

THE STRONG FORM

The strong form of the efficient market hypothesis asserts that not even access to inside information can be expected to result in superior investment performance. Once again, this does not mean that an individual who acts on inside information cannot achieve superior results. It means that these results cannot be expected and that success in one case will tend to be offset by failure in other cases, so over time the investor will not achieve superior results.

This conclusion rests on a very important assumption: Inside information cannot be kept inside! Too many people know about the activities of a firm. This information is discerned by a sufficient number of investors, and the price of the firm's securities adjusts for the informational content of this inside knowledge. Notice that the conclusion that the price of the stock still reflects its intrinsic value does not require that all investors know this additional information. All that is necessary is for a sufficient number to know. Furthermore, the knowledge need not be acquired illegally. It is virtually impossible to keep some information secret, and there is a continual flow of rumors concerning a firm's activities. Denial by the firm is not sufficient to stop this spread of rumors, and when some are later confirmed, it only increases the credibility of future rumors as a possible means to gain inside information.

Although considerable empirical work has been designed to verify both forms of the efficient market hypothesis, these tests seem to verify the weak form.* The use of privileged information may result in superior investment performance, but the use of publicly known information cannot be expected to produce superior investments. Thus, neither technical nor fundamental analysis is of help to the individual investor, because the current price of a stock fully incorporates this information.

It is particularly important that the individual investor understand this conclusion and several of its implications. The first implication is that the market is efficient because investors and financial analysts are using this known information in a rational way. This information is being digested, and its implications for the future performance of the firm are being properly discounted back to the present. Thus, the individual cannot use public information for superior investment results because the investment community is using it! If the investment community did not use this information and the correct valuation models, then the individual could achieve superior investment results. It is the very fact that financial analysts and investors are competent and trying to beat the other that helps to produce the efficient market.

The second implication is that while security markets are efficient, they are not necessarily equally efficient. The hypothesis applies pri-

Even inside information may not produce superior results

Empirical evidence supports the weak form

The hypothesis need not apply to all assets

*For a discussion of this research, see James H. Lorie and Mary T. Hamilton, *The Stock Market — Theories and Evidence*, Homewood, Ill., Richard D. Irwin, Inc., 1973, pp. 70–112.

marily to the large firms with securities listed on organized exchanges. There may be, however, small over-the-counter securities that are fundamentally sound but are not accurately priced. Perhaps the individual investor may be able to identify these undervalued smaller firms.

The third and perhaps most important implication of the efficient market hypothesis applies to an individual's portfolio. The efficient market hypothesis seems to suggest that the individual investor could randomly select a diversified portfolio of securities and earn a return consistent with the market as a whole. Furthermore, once the portfolio has been selected, there is no need to change it. The strategy, then, is to buy and hold. Such a policy offers the additional advantage of minimizing commissions.

The need to match the portfolio with the investor's goals

The problem with this naive policy is that it fails to consider the reasons an investor saves and acquires securities and other assets. The goals behind the portfolio are disregarded, and different goals require different portfolio construction. Furthermore, goals and conditions change, which in turn require changes in an individual's portfolio. Altering the portfolio for the sake of change will probably result in additional commissions and not produce superior investment returns. However, when the investor's goals or financial situation changes, then the portfolio should be altered in a way that is consistent with the new goals and conditions.

The investor should earn a return consistent with the market

The importance to the individual investor of the efficient market hypothesis is not the implication that investment decision making is useless. Instead, it brings to the foreground the environment in which the investor must make decisions. The hypothesis should make the investor realize that investments in securities will not produce superior returns. Rather, the investor should earn a return over a period of time that is consistent with the return earned by the market as a whole. This means that individual investors should devote more time and effort to the specifications of their investment goals and the selection of securities to meet those goals than to the analysis of individual securities. Since such analysis cannot be expected to produce superior returns, it takes resources and time away from the important questions of why we save and invest.

THE INVESTMENT STRATEGY

Define the purpose

In order to construct an optimal portfolio, the investor must start by defining the purpose of the portfolio. There has to be some goal (or goals) to offer guidance for the types of assets that should be included. In addition to the specification of investment goals, the investor should determine his or her willingness to accept risk. Every investor must bear some risk, but individuals' aversion to risk varies. Some people are more capable of enduring the stress and strain associated with risk and may even enjoy some elements of risk taking. This capacity to endure risk may have an important impact on the composition of the portfolio.

After establishing investment goals, the investor should analyze the environment in which he or she exists. Environments obviously vary with individuals, and each affects the portfolio that best meets the individual's needs. The investor needs to be aware of the resources and sources of income with which he or she has to work. After analyzing the environment and resources, the investor can construct a plan designed to fulfill the investment goals within the environmental and financial constraints.

Analyze the environment

THE SPECIFICATION OF INVESTMENT GOALS

The purpose of investing is to transfer purchasing power from the present to the future. A portfolio is a store of value designed to meet the individual investor's reasons for postponing the consumption of goods and services from the present to the future. The investor should determine the purpose for saving (i.e., the goals of the portfolio) before actually deciding on the composition of the portfolio.

Several reasons for saving and investing were offered in the introductory chapter. These include

Possible goals

1. the capacity to meet financial emergencies
2. the desire to finance future purchases of goods and services
3. the need for additional income
4. the desire to leave a sizable estate
5. the inclination to speculate and the enjoyment derived from accumulating and playing the investment game

These are not all of the possible reasons for saving and investing, but they are certainly indicative of several. motivations for constructing a portfolio. The following paragraphs discuss the possible assets that will meet these goals.

The Capacity to Meet Financial Emergencies

While this financial goal can be well defined, planning to have funds to meet financial emergencies involves considerable uncertainty. The investor does not know when (or even if) the money will be needed. Long-term securities that may be used to meet a financial goal that has an identifiable time period are inappropriate to meet the goal of having sufficient funds to deal with emergencies. Assets that are very liquid (i.e., that are easily converted into cash without a loss) should be chosen to fulfill this investment goal. These include

Liquidity and safety are stressed

savings accounts   short-term debt   series EE bonds

Savings accounts and savings certificates that mature quickly (e.g., six months) may be readily converted into cash. While their yields are lower than would be available from debt with a longer maturity, they offer the important advantages of the safety of the principal and the ease of conversion into cash.

Short-term debt investments, such as treasury bills, commercial paper, and series EE bonds, are also excellent investments for funds that are being held for emergencies. Although such investments do not maximize the investor's yield, they are more productive than leaving the money in a checking account. If the investor lacks sufficient funds to buy treasury bills, money market mutual funds offer a viable alternative. Of course, the problem of the amount of the minimum unit of purchase does not apply to series EE bonds, and they offer the additional advantage of deferring income taxes until the funds are needed and the bonds redeemed.

The Desire to Finance Future Purchases

By the nature of emergencies, it is impossible to know when the funds will be needed, but this does not apply to other goods and services. The desire to purchase a specified good or service often has a known time dimension. Financing an education and planning for retirement are both examples of consumption expenditures that will occur at a particular time in the future. Individuals know approximately when their children will be in college or when they will retire. While there may be some deviation in the time of the actual occurrence, the investor knows approximately when these events will happen and can plan now to have the funds to finance the purchase.

Long-term assets and safety are stressed

Consider the financing of a child's college education. If the child is currently eight years old, the funds for a college education will be needed in approximately ten years.* What assets are desirable to meet this particular financial goal? The answer to the question is primarily long-term but relatively safe assets. They should be long-term because the funds will not be needed for many years and such investments tend to offer a superior yield to short-term assets. They should be relatively safe because one should not want to gamble with funds earmarked for this education. What assets are long-term and relatively safe? There are many, including

conservative growth stocks

high-yielding utility stocks

long-term bonds

long-term savings certificates

---

*Although the future cost of the education is unknown, the parents can systematically accumulate assets to begin to meet this anticipated expense.

Long-term growth stocks offer possible appreciation in the investor's capital. Since the emphasis is on the need for funds many years in the future, steady long-term growth is one means to meet his goal. In effect, this strategy suggests that the investor select known growth stocks, such as IBM, rather than riskier stocks that may offer a higher return but require that the investor bear more risk.

Growth stocks

Utility stocks that offer a high yield may also earn a considerable amount of money over time. Stocks with an 8 or 9 per cent annual dividend yield may double an investment in less than nine years. However, the investor cannot spend the dividends as they are received or the amount of savings will not grow. This forced saving may be achieved by opting for the dividend reinvestment plans that many utilities offer their stockholders. Since the investor never receives the cash dividends, they cannot be spent. Hence, such plans offer a painless means to save for a specified goal.

Utilities with generous dividends

Long-term bonds are also an excellent means to save for a certain time period. Since the bonds mature at specified times, the investor can purchase an issue that will be redeemed at the desired time in the future. For example, if the funds are needed after ten years, the investor may buy bonds that mature after ten years. If the investor knows when the money will be needed, a portfolio of bonds may be constructed that matches the maturity dates of the bond and the time when the funds will be required.

Long-term bonds

Savings certificates that are available from commercial banks and other savings institutions also offer the advantages of higher yield and specified maturity dates. In addition, there is no commission charge to acquire them. However, the investor may pay a substantial penalty if the certificates must be redeemed prior to maturity. Therefore, the investor should choose certificates whose maturity date coincides with the time the funds will be needed.

Savings certificates

Each of the aforementioned alternatives requires that the investor choose an individual asset for purchase. The investor may avoid this decision by purchasing shares in an investment company that meets the specific investment goal. Investment companies that specialize in growth or in high-yielding securities offer another means to accumulate funds designed to finance a specific expenditure in the future, such as a college education. Obviously, investment companies that specialize in money market instruments or special situations may not meet this investment goal and should be avoided.

Although the preceding discussion used the financing of a college education as the investor's goal, other similar goals could have been used. For example, the accumulation of funds to help finance retirement is a similar goal. Once again, the investor knows approximately when the event (i.e., retirement) will occur. The portfolio should then be constructed with assets that can be converted into cash at a specified time in the future. This general principle actually applies to any portfolio whose purpose is to meet a goal, the time of which is known with some degree of certainty.

The Need for Additional Future Income

Safety and income

Some investors save and purchase assets so that they may have a flow of income in the future. These investors are not particularly concerned with capital appreciation, but they are concerned with the general safety of their assets. This is especially true if this investment income is to be a primary source of the individual's total income. Although such investors may receive social security payments and other forms of supplemental income, their investment income is extremely important to their well-being. Such investors should choose assets that offer generous income and assure to some extent the safety of the principal. These include

preferred stock

bonds

federal government securities

long-term savings certificates

All of these assets tend to offer generous yields and the relative safety of the principal. The safest is, of course, the long-term debt of the federal government, but these bonds offer returns that are less than those which may be earned on high quality corporate debt, such as bonds issued by AT&T. Preferred stocks are the riskiest of the alternatives listed but may offer the highest yield. These bonds and preferred stock are easily sold should the investor need immediate cash. Long-term savings certificates also offer higher yields than shorter term savings accounts and savings certificates. The saver, however, must pay a penalty if the certificates are redeemed prior to maturity.

Stocks with a history of dividend increments

This investor should also consider common stocks with generous dividends or with a history of dividend increments. While the aforementioned securities may be safer than corporate stock, they do not offer the possibility of growth in income. Such growth may be very desirable, especially during periods of inflation. Without an increase in income, the investor's purchasing power is diminished. Common stocks do offer the possibility of increased dividends, and some companies (e.g., telephone utilities) have a history of annual dividend increments. Such common stocks offer the investor who is primarily concerned with income and the safety of the principal a means to obtain some increment in income for accepting only a modest degree of risk.

The Desire to Leave an Estate

The desire to leave a substantial estate may be fulfilled by virtually any of the assets discussed in this text. However, there is less emphasis on liquidity and a flow of income. Instead, the portfolio should stress assets whose values tend to appreciate over time. These would include

Less need for liquidity and safety

growth stocks

art objects and various collectibles

real estate

convertible bonds

Growth stocks and convertible bonds place emphasis on price appreciation, but they also generate some flow of income. Collectibles, art work, and real estate produce no income in cash but do offer income-in-kind. The quantifiable yield on such investments is limited to price appreciation. If the investor desires to accumulate a sizable estate, he or she should be willing to acquire assets that not only may be very illiquid but also may be somewhat risky. However, if these assets are held for a sufficient time to average out price fluctuations, they should appreciate in value. Although the time of one's death is unknown, an estate portfolio still places emphasis on those assets with potential for long-term growth. Many of these assets would not be appropriate in a portfolio stressing safety and liquidity.

Potential growth is stressed

The Desire to Speculate

Many assets are available that may satisfy an investor's desire to speculate. These include

A large potential return is stressed

poor quality debt

stocks of small and risky companies

options

commodities

collectibles

real estate

Poor quality bonds offer higher potential return as compensation for the additional risk. Debentures, income bonds, even bonds in default may produce additional speculative gains should the company improve its financial position, which will improve the quality of the bonds. There certainly have been many bonds that at one time fell on bad times, yet returned to respectability and rewarded those willing to bear the risk.

Additional risk

Small growth firms

All large companies were small at one time. Although purchasing the shares of small or risky companies may often result in substantial losses (especially if the firm should fail, as many do), the rewards can be substantial if the firm succeeds. Investors who purchased the shares of Coca-Cola, IBM, or Johnson & Johnson when these firms were small and just emerging were well rewarded for bearing this risk. Of course, hindsight is considerably better than foresight; it is extremely difficult to identify which of today's small but growing companies will be the success stories of tomorrow. But it is the possibility of such success that stimulates speculators' willingness to bear the risk and purchase the shares of emerging companies.

Options and commodities

Options and commodity contracts may offer the speculator the greatest satisfaction. While it may take years for poor quality debt to improve or for small companies to grow, the action with options and commodity contracts is very rapid. Both are a means to apply leverage to one's position. The potential for large and sudden price changes is substantial. If the price of the underlying stock changes, the resulting change in the price of the option will be magnified. The same applies to the value of commodity contracts. The small margin requirement magnifies the potential return (or loss) on the speculator's funds. This potential for fast action and large percentage gains increases the appeal of these very risky assets to investors who seek to speculate.

Collectibles

Although not all speculators will invest in collectibles and real estate, these two types of assets offer special appeal to some investors who are willing to bear substantial risk. Investing in these assets requires specialized knowledge, and the possibility of buying a collectible or real estate at a minimal price and then seeing one's appraisal of the asset's potential value prove to be correct should offer special appeal to some investors who are willing to accept the risk for the possibility of a large return.

THE ANALYSIS OF THE INDIVIDUAL'S ENVIRONMENT AND RESOURCES

The need to be aware of one's resources

In addition to specifying their investment goals, individuals should be aware of their environment and financial resources. These differ from person to person, and what may be the correct investment strategy for one individual may not be correct for another. While this seems self-evident, many individuals do not recognize their environment and the resources they have.

Environments differ

One's environment includes such factors as age, health, employment, and family. A young bachelor in good health who is securely employed does not need the same portfolio as a young man with a family, even if his health is excellent and his employment is secure. The more current obligations an individual has (be they debt or family), the greater is the need for a conservative portfolio of assets. Such assets should stress safety and liquidity so that short-term obligations may be met as they occur. In contrast, the young bachelor could afford to bear more risk in the selection of a portfolio.

In addition to the individual's environment, the investor should take an accurate account of resources. This may be done by constructing two lists. One enumerates what is owned and owed, and the other enumerates cash receipts and disbursements. The former is, of course, a balance sheet, whereas the latter is effectively a cash budget.

Enumerate what one owns and owes

The entries for an individual's balance sheet are given in Exhibit 25–1. It lists all of the individual's assets and liabilities. The difference between these assets and liabilities is the individual's net worth (which would be the estate if the individual were to die at the time the balance sheet is constructed). For clarity, the individual should list short-term assets and then long-term assets, and the same should be done with liabilities. In effect, this balance sheet is no different from the balance sheet presented in Chapter 8.

The construction of such a balance sheet is relatively easy. The difficult part is enumerating the individual's assets and placing a value on them. Estimates for personal effects are probably sufficient, but the individual should ascertain the current value of several assets that are not so obvious. These include the present value of one's life insurance, pension plan, and social security death benefits. These are easily omitted in the construction of an individual's balance sheet, but they are very important. If sufficient funds have already accumulated in an individual's life insurance policy or pension plan, the need to save in order to meet one's family obligations in case of death is reduced. The individual, then, can devote more resources to investments that meet other goals.

The problem of placing a value on some assets

The entries in the balance sheet in Exhibit 25–1 are probably more detailed than is necessary for most individuals. Many of the categories of assets and liabilities illustrated in the exhibit do not apply to all individuals. However, it is probably better to be excessively detailed in the construction of the balance sheet so that the individual is better aware of his or her financial situation.

After one enumerates what is owned and owed, the next step is to analyze the flow of income and expenses. This is essentially a cash budget for the individual. An example of the entries for an individual's cash budget is given in Exhibit 25–2. This list of all sources of cash (e.g., salaries, interest, and dividends) and disbursements is probably more detailed than would apply to most investors, but it does show the variety of possible sources and uses of funds. The difference between the receipts and disbursements is the fund that should be profitably invested to meet the financial goals specified by the investor.

Analyze the flow of income and expenses

THE ESTABLISHMENT OF
FINANCIAL PLANS

Establish a financial strategy

After specifying financial goals and analyzing one's financial position, the investor can establish a plan or course of action. This plan is the strategy by which the investor will fulfill the financial goals. While

---

EXHIBIT 25–1. An Individual's Assets and Liabilities

Assets

Current Assets
  Cash and checking accounts
  Savings accounts
  Savings certificates (one year or less to maturity)
  Money market instruments (treasury bills, commercial paper, money market mutual funds)
  Personal effects
Long-term Assets
  Real Estate
    a. House
    b. Land
    c. Other real estate
  Personal Effects
    a. Automobile
    b. Furniture
  Insurance
    a. Cash value of life insurance
    b. Social security death benefits
    c. Cash value of pension
  Securities
    a. Stocks
    b. Bonds
    c. Options
    d. Mortgages receivable
    e. Savings certificates (more than one year to maturity)
  Business Assets
    a. Equipment
    b. Shares in partnerships
    c. Shares in closed corporations
  Other Assets
    a. Gold and silver
    b. Art objects
    c. Antiques
    d. Stamps and coins

Liabilities

Current Liabilities
  Current portion of mortgage
  Credit card payments due
  Current portion of installment loans
  Quarterly estimated income tax payments
  Property taxes
  Annual insurance payments
  Borrowings against securities and insurance
Long-term Debt
  Mortgage
  Installment loans
  Other long-term loans

EXHIBIT 25–2.   An Individual's Receipts and Disbursements

Receipts
  Wages and salaries
  Dividends
  Interest
  Rent
  Repayment of debt owed
  Social security payments
  Pension payments
  Payments from partnerships
                              Total Receipts

Disbursements
  Mortgage payments
  Maintenance of property
  Taxes
  Personal effects (clothing, food, and the like)
  Utilities
  Insurance
  Entertainment and travel
  Gifts
  Transportation
  Installment payments
  Phone
  Furniture
                              Total Disbursements

---

plans will vary among individuals, the importance of such a plan applies to all. It is the means to the end — the means to financial success.

Plans require the establishment of priorities. Those financial goals **Establish priorities** that are more important should be fulfilled first. After investments have been made to satisfy these needs, the next most important goals should be attacked. In this way the investor systematically saves and invests to meet the specified goals. For example, an individual may determine the following goals and their priority:

funds to meet emergencies

funds to finance a child's education

funds to finance retirement

funds for an estate

The initial goal, then, is sufficient liquid assets to cover emergencies (e.g., unemployment or extended illness). After this goal has been met, the investor proceeds to save and accumulate assets designed to finance the college education. The process is continued until all of the goals have been met.

While such planning is the backbone of portfolio construction, the **Financial planning** investor must realize that goals and financial conditions do change. **is the backbone** Such changes may alter the general financial plan. The birth of an addi-

The need to reevaluate the financial plan

tional child, the death of a spouse, a promotion, and many other possible events shape our lives and further alter our financial plans. The individual must be willing to adjust. If one financial plan becomes outmoded or is incorrect, the investor should act rapidly to change the portfolio. This requires that investors be continually aware of their financial situation and environment and of the competition of the assets they own and the liabilities they owe.

Portfolio planning and management are not easy tasks that can be performed casually and infrequently. It is for this reason that many investors allow others who are more versed in the subject to do their financial planning. Trust departments of commercial banks, financial planning consultants, and the managements of investment companies partially relieve the individual of making investment decisions. However, the investor should realize that the establishment of financial goals is still an individual responsibility. Without financial goals, financial consultants cannot help the individual. In addition, the individual must realize that professional money managers cannot perform miracles. Their fees must ultimately come from the indivduals who employ them. This, of course, reduces the return that investors earn on their funds, but it is the price they pay for being relieved of the necessity of making investment decisions.

Investing — an exciting challenge

Individuals who are willing to make their own investment decisions face an exciting challenge. According to the efficient market hypothesis, the return they earn should, on the average, match the return earned by the average investor. However, individuals who manage their own portfolios have the additional satisfaction of making their own decisions. To best make financial decisions, these investors need to be well aware of (1) the alternative investments available to them, (2) their financial goals, and (3) their resources. With this knowledge they can construct a strategy to fulfill their financial goals and still enjoy the excitement associated with investing.

SUMMARY

Investors, especially those who buy and sell securities, operate in very efficient markets. There are sufficient numbers of well-informed financial analysts and investors to assure that security prices measure correctly the current view of a firm's future potential. As new information is learned, it is assimilated and the prices of securities adjust for the impact that this additional information may have on future earnings and dividends.

Since investors buy and sell in efficient markets, there is little that the individual investor can do to beat the market. The efficient market hypothesis suggests that the individual investor cannot use known information to select securities that will consistently outperform the market.

Neither traditional fundamental analysis nor technical analysis is of much help for the sole investor. While inside information may be very useful in the selection of securities that will subsequently earn a superior return, this information is not available to the general investing public.

Since individual investors will not, in all likelihood, be able to beat the market, they should probably devote more time to identifying their financial goals and constructing portfolios that are consistent with these goals. After identifying their reasons for saving and investing, individuals should analyze their financial position to ascertain both their assets and liabilities and the flow of their receipts and disbursements. Then a portfolio can be constructed that is consistent with the individual's goals and resources. While such a portfolio will probably not outperform the return earned on assets of comparable risk, it should help to achieve the individual investor's financial objectives.

Terms to Remember

Efficient market hypothesis: strong form weak form	Financial planning	Short-term assets
	Liquidity	Growth stocks
	Safety	Savings certificates
Inside information	Income	Options
Financial goals	Long-term assets	Valuation

QUESTIONS

1. Why are security markets efficient? Why is fundamental analysis important but not necessarily important for individual investors?

2. What is the primary difference between the weak and strong forms of the efficient market hypothesis?

3. Do the conclusions of the efficient market hypothesis mean that professional security analysts are incompetent? Explain.

4. Why should investors specify their financial goals?

5. Study the portfolio in Exhibit 3–4 in Chapter 3. Comment on its appropriateness for (1) an individual seeking additional income, (2) a speculator, and (3) an individual seeking to build an estate.

6. What types of assets are appropriate holdings for financial emergencies?

7. Why should investors analyze their resources and obligations?

8. What role does financial planning play in the construction of a portfolio?

SELECTED READINGS

Arditti, Fred D., and W. Andrew McCollough: "Can Analysts Distinguish Between Real and Randomly Generated Stock Prices?" *Financial Analysts Journal,* (November–December 1978), pp. 70–74.

Baumol, William J.: *The Stock Market and Economic Efficiency.* New York, Fordham University Press, 1965.

Brealey, Richard A.: *An Introduction to Risk and Return From Common Stocks.* Cambridge, Mass., MIT Press, 1969.

Brealey, Richard A.: *Security Prices in a Competitive Market.* Cambridge, Mass., MIT Press, 1971.

Fama, Eugene F.: "Efficient Capital Markets: A Review of Theory and Empirical Work." *The Journal of Finance,* (May 1970), pp. 383–423.

Hallman, G. Victor, and Jerry S. Rosenbloom: *Personal Financial Planning.* New York, McGraw-Hill Book Co., 1975.

Malkiel, Burton G.: *A Random Walk Down Wall Street.* New York, W. W. Norton & Co., Inc., 1973.

Porter, Thomas, and Durwood Alkire: *Wealth: How to Achieve It!* Reston, Va., Reston Publishing Co., Inc., 1976.

Rukeyser, Louis: *How To Make Money in Wall Street.* Garden City, N.Y., Doubleday & Co., Inc., 1974.

Sokoloff, Kiril: *The Thinking Investor's Guide to the Stock Market.* New York, McGraw-Hill Book Co., 1978.

Van Caspel, Venita: *Money Dynamics — How to Build Financial Independence.* Reston, Va., Reston Publishing Co., Inc., 1975.

Glossary

accelerated depreciation — the writing off of plant and equipment in such a way that most of the cost is recovered in the early years of the asset's life.

accrued interest — interest that has been earned but not received.

acid test — current assets, excluding inventory, divided by current liabilities; a measure of liquidity.

ADRs — American Depository Receipts; receipts issued for foreign securities held by a trustee.

AMEX — American Stock Exchange.

annual report — a financial report sent yearly to a firm's stockholders.

annuity — a series of equal annual payments.

anticipation note — a short-term liability that is to be retired by specified expected revenue (e.g., expected tax receipts).

arbitrage — the simultaneous buying and selling of an asset in two markets to take advantage of price differences.

arrears — cumulative preferred dividends that have not been paid.

assay — a process by which metallic content is determined.

assets — what a firm or individual owns.

auditor's opinion — the opinion of the certified public accountant who analyzes a firm's final statements for their conformity with generally accepted accounting principles.

average collection period — the number of days required to collect accounts receivable.

balance sheet — an enumeration at a point in time of what an economic unit owns and owes and its net worth (equity).

balloon payment — the large, final payment necessary to retire a bond issue.

bar graph — a graph indicating the high, low, and closing prices of a security.

Barron's Confidence Index — an index designed to identify investors' confidence in the level and direction of security prices.

bear market — a market of declining security prices.

bearer bond — a bond with coupons attached or a bond the possession of which denotes ownership.

bearish — an expectation that prices will decline.

best effort — an agreement with an investment banker who does not guarantee the sale of a security but who agrees to make the best effort to sell it.

beta coefficient — a measure of risk; the risk associated with a particular stock relative to the market.

bid and ask — prices at which a security dealer offers to buy and sell stock.

"big board" — the New York Stock Exchange.

bond — a long-term liability with a specified amount of interest and maturity date.

book value — a firm's total assets minus its total liabilities; equity (frequently expressed in per share terms).

broker — an agent who handles buy and sell orders for an investor.

bullish — an expectation that prices will rise.

bull market — a market of rising security prices.

buy, sell, or hold — a brokerage firm's recommendations as to investment strategies for a particular security.

bylaws — a document specifying the relationship between a corporation and its stockholders.

call — an option sold by an individual that entitles the buyer to purchase stock at a specified price within a specified time period.

capital gain — an increase in value of a capital asset, such as a stock.

CBOE — Chicago Board Options Exchange; the first organized secondary market in puts and calls.

certificate of deposit (CD) — a time deposit with a specified maturity date.

charter — a document specifying the relationship between a firm and the state in which it is incorporated.

closed-end investment company — an investment company with a fixed number of shares that are bought and sold in the secondary security markets.

commissions — fees charged by brokers for executing orders.

common stock — a security representing ownership in a corporation.

compound sum of an annuity — the future value of a series of equal annual payments.

compounding — the process by which interest is paid on interest that has been previously earned.

condominium — an apartment that is owned instead of rented.

conglomerate — a diversified firm with interest in unrelated areas of business.

consolidated balance sheet — a parent company's balance sheet, which summarizes and combines the balance sheets of the firm's various subsidiaries.

convertible bond — a bond that may be exchanged for (i.e., converted into) common stock.

convertible preferred stock — preferred stock that may be exchanged for (i.e., converted into) common stock.

cost of debt — the interest rate adjusted for any tax savings.

coupon — the specified interest rate or amount of interest paid by a bond.

coupon bond — a bond with coupons attached that are removed and presented for payment of interest when due.

covered option — an option for which the seller has the securities.

covering — the buying of securities or commodities to close a short position.

credit union — a savings union that borrows from and lends to its members only.

cross-sectional analysis — an analysis of several firms in the same industry.

cumulative preferred stock — a preferred stock whose dividends accumulate if they are not paid.

current asset — an asset that should be converted into cash within 12 months.

current liability — a liability that has to be paid within the next 12 months.

current ratio — current assets divided by current liabilities; a measure of liquidity.

current yield — annual income divided by the current price of the security; annual return.

cyclical industry — an industry whose sales and profits are sensitive to changes in the level of economic activity.

daily limit — the maximum daily change permitted in a commodity's price.

daily range — the maximum daily range permitted in a commodity's price.

day of record — the day on which an investor must own shares in order to receive dividends.

day order — an order placed with a broker that is canceled at the end of the day if it is not executed.

debenture — an unsecured bond.

debt ratio — the ratio of debt to total assets.

declaration day — the day on which a dividend is announced.

default — the failure of a debtor to meet any term of a debt's indenture.

delivery — the receipt of previously purchased securities.

depreciation — the writing off of the cost of a fixed asset over its useful life.

dilution — a reduction in earnings per share that is due to the issuing of new securities.

director — a person who is elected by stockholders to determine the goals and policies of the firm.

discount — the sale of anything below its stated value.

discount broker — a broker who charges lower commissions on security purchases.

discounted bond — a bond that is sold for less than its face amount or principal.

discounting — the process of determining present value.

dispersion — deviation from the average.

distribution day — the day on which a dividend is distributed to stockholders.

diversification — the process of accumulating different securities to reduce the risk of loss.

dividend — a payment to stockholders that is usually in cash but may be in stock or property.

dividend growth model — a valuation model that deals with dividends and their growth properly discounted back to the present.

dividend reinvestment plan — a plan that permits stockholders to have cash dividends reinvested in stock instead of received in cash.

dollar averaging — the purchase of securities at different intervals to reduce the impact of price fluctuations.

Dow Jones industrial average — an average of the stock prices of 30 industrial firms.

Dow theory — a technical approach based on the Dow Jones averages.

earnings per preferred share — the total earnings divided by the number of preferred shares outstanding.

earnings per share (EPS) — the total earnings divided by the number of shares outstanding.

efficient market hypothesis — a theory that security prices correctly measure a firm's future earnings and dividends.

EPS — earnings per share.

equilibrium price — a price that equates supply and demand.

equipment trust certificate — a bond secured by specific equipment.

equity — net worth; investment in a firm by its stockholders.

equity trust — a real estate investment trust that specializes in acquiring real estate for subsequent rental income.

estate tax — a tax on the value of a deceased individual's assets.

ex dividend — the day on which a stock trades exclusive of any dividends.

expected return — the sum of the anticipated dividend yield and capital gains.

extra dividend — a dividend that is in addition to the firm's regular dividend.

face value — the amount of a debt; the principal.

federal agency bonds — debt issued by divisions (i.e., agencies) of the federal government.

Federal Reserve — the central bank of the United States.

financial goal(s) — the purpose(s) of investing.

financial intermediary — a financial institution that borrows from one group and lends to another (e.g., a commercial bank).

financial leverage — the use of borrowed funds to acquire an asset; the use of debt financing.

financial planning — the programs for meeting financial goals.

flat — a description of a bond that trades without accrued interest.

forecasting — the processes of predicting the future.

foreign exchange — foreign moneys or currencies.

full-disclosure laws — the federal and state laws requiring publicly owned firms to disclose financial and other information that may affect the value of their securities.

fundamental approach — the analysis of economic and financial information to identify assets for purchase.

futures contract — an agreement for the future delivery of a commodity at a specified price.

futures price — the price for the future delivery of a commodity.

general obligation bond — a bond whose interest does not depend on the revenue of a specific project; government bonds supported by the full faith and credit of the issuer.

GNP — gross national product; the value of a nation's final goods and services produced during a year.

good-till-canceled order — an order placed with a broker that remains in effect until it is executed by the broker or canceled by the investor.

gross profit margin — sales revenues minus the cost of goods sold.

growth stock — shares of a company whose earnings are expected to grow at an above average rate.

head-and-shoulder pattern — a pattern of security prices that resembles a head and a shoulder.

hedging — the simultaneous buying and selling to reduce risk.

hidden asset — an asset that has appreciated in value but is carried on the balance sheet at a lower value (e.g., at cost).

holding company — a firm that owns securities of other companies.

improved land — land that has been cleared or has had improvements (e.g., curbs, gutters).

income — the flow of money or its equivalent produced by an asset (e.g., dividends, interest).

income bond — a bond whose interest is paid only if it is earned by the firm.

income-in-kind — nonmonetary income (e.g., services received in lieu of cash).

income statement — a statement of profit or loss; a summation of revenues and expenses for a specified time period.

indenture — the document that specifies the terms of a bond issue.

index fund — a mutual fund whose portfolio seeks to duplicate an index of stock prices.

inheritance tax — a tax on what an individual receives from an estate.

inside information — information available only to a firm's management.

insider transaction — the buying or selling of a firm's securities by its managers or by individuals who own more than 5 per cent of the stock.

interest — payment for the use of money.

intrinsic value — an estimation of what an asset is worth.

inventory turnover — the speed with which inventory is sold.

investment banker — an underwriter; a firm that sells new issues of securities to the general public.

investment club — a club whose members make contributions for the purpose of investing.

IRA account — a retirement plan that is available to workers who are not covered by employer-sponsored retirement plans.

irregular dividends — dividend payments that either do not occur at regular intervals or vary in amount.

Keogh account — a retirement plan that is available to self-employed individuals.

Krugerrand — a gold coin consisting of one ounce of gold issued by the Union of South Africa.

leverage — the use of debt financing to increase the return to the equity.

liabilities — what an individual or a firm owes.

limit order — an order to buy or sell at a specified price.

liquidation — the process of converting assets into cash.

liquidity — moneyness; the ease with which assets can be converted into cash without a substantial loss.

liquidity ratios — measures of the safety of current liabilities; indicators of the firm's ability to meet current obligations as they become due.

listed security — a security that is traded on an organized exchange.

loading charge — a fee charged by a mutual fund for selling shares.

long position — owning assets for their income or possible price appreciation.

long term — a period of time greater than one year.

long-term asset — an asset that is expected to last for more than one year (e.g., plant and equipment).

long-term debt — debt that becomes due after one year.

margin — the amount that an investor must put down to buy securities on credit.

margin call — a request by a broker for an investor to place additional funds or securities in an account as collateral against borrowed funds.

marginal tax rate — the tax rate paid on an individual's last dollar of taxable income; an individual's tax bracket.

market order — an order to buy or sell at the current market price.

maturity date — the time at which a debt issue becomes due and the principal must be repaid.

money market fund — mutual funds that specialize in short-term securities.

moral backing — nonobligatory support for a debt issue.

mortgage bond — a bond that is secured by property.

mortgage trust — a real estate investment trust that specializes in loans secured by real estate.

moving average — an average in which the most recent observation is added and the most distant observation is deleted before the average is recomputed.

municipal bond — a bond issued by a state or one of its political subdivisions (see tax-exempt bonds).

mutual fund — an open-end investment company.

mutual savings bank — a savings bank owned by its depositors.

naked option — an option that is sold for which the seller does not have the securities.

NASDAQ — National Association of Security Dealers Automatic Quotation system; quotation system for over-the-counter securities.

net asset value — the asset value of a share in an investment company; total assets minus total liabilities divided by the number of shares outstanding.

net profit margin — a ratio of earnings before interest and taxes to sales.

net worth — equity; book value.

no-load fund — a mutual fund that does not charge a fee for selling shares.

NOW account — a savings account against which negotiable orders of withdrawal may be written.

NYSE index — New York Stock Exchange index; an index of prices of all stocks listed on the exchange.

odd lot — a unit of trading that is smaller than the general unit of sale (e.g., 32 shares).

open-end investment company — a mutual fund; an investment company from which individuals buy shares and to which they resell them.

open market operations — the buying and selling of government securities by the Federal Reserve.

option — the right to buy or sell something at a specified price within a specified time period.

organized exchange — a formal market for buying and selling securities or commodities.

originating house — an investment banker that makes an agreement with a firm to sell a new issue and that forms the syndicate to sell the securities.

over-the-counter market (OTC) — the informal secondary market for unlisted securities.

paper profits — price appreciation that has not been realized.

partnership — an unincorporated business owned by two or more individuals.

payout ratio — the ratio of dividends to earnings.

PE ratio — the ratio of the price of a stock to the earnings per share.

perpetual bond — a debt instrument with no maturity date.

portfolio — a combination of assets owned by an investor.

portfolio risk — the total risk associated with owning a portfolio; the sum of systematic and unsystematic risk.

preemptive rights — the right of current stockholders to maintain their proportionate ownership in the firm.

preferred stock — a class of stock (i.e., equity) that has a prior claim to common stock on the firm's earnings.

premium of a bond — the extent to which a bond's price exceeds the face amount of the debt.

premium of an option — the amount paid for an option that exceeds the option's intrinsic value.

present value — the current worth of a sum to be received in the future.

present value of an annuity — the present worth of a series of equal payments.

principal — the amount owed; the face value of debt.

private placement — the sale of securities to a financial institution.

progressive tax — a tax whose rate increases as the tax base increases.

project note — a short-term tax-exempt note issued through the Department of Housing and Urban Development to finance urban renewal.

prospectus — a document filed with the Securities and Exchange Commission concerning a proposed sale of securities to the general public.

proxy — a written authorization given to someone by a stockholder to vote his or her shares.

put — an option to sell stock at a specified price within a specified time period.

quarterly report — a financial report sent every three months to a firm's stockholders.

random walk hypothesis — see efficient market hypothesis.

range — the high and low prices for a time period, such as the last 12 months.

rate of return — the annual percentage return realized on an investment.

rating systems — classification schemes designed to indicate the risk associated with a particular security.

recapitalization — an alteration in a firm's sources of finance, such as the substitution of long-term debt for equity.

recession — a period of rising unemployment and a declining gross national product.

record date — the day on which an investor must be the registered owner of a share to receive the dividend.

red herring — the preliminary prospectus.

refunding — the act of issuing new debt and using the proceeds to retire existing debt.

registered bond — a bond the ownership of which is registered with the commercial bank that distributes interest payments and principal repayments.

registered representative — a person who buys and sells securities for customers.

registration — the process of filing information with the Securities and Exchange Commission concerning a proposed sale of securities to the general public.

regressive tax — a tax whose rate declines as the tax base increases.

regular dividends — steady dividends that are distributed at regular intervals.

REIT — a real estate investment trust.

required rate of return — the expected return necessary to induce an investor to purchase an asset.

reserves — cash and deposits at the Federal Reserve held by commercial banks against deposit liabilities.

retained earnings — earnings of a firm that have been retained instead of distributed.

return on assets — the ratio of earnings to total assets.

return on equity — the ratio of earnings to stockholders' equity.

revenue bond — a bond whose interest is paid only if the debtor earns sufficient revenue.

rights — an option given to stockholders to buy additional shares at a specified price during a specified time period (e.g., a month).

risk — the possibility of loss; the uncertainty of future returns.

round lot — a general unit of trading in a security (e.g., 100 shares).

safety — little chance of loss of the amount invested.

savings and loan association — a savings bank that specializes in mortgages.

savings certificate — a type of time deposit issued by a bank.

secondary market — a market for buying and selling previously issued securities.

Securities and Exchange Commission (SEC) — the federal government agency that enforces the federal security laws.

semiannual compounding — the payment of interest twice a year.

semilogarithmic paper — graph paper on which one axis is expressed in logarithms.

serial bond — an issue of bonds in which specified bonds mature each year.

series E and EE bonds — savings bonds issued by the federal government in small denominations.

series H and HH bonds — income bonds issued by the federal government.

settlement date — the date on which an investor must pay for a security purchase.

short position — owing assets for possible price deterioration; being short in a security.

short sale — the sale of borrowed securities in anticipation of a price decline.

short term — a period of time less than one year.

sinking fund — a series of periodic payments to retire a bond issue.

SIPC — Security Investors Protection Corporation, which insures investors against failures by brokerage firms.

specialist — a market maker on the New York Stock Exchange who maintains an orderly market in the security.

speculator — an individual who is willing to accept substantial risk for the possibility of a large return.

spot price — the current price of a commodity.

spread — the difference between the bid and ask prices.

Standard & Poor's 500 stock index — an index of prices of 500 stocks.

stock dividend — a dividend paid in stock.

stockholders' equity — equity; stockholders' investment in a firm; the sum of stock, paid-in capital, and retained earnings.

stock split — recapitalization that affects the number of shares outstanding, their par value, the earnings per share, and the price of the stock.

stop loss order — a purchase or sell order designed to limit an investor's loss on a position in a security.

street name — the registration of securities in the broker's name instead of in the buyer's name.

supply of money — the sum of cash, currency, and demand deposits outstanding.

syndicate — a selling group assembled to market an issue of securities.

systematic risk — risk associated with fluctuations in security prices (i.e., the market as a whole).

T-account — an abbreviated balance sheet.

tax credit — a credit against one's tax liabilities, which reduces the amount of taxes owed.

tax-exempt bond — a bond whose interest is excluded from federal income taxation.

tax-exempt fund — a mutual fund that specializes in tax-exempt securities.

technical approach — an analysis of past volume and price behavior to identify assets for purchase.

tender offer — a formal offer by a firm to buy shares at a specified price.

10-K report — a required annual report filed with the Securities and Exchange Commission by a publicly owned firm.

10-Q report — a required quarterly report filed with the Securities and Exchange Commission by a publicly owned firm.

theoretical value as debt — the value of a convertible bond as a debt instrument.

theoretical value as stock — the value of an option in terms of stock.

thin issue — an issue of securities with either a small number of securities in the hands of the general public or a small volume of transactions.

time series analysis — an analysis of a firm over a period of time.

times-interest-earned ratio — the earnings before interest and taxes divided by interest expenses; a coverage ratio that measures the safety of debt.

total return — the sum of dividend yield and capital gains.

transfer agent — a company that maintains the record of a firm's stockholders and transfers shares from seller to buyer.

treasury bills — the short-term debt of the federal government.

treasury bonds — the long-term debt of the federal government.

treasury notes — the intermediate-term debt of the federal government.

treasury stock — stock previously issued but repurchased and held by the firm.

trust department — the division of a financial institution that manages individuals' investments.

trustee — a commercial bank that is appointed to uphold the terms of a bond's indenture.

underwriting — the guaranteeing of the sale of a new issue of securities.

underwriting fees — the cost to a firm of selling an issue of securities through an investment banker.

unimproved land — land that has not been cleared and has not had improvements, such as curbs and gutters.

unsystematic risk — the risk associated with a particular security.

valuation — the process of determining the current worth of an asset.

variable interest rate bond — a long-term bond with a coupon rate that varies with changes in short-term interest rates.

voting rights — the rights of stockholders to vote their shares.

warrant — an option issued by a company to buy stock at a specified price within a specified time period.

working capital — current assets minus current liabilities.

X–O chart — a chart composed of Xs and Os that is used in technical analysis to summarize price movements.

yield curve — the relationship between the time to maturity and yields.

yield to call — the yield earned on a bond from the time it is acquired until the time it is called by the firm.

yield to maturity — the yield earned on a bond from the time it is acquired until the maturity date of the bond.

APPENDIX A

THE COMPOUND VALUE OF ONE DOLLAR

Year	1%	2%	3%	4%	5%	6%	7%
1	1.010	1.020	1.030	1.040	1.050	1.060	1.070
2	1.020	1.040	1.061	1.082	1.102	1.124	1.145
3	1.030	1.061	1.093	1.125	1.158	1.191	1.225
4	1.041	1.082	1.126	1.170	1.216	1.262	1.311
5	1.051	1.104	1.159	1.217	1.276	1.338	1.403
6	1.062	1.126	1.194	1.265	1.340	1.419	1.501
7	1.072	1.149	1.230	1.316	1.407	1.504	1.606
8	1.083	1.172	1.267	1.369	1.477	1.594	1.718
9	1.094	1.195	1.305	1.423	1.551	1.689	1.838
10	1.105	1.219	1.344	1.480	1.629	1.791	1.967
11	1.116	1.243	1.384	1.539	1.710	1.898	2.105
12	1.127	1.268	1.426	1.601	1.796	2.012	2.252
13	1.138	1.294	1.469	1.665	1.886	2.133	2.410
14	1.149	1.319	1.513	1.732	1.980	2.261	2.579
15	1.161	1.346	1.558	1.801	2.079	2.397	2.759
16	1.173	1.373	1.605	1.873	2.183	2.540	2.952
17	1.184	1.400	1.653	1.948	2.292	2.693	3.159
18	1.196	1.428	1.702	2.026	2.407	2.854	3.380
19	1.208	1.457	1.754	2.107	2.527	3.026	3.617
20	1.220	1.486	1.806	2.191	2.653	3.207	3.870
25	1.282	1.641	2.094	2.666	3.386	4.292	5.427
30	1.348	1.811	2.427	3.243	4.322	5.743	7.612

THE COMPOUND VALUE
OF ONE DOLLAR
(Continued)

Year	8%	9%	10%	12%	14%	15%	16%
1	1.080	1.090	1.100	1.120	1.140	1.150	1.160
2	1.166	1.188	1.210	1.254	1.300	1.322	1.346
3	1.260	1.295	1.331	1.405	1.482	1.521	1.561
4	1.360	1.412	1.464	1.574	1.689	1.749	1.811
5	1.469	1.539	1.611	1.762	1.925	2.011	2.100
6	1.587	1.677	1.772	1.974	2.195	2.313	2.436
7	1.714	1.828	1.949	2.211	2.502	2.660	2.826
8	1.851	1.993	2.144	2.476	2.853	3.059	3.278
9	1.999	2.172	2.358	2.773	3.252	3.518	3.803
10	2.159	2.367	2.594	3.106	3.707	4.046	4.411
11	2.332	2.580	2.853	3.479	4.226	4.652	5.117
12	2.518	2.813	3.138	3.896	4.818	5.350	5.936
13	2.720	3.066	3.452	4.363	5.492	6.153	6.886
14	2.937	3.342	3.797	4.887	6.261	7.076	7.988
15	3.172	3.642	4.177	5.474	7.138	8.137	9.266
16	3.426	3.970	4.595	6.130	8.137	9.358	10.748
17	3.700	4.328	5.054	6.866	9.276	10.761	12.468
18	3.996	4.717	5.560	7.690	10.575	12.375	14.463
19	4.316	5.142	6.116	8.613	12.056	14.232	16.777
20	4.661	5.604	6.728	9.646	13.743	16.367	19.461
25	6.848	8.623	10.835	17.000	26.462	32.919	40.874
30	10.063	13.268	17.449	29.960	50.950	66.212	85.850

APPENDIX B

THE PRESENT VALUE OF ONE DOLLAR

Year	1%	2%	3%	4%	5%	6%	7%	8%	9%	10%	12%	14%	15%
1	.990	.980	.971	.962	.952	.943	.935	.926	.917	.909	.893	.877	.870
2	.980	.961	.943	.925	.907	.890	.873	.857	.842	.826	.797	.769	.756
3	.971	.942	.915	.889	.864	.840	.816	.794	.772	.751	.712	.675	.658
4	.961	.924	.889	.855	.823	.792	.763	.735	.708	.683	.636	.592	.572
5	.951	.906	.863	.822	.784	.747	.713	.681	.650	.621	.567	.519	.497
6	.942	.888	.838	.790	.746	.705	.666	.630	.596	.564	.507	.456	.432
7	.933	.871	.813	.760	.711	.665	.623	.583	.547	.513	.452	.400	.376
8	.923	.853	.789	.731	.677	.627	.582	.540	.502	.467	.404	.351	.327
9	.914	.837	.766	.703	.645	.592	.544	.500	.460	.424	.361	.308	.284
10	.905	.820	.744	.676	.614	.558	.508	.463	.422	.386	.322	.270	.247
11	.896	.804	.722	.650	.585	.527	.475	.429	.388	.350	.287	.237	.215
12	.887	.788	.701	.625	.557	.497	.444	.397	.356	.319	.257	.208	.187
13	.879	.773	.681	.601	.530	.469	.415	.368	.326	.290	.229	.182	.163
14	.870	.758	.661	.577	.505	.442	.388	.340	.299	.263	.205	.160	.141
15	.861	.743	.642	.555	.481	.417	.362	.315	.275	.239	.183	.140	.123
16	.853	.728	.623	.534	.458	.394	.339	.292	.252	.218	.163	.123	.107
17	.844	.714	.605	.513	.436	.371	.317	.270	.231	.198	.146	.108	.093
18	.836	.700	.587	.494	.416	.350	.296	.250	.212	.180	.130	.095	.081
19	.828	.686	.570	.475	.396	.331	.276	.232	.194	.164	.116	.083	.070
20	.820	.673	.554	.456	.377	.312	.258	.215	.178	.149	.104	.073	.061
25	.780	.610	.478	.375	.295	.233	.184	.146	.116	.092	.059	.038	.030
30	.742	.552	.412	.308	.231	.174	.131	.099	.075	.057	.033	.020	.015

THE PRESENT VALUE OF ONE DOLLAR (*Continued*)

Year	16%	18%	20%	24%	28%	32%	36%	40%	50%	60%	70%	80%	90%
1	.862	.847	.833	.806	.781	.758	.735	.714	.667	.625	.588	.556	.526
2	.743	.718	.694	.650	.610	.574	.541	.510	.444	.391	.346	.309	.277
3	.641	.609	.579	.524	.477	.435	.398	.364	.296	.244	.204	.171	.146
4	.552	.516	.482	.423	.373	.329	.292	.260	.198	.153	.120	.095	.077
5	.476	.437	.402	.341	.291	.250	.215	.186	.132	.095	.070	.053	.040
6	.410	.370	.335	.275	.227	.189	.158	.133	.088	.060	.041	.029	.021
7	.354	.314	.279	.222	.178	.143	.116	.095	.059	.037	.024	.016	.011
8	.305	.266	.233	.179	.139	.108	.085	.068	.039	.023	.014	.009	.006
9	.263	.226	.194	.144	.108	.082	.063	.048	.026	.015	.008	.005	.003
10	.227	.191	.162	.116	.085	.062	.046	.035	.017	.009	.005	.003	.002
11	.195	.162	.135	.094	.066	.047	.034	.025	.012	.006	.003	.002	.001
12	.168	.137	.112	.076	.052	.036	.025	.018	.008	.004	.002	.001	.001
13	.145	.116	.093	.061	.040	.027	.018	.013	.005	.002	.001	.001	.000
14	.125	.099	.078	.049	.032	.021	.014	.009	.003	.001	.001	.000	.000
15	.108	.084	.065	.040	.025	.016	.010	.006	.002	.001	.000	.000	.000
16	.093	.071	.054	.032	.019	.012	.007	.005	.002	.001	.000	.000	
17	.080	.060	.045	.026	.015	.009	.005	.003	.001	.000	.000		
18	.069	.051	.038	.021	.012	.007	.004	.002	.001	.000	.000		
19	.060	.043	.031	.017	.009	.005	.003	.002	.000	.000			
20	.051	.037	.026	.014	.007	.004	.002	.001	.000	.000			
25	.024	.016	.010	.005	.002	.001	.000	.000					
30	.012	.007	.004	.002	.001	.000	.000						

APPENDIX C

THE SUM OF AN ANNUITY OF ONE DOLLAR FOR *N* YEARS

Year	1%	2%	3%	4%	5%	6%
1	1.000	1.000	1.000	1.000	1.000	1.000
2	2.010	2.020	2.030	2.040	2.050	2.060
3	3.030	3.060	3.091	3.122	3.152	3.184
4	4.060	4.122	4.184	4.246	4.310	4.375
5	5.101	5.204	5.309	5.416	5.526	5.637
6	6.152	6.308	6.468	6.633	6.802	6.975
7	7.214	7.434	7.662	7.898	8.142	8.394
8	8.286	8.583	8.892	9.214	9.549	9.897
9	9.369	9.755	10.159	10.583	11.027	11.491
10	10.462	10.950	11.464	12.006	12.578	13.181
11	11.567	12.169	12.808	13.486	14.207	14.972
12	12.683	13.412	14.192	15.026	15.917	16.870
13	13.809	14.680	15.618	16.627	17.713	18.882
14	14.947	15.974	17.086	18.292	19.599	21.051
15	16.097	17.293	18.599	20.024	21.579	23.276
16	17.258	18.639	20.157	21.825	23.657	25.673
17	18.430	20.012	21.762	23.698	25.840	28.213
18	19.615	21.412	23.414	25.645	28.132	30.906
19	20.811	22.841	25.117	27.671	30.539	33.760
20	22.019	24.297	26.870	29.778	33.066	36.786
25	28.243	32.030	36.459	41.646	47.727	54.865
30	34.785	40.568	47.575	56.085	66.439	79.058

THE SUM OF AN ANNUITY OF ONE DOLLAR FOR *N* YEARS
(*Continued*)

Year	7%	8%	9%	10%	12%	14%
1	1.000	1.000	1.000	1.000	1.000	1.000
2	2.070	2.080	2.090	2.100	2.120	2.140
3	3.215	3.246	3.278	3.310	3.374	3.440
4	4.440	4.506	4.573	4.641	4.770	4.921
5	5.751	5.867	5.985	6.105	6.353	6.610
6	7.153	7.336	7.523	7.716	8.115	8.536
7	8.654	8.923	9.200	9.487	10.089	10.730
8	10.260	10.637	11.028	11.436	12.300	13.233
9	11.978	12.488	13.021	13.579	14.776	16.085
10	13.816	14.487	15.193	15.937	17.549	19.337
11	15.784	16.645	17.560	18.531	20.655	23.044
12	17.888	18.977	20.141	21.384	24.138	27.271
13	20.141	21.495	22.953	24.523	28.029	32.089
14	22.550	24.215	26.019	27.975	32.393	37.581
15	25.129	27.152	29.361	31.772	37.280	43.842
16	27.888	30.324	33.003	35.950	42.753	50.980
17	30.840	33.750	36.974	40.545	48.884	59.118
18	33.999	37.450	41.301	45.599	55.750	68.394
19	37.379	41.446	46.018	51.159	63.440	78.969
20	40.995	45.762	51.160	57.275	72.052	91.025
25	63.249	73.106	84.701	98.347	133.334	181.871
30	94.461	113.283	136.308	164.494	241.333	356.787

APPENDIX D

THE PRESENT VALUE OF AN ANNUITY OF ONE DOLLAR

Year	1%	2%	3%	4%	5%	6%	7%	8%	9%	10%
1	0.990	0.980	0.971	0.962	0.952	0.943	0.935	0.926	0.917	0.909
2	1.970	1.942	1.913	1.886	1.859	1.833	1.808	1.783	1.759	1.736
3	2.941	2.884	2.829	2.775	2.723	2.673	2.624	2.577	2.531	2.487
4	3.902	3.808	3.717	3.630	3.546	3.465	3.387	3.312	3.240	3.170
5	4.853	4.713	4.580	4.452	4.329	4.212	4.100	3.993	3.890	3.791
6	5.795	5.601	5.417	5.242	5.076	4.917	4.766	4.623	4.486	4.355
7	6.728	6.472	6.230	6.002	5.786	5.582	5.389	5.206	5.033	4.868
8	7.652	7.325	7.020	6.733	6.463	6.210	5.971	5.747	5.535	5.335
9	8.566	8.162	7.786	7.435	7.108	6.802	6.515	6.247	5.985	5.759
10	9.471	8.983	8.530	8.111	7.722	7.360	7.024	6.710	6.418	6.145
11	10.368	9.787	9.253	8.760	8.306	7.887	7.499	7.139	6.805	6.495
12	11.255	10.575	9.954	9.385	8.863	8.384	7.943	7.536	7.161	6.814
13	12.134	11.348	10.635	9.986	9.394	8.853	8.358	7.904	7.487	7.103
14	13.004	12.106	11.296	10.563	9.899	9.295	8.745	8.244	7.786	7.367
15	13.865	12.849	11.938	11.118	10.380	9.712	9.108	8.559	8.060	7.606
16	14.718	13.578	12.561	11.652	10.838	10.106	9.447	8.851	8.312	7.824
17	15.562	14.292	13.166	12.166	11.274	10.477	9.763	9.122	8.544	8.022
18	16.398	14.992	13.754	12.659	11.690	10.828	10.059	9.372	8.756	8.201
19	17.226	15.678	14.324	13.134	12.085	11.158	10.336	9.604	8.950	8.365
20	18.046	16.351	14.877	13.590	12.462	11.470	10.594	9.818	9.128	8.514
25	22.023	19.523	17.413	15.622	14.094	12.783	11.654	10.675	9.823	9.077
30	25.808	22.397	19.600	17.292	15.373	13.765	12.409	11.258	10.274	9.427

THE PRESENT VALUE OF AN ANNUITY OF ONE DOLLAR (*Continued*)

Year	12%	14%	16%	18%	20%	24%	28%	32%	36%
1	0.893	0.877	0.862	0.847	0.833	0.806	0.781	0.758	0.735
2	1.690	1.647	1.605	1.566	1.528	1.457	1.392	1.332	1.276
3	2.402	2.322	2.246	2.174	2.106	1.981	1.868	1.766	1.674
4	3.037	2.914	2.798	2.690	2.589	2.404	2.241	2.096	1.966
5	3.605	3.433	3.274	3.127	2.991	2.745	2.532	2.345	2.181
6	4.111	3.889	3.685	3.498	3.326	3.020	2.759	2.534	2.339
7	4.564	4.288	4.039	3.812	3.605	3.242	2.937	2.678	2.455
8	4.968	4.639	4.344	4.078	3.837	3.421	3.076	2.786	2.540
9	5.328	4.946	4.607	4.303	4.031	3.566	3.184	2.868	2.603
10	5.650	5.216	4.833	4.494	4.193	3.682	3.269	2.930	2.650
11	5.988	5.453	5.029	4.656	4.327	3.776	3.335	2.978	2.683
12	6.194	5.660	5.197	4.793	4.439	3.851	3.387	3.013	2.708
13	6.424	5.842	5.342	4.910	4.533	3.912	3.427	3.040	2.727
14	6.628	6.002	5.468	5.008	4.611	3.962	3.459	3.061	2.740
15	6.811	6.142	5.575	5.092	4.675	4.001	3.483	3.076	2.750
16	6.974	6.265	5.669	5.162	4.730	4.003	3.503	3.088	2.758
17	7.120	6.373	5.749	5.222	4.775	4.059	3.518	3.097	2.763
18	7.250	6.467	5.818	5.273	4.812	4.080	3.529	3.104	2.767
19	7.366	6.550	5.877	5.316	4.844	4.097	3.539	3.109	2.770
20	7.469	6.623	5.929	5.353	4.870	4.110	3.546	3.113	2.772
25	7.843	6.873	6.097	5.467	4.948	4.147	3.564	3.122	2.776
30	8.055	7.003	6.177	5.517	4.979	4.160	3.569	3.124	2.778

Index